"An outstanding and timely work. Fuchs is the only person I know who could have produced a book on immigration and ethnicity at once so thorough and thoughtful."

—Milton D. Morris, Director of Research,
Joint Center for Political and Economic Studies

"This book surpasses others that factually survey the new immigration because of its powerful philosophical vision of how immigrant achievements confirm the inclusive principles of American polity."

—Reed Ueda, Tufts University

"I have gained from *The American Kaleidoscope* a deeper appreciation of the diversity that is at once America's greatest strength and the source of some of its most threatening vulnerabilities. Lawrence Fuchs has advanced our efforts to improve the often strained relationships between ethnic groups in America. I will retain his book in my office as an important reference and a valued source of inspiration."

—Daniel K. Inouye, U.S. Senator

"Americans working in various disciplines have long needed a scholar who would effectively, perceptively, and compassionately analyze and compare the experiences of America's national and religious ethnic groups as well as its racial ones. Lawrence Fuchs has accomplished those goals."

—Elliott Barkan
California State College, San Bernardino

THE AMERICAN
KALEIDOSCOPE

Other Books by Lawrence H. Fuchs

The Political Behavior of American Jews
Hawaii Pono
John F. Kennedy and American Catholicism
Those Peculiar Americans
American Ethnic Politics
Family Matters

Lawrence H. Fuchs

THE AMERICAN KALEIDOSCOPE

Race, Ethnicity, and the Civic Culture

Wesleyan University Press

Published by University Press of New England
Hanover and London

The University Press of New England
is a consortium of universities in New England dedicated to publishing
scholarly and trade works by authors from member campuses and elsewhere. The New England imprint signifies uniform standards for publication excellence maintained without exception by the consortium
members. A joint imprint of University Press of New England and a
sponsoring member acknowledges the publishing mission of that university and its support for the dissemination of scholarship throughout
the world. Cited by the American Council of Learned Societies as a
model to be followed, University Press of New England publishes books
under its own imprint and the imprints of Brandeis University, Brown
University, Clark University, University of Connecticut, Dartmouth
College, University of New Hampshire, University of Rhode Island,
Tufts University, University of Vermont, and Wesleyan University.

© 1990 by Lawrence H. Fuchs

Excerpts from "Incident" by Countee Cullen Copyright estate of Ida M.
Cullen, reprinted by permission of GAR Associates, Inc., Agents.

Printed in the United States of America
∞

Library of Congress Cataloging-in-Publication Data
Fuchs, Lawrence H.
   The American kaleidoscope : race, ethnicity, and the civic culture
   Lawrence H. Fuchs. —1st ed.
      p. cm.
   Includes bibliographical references (p.   ).
   ISBN 0-8195-5122-8
   1. United States—Ethnic relations.   2. United States—Race
relations.   I. Title.
E184.A1F83   1990
305.8'00973—dc20   89-21481
                    CIP

5   4   3   2   I

To my immigrant grandparents, Pearl and Philip, Nettie and Norbert, who discovered the United States, and to my grandchildren—Satya, Simon, Jazmin, Megan, Molly, Brian, and Abigail—who I hope will work to make it an ever more humane nation.

From the first appearance of man on earth down to very recent times, the words "stranger," "enemy," were quite or almost synonymous . . . To correct the evils, great and small, which spring from want of sympathy and from positive enmity among strangers, as nations or as individuals, is one of the highest functions of civilization.

—ABRAHAM LINCOLN

Contents

Acknowledgments

I have many to thank for help on this book. After finishing my work as executive director of the staff of the Select Commission on Immigration and Refugee Policy in 1981, I was given an office and support as a guest scholar in the Program of American Society and Politics at the Woodrow Wilson Center of the Smithsonian Institution for several months, where I began this book. Additional support during the past eight years for my work on ethnic pluralism and the civic culture came from the Rockefeller Foundation, the Ford Foundation, the Alfred P. Sloan Foundation, and the Exxon Foundation. The Jaffe Foundation has provided continuous support for secretarial assistance since 1984, and I am particularly grateful, as holder of the Meyer and Walter Jaffe professorship in American Civilization and Politics, to have received that generous assistance. I am also appreciative to the Rockefeller Foundation for my appointment as Scholar in Residence at the splendid Villa Serbelloni at Bellagio in Italy during the summer of 1985.

I am grateful to my secretaries in the American Studies Department at Brandeis, Grace Short and her replacement, Angela Simeone, for their patience. I am indebted to Debra Post, who provided secretarial help on the book during its early stages; I am especially grateful to Christine Stone, whose intelligence and skills and pungent editorial suggestions added a measure of assistance far beyond what should normally be expected in a secretary.

To my research assistants, all former students at Brandeis, I offer a special salute. Thank you: Anaya Balter, Christopher Bean, Alka Gurung, Jill Lennett, Shelly Tenenbaum, and Veljko Vujacic. Ms. Tenenbaum, who has become a scholar of ethnicity, was particularly thoughtful about many ideas in this book.

A slightly different version of chapter 16 appeared in *The Tocqueville Review*, Volume VIII, 1988/89, edited by Jessie R. Pitts (Charlottesville: University Press of Virginia, 1989), with my permission and that of Wesleyan University Press. Some of chapter 23 appeared in 1986 in a booklet published by the American Jewish Committee, *Counting by Race*.

I think the idea for the title of this book may have been planted when I first read John Higham's series of essays, *Send These to Me: Immigrants in Urban America* (1975), where he writes of the United States as a "kaleidoscopic culture." The concept was also used as a title for an exhibition on ethnicity at the Balch Institute in Philadelphia (1976–1987).

I appreciate the many helpful suggestions I received from several scholars: Elliott Barkan, Rodolfo O. de la Garza, Edwin Dorn, Victor Fuchs, Alan Kraut, Virginia Yans-McGlaughlin, David Reimers, Peter Rose, John Stack, Reed Ueda, Stephen Whitfield, and Myron Wiener. An extra tip of the hat to Professors Barkan, Kraut, Reimers, Rose, Stack, and Ueda for having read the entire manuscript. Professor Barkan made dozens of detailed suggestions.

I also thank the staff at Wesleyan University Press for thoughtful assistance. Jeannette Hopkins, one of the most experienced editors of books dealing with race and ethnicity, did not always agree with my interpretations or emphases. But I learned from her tough and thorough comments and queries. Of course, neither she nor any of the scholars acknowledged above should be blamed for errors of mine. John Anderson was a superb copy editor.

A word of thanks also to my agent and friend, the always helpful Gerard McCauley.

To my family, especially my wife, Betty, thanks for your good humor and support.

LAWRENCE H. FUCHS
Meyer and Walter Jaffe Professor of
  American Civilization and Politics
Brandeis University, Waltham

Preface

Since the Second World War the national unity of Americans has been tied increasingly to a strong civic culture that permits and protects expressions of ethnic and religious diversity based on individual rights and that also inhibits and ameliorates conflict among religious, ethnic, and racial groups. It is the civic culture that unites Americans and protects their freedom—including their right to be ethnic.

As a sophomore in college in 1947, recently returned from the U.S. Navy, I read two books that are the godparents of this book, Gunnar Myrdal's *An American Dilemma* and Robert MacIver's *The Web of Government*. By setting forth the case for an American national identity based on unifying political ideals and documenting the failure to live up to those ideals with respect to Negroes, Myrdal issued a call for justice for blacks, not just for their sake but to make our nation whole. That call ultimately led me to join the march from Selma to Montgomery, Alabama, in 1965. Myrdal, a Swede, had little to say about Jews or other religious or nationality groups in the United States (the word "ethnic" was not in use), probably because he assumed, like most liberals, their inexorable assimilation into dominant American culture. MacIver, an immigrant from Britain who had lived and worked in New York City for many years, was much more aware of the persistence of ethnic traditions and loyalties. Democracy, with all of its leveling and assimilating tendencies, he maintained, also allowed for ethnic diversity.

What I took from Myrdal principally was a better understanding of the American creed and of American racism and the too optimistic conclusion that if Americans applied their creed consistently they would overcome racism. What I took from MacIver primarily was the confident belief that racial and immigrant-ethnic group harmony was possible in the U.S., although rarely present elsewhere. The five books I have written on aspects of ethnicity and American unity were shaped in part by my understanding of Myrdal and MacIver. But my confidence in their teachings was shaken by books by three friends and colleagues, all published in 1975.

Warning against the destructive power of ethnic tribalism in *The Idols of the Tribe: Group Identity and Political Change,* Harold Isaacs challenged the view that ethnic mobilization in the U.S. was compatible with national unity. Isaacs wondered, in his last chapter, whether the ethnic patterns emerging in the 1970s—creating "new conflicts, new dilemmas"—would lead to a new pluralistic system, which, by emphasizing group rights, would destroy the very basis for American nationhood, the idea that "one is American only as an individual" and that "the American individual is free to associate with any kind of group to which he feels he belongs, and each such group is free to exist, to function, to live and to grow according to its own genius and its own vitality. It does so on its own . . . in the great private domain where every person retains his own individual freedom of choice." At the end of *Idols of the Tribe,* Isaacs concluded, "The underlying issue is still: Can human existence be made more human, and if so, how? . . . How can we live with our differences without, as always heretofore, being driven by them to tear each other limb from limb?"

The same concern was raised in a different way by Nathan Glazer in *Affirmative Discrimination.* Glazer saw American society drifting away from a pattern in which government generally had abstained from forcing assimilation on newcomers or from attempting to establish some kind of parity among different groups. Of course, that was only one historical pattern of pluralism. There were others, in which government participated in enforcing not parity but inequality between individuals of different groups, usually on the basis of color. Glazer now was worried about the growing tendency to make public policy to compensate members of groups for past injustices to their forebears, a principle that "can be extended indefinitely and make for endless trouble." Warning that "the gravest political consequence is undoubtedly the increasing resentment and hostility between groups that is fueled by special benefits for some," Glazer saw a white backlash gaining momentum. "The implications of the new course," he wrote, "are an increasing consciousness of the significance of group membership, an increasing divisiveness on the basis of race, color and national origin, and a spreading resentment among the disfavored groups against the favored groups."

John Higham acknowledged the recent surge of ethnic consciousness in *Send These to Me: Immigrants in Urban America,* but he wrote also of "pluralistic integration," in which pluralism was "contained within a larger conception of social integration." Higham believed that the creation of a "decent multi-ethnic society" was, next to elimination of the threat of nuclear war, highest on the list of world problems requiring urgent attention in the 1970s. Believing that American life does not permit "a rigidity of group boundaries and a fixity of group commitment," Higham nonetheless acknowledged in the last line of his book a concern much like that expressed by Isaacs and Glazer that Americans had a serious problem "in rediscovering what values can bind together a more and more [and here he gave me the title for this book] kaleidoscopic culture."

Three years later, in 1978, one of my favorite journalists, Theodore H. White, in his autobiography, *In Search of History: A Personal Adventure*— a book that somewhat undermined his reputation for positive thinking— concluded that American unity was threatened by the 1965 amendments to the Immigration and Nationality Act (which had opened up to American membership immigrants from all over the world) and by what he called "the new Jurisprudence of Civil Rights," which was "destined to establish new special privileges for American ethnic groups." Like the others, White insisted that "the polyglot peoples of America had no common heritage but only ideas to bind them together," and he worried, somewhat more urgently than Higham, with a tone as pessimistic as Isaacs', that "America would be transformed" into "a gathering of discretely defined and entitled groups, interests and heritages; or whether it would continue to be a nation. . . ." In the last sentence of his book, he wrote that the old political system "was passing away."

Aspects of the old system were passing away, but they were the parts of the system that were based on the domination of whites over blacks (caste pluralism), of whites over Indians (predatory tribal pluralism), and the restrictions on Asian and Mexican immigrants that kept them from full membership in the civic culture (sojourner pluralism). The system of voluntary pluralism based on individual rights protected by the civic culture was not passing. It flourished because the civic culture itself had become stronger and more inclusive.

I could understand why Harold Isaacs spoke of the 1970s as "a time of confused and chaotic passage," and why later when he was asked by the Ford Foundation to do a survey of the American ethnic landscape he found it all "hugger-mugger," as he wrote in a letter to me, a shorthand term for what Higham had called "a multiplication of small audiences, specialized media, local attachments, and partial identities which play into one another in ways we cannot yet understand," but I did not observe nearly as much confusion and chaos as Harold Isaacs saw, even in 1980 when he wrote his letter.

In my work as a founding member of the Congress of Racial Equality, a member of the advisory board of the Commission on Law and Social Action of the American Jewish Congress in the 1960s, a member of the board of directors of the Mexican-American Legal and Education Defense Fund in the 1970s, and as executive director of the staff of the Select Commission on Immigration and Refugee Policy in the 1980s, I observed that the basic patterns of "pluralistic integration" Higham described were intact and probably stronger than they had ever been.

About six months before the work of the select commission was over in 1981, I read Philip Gleason's essay "American Identity and American-ization," prepared for the *Harvard Encyclopedia of American Ethnic Groups*. Gleason, acknowledging that the American ethnic landscape was chang-ing radically, wondered if any of the older theories of pluralism were adequate to deal with the realities of change. "What the new ethnicity and all the talk of pluralism signify," he wrote, "is that the perennial problematic issue of American nationality is taking on a new configura-tion. It is a continuing task to make a reality out of the ideal proposed in the national motto—*e pluribus unum*. We cannot hope to settle the issue definitively, to finish the task once and for all. But we cannot even begin to do justice to the problem as it is posed in our own time unless we grant the same kind of recognition to the imperative of unity that we give to the reality of diversity." Ending on a note of concern, like Hig-ham's, gently expressed, Gleason reiterated the questions put by Isaacs, Glazer, Higham, and White: Could order, community, and unity be dis-covered in America's rapidly changing ethnic landscape?

In this book it is my intention to provide an understanding of the historical patterns of ethnicity and the contemporary American ethnic landscape, which Higham said in 1975 "we cannot yet understand" but which became much more comprehensible during the 1980s. I also hope to promote an understanding of the ways in which the American national political culture has evolved to manage the "hugger-mugger" about which Isaacs wrote, and by setting forth what the *unum* and the *pluribus* owe to each other to encourage clear thinking about such difficult policy ques-tions as illegal immigration, affirmative action, and language. By doing that, perhaps we will be able to build a stronger and more humane multi-ethnic society, one in which individuals are free to express their ethnic traditions and interests within the framework of a civic culture that, para-doxically, makes ethnic diversity a source of unity instead of the divisive-ness against which Isaacs, White, and others warned.

Part One
THE CIVIC CULTURE AND VOLUNTARY PLURALISM

The bosom of America is open to receive not only the Opulent and respectable Stranger, but the oppressed and persecuted of all Nations and Religions; whom we shall welcome to a participation of all our rights and previleges, if by decency and propriety of conduct they appear to merit the enjoyment.
—GEORGE WASHINGTON

They came here—the exile and the stranger, . . . they made a covenant with this land. Conceived in justice, written in liberty, bound in union, it was meant one day to inspire the hopes of all mankind; and it binds us still. If we keep its terms, we shall flourish.
—LYNDON BAINES JOHNSON

Ethnic diversity a nation does not make, and separatist movements are a source of tension in many multiethnic nations: Sikhs in India, Basques in Spain, Tibetans in China, Albanians in Yugoslavia, Shiites in Lebanon, Estonians in the Soviet Union, the French in Canada, and others. In an effort to achieve stability in such societies, arrangements sometimes are made to divide up power, a president for this group, a prime minister for that, so many seats here and there in a process that used to be called *verzuiling* (columnization or pillarization) in The Netherlands, where until recent decades the Dutch divided leadership positions between Catholics and Protestants.

Lebanon, where top positions usually were explicitly divided between Muslims and Christians in the decades following the Second World War, is the most notorious example of the failure of *verzuiling* to achieve stability. In adjacent Israel, which has special schools for Arab children and seats for Arabs in the Knesset (parliament), the Israelis desperately seek ethnic peace. In other multiethnic, multilingual societies, the interests of language groups are balanced, as in Belgium, which has official language regions with linguistic borders, and Switzerland and Canada, with comparable arrangements. In other multiethnic states, nationality regions are recognized (China has so-called "autonomous regions" and the Soviet Union has a Council of Nationalities), although without necessarily yielding significant power to minorities.[1]

Arrangements to share power, whether symbolic or real, describe var-

I

ious systems of pluralism, ways of drawing boundaries between members of one group and another. Each pluralistic system answers the questions: What kind of boundaries? Toward what goals? Enforced by whom? Whatever the formal power-sharing arrangements, one group usually dominates the others in pluralistic societies, as in Cyprus, where Greeks dominated Turks for a long time, or in Turkey, where Turks still oppress Armenians, or in Japan, where Koreans born in that country are regarded officially as foreigners.

Groups often are kept apart by tightly drawn boundaries. Turkish children born in Germany are not thought of as Germans, the children of Italian workers born in Switzerland are not regarded as Swiss, the children of Ghanaians in Nigeria are Ghanaians still. Insiders usually scorn outsiders, as the Chinese Han people have done, calling them *yemanren* (wild people who do not reason), or the Ethiopians, who label Jews in their midst by the pejorative term *falashas* (strangers). Even when insiders do not disparage outsiders they rarely trust them, as in the case of southern Italians, who often are warned in childhood to be wary of the *forestiere* (foreigner or stranger) or the *straniero* (alien) only a village distant from themselves.

The feeling of "we-ness" that insiders share usually is based on similar physical characteristics, language, and religion. When those characteristics are combined with the memory of a shared historical experience (on Passover all Jews recite "when *we* were slaves in Egypt") and founding myths (God told Abraham to create a new nation), the ties that bind— the cement of nationhood—are particularly strong. Such founding myths, accounting for the origins of a nation and explaining its destiny, usually are tribal (based on genealogy or blood), as with the Abraham story, or the tale of Theseus, the mythical Athenian king who defeated the horrible Minotaur of Crete and united twelve small independent states of Attica, making Athens the capital of the new state. The foundation of Rome was attributed to Romulus, son of Mars, the god of war, who, after having been raised with his brother Remus by a she-wolf, conquered the Sabines and built a new city on the Tiber River on the spot where their lives had been saved. Japan, according to its traditional founding myth, was established because a favorite descendant of the Sun Goddess created the Japanese islands and became the first emperor, from whom all other emperors are descended.

Early in its history, spokesmen for the new American nation explained that the U.S. was created by God as an *asylum* in which *liberty, opportunity,* and *reward for achievement* would prosper. This powerful new myth provided an ideological rationalization for the selfish interest Americans had in recruiting European immigrants to claim the land, fight Indians, and later to work in the mines and factories. It became the founding myth of a new political culture, uniting white Americans from different religious and national backgrounds. Belief in the myth motivated Americans to create new political institutions and practices, which Alexis de Tocqueville saw as the basis of American patriotism in the 1830s.

When Tocqueville asked what made the Americans a nation, he answered that American patriotism was not based on ancient customs and traditions as in other countries. Patriotism in the U.S., he wrote, "grows by the exercise of civil rights." What he called the "patriotism of a republic" was based on the premise that it is possible to interest men (and women) in the welfare of their country by making them participants in its government, and by so doing to enlist their enthusiastic loyalty to the national community. He asked, "How does it happen that in the United States, where the inhabitants have only recently immigrated to the land which they now occupy . . . where, in short, the instinctive love of country can scarcely exist; how does it happen that everyone takes as zealous an interest in the affairs of his township, his county, and the whole state as if they were his own? It is because everyone, in his sphere, takes an active part in the government of society."[2]

To this theme Tocqueville returns again and again; it is the core of his interpretation of American civilization. Immigrants and their children claimed the U.S. for their own and became attached to it through the exercise of civil rights. The freedom of Americans to worship, speak, assemble, and petition their government, and their protection under equal laws (for whites only) bound them in a national community even though their political interests often were diverse. Tocqueville maintained that Americans combined in political and civic associations to effect remedies to problems that in aristocratic or monarchical societies they would have to endure. In lobbying for remedies, they learned the arts of working with others. They formed coalitions, made compromises, and extended their connections and knowledge beyond the small circle of relatives and friends with whom they ordinarily dealt. The capacity of Americans to form associations in order to achieve some public good constantly amazed him. Given political freedom, Americans saw the possibility of changing their own lives for the better by altering some public condition. Self-interest and patriotism went hand in hand.

Tocqueville wrote that political life made the love and practice of association more general. It appeared to teach men and women to work together with those "who otherwise would have always lived apart."[3] Instead of dividing groups from each other, politics in the U.S. appeared to have the paradoxical effect of breaking down barriers and rendering Americans more loyal to the national community. He described political associations as "large free schools, where all the members of the community go to learn the general theory of associations."[4] In their political associations, he wrote, Americans "converse, they listen to one another" and work together in all sorts of undertakings. "Thus it is by the enjoyment of a dangerous freedom that the Americans learn the art of rendering the dangers of freedom less formidable."[5] Freedom of association in political matters, he concluded, at least where rights were extensively practiced, "is not so dangerous to public tranquility as is supposed." Indeed, "it may strengthen the state in the end."[6] The only threat to the state that Tocqueville foresaw would be caused by the inequality of blacks, who, in contrast with white immigrants, were generally excluded from the exercise of civil rights.[7]

Other Europeans saw the American political system—none of them called it a culture, let alone a civic culture—as the most distinctive feature of American life and the one that made Americans a nation. John Stuart Mill, who was influenced by Tocqueville's great work (he reviewed it in 1835 and 1840), saw that by encouraging the practice of civic responsibility, Americans, as vestrymen, jurymen, and electors, lifted their ideas and feelings out of a narrow circle. Mill wrote of Tocqueville that he showed how the American was "made to feel that besides the interests which separate him from his fellow citizens, he has interests which connect him with them; that not only the common weal is his weal but that it partly depends upon his exertion."[8] In his classic work *On Representative Government,* Mill observed, "for political life is indeed in America a most valuable school."[9] Almost all European travelers to the United States, he noted, observed that every American is in some sense a patriot. Paraphrasing Tocqueville without acknowledging him in this instance, he continued, "it is from political discussion and collective political action that one whose daily occupations concentrate his interests in a small circle round himself, learns to feel for and with his fellow citizens, and becomes consciously a member of a great community."

Like Tocqueville, Mill pointed out that when some are excluded from the exercise of civil rights they will become either permanent malcontents "or will feel as one whom the general affairs of society do not concern."[10] Without mentioning American slaves, he pointed out that everyone is degraded in an otherwise free society when some persons are not permitted to participate in its deliberations.

Americans were united not just by the political principles of the republic or even the exercise of civil rights, but also by the symbols and rituals that gave emotional significance to their patriotism: speeches about the Constitution and the Declaration of Independence; celebrations on the Fourth of July; the naming of towns, counties, and cities and the writing of songs to honor the apostles of the American myth (Washington, Jefferson, and later Lincoln). Much later, Americans would add ritual incantations (the Pledge of Allegiance, "God Bless America," "My Country 'Tis of Thee," "The Star-Spangled Banner").

Americans were members of a political community that political scientists Gabriel Almond and Sidney Verba labeled a "civic culture" in 1965, a political culture in which "there is a substantial consensus on the legitimacy of political institutions and the direction and content of public policy, a widespread tolerance of a plurality of interests and belief in their reconcilability, and a widely distributed sense of political competence and mutual trust in the citizenry."[11] When Almond and Verba asked respondents in five democratic countries to list the things about their country of which they were most proud, 85 percent of the American respondents mentioned governmental and political institutions, compared to 46 percent in the British sample, 30 percent of the Mexicans, 7 percent of the Germans, and 3 percent of the Italians. Much more than the others, Americans reported that a good citizen is one who actively participates in community affairs.[12]

The civic culture was based essentially—though Almond and Verba did not make the analysis—on three ideas widely held by the founders of the republic, the ideas that constituted the basis of what they called republicanism: first, that ordinary men and women can be trusted to govern themselves through their elected representatives, who are accountable to the people; second, that all who live in the political community (essentially, adult white males at the time) are eligible to participate in public life as equals; and third, that individuals who comport themselves as good citizens of the civic culture are free to differ from each other in religion and in other aspects of their private lives.

That third idea was the basis for a kind of *voluntary* pluralism in which immigrant settlers from Europe and their progeny were free to maintain affection for and loyalty to their ancestral religions and cultures while at the same time claiming an American identity by embracing the founding myths and participating in the political life of the republic. It was a system of pluralism that began, principally, in colonial Pennsylvania, where immigrants of various nationalities and religious backgrounds moved with relative ease into political life. This new invention of Americans—voluntary pluralism—in which individuals were free to express their ancestral affections and sensibilities, to choose to be ethnic, however and whenever they wished or not at all by moving across group boundaries easily, was sanctioned and protected by a unifying civic culture based on the American founding myth, its institutions, heroes, rules, and rhetoric.

The system would not be severely tested as long as most immigrants were English or Scots. The new republic, as George Washington said in his farewell address, was united by "the same religion, manners, habits and political principles."[13] But differences in religion, habits, and manners proliferated after the immigration of large numbers of Germans (many of whom were Catholic), Scandinavians, and Irish Catholics throughout the last sixty years of the nineteenth century, and of eastern and southern Europeans, a majority of whom were Catholic or Jewish, in the decade before and after the turn of the twentieth century. Political principles remained the core of national community. The new immigrants entered a process of ethnic-Americanization through participation in the political system, and, in so doing, established even more clearly the American civic culture as a basis of American unity.

Chapter One

"TRUE AMERICANISM"
The Foundations of the Civic Culture

JACOB De La Motta was only thirty-one but already a distinguished
doctor with a substantial practice in Savannah, Georgia, and other
cities when he was chosen to give the address at the consecration of
a new synagogue in Savannah on July 21, 1820. The physician wondered
at the good fortune of Jews in the new republic, who, for the first time
in history, "stood on the same eminence with other sects." So taken was
La Motta with his own discourse, in which he praised the Constitution
as the "palladium of our rights," that he sent it to ex-presidents Thomas
Jefferson and James Madison, two of the most distinguished living Americans. Within a month, Madison thanked him for the copy of his talk,
pointing out that the experience of the Jews in Savannah showed that
"equal laws, protecting equal rights, are found, as they ought to be presumed, the best guarantee of loyalty and love of country." A few weeks
later, Jefferson wrote that he saw confirmation of two fundamental truths
in La Motta's letter: "that man can govern himself, and that religious
freedom is the most effectual anodyne against religious dissension: the
maxim of civil government being reversed in that of religion, where its
true form is 'divided we stand, united, we fall.'" The sage of Monticello
hoped that Jews would soon be "taking their seats . . . at the board of
government."[1]

Jews, who had been expelled from every major nation of Europe, and
who, when permitted to live in them, were usually denied fundamental
rights, by 1820 had become active in the politics of several communities
in the U.S.[2] Although they came from different national backgrounds
and religious orientations and were scattered throughout the country,
Jews were developing a surer, clearer sense of their relationship to other
Jews in the country—becoming ethnic—while at the same time developing a growing sense of loyalty to the U.S. in a process of ethnic-
Americanization that was first nurtured mainly in colonial Pennsylvania.

Three Ideas About Immigrants and Membership:
Massachusetts, Virginia, and Pennsylvania

The Pennsylvania idea was that all white European settlers were welcome into the colony on terms of equal rights. Fueled by the desire of

early white settlers for additional immigrants to build a nation and generate prosperity, the Pennsylvania idea would become the basis for U.S. immigration and naturalization policy for white Europeans after the founding of the republic. But the Pennsylvania idea was in competition with two other ideas, the first of which gained prominence in colonial Massachusetts, and the second mainly in the Chesapeake Bay colonies of Virginia and Maryland, called here the Virginia idea. To oversimplify: Pennsylvania sought immigrants who would be good citizens regardless of religious background; Massachusetts wanted as members only those who were religiously pure; and Virginia, with its increasing reliance on a plantation economy, wanted workers as cheaply as it could get them, without necessarily welcoming them to membership in the community.

Early Puritan Massachusetts, believing that the success of its settlement would depend upon the fulfillment of its covenant with God, welcomed only those newcomers who accepted the stringent beliefs and practices of that theocratic community (it turned back sixty English Protestant passengers on the ship *Handmaid* because of insufficient testimony as to their character and godliness).[3] Since the Puritan church was an exclusive fellowship restricted to those who convincingly said they had been redeemed by the saving grace of God and who demonstrated their experience in the ways of grace, not everyone who was permitted to settle was admitted to church membership, a prerequisite for participation in the political community.

The Massachusetts approach became influential in the development of a national ideology of Americanism, but it was too restrictive to form a dominant immigration and naturalization policy for the middle and northern colonies, which sought, not an ideal community (to say nothing of a Utopian one), but capital expansion. Since permanent settlers were valuable economic assets, exclusion of immigrants on the basis of religion seemed to make little economic sense. When local settlers or colonial governors tried to maintain religious exclusivity, investors sometimes countermanded them, as in New Netherlands, where Peter Stuyvesant wanted to bar Jews (and Lutherans) but was obliged to accept them by his sponsors. Maryland, with Catholics in power, excluded Jews from membership; but when a Jewish physician, Jacob Lambrozo, was tried for blasphemy in 1658, he was acquitted and permitted to remain in the colony because he was a useful settler.[4] Later, after Protestants took control of Maryland and established the Church of England there, they decided it was practical to permit Catholic churches to remain open in order to obtain additional settlers.[5]

Boston, where the Puritan Edward Johnson warned in his pamphlet *Wonder-Working Providence* (1654) that immigrants would undermine the holy experiment of the Massachusetts Bay Colony, tried to hold to a sectarian basis for civic membership for a long time, but eventually succumbed to the desire for settlers to the point of accepting Jews, after rigidly excluding them throughout the seventeenth century.[6] In 1649, only twelve days after he arrived in Boston with a cargo, Solomon Franco was "warned out" of town and given six shillings a week for up to ten weeks for subsistence until he could get passage to Holland.[7] The much more prominent Roger Williams, Anne Hutchinson, and the Quaker Mary Dyer were among the dissenting Christians who were forced to leave the colony, and some, including Dyer, were executed for trying to stay.

Long after the hanging of heretics had stopped and Protestant dissenters were numerous, the Massachusetts idea of political membership based on religious affiliation continued to be influential. Before the Hebrew scholar Judah Monis was appointed to teach at Harvard College in 1722, he was compelled to convert publicly from Judaism to Congregationalism.[8] Even as late as 1762, Isaac Moses was "warned out" of Boston, although he later became a well-known patriot and a leader in the New York City Chamber of Commerce. But in the same year, Aaron Lopez, a Jewish merchant who had been denied citizenship in Rhode Island on the ground that "no person who does not profess the Christian Religion can be admitted free of the Colony," was given full citizenship in Boston and allowed to strike the phrase "upon the True Faith of a Christian" when signing his oath.[9] Even Massachusetts began to back away from exclusionary principles to accept immigrants.

Only sixty years after Judah Monis converted in order to be accepted at Harvard, another Boston Jew found it quite easy to live proudly as both a Jew and a prominent citizen in the community. Moses Michael Hays, who helped to found the Boston Atheneum and the First National Bank of Boston and who supported the Massachusetts General Hospital and Harvard, observed the Jewish Sabbath, held religious services in his home (there was no synagogue as yet), and obeyed the Jewish commandment to do justice by inviting the poor to his dinner table.[10] Established churches would remain in New England for several years (in New Hampshire until 1817, in Connecticut until 1818, and in Massachusetts until 1833), and for a long time after, many Americans thought of the U.S. as a Protestant nation and many more thought of it as a Christian nation. But the idea that membership in the American polity should be based on belonging to a particular faith was overwhelmed by the desire for immigrants.

Planters in Virginia and Maryland began to recruit laborers to maximize tobacco profits early in the seventeenth century. Wanting workers and not visible saints, Virginians soon began to import indentured servants regardless of their religious backgrounds, laborers who would serve those who paid their transportation for a period of four to seven years after which they would become free. Emigration to the Chesapeake for one hundred years after 1607 was eight times as large as to New England.[11] The idea of procuring servants to do the dirty jobs and be left outside the political community caught on everywhere. Indentured males outnumbered females six to one. Later, Virginia and all of the South, particularly, would build on the idea of importing workers as cheaply as possible by replacing white indentured servants with black slaves.

By paying for a servant's transportation, Virginia planters became entitled to an additional fifty acres of land. The planters greedily took convicts, vagrants, and paupers from England, Scotland, and Ireland to augment their indentured-servant population. But servants could not be kept as servants forever. When they became free they preferred to work for themselves, taking advantage of the cheap public land available in Virginia and elsewhere. Planters tried to ensure a continuing supply of white indentured workers. Between 1658 and 1666, the Virginia Assembly revised the terms of indenture to give themselves and other masters a longer hold on their workers, essentially adding three additional years to the terms of most servants.[12] For those who ran away and were caught the terms of service were increased by twice the length of time they had been gone, and minor misdemeanors were punished severely, often by adding years of service.[13] Even so, efforts to import and control white servants proved more costly than slavery. One way to counter the restlessness and rebelliousness of freed poor whites was to buy black slaves and at the same time link the hopes of poor whites for a better life to a social, economic, and political system based largely on racism. By the early 1640s, Virginia courts recognized black men and women and their unborn progeny as property. By the 1660s, there were probably more than a thousand slaves in Virginia, at the bottom of a social system, above them a much larger body of white servants and a vast, growing population of freedmen who had finished their terms of service entitled to set up households. Slavery was also a more efficient way of controlling labor; planters "converted to slavery simply by buying slaves instead of servants."[14] Less than 8 percent of the Chesapeake population were black slaves in 1680, but by 1710 25 percent.[15]

The slave system grew everywhere in the colonies, less in Pennsylvania and New England than elsewhere, but especially in the South. A 1680 act in Virginia which called for thirty lashes on the bare back of any Negro or slave who lifted a hand in opposition against any Christian allowed white servants as well as masters and mistresses to bully slaves without fear of retaliation.[16] In 1691, harsh punishment was prescribed for miscegenation between any white man or woman and a Negro, mulatto, or

Indian.[17] In 1705, a new law required masters to give servants ten bushels of Indian corn, thirty shillings of money, and a well-fixed musket at the conclusion of their term and, best of all, fifty acres of land.[18]

Pennsylvania, following the leadership of William Penn in 1681, had by the early eighteenth century established a policy of encouraging immigration of Europeans regardless of their religious background and of admitting them to membership in the civic life of the colony on roughly equal terms with native-born Pennsylvanians. As a result, Pennsylvania became home to Scotch-Irish Presbyterians, Baptists and Presbyterians from Wales, and a variety of German Pietists. German immigrants, particularly, provided a linguistically and culturally diverse population. By the mid-eighteenth century considerable tension existed between Germans and English-speaking groups and between Germans and Scotch-Irish. The colony, in response, instructed its agents to sell no more land to Scotch-Irishmen in the predominantly German counties of Lancaster and York and to offer money to those who were already there if they would move to the Cumberland Valley.[19]

Of the other colonies, New York was most like Pennsylvania in its cultural diversity. Founded by the Dutch, it had had a substantial number of non-English speakers from the beginning. It was not unusual for mid-eighteenth-century Anglo-American politicians in New York to complain that the Hollanders spoke Dutch in public, or that they were clannish and lacked patriotism. Cadwallader Colden, a Scottish-born counselor to the governor, spoke angrily of "dutch boors grossly ignorant and rude who could neither write nor read nor speak English."[20] But Colden, who well understood the need for new settlers, particularly if they were English, warned late in 1761, after he had become lieutenant governor, that if foreigners were made uncomfortable in New York by a difficult naturalization process, they could go easily to other colonies to settle and improve the lands there.[21] The earlier Colden had wanted newcomers to be "like us." The later Colden wanted newcomers to settle in New York whether or not they were "like us." Several leading political figures in Pennsylvania, including Benjamin Franklin, felt similar antipathy to outsiders. Where Colden saw "dutch boors," Franklin complained of "Palatine Boors,"[22] the charge of boorishness based partly on Germans' resistance to speaking English. By 1753 two of the six printing houses run by Germans in Pennsylvania published in English and two partly in English. Franklin was furious that the remaining two continued to publish only in German. "Why should Pennsylvania," he asked, "founded by the English, become a colony of *aliens,* [italics his] who will shortly be so numerous as to Germanize us instead of Anglifying them, and will never adopt our Language or Customs any more than they can acquire our complexion?"²³ Franklin eventually overcame his fears of "German boors" and "superstitious Papists," too.²⁴ Like New York, Pennsylvania wanted settlers for the backcountry.

Unskilled laborers and artisans came not just from Germany but mostly from England, the Scottish highlands, and Ireland (nearly all Protestants). Rampant land speculation drew families—sometimes of substance—not only the single men who came to labor.²⁵ By the time of the Revolution, most of the children and grandchildren of Dutch, French, German, and Swedish immigrants in the colonies spoke English and were otherwise indistinguishable from the children and grandchildren of English settlers, although in Albany, where the Dutch predominated, it was difficult to assemble an English-speaking jury, and several counties in Pennsylvania were overwhelmingly German-speaking.²⁶ Hostility toward speakers of Dutch and German and toward the English-speaking Scotch-Irish, the newest large immigrant group, was widespread, but none of the new-comers were kept from easy naturalization or from participating in pol-itics on roughly equal terms with the native-born. That such persons could be good citizens even though they were Scotch-Irish Presbyterians, French Huguenots, German Pietists, or English Quakers had become a commonly accepted idea.

Can Immigrants Learn New Republican Principles?

It was one thing to welcome immigrants to labor. It was quite another to welcome them as citizens. Even Thomas Jefferson wondered shortly after the Revolution if the new nation could accept large numbers of immigrants and maintain its republican principles. But the Pennsylvania ideal of equal rights for white newcomers had no more eloquent apostles than George Mason, Thomas Paine, and Thomas Jefferson, all of whom came from Virginia, a state that held 40 percent of the slaves in America. Calling the principles that underlie the Declaration of Independence "an expression of the American mind," "the genuine effusion of the soul of our country," Jefferson was nonetheless uncertain that immigrants could learn those principles or practice them easily.²⁷ "Our principles," he wrote in 1781, "are more peculiar than those of any other in the universe," being based on "a composition of the freest principles of the English Consti-tution, with others derived from natural right and natural reason." Against these, "nothing can be more opposed than the maxims of abso-lute monarchies. Yet, from such, we are to expect the greatest number of emigrants."

To underscore his concern about immigration as a potentially royalist or otherwise disruptive force, he wrote of immigrants that "they will bring with them the principles of the governments they leave, imbibed in their early youth; or, if able to throw them off, it will be in exchange for an unbounded licentiousness . . . these principles, with their language, they will transmit to their children. In proportion to their numbers, they will share with us the legislation. They will infuse into it their spirit, warp and bias its directions, and render it a heterogeneous, incoherent, distracted mass."

Issuing a challenge for generations to come, Jefferson asked, "May not our government be more homogeneous, more peaceful, more durable," without large-scale immigration? He queried further, "Suppose twenty million of republican Americans [were] thrown all of a sudden into France, what would be the condition of that kingdom? If it would be more turbulent, less happy, less strong, we may believe that the addition of a half million of foreigners to our present numbers would produce a similar effect here."[28] While skeptical about taking vigorous measures to speed immigration, Jefferson did not oppose it, however, and he later became a champion of easy naturalization, partly for partisan reasons, but also because as the nation expanded it needed more settlers.

Capitalism and territorial expansion were the driving forces behind a wide-open immigration policy. But Americans continued to worry about the potentially divisive effects of immigration. In the early seventeenth century, Boston's John Winthrop had been concerned about religious purity; in mid-eighteenth-century Pennsylvania, Franklin was concerned about linguistic and cultural unity; in 1781, Jefferson's apprehension about immigration was based on a different idea of membership, that Americans were united by a common set of political beliefs. But how could one test the newcomers for political ideology?

Many states required some sign of commitment to the political principles on which the new experiment in self-government depended before admitting immigrants as members of the polity. New York, in language close to that used later in the naturalization law of the federal government, required that any settler who wished to become a citizen "abjure and renounce all allegiance and subjection to all and every foreign king, prince, potentate and state, in all matters ecclesiastical as well as civil."[29] Georgia required an applicant for citizenship (all male) to produce from a circuit or county court judge where he had last resided a certificate verifying "his . . . Attachment to the liberties or Independence of the United States of America, and also of . . . Honesty, Probity and Industry."[30] Some states required signs of commitment beyond an oath of allegiance renouncing old and accepting new political principles before they gave newcomers full membership. Virginia naturalized all white persons who had lived in the state for two years and had "evinced a permanent attachment to the state, by having intermarried with a citizen of the Commonwealth, or a citizen of any other of the United States, or purchased lands to the value of one hundred pounds therein."[31]

Pennsylvania allowed every male foreign settler of good character who took an oath of allegiance to acquire land or other real estate and after a year to become a citizen entitled to all of the rights of natural-born subjects, "except that he shall not be capable of being elected a representative until after two years of residence."[32] Other states made the privileges of naturalized citizens somewhat less than those for the native-born. A white male in South Carolina who resided in the state one year and swore allegiance to it could become a citizen and obtain the privilege of voting for the legislature or the city corporation of Charlestown, but was not eligible for high office unless authorized by a special act of the legislature. In Georgia, a new citizen could not vote for the legislature or hold any office of trust until the completion of a seven-year residence.[33] But these limitations, and others imposed on the rights of Jews to vote in Maryland or to hold office in New Hampshire, were exceptions to the general rule. In contrast to England, where only Protestants who took the sacraments in the Church of England were eligible for naturalization, white male immigrants regardless of their religious affiliation were placed on a clear, fast track to full membership in nearly all of the states of the new nation by the 1830s.

The issues of immigration and naturalization—those crucial questions of membership—were little discussed at the constitutional convention, but such discussion as there was took place within the context of Jefferson's concern for inviting as members only those who believed in the American idea of self-government and who were capable of practicing it. Although his friend James Madison recognized that there might be a danger in having members who had "foreign predilections," he trusted that the general electorate would prevent abuses and he thought it wise "to invite foreigners of merit and republican principles." But there was no certain way to tell which foreigners held republican principles. It was well to argue as Madison did that the new government should be as welcoming as possible to those who "love liberty and wish to partake in its blessings," but what test could be established before issuing the invitation? Franklin, having overcome his earlier doubts about immigration, thought it sufficient proof of fealty to republican ideals and principles of government if individuals had left the countries of their birth and had chosen to live in the new nation.[34] Another Pennsylvanian, Scotland-born James Wilson, whom President Washington would later appoint to the U.S. Supreme Court, referred to the experience of Pennsylvania, where most of the line officers during the Revolution had been foreigners, and noted his own and the foreign birth of other delegates to prove that newcomers could be as devoted to the well-being of a republic as anyone born in the United States.[35]

Some leaders believed that care should be taken to prepare newcomers by extending the waiting period for naturalization and/or holding office. George Mason, in arguing that no male person be qualified for election to the House of Representatives until he had been a citizen for seven years, was afraid that a rich foreign nation such as Great Britain might send over hostile or at least monarchical persons to infiltrate the legislature. Gouverneur Morris argued that the requirement for admission for election to the Senate should be fourteen years, saying that there are degrees of hospitality one ought to give the stranger. Morris was afraid that newcomers would retain attachment to the interests of the countries from which they emigrated, and engage in what much later would be called ethnic lobbying. "Admit a Frenchman into your Senate," he said, "and he will study to increase the commerce of France."[36]

Eventually, a residency requirement of seven years was established for election to the House, with an additional two years for the Senate (on the ground that the upper chamber has a direct responsibility in foreign affairs and two more years would provide even more time to wean immigrants from their foreign loyalties). The only other distinctions made in the Constitution between native-born and naturalized citizens was that the newcomers would not be eligible for the presidency. The basic questions of a waiting period and other requirements for naturalization itself were not included in the Constitution but were left for Congress to establish in a uniform rule of naturalization in 1790.

When Congress debated the issue no one challenged the proposal to restrict naturalization to white persons, and nothing was said about establishing religious, cultural, or linguistic tests for citizenship, making the terms of membership for whites unprecedentedly liberal, while excluding dark-skinned persons altogether. The argument over the length of the period of residency required before being eligible for citizenship was between a short period of one or two years versus none at all. One advocate of no waiting period, a congressman from Virginia, maintained, "We shall be inconsistent with ourselves, if, after boasting of having opened an asylum for the oppressed of all nations . . . we make the terms of admission to the full enjoyment of that asylum so hard as is now proposed. It is nothing to us, whether Jews or Roman Catholics settle amongst us; whether subjects or kings, or citizens of free states wish to reside in the United States, they will find it their interest to be good citizens."[37]

No one in the debate quarreled openly with the idea that Jews or Roman Catholics might make good citizens. Although several states required officeholders to be Christians, no one pressed that position on the convention. Even liberal Pennsylvania required officeholders to swear that they believed in the divine inspiration of the Old and New Testaments, but there would be no such test for federal officeholders. Religious affiliation was not to be the criterion either for holding office or for becoming citizens in the new republic. But several congressmen wanted to make sure that whatever religious beliefs newcomers might profess, they had sufficient time to learn the political principles of the republic before becoming naturalized citizens. Thomas Hartley of Pennsylvania thought that admission to citizenship should be delayed long enough for immigrants to acquire a "firm attachment to the government." Michael Stone of Maryland wanted a term of residence prior to naturalization long enough to guarantee that aliens would "have acquired a taste for this kind of government."[38]

On the other side were those who thought any period of residence unnecessary. Even two years was too long for Senator William Maclay of Pennsylvania, who contrasted his confidence that immigrants would become Americans easily with the more conservative view of New Englanders. Maclay, forgetting the widespread enmity of Pennsylvania's Anglo-Americans toward German immigrants only a few decades earlier, said that "we Pennsylvanians act as if we believed that God made of one blood all families of the earth; but the eastern people seem to think that he made none but New England folks . . . these are the men who affect the greatest fear of being contaminated with foreign manners, customs or vices."[39]

The Pennsylvania Approach Prevails: Equal Rights Regardless of Religion or Nationality

The Pennsylvania approach to procuring worker-citizens prevailed, as the final passage of the 1790 act put newcomers on a swift and unobstructed single path to what amounted to virtually full citizenship by establishing a residence period of two years in the U.S. prior to admission as a citizen (one year in the state where the applicant resided) and proof that "he is a person of good character" who will "support the Constitution of the United States."[40] But the Virginia idea of maintaining a noncitizen labor force also was continued. There would be no entry into the political community by persons of color unless states themselves allowed native-born free blacks to participate.

As immigrants continued to arrive, new arguments were generated about their ability to learn quickly and practice effectively the art of self-government. German Pietists fleeing forced military service, aristocratic French escaping revolutionaries in France, French planters running from

the black revolution in Santa Domingo, and Irish men and women escaping from poverty and English domination each had their critics. Although some were disliked because of differences in language, religion,
or cultural customs, the arguments about immigration and naturalization
again usually were couched in Jeffersonian terms. How capable were the
new immigrants of self-government, it was asked again in 1795 when the
issue of naturalization was debated in Congress for the second time.
Federalist leaders, concerned because most of the newcomers were voting
for the Jeffersonians, had a simple partisan reason for desiring a longer
residency requirement prior to eligibility for naturalization. Many also
clung to the Massachusetts idea that civic membership should be based,
as in other societies, on a close affinity of religious and cultural background to those who already were citizens so as to guarantee a national
unity of values and sensibilities. Senator Maclay was correct in accusing
most New England Federalist leaders of wanting only immigrants who
were linguistically, culturally, and religiously like themselves. The New
Englanders tended to think of themselves as charter members, the original
Anglo-Americans, but when Thomas Sedgewick of Massachusetts argued
for a longer residency requirement, he did not do so on the basis of the
old Puritan idea of religious and cultural exclusivity, but that the newcomers, having been subjects of "despotic, monarchical and aristocratical"
governments would not be qualified "to participate in administering the
sovereignty of our country . . . as soon as they set foot on American
ground," an argument expressed by Jefferson fourteen years earlier.[41]

By 1795, Jefferson and his followers had totally repudiated the charter
member mentality, tending to accept the Pennsylvania view that European
immigrants could learn to become good citizens regardless of their religious or national backgrounds once they came under the influence of the
American environment. Jeffersonians wanted to make certain that immigrants with aristocratic backgrounds would convert to the political
ideology of republicanism before admitting them to citizenship, and they
pushed through a naturalization bill that required any applicant to "make
an express renunciation of his title or order of nobility," comparable to
a stipulation in the old New York statute. It was a measure necessary,
argued William B. Giles of Virginia, to keep aristocrats from subverting
republican government.

Some congressmen, though averse to test oaths, also were concerned
that fugitive nobility would come to the United States in such numbers
as to have undue influence on American politics, and, therefore, Congress
accepted James Madison's position that "when crowds of them [nobility]
come here, they should be forced to renounce everything contrary to the
spirit of the Constitution." In its final version, the bill specified that an
alien at the time of application for citizenship must "absolutely and en-

tirely renounce and abjure all allegiance and fidelity to every foreign prince, potentate, state or sovereignty whatever, and particularly by name, the prince, potentate, state or sovereignty, whereof before he was a citizen or subject."[42]

The Jeffersonians won on the issue of the renunciation of titles, but the Federalists made some headway on lengthening the residency requirement from two to five years in the U.S. while conceding a one-year residency in a state or territory. Although many Anglo-American congressmen may have found the German and Scotch-Irish newcomers distasteful, they explained their call for a longer waiting period in terms of ideology. Samuel Smith, a Maryland Federalist, for example, argued that aliens would need time to acquire "just ideas of our Constitution and the excellence of our institutions before they were admitted to the rights of a citizen."[43] For Federalists, generally, the fear of foreigners remained strong, not just because they usually voted for the opposition candidates but also because many looked, talked, and worshiped differently from the Yankees.

When the Federalists, whose leadership came from New England, took firm control over both executive and legislative branches of the federal government in 1798, they capitalized on growing anti-alien feeling as a result of the so-called "XYZ Affair," which implicated the French in an attempt to bribe American commissioners sent to Paris to negotiate a treaty. Congress quickly pushed through a new naturalization act extending the time necessary for a foreigner to become a citizen from five to fourteen years. An Alien Act, also of 1798, required all foreigners to register with the federal government and allowed the president to deport without trial any alien whom he considered "dangerous to the peace and safety of the United States."[44] Although never enforced, the Alien Act was considered a hostile measure by many Scotch-Irish, Irish, and German immigrants, most of whom, particularly those in the West, already were unsympathetic to the conservative policies of President John Adams.

Only four years later, with the Jeffersonians back in control, the residency requirement was changed again to five years; it has never been altered since. But the Federalists continued to sputter against immigration. Meeting at its Hartford convention in 1812, the party passed a resolution urging a constitutional amendment to bar naturalized citizens from elective and civil office. Although the economic imperatives of nation building made it foolish to cut back on incentives for immigration, the Federalists hoped that by lengthening the time required for naturalization from five years to a much longer period and by restricting the privileges of naturalized citizens they could weaken their increasingly powerful political opponents.

Two years later, furious that the opposition party had made it easy for naturalized foreigners to hold "places of trust, honor or profit" in the government, Federalists cloaked their basic xenophobic feelings and political frustration in the language of republican ideology. By giving jobs to the immigrants, the Federalists charged that the party of Jefferson had provided "an inducement to the malcontent subjects of the Old World to come to these States in quest of executive patronage, and to repay it by an abject devotion to executive measures."[45] The Federalist solution— that no naturalized citizen should be eligible to become a member of the Senate or the House of Representatives or be permitted to hold any civil office in the federal government—was buried as inimical to the overwhelming American urge for expansion, and the Federalist party soon died.

The Ethnic-Americanization of the Germans

The concern of Jefferson and other republican ideologues was understandable, since most of them lived in a world of Anglo-Americans. The debates on immigration and naturalization policy were not informed by the opinions of immigrants, as such debates would be in the twentieth century. Few of the founding fathers were immigrants. James Wilson, a major author of Article Two of the Constitution, was born in Scotland; Alexander Hamilton was born in the West Indies; the second secretary of the treasury, Albert Gallatin, emigrated from Switzerland. More than 95 percent of the leaders of the Revolution, signers of the Declaration of Independence, and authors of the Constitution had English Protestant backgrounds. Not one signer belonged to the largest non-English-speaking immigrant-ethnic group, the Germans. John Jay wrote in the Federalist Papers that "Providence has been pleased to give this one connected country to one united people—a people descended from the same ancestors," even though his own paternal grandfather had been a French Huguenot immigrant and he was Dutch on his mother's side.[46] Neither he, Madison, nor Hamilton had anything to say about the German-speaking communities in the Federalist Papers. Jay had exaggerated the cultural unity of Americans probably in order to buttress his argument for the creation of a national government.

New immigration was slight in the first twenty years of the republic, and Dutch and German—the two most widely used foreign languages— became local curiosities in some areas and died out in others. In the churches, American-born ministers were replacing those from abroad and were introducing English in place of German or Dutch in services, although some Pennsylvania German churches resisted the trend, as they do even now. One looked in vain in Tocqueville's discussions on the press, political associations, the unlimited power of the majority, language and

literature, and public associations for any mention of nationality influences or what would later be called ethnicity. But if Tocqueville had been
German, or if he had returned fifteen years later, he could hardly have
avoided it.[47]

German immigrants and their children, more than any other group,
provided a large-scale early example of the process of ethnic-Americanization, in which ancestral loyalties (religious, linguistic, and cultural) are
changed (and in some ways strengthened) to American circumstances
even as immigrants and their children embrace American political ideals
and participate in American political institutions. More than 50,000 immigrants arrived annually beginning in 1832, the year of Tocqueville's visit,
with the exceptions of 1835 and 1838. In the 1840s, a total of 1,713,251
immigrant arrivals were reported, a large majority of them either Irish or
German. Some Germans remained separate from the larger society, as do
many immigrants from other countries today. In the 1980s, the Hutterite
Brethren, with about six thousand members, the largest Christian communal group, continued to speak German even though they were fluent
in English. It was their strong religious commitment and not their German nationalism that defined their social system and kept them from
social and political assimilation. But the German flavor of the Hutterite
colonies, principally in South Dakota and Montana, was unmistakable,
even though the largest group of immigrants came to South Dakota more
than one hundred years ago.[48]

The Old Order Amish Mennonites, about eighty thousand of whom
lived in twenty states in the 1980s (mainly Pennsylvania, Ohio, and Indiana), kept largely to themselves. With other Germans, they began to
settle in Pennsylvania from 1727 to 1790; a second wave came after 1815 to
Ohio, New York, Indiana, and Illinois. The Amish formed unique farming communities and German enclaves in the U.S. for two and a half
centuries, refraining not only from participation in American politics,
but, under the strict rules of their church, from modern technology and
conveniences.[49] Other German pietistic communal settlements in Harmony (1805) and Economy (1825), Pennsylvania, Zoar, Ohio (1817), and
Amana, Iowa (1843),[50] disappeared. The vast majority of German settlers
in the second quarter of the nineteenth century were not religious pietists
at all. They wanted, not to live entirely apart from American society, but
to be Germans and Americans, too.

Thousands of white European immigrants united around republican
principles, just as Jefferson had hoped they would but feared they might
not. Tocqueville saw that immigrants quickly claimed the principles of
republican government as their own, sharing in the cult of the glorious
Fourth of July (the Declaration of Independence was read aloud on village
greens and main streets) and the worship of "god-like Washington,"

whose birthday was made a national holiday in 1799 and was, like the Fourth of July, an occasion for teachers and preachers to talk about the virtues of American liberty and opportunity.[51] Without using the term, Tocqueville described the civic culture as a unifying set of principles of and practices in government. "It is possible to conceive the surprising liberty that the Americans enjoy," he wrote, and "some idea likewise may be formed of their extreme equality; but the political activity that pervades the United States must be seen to be understood."

No sooner do you set foot upon American ground than you are stunned by a kind of tumult; a confused clamor is heard on every side, and a thousand simultaneous voices demand the satisfaction of their social wants. Everything is in motion around you; here the people of one quarter of a town are met to decide upon the building of a church; there the election of a representative is going on; a little farther, the delegates of a district are hastening to the town in order to consult upon some local improvements; in another place, the laborers of a village quit their plows to deliberate on the project of a road or a public school. Meetings are called for the sole purpose of declaring their disapprobation of the conduct of government; while in other assemblies, citizens salute the authorities of the day as the fathers of their country.[52]

Tocqueville discovered that what distinguished the American national spirit, character, and identity was not sectarian religion or ancestry but a culture of politics. The Americans were not a Protestant nation in the same sense that the French were a Catholic nation, or the Germans a folk. The unifying culture of the U.S. was not religious or racial but political.

One might expect an immigrant from England, someone whose language and political institutions were not dissimilar from those of the Americans, to grasp the idea of the civic culture, as did Frances Wright, a naturalized citizen, who said, "*They* are Americans who, having complied with the Constitutional regulations of the United States . . . wed the principles of America's Declaration to their hearts and render the duties of American citizens practically in their lives."[53] Thousands of Germans sought to establish a new Germany in the American West, but most of them, and especially their children, became German-Americans who embraced and practiced the civic culture.

Between 1850 and 1900, the Germans, who settled principally on farms in the north central and middle Atlantic states, were never less than a quarter of all foreign-born,[54] and during the First World War, when the principal enemy of the U.S. was Germany, they were the largest first-generation immigrant group. At the advent of the Second World War, again with Germany the enemy, there were more first- and second-generation Americans of German origin than of any other nationality.[55] But by then, the vast majority of German-Americans were so assimilated that they were indistinguishable from the descendants of most English immigrants, except perhaps for their names, as in the case of two of the best known battle commanders, Admiral Chester W. Nimitz and General Dwight D. Eisenhower.

A German visitor, Francis J. Grund, who came from Bohemia in the early 1820s, wrote extensively on the process of ethnic-Americanization only three years after Tocqueville had written on democracy in America.[56] He saw that Germans wanted to retain their ties to the German culture, observing that "there are now villages in the states of Pennsylvania and Ohio, and even in the new state of Illinois, where no other language is spoken" but German.[57] He noted that the thousands of immigrants coming annually did not disperse and mix with the Anglo-Americans, "but increased the settlements which are already established by their countrymen, or settle in their immediate neighborhood." The Germans, Grund noted, "hardly feel that they are strangers in the land of their adoption," because they developed the habit "of remaining together, and settling whole townships or villages," making "their exile less painful" and enabling them "to transfer a part of their own country to the vast solitudes of the New World."[58]

The newcomers "find friends, relatives," Grund said, and establish social lives together based on newspapers, churches, schools, food, and the celebration of holidays. Having a substantial number of educated immigrants among them, most Germans lived within largely self-contained ethnic communities. Grund wrote that the newcomers might find that "their officers of justice will be Germans; their physicians and—if they should be so unfortunate as to need them—their lawyers. It will appear to them as if a portion of the land of their fathers had, by some magic, been transplanted to the New World."[59]

Grund wrote about the Germans as if they had come from a common background in the Old Country. Actually, they were divided between Protestants and Catholics, spoke different dialects, and had different regional and political loyalties, but after a short time in the U.S. they went through a process of reconfiguration of their ancestral identity. Immigrants of different backgrounds found it was to their advantage to establish a new identity as ethnic-Americans, although the term obviously had not been invented. The process of reconfiguring their ancestral identity was one other groups would go through, too, including various Filipino and Chinese dialect groups, Italian *paisani,* and Jews from many national backgrounds. For all of them, the reconfiguration of identity became and still is a mechanism for bridging differences and enlarging common interests and habits. It was and is also a way of gaining protection against the surprises and dangers of the new environment, and of making claims within it.

The civic culture, with its principles of separation of church and state and the right of free speech and assembly, facilitated and protected the expression of ancestral cultural values and sensibilities and, in so doing, sanctioned the system of voluntary pluralism by which ethnic groups could mobilize their economic and political interests. In the cities, they formed workers' associations, district and regional societies, fraternal orders, such as German-speaking lodges of the Masons, and Turnvereine (physical culture societies). German debating societies, amateur theatrical groups, and singing societies appeared in the 1830s and 1840s. Pre-Lenten carnivals, outdoor folk fests, and annual German Day celebrations became common. Summer beer gardens and German taverns became gathering places. By 1860, there was approximately one German tavern for every thirty German households in Milwaukee.[60] The German churches and their parochial schools reflected the intention of Germans to remain true to their ancestral culture, and provided a basis for the establishment of the *central-verein* in 1855 as a national union of parish mutual benefit associations.[61]

Economic Self-Interest and Patriotism

The French immigrant Crèvecoeur wrote about the relationship of economic opportunity to national patriotism in the early 1770s, saying that newcomers "ought . . . to love this country much better than that wherein either he or his forefathers were born," because "here the rewards of his industry follow with equal steps the progress of his labour; his labour is founded on the basis of nature, *self interest*. . . . From involuntary idleness, servile dependence, penury, and useless labour, he has passed to toils of a very different nature, *rewarded* by *ample substance*. [italics mine]—This is an American."[62]

Most published letters from English and German and Scandinavian immigrants echoed that theme, and their individual economic success in the new land understandably promoted their love for it. Perhaps the immigrants who were disappointed in the new land did not write as often as those who were pleased. Probably as many as one-third of all immigrants went back to their homelands. Loneliness and illness were common. So was hostility from others. But many who remained told a story of opportunity and reward, as one English immigrant in Virginia did in 1818, writing, "If a man be industrious and steady, he reaps the fruit of his own labor."[63] From Paterson, New Jersey, came an immigrant's report, "to us, who have long been half-starved in England, it appears like a continual feast . . . no fawning, cringing adulation here: the squire and the mechanic converse as familiarly as weavers do in England. We call no man master here."[64] An immigrant writing from Pennsylvania to his brothers and his sisters instructed them that "every industrious farmer may become a freeholder of the United States by paying eighty dollars, being the first installment for a quarter of a section of land; and though he has not a shilling left, he may easily gain as much off the land as will pay the other installments, before they become due. The land being his own, there is no limit to his prosperity; no proud tyrant can lord it over him."[65] Another man from Philadelphia told his family, "I can by my own labor (mind you) procure all the good that this world affords in eating, drinking or clothing; and not work above ten hours a day. For heaven's sake, Father, do come and end your days in a country, where the labouring bee enjoys the honey which he collects."[66] A young man from a small town in Illinois wrote his mother, "I now sit down in a country, where fortune is within my reach. I suffered a little for want of money, but I now look beyond all that. . . . Lands such as you never saw, which you may use for three years, and then it wants no manure. I have purchased one hundred and sixty acres on a fine level plain."[67]

German immigrants wrote home in the same vein. One of them, writing in 1820, said, "No family is so poor that it does not have at least two horses . . . the farmer lives in a situation which is infinitely superior to that of the German farmer of the same property."[68] A woman in Germantown, Pennsylvania, wrote her mother, "I wish you were all as well off as we are now: there is no want of meat and drink here."[69] Germans and other immigrants and their children were the beneficiaries of preemption, a well-established custom by 1800, which consisted of establishing a prior claim on public land by living on it and improving it, and by the Pre-emption Act of 1841, which for fifty years made it possible for any alien intending to become a citizen to preempt a 160-acre farm from the public domain, live on it, and work it, and then buy it at a price no higher than that set at public auction without the trouble of having to go to auction.

Other land acts followed, which made many Germans, among others, capitalists quickly. To bring settlers to Oregon and New Mexico, Congress passed the Donation Act in 1850 to give each citizen settler 320 acres (double the usual), 640 acres to married couples. Wanting to build four transcontinental railroads after the Civil War, the government made huge land grants to investors, who advertised in Europe for settlers to live alongside the line; and during the war, in 1862, Congress passed the Homestead Act to give 160 acres anywhere in the public domain to any citizen or intended citizen who would farm the land for five years. Nothing gave immigrants a stake in American society so quickly as the ownership of land, and German and Scandinavian immigrant beneficiaries of such largess might have asked, as John Fisher, the English immigrant in Michigan did, "is not this a land in which one may be proud to be received as a citicen? . . . Is this not a land in which one may be happy to fix one's destany?"[70]

Francis Grund noted that Germans depended upon Germans for their "principal means of support."[71] Independently owned farms constituted classic examples of family-capitalist organization, usually selling to other Germans what they could not use for themselves. Germans in the cities tended to extend their economic activities with other Germans in a system of ethnic networking that became common for all major immigrant groups in the nineteenth and twentieth centuries. It was not difficult for Germans to succeed in trade, Grund found, because their countrymen preferred to patronize them over others. Although a relatively high proportion of German immigrants became farmers, a majority found work in cities, where families, cousins, and *landsmen* from the same town or region could work together in taverns and other food-related business such as baking, butchering, brewing and distilling. Other services were provided within the German community by restaurant keepers, barbers, dairymen, tailors, and a small number of professionals, such as musicians, teachers, and doctors.

As was true for the vast majority of workers in all large immigrant groups, the work was extremely hard, particularly for unskilled laborers in St. Louis or Detroit (the Irish absorbed most unskilled jobs in New York and Boston), and Germans, especially after the Civil War, formed German trade unions and took a large role in the International Working Men's Association in America, established in 1869 as the branch of the first Communist international. But the vast majority of Germans and their children, like other immigrants, were capitalists par excellence, working, saving, investing as individuals and families, and using ethnic connections to help build a business, provide a service, or supply a need. Even industrial workers, skilled or unskilled, accepted the general American view that economic opportunities would be better for their children.[72]

Grund emphasized economic opportunity in explaining the obvious affection and loyalty that many Germans quickly gave to the U.S. when he asked rhetorically, "what Unites the citizens of a country more effectually than their common stakes of rights and property?"[73] By holding out to all persons (meaning mainly white males) "without distinction of birth of parentage" the hope of acquiring property, the nation bound its newcomers to the polity. But Grund wrote much more about rights than economic opportunity. He was, like Tocqueville, fascinated by the American preoccupation with politics. He also saw the civic culture as pervasive. "Every town and village in America has its peculiar republican government, based on the principle of election, and is, within its own sphere, as free and independent as a sovereign state. . . . Freedom takes its root at home, in the native village or town of an American. . . . In every place, in every walk of life, an American finds some rallying point or centre of political attachment."[74] "The Americans," wrote the German immigrant, "present the singular spectacle of a people united together by no other ties than those of excellent laws and equal justice."[75]

John Quincy Adams wrote to a German baron that newcomers who "cast off the European skin, never to resume it" can expect as citizens "equal rights with those of the natives of the country."[76] Whatever Adams meant by casting off the European skin, he said nothing about abandoning the German language or giving up beer-drinking, or modifying the German Christmas (which soon became popular in America), or about converting from Lutheranism to Congregationalism. Voluntary pluralism was not only compatible with patriotism but reinforced it, as in the case of Dr. Jacob De La Motta, who extolled the Constitution and republican principles—in effect, the civic culture—because it guaranteed his freedom to be a Jew.

In the process of ethnic-Americanization, the Germans, as other immigrant groups would also do, not only created ethnic organizations based on American models, such as the volunteer fire militia companies and Masonic lodges, they also joined patriotic fraternal associations that included non-Germans, such as the Improved Order of Redmen, which preached "an ultra-patriotic Americanism connected with the republican iconography of the American Revolution."[77] Like other self-consciously Americanist organizations, the Improved Order of Redmen used the name and symbols of Indians, an ugly travesty from an Indian point of view, as a way by which immigrants could quickly claim common ground with other whites who had come before them.

An offshoot of an earlier organization, the order, with about nineteen tribes in Maryland, Virginia, the District of Columbia, Delaware, and Pennsylvania, and about 1,300 members by 1844–1845, had by midcentury grown to forty-five tribes and 3,200 members. Americanist in rhetoric and symbol, it concentrated mainly on social and fraternal activities, paying benefits to members, widows, and orphans. It had a disproportionate number of German-American leaders, and by June 1850 seven of the sixteen active chapters in Philadelphia were composed of German-Americans, six of which conducted their affairs in German.[78] Eventually, the German chapters split off to create their own Order of Redmen, a fraternity of German-Americans, because they resented efforts on the part of the Great Council to restrict the use of German and to dampen the enthusiasm of German-Americans for meeting in taverns and accompanying funeral processions with brass band music.[79]

The period 1830–1860 saw the emergence of ethnic-American leaders, persons tied by affection and culture to other immigrants and their children but who also participated broadly in American civic and political life. Victor Greene has identified several such immigrant leaders among the Germans. In Charleston, South Carolina, Johann Andreas Wagener became a real estate agent for Germans seeking property and a notary public to those needing official interpretation.[80] He took the lead in building the Charleston German Society and participated in starting a German Masonic lodge, a group theater, and a charity association. But he also urged immigrants to be Americans and to utilize their political rights. Celebrating the American idea of self-government, he saw ethnic organizations as a way to make effective American citizens.

Charles Reemelin, a journalist and politician in Cincinnati in the 1840s, fought to preserve the German language and established the first German Society. By 1848 he had been elected three times to the Ohio legislature and served as a representative to the state constitutional convention, arguing always that the preservation of immigrant cultures and languages would make the newcomers more loyal to the nation's democratic ideals.[81]

According to Greene, the most successful German-American leader in the 1840s and 1850s was Francis Arnold Hoffman of northern Illinois and southern Wisconsin. Minister, teacher, journalist, banker, and politician and a successful recruiter of German immigrants for the Illinois Central Railroad in later years, he was elected lieutenant governor of Illinois during the Civil War. Like other ethnic-American leaders, he was a vigorous advocate of preserving the old culture while urging his fellow ethnics to practice American citizenship and become loyal to the new government.[82] In Milwaukee, Dr. Franz Huebshmann, a doctor, organized several German cultural societies and founded Milwaukee's first German newspaper, aiming to mobilize Germans into an active voting group. He pushed for a liberal suffrage provision for foreigners in the new state constitution and for German-speaking clerks in the post office, and fought successfully against attempts by Anglo-Americans to impose restrictions on the sale of beer. While fighting for the interests of Germans and German-Americans, he preached love for "our new free Fatherland, the country of free elections . . . freedom, equality and independence."[83]

These ethnic-American leaders often began their public careers by defending what others saw as parochial German interests. But very quickly they illustrated Tocqueville's central principle that participation in American civic life, understandably driven by parochial interests at first, often leads to a wider patriotism. Ethnic politicians must form coalitions to advance the interests of their constituents. They must use the rhetoric and symbols, and generally obey the rules, of the common civic culture.

In the city of Buffalo in the 1830s and 1840s, German Protestants tried to establish a public school in which some instruction would be in German as was permitted in several states.[84] Having just come to Buffalo in the 1830s, the Germans were fragmented by differences in religion and regional background. The religious difference was particularly important, because German Catholics were less interested in having German taught in the public schools than in gaining support for their parochial schools, although both won the city council's agreement to publish its proceedings in German. The immediate battle over the creation of a neighborhood school that offered instruction in German was lost, because of the Protestant-Catholic split; but as a result of the campaign two German immigrants became active in the Democratic party and the political influence of German-Americans in Buffalo generally increased.[85]

Francis Grund saw that influence growing elsewhere. Germans were so numerous in Pennsylvania in the early 1830s that he thought none but a German-American would have a chance at being elected governor. In Ohio, Maryland, Illinois, and New York, Germans were voting in increasing numbers. In New York City, he noted regarding the mayoral election that "the German vote becomes a matter of great solicitude with politicians of all ranks and persuasions."[86] German newspapers (thirty alone in Pennsylvania) were full of political news. Grund himself wrote a campaign biography of presidential candidate William Henry Harrison.[87]

The Anglo-American nativists of the 1850s did not appreciate attempts by Germans to advance their cultural and linguistic interests in the name of Americanism. The Massachusetts idea was still strong, not only in New England but also among transplanted New Englanders in the Midwest. In his farewell address, George Washington had said the Americans were united by "the same religion, manners, habits and political principles." But now there were a great many people whose manners and habits, and in some cases religion, were different. Nativists saw those differences as compromising their capacity for Americanization. But under the rules of naturalization and the political system, nothing could stop Germans from claiming an American identity as their own. Phillip Schaff, an immigrant active in the movement to Americanize the German church for more than thirty years in the mid-nineteenth century, wrote in 1855 that "the American's digestive power is really astonishing. How many thousands and millions of Europeans has his stomach already received! And yet he has only grown firmer and healthier thereby."[88] He saw that "over this confused diversity there broods after all a higher unity."[89]

Abraham Lincoln, with his considerable experience in electoral politics, observed in 1860 that even though the immigrants of his time, the largest group of which were German, could not identify personally with the Revolution and the early days of the republic, they felt "a part of us . . ." because "when they look through that old Declaration of Independence, they find that those old men say that 'we hold these truths to be self evident, that all men are created equal,' and then they feel . . . that they have a right to claim it as though they were blood of the blood and flesh of the flesh of the men who wrote the Declaration of Independence," and, Lincoln concluded, "so they are."[90]

Lincoln already had become friends with Carl Schurz, a German immigrant who helped to organize the new Republican party in Wisconsin in 1856, only four years after he had arrived. Still not a citizen, Schurz was almost elected lieutenant governor of that state in 1857. He would later serve as a diplomat, a general, as a U.S. senator, and as secretary of the interior. In 1859, he was invited to give a speech in Boston's cradle of revolution, Faneuil Hall; he spoke as a newly naturalized citizen and in a thick German accent on "True Americanism."

In the heartland of the Americanist movement and aware of Massachusetts's preoccupation with Catholic immigration, Schurz praised the founding myth of the U.S. as an asylum for those seeking freedom and opportunity regardless of their nationality or religion. He proudly claimed the heritage of Bunker Hill, Charlestown, Lexington, John Hancock, and Benjamin Franklin as his own, and asserted that the nation had been founded as a "great colony of *free humanity* which has not old England alone but the *world* for its mother country." "True Americanism," he maintained, is based on belief in "that system of government, which makes the protection of individual rights a matter of common interest."[91] This idea, "liberty and equal rights common to all," said Schurz, was the incentive for all immigrants, including Irish Catholics, to love their adopted country. "Around the banner of liberty . . . all the languages of civilized mankind are spoken, every creed is protected, every right is sacred."[92]

The German story of ethnic-Americanization would be repeated in roughly the same manner by all other major ethnic groups who came voluntarily. A minority of immigrants and their children would separate themselves from the mainstream and live in small ethnic enclaves for at least two or three generations. A large majority, after establishing ethnic churches, fraternal and mutual aid associations, and ethnic economic networks, would begin to participate in the wider economic marketplace and in the arenas of American politics, and become strongly patriotic in the process.

By the mid-twentieth century, German-Americans would become the only large ethnic group to disappear as a serious ethnic political force, partly because of anti-German sentiment during the First World War but also because of the passage of time and extensive intermarriage. Yet from the earliest days of the republic through the nineteenth century, no immigrant-ethnic group, including the Irish, had a larger ethnic press.

Between 1862 and 1945, forty-three German-born Americans were elected to Congress; most had worked their way through the civic culture as elected officials in their home towns or states.[93] In examining the careers of seven who were explicitly German-American leaders when they ran for office, Willi Paul Adams found that

the "ethnic" politician who . . . wanted to be an effective servant of his constituency could not limit himself to act as ambassador of the ethnic group that voted him into office. He had to participate fully in the all-American political game, and he was likely to be forced by his hometown newspapers to explain his moves to his constituents, and by doing so he educated them in American ways. By achieving the ultimate, getting a World's Fair to your home town, as St. Louis Congressman Richard Bartholdt did in 1904, you scored a point for your group by doing something for the whole community.[94]

Politicians like Bartholdt were quintessential examples of ethnic-Americanization. Representing German-American sensibilities and interests to a wider audience, they expressed and taught the principles of the civic culture to their own constituents. It was Bartholdt who persuaded Congress to appropriate money to erect a statue of General von Steuben, a hero of the Revolution, across from the White House next to those of Lafayette and Rochambeau so that future generations would be "reminded of what the men of German blood had contributed to the cause of American independence."[95] The example was repeated on a lesser scale in the naming of streets, squares, and smaller monuments in cities and towns throughout the country after Poles, Jews, Italians, Irish, Swedes, Norwegians, African-Americans, and now Hispanics and East Asians to symbolize the contribution of the diversity of Americans in defending American freedom in successive wars.

The Civil Religion Sanctifies the Civic Culture

By saying that every right is "sacred," Carl Schurz had adopted the vocabulary of the civic culture's own religion. Twenty-five years earlier, Francis Grund had written that "their political doctrines have become the religion and the confession of the people . . . like the truths of Christianity, they have their apostles and their martyrs."[96] Americans transmit their political principles as "their faith to their children," and "every newcomer is initiated into its creed, and soon becomes a convert to it; for if he should not, they would shun him as given to idolatry."[97] Liberty, said Grund, was "not only the bond of union," but also "the confession, the religion, the life of Americans."[98]

The religion of republicanism was something quite different from sectarian religions. While other nations felt chosen or blessed by God or gods, Americans were evolving what twentieth-century scholars would call a "civil religion,"[99] in which they felt a special mission to live up to the ideals embodied in the Declaration of Independence and attributed to the authority of God (*"they are endowed by their Creator* with certain inalienable Rights . . ."). Jews of old had covenanted to follow the laws of Yahweh. The Americans, in accepting their blessings, took on other obligations. Swearing allegiance to the Constitution, paying homage to the almost sainted Washington and to the Declaration of Independence, they, by implication, promised to fulfill the founding myth of the nation as a divinely inspired asylum for those who sought liberty and opportunity.

The Puritans of early colonial New England preached that they had been chosen to effectuate a divine plan for the salvation of souls. The apostles and prophets of the new republic preached that it had been chosen to save refugees and immigrants from tyranny and want. No one before had described their *nation,* as Washington did, as "an Asylum . . . to the oppressed and needy of the Earth."[100] Jefferson asked, "Shall oppressed humanity find no asylum on the globe?" when arguing for a short period of residency for aliens to become eligible for citizenship.[101] Not only was "the bosom of America," in Washington's maternal phrase, "open to receive . . . the oppressed and persecuted of all Nations and Religions," but they were "welcome to a participation of all our rights and privileges."[102]

James Otis wrote, "There can be no prescription old enough to supersede the law of Nature and the grant of God Almighty, who has given to all men a national right to be free."[103] The spread of liberty to all, justified as a natural, God-given right, became the American national mission. That sense of mission pushed Americans toward a powerful emotional and spiritual national patriotism. Franklin called the Revolution a "glorious task assigned to us by Providence," and Adams considered the settlement of the American colonies "as the opening of a grand scene and design in Providence for the illumination of the ignorant and the emancipation of the slavish part of mankind all over the earth."[104] Washington wrote to the Jewish congregations of Philadelphia, New York, Charleston, and Richmond that "The power and goodness of the Almighty were strongly manifested in the events of our late glorious revolution. —and his kind interposition in our behalf has been no less visible in the establishment of our present equal government."[105] Jefferson wrote to a friend in 1787 during deliberations on the new Constitution, "Our experiment will be that men may be trusted to govern themselves without a master. Could the contrary of this be proved, I should conclude, either that there is no God, or that he is a malevolent being."[106]

Not just the politicians but also ministers and educators believed that the American experiment in government was providential. Samuel Cooper declared in 1790, upon the inauguration of the new Massachusetts Constitution, that America was a new Israel, designed as "a theater for the display of some of the most astounding dispensations of His Providence." The new constitution was a thing of beauty and godliness, maintained Cooper, because the power of the government was so intricately balanced as to protect liberty. The president of Yale College, Ezra Stiles, preached before the General Assembly of Connecticut in 1783, singing hosannahs to the new Zion: "this will be a great, a very great nation . . . when the Lord should have made his American Israel high above all nations which He has made, in numbers, and in praise, and in name, and in honor!"[107] Two generations later, Phillips Brooks said, "I do not know how a man can be an American and not get something with regard to God's purpose as to this great land."[108]

The American experiment in representative self-government was blessed, but the congregation—the members of the polity—were covenanted as partners of God in fulfilling the promise of the blessing. The civic culture, with its emphasis on individual choice and voluntary pluralism, made it possible for sectarian religious groups to go unmolested even if they did not participate in the republic. Germans provided some of the best examples of such groups, such as the Old Order Amish, who chose not to vote or run for office or even participate in the wider economic marketplace. They governed themselves without becoming governors of the republic. But the vast majority of immigrants and their children embraced the vocabulary, liturgy, and icons of the civil religion as they participated increasingly in the civic culture, and they did it while holding on to their ancestral sectarian religions.

In the early 1770s, Crèvecoeur observed that Americans were much more religious than Europeans. But for the vast majority of immigrants and their descendants, sectarian religion was put in the service of the civic culture. By the early decades of the republic, some Jewish congregations had already altered their liturgy to pray in their Sabbath service for the president and the people of the United States, the "citizens of one common country."[109] In Worcester, Massachusetts, in the 1890s, Swedes mingled their hymns and "The Star-Spangled Banner" in celebrating Independence Day. In 1896, a divinity student spoke on the relationship of the American Revolution to Christ's message of liberty to the world.[110] The "public religion," as Franklin called it, promoted a general disposition to be religious as a sign that one was a good American, a believer in the providential mission of the American nation. This new patriotic religion, the "religion of democracy," as Lord Bryce called it in the late nineteenth century,[111] did not replace sectarian religions but, paradoxically, encouraged sectarian religious affiliation while uniting sectarians in feelings of national patriotism which helped to blur the edges of doctrinal differences.

Sectarian religions did not hold the passion of their adherents as much as they did in Europe, but, as Grund observed, the promotion of religion seemed "essential to the Constitution" of Americans. "Religion presides over their councils, aids in the execution of the laws, and adds to the dignity of the judges."[112] Here was the most amazing paradox of all. Crèvecoeur observed that religious freedom led to a kind of religious "indifferentism."[113] The modern word would be "toleration," as exemplified by Jefferson's remarks during the debate over the proposal to disestablish the Anglican Church in Virginia. "It does me no injury," he said, "for my neighbor to say there are twenty gods, or no god. It neither picks my pocket nor breaks my leg."[114]

The separation of state and church was strengthened in the ensuing years: disestablishment in Virginia (1788); the proclamation of religious freedom in the Northwest Ordinance as policy for the territories and new states (1787); the passage of the Constitution with a sixth article barring a religious test for holding public office (1789) and a First Amendment prohibiting Congress from making any law respecting the establishment of religion or prohibiting its free exercise (1791).

Toleration meant that it was hard for foreign visitors to tell Presbyterians and Congregationalists apart, and even Baptists and Presbyterians seemed to converge in doctrinal and organizational matters, but it did not mean toleration for the village atheist. Grund, who wrote that it was "with the solemnities of religion that the Declaration of Independence is yet annually read to the people from the pulpit," and that "Americans look upon religion as a promoter of civil and political liberty," also noted that Americans "should belong to some persuasion or other, lest his fellow-citizens should consider him an outcast from society."[115] Almost 125 years later, President Dwight D. Eisenhower, a descendant of a sectarian German Pietist family, said Americans should belong to some religious group but that it did not matter which one.

In accepting the Pennsylvania idea that European immigrants could become members of the polity on a basis of equal rights with native-born citizens regardless of the country they came from or the religion they believed in, Americans laid the basis for the civic culture that emerged in the early decades of the Republic: Article VI of the Constitution (prohibition of a religious test for holding any office or public trust); the First Amendment (separation of church and state, freedom of religion, freedom of speech); and later the Fourteenth Amendment (equal protection of the laws). But not all of the Massachusetts idea had been lost. The view that entry into political membership should be based on one's religious affiliation had been defeated, but it would surface repeatedly in opposition to Irish Catholic immigration and naturalization. The view of the Puritans that the settlement of the new land was providential and that the settlers had entered into a covenant with God to create a new life for men and women led to the sanctification of the civic culture by the civil religion. Massachusetts could claim a large share in the origins of the civil religion, including the national motto ("In God We Trust"); the references to divine guidance and inspiration in major presidential speeches; the prayers that open every session of Congress; the references to God in the Pledge of Allegiance and in patriotic songs ("My Country 'Tis of Thee," "America the Beautiful," "The Star-Spangled Banner," and "God Bless America"). The civic culture was born in Pennsylvania; the civil religion had its origins in theocratic Massachusetts.

By 1845, membership in the civic culture was still limited to white persons, a large majority of whom were Protestants. In the South, about 40 percent of the population was enslaved. Slavery was a massive contradiction to the ideals, principles, and institutions of the civic culture. But slave revolts were put down ruthlessly. Racism—belief in the inherent inferiority of persons of color—enabled most whites to ignore or even rationalize the contradiction. Some faced it and feared its consequences. Tocqueville saw conflict between whites and blacks in the South as inevitable. He called it a "danger" which "perpetually haunts the imagination of Americans, like a painful dream."[116] Grund saw the situation of free blacks in the North as worse than that of enslaved blacks. Whites, he predicted, would drive them to the meanest employment and their eventual ruin.[117] The sympathy of Tocqueville and Grund for blacks was distant, even cold, for they were enamored with another story, that of white Americans' democracy.

Chapter Two

"REINFORCEMENTS TO REPUBLICANISM"
Irish Catholic Response to the Civic Culture

O
N THE evening of September 12, 1960, before several hundred Protestant ministers and laymen in the Crystal Ballroom of the Rice Hotel in Houston, John F. Kennedy gave the clearest and most eloquent statement ever made by a presidential candidate on religion and politics in American life. A minister who was present reflected that the meeting had had many of the characteristics of an "inquisition." Although Kennedy was a fourth-generation American, grandson of a mayor of Boston, son of an ambassador to England, and a U.S. senator who had sworn allegiance to the American Constitution, as a Catholic, he had to prove that he was American enough to hold the presidency.

Kennedy had been reassured by his friend John Wright, Catholic bishop of Pittsburgh, that, contrary to public belief, no public act of a president could lead to his excommunication and that he had not, as a Catholic, sworn allegiance to the Pope. "I am not the Catholic candidate for President," Kennedy told the clergymen, "I am the Democratic Party's candidate for President, who happens also to be a Catholic. I do not speak for my Church on public matters, and the Church does not speak for me." When Kennedy was asked by a minister to appeal to Richard Cardinal Cushing to present his views on church and state to the Vatican so that they might become the authorized views of all Roman Catholics in the United States, the candidate replied, "As I do not accept the right of, as I said, any ecclesiastical official to tell me what I should do in the sphere of my public responsibility as an elected official, I do not propose also to ask Cardinal Cushing to ask the Vatican to take some action." Applause burst from the audience; the minister rose to state his admiration for Kennedy's courage, but doubted that the senator's views represented the position of his church. The candidate shot back: "I believe I am stating the viewpoint that Catholics in this country hold toward that happy relationship which exists between church and state." The minister responded, "Let me ask you, sir, do you state it with the approval of the Vatican?" Kennedy replied, "I don't have to have approval."[1]

Kennedy shared Jefferson's view on religious freedom and separation of church and state. Religious freedom had become a main foundation of voluntary pluralism by the 1830s, but its champions had never contemplated a challenge of the magnitude presented by Irish Catholic immigration in the years following the Irish potato blight of 1845–1847. Several of the founders of the new republic who believed so strongly in religious freedom for Protestants held deep and persistent anti-Catholic prejudices. Only thirty years before the Declaration of Independence and twenty-seven years before the passage of the Virginia Statute to Disestablish the Anglican Religion, Virginia's House of Burgesses prevented Catholics from acting as guardians, or serving as witnesses, congregating in large groups, carrying arms, or even keeping a horse valued at more than five pounds.[2] Fear of Catholicism was so great that when Great Britain passed the Quebec Act in 1774 extending toleration to Catholics in Quebec and to French settlers of the Ohio Valley, Alexander Hamilton complained that the English threatened New York with Popery.

The anti-Catholic sentiments of such republicans as John Jay, Patrick Henry, and John Adams were bolstered by the opposition of the Church in Europe to movements for self-government. Jay was astonished that "a British Parliament should ever consent to establish in that country [Canada] a religion that has deluged your island in blood and dispersed impiety, bigotry, persecution, murder and rebellion throughout every part of the world."[3] In South Carolina, an effigy of the Pope was burned in a bonfire fueled with English tea leaves; in Maryland, a double land tax was levied on Catholics. Boston (where Paul Revere produced anti-Catholic engravings) and other American towns revived the American holiday "Pope Day," which featured a large parade that ended in the burning of an effigy of the Pope.[4]

On the eve of the Revolution, Catholics, small in number, were easy to assimilate, according to Crèvecoeur. Writing about life on the New York frontier perhaps only a year or two before Jay's fulminations against the Quebec Act, he saw "strict modes of Christianity" abandoned because each man, preoccupied with his own land, horses, and produce, lost interest in pushing his religious views on others. "How does it concern the welfare of the country, or of the provinces at large, what this man's religious sentiments are, or really whether he has any religion at all?" asked Crèvecoeur in a query similar to Jefferson's remark a few years later that it neither picked his pocket nor broke his leg if his neighbors worshiped twenty gods or no god.[5] Confidently predicting that religious indifference and tolerance would grow from generation to generation, Crèvecoeur did not foresee the immigration of huge numbers of Irish Catholics to the growing cities of America.

Crèvecoeur's prediction held for about forty years. Although public celebrations on behalf of freedom preceding and during the Revolution often included diatribes against the Pope, the virtually unanimous support that the small number of American Catholic leaders gave to the cause of independence and the assistance of France against England inhibited anti-Catholic attacks. The practical requirements of organizing an insurrection and then a revolution also undermined anti-Catholicism. The same First Continental Congress that resented the Quebec Act invited the *Quebecois* to join with them in fighting the British. Later, Benjamin Franklin, who attempted to involve the *Quebecois* with the Continental Army, visited Ireland to cultivate the friendship of leaders of the fight for Catholic emancipation there and persuaded Congress to send a message of solidarity to Catholics in Ireland. The Revolutionary leaders were practical men who wanted to win their independence; they had no trouble accepting the help of France, one of the most Catholic nations in Europe.

After the war, American patriots no longer warned that Jesuits were the advance agents of the Pope and conspiring to destroy American liberties; now they denounced the Loyalist newspapers that reflected anxieties born of vanished privileges and status.[6] Although seven state constitutions forbade Catholics to hold office, the federal Constitution (two Catholics were among the signers) prohibited imposition of any religious test of officeholders in the new government, and the First Amendment made it unconstitutional for Congress to make any law "respecting an establishment of religion, or prohibiting the free exercise thereof." Numbering only about 35,000 in 1790, Catholics were not seen as a potential problem in the new nation even while Catholicism itself was often denounced.[7]

Guarding the Civic Culture: What to Do About Catholic Immigration

By 1820 there were 200,000 Catholics in the U.S. Hostility arose, particularly after the first provincial council of Catholic bishops in 1829 urged the establishment of Catholic schools in each community to be supported by public funds as were the secular common schools, and as unemployment in Ireland stimulated the exodus of slightly more than 200,000 immigrants to the U.S. during the decade of the 1830s. Exhortations to Catholics by Protestant ministers to read the Protestant Bible, to discover the Gospel, and to witness for Christ were frequently linked to attacks on the papacy as a symbol of tyrannical power.

From the perspective of Protestant militants, the Roman Catholic church was an enemy of freedom because it did not accept churches as voluntary associations or the idea that an individual encounter with God without the intervention of priests and sacraments was the way to salvation. The Catholic church could not claim to be free from the authority and dictation of foreigners who were seen as enemies of personal liberty and of the institutions that had been designed to protect and extend it.

Yet, Tocqueville wrote of religious peace in the United States in 1833 and, from a European perspective, he was largely right. In 1835, Roger Taney, a devout Roman Catholic, was appointed and confirmed as Chief Justice of the U.S. Supreme Court. But the general religious harmony of the 1830s was marred by incidents in Philadelphia and in other cities and would be shattered in the next two decades when the potato blight of 1845–1847 left hundreds of thousands dead or starving in Ireland. The number of immigrants jumped from 200,000 in the 1830s to 781,000 in the 1840s and 914,000 in the following decade. The vast majority would not even have qualified as immigrants in the 1980s, on several grounds— poverty, illness, and no family relations. But the mid-nineteenth century American appetite for settlers and laborers was insatiable.

Most Irish crowded into wretched tenements in the cities or shacks in the marshlands or outlying districts, and were frequently plagued by disease and drink. Many entered almshouses, mental institutions, and prisons (by mid-century, more than half of the criminal offenses recorded in the U.S. were committed by immigrants, mostly by the Irish). Often willing to work at hauling heavy loads, cleaning stables, and sweeping streets for wages lower than those acceptable to many native-born Americans, they would have provoked the antagonism of poor, unskilled native workers even if they had not practiced a "foreign" religion with its statues, crucifixes, and ornate vestments.

There was street fighting in several cities between poor Catholics and Protestants in the 1830s and 1840s, burning of churches, and stoning of houses. But cheap labor was badly needed to work in the factories and mines, to build the bridges and roads, and to serve as domestics in the homes of the affluent. If upper- and upper-middle-class Whigs wanted the Irish to do the dirty jobs, leaders of the Democratic party wanted their votes. The Democratic platforms of 1840, 1844, 1848, and 1852, employing the language of the civic culture, praised "the liberal principles embodied by Jefferson in the Declaration of Independence and sanctioned in the Constitution, which makes ours the land of liberty, and the asylum of the oppressed of every nation" in opposition to nativist efforts to lengthen the waiting time of newcomers for naturalization and to restrict their privileges as citizens.[8]

By 1850, the Irish constituted 42 percent of the foreign-born population in the U.S. The Catholic population reached two million. One thousand priests served nearly fifteen hundred churches and Mass stations, ruled by a hierarchy of thirty-five bishops, mostly Irish; the Irish became a target of Anglo-American Protestant attacks. Anti-Catholic agitation between 1830 and 1850 was based on a mixture of xenophobic, sectarian, and economic, as well as ideological fears, but it was often couched in patriotic slogans about the defense of Americanism. "They come here ignorant and poor, without a knowledge of our institutions," intoned *The New England Magazine* in 1834.[9] A U.S. House of Representatives Report in 1838, speaking of the new Irish immigrants, insisted, "The character of our free institutions was not adapted for such citizens; nor did the framers of those institutions contemplate the nature and mental character of the bulk of those who have since blotted our country."[10]

Some of the Americanizers were confident that even though the Irish belonged to a church that seemed idolatrous and were used to servile dependence, they could adapt to American society if given the opportunity. A Dartmouth professor speaking before the 1841 annual meeting of the New England Society (a fraternal, charitable organization open to native-born New Englanders or their sons resident in New York) argued that the "common institutions of government and education" in the U.S. created a uniform national character that obliterated differences of class, region, and even religion.[11] The common culture—he did not call it the "civic culture"—would make immigrants into Americans. But others were just as certain that the avarice of employers for cheap laborers and the lust of Democratic party leaders for servile followers threatened the foundations of the American republic.

The American inventor and painter, and the first president of the National Academy of Arts and Design, Samuel F. B. Morse, tried to sound an alarm in 1835 with a pamphlet, *Imminent Dangers to the Free Institutions of the United States Through Foreign Immigration,* that pointed to the immigration of Catholics as a dire threat to free institutions. He reminded readers of Jefferson's worry that foreigners would bring foreign principles of government with them and might render American legislation into "a heterogeneous, incoherent, distracted mass."[12] In days past, immigration had not been threatening, argued Morse, because immigrants had come "from the ranks of the learned and the good, from the enlightened mechanic and artisan, and intelligent husbandmen." Forgetting the large numbers of paupers and convicts who had emigrated from Europe throughout the seventeenth and into the eighteenth centuries, Morse maintained that Europe had sent "real lovers of liberty, to the benefit of America." But "*now,*" Morse claimed, "emigrants are selected for a service to their tyrants, and by their tyrants, not for their affinity to liberty, but for their mental servitude, and their docility in obeying the orders of their priests."[13]

It was an argument that spurred the rise of the native American movement, whose leaders called for a long residency requirement for immigrants before naturalization. Some proposed a constitutional amendment to keep naturalized citizens from holding office. Still, few nativists argued that immigration should be stopped altogether. Immigrants were needed as workers. The principal goal of the Americanists was to allow the Irish full citizenship only when they were ready to participate in a republican form of government. One member of Congress, a representative of the American Republican (nativist) party from Pennsylvania, urged that "we be faithful to our own creed of freedom, . . . by asking that the alien shall be naturalized in mind, in heart, in soul, by a residence sufficiently long to wean him from his first love, and engraft on his understanding the knowledge that dignifies a free man."[14] The problem, from the nativist point of view, was, in Morse's words, "that popery is opposed in its very nature to Democratic Republicanism; and it is, therefore, as a political system, as well as a religious, opposed to civil and religious liberty and consequently to our form of government."[15]

Many Americans were appalled when Monsignor Gaetano Bedini, who had helped squelch the uprisings of 1848 and 1849 in Italy and who was associated with the resurgence of monarchy there, was sent to settle a controversy within the Catholic communities of Buffalo and Philadelphia on whether church property should be legally held in trusteeship by the laity or, as Rome directed, by the clergy. Here was Bedini, an official of the Roman Catholic church, telling American citizens what they should do. He was burned in effigy in Boston and Baltimore, manhandled as he entered the bishop's carriage in Pittsburgh, and saved from possible assassination in Wheeling, West Virginia, only by quick action of several hundred armed Irishmen who guarded him and the churches of the city.[16]

The Americanist movement of the 1840s and 1850s was fueled not just by fear of Rome but also by the separatism of the church, which established Catholic parochial schools to guard the young and keep them faithful. One political response to the growing numbers of Catholics was the formation of a Nativist party, which in New York City published a newspaper entitled *Spirit of Seventy-Six*; it elected a mayor and the entire common council of New York City in 1837. It led, in turn, to the American Republican party, which was swept into office in the city in 1844 on an explicitly anti-Catholic platform,[17] and established branches in every county in New York State and New Jersey and in the cities of Boston and Charleston, South Carolina. The American Republicans changed their name to the Native American party and embraced a program of positive reform as well as antiforeignism and anti-Catholicism.

In the 1850s, the Know-Nothing party, the only xenophobic, nativist party to win substantial power in national and state elections, was organized. It was officially called The Order of the Star-Spangled Banner and appeared on the ballot as the American Party.[18] Believing that Catholicism was a foreign conspiracy bent on destroying American institutions, its members were sworn to exclude all immigrants "and Roman Catholics in particular" from places of trust, profit, or honor. No one who was a Catholic or even married to one could join.[19]

Americanists intended to guard the gates of republicanism by having the newcomers wait twenty-one years before becoming eligible for naturalization and by placing an absolute bar against their holding public office.[20] The success of their appeal was phenomenal, and in the state legislative elections of 1854 the new party carried Massachusetts, Delaware, and, in alliance with the Whigs, Pennsylvania.[21] In Massachusetts, the governor and all state officers were Know-Nothings, as was the state senate and all but two of 378 members of the state house of representatives. In the fall election, about seventy-five party members were elected to Congress, and in the next year, major state offices in Rhode Island, New Hampshire, and Connecticut were won by nativists.[22] By 1856, seven governors, eight U.S. senators, and 104 members of the U.S. House of Representatives who campaigned on the American Party platform were elected. Talk of a Know-Nothing president became commonplace.

Most leaders of the Democratic party itself resisted anti-Catholic hysteria and made a strong appeal for immigrant support. The party platform in 1856, faithful to the Pennsylvania idea of American nationality, insisted that "no party can justly be deemed national, Constitutional, or in accordance with American principles which bases its exclusive organization upon religious opinions and accidental birthplace." Opposing what it called a "crusade . . . against Catholics and foreign born," the platform denounced it as not "in unison with the spirit of toleration and enlarged freedom which peculiarly distinguishes the American system of popular government."[23]

The platform was right and wrong. The Pennsylvania approach of "toleration and enlarged freedom" was an important feature of American life in the 1850s. But Massachusetts disbanded Irish military companies and kept the Irish from the police force and state agencies, an approach of those who believed they were protecting republicanism. But even in Massachusetts, no action was taken to restrict the voting of immigrants, as many Know-Nothing leaders had demanded. The militant attacks of the Americanists had diminishing appeal to politicians, especially in states where a growing number of newcomers voted. But the most important reason for the demise of the American Party was the rise of a wrenching debate over slavery.

Millard Fillmore, American Party nominee for the presidency in 1856, was viewed in the North as a champion of slavery. He had signed the Fugitive Slave Law in 1850 as president. New England nativists, perhaps discouraged by the excesses of some leaders, were disgusted by the nomination of Fillmore, and although the American Party polled about 25 percent of the votes nationally, it won a majority only in Maryland. As the conflict over slavery intensified, religious passions and the debate over the period of residency required for aliens to become citizens receded; the American Party disappeared, and with it the issue of a religious test for membership in the American polity.

The urban Irish opposed the cause of abolition; Irish rioted against the draft law in New York City in July 1863, and rumors arose of papal conspiracy to destroy republican government. But these were largely forgotten as the Civil War ended. More likely to be remembered were the heroes of General Thomas Meagher's Irish Brigade, two-thirds of whom had been killed in the battle of Fredericksburg, and the thousands of Catholic soldiers who fought in the Union Army. Americans hardly noticed when Pope Pius IX in 1864 issued a series of eighty propositions as the Syllabus of Errors, among them the "error" that "the Pope may and must reconcile himself and adapt himself to progress, liberalism, and modern civilization."[24] In later decades, anti-Catholicism would surface again in a national movement in the form of the American Protective Association and the Ku Klux Klan.

The Irish Response: Americanization Through Politics

The Irish were well on their way toward becoming Irish-Americans just as the Germans were becoming German-Americans, even though, unlike the Germans, they were overwhelmingly poor and suffered from high rates of family separation, crime, and disease. The story of the Americanization of Irish Catholics is without parallel, not just because of their desperate economic circumstances but because the civic culture of the Americans was formed to such a large extent on the basis of principles antithetical to Irish Catholic culture in the early and mid-nineteenth century. Altogether, about nine million Irish immigrants came to the United States, nine-tenths of them of Roman Catholic background.[25] They provided a severe test of the capacity of the civic culture to permit and sanction voluntary pluralism while unifying newcomers around republican principles. Most of the Irish did not speak a foreign language, but they might just as well have, so suspect were their strange habits, manners, and authoritarian religion. Yet, they proved that it was possible for immigrant-ethnic groups to retain separate communal, cultural, and educational institutions even as they participated increasingly in the nation's wider economic and political life.

If language had been the principal political issue for the Germans, Catholic education was the Irish issue. Even before the great famine migrations, when there were relatively few Irish Catholics in the U.S., the Catholic church pressed the issue of Protestant influence in the schools, although its only power at the time lay in the votes of naturalized immigrants and, later, of their children. In an important political struggle in New York City in the late 1830s, the Irish pressed their sectarian interests, not only becoming more Americanized in the process but also strengthening one of the most important principles of the civic culture, the separation of church and state. Catholics in New York objected because a Protestant sectarian organization, the Public School Society, ran the common schools of the city and used books with an anti-Catholic slant. When, in 1840, Catholics petitioned for a share of the school funds to support their own sectarian schools, Protestants successfully rebuffed their efforts through both the Whig and Democratic parties. Many Protestants saw in the Catholic opposition to the common schools an unwillingness to let their children become Americanized.[26]

In this struggle, unable to win sufficient support from the major parties, Bishop John Hughes led Irish Catholics in advancing Catholic nominees independent of the established political parties, for three assembly seats and two for the state senate. Catholics pressed their case on the ground of equal rights. When a large crowd assembled on October 29, 1840, they came, as their advertisement said, as "the friends of civil and religious freedom."[27] When Bishop Hughes urged his listeners to use politics to protect their interests, he employed the language of the civic culture: "You now, for the first time, find yourselves in the position to vote at least for yourselves . . . now you are determined to uphold, with your own votes, your own rights . . . go, like free men, with dignity and calmness, entertaining due respect for your fellow-citizens and their opinions, and deposit your votes."[28] The chemistry of ethnic Americanization was at work. The Irish organized, petitioned, and voted to get their view across. Although the independent Irish Catholic ticket lost, with only two thousand votes, Catholic votes made the difference between success and defeat for the ten Democratic candidates for assembly whom Catholics endorsed. Irish Catholics had demonstrated to Tammany Hall, New York City's Democratic organization, that it needed Catholic support to win. Upstate New York Democrats were impressed when Hughes presented a petition to the legislature bearing the names of thirteen thousand Catholics in support of a bill to put New York schools under the jurisdiction of the state rather than the Public School Society.[29] Funds were not authorized by the legislature for parochial schools, but in the next election New York City Catholics put up their own candidates for mayor and the common council. Although not elected, they presented a threat to the Democrats, whose state leaders pressured the legislature to establish, for the first time, a school system directly controlled by the people and entirely financed from the public treasury—a full *public* school system—in what was a major victory for the separation of church and state.

The outcome had vast implications for the evolution of voluntary pluralism. While the New York legislature had voted not to subsidize Irish Catholic parochial schools, it did agree to try to remove the Protestant influence from the public schools, and, by 1844, Bible reading was excluded from thirty-one of the city's public schools.[30] There was nothing to stop the Irish or other national Catholic groups from establishing their own parochial schools if they would pay for them.

Irish Catholics had set a precedent for other ethnic-religious groups: negotiate, bargain, and work within the system. Effective in endorsing Democratic candidates but relatively ineffective in advancing an independent Catholic party, they inadvertently established a presumption against presenting an explicitly religious or ethnic slate in future elections. Claiming American values and institutions as their own and employing the rhetoric of the civic culture, Irish Catholics illustrated Tocqueville's proposition that patriotism is nurtured and reinforced by participation in the political process.

Irish Catholics had known politics in the old country, where the rules were rigged against them. In the U.S., where every vote was equal, sheer numbers counted most. The Democratic party's appeal was primarily to those trying to acquire property and status. It was the natural home for the Irish, although in Philadelphia Irish building contractors were tied into the Republican machine. The most strident anti-Catholics were found overwhelmingly among the Know-Nothings, the Whigs, and factional predecessors of the Republican party. In return for Irish votes, the Democrats of New York, Philadelphia, Boston, and dozens of other cities offered jobs in the party, protection against riots, recognition of Irish culture and nationalism, as in the sponsorship of a major Saint Patrick's Day parade or party, and, as Kirby A. Miller has written, "a sense of belonging to a powerful, *American* institution."[31] Irish political clubs were set up in Irish grog shops and by street gangs and in volunteer fire companies. The use of repeater voters was common among the Irish, who were taught the practice by non-Irish (usually Anglo-American) political leaders, like New York's Boss Tweed in the 1860s. Politics became a principal route to municipal jobs, and, for those who could be elected to a moderately important office, it meant a decent income and life-style, too. Before the arrival of large numbers of Irish Catholics, Boston was one of the most tranquil, best governed, and most homogeneous cities in the world, with, in 1845, fewer than ten thousand industrial workers in a population of 165,000.[32] Class differences existed, of course; blacks, nearly always at the bottom, lived in "nigger hill" behind the State House and in the North End near poor whites, most of whom lived around Fort Hill. But there was little poverty in the city, the crime rate was less than in cities of comparable size, and standards of public health were relatively high. Harriet Martineau, a visitor from England, wrote, "I know no large city where there is so much mutual helpfulness, so little neglect and ignorance of the concerns of other classes."[33] Then came the famine Irish, and, as Oscar Handlin has shown, they quickly formed an urban proletariat, a laboring class exploited through exorbitant rents for miserable tenement apartments, low wages, and grinding, menial work. Disease and crime followed.

Yankee Protestants were not entirely without sympathy. Yankee doctors treated the Irish victims of the cholera epidemic of 1849, in which five hundred persons perished. Yankee Protestants supported the St. Vincent Female Orphan Asylum, which cared for children who had lost both parents during the epidemic. A Harvard graduate and former Episcopalian minister founded the House of the Angel Guardian in the North End in 1851 as a "moral restaurant" for "intractable" Catholic children who had appeared before municipal court judges and others whose parents and guardians were willing to commit them there.[34] But Yankee Boston generally felt outrage, shock, and disdain for the Irish. By the late 1840s and early 1850s the Irish accounted for 97 percent of the residents in the Deer Island almshouse, 75 percent of the prisoners in the county jail, 90 percent of Boston's truants and vagabonds, and 58 percent of its paupers.[35]

The Irish themselves, through church and charitable organizations, tried to deal with the survival needs of children growing up in homes headed by women[36] and created such charitable institutions as the Working Boys' Home in the North End and the Carney Hospital, founded by a wealthy Irish merchant, which set aside a ward for abandoned infants and unwed mothers. By the 1870s the Irish "were no longer the illiterate, impoverished peasants who had dragged themselves ashore,"[37] but an estimated 22 percent of Irish households in 1870 still struggled in desperate poverty.[38] With more than 26 percent of the population in Boston, 24 percent in New York, 25 percent in Jersey City, and 19 percent in St. Louis, Pittsburgh, and Providence, the Irish Catholics established churches, sodalities, Holy Name societies, and social, athletic, and community organizations connected to the church.[39] In addition to the network of parishes and parochial schools, they organized fraternities, labor unions, volunteer fire departments, orphanages, homes for the elderly, and temperance halls. Such organizations provided solace and comfort for immigrants and their children, and often served as bases from which the Irish Catholics could express their interests and make their claims in the polity. The most important communal organization of all for the Irish in Boston, New York, and other cities, next to the church itself, was the Democratic party, and for Irish men, the party probably was more important than the church. In and through the party they found sociability, jobs, and a way to claim an American identity.

The Irish were at least as eager to embrace their new country as the Germans. Even at the height of the Americanist–Know Nothing fervor in 1856, an Irish Catholic immigrant standing on the steps of the Capitol in Washington, D.C., recorded his awe at seeing about him "signs of incorruptible liberty." Writing of the Capitol, he said, "I prayed fervently for its perpetuation and invincibility, as I considered it the shield of the oppressed, the dread of tyrants, and the nucleus of *our* glorious Constitution [italics mine]."[40]

The Catholic press in the mid-nineteenth century reflected the hunger of the Irish to be accepted as Americans.[41] The first major editor of the leading Catholic newspaper, *The Pilot* of Boston, Patrick Donahoe, fought to protect Irish Catholics; he urged his readers to become citizens and to get involved in politics.[42] Speaking very much as Carl Schurz had to the Germans, Donahoe urged the Irish of Boston and the surrounding area not to anglicize their names but to be proud of every aspect of their Irish ancestry even as they gained self-respect by becoming citizens and voting. He saw the immigrants as continual " 'reinforcements to the principle of our republicanism' with 'a strong hatred of monarchy' and a 'natural love for this sheltering democracy.' "[43]

It was advice followed by a succession of Boston politicians. The first great South Boston Irish politician, Patrick Collins, found (in Victor Greene's phrase) "that America offered a universal ideology that he and his countrymen could share."[44] So strong was Collins's Irish identity that he joined the Fenian Brotherhood, the Irish-American revolutionary organization, although he did not accompany them in their raid into Canada, reasoning that immigrants should not fight in wars that had not been declared by Congress. An Irish nationalist, he was also an active Democratic party politician, preaching what he called the "genius of republicanism" to all who would listen.[45]

Collins did not hold elective office in Boston (President Cleveland appointed him consul-general in London in 1892), but Hugh O'Brien, John Fitzgerald, and James Michael Curley did. The nativists of the 1850s had warned that one day the Bridgets and Patricks down below in the kitchen would rule the city of Boston, but there had been only one Irish policeman in the entire city before the Civil War. By 1869, there were nearly forty. In 1871, there were forty-five, and by 1900, one hundred.[46] In the prewar years there had never been an Irishman on Boston's eight-man board of aldermen and only one on the forty-eight-person common council. By 1870, there were a half dozen on the common council and one alderman.

In 1884, the Irish-born Hugh O'Brien was elected Mayor of Boston; he was reelected for four consecutive terms. Since he could win only with Yankee votes, he was careful not to identify too strongly with his Irish constituents, although later he made an occasional gesture, such as shutting down the Boston public library on St. Patrick's Day.

By 1906, when John Fitzgerald was elected mayor, all of the major political bosses of the city were Irish, and many Irish-Americans ran for city and state office. "Honey Fitz," as he was called, had no reticence in making strong local ethnic appeals and attacking his opponents as tools of the merchants of Boston. If O'Brien had been a conservative and dependable Irishman, someone the Brahmins could use to broker their interests, Fitzgerald was outrageously Irish. Before his election as mayor, he was sent to Congress, one of three Catholics in the national legislative body.[47] As mayor he became a champion not of the poor Irish alone, but of an increasing number of Jewish and Italian immigrants for whom, when in Congress, he had opposed immigration restriction. Opposed by the Brahmin Good Government Association, he was turned out of office in 1907, but he won again in 1910, despite denunciations of the "evils of Fitzgeraldism."[48] Fitzgerald's oldest daughter, Rose, married Joseph Patrick Kennedy, the son of another of Boston's political bosses, Patrick J. Kennedy of the East End, and the father of President John Fitzgerald Kennedy.

Most Brahmins intensely disliked Fitzgerald's successor, James Michael Curley. Born of poor immigrant parents, with no formal education beyond grammar school, Curley had followed much the same path as Fitzgerald; he had worked his way up in politics in Roxbury to become a local ward boss, member of the common council, representative in the state legislature, alderman, and then member of the city council. Like Fitzgerald, he was elected to Congress and, like Fitzgerald, after just one term in Washington, he ran for mayor. He appealed to all of the ethnics, whom he used to call the "newer races," but especially his own, the Irish, when he labeled the Good Government Association as "Goo-Goos" and Boston's Yankee business leaders as "the State Street Wrecking Crew."[49]

While Curley's basic appeal was to the poor, he was extremely knowledgeable about a large range of subjects and a brilliant orator, who clasped to his bosom all of the icons, symbols, and rituals of the American republic. He was the Andrew Jackson of Boston's city hall, opening the corridors and staircases to voters looking for jobs and favors of every description. As Jackson had represented the triumph of democracy for the backwoods frontiersman, the Scotch-Irish Presbyterians from whom he came, so the election of Curley was the triumph of the Irish Catholics and a sign to the Italian, Jewish, Portuguese, Polish, and other immigrants who now flooded the city of the possibilities of power. Curley dominated Boston politics for more than thirty years, serving as mayor for four terms, as congressman twice, and governor once; he built playgrounds, parks, and bathhouses, tore down slums, and paved streets for the benefit of ethnic neighborhoods at a high cost to Boston's business community, whose downtown financial district was largely neglected. Eventually, he went to prison for five months in 1945 after being convicted of using the mails to defraud. (His sentence was commuted by President Harry Truman and he returned to finish his term.)

By his own admission, Curley was a rogue,[50] but he also was an ardent and even eloquent spokesman for the civic culture and civil religion. Like Schurz, who identified with the Yankee heroes of the Revolution in his speech on "true Americanism" at Faneuil Hall, Curley loved to praise the revolutionary heroes of the Brahmins as his own. Preaching the virtues of Americanism in a Faneuil Hall speech, he called Boston the "mother city of liberty." He welcomed visitors to the city, which he said was "dedicated to . . . the doctrine of equality expressed in civil, political and religious liberty," a city where they could visit the Old South Church, "sacred to the memory of John Hancock and Samuel Adams." Never mind that Hancock and Adams shared the hatred of papism common to Boston in their day, or that leading Brahmins excluded the Irish from the banks and businesses and social clubs they controlled. Curley told visitors that after they had drunk "from freedom's fountain in Boston" they should "go forth as zealous missionaries determined to teach by individual example the lesson of the [founding] fathers."[51]

There was no inconsistency in Curley's mind between obeying the teachings of the church and its vicar, the Pope, and those of America's civil religion and its prophets and martyrs. Visiting the Lincoln Memorial in 1923, Mayor Curley preached: "America has ever been the object of divine favor, a factor in the divine scheme of human betterment." God had sent Washington "in that darkest hour when we were most weak," and when the "struggle and sacrifice for human rights and the blessings of liberty and quality were about to be lost, He sent us a savior—Lincoln."[52]

Jefferson's concern that large numbers of badly educated immigrants used to tyranny might make poor material for citizens in a self-governing republic had not been entirely without foundation. Curley was a crook, after all, as were some of the Yankee bosses who preceded the Irish in Tammany Hall in New York. But no group took as rapidly to American politics as the Irish; and once in it, the Irish Catholics appropriated its heroes and symbols, articulated and embellished its litanies, and played by its fundamental rules. The Yankees who worried that the Irish could never overcome habits of servile dependence had underestimated the power of the civic culture to shape its citizens.

The Civic Culture and the Irish

At the height of the controversy over whether or not Irish Catholics could make good Americans, the New York *Irish-American* urged the preservation of an Irish identity in the United States; if they kept in mind "what was good and honorable and virtuous in the old land," they would best be able to teach their children "to adopt and love what is good and noble in the new."[53] The Boston *Pilot,* then a secular Irish paper, warned against self-hatred, "a moral deformity of the worst description," and advocated the preservation of Irish social customs and of the Gaelic language, but no Irish leader advocated changing the First Amendment with its protections for freedom of speech and religion and its guarantee to the Catholic minority, among others, that church and state would be separated.

Irish social organizations continued to grow in the late 1850s and into the 1860s. Irish churches and the Irish press continued to flourish. Irish nationalism intensified, resulting in attacks on cooperation between England and the United States, even in something as obviously constructive as the opening of the Atlantic cable.[54] Irish-American nationalism, reflected in the activities of the Fenian Brotherhood and the Irish press, peaked between 1870 and 1890,[55] and both cultural and political nationalism waned over time.

So strong was the acceptance by Irish Catholics of principles of American freedom that American bishops at the First Vatican Council in 1869–1870 spoke in opposition to two dogmatic constitutions aimed at protecting their church against the dynamic changes sweeping the Western world. A growing number of priests and bishops felt no conflict between the American emphasis on freedom and Roman Catholicism, despite the Syllabus of Errors and the doctrine of papal infallibility.

The leading Americanizers were Archbishop James Gibbons of Baltimore, who was elevated to the cardinalate in 1886 and became a consultant to presidents and a friend to Protestant and Jewish causes, and Archbishop John Ireland of Minneapolis and St. Paul, who spoke bluntly and loudly about the universal validity of separation of church and state and of democracy. Ireland became more outspoken as the Americanizers within the American church gained influence, despite an implicit warning issued by Pope Leo XIII in an encyclical in 1888, *Libertas praestantissimum,* which condemned unconditional freedom of thought, speech, and worship. Catholic Americanists virtually ignored the encyclical. Many probably agreed with Father Isaac Hecker, who pointed out that the Pope was writing mainly for the people of an "eastern" mentality and intended no limitation on American ideas of liberty.[56]

Catholic Americanists believed not just in the value of freedom for

America but in the mission to spread that value to other countries. They were as imbued with the spirit of America's civic culture as non-Catholics were, and Archbishop Ireland, the loudest apostle of Americanism, had boasted in several lectures in Paris that if Frenchmen would emulate American Catholics they would achieve success over antireligious forces. In Rome and in Europe, in response, conservative church leaders and theologians began to speak of the heresy of Americanism, and in 1885 Pope Leo issued a long-awaited encyclical to the church in America. *Longinque Oceani* made it plain that even if many of his friends and children in America had forgotten the Syllabus of Errors, he had not. He expressed satisfaction with the growth of the church in the U.S.—there were now more than twelve million Catholics—but warned that "it would be erroneous to draw the conclusion that in America is to be sought the type of the most desirable state of the Church," or that it would be expedient for church and state to be "dissevered and divorced in other countries as in America." Almost all of the priests or bishops who urged reform on the European Continent—whatever the reform—were calling themselves or were being called "Americanists."

European Catholics were on warning not to become like the Americans. But in the U.S. most Catholics accepted the idea of a strong separation between church and state, especially after the election of John F. Kennedy. "I am wholly opposed," he had told the ministers in Houston in the 1960 campaign, "to the state being used by any religious group, Catholic or Protestant, to compel, prohibit or persecute the free exercise of any other religion. And that goes for any persecution at any time, by anyone, in any country."[57] In the U.S. the Americanist Catholics had clearly triumphed.

So strongly had the idea of individual freedom become identified with American life that at the Second Vatican Council in 1965 the declaration on religious liberty was commonly referred to as the "American Schema." Its chief author was John Courtney Murray, and its most powerful support came from American bishops against key figures in the Roman curia, Spanish bishops, and southern Italian prelates. In previous papal encyclicals and other expressions of Catholic theology, religious liberty was something to be tolerated in the interests of civic peace. There were no rights of conscience to be recognized in conflict with the one, true church, which, whenever possible, was to be favored over other religions. Millions of American Catholics had, in effect, repudiated that position. For two decades before the Second Vatican Council, Father Murray argued that it was impossible to separate religious freedom from civil freedom and that persons in error have rights which must be respected by church as well as state.[58]

By the 1980s, Father Murray's position had been embraced by the vast majority of American Irish Catholics. It was an outcome that Jefferson, with his fear of hierarchical religions, could not have predicted, and one that Tocqueville, who had prophesied either the demise of the Catholic church in the U.S. or, more likely, the absorption of Protestants into it, explicitly rejected. But neither Protestants nor Catholics disappeared. Some crossed over; others dropped out. They intermarried. More typically, Protestants and Catholics maintained their ancestral religious affiliations while finding it possible to share with and borrow from each other in an ever-moving American ethnic kaleidoscope. James Michael Curley once boasted that Brahmin politician Leverett Saltonstall, a popular Republican politician in Massachusetts and a Unitarian, who learned early in his career that the vote of an Irish Catholic was just as good as that of a Yankee Protestant, joined the charitable Irish society of Boston before Curley did.[59]

Because the Irish were the largest Catholic group and spoke English, they dominated the Roman Catholic church in America throughout the century and helped to integrate other European Catholics into American culture. Since the Germans, Poles, Italians, and other groups spoke different languages and interpreted Catholicism in national terms, many chafed at what they thought was Irish inhospitableness. The Italians, with their emphasis on the occult, mystery, and passion, could hardly be expected to warm to the ascetic Irish approach to religion. The Germans, with their stress on language and culture, often scorned the Irish as an inferior people. And the Poles saw their own faith as inextricably linked with the destiny of their fatherland.[60] Each group developed national fraternal associations and, in some cases, national religious organizations as well, and always local parishes of the national church.

German Catholics had opened a parish of their own in Philadelphia as early as 1790. The German Catholic population increased fourteenfold between 1840 and 1870, by which year one of four Catholics was of German stock. But by 1916, during the First World War, only one of ten Catholics worshiped in a church that used the German language.[61] German and other national church movements failed to win support in Rome because they did not have the backing of the dominant Irish-American leaders. German Catholics established their own parochial schools, benefit societies, and other organizations to help them adjust to the American environment, but those who tried to form a national church were frustrated by the U.S. and Roman hierarchies.

Resenting the domination of the Irish, a group of American German Catholics in 1890 asked Rome for a national clergy, for national schools, and proportional representation in the hierarchy for each U.S. nationality. The plan was denounced in the U.S. Senate and by President Benjamin

Harrison, but, more important for the ears of Rome, it was opposed vigorously by the Irish Catholic bishops, who constituted half of the U.S. total. (Only 14 percent of American bishops were German.)[62] Where the Germans did gain control over the church, as in Wisconsin, they began to behave like the Irish in their relationship to recently arrived groups, in this case, Polish Catholics. What the Germans thought of as justifiable pluralism in the 1880s, they disparaged as Polish parochialism in the 1900s. In 1904, some Poles formed an independent Polish National Church, which eventually claimed twenty-four churches and 28,200 communicants.

Many of the Irish Catholic bishops became apostles of Americanism, not only preventing the development of separatist movements linked to foreign languages and cultures, but, imbued with the ideals of the civic culture and the civil religion, becoming super-American patriots in the process. Nevertheless, just as Protestant ministers had done before them, they often displayed the narrower, parochial side of the civil religion. Archbishop O'Connell of Boston, writing to Archbishop Ireland, defended the sweeping of Catholic Spain from Cuba by American forces. It was good to replace "the meanness and narrowness of old Europe," he wrote, with "the freedom of America." O'Connell believed that "America is God's apostle in Modern times," and that its imperial advance reflected "God's way of developing the world."[63] Some Catholics, lay and clerical, became nativist bigots, too. They, particularly the Irish, flocked disproportionately to the banner of Senator Joseph McCarthy of Wisconsin in his hysterical anti-Communist crusade in the early 1950s. Ironically, the Ku Klux Klan, which had originally seen Catholics as unfit to become Americans, elected a Catholic as its Grand Wizard in 1986.[64] More significantly, by the 1980s, Catholics played a major role in defending the ideals and principles of the Declaration of Independence and the Constitution—three Roman Catholics, two of them Irish, sat as guardians of the civic culture on the U.S. Supreme Court. In all of U.S. history, no president, no speaker of the House of Representatives, and no justice of the Supreme Court have been more ardent defenders of civil liberties, religious freedom, and voluntary pluralism than President Kennedy, Speaker Thomas P. O'Neill and Justice William J. Brennan, all descendants of nineteenth-century Irish immigrants and members of the Catholic church.

Probably less than one percent of the population at the time the Constitution was written, Roman Catholics were more than 20 percent by 1920. The United States had not become Roman Catholic, as many had feared; Roman Catholics had become American. By supporting the principle of separation of church and state, the Irish also contributed to the ideal of a civic culture as the basis of American identity by successfully challenging the assumption that Americanism was synonymous with Protestantism.

Thomas D'Arcy McGee, the Irish-born editor of *The Celt,* in the 1850s challenged the view that American character was fixed at the time of the Revolution: he said "American nationality" was "like a chemical solution" that "might contain independent elements, and yet form a whole, which would be different from, and better than any of them."[65]

Yet the Irish-dominated church was still seen by many Americans as a menace right up until the election of Kennedy in 1960. But by the 1980s, when perhaps almost half of the continuing flow of immigration to the U.S. was Catholic, there was virtually no discussion of a Catholic menace. The Americans had discovered something which, while difficult to export, clearly worked in their own environment. The permission to maintain traditional religious and cultural loyalties helped to bind immigrants and their children to the American political culture. By making it easy to join the polity, by defining nationality in essentially political terms, the *unum* had ensured the allegiance of the *pluribus.*

Chapter Three

MORE SLOVENIAN AND MORE AMERICAN
How the Hyphen Unites

O N A cold, misty April 19, 1875, President Ulysses S. Grant and key members of his cabinet joined the centennial celebration of the beginning of the American Revolution at Concord and Lexington, Massachusetts, where they listened to speeches made by illustrious Anglo-Americans, among them Ralph Waldo Emerson, Julia Ward Howe, James Russell Lowell, and John Greenleaf Whittier. It was a high moment for the Anglo-American leadership of Massachusetts, who were reminded by Thomas Merriam Stetson, the master of ceremonies of the festive day in Lexington, that the fallen heroes of Lexington and Concord all had English names. Speaking of the martyrs of the Revolution, Stetson called their courageous stand against the larger British force "the flower and consummation of principles that were long ripening in the clear-sighted, liberty-loving, Anglo-Saxon mind."[1]

The Anglo-Americans, especially in New England, thought of themselves as charter members of the republic. Americans from other backgrounds were relative newcomers, and persons of color, despite the Thirteenth, Fourteenth, and Fifteenth Amendments, still were treated essentially as outsiders, and within a few years after the centennial their position as outsiders would be more sharply defined. With the end of Reconstruction, blacks in the South were relegated to the position of a subjugated, segregated rural proletariat. Chinese laborers were excluded from immigrating to the United States in 1882, and the Dawes Act was passed in 1887 in an attempt to assimilate Native Americans (Indians) by breaking up tribal lands.

By the time of the centennial in 1875, however, probably most Anglo-Americans accepted the necessity of immigration from northern and western Europe. Employers greedily sought white immigrant labor, and the Republican party platforms of 1864 and 1868 made explicit the connection between capital expansion and the venerable myth of asylum by asserting that "foreign immigration, which in the past has added so much to the wealth, development of resources, and increase of power to this nation—the asylum of the oppressed of all nations—should be fostered and encouraged by a just policy."[2] Immigrants from Germany kept coming in large numbers (718,182 between 1871 and 1880, totaling more than one-quarter of all immigrants and a third of those from Europe), and German-speaking enclaves existed all over the Midwest, but their arrival did not often raise the sharp anxieties that Benjamin Franklin and other Anglo-Americans had expressed in the mid-eighteenth century when they said such immigrants might "Germanize us." Immigration from Ireland, while substantial (436,871 in the 1870s), had been halved in the twenty-year period between 1861 and 1880 from the previous twenty years, and the percentage of Irish compared with other immigrants had gone down steadily since the 1850s.[3]

The Irish still aroused hostility even though mine operators, railroad owners, small manufacturers, and a growing number of Americans in commerce and the professions had grown used to having them fill a variety of unskilled and semiskilled jobs. They were more threatening to Anglo-Americans than Germans or Scandinavians not just because they were Catholic (a substantial number of Germans were Catholic, too) but also because, poor and unskilled, they crowded into the cities of the Northeast, where their presence was linked to alcoholism and other diseases, and to crime.

Northern Europe accounted for 90 percent of all immigration in the 1860s and 80 percent in the 1870s, but as the numbers from Ireland went down, those from Scandinavia went up, almost doubling between 1871 and 1880 over the previous decade. Scandinavians were overwhelmingly Protestant, and a large number, like the Germans, moved to the Midwest, where almost everyone came from somewhere else. Their arrival met relatively little opposition; even though they spoke their ancestral languages at home and sometimes in school, they entered the political life of their communities and, as did the Germans, established ethnic associations in the American pattern of voluntary ethnic pluralism.

Immigration from Southern and Eastern Europe

With continued confinement of free blacks to the coercive, segregated labor system of the South and with continued exclusion of Chinese laborers from immigration, the leaders of American industry and commerce in the North looked to European immigrants to keep the cost of labor low. Immigrant labor was cheap for many reasons. A high proportion were young, single men who brought no children for the state to educate. As noncitizens, they were subject to deportation for at least five years, and, lacking language skills in most cases, they also lacked mobility. Native-born workers, on the other hand, were organizing in unions, demanding a shorter work day and work week and higher wages. With the number of immigrants from northern Europe going down (in the last four years of the 1870s never above 177,826 [1879] in any year), employers and labor contractors began to look to southern and eastern Europe for workers. In the 1880s, the number of immigrants more than doubled over the previous ten years (2,271,925 to 4,735,484), and net migration as a percentage of American population growth rose from slightly more than 25 percent to over 40 percent in the same decade.[4] American capital looked for labor in southern Italy, where large numbers of unemployed and underemployed single men were willing to come to the U.S. to build roads, buildings, and reservoirs. They took jobs in what economists would later call a secondary labor market—low-skilled, heavy-muscle, often temporary jobs segregated from mainstream economic opportunities. During the 1880s, immigration from Italy, nearly all of it from the poor south, jumped six times over what it had been in the 1870s. It doubled again in the decade of the 1890s to 651,893, and quadrupled from 1901 through 1910 to 2,450,877.

Russia and other eastern European countries provided another source of workers. From the decade of the 1870s to the decade of the 1890s the number of immigrants from Russia, most of them Jews, increased more than ten times, from nearly 40,000 to 505,290; from 1901 through 1910 (when Poles were counted among Russians, Austro-Hungarians, and Germans) the number of immigrants admitted to the U.S. grew to 1,597,306. The percentage of all European immigrants who came from the east and south of Europe rose steadily from nearly 20 percent in the decade of the 1880s to 53 percent in the 1890s and 75 percent from 1901 through 1910 as the exploding industrial revolution in the United States called for workers in the Midwest as well as in the North.[5]

Most immigrants were Catholics, including Italians, Poles, and Slavs. Along with a substantial number of Greeks and Jews, these were peoples whose languages, appearance, customs, and religions combined with their poverty to mark them clearly as outsiders. That the composition of immigration changed so drastically—in the 1870s one of every four immigrants from Europe was from the United Kingdom, in the 1880s, one of every eight—gave rise once more to apprehensions for the preservation of American identity and unity.

Guarding the Gates: A Racial View of American Identity

But what was the essence of American identity? On what did American unity depend? For Jefferson, American identity was a matter of American ideology, and American unity depended upon newcomers embracing the principles that gave rise to and sustained self-government. He had said nothing about nationality or race. But for the forty years between 1880 and 1920, a period of almost continual national debate over the meaning of American identity and unity, Jeffersonian arguments were mixed in a potpourri of concerns about class, culture, and race.

As always, skilled, semiskilled, and unskilled native-born workers worried about the negative effect that immigrants would have on wages and working conditions. Often confined to city neighborhoods where their children were obliged to attend school with the children of immigrants, native-born workers were much more likely than high-level managers or employers to be upset by the strange ways of the newcomers. But the antiimmigrant appeal was widespread, reaching into the rural South, where there were few immigrants, to small towns in the Midwest, and to the upper reaches of Beacon Hill and the Back Bay, where the Brahmins of Boston kept the Massachusetts idea alive despite and perhaps because of the rising power of the Irish.

Woodrow Wilson, professor of government at Princeton University, observed in 1901 that earlier in the nineteenth century "men of the sturdy stocks of the north of Europe" made up the main force of immigrants, but now "multitudes of men of the lowest class from the south of Italy and men of the meaner sort out of Hungary and Poland" who had "neither skill nor energy nor an initiative of quick intelligence" were coming in such huge numbers "as if the countries of the south of Europe were disburdening themselves of the more sordid and hapless elements of their population."[6] Complementing the image of Europe disgorging huge unwanted populations was the picture of an American gate that was open and unguarded. "Wide open and unguarded stand our gates," warned Thomas Bailey Aldrich in a poem in the *Atlantic Monthly* in 1892, "and through them presses a wild, a motley throng" who "bring with them unknown gods and rites." Appealing to the American goddess of liberty, he concluded, "O! Liberty! White Goddess! . . . Lift the downtrodden, but with the hand of steel / Stay those who to thy sacred portals come / To waste thy gifts of freedom."[7]

The fears expressed by Wilson and Aldrich were echoed in editorial pages, labor union halls, and political rallies, and in pseudoscientific thinking about race and culture. A former dean of the Lawrence College of Science at Harvard, Nathaniel Shaler, explained patiently in a book about Jews, blacks, and other outsiders that Jews could "never become effectively reconciled with any Christian society."[8] Jews, said Shaler, will never make good Americans because "they are to our race a very unpleasant people . . . socially impossible."[9]

Shaler did not call for a complete ban on immigration of Jews, only of "the degraded" among them, along with "such composite folk as the southern Italians and those from the lower Danube and the Balkan Peninsula."[10] Despite such commonly held attitudes, the tremendous growth of the American economy sustained the demand for cheap immigrant labor. Industrial interests, in particular, resisted restrictionist proposals, and in 1907 the National Association of Manufacturers called for a loosening of the existing minor controls on immigration. Immigrant-ethnic groups, already adapted to the American pattern of voluntary ethnic pluralism, mobilized against immigration restriction in 1907. The Ancient Order of the Hibernians, for example, signed an agreement with the largest ethnic organization in the nation, the German-American Alliance (more than a million and a half members) to oppose all immigration restriction.[11] In 1907, the year of greatest immigration to the U.S., more immigrants were admitted lawfully (1,385,459) than in any single year before or since, the third year in a row in which more than a million immigrants had arrived. The sheer volume of immigration (the previous decade, 1891–1900, saw an annual average of 370,000) gave impetus to restriction.

The Immigration Restriction League, founded in 1894 by five Boston-born-and-bred graduates of Harvard College who believed with utmost certainty that they were defending Americanism, brought back the Massachusetts idea once again. Americans had built a glorious city on the hill, now a representative self-governing republic. The descendants of those who had been there at the creation felt obliged to protect it from contamination. Grossly exaggerating the differences between the newcomers and older groups of immigrants, one professor of education at Stanford University saw the eastern and southern Europeans as "lacking in self reliance and initiative, and not possessing the Anglo-Teutonic conceptions of law, order and government." Their arrival, he asserted, had already tended "to corrupt our civic life."[12]

The plea for immigration restriction met strong political opposition—from employers wanting more muscle, ethnics wanting more brothers and sisters, and a growing band of social workers and politicians wanting more clients. Minor restrictions and reforms led to the banning of prostitutes and convicts (1875), of lunatics and those likely to become public charges (1882), and of contract laborers (1885). When Congress, for the first time, placed all immigration under federal authority, steamship companies were obliged to carry back to Europe those passengers rejected by U.S. inspectors (1891). The 1891 act also provided for deporting aliens already in the U.S., stipulating that any alien who became a public charge "from causes existing prior to his landing" could be expelled within a year after arrival.

The principal legislative objective of the Immigration Restriction League was a literacy test, first proposed in 1887, requiring all male adult applicants for immigration to read and write their own language. The standoff between the pro- and anti-immigration forces was reflected in the schizophrenic immigration bill of 1907, which gave the secretary of commerce the power to admit immigrants in borderline cases if he deemed them needed for the work force, and which required immigrants to pay a head tax of four dollars, twice the amount prescribed before. The most important part of the legislation was the creation of an immigration commission, a tripartite body consisting of three U.S. senators, three members of the House of Representatives, and three appointed by the president, Theodore Roosevelt. Reporting three years later on December 5, 1910, the commission recommended, with only one dissent, a two-decades-old proposal of a reading and writing test "as the most feasible single method of restricting undesirable immigration," a proposal that had passed the Congress in 1897 only to be vetoed by President Cleveland.[13]

With so many conflicting pressures, the political parties straddled the issue of immigration in the early 1900s. Both Republican and Democratic party platforms promised a continuation of the exclusion of Chinese labor but were uncertain about European immigration until 1912, when the Republicans pledged "the enactment of appropriate laws to give relief from the constantly growing evil of induced or undesirable immigration, which is inimical to the progress and welfare of the people of the United States."[14] The Democrats, increasingly dependent on ethnic-immigrant votes, did not join the growing call for restriction, though in their 1916 platform they took a swipe at German, Irish, and other ethnic anti-preparedness groups when they condemned "combinations of individuals in this country, of whatever nationality or descent, who agree and conspire together for the purpose of embarrassing or weakening our government or of improperly influencing or coercing our public representatives in dealing or negotiating with any foreign power."[15]

As the United States reacted to the war among the European powers, a growing number of Americans became concerned about hyphenates whose affection for the old countries might make them something less than 100 percent loyal. The Prohibition party in 1916 said in classic civic culture terms, "We stand for Americanism. We believe this country was created for a great mission among the nations of the earth. We rejoice in the fact that it has offered asylum to the oppressed of other lands. . . . But he who loves another land more than this is not fit for citizenship here."[16] Growing mistrust of immigrants led in 1917 to the passage of the literacy test over Wilson's veto.[17] (Wilson, now a Democratic president dependent upon the political support of most of the ethnics, had changed his stance since 1901.)

With the entry of the U.S. into the First World War, immigration was drastically diminished, and restriction was no longer an immediate issue. The war unleashed a frenzy of antiforeign feeling, much of it directed against the Germans, who until that time had maintained a large network of German-language clubs, newspapers, and churches in the U.S. All "foreign" religions and cultures were attacked, especially by a revived Ku Klux Klan and particularly in the South, the Midwest, and the Far West, where many small-town and rural Protestant Americans saw the Klan as defending American purity against what was seen as the growing power of big-city Catholics and Jews. Examples of hysteria were legion. Tom Watson of Georgia campaigned successfully for a seat in the U.S. Senate, claiming that Wilson had become a tool of the Pope. The governor of Florida warned that the Pope planned to invade the Sunshine State and to transfer the Vatican there. Several itinerant preachers for the Klan warned against a Roman plot to destroy the only true Christian nation, and the Grand Dragon of the Klan in Oregon told its members that it must work actively to keep the country from a takeover by immigrants.[18]

The literacy test did not curb the large flow of immigrants from eastern and southern Europe, and in 1921 Congress, following another recommendation of the Immigration Commission (1907–1910), passed into law a provisional measure for strict quotas on each European nation. The act established an annual ceiling of 355,000 on European immigration and limited the number of immigrants of each nationality annually to 3 percent of the number of foreign-born persons of that nationality resident in the U.S. at the time of the 1910 census. This first quota act was extended for two years, but in 1924 came passage of what was heralded as a permanent solution to immigration problems, the Johnson-Reed Act, more commonly known as the National Origins Act. It provided for an annual limit of 150,000 Europeans (plus the wives, parents, and minor children of U.S. citizens), a complete prohibition on Japanese immigration, the issuance and counting of visas against quotas abroad rather than on arrival, and the development of quotas based on the numerical contribution of each nationality to the overall U.S. population rather than on the foreign-born population.

Recognizing that it would take some time to develop new quotas, the bill provided as a stopgap measure for the annual admission of immigrants to be no more than 2 percent of each nationality's proportion of the foreign-born U.S. population in 1890. The old Pennsylvania approach of accepting as Americans white Europeans regardless of their national background was repudiated. Use of the 1890 instead of the 1910 census meant a reduction in the annual Italian quota from 42,000 to about 4,000; in the Polish quota from 31,000 to 6,000; and in the Greek quota from 3,000 to 100. The commissioner of immigration reported, one year after the 1924 legislation took effect, that virtually all immigrants now "looked exactly like Americans."[19]

Immigration from southern and eastern Europe now slowed to a trickle. Would the newcomers from eastern and southern Europe who had already arrived become Americans, or constitute some foreign, undigestible irritant in American society? Holding fast to the idea that American identity was based on conformity to the culture and religion of the earliest American settlers, many restrictionists saw in ethnic churches, fairs, songs, food, and dozens of other manifestations of voluntary ethnic pluralism ample proof that the newcomers were not becoming American. Madison Grant, whose book *The Passing of the Great Race* (1916) had issued an urgent call for restriction, wrote in 1925 that "the example of the Pennsylvania Germans [Amish] shows us that it will take centuries before the foreigners now become Americans." And observing the community of Hamtramck, in Detroit, where he alleged a mass meeting of Polish residents demanded Polish rule, he concluded, "there certainly was no 'melting pot' in Hamtramck."[20]

"The myth of the melting pot has been discredited," said Albert Johnson, a principal author of the 1924 National Origins immigration legislation.[21] In 1926, Henry Pratt Fairchild in *The Melting Pot Mistake* saw "the native and the foreigner . . . growing steadily farther and farther apart, and the spheres in which they move . . . growing more and more distinct and irreconcilable."[22] Efforts to Americanize the newcomers, no matter how well-intentioned, were doomed to fail, argued Fairchild, because the deepest feelings of love and affection of immigrants lay understandably with their ancestral homelands.

Efforts to Americanize the Newcomers

The Americanization movement Fairchild thought futile had been hard at work even before July 4, 1915, when the first official national Americanization Day was held, with the motto, "Many Peoples, But One Nation"[23] (soon to be replaced by "America First"). The leaders of the movement acted on the assumption that immigrants from southern and eastern Europe and their children could be remade by the American environment, just as immigrants from the north and west of Europe, including impoverished and despised Irish Catholics, had been remade in the nineteenth century. Wilson's secretary of the interior, Franklin Lane, whose department issued an *Americanization Bulletin* during 1918 and 1919, wrote that in "fashioning a new people . . . we are doing the unprecedented thing in saying that Slav, Teuton, Celt and the other races that make up the civilized world are capable of being blended here."[24]

Education in a variety of settings was the chief strategy of the Americanizers. As early as 1907, New Jersey passed legislation to support evening classes in English and civics for the foreign-born, and a new organization called the North American Civic League for Immigrants was created "to improve the environment and the spirit of America, the knowledge of America, and the love of America and one's fellow men into the millions gathered and gathering here from the ends of the earth."[25] A nonsectarian organization that sought support from Protestants, Catholics, and Jews, the league selected Boston, site of antiimmigrant agitation, and then the second-largest port of entry to the U.S., in which to begin its program of education in English and good citizenship.[26] By the end of the first year, it had organized committees in thirty-six cities in nine states to assist in its program of assimilation; eighteen of the committees were in Massachusetts. Granted space by the federal government in the new immigration station in Boston, it enlarged its role as a coordinating organization, becoming a repository of information on immigration aid societies, immigration boarding houses, the character and availability of interpreters, and other services, and published a series of messages stressing patriotic themes for newcomers to the United States in nine foreign languages, including Yiddish, Arabic, and Finnish.

Similar to the North American Civic League was an organization developed in Chicago in 1908 called the League for the Protection of Immigrants (the Immigrants Protective League by 1910), which also sponsored programs to welcome newcomers and to educate them in American ways.[27] In New York, a special gubernatorial commission, after finding evidence of considerable exploitation of and discrimination against immigrants, recommended establishment of a Bureau of Industries and Immigration to promote the effective employment of immigrants and their development as useful citizens, a recommendation that was enacted in 1910.[28]

Many social clubs such as the General Federation of Women's Clubs and the National Society of the Daughters of the American Revolution, labor unions such as the American Federation of Labor and the United Mine Workers, and business organizations such as the Chamber of Commerce joined schools and other agencies of government in the Americanization movement. Industry participated, partly because it believed that the failure of immigrants to learn English resulted in an economic loss. Henry Ford set up classes in his plants and required attendance of his five thousand non-English-speaking employees. The International Harvester Company produced its own lesson plans for the non-English-speaking workers in its plants, which clearly taught more than English. The first plan read:

I hear the whistle. I must hurry.
I hear the five minute whistle.
It is time to go into the shop . . .
I change my clothes and get ready to work . . .
I work until the whistle blows to quit.
I leave my place nice and clean.

I put all my clothes in the locker.
I must go home.[29]

The first report issued by the Bureau of Industries and Immigration in New York in 1912 stressed the importance of ensuring liberty and justice. In 1914 the Federal Bureau of Naturalization sponsored citizenship classes throughout the public schools. Its program brought candidates for citizenship together with naturalized citizens for patriotic exercises.[30] By 1919, the Bureau of Immigration reported that 2,240 communities were conducting classes for immigrants. That year, the bureau entered into an agreement with the National Council of the Boy Scouts of America, in which the Scouts were pledged to serve as guides and ushers in citizenship receptions. Many states followed the lead of the national government in setting up departments or bureaus of Americanization, and some state boards of education conducted special training courses for Americanization teachers.[31]

At the height of the Americanization movement in 1921, the National Society of the Daughters of the American Revolution published a *Manual of the United States: For the Information of Immigrants and Foreigners* in English and seventeen other languages, which in its first four editions was distributed in two million copies throughout the nation.[32] The general tone of the booklet was welcoming: "To the men and women who come from far-off lands to seek a new home in America and become its loyal supporters as good citizens, the Daughters of the American Revolution extend a cordial welcome." Citizenship was the key, according to the DAR. "We ask you to make yourselves worthy to become a citizen of our country, to study its history, to become acquainted with its literature, its traditions and its laws. . . . It is a proud honor to have American citizenship conferred upon you. It is more honorable to deserve such citizenship," wrote a past president-general in her address of welcome. She invited the outsiders "to share in this citizenship when you have learned its duties and privileges," promising them that "this is a land of equal opportunity for all. We offer you these equal opportunities."[33]

The DAR booklet made it clear that becoming an American was a matter of belief and faith and not ancestry, at least if one was white and from Europe, or possibly Japanese, since immigration from Japan between 1900 and 1920 justified one booklet in Japanese even though Japanese nationals were ineligible for citizenship (Japanese immigration would be banned three years after publication of the booklet). Immigrants should "make themselves worthy to receive the great gift of American citizenship; to become *true Americans* in heart and soul."[34] The booklet advised that there must be some visible sign of what was in one's heart and soul, and that the best way to show it was to learn English. Immigrants were urged to study the problems of government. "Then you will be the kind of citizen America needs."[35] The advantages of citizenship, voting, holding public office, obtaining passports, and other benefits were stressed. In exchange for these benefits, the immigrant citizen was advised to vote, accept jury duty enthusiastically, and pay taxes without evasion.

For the European immigrant, the path to citizenship was still clear, quick, and simple. The obligations of citizenship, far from being onerous, called for participation in the American system of self-government. The DAR was not asking newcomers to abandon feelings of affection for their old countries. "America does not ask you to forget your old home," said the booklet. But in taking the oath of allegiance to the United States, new citizens must promise to give up allegiance "to your former country. . . . You cannot have two countries."[36]

The DAR did not have cause to doubt the immigrants on the question of political allegiance. It was not a major issue for most of those who came from southern Italy, who hated the oppressive rule of the north, or of Jews who came from Russia or Poland or Austria-Hungary, where anti-Semitism was vicious, or even of the Slavs, Poles, Lithuanians, and others from eastern Europe, whose old-country allegiances were religious and cultural much more than political. The problem for immigrants was rather the anguish of trying to be understood in a foreign language, of being mocked for strange customs, of having to listen to an Irish priest and not understanding a word he said, of being shocked by the newly irreverent behavior of children, and of being unable to adjust from a peasant life to industrial work. The problem was the pain of separating from one's loved ones and then sometimes of broken marriages in the new country. The anguish was about the danger of losing cultural and religious loyalties and sensibilities, the fear of acquiring in America what one immigrant called a "flavorless . . . soul."[37] Even though they still felt like strangers in the new country, sometimes strangers even to their children, they often felt cut off from the old world, too.

Acceptance into the political community was tainted by inhospitable actions toward expressions of ethnicity, and during and for several years after the war, German-Americans especially did not feel it was safe to show the hyphen because many Americanizers scorned the newcomers as un-American when they showed pride in things German. Charles Heartman, an American writer of German birth and an advocate of immigration from Germany, urged that "when they come, let them be cut off from German influence, from a German press, from a German club."[38] Another German-American, Gustavus Ohlinger, acquiescing in the view that cultural pride was a sign of political disloyalty, denounced a speech given in Milwaukee to ten thousand German-Americans by the president of the German-American National Alliance, who had told his audience not to permit "our two thousand year culture to be trodden down in this land," and exhorted them to "remember . . . the benefits of *German Kultur*."[39] Such attitudes, Ohlinger pointed out, had led to insistence by Germans and other groups in Chicago for public school instruction in their own languages, which could only lead to "racial feuds" that would "disrupt the country and make it a heterogeneous mass of warring factions."[40] From 1917 to 1923, twenty-three German Catholic publications were discontinued and the two-million-member National German-American Alliance, organized in 1901 to promote German culture in America and the interests of German-Americans, had to disband in 1918.

Japanese, Chinese, Scandinavian, Greek, and Hebrew language schools also were under constant attack, but most immigrants who stayed in the United States (about a third went back) began to replicate the pattern of voluntary ethnic pluralism established by the Germans, Dutch, Scandinavians, Scotch-Irish, Irish, and English themselves in earlier years. Armenians, Greeks, and Albanians established their own orthodox churches, the Polish, Italian, and German Catholics their own parishes, and nationality groups among the Jews created their own small synagogues in an effort to keep fellow countrymen together and make the transition easier to the strange and often hostile new world. Ethnic-group leaders opposed attempts in the Americanization movement in the early 1920s to disparage foreign cultures, such as state laws forbidding the teaching of foreign languages. Making a defense in terms of American ideals, a Polish-language newspaper asserted, "It is deplorable that so many Americans object so much to foreign customs. It smacks decidedly of Prussianism, and is not quite at all in accordance with American ideals of freedom."[41] A Hungarian paper said that "Americanization does not mean the suppression of foreign languages." An Italian newspaper said that "Americanization is an ugly word," if "it means to proselytize by making the foreign born forget his mother country and mother tongue."[42]

However much immigrants felt hostility from native-born Americans, they usually were welcomed by presidents from Grover Cleveland to Woodrow Wilson. One can imagine the joy felt by Jews when President William McKinley appeared on September 16, 1897, with his cabinet for the laying of a cornerstone for a Washington synagogue[43] or the excitement of five thousand newly naturalized citizens as they listened to a speech by President Wilson at Convention Hall in Philadelphia on May 10, 1915, where facing the new citizens were great flags draped on twenty pillars, festoons of bunting, and a wreath thirty feet in diameter below electric lighted letters: "Welcome to a government of the people, by the people, for the people." Several ethnic groups petitioned Wilson for special celebrations to enable the foreign-born to demonstrate their loyalty.

On July 4, 1918, thirty-three nationalities sent representatives on a pilgrimage to the Washington Monument as the president's guests, and parades, pageants, and mass meetings celebrating American freedom were held all over the country.[44] Nonetheless, most immigrants did not rush to naturalization. Their first interest was in making a living, and a second interest for perhaps a majority was in returning home. The story of one immigrant, which came to the author in a cigar box found by a colleague, probably was typical of many of the single male sojourners from southern Italy who came to the U.S. to work, with the expectation of returning home. Salvatore DeMeo, whose passport listed him as a *contadini* (peasant), came from Castellonorato in the province of Latina to Waltham, Massachusetts in 1894. After working as a day laborer he obtained a job in the Waltham mill and made enough money to travel back and forth to Italy in 1919, 1928, and 1929, a classic sojourner pattern. Not until 1930, eleven years after his arrival, did he decide to stay. For three years he took courses in English on American citizenship, receiving credit for 312 hours of instruction. In the Corona cigar box in which his naturalization and other certificates were found neatly folded in a looseleaf binder, DeMeo also kept the Waltham book of American citizenship, a sixty-seven-page manual outlining basic facts of American history, city, county, and state governments, presented in a question-and-answer format. In DeMeo's well-worn booklet he was told that being 100 percent American does not depend on where one's grandfather was born but on obeying the laws of the United States. "All residents of America should become citizens of America. . . . America needs all the wisdom of all the people who live under her flag."[45] Underlined were the words that told the naturalized citizen to vote every year, "not just when he feels like it." He should examine the records of the men running for office and "vote for what I believe in my own heart is right, and for the best man, no matter what his race or creed or ancestry."[46]

In the very year in which DeMeo began taking his citizenship course, 1930, President Herbert Hoover responded to a criticism from Italian-born mayor Fiorello LaGuardia of New York by telling him, "you should go back to where you belong and advise Mussolini on how to make good honest citizens in Italy. The Italians are predominantly our murderers and bootleggers . . . like a lot of other foreign spawn, you do not appreciate the country which supports and tolerates you."[47] It was an outrageous expression of bigotry against a man who, in addition to being a distinguished mayor of the largest and most important city in the country, had flown in the U.S. Air Force in the First World War and in the Second would play a major role in directing the national war effort. Did Hoover make LaGuardia feel like an outsider? Probably not. Like many other talented immigrants from eastern and southern Europe, he found it easy to claim membership in the American civic culture because its ideals, symbols, and founding myth did not require him to stop feeling Italian, something that Hoover had forgotten.

Italians and Jews Claim Their American Identity

LaGuardia was thoroughly assimilated. No one would necessarily know that he was foreign born. But there were some who actually claimed an American identity even though they were fresh off the boat. What accounted for the fact that foreign-speaking and -acting newcomers felt a direct relationship to the founding fathers? Lincoln had already given that answer in 1860 when he pointed out that though immigrants could not claim ancestors who made the Revolution or founded the republic, they "felt a part of us" because those who wrote the ideals expressed in the Declaration of Independence meant them for all people for all time. That is why the newcomers had the right to claim them as forefathers "as though they were the blood of the blood and flesh of the flesh of the men who wrote the Declaration."[48]

Perhaps Lincoln understood so well because he wanted German votes, or perhaps because of his friendship with Carl Schurz, who had spoken on "True Americanism" at Faneuil Hall only a year earlier, or because of his own wisdom. Whatever the reason, Lincoln understood that generations of newcomers from all parts of the globe spoke of "our forefathers, who brought forth this nation" as if they were truly related to the heroes of the Revolution and the early republic, just as Jews and non-Jewish guests speak on Passover of coming out of Egypt from slavery as if they were physically there in the desert about fifteen hundred years before Christ's birth. American ideals and principles were universal and could be claimed by anyone, as could the symbols, rituals, and heroes connected to those ideals. Crèvecoeur had written of "our *alma mater.*" An Irish immigrant marveled at "our glorious Constitution." Schurz spoke of "our institutions."

The eastern and southern Europeans claimed American heroes and legends as theirs, too. The scions of Brahmin families in New England often looked at the newcomers and thought that they could not possibly understand all that had gone into the making of free American institutions. To Henry Adams in 1911, a new society was being formed, and he felt powerless to deal with it "and its entire unconsciousness that I . . . or George Washington ever existed."[49] Adams totally misunderstood the power of the ideas of his New England ancestors. But only a few years later, a young Jewish immigrant woman, Mary Antin, wrote of "our forefathers" in a series of articles in the *Atlantic Monthly*. Writing that "George Washington himself could not mean more than I when he said, 'my country' after I once felt it," she explained that "for the country was for all citizens, and *I was a citizen,* and when we stood up to sing 'America!' I shouted the words with all my might."[50] Antin would walk the steps of the Boston public library, not far from her tenement home, lingering to read the carved inscription: *Public Library—Built By The People—Free To All.* Calling it her "palace" because she was a citizen, she would say to herself repeatedly as she watched the scholars and the "fine-browed women" and their children going in and out of the library, "this is mine . . . this is ours."[51]

Probably Antin did not know that Asian immigrants were ineligible for citizenship, although she wrote of the boys in her neighborhood making fun of a "Chinaman." Perhaps she did not know of the decimation of the Indians, and that those who lived on reservations were still ineligible for citizenship, or of the misery of many native Hawaiians following annexation of the islands by the U.S. She must have been aware that most blacks were denied even the most elemental of rights, including the right to vote, through systematic oppression and intimidation throughout the South and even in many places in the North. But she did not mention blacks. She certainly had knowledge of the mounting opposition of Anglo-Americans to immigrants and immigration, and of the deep resentment they felt against such upstarts as herself, a Jew, no less, a member of the hated tribe, claiming to be an American on equal terms with others.

Only six years after publication of Antin's book, another Russian Jewish immigrant, Jacob Abrams, when questioned about his anarchist beliefs by Judge Henry Delamar Clayton, Jr., a fifth-generation American, began his reply, "When our forefathers of the American Revolution—" At that point, Judge Clayton exclaimed, "Your what?" Again, Abrams said, "My forefathers," whereupon the judge asked incredulously if he meant to refer "to the fathers of this nation as your forefathers?"[52]

Clayton did not believe that the First Amendment was for naturalized citizens. Two years before the Abrams case, when he empaneled a grand jury in New York City, the judge had declared that "naturalized citizens who unfairly criticize the government should get off the face of the earth, or at least go back to the country they left. . . . I have no sympathy with any naturalized citizen who is given to carping criticism of this Government."[53] But Abrams was not even a citizen. How dare he speak of "our forefathers"! Twice Clayton asked, "Why don't you go back to Russia?"[54] Later in the trial, the judge recalled Abrams's use of the term "our forefathers": "I said, What? You were born in Russia and came here four or five years ago and not a citizen, an anarchist, who can never become a citizen. Our forefathers . . . why, just look at it."[55] Abrams undoubtedly sensed that the forefathers' ideals were his.

The ardent patriotism of immigrant Mary Antin became commonplace, as Jewish, Greek, Polish, and other ethnic organizations sponsored naturalization classes and "I Am an American Day" and encouraged new-comers, especially their children, to participate in the civic life of their communities. But the claiming of America was much less dramatic for the vast majority of eastern and southern European immigrants, a large portion of whom were too busy surviving to even apply for naturalization.

Salvatore DeMeo was more typical of most immigrants than Mary Antin, although DeMeo also began acting like an American even before he became a citizen, despite his trips to and from Italy. Having made deposits regularly in the Waltham Savings Bank during the 1920s, he had accumulated nearly four thousand dollars in 1929, only three months after his last return from Italy. After the onset of the Depression and the closing of the banks, he quickly discovered that he had rights under Massachusetts law to recover some money from the Waltham Trust Company, another bank in which he had funds, and then in liquidation. He joined other depositors in a legal struggle and recovered $408.60, or 74.4 percent of his original balance, facts I discovered from papers found in the cigar box with George Washington's profile stamped on its cover. DeMeo and millions like him quietly went about the business of becoming Americans, even as they maintained some of the religious practices, culinary preferences, and family values of the old country. In that respect, they were no different than the Anglo-Americans themselves, with their Presbyterian and Anglican rites, scones, puddings, and English and Scottish music and dance. Cultural and religious prejudices were commonplace among all groups, but the prejudices of the Anglo-Americans had greater significance because they had more power of all kinds, including cultural power.

Randolph Bourne, a rebellious descendant of English settlers, wrote in 1916, at a time of growing hostility toward newcomers from southern and eastern Europe, that "the truth is that no more tenacious cultural allegiance to the mother country has been shown by any alien nation than by the ruling class of Anglo-Saxon descendants in these American states. English snobberies, English religion, English literary styles, English literary references and canons, English ethics, English superiorities, have been the cultural food we have drunk in from our mothers' breasts."[56]

Strengthening the Civic Culture Through Voluntary Pluralism

Those who thought of themselves as charter members could not logically have their political ideology and deny cultural diversity too. The ideology that led to First Amendment freedoms and Fourteenth Amendment protections ensured the development of cultural diversity. Even amid the ethnic and religious bigotry of what John Higham called "the tribal Twenties,"[57] as in the mining town of West Frankfurt in southern Illinois, where crowds rushed into the Italian district, "dragged cowering residents from their homes, clubbed and stoned them, and set fire to their dwellings,"[58] a white and essentially Anglo-Saxon U.S. Supreme Court upheld that principle of the civic culture—freedom of religion and of association in all things private—that gave birth to and protected voluntary ethnic pluralism.

In a series of three landmark decisions, Justice J. C. McReynolds made it clear that although he sympathized with the cultural conformists, it was his and the Court's responsibility to uphold the principles of freedom that led to expressions of ethnic and religious diversity. In 1919, Nebraska passed a law forbidding the teaching of modern foreign languages to children between eight and sixteen. The special intention of the law, like others passed in South Dakota and Iowa, was to eliminate the German language, particularly in church-related schools run by German-Americans, but the overall effect of the law would have been to disparage the foreign languages and cultures of several other immigrant groups as well. Although the supreme courts of Iowa, Ohio, and Nebraska upheld such acts as constitutional on the broad ground that the legislature could decide what the common welfare demanded, McReynolds, speaking for the U.S. Supreme Court, said that the states had acted unconstitutionally.

The Court was sympathetic to the desire of the legislature "to foster a homogeneous people with American ideals, prepared readily to understand current discussions of civic matters. . . ." It was cognizant of the fact that "the foreign born population is very large, that certain communities use foreign words, follow foreign leaders, move in a foreign atmosphere, and that the children are thereby hindered from becoming citizens of the most useful type." However, while a law to prohibit the teaching of foreign languages in the schools would have been fine in ancient Sparta, where the education of males to be ideal citizens was entrusted to official guardians, it was not for the U.S. McReynolds asserted that Spartan ideas on "the relation between individual and state were wholly different from those upon which our institutions rest." "The protection of the Constitution," the Court insisted, "extends to all, to those who speak other languages as well as to those born with English on the tongue."[59]

Two other decisions also strengthened the idea that Americans were united by their loyalty to a civic and not a religious, linguistic, or other characteristic of a tribal culture. In 1922, Oregon passed a law requiring all students to attend public schools; the intent was to stamp out Catholic and other parochial religious schools. Sued by the Society of Sisters, a Catholic order, the plaintiffs, having lost their case in the Oregon Supreme Court, appealed to the U.S. Supreme Court; they were supported by, as *amici curiae,* the American Jewish Committee, the Seventh-Day Adventists, and the Domestic and Foreign Missionary Society for the

Protestant Episcopal Church. Justice McReynolds, and the majority opinion, upheld the right of Americans to send their children to private or parochial schools. In what are essentially private matters, the Court ruled, diversity is protected by the Constitution. The freedoms given all Americans prevent the state from taking actions "to standardize its children. . . . The child is not the mere creature of the state; those who nurture him and direct his destiny have the right, coupled with the high duty, to recognize and prepare him for additional obligation."[60]

The conception of American identity as based on membership in a civic culture had an even more difficult test three years later, in 1926, when the Court heard arguments on a law in the Territory of Hawaii on whether private language schools were free to shape their own curricula if they complied with the requirements of the public schools. Even some empathic social workers and teachers in Hawaii were worried that Nisei children, by the mid-1920s more numerous than Caucasian children in the public schools, might resist Americanization. A large proportion of Japanese-American children continued to speak Japanese in their homes; a majority attended Japanese-language schools, sometimes getting up as early as four a.m. to go to schools that also taught Japanese values, customs, and history; some were even taught to venerate the emperor of Japan as a semideity.

The Hawaii legislature attempted to regulate the language schools through strict examinations for teachers and oversight of curricula. After several years of litigation in the territorial and federal courts, the U.S. Supreme Court held that the laws regarding the language schools were unconstitutional. After noting that there were 163 foreign-language schools in the territory (nine Korean, seven Chinese, and the remainder Japanese), Justice McReynolds found, this time under the Fifth Amendment, that an action by the territory to deprive parents of the right to raise their children through special language schools could not be sanctioned even though such schools encouraged an understanding and love of foreign ancestral languages and cultures.[61] The practical effect of these three decisions was to encourage American patriotism not by stamping out old-culture sensibilities, as the cultural conformists wished and as many of the children of immigrants actually tried to do, but by giving legal permission to immigrants to carry on their ethnic traditions.

When the Danish immigrant journalist Jacob A. Riis concluded his autobiography in 1902 with a panegyric to the American flag and the ideals for which it stood, he also wrote of his love for the Danish countryside and of the Danish king. But as a Scandinavian he had not faced the attacks of the cultural conformists as did immigrants from eastern and southern Europe one or two decades later.[62]

Explaining how the hyphen unites an old identity with a new one,

Slovenian-born journalist Louis Adamic said that the chemistry of the hyphen intensified both feelings. In his autobiography, *My America,* Adamic told of returning to the village in which he was born and being asked, "Do you consider yourself an American or a Slovenian?" The answer came swiftly that Adamic believed himself to be an American, "not only legally and technically but actually," adding, "I sometimes think I am more American than a great many of them." Then Adamic must have confused many of the villagers when he remarked, "I am also a Slovenian . . . and I would say that I am an American of Slovenian birth; but, if you like it better, you can consider me as a Slovenian who went to America when he was not quite fifteen and became an American. . . . there is no conflict in me between my original Slovenian blood or background and my being an American."[63] Even though he lost fluency in his mother tongue, *slovenstvo* (which means deep love for and loyalty to Slovenian traditions) had become a powerful part of his being. It was the genius of America, he said, to give room for him to find and give "the essentials of it [*slovenstvo*] wider and fuller expression than I could probably ever have found had I remained at home."[64]

The hyphen had triumphed, not in defiance of Americanism but as an expression of it. Paradoxically, the arrival of millions of immigrants from Europe and hundreds of thousands from Asia strengthened the Jeffersonian idea that Americans are held together by common beliefs and practices in self-government. The cultural and racial conformists kept looking to Europe for models of national identity and not to the American experience itself. When Henry Pratt Fairchild argued in 1926 that the melting pot had been a huge mistake, he also insisted that the Americanization movement was bound to fail because it was based on the idea that assimilation could be produced by a program of citizenship. Because he did not understand that the civic culture was the unifying culture of Americans, he was certain that the newcomers would, when put to the test, revert to an atavistic allegiance to their ancestral nations. To make his point clear, he asked:

Suppose that you, John Smith, native American of old New England stock . . . had received an attractive offer of a business position in Germany. . . . you soon became fluent in the language . . . attended German opera, read German books, took part in religious services in German churches, spent your evenings in German beer gardens, and by every means got as near to the heart of the German people as possible. Your children, born in Germany, went to German schools, played with German children, spoke German more readily than English, were never taken to visit the United States.[65]

Then Fairchild asked, suppose war broke out between the U.S. and Germany. Would your children fight for the Germans? To Fairchild, the question was rhetorical. Of course, he insisted, John Smith would not urge his children to enlist in the German army. He would expect his children to feel allegiance to the homeland of their ancestors, "and however painful the act of turning their backs upon friends and associations, to respond unreservedly to the ultimate appeal of nationality."[66]

It did not work that way in the U.S. Crowding into their own ghettoes, some Italian immigrants wore horns of gold or coral along with a religious medal under their shirts.[67] But that did not keep them from participating in citizenship classes given by the Sons of Italy and other organizations. By 1927, there were five hundred Polish Roman Catholic grade schools. But that did not keep the Poles from expressing a fierce American patriotism.[68] In the 1880s in Worcester, Massachusetts, the Ancient Order of the Hibernians, an Irish nationalist society, held a picnic on July 4, in which the exuberance of the Irish served "both as a preservation of Irish customs and a defense of American freedoms."[69] Worcester Swedes' Independence Day picnics in the 1890s attracted about 4,600 out of a total Swedish-American population of 11,000. They began with services at one of eight Swedish Protestant churches, and ended at the picnic with patriotic speeches, sometimes in Swedish. All ethnic groups of Worcester "used the Fourth as an occasion to assert their particular identity and values," even as they celebrated their American freedoms.[70] The sojourner French Canadians of Worcester, more insular than the Irish or the Swedes, tended to celebrate St. Jean Baptiste Day rather than the American Independence Day, and when they did observe the Fourth "they generally demonstrated more of an ethnic than an American identity." But those who were interested in settling in the U.S. permanently, such as members of the Ward Three Naturalization Club, celebrated the Fourth of July without giving up their love for the French language and culture.[71]

Of all the new European groups, the Jews provided the sharpest refutation of those who argued that American identity was based on one kind of religion and/or culture. In the U.S., Jews would build hospitals, orphanages, cemeteries, schools, fraternal societies, and communal institutions just as they had in Poland, Russia, and other European countries. But now there was a difference. For the first time in the history of their diaspora they experienced not mere toleration as a group but the protection of equal rights as individuals. Often they felt the sting of anti-Semitism, and many drifted or wrenched themselves away from the older Orthodox practices and from the Yiddish language, partly because of the pressures they felt to be culturally like most Americans. Those who maintained a fierce pride in their Jewish identity illustrated Tocqueville's principle that "patriotism grows by the exercise of civil rights." Jewish leaders who in 1916 filed a complaint against the School Committee of Boston because Jewish children were forced to sing Christmas carols in the public schools argued on grounds of patriotic civic culture principles, including the First Amendment.[72]

Thesis

Old-world traits were transplanted, to borrow from the title of the first major sociological analysis of immigration, but the authors of the study argued that assimilation was inexorable in the United States.[73] Robert Park and Herbert Miller were right with respect to political assimilation. But they underestimated the ability of ethnic-Americans to nurture, sustain, and re-create their religious and cultural inheritance in new forms of ethnicity in an ever-changing kaleidoscope. Horace Kallen, the son of a rabbi from Germany, not only saw that possibility but argued its merit in a 1915 article in the New York weekly, *The Nation*.[74] Even Kallen at first did not understand the totally voluntary nature of ethnic-Americanism when he argued that it was necessary for the U.S. to become "a federation or commonwealth of nationalities" in order to ensure cultural democracy.

Such a federation was out of the question. If it had occurred, the very basis of American unity—equal rights of individuals—would have been vitiated for the more traditional approach of other nations to group pluralism in which the identity and rights of the individual are derived from his or her membership in a group. That Kallen did not grasp the essence of voluntary pluralism—no one used the phrase—as a diversity based on the free choice of individuals united by a common civic culture was hardly surprising, since it had never existed in his or anyone else's experience before. But Kallen, influenced by the criticism of John Dewey, whose commitment was to individuality and diversity, quickly backed away from the appeal for a "federal republic" of nationalities or "a federation or commonwealth of national cultures." By 1924, he was using the term "cultural pluralism" and defining it as a "fellowship of freedom and co-operation" that would result in a "national fellowship of cultural diversities," describing, in effect, what is here called voluntary pluralism.[75]

The eastern and southern European immigrants answered Jefferson's question as to whether the country would become "more turbulent" because of massive immigration. The U.S. was not notably more turbulent because of their arrival. Most of the major episodes of internal violence in American history—Shay's Rebellion, the Whiskey Rebellion, Dorr's Rebellion, and the Civil War itself—occurred long before they came, and most of the labor and racial violence of the twentieth century would have occurred without them. Their presence actually helped to make Americans more aware of the civic basis of their national identity. In the period of heaviest migration from eastern and southern Europe (1881–1924), the Washington Monument was dedicated (1884), the centennial of the adoption of the Constitution was celebrated (1887), the pledge of allegiance to the American flag was adopted (1892), and the Lincoln Memorial was dedicated (1922).

Entry into the U.S. had been made much more difficult with the passage of the Immigration Law of 1924 based on a new version of the old Massachusetts idea of excluding people thought to be difficult to assimilate because of their nationality and religion. But the gates were kept open long enough to prove that the Pennsylvania idea worked for the nation. Immigrants actually helped to strengthen and more sharply define the civic culture, encouraging a voluntary ethnic pluralism within the framework of civic unity that was different from anything the world had ever known.

Part Two

OUTSIDE THE CIVIC CULTURE
The Coercive Pluralisms

The American minorities can be placed on a kind of color wheel. For example, when we think of the American boy, we don't usually think of a Spanish, Turkish, a Greek or a Mexican type, still less of an Oriental type. We usually think of someone who is kind of a cross between the Teuton and the Celt.

—JAMES BALDWIN

European immigrants and their children, most of whom enthusiastically embraced the civic culture and its system of voluntary pluralism, kept non-Europeans from membership in the American polity by maintaining other systems of pluralism. The first such system was tribal pluralism. Euro-American settlers regarded native American Indians as different and lesser creatures, living in different societies, worshiping different gods, embracing different myths. Sometimes Indians were receptive to the European newcomers: Indians* along the Carolina coast were friendly in their first encounters with the Europeans. Other Native Americans were hostile, as when Powhaton captured John Smith near Jamestown in 1607. Some whites were assimilated into Indian tribes, and some Native Americans assimilated into Euro-American society. But, generally, the boundaries between them were rigidly maintained by mutual desire.

Indians often resisted the presence or incursion of whites, and most of the whites believed the Indians were savages. With Euro-Americans gaining in numbers and power, they were in a position to decide whether tribal pluralism would be based on mutual accommodation and negotiation or on force, and they increasingly opted for force. Native Americans, with few exceptions, did not seek admission to the Euro-American civic culture. Whites could not enslave the Indians or otherwise compel their labor, and they did not want them to mix in their own society.

*The term "Native Americans" is preferred over "Indians" by the leaders of many North American tribes. I use both terms in this book, and prefer "Indians" where I wish to distinguish native American Indians from Aleuts, Eskimos, and Hawaiians, who also settled in what is now the United States long before the Europeans arrived.

One of the most fundamental constants in human history is the desire of insiders to arrange for outsiders—"outside" usually marked by ethnicity, language, religion, or some combination of these—to do the most menial work. Euro-Americans imported African slaves, thereby creating a coerced labor force of blacks* and their descendants throughout most of American history under a system of slavery, of involuntary caste pluralism. Spokespersons for African-Americans, who had lost their ancestral African cultures, talked repeatedly with bitterness of their exclusion from the civic culture and, for the most part, claimed their right to belong to it. Native Americans, while defeated and oppressed, remained in their own cultures. Caste pluralism, in the form of slavery, was maintained in the South up to Emancipation and in the form of severe segregation up to the Second World War and beyond. Its effects lingered even after systematic segregation was substantially dismantled everywhere.

Sojourner pluralism, a system designed by Euro-Americans for immigrants regarded as temporary residents, was applied principally to two groups of non-European immigrants in the West and Southwest. Established after the Civil War and in the decades that followed, this form of pluralism was intended to meet the labor needs of an expanding American economy without having to admit nonwhite immigrant laborers to the civic culture. Workers from the Far East, who were kept ineligible for citizenship, were expected to return home following their terms of labor. Workers from Mexico were permitted to come back and forth across the border, moving north as American employers sought their labor, then were encouraged or compelled to return south as the demand for their labor diminished.

Sojourner pluralism was far less restrictive than caste pluralism, and the children of sojourners who remained to become settlers for the most part entered the civic culture and its system of voluntary pluralism in a fashion similar to the children of European immigrant settlers. Like them, they embraced the American founding myth, with its dream of opportunity for all based on equal rights. African-Americans also treasured that ideal. Writing in 1903, W. E. B. Du Bois said there were "no truer exponents of the pure human spirit of the Declaration of Independence than the American Negroes."[1] But blacks were denied the promise of the Declaration.

The white Anglo-Saxon charter members of the government of the

---

*In this book, I use the term "blacks" extensively, for reasons that are made clear in chapter 9, and also occasionally "Negroes," the term preferred by most blacks in the first sixty-plus years of this century. I personally prefer the term "African-Americans," having taught a course on the African-American experience at Brandeis for many years, and I often use it here. That term is apparently coming into wider use.

United States had created an idea of national membership based on equal rights for all, but the systems of sojourner pluralism and, to a much greater degree, that of caste pluralism contradicted that ideal. Not until the 1960s–1980s would the Euro-American determination to maintain a racially exclusive civic culture be abandoned.

Chapter Four

"GO BACK TO THE COUNTRY FROM WHENCE YOU CAME"
Predatory Pluralism and the Native American Response

W HEN in the early nineteenth century Pawnee Indians first encountered Anglo-Americans, the whites proposed a treaty,
promising blankets, guns, and knives made of steel in exchange
for land. The head chief of the Pawnees declined the offer. His robe
would keep him warm, even in winter; his arrows would kill cattle, his
stone knife would cut meat for eating. "Go back to the country from
whence you came," he said, "We do not want your presents, and we do
not want you to come into our country."[1]

There was no question of assimilation or integration. "The Great Spirit
has made us all," the Seneca chief Red Jacket said in 1805, "but he has
made a great difference between his red and white children."[2] The whites
agreed.

The early encounters between the English settlers and the Indians on
the East Coast in the seventeenth century established the terms of the
American system of tribal pluralism throughout the eighteenth and nineteenth centuries and much of the twentieth. Although early white settlers
tried and usually failed to get Indians to work for them, they did not
want their labor first of all. They desired their land. To possess the land
became their overwhelming obsession. They negotiated for it or they
seized it. Coercion became the dominant strategy of acquisition. If Indians refused the colonists' offers for land or resisted their incursions into
Indian lands they were pushed out, or even captured and held or sold as
slaves. Roger Williams thought that the Massachusetts Bay Colony belonged to the Indians. He would have established a system of pluralism
based on respect for the tribal integrity of the indigenous population.
William Penn bought title from the Indians. But Williams and Penn were
exceptions.

The authors of the American Constitution made the Indians' position
clear. They, not the colonists, were the outsiders. Most Indians were not
taxed and not counted as part of the population that determined appor-

tionment of representatives. Congress was granted the power to regulate commerce not only with foreign nations but also with Indian tribes. They were, in effect, aliens in their own lands. Still, Indians were a force to be reckoned with, and making war against them was not always the most effective policy. Where conquest was not likely except at great cost, negotiation made sense. Beginning in 1778, when the first treaty was signed between the Continental Congress and an Indian nation (the Delaware), and until the treaty system was abrogated in 1871, the U.S. government negotiated nearly four hundred treaties with Indian nations.

Many treaties conceded that some land should remain Indian and agreed that certain fishing and hunting rights be maintained. But substantial acreage was gained without a fight. Whites clothed their avarice in high-minded phrases about fair treatment. The Northwest Ordinance of 1787, which established a system for incorporating western territories as states, affirmed an Indian policy based on "good faith"; Indian "lands and property shall never be taken from them without their consent; and in their property, rights and liberty, they shall never be invaded or disturbed, unless in just and lawful ways authorized by Congress." The promise of good faith was never fulfilled. The white settlers ignored it as they pushed the frontier farther west. The Congress was left to decide what is "just and lawful," but Congress most often responded to political pressures emanating from land-hungry whites.

The ambiguous and shifting positions of Thomas Jefferson reflected the continuing (albeit tenuous) hold of the ideals of the Northwest Ordinance but even more the general white attitude of disdain for Indians and lust for their lands. One year before the ordinance, Jefferson embraced the view of tribal rights in a letter to a European friend. "It may be regarded as certain, that not a foot of land will ever be taken from the Indians, without their consent. The sacredness of their rights is felt by all thinking persons in America."[3] Ten years earlier, when the Indians were labeled "merciless savages" in the Declaration of Independence, he also wrote that "nothing will reduce those wretches so soon as pushing the war into the heart of their country. But I would not stop there. I would never cease pursuing them while one of them remained on this side of the Mississippi."[4] By the time Jefferson became president, he had abandoned both his 1776 and his 1786 positions and had been converted to an assimilationist approach. Writing to Andrew Jackson, he advocated that the Indians be guided "to an agricultural way of life. . . . In leading them thus to . . . civilization . . . I trust and believe we are acting for their greatest good."[5] By his second inaugural address in 1805, Jefferson was still an assimilationist: "Humanity enjoins us to teach them agriculture and the domestic arts." But, concerned that Indians would oppose his policies, he complained that they had "a sanctimonious reverence for the customs of their ancestors."[6] He then abandoned the policy of assimilation and ordered his representatives on the frontier to acquire all Indian lands east of the Mississippi. By 1808, Jefferson told some Cherokees who wished to retain their lands in the upper South and become citizens of the United States that it would not work. He urged them to move west of the Mississippi. By 1812, he had reverted to his 1776 position, predicting that the Indians "will relapse into barbarism and misery . . . and we shall be obliged to drive them with the beasts of the forests into the Stony [Rocky] Mountains."[7]

Andrew Jackson both reflected and stimulated the hostility of whites on the frontier toward the Indians. In 1833, in his second inaugural address, he justified a policy of white expansion: "What good man would prefer a country covered with forests and ranged by a few thousand savages to our extensive Republic, studded with cities, towns, and prosperous farms, embellished with all the improvements which art can devise or industry execute, occupied by more than twelve million happy people, and filled with all the blessings of liberty, civilization and religion?"[8]

The tidewater planters and rich merchants on the East Coast, who sought peace with the Indians, were losing to the democracy of the Jeffersonians and Jacksonians. The Federalists, who had wanted peace on the frontier, failed to win the frontiersmen's votes and hence sputtered out as a political party, effectively removing Northwest Ordinance sentiments as a force in making Indian policy. Their influence persisted, however, on the U.S. Supreme Court, where one of their principal leaders, John Marshall, sat as chief justice. Marshall interpreted constitutional law as consistent with the promises of the Northwest Ordinance that called for a benign form of tribal pluralism. In 1831, the Marshall Court listened to a complaint from the Council of the Cherokees against the Georgia Guard, which had carried out provisions of a series of harsh state laws against the Cherokees. The guard had terrorized them, put them in chains, tied them to trees, and thrown them into jails. The Cherokee nations sought to qualify as a "foreign state" in order to appeal to the Court's jurisdiction. When, in *Cherokee Nation* v. *Georgia* (1831), the court refused jurisdiction, Marshall asserted in benevolent paternalistic *obiter dicta* that the Indian nation is "a distinct political society . . . capable of managing its own affairs and governing itself." Such societies are "domestic dependent nations," whose "relation to the United States resembles that of a ward to his guardian."

The repressive laws against the Cherokees were tested again the following year, when representatives of the American Board of Missionaries on Cherokee land, who refused to take an oath of allegiance to the state, were arrested by the Georgia Guard, convicted, and sent to prison. This time Marshall, writing for the Court, did assume jurisdiction, and in *Worcester* v. *Georgia* (1832) established that the Cherokee nation "is a distinct community occupying its own territory, with boundaries accurately described, and which the citizens of Georgia have no right to enter, but with the assent of the Cherokees themselves, or in conformity with treaties and with acts of Congress."[9]

Marshall's pronouncements clearly had not reflected the election returns. On the frontier, the policies of removal and extinction—the predatory version of tribal pluralism—were far more popular than his legalisms. Jackson had led the campaign for the Congressional Removal Act of 1830, which authorized expelling eastern tribes from their lands in exchange for guaranteed land west of the Mississippi River. A few of the Cherokee nation leaders, acting without the approval of the tribal government, sought to avoid open conflict by agreeing to a treaty that ceded their eastern homeland in exchange for western land. The rest—about three-quarters—of the Cherokees refused to leave and were forced to take a long march to what is now northeastern Oklahoma, when about four thousand died on "the trail of tears."

Between 1810 and 1821, more than a half million Euro-American settlers poured into Kentucky, Tennessee, Alabama, Mississippi, and Louisiana; almost a half million others moved into Ohio, Indiana, Illinois, and Missouri. Many were squatters, "pre-emptors," who found land, farmed it, and claimed it as their own. In 1841, Congress legalized this widespread practice through the Pre-emption Act. One hundred thousand Indians, removed from the East before the Civil War, obliged western tribes to give up hunting grounds to make room for them and eventually for more whites.

One Norwegian settler wrote home in 1835 about his success in planting "Indian corn" in New York State. But he could purchase public land in Illinois at $1.25 an acre, and planned to move there. In the U.S., "whether native born or foreign, a man is free to do with it [land] what he pleases." He urged a friend to emigrate: "Even if many more come, there will still be room for all."[10] The frontier to him was a symbol of the American founding myth of asylum and freedom. But to the Sauk-Fox leader Black Hawk, settlers were liars and cheats. "We told them to let us alone; but they followed on and beset our paths, and they coiled themselves among us like the snake."[11]

Millions of acres were granted to whites through the Homestead Act of 1862 and, indirectly, through land grants to the railroads after the Civil War. In the Northwest, the Oregon Donation Act encouraged raids on Indian lands. In Texas, savage wars were fought by Comanches against the Texas Rangers and the American cavalry; in Colorado, Indians fought for their ground against gold prospectors; in Kansas and Nebraska, they gave up most of their land through treaties.

Confined by treaty and harassment to reservations after the Civil War, many tribes swept across the plains and waged war so effectively against the U.S. Army that General William T. Sherman, the Civil War hero, said fifty Indians could hold off three thousand soldiers. On the plains, white hunters' relentless slaughter of the buffalo to feed laborers on the railroads and to get hides to sell defeated the Indians. Between the end of the Civil War and 1885, when the buffalo became nearly extinct, the Indians in North America, whose population may have been as high as twelve to fifteen million north of the Rio Grande in 1491, were reduced to fewer than 250,000, and to 210,000 by the 1920 census.

Driven back to reservations, decimated by war, disease, and consequent social disorganization, the Indians were unable to prevent the declaration by Congress, in 1871, that "hereafter, no Indian nation or tribe within the territory of the United States shall be acknowledged or recognized as an independent nation, tribe or power with whom the United States may contract by treaty." Tribal pluralism based on mutual respect, envisioned by the Northwest Ordinance, had long since been abandoned and predatory tribal pluralism was no longer needed, although several Indian massacres lay ahead. Some whites sympathetic to the Indians' plight concluded that the "Indian problem" could only be solved if Indians left the reservations altogether and deserted tribal life. Schools were established for Indian children (the most famous, in Carlisle, Pennsylvania) and were deliberately located far from Indian communities to separate Indian children from their parents' way of life.[12]

The goals of assimilation and rejection of tribal pluralism led to the breakup of the reservations through allotment of plots of land to individual Indian families. The General Allotment Act of 1887, or the Dawes Act (named after Senator Henry Dawes of Massachusetts, chairman of the Senate Indian Affairs Committee), gave the president authority not only to distribute a reservation among Indian families but also to permit white settlers to take over unallotted surplus land. Although some tribes—including the five tribes in the so-called "Indian Territory" of Oklahoma, earlier removed from the East, and the Osage—were exempted at first because of their strong resistance to the allotment scheme, most Indians on reservations were subject to allotment, and after passage of the Curtis Act in 1898 virtually all Indians, including the five tribes not on reservations, became eligible for allotments of public land.

Advertising himself as a friend of Indians, President Theodore Roosevelt wrote to Chief No Shirt that if Indians would only work hard and earn their living they could become rich and successful just like whites.[13]

But most Indians were unpersuaded. They preferred to keep tribal identities. The old Potawatami Chief Simon Pokagon pulled a red, white, and blue rope to ring a new Liberty Bell at the 1893 World's Columbian Exposition, but most rejected white overtures.[14] Even though they were now few in number, psychologically demoralized, and physically weak, they resisted assimilation just as they had fought against removal and conquest. But, unable to function effectively as individual landowners on the terms set by the highly individualistic, competitive market society, most sold the land allotted to them or lost it through foreclosure. In forty-five years land still in Indian ownership was reduced by more than half. Instead of becoming independent farmers, large numbers of Indians became landless and penniless on the most arid land of the West.

The climax of the campaign to assimilate by separating them from their trust relationship with the federal government came in 1924 when Congress granted citizenship to all Indians (more than half already had citizenship), partly in recognition of their services in the armed forces in the war. But the policy of assimilation was pronounced a failure in a 1928 study of the Institute of Government Research (Brookings Institution). A report, known after the project's director, Lewis Merriam, as the Merriam Report, opposed forced assimilation. After the 1932 election its recommendations found a sympathetic hearing in the Roosevelt administration, particularly from the commissioner of Indian affairs, John Collier, a white man who had worked for the Indian cause for many years and whose proposals for recognizing anew the right of Indian tribes to be distinct functioning political entities were embodied in the Indian Reorganization Act of 1934. Funds were allocated to buy back some of the land lost through the allotment policy (ninety million acres, or two-thirds of the land held by the Indians in 1887), and reservations were urged to enact tribal constitutions to enable them to fulfill the functions of self-governing nations once more.[15]

But Indian reorganization, based in large measure on the philosophy and promise of a just system of pluralism linked to the territorial integrity of tribes, was not honored consistently. The Bureau of Indian Affairs, the federal agency charged with fulfilling the government's trust responsibility, leased Indian land to outside companies under contracts that did not protect Indian rights and sometimes even were signed without knowledge or consent of the Indians themselves. And the bureau bowed to congressional pressure for assimilation by continuing the Indian boarding school system, which sometimes took Indian children away from their parents for many years at a time and kept them from learning about their traditional cultures or languages.

In 1953, less than two decades after passage of the Indian Reorganization Act, the House of Representatives passed a resolution proclaiming as the policy of the United States the speedy abolition of federal supervision over the tribes and subjection of Indians to the same laws, privileges, and responsibilities as all other citizens of the U.S. A process aptly known as "termination" had begun. The resolution spoke of giving Indians "equal rights" and of "freeing them from all the disabilities and limitations specifically applicable to Indians."[16] But, subject to state taxes and hunting and fishing laws, Indians would lose federal protection over their lands and the right to self-governing sovereign status.

Not until the 1970s and 1980s did white Americans return to support for tribal pluralism, based upon the original promise of the Northwest Ordinance and the judicial opinions of John Marshall. The American civil rights consciousness was responsible, in part; so was the growing recognition among whites of the history of oppression of the Indian tribes and also the new assertiveness of Indians themselves in claiming their rights both as American citizens and as members of tribes that possessed a unique relationship to the polity as a whole.

Chapter Five

"THIS FOURTH OF JULY IS YOURS"
African-Americans and Caste Pluralism

SPEAKING on July 4, 1853, Frederick Douglass complained: "I am not included within the pale of this glorious anniversary . . . this Fourth of July is yours, not mine."[1] By 1853, most free African-Americans were excluded from meaningful participation in the civic culture and from skilled or middle-class occupations.

Slavery based on race began soon after the first settlers came, when whites treated their black and their white indentured servants in a radically different manner. Of three runaway servants caught in Virginia in 1640, two, who were white, were sentenced to an extension of four years in their period of servitude, but the third, who was black, was sentenced to servitude for life. In 1662, Virginia declared that the status of offspring of a white man and a Negro woman would follow that of the mother. Two years later, Maryland prohibited intermarriage between the races; in 1690, South Carolina declared slaves to be real estate.[2] By 1700, when blacks were transported in large numbers, slavery was well established.

The expansion of slavery and the tightening of controls on slaves in the South was fueled at first by profits in rice, indigo, and tobacco, and then especially in cotton. In the South in the seventeenth and much of the eighteenth century, slavery was supported also by the interests of New England merchants and shipbuilders, who profited from the slave trade. Slavery became entrenched in the North as well, if on a more modest scale. In 1704, the governor of Connecticut reported that all children born of Negro bondswomen were born in servitude; thirteen years later, African-Americans were barred from holding land in Connecticut. In New York, trade with blacks was prohibited by 1702; in New York City, slaves were forbidden to be on the streets after sundown and were not allowed to appear as witnesses at the trial of a free person.

The Early Agreement to Exclude Blacks from Participation in the Republic

By 1775, nine-tenths of the half million Negroes in the colonies lived in the South. Indentured servants and redemptionists could become members of the polity once they discharged their contracts, but slaves had no contract. Locked into a caste relationship, they were compelled to work at the most brutal, lowly, and unrewarding of jobs. The sons and daughters of indentured servants could go off to the West and claim land. Slaves could go nowhere without their masters' authority.

Even the most illustrious of the founding fathers—John Adams, Benjamin Franklin, George Washington, Thomas Jefferson, and James Madison—all but Franklin later Presidents of the United States—saw no way to overturn the slave system when the Constitution was written in 1787. Washington, Jefferson, and Madison agreed on slavery with those other Virginians who spoke so eloquently of liberty and freedom, George Mason and Patrick Henry. The difficulties would be too great should we be deprived of slaves, said Mason, while denouncing slavery as immoral and warning of its terrible consequences. "I deplore slavery," said Henry, but "prudence forbids its abolition."[3] Adams of Massachusetts not only deplored slavery but refused to own slaves even "when the best men in my vicinity thought it not inconsistent with their character" and even "when they were very cheap."[4] Franklin, who came from multiethnic Pennsylvania, grew up in a household in Boston that had no Negro slaves or servants. Even before the Revolution, he expressed the hope that the slave trade could be ended.[5] But not until after the Revolution, especially in the last few years of his life, when he was president of the Pennsylvania Abolition Society, did he take a strong stand on the issue. In his last public act, Franklin wrote a memorial to the first Congress of the United States to promote the abolition of slavery, but the Congress, after a debate that lasted nearly a month, put it aside.

Washington's views were more commonly held. Slavery is immoral; slaves have the right to be free; we have come to depend on them as a source of labor that we cannot do without; therefore, we cannot abolish slavery. He wrote and said repeatedly that he hated slavery and wished it could be abolished gradually, but he was certain that to set the slaves free at once would produce "inconvenience and mischief."[6] He often said that he wished never to buy another slave, yet he found that circumstances required such purchases.[7] At the Constitutional Convention, where he presided, he appears to have remained aloof from the debate on slavery (Georgia and South Carolina insisted that nothing be done to touch it and that slaves be counted for purposes of representation). As president, he told a Quaker visitor that he thought it best for him not to comment publicly on the question of slavery since the issue of its abolition might come before him for an official decision.[8] His own slaves constituted so much a portion of his estate that he thought he could not afford to free them, and at the time of his death he owned 317 slaves.[9]

The new Constitution recognized slavery by specifying that every slave should count as three-fifths of a person for purposes of apportioning representatives, by stipulating that the Congress could not prohibit the slave trade until 1808, and by insisting that no slave held under the laws of one state escaping into another could be discharged from slavery. But the authors of the Constitution themselves recoiled from the word "slave." They wrote of "three-fifths of all other persons" and of "the migration or importation of such persons as any of the states now existing shall think proper to admit" and that "no person held to service or labor in one state, . . ." So odious was the term "slavery" that the term "service or labor" is repeated three times in order to avoid it.

Madison and Jefferson both agreed with Washington on slavery's moral evils, Madison writing in Federalist Paper No. 42 that the hope of ending the slave trade in twenty years "ought to be considered as a great point gained in favor of humanity."[10] Madison lamented, "happy would it be for the unfortunate African, if an equal prospect lay before them of being redeemed from the oppression of their European brethren."[11] But in what sense were they "brethren"? He voted in the first Congress for a naturalization law that admitted only whites to citizenship, and neither he nor Jefferson released all of their slaves to freedom.

As president, Madison tried his best to enforce the ending of the slave trade in 1808. In his later years, he tended to favor the idea of colonization, with the agreement of slave owners, of course: he believed the western territories would be better for colonization than Africa, and he accepted the presidency of the Colonization Society. To end slavery would be to erase a "blot from our Republican character,"[12] he said, but, as late as 1833, he wrote to Henry Clay that slavery had become inextricably woven into the economy of that republic, and that he did not think Northerners would meddle in the institution because, as merchants, ship owners, and manufacturers, they had an interest in preserving the union with the slaveholding states.

Although Jefferson understood as keenly as Madison and Washington the moral degradation of slavery, he wrote more than they did on the character and the qualities of blacks, to their disadvantage. He loved liberty, anguished about slavery, but believed blacks intellectually, spiritually, and physically inferior to whites.[13] After the Revolution, he hoped for a total emancipation and the abolition of the slave trade; yet, like Washington and Madison, he doubted that the two races could ever live peaceably side by side. The answer to the problem, he thought, was in the colonization of blacks in Africa or in some other far place.[14] Jefferson made his opposition to slavery public in a message to Congress on December 2, 1808, when he spoke of the impending end of the slave trade as preventing "those violations of human rights which have been so long continued on the unoffending inhabitants of Africa."[15] He worked hard to see the passage of a strong act to implement the proscription put into the Constitution.

The passage of the famous act of 1807 probably could not have occurred without Jefferson's energetic leadership. But by that time, 400,000 slaves had been transported to North America. They, along with their descendants, might be kept as slaves for as long as they lived. Even with the virtual end of the transatlantic traffic, the institution had become firmly entrenched in the South with the invention of the cotton gin in 1793 and the insatiable demand for cotton of Britain's textile industry. By 1820, cotton was grown extensively in Tennessee, Alabama, Louisiana, Mississippi, Georgia, and South Carolina. White settlers pushed Indians out of their ancestral territories, and as production soared in the black belt— the rich, dark-soiled heartland of the expanding cotton kingdom—many small farmers became large landholders and slaveholders.

The ideology of Jeffersonian republicanism created problems for the institution of slavery. Pitted against the ideal of God-given human rights was the rationalization that slaves were not morally fit for freedom. The new nation could not make up its mind about the extension of slavery. Its policies veered in fits and starts away from sanctioning it to disapprobation and back to approval again. The Northwest Ordinance had prohibited slavery in the Northwest Territories in 1787; the Missouri Compromise in 1820 admitted Missouri as a slave state but prohibited slavery north of 36 degrees and 30 minutes forever; the compromise of 1850 admitted California as a free state but allowed Utah and New Mexico to enter the Union with slavery if their constitutions so determined; the Kansas-Nebraska Act in 1854 undermined the Missouri Compromise by permitting the people of the territories of Kansas and Nebraska to decide for themselves whether they would come into the Union as slave or free states.

If economic greed caused slavery to spread, the theory of racial inferiority justified it. As the slave population grew in the South, whites enforced slavery with increasing rigor. Slave codes often forbade slaves to own anything in their own right or dispose in any way of the product of their industry; no slave was to be admitted as a witness in either criminal or civil matters, for or against a white person; in many jurisdictions it was not a crime to kill a slave; husbands and wives, parents and children were often separated at the auction block; floggings were common.[16]

Even at the height of the power of the slave system, blacks were not a caste in the sense of the Untouchables of India or the Eta of Japan, who worked only at certain stigmatized jobs as their fathers and ancestors had for generations. Some blacks were free, even in the South, and worked at jobs that required education and a high degree of skill. Even among the slaves, some were entrusted with important responsibilities within the households of white planters. Far from being untouchable, thousands served as the nurses and confidantes of white children, and tens of thousands more were mistresses to white owners. Unlike low castes elsewhere, they knew the possibilities of freedom. They also knew a religion that, in the Old Testament, called not for acceptance of but resistance to injustice.

There were many ways to resist: doing a poor job; feigning illness; self-mutilation; killing overseers and masters in the woods or poisoning them; self-starvation; running away; and even slave revolts in the face of impossible odds. Whenever a major revolt took place, the noose of slavery was tightened. The names of Gabriel Prosser, Denmark Vesey, and Nat Turner, the three most famous leaders of slave revolts, seized white Southerners with fear. Prosser, a slave, led the first of these nineteenth-century revolts in 1800, when a thousand slaves met six miles outside Richmond, armed with clubs, swords, and other crude weapons, to march on the city. Vesey, a free man who worked as a carpenter in Charleston, plotted his revolt for years, but although perhaps as many as nine thousand slaves were involved, it was easily beaten down before it started in July 1822. Nat Turner selected the Fourth of July as his day of revolution, but illness postponed the action until August 21. Within twenty-four hours sixty whites were killed, after which the blacks were overtaken and captured by state and federal troops.[17]

Following each rebellion, there was a flurry of action by whites to intimidate slaves, free blacks, and white sympathizers. In 1845, a Kentucky man was sentenced to fifteen years' imprisonment for having brought to freedom three runaway slaves. In 1850, the Fugitive Slave Law laid heavy fines and imprisonment on anyone who harbored or concealed a fugitive slave. But the most significant sanction for slavery came in the Supreme Court's decision in 1857 in *Dred Scott* v. *Sanford*.

In that year, when a quarter of a million immigrants arrived in the United States and when Carl Schurz, not yet a citizen, was almost elected lieutenant governor of Wisconsin, the U.S. Supreme Court declared that since blacks were not citizens they did not have the right to sue in court and a citizen-master could take his slave property wherever he liked, even to states that did not recognize slavery, without giving up total control. Dred Scott, a Missouri slave who had been taken by his master to live in free Illinois, could not sue for his freedom after returning to Missouri because he had never been released from slavery by his master. Frederick Douglass saw in the Supreme Court's harsh decision the possibility that it would become "one necessary link in the chain of events preparatory to the complete overthrow of the slave system."[18] The Civil War was only four years away.

The ambiguities of the caste system were most apparent with respect to free blacks, even before the Civil War. At the end of the Revolution, when free African-Americans constituted less than 4 percent of the black population in the South, the laws against them were relatively mild. But as Southerners became more fearful of slave revolts, one southern state after another disenfranchised free blacks, barred them from military service, and prohibited them from testifying against white persons. They were subject to search without a warrant and to trial without jury for all but capital crimes; they were not permitted to assemble and were forbidden to carry arms; they were kept from professions and many trades by high license fees and physical intimidation; some states required them to register and carry freedom papers; and, of course, they could not marry out of their caste. They lived in constant danger of being kidnapped or being forced back into slavery by the courts. As historian John Hope Franklin has written, "one slip or ignorance of the law would send them back into the ranks of slaves."[19]

That the vast majority of them were essentially outside of the civic culture was clear from laws regulating their freedom of movement. By 1835, most southern and many northern states had restricted or prohibited free immigration by blacks; the right of assembly had been taken away from almost all free Negroes in the South. Blacks generally could own land (except in Georgia up until 1818), but in 1826 Congress denied them preemption rights on public lands.[20] Even in the North, some states did not allow free African-Americans to testify in cases involving white persons, and their children either attended segregated schools or were not permitted into public schools.

Both northern and southern states began to disenfranchise free blacks at the beginning of the nineteenth century, and probably more than 90 percent were not permitted to vote during the several decades prior to the Civil War.[21] Even in liberal Pennsylvania, where the law permitted blacks to vote until 1838, when the franchise was restricted to white males, blacks did not vote out of fear, according to an informant of Alexis de Tocqueville. When the French visitor was surprised in 1832 to find no blacks voting in a state founded by Quakers and celebrated for its toleration, he asked the Pennsylvanian whether it was fair that blacks should not vote, since they paid taxes. The answer came that of course blacks had the right to vote but they voluntarily abstained. Tocqueville, exclaiming on their extraordinary modesty, was told that they were "afraid of being maltreated" and that "the magistrates are unable to protect them in the exercise of their legal rights."[22]

African-Americans generally were denied the benefits of federal land policy. An opinion from the attorney general's office was necessary to qualify free Negroes for the benefit of the Pre-Emption Act of 1841, and in the 1850s they were frequently excluded from homesteading legislation. From 1810 until 1862, federal law excluded Negroes from the postal service. But nothing so clearly symbolized the caste status of all blacks—free or slave—as the Dred Scott decision. Up to that decision, African-Americans were considered citizens in many northern states, even though they were excluded from suffrage and holding office, in the same way that women and children were considered citizens. They had rights to property, liberty of person, freedom of speech, and access to the courts. After Dred Scott, it was uncertain whether free blacks who had not been citizens at the time of the creation of the Union enjoyed any rights guaranteed by the Constitution. The case was complicated because Scott had not only lived in Illinois with his owner but had also been sold to an abolitionist family in New York. Since the Missouri Supreme Court had declared Scott to be a slave, the justices could have decided that Scott had no status as a citizen or an alien. Instead, Chief Justice Taney and five other justices ruled that because Scott was a black man he could not be a citizen of the U.S. within the meaning of the Constitution because no state could on its own "introduce a new member into the political community created by the Constitution of the United States."[23]

It was a convoluted decision intended to tighten the boundaries of caste. Taney made up a theory that all Negroes were meant to be excluded from the political community by the Constitution through its clauses respecting the slave trade and the extradition of fugitives, even though those provisions applied only to slaves. Taney somehow saw confirmation of his theory in the explicit restriction barring naturalization to all but white aliens in statutes passed from 1790 on. The decision, in effect, held that those who created the Union in 1789 formed a closed community that restricted membership to their descendants and to aliens (only whites) brought in by the process of naturalization.[24] Taney was wrong in history and in law, but it would take a civil war to affirm citizenship for blacks and the principles of membership in the political community by right of birth.

As Richard Wade has shown, regulations in southern cities controlling the movement and behavior of Negroes tended to be the same for free and bonded blacks.[25] In Baltimore in 1850, 90 free Negroes joined 126 whites in petitioning for a school to prepare free blacks for "those humble stations in the community to which they are confined by the necessities of their situation."[26] The system chose white labor—including Irish and German immigrants—over blacks for higher-status jobs. Once free, Ira Berlin has shown, blacks in the South were confined to the bottom of the social order, "despised by whites, burdened with increasingly oppressive racial proscriptions, and subjected to verbal and physical abuse."[27]

The number of free blacks grew in the decades before the Civil War. By 1830, there were 319,000 in the U.S., thirty years later 488,000, 44 percent in the South, 46 percent in the North, the remainder in the south central states and the West.[28] In the face of almost every form of discrimination, including segregated schools, free African-Americans worked in a diversity of occupations, to that extent modifying the fundamental objective of caste. John Hope Franklin has written that "almost every community had its free Negro carpenters, barbers, cabinetmakers, and brick masons; many had shopkeepers, salesmen, and clerks, even where it was in violation of the law."[29] Some free blacks owned extensive property, including slaves in a few cases, and many developed fraternal and charitable organizations in the tradition of ethnic voluntary pluralism, particularly in the North, where they also established and joined abolitionist societies. A tiny number went to predominantly white colleges. Some became writers, poets, and physicians. But while caste pluralism was not airtight, it worked largely as it was intended until passage of the Thirteenth Amendment in 1865 abolished slavery.

The Changing Nature of Caste After Emancipation

Encouraged by emancipation and the adoption of the Thirteenth Amendment, African-Americans formed state associations of the National Equal Rights League; they lobbied to end policies of racial segregation and discrimination in many states; and, in some places, they won. In Iowa, the Negro Exclusion Law was repealed; in Ohio, the legislature provided that impoverished colored persons could be eligible for relief; in Illinois, the ban on the testimony of blacks in state courts was ended. Impressive reforms were achieved in the upper midwestern states in 1864 and 1865. Nevertheless, the situation in Indiana probably was more typical of the North's determination to exclude blacks from basic rights. In September of 1865, the governor of Indiana pointed without shame to the fact that blacks were not only excluded from voting but from testifying in courts of justice; they even were kept from public schools and from acquiring title to land.

In 1864, even after Lincoln's Emancipation Proclamation, Congress continued its traditional policy of disenfranchising blacks in the territories and the District of Columbia; in 1865, it voted to perpetuate racial segregation in the Union army and in the public school system of the Capital; even in the midwestern states of Iowa, Minnesota, and Michigan, where blacks were few and where sentiment for equality was as strong as anywhere in the country, the state legislatures permitted cities and towns to establish segregated school systems.[30]

Because the Thirteenth Amendment said little about the position of blacks as members of society other than that they were free, a Reconstructionist Congress passed the Civil Rights Act of 1866, which specified that they would have fundamental rights as citizens of every state and territory in the U.S. They could enforce contracts, sue, give evidence, deal in property, and have the benefit of laws to protect their persons and property the same as white citizens. When doubt was raised about the constitutionality of the Civil Rights Act of 1866, Congress met to consider a Fourteenth Amendment. The amendment later would become (along with the First Amendment) the fundamental charter of human rights in American society—the crux and the fulcrum of the redefined and expanded civic culture of the 1970s and 1980s. Opposition, even in the North, was strong. Senator Thomas Hendricks of Indiana argued that white men "had a right to exclude the colored man if they saw fit . . . this is a white man's government, made by the white man for the white man."[31] In the House of Representatives, Andrew Rogers of New Jersey echoed that view: "Sir, I want it distinctly understood that the American people believe that this government was made for white men and white women."[32]

Passage of the Fourteenth Amendment, and its ratification by the states, and of subsequent civil rights legislation by Congress was made possible by the political dominance of radical Republicans and the occupation of reconstructed southern states by Union troops.

Caste pluralism was abolished on paper under the cover of Union bayonets, mainly by men such as Senators Charles Sumner of Massachusetts and Daniel Cook of New Hampshire, who had little to do with blacks in their daily lives and who were not in a position to enforce the laws they wrote. The most far-reaching amendment to the Constitution ever enacted, the Fourteenth Amendment provided, in Section I, that any *person* born or naturalized in the U.S. is a citizen of the U.S. and of the state wherein he or she resides. Then, in what became the basis of the civil rights revolution of the 1960s and 1970s, the amendment stipulated that "no state shall make or enforce any law which shall abridge the privileges or immunities of citizens in the United States; nor shall any state deprive any person of life, liberty or property, without due process of law; nor to deny any person within its jurisdiction the equal protection of the laws."

Even after passage of the Fourteenth Amendment, citizenship in the Deep South did not mean the end of terror for blacks. Reconstructionist Representative Samuel McKee of Kentucky pointed out in 1869 that in his state the Ku Klux Klan was on the rampage against blacks, committing "assassinations by night and by day," without a single case on the record of anyone having been arrested or punished for these crimes. "Today I can walk in broad daylight into the cabin of any colored man and rob him of all he possesses in the presence of all his family, and there is no court of Kentucky that will convict me; today I can enter the church where one of the colored ministers preaches to his flock, and in the presence of his own congregation, drag him from the altar and murder him on the spot, and there is no court of Kentucky that can convict me unless a white person saw the deed."[33]

McKee was speaking in favor of the Fifteenth Amendment to the Constitution, which provided that "the right of citizens of the United States to vote shall not be denied or abridged by the United States or by any state on account of race, color, or previous condition of servitude." The Fourteenth had decided citizenship, but the question of suffrage remained open, since states had total responsibility for specifying voting qualifications. McKee's point was that citizenship meant nothing without the right to vote, a position echoed in the other chamber by Reconstructionist Senator Adonijah Welch of Florida, who argued that blacks would never be truly free without political power.[34] Other senators argued back that blacks were incompetent to vote; but the Fifteenth Amendment, like the Fourteenth, was passed by a Congress controlled by radical Republicans, including some from the formerly rebellious states occupied by Union troops and now under Reconstruction.

At the time of ratification of the Fifteenth Amendment in 1869, only seven northern states had acted to give African-Americans the vote, and not one state with a large black population outside the South had done so. The former slaves were citizens who were protected in certain fundamental rights; but when the Supreme Court cast doubt on the full sweep of the Fourteenth Amendment in 1873, the Reconstructionist Congress passed the Civil Rights Act of 1875, the most sweeping legislation of its kind until 1964, asserting, among other things, that all citizens "of every race and color" were entitled to equal enjoyment of public accommodations.

The amendments and laws of the post–Civil War Congresses and ratifying legislatures in the states—the acts of the victors in war—were on the books. But what of the real constitution, the feelings, opinions, and behavior of the American people? And what of the willingness of the U.S. Supreme Court to give meaning to those words in such a way as to affect the everyday lives of blacks? In 1870, Congress had passed a bill directed specifically at the Ku Klux Klan, making it an offense for two or more persons to go in disguise with the intent of intimidating any citizen from exercising or enjoying any right or privilege secured by the Constitution or the laws, but, in a decision only one year after passage of the Civil Rights Act of 1875, the Supreme Court said that only the State of Louisiana, and not the United States Congress, could guarantee the rights of its citizens.[35] The Court declared the Civil Rights Act of 1875 unconstitutional, saying that only state action denying equal protection of the laws was prohibited by Congress in the Fourteenth Amendment. Private citizens who owned theaters or hotels could deny their facilities to blacks if they wished.[36] By 1892, the year in which Ellis Island was opened as a gateway for what would become more than ten million immigrants, ten southern states had passed laws separating blacks from whites on trains. In 1895, the Supreme Court, citing an 1849 decision of the Massachusetts Supreme Court allowing segregation in the schools in that state, concluded in the infamous *Plessy* v. *Ferguson* case that segregation on railroads as prescribed by a Louisiana statute of 1890 did not deny equal protection of the laws.[37]

In his dissent, Justice John Harlan set the standard to which the Court would return in 1954, more than half a century later. But his was a lonely voice in asserting that "the law regards man as man, and takes no account of his surroundings or of his color when his civil rights as guaranteed by the supreme law of the land are involved." Harlan acknowledged that the white race was dominant in education, wealth, and power, but that did not justify whites' denying basic, fundamental rights to blacks since those rights were now clearly guaranteed to all persons in the U.S. Segregation on railroads put "the brand of servitude and degradation upon a large class of our fellow-citizens, our equals before the law." Then, in the standard which he set for generations to come, Harlan expressed a view probably of only a small minority of the American people. "There is no caste," he wrote. "Our Constitution is color blind."[38]

The real constitution, the deep and wide consensus of the American people on the position of blacks in American life, was far from color-blind. Almost twenty years before *Plessy,* the American people acquiesced in a deal that elected Republican Rutherford B. Hayes president in 1877 in exchange for removal of federal troops from the South and the end of Reconstruction. Soon, many blacks who attempted to vote were terrorized and states began to enact statutes to institutionalize blacks' exclusion from the political process. Louisiana passed the first of the famous "grandfather clauses," under which the right to vote was given to all male citizens whose fathers or grandfathers had been able to vote on January 1, 1867. Schools were segregated, and curfews applying exclusively to blacks were imposed.[39]

Keeping blacks in a servile state meant the vast majority remained landless and constantly in debt. Those who owned their own farms were maintained in a dependent state through the lien system of farm financing, though it actually burdened many more poor white farmers than blacks. Rational economic behavior might have led the much larger number of poor whites to join forces with blacks against the system,[40] but most whites "never questioned the sacredness of caste, never stopped wanting the greatest subordination of 'idle and unreliable' black labor." As one labor historian of late-nineteenth-century Georgia put it, "whether planter or poor, whites continued to believe that a proper caste system would assure their own prosperity."[41]

Within twenty years of *Plessy*, the evidence of racial caste was everywhere in the South. Restaurants, drinking fountains, theaters, circuses, hospital floors, barber shops, juries, public parks, schools, and all manner of public accommodations were racially segregated. Although class divisions among whites were strong, there was nearly universal agreement among whites that blacks should be confined by what one historian of the South has called an "inherited, inflexible system with a literal moral authority."[42]

With the end of Reconstruction, the lives of many blacks became more precarious than under slavery. As blacks moved from the South to the North and West, racial animosity increased in both sections. The burning of homes and churches and individual acts of unprovoked violence were commonplace in the North against African-Americans, who were driven out of many cities, and violence against blacks reached new levels of terror in the South with the rise of the Ku Klux Klan and the Knights of the White Camelia.[43]

Terrorist attacks on freed blacks in the South appeared to succeed with the support or acquiescence of the vast majority of whites. After 1870, terrorist intimidation kept blacks from the polls. Houses were burned, crops destroyed, and blacks were whipped and lynched for voting Republican. Lynching became the ultimate sanction against blacks who were so uppity as to agitate for voting rights. The prevalent view was that blacks of any station, even those who owned property and went to college, should not vote. One Mississippi senator exclaimed, "I am just as opposed to Booker Washington as a voter, with all his Anglo-Saxon reinforcements, as I am to the coconut-headed, chocolate-colored, typical little coon Andy Dotson who blacks my shoes every morning. Neither is fit to perform the supreme function of citizenship."[44]

Caste followed American blacks into the armed services in the First World War when all units were segregated. Following the lure of freedom and opportunity, one million blacks moved from the South to the North between 1915 and 1925, leaving the caste system of the South for a different kind of caste in the North. As was true whenever large numbers moved to the North in search of jobs, violent racial clashes became common, the worst of them in 1919 in Chicago and East St. Louis, Illinois, where at least forty Negroes were killed.[45] The violence was massive in cities throughout the country (more than twenty-five race riots in urban centers) in the "Red Summer" of 1919. It was one thing to draft blacks or hire them to fight in a war; it was another to let them work alongside whites in jobs that held some status and paid decent wages.[46] One of

America's most noted satirists, Finley Peter Dunne, wondered if blacks would not be better off with the Cotton Belt than a belt on the neck from a policeman's club. Dunne's barroom philosopher, Mr. Dooley, asked his friend Hennessey, "I used to be all broke up about Uncle Tom, but cud I give him a job tendin' bar in this here liquor store?"[47]

African-American soldiers who returned from the war could not get jobs, for example, in a white man's liquor store in Chicago or New York. Yet, there was reason to escape from the South, where some blacks had been lynched in their uniforms in the terrible summer of 1919. Even public-spirited social workers in many cases appear not to have advanced beyond Jefferson's view about the inherent inferiority of blacks. It was a time when blaming the victim was accepted as an explanation for caste or, at the least, second-class citizenship for African-Americans. C. Vann Woodward wrote that public-spirited professionals "laid great stress on the alarming increase in Negro crime as the race flocked to the cities and packed into crowded, filthy sums. Convinced that the race was rapidly deteriorating in morals and manners, in health and efficiency . . . they resolved that the Negro was incapable of self government, unworthy of the franchise."[48]

When Woodrow Wilson, a self-proclaimed reformer and progressive, was elected president, the hopes of African-Americans, who seem to have shifted to the Democratic candidate in the 1912 election, were raised. But Wilson actually strengthened the caste system by reintroducing segregation in several federal departments. At least three of his cabinet members were sympathetic to the arguments of the so-called "National Democratic Fair Play Association," to the effect that great harm would come to the country if the 24,500 blacks employed by the federal government were permitted to continue to work in integrated settings among their 465,000 white fellow employees.[49]

Wilson staunchly defended the official policy of segregation in personal letters to his old friend Oswald Garrison Villard, the publisher, who was an activist in the National Association for the Advancement of Colored People. He told a Negro delegation that federal segregation was necessary because of friction between blacks and whites. Leading the delegation was William Monroe Trotter, one of the founders of the Niagara Movement (the civil rights organization begun in 1905 on the Canadian side of Niagara Falls that led to the founding of the NAACP) and editor of an African-American paper, the *Boston Guardian*. He told the president that unless the policy of segregation was changed Wilson would lose Negro support at the polls. Wilson dismissed Trotter's words as an empty threat, and the federal government continued a policy of segregating blacks in "the less desirable rooms, the inconveniently located lavatories, the poorly lit alcoves."[50]

Washington, D.C., was essentially a southern city, but segregation increased in northern cities as well. There was, in Stanley Lieberson's phrase, "a hardening in white attitudes toward black schooling" in the 1920s, as more blacks moved to the North.[51] In Cleveland, for example, the curricula for predominantly black schools and classes shifted away from academic subjects to vocational training. More emphasis was placed on sewing, cooking, manual labor, foundry and sheet and metal work. Central High School, which was serving 61 percent of Cleveland's black high school students by 1930, provided mathematics instruction to fewer than half of its tenth graders; it dropped classes in Spanish, German, bookkeeping, and stenography, and in its home economics classes emphasized laundry work.[52] Blacks with high school degrees found themselves relegated to lowest-status jobs. Education provided little reward for blacks as compared to whites, especially after the onset of the Great Depression.[53]

The Depression: Tightening the Boundaries of Caste

During the great industrial expansion in the North between 1910 and 1930, the black male labor force in the region more than doubled to 480,000.[54] Many became longshoremen, garage workers, truck drivers, and deliverymen. Others found jobs in the iron, steel, machinery, automobile, and railroad industries. In railroads, they were kept at unskilled work. Even before 1910, they had entered several industries as strikebreakers, working the docks in Baltimore, and in the iron and steel industries in western Pennsylvania.[55] In Detroit, the Ford Motor Company offered a wide range of blue-collar jobs to black workers beginning in the 1920s; they were later organized by the United Auto Workers of America.[56] In industries such as utility companies blacks were not hired at all.

Even in the North, blacks were shut out from craft labor unions and often were forced to establish unions of their own.[57] Exceptions rarely did more than blunt the edge of the color line, even in industrial unions. Although the Amalgamated Meat Cutters and Butcher Workers Union admitted blacks on the basis of equality with whites, many of the other twelve crafts in the packing industry excluded them.[58] Between 1882 and 1900 there were at least fifty strikes by whites against the hiring of blacks, which, according to labor historian Herbert Hill, kept them from highly paid skilled work in most industries for decades to come.[59] "The less attractive and lower paid jobs" went "to the black man."[60]

One union that appeared to open opportunity to blacks in the late 1920s was the Jewish-led International Ladies' Garment Workers' Union, but, in Philadelphia, some native-born American white women refused to work alongside blacks. In New York, where Jews were particularly active in the ILGWU and where a disproportionate number of blacks were West Indian immigrants, blacks occasionally were elected shop chairmen and used as organizers.[61] But even in that most liberal of unions, the top leadership was white until the 1970s, and Hill's statement that in the early decades of the twentieth century "the aim of white labor organizations to restrict black workers to the lowest rungs of the job ladder was increasingly successful" has been amply documented.[62]

The Depression ravaged most of the economic gains blacks had made in the early 1920s. John Bodnar's study of a small steel town shows how the position of blacks, which in 1920 had been stronger there than that of Slavs and Italians, was considerably weakened as blacks became more numerous. Although a greater percentage of blacks than Slavs and Italians were semiskilled in 1920, 40 percent of the Slavs and Italians had become semiskilled by 1939, compared to 27 percent of the blacks.[63]

Unemployment actually was higher in the North than in the South during the Depression, but southern blacks continued to migrate, although at a much lower rate than in the previous ten years. In the North, blacks had more personal freedom, better wages if they could find a job, and a modicum of government relief if they could not. The caste system itself could be challenged openly, at least by intellectuals, teachers, and social workers and some politicians who courted African-American voters. But in the North blacks were segregated in the most deteriorated neighborhoods, where, unaccustomed to northern winters and separated from family and often from their church and professional black leadership, blacks were in some ways worse off than they had been in the South. As early as October 1933, as many as 40 percent of blacks in several large urban centers were on relief, three or four times as many as whites, and by the late 1930s, when sociologists St. Clair Drake and Horace R. Cayton made their intensive study of blacks in Chicago, the situation had become even worse.[64]

Drake and Cayton found that "caste" existed in "watered down form" in Chicago and elsewhere in the North.[65] By the mid-1930s, white Chicago was organized to keep Negroes in their place. Three such groups were some American Federation of Labor unions in skilled trades, certain railroad brotherhoods, and, most important, an association of neighborhood property owners in alliance with the Chicago Real Estate Board and the Chicago Title and Trust Company.[66] Blacks in Chicago made gains in voting and political power; yet, the overwhelming majority were still subordinated to menial jobs if employed at all, and they were the first fired and the last hired. Those few African-Americans who did what the authors called "clean work" were almost entirely confined to the black ghetto, and, even before the Depression, more than twenty-five of every hundred Negro men and fifty-six of every hundred Negro women were doing some kind of servant work, or four times their proportionate share.[67] Those men working at manual labor were confined overwhelmingly to the lowest-paid, dirtiest, and heaviest of jobs.[68] That was the main point of caste! The black poet Langston Hughes wrote sardonically in 1936, "I am the Negro, servant to you all."[69]

When other sociologists studied ethnic and racial groups in the North after 1925, they found African-Americans often excluded from mainstream institutions. Robert S. Lynd and Helen Merrell Lynd reported that in Muncie, Indiana, in 1925, although no Jews were members of the Rotary Club, Jewish merchants mingled freely with other businessmen in the smaller civic clubs. But blacks were excluded not only from all civic clubs but also from the larger movie houses, the YMCA, and the YWCA. Black children were restricted to their own corner of the park for play.[70] Returning in the mid-1930s, the Lynds found that "business-class Middletown tolerates the Negro population complacently as a convenient instrument for getting certain types of dirty work done for low wages." Blacks were not permitted to become machinists, and an official in a large automobile plant told the Lynds that they had no Negroes at all because it would be degrading for white men to do the same kind of work as blacks.[71]

The doubling and tripling of black populations in northern cities in the 1920s resulted in an intensification of public school segregation. There had been few blacks in the schools of Chicago and Pittsburgh at the turn of the century; by 1930, the great majority of black pupils and teachers learned and worked in overwhelmingly black schools in Chicago and Pittsburgh, and also in Milwaukee, New York, Cleveland, Detroit, and certain other cities.[72] Segregation in the schools was an index of increased residential segregation. In some cities, Cleveland among them, blacks had earlier been less segregated residentially than immigrant-ethnic groups— in 1910, Italians had been more segregated than African-Americans. Ten years later blacks had become the most segregated group.[73]

At the onset of the Depression, almost nine out of ten blacks still lived in the South, where the informal rules and etiquette of caste were tight and where "the white southerner might readily be branded a race traitor if he shook a Negro's hand or called a colored person 'Mr.' or 'Mrs.'"[74] The term "caste" was used extensively by sociologists and other scholars who studied the South in the 1930s. Research sponsored by the Commission on Interracial Cooperation, which later became the Southern Regional Council, concentrated on the impact of the New Deal on southern agriculture and on the life of southern blacks. When the North Carolinian Arthur Raper, then research and field secretary of the Commission, made a systematic study of Greene and Macon counties in Georgia

in the early 1930s, he learned that all of the instruments of caste pluralism—social indignity, physical brutality, educational deprivation, and political exclusion—combined to keep the vast majority of blacks confined
to the most menial kinds of work. Some blacks in the North were being
drawn into a new national industrial economy, but in the South only one
out of every ten who farmed owned any land, "and scarcely half of these
have enough to make a living on." Of the 90 percent who owned no
land, half were sharecroppers without work animals, plows, or farm
equipment of their own, and a fourth were farm wage hands.[75]

Education and politics, which had provided hope to so many immigrants and their children, gave very little to African-Americans. Education
in the Black Belt counties of the South resembled that of Georgia's Greene
County, where blacks of high school age outnumbered whites; only one
black school provided even ninth-grade work, compared to three four-
year and four two-year high schools for whites.[76] As for the Fifteenth
Amendment, Raper wrote in 1936, "It is the expressed belief of nearly all
the white people in these counties that the Negro should not be allowed
to vote, especially in local elections, and if necessary, force should be used
to keep them from the polls."[77] As a result, practically no blacks voted in
county and state elections, and only a few in national elections.

John Dollard, a Yale psychologist, conducted a highly personal, eth-
nographic research study in a small town in Mississippi just large enough
to qualify as an urban area (more than 2,500 people). In his 1937 book,
Caste and Class in a Southern Town, Dollard described "Niggertown," a
community of ramshackle housing and only two paved streets for 1,500
people.[78] Before the Depression, blacks there had owned some businesses,
and more land; there had even been a black-run bank. By the time Dollard
arrived, all of these acquisitions were gone. Dollard used the word "caste"
to describe the condition of blacks, who were subjugated and excluded
by whites from institutions of education, religion, and politics.[79]

Caste was enforced by the rules of social relations. Of all the whites in
town, only Jewish merchants, themselves a tiny minority, appeared to
give blacks a modicum of courtesy.[80] Dollard saw education as the only
opening; if white teachers were permitted to encourage learning among
blacks, he believed that the system of caste might eventually be undermined.[81] But, as Raper had reported one year earlier in Georgia, segregated schools for blacks were inferior, and education was ineffective as a
means of breaking the rules of caste since it was also a reflection of it.[82]

Two years after Dollard's book, another study of the Deep South was
published, anthropologist Hortense Powdermaker's *After Freedom.*[83] It
described life in a Mississippi town disguised by the name "Cottonville."
Elliott M. Rudwick, in his preface to the later, 1967, edition, called Cottonville "a caste-like social system." Like Dollard, Powdermaker found

some class distinctions among the Negroes, but only three owned automobiles, one of them an illiterate ex-bootlegger.[84] No matter what the status of black ministers or teachers within the black community, they were still just "boy" to whites who met them on the street in Cottonville. Powdermaker told of one fairly prosperous, dignified man in his late fifties, a highly respected member of the church, who was stopped by a young white woman who was having trouble with her car. Although she knew his name very well, she called him "boy," repeating it sharply as she ordered him about "in rendering her this unpaid service."[85]

What Powdermaker, Dollard, and Raper described was a social system based overwhelmingly on racial lines. They acknowledged certain deviations from the rules. Some white men had black mistresses; some African-Americans owned land; a few white teachers tried to instill ambition and hope in their black students. But these exceptions were too rare in the South to constitute a fundamental challenge to the pervasive system of caste.

Of all the studies by social scientists of the condition of blacks in the U.S. in the late 1930s and early 1940s, the most influential by far was the Carnegie study conducted by economist Gunnar Myrdal and his large staff of researchers. He, too, used the word "caste" to characterize the position of blacks, in the South particularly. The principal significance of black migration north and west, Myrdal wrote, was separation from "the full blown caste system of the South." He and his associates found effects of caste in the North as well.[86] He insisted that it was a mistake to talk about both ethnics and blacks as minority groups because such a term failed "to make a distinction between the *temporary* social disabilities of recent light-skinned immigrants and the *permanent* disabilities of Negroes and other colored people."[87] The American definition of Negro as anyone who had the slightest amount of black blood made the caste line "absolutely rigid."[88] Blacks were subject to certain disabilities solely because they were Negroes, no matter the actual color of their skin or how well educated they were.

The point of caste was absolutely clear, Myrdal believed. It was to keep blacks in servile jobs. Middle- and upper-class occupations were almost all closed to Negroes. Young Negro women had practically no chance of getting employment as stenographers or secretaries, as sales clerks in department stores, or as telephone operators outside of businesses run by Negroes for Negroes. Even as late as the mid-1930s, blacks in such jobs were only two-thirds of one percent of all female workers. To surmount discrimination, some of the lightest-colored Negroes in the North "passed" into white life from nine to five in order to earn a living, while maintaining their social and family life among blacks.[89] But most blacks could not pretend to be white, and with rare exceptions they were locked into jobs intended for their caste.

A minority of blacks—mostly teachers and ministers but also undertakers and beauticians—were professionals who served blacks. By 1910, blacks in the professions and blacks with business and white-collar jobs equaled only 7 percent of the total black labor force, compared to 6 percent twenty years earlier.[90] Many of those who were professionals despised segregation; nevertheless, they had a vested interest in caste, which gave them control over certain markets. In the Depression, even the slight gains by blacks in the workplace and schools were sharply reversed. Only in the field of politics in the North did blacks gain some slight ground.

Black Political Action Before the Second World War

Blacks seeking to change the system of caste could employ patience, accommodation, and self-help, as advocated by the influence of Booker T. Washington; or they could protest through political action; or they could opt for some form of black separatism. Protesters had to do their share of accommodating. Accommodators occasionally protested. Both groups shared a belief in the promise of America's civic culture; they saw its caste system as remediable. The American system differed from the traditional caste systems of India or Nepal in that it was at odds with the dominant religion of society—Christianity's biblical prophetic emphasis on justice—and with the basic tenets of the American civil religion.

When the brilliant poet and essayist Langston Hughes wrote in 1926, "I, too, sing America," and ten years later, "America will be an ever-living seed, Its dream lies deep in the heart of me,"[91] he repeated the faith in America expressed by all of the major black protest leaders from Frederick Douglass on. When Douglass protested in 1853 that "this Fourth of July is *yours*, not mine," he was not rejecting the promise of the Declaration of Independence or the political institutions created by the Constitution, for, speaking in Scotland six years earlier, he had said, "I love the Declaration of Independence."[92] Black abolitionist organizations, conventions, and other protest movements existed wherever large groups of blacks lived in the North. With the spread of the black codes in the South and the imposition of Jim Crow ideas everywhere, African-American leaders who formed the Niagara Movement declared, "We will not be satisfied to take one jot or tittle less than our full manhood rights. We claim for ourselves every single right that belongs to a free born American, political, civil and social; and until we get these rights we will never cease to protest and assail the ears of America."[93]

In 1910, the leaders of the Movement helped to form the National

Association for the Advancement of Colored People, whose platform proclaimed integration as the central goal of blacks. "We do not believe in the color line against either white or black," asserted the NAACP, calling America a "failure" if it continued to exclude blacks from political, economic or social equality.[94] The principal intellectual inspiration of the NAACP was W. E. B. Du Bois. There have been few scholars in American history who have been as original, prolific, and influential. Born of African, French, and Dutch ancestry in Great Barrington, Massachusetts, in 1868, he eventually joined the Communist party in 1961 and became a Ghanaian citizen a year later, a disillusioned man whose earlier dreams of an integrated society had been shattered. But long before that he had asked whites: "Your country? How come it's yours? Before the Pilgrims landed, we were here . . . would America have been America without her Negro people?"[95]

Other African-Americans repudiated American society altogether. They could not say to whites, as Indians had said, "Go back to the land from whence you came," but they could call for their own return to Africa or for the creation of a national home for black Americans elsewhere. Some blacks, and many whites too, fantasied a kind of racial territorial pluralism in which blacks would be given a state or a nation within the U.S. The high point of the black nationalist movement came at the end of the First World War, when Marcus Garvey, a Jamaican-born immigrant to Harlem, began to organize blacks into The Universal Negro Improvement Association, with the goal of building institutions under the control of blacks.[96] It was the biggest and most successful of all of the black separatist movements, but it was based on a false premise: that most African-Americans did not share the goal of an integrated society.

Garvey inspired a sense of pride and a confidence that black Americans could take control of their own destiny, but separatism was not the goal of most blacks. One said the trouble with Garvey was that "he assumed we were not first and last of all Americans." Another reported, "this was my country, and I would rather fight for what I have here than go back to Africa."[97] Garvey, who had never actually called for most American blacks to return to Africa, was convicted of using the mails fraudulently. The movement withered, but Garvey's ideal of self-direction and self-esteem would surface again in the call for black pride in the 1960s.

The ability of blacks to effect change through politics was sharply limited, of course, by caste, particularly in the South. As a consequence, a form of black leadership emerged that Myrdal and his colleagues described as "accommodating."[98] A former slave, Booker T. Washington, one of the few "accommodating" leaders to achieve a national forum and reputation, promised whites that blacks would be patient; he asked whites for support and money to build the educational and economic skills necessary for genuine integration of blacks into American society. He asked blacks also to be patient, promised that with the cooperation of whites the worst of their miseries and burdens would be relieved and they and their children would be trained to take advantage of the opportunities freedom would one day offer. Blacks who followed Washington's strategy negotiated with whites for benefits and jobs in the political system; they promised to deliver compliance with that system, and, in the North, they promised votes, as well. Their achievements were ultimately limited by their utter dependence on the power and indulgence of whites.

Booker T. Washington was unhesitating in his insistence that blacks should and would achieve the goal of full equality. Before the Second World War, the accommodation model was followed by most black leaders in the North. "Negro protest," wrote Myrdal, "is shut in by caste."[99] Even in the northern cities, blacks, a small minority unable to make a critical difference in citywide elections or state politics, tended to be dependent on white leaders for favors and spoils. Black northern politicians had some bargaining power in pushing white city governments to act. Still, northern urban political machines in a number of cities were run by sleazy officials who aided in corrupting aspiring black politicians. In Chicago, for example, the northern city with the highest proportion of African-Americans, Oscar DePriest, elected alderman in 1915 and in 1928 elected as the first northern Negro congressman, was, according to Harold F. Gosnell's landmark study of Chicago politics, tightly tied to the black underworld.[100]

Gosnell's intricate analysis of the workings of the Chicago government revealed that for blacks city government was only to a slight extent an instrument of economic mobility. Less than one percent of Chicago firemen and only 2.7 percent of policemen were black in 1932 in a city already 7 percent black. Two and a half percent of public school teachers in Chicago were black by 1934, up from one-half of one percent in 1910; only minuscule progress in that regard had been made in more than a generation. Although blacks in 1932 held 6.4 percent of all the classified civil service positions in Chicago, they worked disproportionately as janitors and as unskilled laborers in other jobs in the city government, just as they did in the private sector.[101] Blacks in Chicago may have been better off economically and politically than blacks in the South, Gosnell concluded, but they were still subject to official and semiofficial coercion. Negro politicians had been unable or unwilling to prevent police brutality, to secure decent housing, or even to hinder black police officers from adapting to "the exploitative patterns of behavior found in the department."[102]

Because of their impotence at the local level, African-Americans in the 1920s had little influence on national politics. Historian John Hope Franklin has written of instances of the increased black influence in politics in those decades, as when blacks strongly opposed confirmation of John J. Parker to the U.S. Supreme Court and possibly influenced his rejection by the Senate in 1930. Blacks also organized to influence the outcome of senatorial campaigns in Ohio and California in what Franklin called "political regeneration."[103]

Republican presidents Warren Harding, Calvin Coolidge, and Herbert Hoover for their part had done little to encourage the participation of blacks in the political process broadly except on demeaning terms; only slightly more was done nationally under the administration of Franklin D. Roosevelt. Roosevelt did appoint more than a dozen African-Americans to subcabinet and somewhat lesser positions in Washington. Most benefits blacks received from the New Deal came from programs designed to help the poor. A number of the few black delegates to the Republican conventions in the 1920s and 1930s were hired sycophants or members of corrupt city machines. Democrats had elected no black delegates at all to their national convention in 1928, where the few black alternates were separated from whites by chicken wire. Nor were there any African-American delegates at the 1932 convention, where Roosevelt was first nominated, though some blacks were elected to the legislatures of ten states in that year's elections. Virtually nothing was done to attack the structure of racial caste itself until the Second World War.[104]

In the arts, one area where African-American accomplishments and recognition by whites could not be wholly constrained, black achievements over a twenty-year period from about 1915 to 1935 were impressive. Probably never before had any one ethnic group in the U.S. created in such a short period of time in one city the literary, musical, and artistic record of the "Harlem Renaissance" in New York.[105] But the Depression blotted out the glittering eminence of that black renaissance, and for all of the brilliance and protest in the poetry of such men as Claude McKay, Countee Cullen, and Langston Hughes, caste pluralism in the form of racial segregation remained substantially intact right up to and through the war.

No national report proclaiming caste pluralism to be a failure appeared to match the Merriam Report of 1929 denouncing the policy of forced assimilation of Indians until Myrdal's *An American Dilemma,* published in 1944. Nor was any legislation passed to improve the status of blacks comparable to the Indian Reorganization Act of 1934, which recognized Indian tribal rights. As devastating as life for reservation Indians had become—infant mortality, disease, alcoholism, and other forms of morbidity were higher for Indians than for any other group, including blacks—official brutality no longer was condoned toward Indians as it was in the South against African-Americans. Lynchings of blacks in the

South frequently went unpunished even into the 1930s, although not as many occurred as in past years (the worst year was 1892, when 154 blacks were lynched). And, only occasionally, as in the famous Scottsboro, Alabama, case of 1931, did northern intervention prevent the execution of blacks who had been wrongly accused of capital crimes. Typically, blacks held were brutalized in segregated, crowded jails.[106]

By 1941 and the war, caste pluralism still locked out the vast majority of blacks from the civic culture. In 1940, only one out of twenty black males was employed in a white-collar occupation, compared to one out of three white males. Six of ten employed black women worked as maids; one of ten white women did so. In Chicago, where blacks were 8 percent of the labor force, they were 22 percent of the unemployed. Government employment practices, local and national, were based to a large extent on caste. The five southern states in which African-Americans were more than a third of the population employed not a single African-American policeman. Blacks could not enlist in the Marines or in the Air Force; the Navy accepted them only in menial jobs. The Army was segregated, and no black officer was permitted to outrank any white man in the same unit. Every state in the South, where three-quarters of the African-Americans in the nation lived, as well as a number of states in the North, outlawed intermarriage.[107] Caste pluralism was enforced by law, by hiring practices, and by public discourse and social etiquette. Southern whites still called adult African-Americans by their first names or "boy" or "girl."

That was the situation in January 1941 when A. Philip Randolph, the head of the Brotherhood of Sleeping Car Porters, proposed a march on Washington, D.C., to demand that the U.S. government (which had passed a law drafting black as well as white men into the armed services) ban discrimination in defense industries. President Roosevelt tried to have the march called off, but Randolph persisted. Just as marchers were preparing to board trains for the capital, on June 25, 1941, the president issued Executive Order 8802, banning discrimination in defense industries or in government "because of race, creed, color or national origin." The civil rights revolution had begun. Probably no one—perhaps not even A. Philip Randolph himself—could have predicted the dismantling of the formal structure of caste that would take place in the 1960s and 1970s.

Chapter Six

"I GO SAD AND HEAVY HEARTED"
Sojourner Pluralism for Asians and Mexicans

MEXICAN workers in the United States in the 1920s sang a *corrido*, a Mexican ballad, "An Emigrant's Farewell," telling of the anguish of a young man about to leave for the United States to work. "I bear you in my heart," he sang about Mexico, his family, and the beloved Virgin of Guadalupe, lamenting, "I go sad and heavy hearted, / To suffer and endure / . . ."[1] It was an immigrant's lament not limited to Mexicans. Millions of male sojourners, and later females, too, came from Asia, Europe, Canada, the Caribbean Islands, and the Azores to the U.S. on a lonely journey in search of work. But of all the sojourner immigrants, two large groups—Asians and Mexicans—had in common an extended history of systematic labor exploitation enforced with the cooperation of national and state governments, the local police, and the system of justice.

The U.S. conquest of more than half of Mexico was preceded by the revolt of Euro-Americans in Texas in 1837, leading to its annexation in 1845. Some of the Americans had been invited to settle in Texas. Many more came as illegal aliens, and, by 1830, Americans outnumbered Mexicans in Texas by two to one. The American cry for manifest destiny, driven largely by racism, anti-Catholic bigotry, land hunger, and the desire to expand slavery into new territories, led to the invasion of Mexico and the conquest of a vast land area with a relatively small number of indigenous people.

The treaty of Guadalupe Hidalgo (1848), which brought the war between the two nations to a formal close, forced Mexico to cede what eventually became California, New Mexico, Nevada, and parts of Colorado, Arizona, and Utah. Those Mexicans who chose to remain for one year in what was now U.S. territory were granted American citizenship. As interpreted by Mexico, protocols to the treaty signed by U.S. emissaries guaranteed to the Mexicans land and water rights and religious and cultural integrity. The American government took the position that since the protocols were not part of the treaty itself, they were not binding. But the U.S. established a system for adjudicating land claims, and a majority of initial claims were approved. Despite that system, Mexicans in the conquered territory lost a substantial amount of property to Euro-

Americans through extralegal means within two decades. Bad feelings between the two groups, generated by arguments about land, cultural tensions, and racism, led to recurring conflicts, especially on the border, where the resistance of Mexicans to what was seen as American colonization was extensive.[2] The Americans blamed *banditos*. The Mexicans complained of "gringo justice."

The treaty of Guadalupe Hidalgo became the basis for subsequent land claims by Mexican-Americans in south Texas, New Mexico, and southern California and for assertions that Mexican-Americans were a colonized people, as Indians were. But nearly all Indians in the U.S. today are descendants of tribes who made treaties with the U.S. government, and all but a small minority of Mexican-Americans descend from immigrants who arrived long after the treaty of Guadalupe Hidalgo was signed.

The vast majority of Mexicans who came to work in the U.S. thought of themselves as Mexican sojourners in a foreign country. What was distinctive about their experience and that of most Asian immigrants was the extent to which they were confined in systems of pluralism intended to coerce their labor.

Cooperation between local police and employers in controlling workers was common in industrial America, as in the coal fields of Appalachia, where native-born Americans as well were exploited by the coal companies with the help of the police throughout much of this century. But only in the case of the Asians and Mexicans were there national policies to keep such groups of immigrant workers in their place. Other sojourners, such as Italians, Greeks, Turks, Poles, West Indians, French Canadians, and Cape Verdeans who went back and forth to their homelands, were not subject to widely enforced systems of sojourner pluralism that made Asian and Mexican workers particularly vulnerable to employer abuse.

Sojourner pluralism was far less rigidly restrictive than the caste pluralism that restricted black Americans, and in every decade a number of Asian and Mexican immigrants broke through the boundaries intended to keep them in unskilled and servile jobs. The U.S. was a land of opportunity as well as exploitation for sojourners. Chinese immigrants of the turn of the century spoke of California as "the golden mountain," even as Jewish immigrants called America "the golden land." Eighty years later, one of the most popular ballads on Spanish-language radio in Texas told of a poor young Mexican woman who waded across the Rio Grande without money, found her boyfriend with a blonde girlfriend, frightened them away with a gun, then married a Hollywood producer and bought a ranch.[3]

Many sojourners succeeded beyond what would have been possible at home. But the vast majority, at least for a while, were confined by law and custom in menial jobs. When they were no longer needed, they were expected to go home voluntarily or be sent home. The coercion of their labor rested on their being socially stigmatized as racially and morally inferior and the imposition of political and legal restrictions.

The linchpin in the system of sojourner pluralism for imported workers from Asia was the Naturalization Law dating back to 1790 that made them ineligible for citizenship. Mexican workers, who came in extraordinarily large numbers illegally, were vulnerable to employer control because so many were working without authorization.

Keeping Asian Sojourners in Their Place

From 1850 to 1934, employers in Hawaii and on the West Coast sought laborers successively from China, Japan, Korea, and the Philippines. They preferred single males who would work hard, fast, and cheap at the most menial jobs. During the 1870 congressional debate on the law that provided for naturalization of persons of African descent, Republican Senator Charles Sumner of Massachusetts proposed an amendment to permit naturalization for other nonwhites as well. But senators from western states, determined to exclude Chinese from citizenship, led an overwhelming defeat of Sumner's motion.[4] The Chinese were, as the Democratic party platform of 1884 later said, "unfitted by habits, training, religion or kindred . . . for the citizenship which our laws confer."[5] The writers of the platform had insisted that "the liberal principles embodied by Jefferson in the Declaration of Independence, and sanctioned in the Constitution, . . . makes ours the land of liberty and the asylum of the oppressed of every Nation," but the Chinese were seen, as nativists saw the Irish in the 1850s, as being incapable of becoming members of a self-governing republic.

Something else beyond "habits, training, religion or kindred" kept the Chinese outsiders. That something else was race. Popular literature, political speeches, and government reports tended to stigmatize Chinese as immoral by nature. "Celestials," "Mongolians," "coolies," and "chinks," they were portrayed as racially habituated to filth, disease, and immorality, themes stressed in a half dozen popular magazines in the 1850s and 1860s.[6] One California senator asked, "Can we stand all the vices, all the diseases, all the mischief that infect humanity the world over and retain our American civilization?"[7] "It is my deliberate opinion," said one popular writer, "that the Chinese are, morally, the most debased people on the face of the earth."[8] An 1865 New York Times editorial said, "We have four million of degraded negroes in the South . . . and if there were to be a flood-tide of Chinese population—a population befouled with all the social vices, with no knowledge or appreciation of free institutions or Consti-

tutional liberty, with heathenish souls and heathenish propensities . . .
we should be prepared to bid farewell to republicanism and democracy."[9]

A state senate investigator in California in 1876 reported that five or six
Chinese were sleeping in spaces only six feet wide and six feet long in
rooms at the Globe Hotel in San Francisco. One policeman, who reported
seeing seventy-five in a room, also told of two hundred houses of pros-
titution and a great many gambling houses in a six-by-eight-block area.[10]
One San Franciscan gave testimony that he went into places "so filthy
and dirty I cannot see how these people live there." He concluded, "the
houses would be unfit for the occupation of white people, for I do not
see how it would be possible to cleanse them, unless you burn up the
whole quarter, and even then, I doubt whether you can get rid of the
filth."[11]

What the report did not add was that the Chinese were often energetic,
enterprising individuals, many of whom had opened stores in cities
throughout the West and in Hawaii. Many sent home remittances to
support their families. Crowded quarters often housed bachelors trying
to create extended families of their own. They resorted to opium and
prostitutes as white American men in similar circumstances used alcohol
and prostitutes, as a relief from the misery of separation from their families.

The racist stigmatizing of the Chinese, and of the Japanese, Koreans,
Filipinos, and Mexicans, reinforced their exclusion from political rights
and their maltreatment by the legal system. An older California law that
prohibited blacks, mulattoes, or Indians from giving evidence for or
against a white person was interpreted by the California Supreme Court
in 1854 as applying to all nonwhites, including Chinese. After all, said the
chief justice, if Chinese were permitted to testify, "we might soon see
them at the polls, in the jury box, upon the bench, and in our legislative
halls."[12]

The ruling and others like it, in effect, sanctioned many brutal attacks
against Chinese. When, in 1869, 350 members of the Miners Union at
Gold Hill, Nevada, raided the living quarters of Chinese railroad workers,
the county sheriff made no effort to stop them.[13] Another sheriff told
white men around a mill camp that they were free to take the law into
their own hands if they suspected any Chinese men of robbery, and they
did. They hanged two to a derrick until nearly dead and, unable to obtain
their confessions, drove them out of the area.[14] On Thanksgiving Day in
1877 in San Francisco, seven thousand white marchers, many carrying
American flags, paraded against Chinese labor. A popular poster held
aloft showed a large boot in close proximity to a flying Chinaman.[15] In

1886, in Rock Springs, Wyoming, a night attack by 150 armed white men plundered and burned the homes of Chinese strikebreakers and killed twenty-eight.[16] Chinese workers were driven from Tacoma and Seattle and from the San Joaquin Valley in California, where they were taken to the railroad station and loaded onto departing trains.[17]

Eastern and southern European immigrants also were frequently harassed, and there were instances of violence, and even murder, against them, the most notable the lynching of Italian prisoners in New Orleans in 1890. But the law generally was on the side of the Europeans, and in the New Orleans case the U.S. government paid indemnities to families of the murdered prisoners.[18] Chinese were often intimidated by U.S. marshals, who would surround a community, herd them together, and demand that they produce their registration certificates. Later, Japanese and Filipinos in Hawaii were systematically intimidated by the police and courts when they struck for better wages and working conditions.[19]

The contrast between the treatment of Chinese sojourners as outsiders and European immigrants as potential citizens was stark. At the same time that police authorities and immigration inspectors chased the Chinese in the West, German and Scandinavian aliens in Wisconsin, Wyoming, and Nebraska were being urged to vote (seven states had laws permitting alien suffrage up to the outbreak of the First World War). At the very time the California constitution of 1878–1879 stipulated that "no alien ineligible to become a citizen of the United States shall ever be employed on any state, county, municipal or other public work in this state,"[20] more than fifty Irish Catholics served on the Boston police force; and, in five years, the immigrant Hugh O'Brien would be elected to the first of five terms as mayor. Keeping the Asians from citizenship and from voting also kept them from owning land or obtaining licenses. In Hawaii, where the plantation oligarchy nourished a tradition of noblesse oblige and where laws were less restrictive than in California, the head of the Hawaiian Sugar Planters' Association said in 1910 that "up to the present time the Asiatic has had only an economic value. . . . So far as the institutions, laws, customs, and language of the permanent population go, his presence is no more felt than is that of the cattle on the ranges."[21]

More than 322,000 Cantonese-speaking male peasants arrived in the U.S. between 1850 and 1882 to work on American railroads, in mines, on plantations, at logging camps, in vineyards, orchards, and ranches. By the late 1870s, it was clear that tens of thousands of them would neither return home nor be confined to servile labor. In 1882, when nearly forty thousand Chinese nationals arrived and only ten thousand went home, Congress decided to oblige employers to look elsewhere for muscle by passing the first law to exclude Chinese laborers. (In no other year in the nineteenth century would there be a net immigration of Chinese.)

Not long after the exclusion of Chinese laborers in 1882, employers sought temporary alien workers among the Japanese, who, like the Chinese in Hawaii, worked on sugar and pineapple plantations there, and who in California on farms, worked in collectives or labor gangs, and in towns in domestic service. The Japanese differed from the Chinese and Filipinos in that Japanese men were often joined by wives, and eventually 80 percent of the issei (foreign-born generation) had families in the U.S. As their numbers grew, state laws were passed to keep the Japanese in their place. State antimiscegenation laws were generally applied to Asians on the mainland, but in 1905, California passed a statute aimed specifically at preventing intermarriage between Caucasians and Japanese. One witness testified that he knew of a Japanese who lived with a white woman. "In that woman's arms is a baby. What is that baby? It isn't Japanese. It isn't white. I'll tell you what it is," he said. "It is the germ of the mightiest problem that ever faced this state." It would make, he said, the black problem of the South "look simple."[22]

In order to keep the Japanese and Chinese as sojourners and to discourage settlement, in 1907, Congress provided that any American woman who married a foreigner—keeping in mind that only Asians were ineligible to become Americans—would automatically take the nationality of her husband. Although that law was repealed in 1922, female citizens who married aliens who were ineligible for citizenship were deprived of their own citizenship until 1931, a rule that discouraged women from marrying Asians even in states with no antimiscegenation law. Since the ratio of male to female sojourners was enormous, especially for the Chinese (twenty-six to one in 1890) and Filipinos (ten to one in 1910), such legislation kept many newcomers from marriage at all, and hence from becoming parents of American-born children.[23]

As a growing number of Japanese sojourners became settlers, the cry of restriction arose once more, and in 1907 the imperial government of Japan agreed to impose limitations on Japanese emigration rather than suffer the indignity of a Japanese exclusion statute. It was not enough to restrict immigration; it became increasingly necessary to enforce the system of sojourner pluralism against Japanese already here. After the Japanese farmers achieved considerable success, California, in 1913, passed an Alien Land Law that prohibited aliens who were ineligible for citizenship from owning land, although they were allowed to rent it.[24]

Efforts to enforce sojourner pluralism were only mildly successful. Despite limitations, the Japanese by the early 1920s were producing most of the berries, celery, asparagus, and onions raised in California. Despite the strong hostility toward them, they were able to increase their role in agriculture.[25] Their numbers were not large (only 80,000 Japanese and 20,000 Chinese immigrated into the U.S. between 1911 and 1920), but because of their success in agriculture and other work, overt white racism became more blatant. "California was given by God to a white people," said the president of the Native Sons of the Golden West in 1920, "and with God's strength we want to keep it as he gave it to us."[26]

The sugar planters and other *haole* (Caucasian) leaders in Hawaii also were concerned about the success of the Japanese workers, who by 1920 constituted more than 30 percent of the territory's population. Unlike the California farmers, who were beginning to look to Mexicans to replace the Chinese and Japanese, the employers of Hawaii implored Congress to permit importation of large numbers of Chinese "coolie" laborers, once again under contract and at low cost. After a Japanese plantation strike in 1920, the most powerful men in Hawaii for two years importuned Congress for a permanent system of rotating peonage, but the planters underestimated the growing influence of Hawaii's small (off-plantation) labor movement with the mainland's American Federation of Labor and through it with Congress, and the planters were turned down.[27]

Walter Dillingham and other leaders in Hawaii argued that it was impossible for the Japanese or their children to become Americans. When the Californian executive secretary of the National Committee on American-Japanese Relations testified before Congress on exclusion of Asian immigration, he insisted that if Asians were permitted to emigrate they would create a race problem like that faced by the whites in the South. When he made that argument to officials in the Japanese government, he said, "they saw the point instantly."[28] Of course the Japanese understood it. Caucasian farmers would not have been permitted in Japan; nor were Chinese and Koreans in Japan allowed to assume any significant roles in the country.

The attorney general of California warned the U.S. Senate committee that "If the Negro had had the capacity, the efficiency, the ambition, the energy, and the power to accomplish possessed by the Japanese, all south of the Mason-Dixon would long ago have been entirely black. . . . the white American will not live upon conditions of equality with the Negro, nor with the Japanese, nor with the Chinese, nor with the Hindu."[29] The warning reflected a considerable degree of intellectual confusion. Blacks were disparaged and thought unfit for full membership in the American polity because of their inferiority. They were seen as lazy and stupid. The Japanese were seen as superhuman; yet in 1924 Congress agreed that all Asians should be barred from immigration.

Following the agreement between the U.S. and Japan in 1907 to limit Japanese immigration and especially after passage of legislation in 1924 barring Japanese, Chinese, and other aliens ineligible for citizenship from immigrating, employers sought workers from the Philippines, a territory of the United States. As the latest sojourner aliens ineligible for citizenship, Filipinos were pushed to the bottom of the system of stratified sojourner pluralism in the West and in Hawaii. From 1909 through 1931, about 113,000 Filipinos came to Hawaii, of whom 55,000 remained in the islands, 39,000 returned to their homelands, and 18,600 moved on to the West Coast to join the 20,000 Filipinos who had gone directly to the mainland. In Hawaii, they worked mainly in the sugar cane mills and fields and on pineapple plantations. In West Coast states (most numerous in California), they took menial service jobs during the winter in hotels and restaurants or as domestic servants, and in the spring as migrant farm workers.

As bad as the situation was for Chinese and Japanese aliens in the 1930s, it was worse for Filipinos. On the plantations in Hawaii, Filipinos made less money for the same work. Without the protection of federal collective bargaining laws, Filipino and other workers in Hawaii were extremely vulnerable to retaliation for strikes. During a 1924 strike on the Hawaiian island of Kauai, sixteen Filipinos were killed.[30] But Filipino life was generally better in the plantation camps in Hawaii than on the West Coast, where, like the Mexicans in the Southwest, Filipinos provided a cheap, expendable work force of bus boys, dishwashers, toilet cleaners, ranch and cannery workers, and pickers of grapes, lettuce, asparagus, pears, and a dozen other vegetables and fruits that fed America. Growers came to depend on such workers and employed railroad detectives, town and county policemen, and agents to help control them. Often brutalized by whites and each other, they moved with the crop seasons in a world of Chinese gambling houses, Japanese hotels, dance halls, small-time gangsters and petty racketeers, pimps and prostitutes of every hue and several nationalities. They suffered with tuberculosis and slept, ate, fought with, and nursed each other ten in a room in cheap boardinghouses in Honolulu, Seattle, Los Angeles, Stockton, Bakersfield, and a dozen other cities in the West and Southwest.

As nonwhite males ineligible for citizenship (the 1930 ratio of males to females in California was fourteen to one) and denied federal relief benefits until 1937, Filipinos, more than the Chinese and Japanese or even the Mexicans, were kept in a servile labor class. But they kept coming to the U.S. until 1934, when Congress established a quota of fifty Filipino immigrants per year in the Philippines Independence Act. With the Depression, these sojourner-workers had become expendable. But, as intending sojourners often do, a large number remained, and by the 1950s and early 1960s, they, and especially Mexicans, were the core of the agricultural work force in California and in Hawaii, where they constituted the largest single ethnic group of plantation workers.

Mexican Sojourners: Turning the Spigot On and Off

Filipinos were easily replaced by Mexicans in California, and for the other border states, Mexico was the obvious source for a steady supply of inexpensive and exploitable labor. An informal system of Mexican sojourner pluralism emerged in the 1890s after U.S. immigration laws excluded Chinese laborers. For several decades before the beginning of large-scale migrations from Mexico in 1897, exploitation had driven farm laborers deep into poverty. The displacement of small farmers by the expansion of large ranches increased the number seeking work as laborers. Railroad development in northern Mexico, where peons could earn three times as much as in the south, brought many closer to the U.S. Soon, knowledge that American wages could be anywhere from four to fifteen times as high as in rural Mexico enticed increasing numbers to cross the border.[31] Under 1902 congressional legislation, construction of large federally funded reservoirs encouraged labor-intensive irrigated farming, especially in Texas and California. After the Mexican Revolution of 1910, hundreds of thousands fled north. Between 1910 and 1930, 10 percent of the population of Mexico had emigrated to the U.S.; about 685,000 were legal immigrants, an unknown but possibly a larger number illegal immigrants. There were no numerical restrictions on immigration within the western hemisphere, but many Mexicans avoided immigration fees, visas, and various exclusionary tests, including the requirement that they not become public charges, and, after 1917, the literacy test, and hence were in the U.S. illegally. How many illegal aliens came to the U.S. for any one period is impossible to say, but the commissioner general for immigration estimated in 1911 that from 1900 to 1910 ten to twenty times as many "unofficial immigrants" came north from Mexico than entered legally. Although there was no way of knowing how many entered illegally, the number, while no doubt exaggerated, was probably substantial.[32]

From an employer point of view, the system was almost flawless. The large number of illegal aliens who came to work provided a strong supply of vulnerable workers who would accept depressed wages and labor standards, thereby keeping employer costs down and preventing formation of any effective labor organization. The growers of perishable fruits and vegetables particularly appreciated a loose labor market since they never knew how many workers they would need, depending upon the vagaries of weather. Nor were they pushed to invest in labor-saving equipment or to spend more for domestic labor. Those Americans who used low-cost, foreign unskilled help for menial tasks, such as hospital orderlies, dish-washers, and housemaids, directly benefited from their presence, and American consumers paid less for their produce. Only American farm workers, an especially weak group politically, suffered directly from the competition. Hence, growers could rely on the flow of undocumented labor and also on the cooperation of government in managing that flow as their needs required.

French Canadian workers who came to New England throughout the late nineteenth and early twentieth centuries were most like the Mexicans in the ease with which they moved back and forth across the border, in their reluctance to put down roots in American life, in their strong sense of cultural identity with their homeland, and in their difficulty in acquir-ing English literacy and fluency. But there were also differences between the two groups. French Canadians were lighter in skin color, and they came to an area where labor unions were relatively strong and where there were large numbers of immigrants from other countries who had already become active participants in American life.

Sojourners from Puerto Rico, like Mexicans in the Southwest, moved frequently back and forth from the mainland. They also had difficulty in acquiring effective use of English. And they, too, suffered from racial prejudice. Large growers' associations often negotiated contracts for Puerto Rican farm workers, after 1948 with the migration division of the Puerto Rican government's Department of Labor. But compared to Mex-icans, the scale of migration was small, and Puerto Ricans working in the post–Second World War era were American citizens with recourse to protection from the Constitution and laws of the U.S., especially in the civil rights era.[33]

Puerto Ricans, French Canadians, and Mexicans shared a sojourner mentality. Armando B. Rendon, a Chicano activist of the 1960s, explained that few Mexicans would buy a house, even when it was to their economic advantage, because most believed they would return soon to Mexico. Others shied away from adult education courses. What sense did it make to learn English if they were returning home? Politics was for those who had a future and a stake in the country. Even lawful resident aliens saw little point in being naturalized. Families as far away as Chicago and New York visited their Mexican home towns at least once and sometimes twice a year for a few weeks on vacation.[34]

By the 1980s, research on the effects of the sojourner mentality of illegal aliens had become more sophisticated, confirming Rendon's impression-istic interpretation.[35] The sojourner mentality was well suited to the needs of growers, ranchers, and other employers of unskilled labor in the Southwest and elsewhere; it made it easier for whites generally to think of Mexicans as stoop labor or "wetbacks" or in racist terms as "greasers," and not as persons. Anglo-Europeans could accept the need for sudden roundups, deportations, and contract labor programs and ignore the miserable conditions under which Mexicans and Mexican-Americans often lived and worked.

The circular pattern of Mexican migration, driven in large measure by employer demand with the cooperation of the government, was entrenched early in the century. When workers reached a certain savings goal or when they could not adapt or were terribly lonely for relatives or friends, or a combination of these, they often returned home on their own. The system of sojourner pluralism was distinctive in the Southwest to the extent of government cooperation in amending and administering the immigration law for the benefit of employers without regard to the immigration statutes. For example, the Immigration Acts of 1903 and 1907 imposed head taxes of two dollars and four dollars on immigrants, except for Mexicans, ensuring the Southern Pacific Railroad and others a steady supply of Mexican workers.[36] Laws forbidding entry of contract laborers, the diseased, the insane, and certain classes of criminals were enforced weakly in order to cater to western employers' need for labor; and until 1908, the U.S. Bureau of Immigration did not even bother to count incoming Mexicans except for the few who said they intended to remain permanently.[37] When workers were no longer needed, they would be repatriated, as in the recession of 1907, when several thousand railroad track laborers in California lost their jobs. Mexican officials cooperated with the railroad, which gave workers free transportation to the border city of Juárez, where they received food and free rail passes back to their homes.[38]

By 1917, when the U.S. enacted the most restrictive (so far) immigration statute in its history, including a literacy test, the law made a special exception for employers in the West. It authorized the secretary of labor to permit otherwise inadmissible persons to enter the country as temporary workers, and in May 1917 the first *bracero* program for Mexican workers was created (later expanded to allow some to be employed in nonfarm work). Regulations called for the *braceros* to return home after their work was done, but the rules were incompletely enforced; of the 76,862 Mexican workers admitted under the program, only 34,922 returned home.[39]

Labor recruiting agencies, deprived of European workers after the restrictive immigration legislation of 1921 and 1924, sought Mexicans for outside the West as well. Because of its central position in the midwestern railroad system, in the 1920s Chicago became a central point for Mexican labor. In 1927, sixteen labor contractors reported that they had placed

lots of land, little labor

75,400 Mexicans in jobs in the Chicago area alone for a fee the employers paid them. A less expensive way for employers to obtain labor was to use smugglers, "coyotes," who, operating along the border, put the workers on a train for Chicago, after which the employer sent the coyote a check for each worker who arrived.[40]

Once in Chicago and other cities, Mexicans were outside the system of sojourner pluralism enforced in behalf of growers and ranchers in the Southwest and California. In the East and Midwest, there was the possibility of joining strong labor unions, and the situation of Mexicans in Chicago or Detroit resembled that of other sojourners in the North and Midwest, as, for example, dark-skinned West Indians who came to the mainland, many illegally.

The system was particularly brutal in Texas, where around the turn of the century vigilante bands attacked Mexicans and Mexican-Americans.[41] By the early twentieth century, Texas Rangers had replaced the local police as principal enforcers of the system of sojourner pluralism, and later, the Border Patrol of the U.S. Immigration and Naturalization Service and local police forces took over from the Rangers. Although the Border Patrol itself was not brutal, it developed informal arrangements of cooperation with agricultural employers from the 1920s on through the 1950s. The INS would go easy on enforcement until picking time was over, making only a few raids to indicate that they were doing their job in order to justify federal appropriations. Sympathetic to the needs of the local economy and amenable to political pressures, the INS stepped up enforcement as in its crackdown after the "wetback strikes" of 1951 and 1952.[42]

Turning the spigot that controlled the labor supply on and off with the cooperation of the authorities was a well-established pattern of labor control by the 1920s. At crop-picking time, workers would go north from Mexico. At slack periods and especially at Christmas, they would go home. When employer desires for Mexican labor waned in 1928, U.S. authorities cooperated in keeping Mexicans out by applying the literacy test enacted by Congress in 1917, previously ignored for Mexicans for years. With the onset of the Depression, between 1929 and 1934 more than 400,000 Mexicans were sent home without formal deportation proceedings, including thousands of U.S. citizens of Mexican descent who were deported illegally.[43]

The vulnerability of the sojourner Mexican workers was not diminished by the fact that many labor contractors themselves were Mexicans. Italian, Greek, Filipino, and labor contractors of other nationalities also held enormous power in the system of sojourner labor recruitment. But in the Southwest, where so many workers were smuggled in illegally, the possibilities for corruption and abuse by contractors probably were greater than in other parts of the country. In his autobiography, *Barrio Boy*, Ernesto Galarza, a leader of the Chicano movement in the 1960s, told of going to work for a rancher near Sacramento after being hired by a contractor who never discussed working conditions or wages or even how much Galarza would be charged for his meals. The contractor "could fire a man and his family on the spot and make them wait days for their wages. . . . the worst thing one could do was to ask for fresh water on the job, regardless of the heat of the day; instead of ice water, given freely, the crews were expected to buy sodas at twice the price in town, sold by the contractor himself."[44]

The political control of Mexicans was easiest at the border, where the movement back and forth was constant. Even Mexican-American citizens who lived near the border seldom felt enfranchised. In Hidalgo, Starr, Cameron, and Duvall counties, local Anglo political machines that developed in the late nineteenth century effectively controlled the votes of Mexican-Americans. Although political boss rule of European immigrants was developing in the big cities of the Northeast and Midwest, too, with machines usually run not by Anglos but by ethnics themselves who asserted group interests in the name of American rights, Mexican-American politicians on the Texas border tended to follow an older Mexican pattern of exchanging their votes for favors, this time from Anglos.

The most influential of all Anglo-American bosses in south Texas, James Wells, explained that Mexican-Americans asked ranch managers who they should vote for because they were totally dependent on them; ranchers protected their servants and workers with jobs, help with the law, loans, and other favors, and, therefore, expected the *peons* to vote at their direction as a form of compensation.[45] Since most of the Mexican-Americans worked as ranch hands, farm laborers or sharecroppers or small farmers with little expectation of advancement, and most expected to go home someday, it is not surprising that they did not develop an independent ethnic-American political stance.[46]

The Big Bracero Program

At the beginning of the Second World War, the system of sojourner pluralism in the Southwest seemed about to come to an end. The American Dust Bowl migrants—Okies and others—who contributed about half of all migratory workers in western agriculture in the 1930s, were now entering the armed services or working in expanding defense industries in West Coast cities. Also, unemployment and underemployment in Mexico were relatively low in 1941 and early 1942, and the supply of migratory workers was reduced. Growers asked the federal government to help them procure Mexican workers as was done during the First World War. Mexico, unhappy with the way Americans had handled repatriation in the 1930s, was at first reluctant to supply workers.

After Mexico declared war on the Axis powers, Mexico and the U.S. worked out a new *bracero* program; an executive agreement signed in July 1942 pledged that workers would not be used to displace American workers or to lower wages and that Mexican workers would receive minimum guarantees on wages and working conditions. Nevertheless, employers found it easy to evade these commitments without much interference. In fact, the *bracero* program was evidence of the willingness of the U.S. government to subsidize Southwest and California agriculture with cheap labor. *Braceros,* essentially limited to the agricultural sector, free from the draft, and unable to join unions, cost less than an average of $500 a year each in wartime wages.[47] Many employers, especially in Texas, which did not participate in the *bracero* program, continued to hire Mexican illegal aliens, partly because sophisticated irrigation systems added 7,500,000 acres to the agricultural lands of seventeen western states between 1945 and 1955, stimulating a substantial increase in demand for Mexican workers.

Smuggling aliens became a highly profitable business. Between 1947 and 1955, more than 4,300,000 Mexican nationals were apprehended.[48] But the Border Patrol's enforcement practices varied to meet employer needs. The Immigration Service began a practice known as "drying out," which involved giving undocumented workers employed by American farmers identification slips, then deporting them, and allowing them to reenter the U.S. legally. The technique was used extensively in 1949, when 87,000 of the 280,000 aliens deported were "dried out," and in 1950, when 96,000 of 459,000 were allowed to reenter this way.

To employers, the drying-out system was not as reliable as the *bracero* program, and therefore, at the beginning of the Korean War in 1951, Public Law 78 established a third *bracero* program in which the Department of Labor became the labor contractor. The new *bracero* program did not stanch the accelerating flow of illegal aliens. Returning *braceros* became recruiting agents for growers by recounting the opportunities to earn good money in the U.S. Many illegal aliens were ex-*braceros* or relatives of *braceros.* The program, it turned out, was not just a replacement for illegal migration but a stimulus to it.[49] The Border Patrol could now vigorously apprehend aliens (875,000 were caught in 1953), while employers could continue to count on large numbers getting across.

The number of illegal aliens alarmed organized labor, which saw illegal aliens increasingly employed in industrial occupations, and also those who saw illegal crossings as a threat to U.S. sovereignty. But labor did not have enough political muscle to gain a law to penalize employers of illegal aliens. When the liberal Senator Paul Douglas (D-Illinois) offered an amendment to the 1952 Immigration and Nationality Act to provide such penalties, it was defeated overwhelmingly by a vote of sixty-nine to twelve.[50] Congress did make it illegal to harbor an undocumented alien, but specifically provided that employment was not harboring, a provision that became known as the "Texas proviso" in recognition of the benefit it brought to employers in Texas and the Southwest.

The Eisenhower administration launched "Operation Wetback" in June 1954. Special mobile forces of the Immigration and Naturalization Service began sweep operations in California and Texas. Light planes were used to find illegal aliens and to direct ground teams, and transport planes airlifted aliens to staging areas for prompt return to Mexico. Some 1,075,000 undocumented aliens were rounded up, but Operation Wetback was more symbolic than real in dealing with illegal migration. Periodic roundups did not constitute a long-term enforcement strategy. Roundups also led to violations of the civil rights of Mexican-Americans. Thousands of Mexican-American citizens as well as resident aliens were arrested and detained, and some even were deported illegally. Raids took place not just in factories and restaurants, but in apartments and homes, and some Mexicans eligible for naturalization did not apply, afraid they might be deported. Mexican-Americans were stopped on the streets or searched at highway checkpoints and asked to prove their legal right to be in the U.S. Some families were separated when fathers and husbands were deported, many of them American citizens.[51]

Because of the Texas proviso and the *bracero* program, employers themselves could tolerate the roundups and summary deportations. (Of the 3,075,000 *mojados* deported between 1950 and 1955, only 63,000 went through formal deportation proceedings.) Between 1955 and 1959, when an average 430,000 *braceros* entered annually, *braceros* were about one-quarter of all the farm workers hired in Texas, California, Arizona, and New Mexico, and in 1960 they accounted for 26 percent of the nation's seasonal agricultural labor force.[52] *Bracero* wages tended to become the norm. Farmers discouraged employment of domestic labor as in the San Joaquin Valley in 1960, where the tomato harvest employed 1,530 *braceros* for the harvest and only 860 citizens and resident aliens, including Mexican-Americans.[53]

The existence of the *braceros* enfeebled efforts in the 1950s and the early 1960s to establish a strong union. The Southern Tenant Farmers' Union, which in 1945 had become the AFL's National Farm Labor Union, conducted a 1950 strike near Tracy in San Joaquin County, where most of the canning tomatoes in California were grown, to protest a wage cut for tomato pickers. Its weakness was quickly exposed: Teamster truck drivers refused to respect the picket lines; illegal aliens, a large number of whom were employed by the tomato growers, continued on the job; and two thousand *braceros* were brought in under the protection of the California Highway Patrol and local police escort.[54]

Nowhere but in the Southwest would a major, powerful union such as the Teamsters not respect a picket line in 1950, and nowhere else would officials of the national government act as a conduit to supply workers for employers. When the NFLU struck the Imperial Valley cantaloupe harvest in April 1951, it was virtually defeated before it started. The U.S. Border Patrol, in typical cooperation with the growers, was lax in stopping the flow of illegal aliens. When the new leader of the NFLU, Ernesto Galarza, persuaded five hundred Mexican-American workers to strike the cantaloupe growers in 1952, the growers' association, having anticipated such an emergency, simply transferred extra *bracero* workers they had already brought to the valley from employers who did not need them to those who were being struck. Galarza's protest to the U.S. Justice Department that such an action violated the law that made it illegal to fill jobs vacated by a strike or a lockout was met with a promise to investigate, but soon the cantaloupe harvest was over.[55]

No agricultural workers' strike could be won in the Southwest in the 1950s and early 1960s as long as the *bracero* program was in effect. Strikers did not have unemployment insurance against lost wages, and when the strike was over, they found their jobs permanently filled by *braceros*. The established trade unions, largely indifferent to agricultural workers, had other important battles to fight. The U.S. Department of Labor gave low priority to the farm workers, a large proportion of whom were Mexican-Americans.

By the late 1950s and the early 1960s a new postwar generation of liberal politicians influenced by the civil rights movement began to listen to stories of exploitation and terrible living conditions, and they began to feel increasing pressure from a mainstream labor movement somewhat more sympathetic to the farm workers than before. When on September 17, 1963, the driver of a makeshift truck full of *braceros* drove into the path of a speeding Southern Pacific freight train in the Salinas Valley, killing thirty-two workers, Galarza was hired by the Education and Labor Committee of the U.S. House of Representatives to investigate the conditions under which *braceros* worked.[56] The report appeared in spring of 1964, shortly before a combination of labor and liberal interests in Congress allowed the *braceros* program to terminate.

Employers of the West and Southwest increased their reliance on illegal aliens once more, supplemented at the borders by a large increase in the use of commuter labor. The commuters carried work authorization cards. Some crossed the border daily to work; others moved farther inland and returned to their homes in Mexico during the off season of the industry in which they were employed. The daily commuter became a new kind of *bracero*; by 1970 approximately 70,000 were working in American border cities.[57]

Illegal alien workers may have supplied about 10 percent of the labor force in counties along the border. Many undocumented workers cooperated with employers in avoiding income and payroll taxes. Some employers failed to make contributions to Social Security or disability insurance, saving up to 20 percent of their wage costs.[58] Some workers were paid less than minimum wages, but they did not complain about that, or about overtime work or inadequate safety and health standards or the absence of fringe benefits. Particularly unscrupulous employers turned in their own illegal alien workers to avoid meeting a payroll. All around, the cost-benefit advantages to employers were considerable—undocumented Mexican nationals, according to one study, accomplished more during each hour worked on certain jobs than American workers and often worked more hours per week or per year.[59]

Without *braceros,* the employer appetite for illegal aliens grew. In 1965, the first post-*bracero* year, there were only 110,000 apprehensions of illegal aliens. After 1976, when a new law placed a 20,000 limit on immigration from all countries in the western hemisphere (except for immediate relatives of U.S. citizens), the pressure to migrate illegally was increased for Mexicans. From 1977 through 1987, the number captured rose above one million annually in all but three years.[60] Although the vast majority caught at the border were Mexicans, only about 50 to 60 percent of illegal aliens in the U.S. came from Mexico, the rest from other Latin American countries, Asia, and even Europe. The best estimate of the illegal population in the U.S. in 1978 was between 3.5 million and 6 million.[61]

Most illegal aliens (70 to 80 percent) did not work in agriculture at all. Even Mexican nationals increasingly bypassed low-wage farm jobs and went directly to the cities—Los Angeles was the principal center—to perform a variety of jobs in restaurants, the garment industry, light manufacturing, construction, and even in white-collar jobs. With many points of access along the two-thousand-mile border, it was extremely difficult through conventional enforcement methods to keep Mexican nationals out.

In some respects, the system of sojourner pluralism worked the way employers of Mexican nationals intended. Their availability kept the labor markets loose in the West and Southwest. When a labor surplus was no longer needed, as during the Depression, the foreigners lost their jobs. So many Mexican nationals were returned home or chose to go back during the 1930s that the total number of Mexican-born persons in the U.S. was only 377,000 in 1940.[62] The total number of Asian-born nationals was even smaller. But in some ways, the system did not work as

intended. The children of those Mexican and Asian immigrants who remained in the U.S. were natural-born citizens, a large proportion of
whom succeeded in obtaining work of much higher status than the menial
tasks assigned to their parents. Almost 700,000 Americans born of Mexican parentage lived in the U.S. in 1940.[63] Most of the 285,000 Japanese,
106,000 Chinese, and 100,000 Filipinos had been born here.[64] The opportunities available to Asian-Americans and Mexican-Americans were
not as ample as those available to the children and grandchildren of European immigrants, but they were not nearly as restricted as those of
native-born black Americans stigmatized by racially based caste.

Chapter Seven

"THE ROAD OF HOPE"
Asians and Mexicans Find Cracks in the System

THE dynamic economic expansion of the West and Southwest in the late nineteenth and early twentieth century opened cracks in the system of sojourner pluralism for East Asian and Mexican sojourners, a substantial portion of whom became settlers. Although the circumstances of the two groups were different in several respects—the Asians lived far from home for many years, often in a highly insulated bachelor society surrounded by a totally foreign culture—many in both groups found the boundaries of sojourner pluralism, while restrictive, permeable. As a consequence, there was more mobility for them and especially for their children than for black Americans. Most blacks could not move from town to town or open up a laundry, a restaurant, or any other small business that served whites without threatening an entire social system.

Cracks in the System: The Chinese

Probably most of the sojourners from China who stayed in the U.S. performed relatively servile or menial work all their lives, but a significant minority became independent businessmen or farmers. A major opportunity to acquire land in Hawaii, an opportunity not available in California, resulted from the tradition of racial and ethnic intermarriage in the islands. Many Chinese married local native Hawaiian women and became rice farmers, an industry they soon dominated. Many others left the plantations for Honolulu, where they became skilled workers and small entrepreneurs. Of the 692 firms listed in the Honolulu Business Directory in 1886, 219 were Chinese-owned.[1]

Conditions generally were more restrictive in California, where Chinese miners were expelled from many towns and were compelled to pay a foreign miners' tax, originally designed to keep Mexican and Chilean miners away, later assessed only on the Chinese.[2] Nonetheless, the booming, diversified economy of the West created many possibilities for entrepreneurial activity, even for the despised and extremely poor Chinese immigrants. After the building of the Central Pacific Railroad, on which some ten thousand Chinese worked, many sought employment in agriculture and construction, others became cooks and laundrymen. Soon, Chinese were engaged in all sorts of capitalistic activities. In 1880, 11.8 percent of the Chinese in San Francisco either were merchants themselves or were employed by them. Laundrymen were another 10 percent, and independent skilled craftsmen over 7 percent.[3] As early as 1890, the Chinese had twice their share of shopkeepers on the mainland relative to the general population, and by 1920 more than three and a half times their share.[4] In that year, 48 percent of all Chinese in the U.S. were in small business, 27 percent providing personal services, and 11 percent in agriculture.[5]

For six or seven decades, Chinese were active participants in California's agricultural development, as cooks, tenant farmers, or vegetable peddlers, and also as owner-operators of farms and as commission merchants, positions that gave them considerable control over their own lives.[6] Their entrepreneurial drive proved remunerative in an economy where production of raw materials was more important than manufacture of finished goods. Individuals with little capital but a great deal of energy and a willingness to take risks could achieve a measure of economic success.[7]

In acquiring capital to start a business, individual Chinese were often helped by the *huiguan,* local associations based on organizations that had existed in China for hundreds of years or, in Hawaii, by immigrants from the same district. Led by merchants, the *huis,* as they were called, performed social and charitable functions, mediated disputes, and provided protection. Some of them functioned as rotating credit associations to aid members in going into business for themselves. *Hui* members would put a certain amount of money into a common pool. Then they would compete by some method, often by lot, for the right to use the entire sum to start a small business. Members would meet again the next month, and those who had not yet had their turn would continue the process until every member of the *hui* had a chance to use the pool.[8]

Even without assistance from *huis,* Chinese laborers often were able to bid up the price of their labor because the supply of workers in the late nineteenth century was still relatively short in times of rapid economic expansion. Once having amassed a small amount of capital, an entrepreneur could quickly establish a business with a limited but sure Chinese clientele, in which his familiarity with the language enabled him to serve customers in ways difficult or impossible for whites. There are thousands of stereotypical stories of such entrepreneurship: Lee Bing began working as a dishwasher and janitor in the Walnut Grove Hotel, then took the place of a Chinese cook and received an increase in salary from $20 to $60 a month, which eventually enabled him to save enough money to buy a restaurant of his own in partnership with another Chinese man. Subsequently, he became a partner in a hardware store and a drugstore, and bought a share in the Shang Loi gambling house, where he served Chinese only.[9]

The Chinese also were able to establish niches in the agricultural economy of California in the late nineteenth and early twentieth century. The Chinese renter of land in the Sacramento Valley in the 1870s, knowing his value to the owner of the land, would insist on hiring two or three Chinese to help him at wages of at least $1 a day.[10] The whites may have dominated all sectors of the economy, but they had to call on Chinese middlemen to help them recruit and manage Chinese labor because industrial and agribusiness expansion accelerated so rapidly.[11] And the labor was paid relatively well. For example, in the 1870s and 1880s, when a farm laborer could save $8 to $15 a month, Chinese who rented land actually earned more than whites who rented land in the South and much more than blacks.[12] When other industries expanded, the price of their labor was bid up, as in the canneries of Contra Costa County, California, where they earned more than white women.[13]

Merchants in all kinds of businesses and entrepreneurs in vice industries could accumulate capital and develop a sense of self-direction impossible for all but a few African-Americans under caste pluralism.[14] After passage of the Chinese Exclusion Acts and as agriculture became more diversified, the labor of Chinese was more valuable than before, with growers depending on them for their skills as pruners of fruit trees and as fruit packers.[15] At one point in 1884, farmers agreed to bring in blacks to replace Chinese hop pickers who were striking in Kern County, but on second thought the farmers decided against what they saw as a dangerous experiment.[16]

The main opportunities both in Hawaii and on the West Coast were not in agriculture; they were in the dynamic, expanding nonagricultural economy of the fastest-growing portion of the U.S. Capitalism itself undermined the structure of sojourner pluralism as it applied to the Chinese, even when the overwhelming majority thought of themselves as strangers. When more married and established families, they, and especially their children, became ethnic-Americans with a stake in the larger society.

A growing number of Chinese developed strategies for claiming citizenship, the most important of which was to assert citizenship by birth or by "derivation." The U.S. Supreme Court had decided in 1898 that a person born in the U.S. of Chinese parents was an American citizen by birth, and therefore eligible for reentry after visiting China. Two years later, the Court ruled that the wives and children of Chinese merchants were entitled to come to the U.S.[17]

Those decisions increased the number of Chinese admitted as citizens between 1920 and 1940 to 71,040, compared to only 66,039 aliens. When records were burned in the San Francisco earthquake in 1906, many

Chinese were able to allege, even if some fraudulently, that they had been born in the U.S. Once armed with citizenship, a father could claim citizenship for his Chinese-born children too. After subsequent trips to China, the father upon his return would report the birth of a son or two (more than four hundred sons to one daughter were reported). Often extra sons were reported, opening such slots for sale to boys who had no family connections in the U.S.[18]

With the admission of women in the early twentieth century and some intermarriage (particularly in Hawaii, where it was extensive), the ratio of Chinese males to females, while still one-sided, went steadily down between 1900 and 1930, when one of every five Chinese in the U.S. was a female.[19] With a more stable family and community life, the Chinese and their children established organizations typical of those created by European immigrants and their children in the process of ethnic-Americanization.

The earliest organizations were fraternal, such as the Native Sons of the Golden State, founded in San Francisco in 1895 and renamed the Chinese-American Citizens' Alliance in 1905. It grew rapidly in membership, with branches in a half dozen cities in the East and Midwest by 1915. With its primary headquarters in San Francisco, it fought against discriminatory immigration laws and segregation in the public schools and encouraged Chinese-Americans to participate in politics. In 1924, the CACA began publishing *The Chinese Times* in San Francisco in Chinese, and eleven years later American-born Chinese founded *The Chinese Digest* in the same city, the first Chinese-American newspaper in English. By 1921, five Chinese YMCAs and three YWCAs had been established. Many Chinese-Americans celebrated Independence Day and Thanksgiving, the great holidays of the civic culture.

After the First World War, Chinese-Americans became much more active politically, successfully defeating anti-Chinese politicians and conducting an effective campaign in support of Roosevelt's candidacy in 1936. By then, the sojourner period was over. The majority of the Chinese in the U.S. had been born here. Chinese-Americans had been elected to many offices in Hawaii and even on the West Coast, and in 1954, in a typical example of ethnic-Americanization, a Chinese-American Democratic club was established as a counterpoint to the CACA, which had become markedly Republican.[20]

Cracks in the System: The Japanese

A substantial portion of the Japanese who remained in the U.S. also broke the bounds of sojourner pluralism. As with the Chinese, the Japanese in California were to some extent able to control the labor supply desired by white farmers, who preferred to lease their holdings to Japanese tenants as a way of obtaining a steady stream of labor and of turning over to the tenants the responsibility of procuring workers.[21] Small businesses emerged with the transfer of immigrant labor from white-owned enterprises to those of Japanese entrepreneurs, who entered businesses that required virtually no capital, such as the leasing of orchards. By 1909, the most common Japanese businesses in California were labor contracting, lodgings, and restaurants.

Entrepreneurial capitalism worked for a large number of Japanese sojourners—who had an advantage over the Chinese in being able to put women and children to work, too—partly because of economic growth in Hawaii and especially in California, but also because of their frugal habits. The issei operated farms that were much smaller than the average, but every inch of land was used. Community cooperation was exemplified in the *tanomoshi*, rotating credit associations, whose members often came from the same prefecture in Japan.[22] The *tanomoshi*, which literally means "to ask for help," constituted a mutual aid system, like the Chinese *hui*, in which individuals contributed money to help members save, invest, and obtain credit, a system particularly helpful since banks frequently refused loans to the Japanese. With the help of *tanomoshi*, Japanese men started small businesses in Hawaii and on the mainland,[23] including rooming houses, restaurants, and laundries, which catered mainly to Japanese, relied upon Japanese suppliers, and were serviced by Japanese workmen. Like several other immigrant groups, the Japanese used credit associations as an effective adaptation of a homeland institution.[24]

In addition to credit unions, the Japanese organized employer and professional associations. By the 1920s, thirty-six farmers' organizations combined to form the Japanese Agricultural Association and California Farmers' Cooperative in northern and central California. Other lines of work had corresponding associations, for example, a southern California Japanese Physicians' and Surgeons' Association of fewer than fifteen members, which nonetheless published a journal.[25]

Like Jewish immigrants on the East Coast in the early 1900s, Japanese entrepreneurs worked with slight profit margins, and they often failed. Also like the Jews, a surprising number surmounted prejudice and hostility by generating business activity among their own kind. In southern California, Japanese growers sold to Japanese wholesalers, who sold to Japanese retailers. The growers obtained financing from the wholesalers instead of from banks, and looked to the wholesalers for fertilizer, seed, and equipment in return for the produce they raised.[26]

Even in Hawaii, where the economy was much less diversified, the Japanese could not be kept in the lowest-status jobs on the plantation. By 1901, they had gone into fishing and rice planting and dominated the coffee farms of Kona on the big island of Hawaii. The Japanese moved into skilled and semiskilled trades on the plantations; by 1901 their participation in the mechanical trades was extensive. Although their average wage was below that of Hawaiians and Portuguese and considerably below that of Caucasians for the same work, especially on the plantations, many took their new skills to Honolulu and other towns. Between 1890 and 1910, the percentage of Japanese working as laborers went down from 92 percent to 67; it was only 58 percent in 1920. Ten years later, there were 1,835 Japanese retailers in Hawaii, operating 49 percent of the retail stores of the territory.[27] Although the Japanese still had slightly more than their share of common laborers among the gainfully employed nationally, their mobility in Hawaii appears to have been approximately like that reported for immigrants in northeastern and midwestern cities.[28]

As with the Chinese, there were thousands of anecdotes of creative entrepreneurship in the face of prejudice and the legal impediments of sojourner pluralism. One Okinawan man quit work on the plantation and invested his small savings in a ramshackle store that sold soft drinks. In 1925, his wife obtained a license to drive a taxi, becoming the first woman taxi driver on Maui. When their turn came to receive money from the *tanomoshi,* they built a house to put up guests for the night and served them breakfast and lunch. Their next step was to borrow $2,000 and open a gasoline station, and after that, in 1928, they established a mortuary.[29] That Okinawans could overcome the restrictions of sojourner pluralism revealed the extraordinary possibilities of entrepreneurial capitalism, even in the plantation-dominated, oligarchically controlled territory of Hawaii, for they had to overcome prejudice against them by Japanese from the inner islands of Japan, the Naichi, as well as the hostility of the whites. Capitalism, which had brought the Okinawans and the Naichi to Hawaii and California, where they were expected to remain in servile jobs until they were no longer wanted, paradoxically offered them a way out of those jobs.

Under the 1907 U.S.-Japan agreement, in which the government of Japan agreed to restrain emigration, the Japanese already in the U.S. were able to send for picture brides. Once they had wives and children here, they behaved much more like European settler immigrants, seeing possibilities for the future and investing their energy and capital *"kodomo no tame ni"* (for the sake of the children).[30] Like the Chinese, Japanese settlers found ways to bend and evade the rules of sojourner pluralism. Some Chinese purchased land in California, bypassing the Alien Land Law by setting up corporations for those eligible to own land who owned it in name only.[31] Japanese settlers used straw buyers among whites and turned ownership over to their children, who, having been born in the U.S., had all the rights of citizens; thus settlers got around laws in twelve states that prohibited aliens who were ineligible for citizenship from owning agricultural property.

Once most of the Japanese in the U.S. had become settlers, they began to create the typical institutions established by other ethnic-Americans, including ethnic newspapers and civic and political clubs. Their own cultural predispositions encouraged self-restraint, but, with the birth of Japanese-American children, even some issei (the immigrant generation) became involved in American-style protest movements. An issei news-paper editor, Fred Makino, founded *The Hawaii Hochi* in 1912, a journal that took enormous pride in protecting Japanese culture while, at the same time, asserting the full rights of Japanese-Americans as Americans. Makino's militancy was seen as un-American by the *haole* oligarchy in Hawaii, but it was quintessentially American and un-Japanese in its in-sistence that the American promise of equal rights be extended to the newcomers from the Far East just as it had been to the newcomers from Europe, an attitude that stimulated in the nisei generation increasing participation in integrated churches, Scout organizations, and other com-munity groups. It also led in the 1920s to formation of many organizations in Hawaii and California, with names that usually included "loyalty league" or "citizens' league." These groups combined into a national Japanese-American Citizens' League in 1930.[32] The Japanese had begun to provide yet another example of Tocqueville's maxim that patriotism grows by the exercise of civil rights.

Cracks in the System: The Mexicans

The situation of Mexican sojourners was much more complex than that of the Asians. Large numbers came in legally as well as illegally, and, unlike the Asians, those who had immigrated lawfully could choose to become citizens. All Mexicans living in the territories acquired from Mex-ico in the treaties of 1848 and 1853 following the Mexican War had been granted citizenship. In 1897, a U.S. district court ruled that the skin color of Mexicans was irrelevant to the issue of naturalization. The vast majority, however, had no interest in citizenship. Why bother to become an Amer-ican citizen when the land one loved, the land of family, language, and *la raza* (the people or race) was so close by? Partly for this reason, the economic and social mobility of Mexican sojourners and even of Mexican-Americans was slower than that of immigrants and their children from Asia. The success of second- and third-generation Mexican-Americans was, however, disguised by aggregate statistics because large migrations of Mexicans continued to enter long after Asian immigration had been reduced to a trickle. Mexican-Americans began to develop roots and loy-alties in the U.S. Many did not want to be identified with Mexican immigrants. By the 1920s and even more in the 1940s, there were signs of geographic and economic mobility for Mexican-Americans more typical of Euro-American populations than of native-born black Americans.[33]

Two out of three Mexican men were either farm laborers or other laborers in 1930; one in fifteen was a craftsman. When workers moved to nonborder states, especially to Colorado, Illinois, and Michigan, where the pay was better for farm work, there were also opportunities to obtain other kinds of jobs. By 1928, Chicago had a small middle class of Mexican-Americans and some Mexicans who had begun life in the U.S. as manual laborers and had then established more than two hundred businesses.[34] By 1948, some workers in California were earning $2.83 a day picking beans, others $5.50 a day in the steel industry in Chicago, still others, from $8 to $14 a day as bricklayers in Texas.[35]

Despite hardships and prejudice, possibilities for entrepreneurial activity existed for Mexicans who became settlers. It was difficult to break sojourner habits, but many of them did, and as with the Chinese and Japanese, there are countless stories of Mexican immigrants, illegal and legal, who succeeded against the odds.

One young man who crossed the Rio Grande at the age of fourteen was apprehended by *la migra* (the Immigration Border Patrol) and was deported. But he soon crossed the river again, and this time eluded capture, teaching himself English at night while washing dishes, picking cotton, and cleaning floors during the day. By the time the law caught up with him ten years later, he had an American wife, a home, and a good job. Given sixty days to get his Mexican papers in order, he reentered the U.S. legally, eventually became a citizen, and sent all of his five children to college.[36]

There was even the possibility of breaking out of the system of sojourner pluralism in south Texas, where it was enforced more rigorously than anywhere else. In the late 1940s and early 1950s, migrant families followed the cotton harvest from the Rio Grande Valley in Edinburg, Texas, up the road to Robstown to El Campo, Hillsboro, or perhaps Waxahachie in west Texas and then to the final destination in Petersburg or Lubbock. The work was grueling, from sunup to sundown, especially in Hillsboro. The mosquitoes were fierce in El Campo, the water extremely salty in Robstown, and babies there became ill. The firetrap shacks in which most migrants lived were infested by ants, yellow jackets, cockroaches, and rats. Yet, some of the migrant workers called the road from Edinburg to Lubbock "the road of hope," and it was in such a migrant family that Jesus Luna grew up, going to school only sporadically because the family moved with the harvests and the authorities were lax in enforcing the school attendance laws. Young Jesus told his parents that if they left to travel the road of hope once more he would remain in

Edinburg with one of his aunts and attend school there. His mother and father decided to stay. Because mother and father and all four children had worked at picking cotton over the years, Jesus's father was able to stay put in Edinburg and purchase two lots and a truck. Jesus became an excellent student, and later, to the pride of his parents, attended college and graduate school. The Luna family were no longer sojourners, and in 1973 Jesus reported, "Dad and Mom now take an interest in how the children are doing in school and who is running in local politics."[37]

The Lunas and other Mexican settlers saved and invested for the sake of the children, building communities of Mexican-Americans and Mexicans called *colonias,* the largest of which was in Los Angeles, where more than 200,000 Mexicans had settled. Between 1900 and 1940, hardly a town of any size—Delano, Hanford, Brawley, Sacramento, San Diego, Fresno—failed to acquire its Mexican *colonia* on the weathered side of the railroad tracks.[38] As more Mexican nationals became settlers, economic mobility increased for themselves and especially their children. By 1950, when two-thirds of the Mexican-origin population in the U.S. had been born there, the proportion of craftsmen had more than doubled over 1930, and the percentage of sales, clerical, and professional employees had almost doubled.[39] By 1970, less than one-quarter of all Mexican-Americans were employed in relatively unskilled occupations, and almost as many were employed as craftspersons. Fewer than one percent were professional workers in 1930; one in twenty was a professional worker by 1970.[40]

Comparisons between Mexican-American men born in the U.S. and Mexican-born men showed that, despite the restrictions, many of the children of those who settled were able to go beyond them. More than 15 percent of the Mexican-born men were employed as farm laborers, less than 8 percent of the sons, and 3 percent of the grandchildren. The second generation of Mexican-Americans born in the U.S. had a median education of 11.1 years, two years more than for first-generation U.S.-born Mexican-Americans and almost double that of Mexican nationals in the U.S. (5.8 years).[41]

Thomas Sowell observed in 1981 that wherever there was a settled Mexican-American community, the income was much higher than in areas where there were a higher proportion of newcomers and transients. Mexicans and Mexican-Americans in metropolitan Detroit, for example, earned more than double the income of Mexicans in the metropolitan area of Laredo or Brownsville, a substantial gap even when wage differentials between those cities were taken into account.[42] Overall, family income for Mexicans and Mexican-Americans was much less than the national average in the post–Second World War years; but comparisons of aggregate statistics were misleading. Family income was down for

Mexicans and Mexican-Americans for many reasons. Labor-force participation rates among Mexican-American females was much lower than for either black or white women, thereby reducing household income. The Mexican-American and Mexican populations together were much younger than the average in the U.S., also reducing reported household income.

Actually, the incomes of Mexican-Americans age twenty-five and up were very close to the incomes of other Americans at the same educational level. When the American children and grandchildren of Mexican immigrants went to school and learned English, they performed well and later showed the occupational mobility so often seen among the children of immigrants generally. Later, however, in the 1980s, some disquieting statistics emerged about increased segregation of Mexicans and other Hispanic-Americans in the U.S. public schools and about a growing dropout rate for children from Spanish-speaking homes. But the general conclusions on mobility for Mexican-Americans in the postwar era was unambiguous: legal aliens had more success than illegal aliens; settlers did better than sojourners; and the grandchildren and children of immigrants did better than their parents.

Opportunities for Blacks and Asians and Mexicans Compared

In explaining the relative success of immigrants compared to African-Americans, some scholars have stressed the internal resources of the immigrants themselves, particularly their cultural values.[43] Others, such as Stanley Lieberson, have emphasized the vast difference between the opportunities presented to blacks and immigrants.[44] An examination of the experiences of the sojourners from Mexico and Asia who became settlers in the U.S. makes it obvious that both factors were important.

The Chinese transplanted the *huis* from China to the U.S., where they often provided an excellent means of capital formation to encourage entrepreneurship. The Japanese had the *tanomoshis,* and dozens of Mexican-American *mutualistas* (mutual aid societies) were formed in the U.S. in the early 1900s to provide assistance to families in need, mediate disputes, and organize social activities, although, unlike the *huis* and *tanomoshis,* they were not used to provide capital to form new enterprises.[45] The cultural emphasis by the Japanese and the Chinese on savings, frugality, and self-restraint undoubtedly preserved capital in a way that spurred economic mobility for the second and third generations. The pride of all three groups in their own versions of *la raza*—a strong sense of peoplehood based on a distinctive history and culture—undoubtedly encouraged self-confidence in facing prejudice and discrimination in the U.S. The fact that these immigrants had made the decision to emigrate and then the extremely important decision to stay and raise their children in a new country also reflected a sense of direction and control over their lives. Internal resources were important to the immigrants, but there also was a vast difference between the opportunities presented to them and those available to native-born American Indians and blacks. No matter how badly they were disparaged or how strong was the intention to confine them to servile jobs, there were large cracks in the system of sojourner pluralism that did not exist under the rules of caste. Segregation was imposed far more rigidly on blacks; the immigrants received help from foreign governments in dealing with the hostility of employers; many white teachers and social workers encouraged the children of immigrants. Immigrants' belief that through their actions they could improve life chances for their children and their children's children gave them a tremendous psychological advantage over African-Americans, who had inherited at least a half dozen generations of subjugation under caste and whose own actions for self-improvement were blocked at almost every turn.

By the early 1900s, when Jim Crow laws were being enforced vigorously against African-Americans in the South, attempts to segregate Mexicans and Asians in the West and Southwest had ambiguous results. The African-American press reported that all Mexicans and Asians were permitted to ride in whites-only streetcars and trains and attend first-class theaters in the white sections, at the same time that even well-educated, prominent blacks could not.[46] All schools in the South attended by blacks were segregated right up to the mid and late 1950s. Until the civil rights movement, parents had no hope of change. But by 1905, the policy of the board of education in San Francisco to segregate Chinese high school students had already broken down when Chinese parents threatened to boycott the elementary school and cause a significant loss of state financial aid. In the following year, President Theodore Roosevelt, under pressure from the imperial government of Japan, condemned San Francisco's policy of keeping Japanese students from the public schools. Within a few years, they were attending those schools, and by 1920 the vast majority went to schools with whites.[47]

Segregation of Mexican-American children in the public schools of California and the Southwest was fairly well established by the mid-1920s, but it was done through the assignment of school districts rather than by state law, and it was not uniformly applied, as it was for blacks in the South. In California, some districts chose not to separate children of Mexican descent, and even in segregated districts some Mexican children were allowed to attend white schools.[48] In Texas, where discrimination against Mexicans was the most severe of anyplace in the country, the vast majority of Mexican and Mexican-American children went to segregated schools, but not as a matter of law as was true for blacks.[49] In Houston and other cities, Mexicans and Mexican-Americans sometimes created their own parochial schools, such as Our Lady of Guadalupe School in Houston, which, unlike the segregated black public schools everywhere, established high expectations for the students and made rigorous demands on them.[50]

The realities of informal or unofficial segregation were cruel: Mexican-American children were turned away from white swimming pools; Mexican-Americans were sometimes denied service at good Anglo restaurants; and Mexican-Americans were discouraged from moving into better neighborhoods. But when these established patterns of discrimination against Mexicans in Texas conflicted with American war goals in 1944, the Texas legislature passed the Caucasian Race Resolution, naming Mexicans and Mexican-Americans officially as Caucasians and indicating that all Caucasians, including Mexicans, should have equal rights in public places of business and amusement.[51] Twenty-five years later, scholars would show that except for Puerto Ricans, the levels of Hispanic-Anglo segregation generally were much lower than for blacks and whites, and were reduced over time. Whereas a rise in socioeconomic status was associated with a weakening of residential segregation nationally for Mexican-Americans, it was not for blacks.[52]

The children of Asian immigrants were even less segregated in schools and neighborhoods than those of Mexicans. In Hawaii, extensive intermarriage between *haoles* and Hawaiians made virtually impossible any establishment of racially segregated public schools. With the introduction of a normal school to train teachers in Hawaii in the early twentieth century, many Chinese and Japanese parents urged their children to attend and become teachers. By the mid-1920s, Asian-American youngsters were attending schools in largely integrated settings, and almost 15 percent of schoolteachers in Hawaii were of Chinese origin, more than double the proportion of the Chinese population in the islands. They taught in non-segregated schools, in contrast, for example, to Chicago, where by 1934 only 2.5 percent of the public school teachers were African-American, although teaching in a city already 7 percent black.[53] Efforts by whites to segregate the Japanese in California and other mainland states were remarkably unsuccessful, not only in schools but also by neighborhoods. As early as 1915, a national study reported that only one-third of the nisei respondents lived in predominantly Japanese-American neighborhoods. The proportion of nisei living in mixed neighborhoods or mainly non-Japanese neighborhoods subsequently increased in every subsequent decade without exception.[54]

Japanese, Chinese, and Filipinos even escaped the antimiscegenation statutes of several mainland states, probably because they were difficult to enforce, but also because they were not made to apply to them by the courts in every state. In Louisiana, for example, the state supreme court in 1938 decided that African ancestry was the only definition of color.[55] In a subsequent decision, the court made it plain that to be a Filipino was not to be colored, but white. It made no difference that some Filipinos had much darker skin color than some African-Americans. That was, of course, the whole point of caste, to confine people by blood lines (not by color alone) in a subjugated status.[56]

The foreign national status of the sojourners also gave them a measure of protection native-born black Americans did not have. On several occasions Asian governments and Mexico intervened in order to help their nationals in the U.S. Even the earliest Chinese sojourners received some protection under the Burlingame Treaty between China and the U.S. (1868), which promised that Chinese subjects visiting or residing in the U.S. should "enjoy the same privileges, immunities and exemptions in respect to travel or residence, as may be enjoyed by the citizens or subjects of the most favored nation." The treaty did not prevent atrocities against the Chinese, such as the killing of twenty-one in Los Angeles in 1871 and the massacre of twenty-eight in Rock Springs, Wyoming, in 1885. But it occasionally helped, as when the Chinese minister to the U.S. protested the lawless treatment of Chinese nationals in Seattle and the federal government responded by threatening to send federal troops to protect them,[57] and when in 1905 communities in China organized to boycott American goods to force improvement in the treatment of Chinese in the U.S.[58]

Treaty rights were relied upon by a federal circuit court to strike down some of the most blatant anti-Chinese provisions in California's constitution and in laws that had been passed in 1880. One such law authorized local authorities to prevent Chinese from obtaining licenses for business and occupational purposes; another barred them from commercial fishing. "To exclude the Chinamen from fishing in the waters of the state . . ." said the federal court, "while the Germans, Italians, Englishmen, and Irishmen, who otherwise stand upon the same footing, are permitted to fish . . . is to prevent him from enjoying the same privileges as are 'enjoyed by the citizens or subjects of the most favored nation.'"[59] In 1900, the U.S. Supreme Court ruled that Chinese merchants had treaty rights to bring wives and minor children into the country.

An agreement in 1885 for the importation of Japanese agricultural workers provided for the right of inspection by the Japanese government, and at least one inspector warned against the coercive methods of plantation managers.[60] In 1906, the year when President Roosevelt intervened under pressure by the Japanese government to stop the segregation of Japanese and Japanese-American students in the San Francisco schools, he also dismissed an entire battalion of native-born black troops without honor and disqualified its members for service in either the military or the civil government merely because of some allegations made against certain of its members.

Mexican nationals could not depend upon a strong government to intervene on their behalf, but Mexico City did try to protect its emigrants in the years following the 1910 Mexican Revolution. Mexican consular officials often played an important role in the social, cultural, and, to some extent, political lives of the Mexican population in California. In 1918, a Mexican consul, after investigating the Spreckles Sugar Company and finding that the men in the camps worked open-ended hours for irregular pay, poor food, and unfit housing, pushed Spreckles, which badly needed the Mexican workers, to negotiate a new contract calling for increased pay.[61] Other consuls took comparable action. When a road-building firm in Hayden, Arizona, went bankrupt in the course of a construction project, the Mexican consul in Tucson gained some of the wages owed to Mexican men by obtaining a lien on the employer's property.[62] In other cases, Mexican officials helped migrant workers and families receive unemployment compensation, severance pay, and death benefits.

The proximity of workers to their home country meant they could maintain an open and lively interest in homeland politics. Mexicans in the U.S. in 1928 flocked to hear Mexican presidential candidate José Vasconcelos speak out against the racism of American labor unions and the anti-Mexican activities of the Ku Klux Klan. Periodically, Mexican officials criticized the federal government's deportation methods and intervened on behalf of Mexican citizens in the U.S. in cases involving racial school segregation; they even helped Mexican farm workers build labor unions in southern California.[63]

Support also came for foreign nationals and their children from a great many social workers and teachers who looked upon the immigrants and especially their children as material to be molded into American citizens. Children of immigrants were preached to about the possibility of success, sometimes even when their parents followed the migrant path or lived in a slum *barrio* because progressive teachers were always anxious to participate in the Americanization of the children of immigrants. The best that the white teachers or social workers in the South who tried to help blacks could do was to encourage them to adapt to the system of racial caste. Blacks in the South who had wonderful, dedicated African-American teachers could expect success only within the segregated system of caste. Children might become teachers themselves someday, or ministers, or even in a few exceptional cases lawyers or doctors, but all the people for whom and with whom they would work would be black. Even in the North, white teachers often thought it unrealistic to try to encourage their black students. An often-repeated anecdote about Malcolm X probably was typical. When he told his high school English teacher in Lansing, Michigan, that he would like to be a lawyer, the instructor urged him to be realistic. He quoted him as saying, "A lawyer—that's no realistic goal for a nigger. You need to think about something you *can* be."[64] American history had a different meaning for African-American children than for the children of immigrants. Blacks who heard teachers talk about the American ideal of equality and the American dream of success knew better than to believe them. One black woman, writing about an elementary school history lesson in North Philadelphia around 1930, remembered, "school was dreadful. . . . We heard that George Washington never told a lie, that the Indians were savages, that . . . slaves were happy, because they were brought here to be civilized."[65] How, she asked, could she believe books and teachers that told blatant lies?

The progressive *haole* teachers at McKinley High School in Honolulu, often called "Tokyo High" in the 1920s and 1930s, constantly pressed the American dream of success on their Japanese, Chinese, Filipino, and Korean students. For many of them the dream seemed real. In a survey of seventh- and eighth-grade pupils at seventeen plantation schools in 1929, 8 percent of the youngsters said they wanted to be engineers, 11 percent doctors, lawyers, or teachers, 8 percent farmers, 12 percent businessmen, and only 1.7 percent laborers. At Kauai High School, more than 60 percent Japanese-American and less than 5 percent *haole*, half of the male students said they wanted to become professionals and another 20 percent businessmen. One boy, hoping to become a teacher, wrote, "When my father came from Japan, he was handicapped in his work. I intend to go to school to get an education and lead a better life and live up to the ideals of an American."[66]

Mexican-American Richard Rodriguez remembered that his nun teacher read from the biographies of early American presidents and that the red and white poster over the nun's desk said, "Open the doors of your mind with books."[67] Rodriguez's father had come as a sojourner (he really wanted to move on to Australia) and found unskilled work in San Francisco in a cannery and later in a warehouse. The supervisor hated Mexicans, and Chinese, too, and there was no union. Like the father of Jesus Luna, Rodriguez's father put his son in a school where teachers stimulated his imagination and ambition, leading him eventually to a Ph.D. and success as a writer.

There were even exceptional teachers who tried to show respect for the cultural backgrounds of their young ethnic pupils, something that almost never happened for black children. Ernesto Galarza, who came to the U.S. during the Mexican Revolution in 1910, wrote that children in his school were marched from the playground to the principal's office "for calling someone a Wop, a Chink, a Dago or a Greaser." At Lincoln elementary school in San Francisco, "making us into Americans did not mean scrubbing away what made us originally foreign." The teachers actually tried to pronounce the children's names correctly in Spanish or Japanese, and at that school no one was scolded or punished for speaking in his native tongue on the playground.[68]

In many schools in Hawaii and on the mainland, however, children were made to feel ashamed of their backgrounds. At the other extreme from Galarza's experience were schools and teachers that showed no respect for Mexican language and culture and who treated Mexican-American children as inherently inferior.[69] In Starr and Duval counties in Texas on the Mexican border, Mexican-American children went to schools that probably were as segregated and otherwise impoverished as most of those in the South; and those children had the added handicap of coming from homes in which English was not commonly spoken. But many who stayed put long enough in any one school probably met at least one teacher along the way who told them that by trying hard they might become successful in a world beyond the confines of their *barrios* or *colonias*.

The children of immigrant sojourners also often were encouraged by social workers in the church or settlement houses. Priests and secular social workers warmed to the task of shaping the newcomers into Americans.[70] Nothing comparable existed for African-Americans to the network of settlement houses and other organizations that participated in the Americanization movement in the first few decades of the twentieth century, and despite the relentless cry of "yellow peril" heard from whites during the three decades that preceded the Second World War, Japanese and Chinese in cities and towns sometimes were seen as fit material for Americanization. The International Institute in San Francisco organized a Japanese girls' club and taught Japanese women about American politics. As early as 1927, its Japanese Center published a bulletin with columns in both English and Japanese to help immigrants and their children adapt to and succeed in American life; similar efforts were made to work with the Chinese, Mexican, and Filipino communities.[71] The Japanese in San Francisco may have had available the citizenship pamphlet published by the Daughters of the American Revolution in 1920, which included a Japanese version, presumably for the nisei (already citizens by virtue of having been born in the U.S.), who were urged to vote, run for office, and serve as jurors.[72]

One of the most striking differences between the situation of sojourners and their children throughout the first half of the twentieth century and that of blacks in the South was the opportunity for sojourners to organize to demand better working conditions. In a striking phrase, the Bureau of Labor Statistics in 1900 reported that Chinese workers were becoming "Americanized to the extent of enforcing such demands in some cases through the medium of labor organization."[73] The immigrants struck against bad conditions and low pay, something unthinkable for the black sharecroppers and tenant farmers of the South. As soon as Japanese workers learned about the annexation of Hawaii and were made aware that they were covered by American laws, they organized strikes that compelled a general wage increase of about 10 percent.[74]

The relative powerlessness of black workers in the South was signified by a series of events in the first few years of the century. In 1903, when Jim Crow policies governed the AFL-CIO, Mexican workers joined Japanese laborers in a strike in Ventura, California. In 1905, the year after an outbreak of an epidemic of race riots, W. E. B. Du Bois met with a group of African-Americans in Niagara Falls, Canada, to draw up a platform to demand freedom of speech, recognition of the basic principles of human brotherhood, and respect for the black working man. In the same year, a group of Japanese actors in Hawaii wrote and produced three plays protesting the condition of workers there, one of which stressed the opulence of the plantation manager. Although the sheriff of Oahu arrested five of the seven actors in the company, audiences in Honolulu saw the dramas.[75] It was a kind of demonstration of ethnic resistance and solidarity on the spot that was impossible for blacks in the South if they wanted to work (or even live).

In 1906, when rioting whites in Atlanta looted and burned the houses of blacks, closed factories, and killed four of them while injuring many more, Mexican workers played a major role in the Anaconda strike in the copper mines of Sonora, California. Although the strike was beaten back (federal troops were used), many Mexicans, continuing to insist on their rights, helped to create the California State Federation of Labor in 1910. After their defeat in the Imperial Valley cantaloupe strike of 1928, Mexican workers continued to participate in other strikes organized in the mid-1930s.[76] Filipinos in Hawaii fought back following the death of sixteen strikers in 1916 at Hanapepe, Kauai. In 1924, they struck on twenty-three of forty-five plantations, and in March 1932 more than one thousand Filipinos attended a rally in Honolulu protesting unemployment, the high cost of living, and the lack of opportunity in the islands. Nothing like that massive protest would have been tolerated under the rules of racial caste in the Deep South.[77]

Mexican-American civil rights organizations established their various headquarters in Texas in the heart of their civil rights struggle. La Socie-

dad Alianza Hispano-American (The Hispanic-American Alliance), organized in 1894, spread throughout the Southwest and into midwestern
and other western states, eventually reaching a membership of 20,000.
In 1910, when Jim Crow laws were thoroughly entrenched in the South
and blacks were effectively shut out from any voting power, the Alianza
met in El Paso, where two hundred delegates were welcomed by the
mayor before discussing their agenda of political action.[78] Other statewide
organizations in Texas pushed for civil rights and representation for Mexican-Americans. The League of United Latin-American Citizens (LU-
LAC), formed in 1929 in Texas, quickly achieved a national membership.
It emphasized its opposition to discrimination and segregation, and
stressed the importance of entering into mainstream American society.
More than any other Mexican organization, it was typical of the immi-
grant-settler voluntary organizations of the 1920s, which emphasized hyphenated Americanism, combining a love and admiration for ancestral
cultures with commitment to American citizenship.[79]

Although the National Association for the Advancement of Colored
People had chapters in the South, W. E. B. Du Bois and the NAACP's
magazine *The Crisis* had to campaign from an office in the North, whereas
Fred Makino, the editor of the *Hawaii Hochi,* led the successful fight to
protect Japanese-language schools in Honolulu. While Chinese-, Japa-
nese-, and Mexican-American civil rights and lobbying organizations had
national headquarters in the very cities where large numbers of their
constituents lived, the NAACP, the Urban League, and other black protest organizations had to issue their programs mainly from New York
City.

Ethnic Stratification: When Sojourners and Blacks Met

Wherever Mexicans and Asians or their children intermingled with
blacks, they usually learned that they were permitted to do things forbidden to blacks. When Chinese were imported to the Deep South under
contract after the Civil War, they stopped work, openly rebelled, or left
the plantation in search of better opportunities when they decided their
contracts were being violated. Settling in nearby towns and cities in non-
Chinese areas, they left the cotton fields of northwest Mississippi and the
region around Augusta, Georgia, to become merchants (mainly small
grocers) in small towns along the Mississippi River from Memphis to
Vicksburg and rapidly improved their economic position because they
were not subject to the same rules of caste pluralism as were blacks.[80]

In east Texas in 1907 and 1908, an investigation for the Immigration
Commission found Japanese farmers who employed, as he put it, "Americans and Negroes."[81] That the Immigration Commission investigator

thought of "white" as synonymous with "American" is not surprising, but that the Japanese employed whites at all—unthinkable for black farmers—revealed the gulf between the status of black Americans and Japanese. In the early 1890s, Mexicans started coming into the Beeville area of Texas to compete for jobs with unskilled blacks. When white employers showed a definite preference for Mexicans, blacks raided the Mexican camp to frighten them away, but "whites sympathized instinctively with the Mexicans," according to the local newspaper.[82]

When sociologist Gerald Suttles studied blacks, Italians, Puerto Ricans, and Mexicans in the Addams area of Chicago in the early 1960s, he found that blacks faced "every sort of misgiving, suspicion, and fear."[83] More than any other group, African-Americans were segregated and dependent on welfare. Blacks even were excluded from organized crime because the Italians held a monopoly on it.[84] Mexican-origin Chicagoans were not much better off in the social order of the slum, but they had more extensive interaction with nonblacks, especially Italians. Mexicans, according to Suttles, were a "people in the middle."[85] There were many fewer Mexicans and Mexican-Americans in Chicago in the 1920s through 1940 than in the 1960s, but the social order of the slum then probably was not much different from the area Suttles studied. Regardless of the status of the migrants and their children, and no matter how difficult their circumstances, they were positioned above blacks.

Mexican and Chinese immigrants knew that blacks were at the bottom, and the bottom was determined by the kinds of jobs one was assigned. One Chinese immigrant said that in France in the Second World War Chinese laborers who had been imported to work on the railroad were assigned to the worst jobs. After work, he said, they were pushed into a stockade where they had no freedom but were simply locked up "sort of like a bunch of cattle or a bunch of horses and probably when their contracts are finished, they'll load them onto freight boats and ship them back." They were, he said, "like the colored people, they were nothing but scavengers, they were doing scavenger work."[86]

Mexicans and Asians brought their own prejudices against dark color with them. Richard Rodriguez tells of the hostility in his family toward skin that was too pale or too dark. An aunt often called her dark child "me feito" (my little ugly one). Children born dark had their faces treated with a mixture of egg white and lemon juice concentrate. Black people, Rodriguez noted, seemed to get the worst jobs, as in Sacramento, where all of the garbage men were Negroes. His mother, feeling sorry for black Americans, would remark, "How the Gringos mistreat them." She knew that it was particularly bad to be black in America because her brother had been dark. The gringos kept him digging all day in a construction job, doing the dirtiest work, and paid him next to nothing. "But what could he do? Report them? We weren't citizens then. He didn't even know English." "And he was dark."[87]

Filipinos also were given the dirtiest jobs. Of all the sojourner groups, the Filipinos before the Second World War had the fewest opportunities. In Hawaii in 1930, where most lived, only 5 percent had nonplantation jobs.[88] But plantation paternalism in Hawaii made their life more secure and stable than on the West Coast, where single Filipino men held menial jobs and often were subject to ruthless exploitation. Filipinos also knew that blacks were at the bottom of the system of stratified pluralism that served the whites of the West and Southwest. In any contest between Filipinos and African-Americans, employers tended to favor the Asians, as when the Pullman Company hired relatively well educated Filipinos in the 1920s, partly in an effort to destroy A. Philip Randolph's attempts to organize black railroad workers.[89]

Carlos Bulosan, a young Filipino migrant worker, who suffered all of the common indignities Filipinos experienced on the West Coast, including police brutality, mentions blacks four times in his 1943 autobiography. Once, he listened to a young black man play a harmonica in a boxcar as they moved in search of a job. The other three times were examples of exploitation of blacks. Once, he sold a black man bedsheets he had stolen from a rooming house; on another occasion, his brother gave him ten cents to offer a Negro bootblack whom he had not paid earlier for shining his shoes; in the last instance, he and a Filipino friend let a black man on the bus take the blame for their not having paid the bus fare.[90]

The stories hardly constitute proof of the subordinate position of African-Americans in the ethnic pecking order of the West Coast, and there probably are numerous anecdotes of blacks cheating Filipinos in California in the 1930s, too. The point is not that blacks were always in a position clearly subordinate to Filipinos but that, despite several generations of freedom, the stigma of caste pluralism followed them to such an extent that they probably were even more vulnerable than the latest and poorest sojourner workers, many of whom spoke English badly, and most of whom had been in the U.S. for only a short time.

In his wanderings, Bulosan was befriended by a half dozen white women of various ages—something that was highly unlikely for a black in his position—and he began to see possibilities for changing his life. When he started a small school for Filipino and Mexican migrants in California, Bulosan taught about "the growth of democracy in the United States," a land of immigrants who had built the nation. When he spoke of the American dream he wrote of his migrant-worker students that "their eyes glowed with a new faith . . . they nodded with deep reverence."[91] The American dream had been a nightmare for most Filipino workers, but they heard the stories of how other immigrants and their children made the dream a reality. Bulosan identified with the experience of the Euro-Americans who had come to this country as immigrants, sometimes as settlers, other times as sojourners, sometimes illegally and more often legally, but often with choices available that would not have been possible in their home countries and that were denied to most American-born blacks, who had nowhere else to go.

Understandably, the pages of African-American newspapers were harsh in their attacks on Mexicans and Asians between 1900 and 1935. Booker T. Washington thought the Chinese particularly objectionable; unlike blacks, he said, they could never be assimilated to occidental civilization.[92] African-American leaders were extremely negative toward Mexican immigrant workers, too, because they saw Mexican laborers taking jobs on farms and railroads and as busboys, cooks, and garbage men which were previously held by blacks.[93] In 1928, the African-American journalist George Schuyler wondered, "If the million Mexicans who have entered the country have not displaced Negro workers, whom have they displaced?"[94] The question was not entirely fair. There was not a fixed number of jobs in an expanding American economy. But it was valid, at least in part, because where the immigrants did compete with blacks for jobs, employers tended to favor them. The rules of caste were much stronger than those intended to keep sojourners in their place, but it would take a revolution by blacks against caste to enable the children and grandchildren of sojourners from Mexico and Asia to assert their full rights as Americans effectively.

Part Three

THE OUTSIDERS MOVE IN
The Triumph of the Civic Culture

O, let America be America again—
The land that never has been yet—
And yet must be—
The land where every man is free.
The land that's mine—
The poor man's, Indian's, Negro's, ME—
Who made America . . .
                    —LANGSTON HUGHES

Not all blacks or Mexican and Asian sojourners or Indians were kept entirely outside of the civic culture and its system of voluntary pluralism in the decades preceding the Second World War. But coercive official systems of pluralism—caste, tribal, and sojourner—continued to limit the opportunities of most persons of color in the U.S. up to the Second World War and beyond.

The war led to the revivification of the American founding myth, its ideals and institutions, and to a much sharper focus on the failure of Americans to live up to those ideals. It induced a spirit of national co-operation and unity, partly because the labor and military service of persons of color had become more valuable than it had ever been before. It made possible the black revolution to dismantle the official system of caste pluralism altogether. That revolution had a profound impact on the human rights consciousness of most Americans and stimulated movements for ethnic pride and power among Indians, Asian-Americans, Mexican-Americans, and other ethnic groups. Following the dismantling of the formal structure of caste, American Indians obliged the U.S. to redefine tribal pluralism on a basis of much greater respect for the integrity of Indian tribal identities. Congress also took several measures to combat the systems of sojourner pluralism that had limited freedom and opportunity for Asian-Americans and Mexican-Americans.

As a result, the system of voluntary pluralism began to work more effectively for persons of color. The political participation of blacks, Asian- and Mexican-Americans, and Indians increased substantially. Those formerly kept from participation in the civic culture often became its most articulate and passionate proponents. They showed, as white immigrant-ethnic groups had done before them, that the exercise of civil rights

149

promotes an attachment to those symbols, values, and institutions that most clearly embody the founding myth. Because of their struggle, the ideal of equal opportunity based on equal rights for all became more securely built into the laws, court decisions, and regulations of the nation than ever before. Inequalities related to ethnicity and especially to color remained severe as the 1980s closed, but they were no longer assured through coercive systems of pluralism.

Chapter Eight

"DO YOU UNDERSTAND YOUR OWN LANGUAGE?"

Black Americans' Attack on Caste

BLACKS rebelled against slavery and caste almost from the beginning of their history in North America, but more than two hundred slave rebellions were swiftly and ruthlessly punished.[1] Free blacks, free but excluded from the civic culture, protested but usually in vain. "We are *natives* of this country; we only ask that we be treated as well as *foreigners*,"[2] pleaded one such free black, Peter Williams, pastor of St. Phillip's Episcopal Church in New York in 1819. North Carolina–born David Walker, living as a free man in Boston in 1828, wanted to know how the U.S. could call itself a republic of liberty when he could not even find a man of color "who holds the low office of a Constable, or one who sits in a Juror Box."[3]

In addition to the stringent rules of racial caste, the situation of blacks was utterly different from that of immigrants in that they could not even return to an identifiable homeland from which their ancestors came. Only America was their home now. "This land," wrote Walker, "which we have watered with our *tears* and our *blood* is now our mother country." Walker pleaded of white Americans, "Do you understand your own language? Here your language proclaimed to the world, July Fourth, 1776, 'We hold these truths to be self-evident, that ALL *men are created* EQUAL!!' "[4]

In their struggle to dismantle the structure of caste pluralism, black protest leaders appealed to the redemptive message of America's civil religion, the nation's God-given destiny to liberate mankind. By enslaving blacks it had steeped itself in sin. To continue slavery would quickly bring down the wrath of God, as George Mason and Thomas Jefferson, Virginian slave owners and champions of human rights, had acknowledged. If Americans failed to abolish slavery, Frederick Douglass warned his white audiences, "your fathers will have fought and bled in vain . . . and American Republicanism will become a hissing and a byword to a mocking earth!"[5] W. E. B. Du Bois urged America in the twentieth century to "awake!" "Put on thy strength, America—put on thy beautiful robes . . . let *us* [italics mine] be true to our mission."[6] But the walls of caste were not shattered until the 1960s and 1970s, after the embittered Du Bois had given up on the American dream and become a Communist and moved to Ghana.

Writing in 1942, before the race riots in Detroit and Harlem of 1943, Gunnar Myrdal was confident that the spread of education combined with the growing acceptance of the impartial administration of justice and the repudiation of racial theories of caste would lead to improved conditions for blacks.[7] All three factors not only led to better conditions for blacks but also contributed to the ultimate success of the civil rights revolution; so did four other developments that were less predictable at the time Myrdal wrote *An American Dilemma*: the emergence of television nightly news programs, by which Americans were forced to face the ugliest aspects of white racism; the role of churches, primarily the black churches, as a moral influence in politics, around the issue of race, and the appearance of one particular churchman and charismatic leader, the Reverend Martin Luther King, Jr.; the ideological competition between the U.S. and the Soviet Union, which forced Americans, and particularly American leaders, to look at domestic politics as a part of an international struggle; and the ability of the executive branch of the federal government to quickly mobilize the military within hours to enforce the orders of federal courts to abolish legal segregation.

Dismantling Caste in the Courts

Myrdal was right in predicting that the courts would take a more active role in opposing caste. "The Negroes," he said, "are awarded the law as a weapon in the caste struggle."[8] When Justice John Harlan wrote in his famous dissent in *Plessy* v. *Ferguson* in 1896 that "the law regards man as man, and takes no account of his surroundings or of his color when his civil rights as guaranteed by the supreme law of the land are involved,"[9] he was pronouncing a goal and not describing reality. Few people were listening to him at the time, and only marginal progress was made by the courts in attacking the structure of caste in the decades that followed. The Court's insistence in *Plessy* that segregation did not destroy the legal equality of the two races was basic law in the country until 1954. Throughout the South, the law backed the segregation of blacks from whites in churches, schools, hospitals, prisons, insane asylums, parks, theaters, hotels, restaurants, barber shops, drinking fountains, rest rooms, and even in courtrooms.[10] Not until the 1970s did the last holdout states repeal their antimiscegenation laws, although such laws had not been enforceable since 1967 when the Supreme Court nullified them.[11]

Only in higher education and primary elections had the courts whittled at the margins of caste by the time Myrdal's book was published in 1944.

In 1938, the Court made its first attack on caste in education, ruling that the University of Missouri could not refuse admission to its law school of a qualified applicant because he was black (*Missouri ex. rel. Gaines* v. *Canada,* 305 U.S. 337). And in 1941, just a year before Myrdal's assessment of the promise of American law, the Court challenged the Democratic party's exclusion of blacks in the South from voting in primary elections (*United States* v. *Classic,* 313 U.S. 299). In 1935, the Supreme Court had ruled in *Grovey* v. *Townsend* (295 U.S. 45) that exclusion of blacks from membership in the Texas Democratic party did not violate the Fourteenth Amendment because it was private and not state action. In the *Classic* case, the Court observed that in the South the Democratic primary was the only election in which there was any contest, a fact that gave Congress the power to regulate primaries to nominate candidates for federal offices.

Encouraged by the decisions in the *Classic* and *Missouri* cases, the NAACP began to press other cases in an effort to achieve equal rights for African-Americans in political access, education, and interstate transportation. *Grovey* v. *Townsend* was overthrown in 1944 when the Court ruled that action by the Democratic party of Texas to exclude a Negro voter from voting in the primary violated both the Fourteenth and Fifteenth Amendments because the primary had become a part of the machinery for choosing public officials (*Smith* v. *Allwright,* 321 U.S. 649).

The decision in *Smith* v. *Allwright* did not result in immediate admission of Negroes to the Democratic party throughout the South. In the face of repeated court decisions, southern states reverted to a variety of dodges to keep African-Americans from voting in the Democratic primaries. But the NAACP persevered, and as barriers fell one by one, Negro voting in southern primary and general elections increased slightly in the 1950s. When the South tried to block that development, federal action was increased; mild Voting Rights Acts were passed in 1957 and 1960, but not until 1965 was a comprehensive and effective statute passed.

Building on the 1938 Missouri decision, which obliged the state university law school to accept a black student, the Supreme Court ruled in 1950 that a separate black law school did not provide equal educational opportunity (*Sweatt* v. *Painter,* 339 U.S. 629, 1950). When the University of Oklahoma admitted a black graduate student pursuant to a lower federal court order but segregated him from white students, the Court ruled, also in 1950, that such segregation was unconstitutional. Even if the student had the same books and professors, he was being denied equal protection of the law (*McLaurin* v. *Oklahoma,* 339 U.S. 637).

The NAACP now challenged segregation in the public elementary and high schools in Kansas, South Carolina, Virginia, and Delaware. Considering these cases together in May 1954 in *Brown* v. *Board of Education of Topeka* (347 U.S. 43), the Court delivered a huge blow to the system of caste by ruling that segregation in public education was inherently unequal and in violation of the Fourteenth Amendment.

But it would take much more than court decisions to break the racism that sustained the structure of caste. In 1944, ten years before the *Brown* decision and the year of publication of *An American Dilemma,* the National Opinion Research Center at the University of Denver, in an intensive poll on racial attitudes, found that a majority of whites thought that white people should have the first chance at any kind of job over Negroes (52 percent, with 6 percent undecided); only a minority thought that "some restaurants in this town should serve both Negro and white people" (46 percent); and 64 percent of whites in the North and West and 85 percent in the South "would object to Negroes as neighbors."[12]

When asked, "If Negroes could get more kinds of jobs than they can now, do you think they would want to go more places white people go?" 65 percent answered yes; of these, only one-third thought that would be "all right."[13] Fifteen years later, a white man, John Howard Griffin, shaved his head, darkened his skin, and set out to discover what it was like to be a black man in the South; it was five years after the *Brown* decision and four years after the Montgomery boycott. He learned firsthand of the depth of Christian commitment among African-Americans when one poor black man who let him stay overnight said of the whites, "when we stop loving them, that's when they win."[14] But mostly he learned how deep and pervasive white racism still was, as when, in Poplarville, Mississippi, a grand jury refused to consider evidence the FBI supplied against persons accused of lynching a young black man.[15]

The Decline of Racial Ideology in the Second World War

The Court could make its decisions, but white men and women in courthouses, statehouses, and in the White House would have to enforce them. Blacks might start a revolution, but without white allies it would fail. And as long as whites generally believed in the racial inferiority of blacks, the rationalization for caste was easily at hand. Probably more than any single factor, the rise of Adolf Hitler and his maniacal racism provided impetus for Americans to examine their own attitudes on race. That reexamination began among intellectuals during the war but probably had its greatest impact in the postwar years when news of the Nazi Holocaust against the Jews and others became widespread. Hitler, in effect, forced Americans not only to practice more democracy in race relations in order to mobilize every American to fight the war, but provoked a new literature on race relations to undermine older social science theories about the claimed superiority of Nordic peoples.

In the midst of the war, anthropologist Ruth Benedict published her widely acclaimed *Race, Science and Politics,* and joined several other social scientists in forming the Public Affairs Committee, which turned out a series of popular pamphlets arguing the scientific basis for racial equality.[16] In 1942, the committee published a booklet on *The Negro and the War Effort,* which was distributed in universities and schools; it detailed the contributions that blacks were making in the war.[17] The basic ideas in Benedict's book were reprinted in 1943 in another Public Affairs Committee pamphlet, *The Races of Mankind,* for which the demand was so great that five printings were needed in fewer than six months.[18] The Benedict study pointed out the necessity for all Americans to pull together to win a final victory against Hitler. Since, as the pamphlet maintained, racism was totally unscientific, "the United States should clean its own house" and "stand unashamed before the Nazis and condemn, without confusion, their doctrines of a Master Race."[19]

Several organizations were formed to produce greater racial cooperation. The Council Against Intolerance in America introduced curricula in the schools; the Council on Intercultural Relations publicized the contribution of black Americans to American life. For twenty years, white and African-American leaders in the South had worked through the Commission on Interracial Cooperation; during the war its programs took on greater significance. Several unions, including the National Maritime Union and the United Auto Workers, moved more rapidly to promote an interracial work force. A number of churches and foundations developed programs to combat racism.[20]

Never before had the nation been so dependent upon black citizens for success in war. Never before had American leaders appealed to whites to accept black men and women as first-class citizens to advance a war effort. When the National War Labor Board issued an order in 1943 abolishing wage differentials based on race, it insisted that "the *Negro is necessary for winning the war*" and pointed out that the treatment of Negroes by whites is "a test of our sincerity in the cause for which we are fighting."[21]

The war not only forced a change in the thinking of whites about race, but it also created major new circumstances for blacks themselves. Never before had they been exposed to so many different peoples from various walks of life in different lands, or been given the opportunity to play leadership roles. Until the war, African-Americans might volunteer for service in the Coast Guard and Navy only as menial workers; the Marine Corps had admitted whites only; so had the Army Air Corps and the Army artillery, engineer, signal, and tank corps. But the Selective Service Act of September 14, 1940, forbade discrimination against persons on account of race or color.

The newest service, the Army Air Force, recruited and trained blacks for jobs heretofore reserved exclusively for whites, such as pilots, mechanics, and technical aviation specialists. In 1943, with about eight thousand African-Americans already in the Air Force, a decision was made to accept blacks on an integrated basis at the Air Force's officer training school at Miami.[22] The first (segregated) black flying unit—the 99th Pursuit Squadron—flew 3,277 sorties and won a special commendation from the Air Force commanding general.

The Navy, which had previously used blacks only for servants, restricted them to shore duty until 1944, but between 1944 and 1945 progress was made in eliminating segregation in most training activities and the Navy announced its intention to assign blacks in all ratings to auxiliary vessels to up to 10 percent of the ship's complement. The decision came late in the war, and so habituated had the Navy become to race-designated caste that at the war's end 95 percent of all African-Americans in the Navy were still messmen.[23] The Army at first resisted efforts to integrate the troops or even to use blacks in combat situations. Field commanders refused to accept black soldiers trained for combat. But thousands of African-Americans eventually did fight on the ground and in the air, though in segregated units, and toward the end of the war volunteer African-American platoons were integrated into white infantry regiments and came under heavy fire in Germany.[24] There were nine black field artillery battalions in combat in Europe, one of which was honored for its distinctive contribution in the Battle of the Bulge. African-American antiaircraft units fought in Burma, on Normandy Beach, in Italy, and in North Africa. The all-black 761st Tank Battalion was praised for "conspicuous courage" after the attack on Omaha Beach, October 10, 1944.

The black men who landed on Omaha Beach or flew long-range fighter bombers over Munich were not likely to comply with the rules of caste at the war's end. They had become restless. A survey of enlisted men in 1944 showed that one-third of blacks, compared to only one-fifth of whites, were planning to move somewhere else other than their home town or city when the war was over. By 1950, more than half of the African-American population of the Northeast, North Central, and West had been born in other regions.[25] Between 1955 and 1960, the South lost more than three million in population through interregional migration, a disproportionate number of whom were black. Mississippi alone had a net out-migration of 325,000 blacks.[26] But there was considerable migration within the South, too, as blacks moved from rural areas to the cities; by 1960, eight of the eighteen cities with more than 100,000 blacks were in the South.[27]

African-Americans were now located in places where they were more likely to join labor unions, participate in elections, or join older black civil rights organizations such as the NAACP and the National Urban League or the new Congress of Racial Equality (1941), which pioneered in organizing nonviolent boycotts and demonstrations in the 1940s. They were more likely to read African-American newspapers, like the *Pittsburgh Courier*, which had launched a militant campaign for a double victory in the war: victory overseas against dictators and victory at home for freedom from oppression. A million black veterans returned from the war, and a large number were unwilling to accept the status quo. Many had suffered racial slurs and even physical attacks when stationed in the South. Whatever their experience with white racism during the war, they were readier than ever to speak out against it.

The conditions were ripe for radical change: a sympathetic justice system; the discrediting of racist theories among intellectuals; the education of whites by teachers who scorned racism; the need of the nation to present a picture of genuine freedom and of a united country in international affairs; and the growing dissatisfaction, restlessness, and political participation of African-Americans. Located increasingly in the cities, black pressure groups, black newspapers, and black leaders were more likely to be listened to by presidential candidates, especially Democrats, whose base of support came from northern and midwestern industrial and urban centers where African-American voters constituted significant potential power.

Never in American history had white political leaders, even those most sympathetic to the plight of blacks, taken the initiative to dismantle caste in the face of widespread white support for it. Major actions toward equality by the best-intentioned presidents had been taken only in national emergencies or under extreme political pressure. George Washington ordered the recruitment of free blacks in the Revolutionary Army only after the British had promised freedom to all blacks who would join them. Lincoln would have gone along with slavery to save the Union, but under exigencies of war issued the Emancipation Proclamation as a strategic military measure in states controlled by southern forces. Franklin Roosevelt, champion of the poor but immobilized by the opposition of southern leaders in the U.S. Senate, never took a position on a federal antilynching bill. Only when A. Philip Randolph threatened to lead 100,000 blacks on a march on Washington in June 1941 did the president, after first refusing, agree to issue an executive order ending discrimination by defense contractors. Roosevelt still balked at desegregating the armed forces—believing it would wreak havoc on the morale of white soldiers and sailors. Halting steps toward integration in the armed forces during the war were made under intense lobbying pressure from African-American organizations and newspapers, but only when Randolph called for black and white youths to boycott the draft in 1947 did President Harry S

Truman in July 1948 issue an executive order to effect equality of treatment in the services as quickly as possible. It would take a black American revolution to force John F. Kennedy and Lyndon B. Johnson to become active, vigorous advocates of sweeping measures to dismantle caste in the United States.

The Black Revolution, Martin Luther King, Jr., and the Civil Religion

In the 1950s and 1960s, conditions for a genuine revolution, the up-rooting of the entire system of caste, were more propitious than they had ever been before, but the obstacles were so formidable that it might not have succeeded had it not been for the leadership of Martin Luther King, Jr., who made the principles and heroes of the civic culture and civil religion his text and television his pulpit. Like Walker and Douglass, King reminded Americans of the founding myth of the republic and its sacred text, the Constitution, but he added something more, a strategy of massive nonviolent resistance learned from Gandhi and advocated by black pacifist leader Bayard Rustin, who became the major tactician of the civil rights revolution under King.

The tactic of active nonviolent resistance was used first in a large, public way in Montgomery, Alabama, in 1955, when Mrs. Rosa Parks refused to give up her seat to a white passenger on a bus. The head of the local NAACP, E. D. Nixon, called for blacks to boycott the buses, and forty thousand responded in two days. Martin Luther King, at twenty-six the newest minister in town and the most articulate, was asked to head the boycott. He hesitated but then agreed, praising "the glory of America with all of its faults." If the boycott is wrong, he said, "the Constitution is wrong, God Almighty is wrong."[28]

Boycotts, sit-ins, and other displays of nonviolent resistance were superb for television. Black Americans espousing the ideals of the civic culture and the civil religion became heroes to many whites who were shocked to see on TV the violence of other whites against black Americans. The Reverend Fred Shuttlesworth, looking back on the movement's early days, said, "We felt we could shame America."[29]

The force of white power was applied to stop the movement in Montgomery. Whites who supported the bus boycott, such as Clifford Durr, a lawyer, and Aubrey Williams, publisher of *The Southern Farmer*, both well-connected southern Democrats, were themselves boycotted, Durr by clients and Williams by advertisers. The Ku Klux Klan held rallies throughout the South, and the NAACP was shut down in Alabama. Even though buses had been desegregated in several southern cities as a result of lawsuits and threats of boycott (Little Rock, Richmond, and Dallas), it took eleven months for the boycott to win in Montgomery; but when it did, the first major victory of the civil rights revolution had been won.

In the last lines of a musical comedy called *Rags*, which had a short run on Broadway in 1986, an immigrant socialist labor organizer, when asked by her husband what was happening that made her so assertive about her rights, answered, "America is happening to me!" America was happening to blacks in the late 1950s and in the 1960s. One of the organizers of the boycott, Jo Ann Robinson, explained that the victory in Montgomery meant to her that she no longer felt like an alien in another man's country. The whites had been forced to give the blacks "a part of our own citizenship." She now had the feeling that "America is a great country and we are going to do more to make it greater."[30]

King's message was not fundamentally different from that of earlier African-American leaders, but Douglass, Washington, and Du Bois were not preachers. As a preacher, King could galvanize other preachers and also produce a response from masses of blacks when he talked about sin and redemption in America, the power to love, and the struggle to reach the promised land. Legions of church leaders, responding to rhetoric that was pure civil religion, worked with King to organize the major army of the revolution, the Southern Christian Leadership Conference, to "redeem the soul of America," as the biographer of the SCLC had written.[31] Christian rhetoric and imagery and his own sense of potential martyrdom were never far from King's thoughts or lips. As one of his biographers wrote, King saw himself as "bearing the cross."[32]

The Civil Rights Revolution on Television

The revolution's objectives had the blessing of the Supreme Court. It had an army of African-Americans ready to fight; it had potential white allies, growing in number. Soon, in "We Shall Overcome," it would have its anthem. But to put effective pressure on the executive branch to enforce the Constitution, it needed a series of victorious battles like the Montgomery bus boycott. King had just returned from India in the fall of 1957, more convinced than ever of the validity of Gandhian tactics. His principal projects were a joint fund-raising drive in the North with the NAACP and a large voter registration campaign in the South, the Crusade for Citizenship. African-American registration in the South was barely over a million, and King had set a goal of five million.[33] But the next battle of the revolution was shaping without him in Little Rock, Arkansas.

When it was announced that nine black youngsters would attend Central High School in Little Rock under an order of the court, Governor Orval Faubus of Arkansas called out the National Guard with instructions to admit whites only. The black children were turned back; but they clearly had the law on their side, for the Supreme Court had decided three years earlier in *Brown* v. *Board of Education* to integrate the public schools. But Faubus, with white public opinion strongly behind him, would not budge. Television news showed mobs of whites threatening the children as they tried again to reenter the school, this time going in through a side door. Millions of Americans could see Alex Wilson, a black ex-Marine, hit on the head by a screaming white man wielding a brick. President Dwight D. Eisenhower, who had refused to meet with King to discuss racial violence in the South and who several weeks earlier had said he could not possibly imagine "any set of circumstances that would ever induce me to send federal troops . . . into any area to enforce the orders of a federal court," was obliged to send in the paratroopers of the 101st Airborne Division of the Army to end mob rule.[34] No president could allow a state governor to defy the federal law in the age of television; for the first time since Reconstruction, the federal government had mobilized force to attack the system of caste. With the help of jeeps, helicopters, army cars, and personal escorts from the 101st Airborne, all shown on television, the children made it to school.

Just as Jo Ann Robinson had shown in Montgomery, so the youngsters in Little Rock exemplified Tocqueville's proposition that participation in the exercise of one's rights encourages patriotism. A special Thanksgiving dinner was filmed for television during which the students held a press conference articulating the rhetoric of the civic culture. One student, Gloria Ray, said she was thankful for "being a citizen in a country where the federal government respects and protects the rights of all of its citizens." Kenneth Roberts, in an effort to remind viewers that American prestige and power in the world were at stake in the struggle of students to achieve their constitutional rights, said he knew that the Communists enjoyed taking advantage of situations such as existed in Little Rock "to twist the minds of people" around the world, but he was "thankful that in America their actions are being foiled in the efforts of many democratic-minded citizens." Eleven years after the Little Rock confrontation, one of the students, Melba Pallilo Beals, recalled that she felt "pride and hope" and that she had "a reason to salute the flag."[35]

On February 1, 1960, four black college students in Greensboro, North Carolina, sat down at a lunch counter reserved for whites and refused to leave, starting a movement known as "sit-ins." When, under the leadership of John Lewis, black and white students remained seated at a downtown Nashville lunch counter, a gang of whites attacked the nonviolent students. After the police arrested the first group of students, a second wave came, and then a third, and then more. Within two months there were sit-ins in sixty-nine cities from Greensboro to San Antonio, and a

new tactic, a national boycott of chain stores, was organized; it was substantially effective within a month in Nashville and other southern cities.

Once again, the violent reaction of some whites resisting the peaceful
revolution was shown on television, when dynamite destroyed the home
of a black city councillor in Nashville. The bombing led to the first major
march of the movement, when four thousand people filled Jefferson Avenue. Television recorded the face-to-face confrontation of the Reverend
C. T. Vivian and Diane Nash, a leader of the black students, with Nashville's Mayor Ben West, who acknowledged for a national TV audience
on the steps of the courthouse that it was wrong to sell merchandise to
African-Americans and yet to deny them service. Three weeks later, the
battle of Nashville was over when blacks were served in downtown stores
at integrated lunch counters.

The next campaign was organized by the Congress of Racial Equality
and the new Student Nonviolent Coordinating Committee (formed in
1960). On May 4, 1961, seven whites and six blacks—freedom riders—left
from Washington on a bus to New Orleans. On the Atlanta-to-Birming-
ham segment of the trip, just outside Anniston, Alabama, a white mob
firebombed the lead bus and blocked the exits; twelve of the riders were
injured. A mob of Klansmen met the second bus in Birmingham; one
white rider, Jim Peck, was badly beaten. Alabama's governor, John Patterson, tried to intimidate the riders by accusing them of creating a riot,
but the SNCC leaders continued on to Louisiana.

Since the Supreme Court had ruled against segregation in interstate
transportation Attorney General Robert Kennedy tried to put pressure
on Governor Patterson and the Greyhound Bus Company to give protection to the riders. When the Alabama director of public safety gave
assurances of protection to Kennedy, twenty-one freedom riders, led by
John Lewis, left Birmingham for Montgomery. But the protection broke
down and a white mob met the riders in Montgomery, shouting, "Kill
the niggers." A black man was beaten so badly on the head that he became
permanently insensible. A young white freedom rider, also beaten badly,
appeared on television swathed in bandages to plead that "segregation
must be broken down."[36]

Attorney General Kennedy then sent six hundred marshals to protect
the riders. Martin Luther King flew to the city to lead a rally at the First
Baptist Church in Montgomery. Governor Patterson refused to guarantee
King's safety even as a white mob gathered outside the church. When
the mob, which outnumbered the federal marshals, became violent, Patterson was forced to declare martial law and ordered the National Guard
to keep peace. Two busloads of freedom riders then renewed their trip,
protected by helicopters, the Alabama guard, and police cars until they
reached Jackson, Mississippi, where they were arrested, accused of tres-

passing, and sentenced to sixty days in the state penitentiary. The freedom riders kept coming to Jackson until three hundred had been arrested and the Interstate Commerce Commission finally issued regulations implementing the ban on segregation in interstate travel.

In Oxford, Mississippi, in 1960, James Meredith attempted to register as a student at the University of Mississippi. Governor Ross Barnett, who had boasted, "I'm a Mississippi segregationist and I'm proud of it," personally denied Meredith registration on two occasions. The new president, John F. Kennedy, who had told the Democratic national convention the previous year that the security of the country and its place in world affairs were threatened when children in America were denied civil rights, sent more than four hundred U.S. marshals to enroll Meredith in the face of threatened white mob action. The marshals were not a sufficient force and the campus was turned into a battlefield, with rioters using guns and Molotov cocktails, frequently targeting representatives of the media, and actually wounding thirty-five marshals and killing one French journalist and an Oxford worker before Kennedy called in the troops and Meredith was enrolled.

The next major televised event took place in Birmingham, Alabama, one of the most segregated and most violent of southern cities. Birmingham whites had bombed the house and the church of the Reverend Fred Shuttlesworth in 1956 after he had demanded the desegregation of buses. Shuttlesworth was attacked again in September 1957 when he tried to enroll his children in a white school. In 1961, freedom riders had been attacked on Mothers' Day at the bus station without protection from the local police. King came to Birmingham in April 1963 to lead sit-ins; after five to six hundred demonstrators were arrested, the state court ordered an end to demonstrations. But money was now gone from the SCLC treasury, the federal government seemed indifferent, King was in jail, and seven white Alabama clergymen wrote an appeal to call off the demonstrations.

King's answer, the famous "Letter from Birmingham Jail" of April 16, 1963, rejected the accusation that his activities were "unwise and untimely." "Freedom is never voluntarily given by the oppressor; it must be demanded by the oppressed . . . we have waited for more than 340 years for our Constitutional and God-given rights," said King, who pointed out that "we have not made a single gain in civil rights without determined legal and nonviolent pressure."[37] Rather than wait, King approved of a nonviolent march of high school children on May 2; seven hundred were arrested. The next day, more than a thousand children showed up at the Sixteenth Street Church to march again. When Birmingham's police chief, Bull Connor, brought out the fire department and hoses and police dogs to break up the march before it got started, millions of Americans watched on television as Connor's white tank rode through the streets to try to intimidate the crowd and as water was shot at one hundred pounds of pressure per square inch by Birmingham's firemen against defenseless black children.

By the fifth day of the children's campaign, the fire hoses and the dogs were still appearing on the nightly news. Two thousand youngsters were in jail, and fighting had broken out between whites and blacks in the streets. Behind the scenes a city official named David Vann met with key business leaders and a representative of the Justice Department to reach an agreement with Shuttlesworth. Thirty-eight days after the movement had begun, an agreement was signed ending segregation at the lunch counters and providing for the hiring of blacks as clerks in downtown stores. But the announcement of the agreement precipitated more violence by whites, including the bombing of King's hotel room and police beatings of blacks who had gathered at the hotel.

Revolution in the Minds of Whites and Blacks

There were three revolutions. The first was in the buses, in the schools, on the courthouse steps, and at the lunch counters of southern cities, where, with the help of the federal courts and the executive branch of government, African-Americans were dismantling the legal structure of caste. The second was in the minds of white men and women, who, having been instructed about racism in the war against Hitler, were now learning the lessons of racism in America. The third was in the minds of black men and women, who, repudiating the psychological stigma of powerlessness inflicted on them by caste for generations, now became more determined (and more hopeful) to bring about an end to caste pluralism. By 1963, the opinions of whites, as reflected in a Louis Harris–Newsweek survey, showed a massive shift away from the racist views recorded by the National Opinion Research Center in 1944. Whereas 43 percent of whites said in 1944 that it would not be acceptable to work at a place where Negroes worked, even if they had comparable training, only 17 percent in 1963 (31 percent in the South) said they would object to working next to a Negro on the job.[38] In 1944, only fifty-one out of every hundred whites said they would eat in a restaurant that served both Negroes and whites, but nineteen years later only 20 percent said they would object to sitting next to a Negro at a lunch counter.[39] Whereas in 1944 only 22 percent said having Negro neighbors would be all right, 59 percent in 1963 thought it would be all right for a child to bring a Negro friend home to supper and 49 percent thought a Negro family next door would be okay.[40]

The 1963 poll also showed that a large majority of African-Americans supported King's strategies and tactics. More than four out of five of all blacks believed that the demonstrations had done some good because they had awakened whites; brought about integration; shown that Negroes were determined to fight for what belonged to them; helped to obtain equal rights; and reinforced a unity of purpose among Negroes.[41] Seventy-nine percent of middle- and upper-income blacks in the South reported that they actually had stopped buying at a store, 30 percent had marched in a demonstration, 28 percent had taken part in a sit-in, and 15 percent had gone to jail. In the North, 63 percent of middle- and upper-income blacks had stopped buying at a store, 44 percent had marched in a demonstration, 12 percent had taken part in a sit-in, and 2 percent had gone to jail.[42] Sixty percent of all blacks outside the South and 44 percent in the South said they would march in a demonstration. Fifty-nine percent outside the South and 42 percent in the South would take part in a sit-in. Fifty-two percent in the North and West were willing to go to jail, as were 43 percent in the South, where the threat was much more real. Fifty-four percent outside the South would picket a store, 40 percent in the South would.[43]

More than three-quarters of the blacks polled saw dangers in demonstrations, including imprisonment, physical impairment, and loss of life.[44] Nevertheless, of all the answers to the Louis Harris–*Newsweek* survey, the one that probably gave King the most satisfaction was that a large majority of blacks favored nonviolence as a revolutionary strategy. African-Americans said that they could win more by nonviolence, that God was on their side, and that a democratic form of government will achieve "our aim." Only 14 percent indicated that nonviolence had failed; 10 percent said a resort to force might become necessary.[45]

Without television depicting the involvement of whites in demonstrations, without the use of federal troops and marshals by American presidents, and without leaders such as King to articulate their cause, it is doubtful that such a large majority of adult blacks would have gained the courage and optimism revealed in the Louis Harris–*Newsweek* poll. But an army cannot be commanded via television, and church leaders, especially blacks, throughout the country formed a network of lieutenants and captains who mobilized troops for demonstrations, letter-writing, and fund-raising campaigns. Almost three out of every four blacks said they went to church at least two or three times a month, 49 percent at least once a week. When asked to assess the extent to which his or her minister in church was assisting the cause, 47 percent said "helping a lot" and only 5 percent said "not at all."[46]

The Presidential Response: Kennedy and Johnson

The combination of growing white support and African-American activism reflected in the Louis Harris–*Newsweek* survey pushed President Kennedy to submit a major civil rights bill in the spring of 1963. Kennedy, who had been elected by a narrow margin and with solid black support, had moved cautiously on civil rights legislation, believing his entire program could be held hostage by southern legislators. His caution contrasted with the 1960 Democratic platform, which contained the most far-reaching pledges for legislation and executive civil rights action ever made by a political party. With the Congress narrowly divided on many of the president's priority programs, the best Kennedy thought he could do in 1961 was to push for an extension of the Civil Rights Commission (created in 1957), issue an executive order establishing the President's Committee on Equal Employment Opportunity to combat racial discrimination in employment policies of government agencies and private firms holding government contracts, and to get the Department of Justice to step up antidiscrimination suits in interstate transportation and education.

Kennedy had not made good on his 1960 campaign promise to issue an executive order putting an end to racial discrimination in federally assisted housing; nor did he press for civil rights bills. Again in 1962, the Kennedy administration sidestepped proposals for general civil rights legislation, but did support a proposed constitutional amendment to outlaw the poll tax as a voting requirement in federal elections and primaries. The poll tax amendment passed and eventually became the Twenty-Fourth Amendment in 1964, but its only real effect was in the five states that still had a poll tax—Alabama, Arkansas, Mississippi, Texas, and Virginia. A Fair Employment Practices Committee bill that would have established the committee on a permanent legislative footing did not even reach the floor of the House.

It took the national domestic crisis of 1963 to force the president to propose new, far-reaching legislation. By the summer, demonstrations had taken place in eight hundred cities and towns, climaxed by the famous March on Washington. Once more, A. Philip Randolph decided that it was necessary to bring moral pressure on the government to act by holding a march on Washington. He did not bargain with or threaten President Kennedy as he had Roosevelt and Truman. Now, the momentum of the revolution was such that the president joined it in public. On June 11, only six weeks before *Newsweek* published the Louis Harris survey, he made his strongest statement on civil rights, declaring that "race has no place in American life or law." "We are confronted primarily with a moral issue," he said. Then, adopting the rhetoric of the civil religion, he maintained, "It is as old as the Scriptures and is as clear as the American Constitution." Pointing out that it was impossible to preach freedom around the world and maintain a caste system for Negroes, he argued that "the events in Birmingham and elsewhere have so increased the cries for equality that no city or State or legislative body can prudently choose to ignore them." Only hours after Kennedy's televised speech—in which he called the movement a "revolution"—the NAACP's field director in Mississippi, Medgar Evers, was shot in the back as he returned home to his wife and children.

Kennedy's exhortation was strong, but it would take the March on Washington, more violence against blacks, more demonstrations, and the martyrdom of the president himself in November to get the civil rights legislation passed. The symbolic march of a quarter of a million Americans from the Washington Monument to the Lincoln Memorial on August 28 was culminated by the greatest of Martin Luther King, Jr.'s speeches, one probably seen by more Americans than any ever made before. Filling his speech with the language of the civic culture and the civil religion, King appealed to all Americans to live up to the founding myth of the republic. His text, like Kennedy's, was based on the Constitution and the Scriptures. Only a few weeks after King's great speech, violence came again to Birmingham when a bomb exploded at the Sixteenth Street Baptist church, killing four young black girls. Once more, brutality shown by whites resisting the black struggle—television carried both stories— helped to mobilize whites and blacks for the cause. In Mississippi, Evers's death brought thousands into the movement who had never participated before.

In the summer of 1964, "Freedom Summer," Bob Moses and James Forman led a thousand teachers, students, and lawyers, all volunteers, into the northwest delta counties of Mississippi to organize community programs and summer schools, and especially to register voters in an area where few blacks had ever voted. The murder of three young civil rights volunteers, black Mississippian James Chaney and two whites from the North, Andrew Goodman and Michael Schwerner, once again impressed on a watching nation the viciousness of those who intended to maintain the caste system based on race in the South. Eighty volunteers were beaten that summer, but the students and professionals were not intimidated. Encouraged by the decision of the Senate on June 10, 1964, to invoke cloture to prevent a filibuster against the Civil Rights Bill, nearly 60,000 Mississippians, all of them black, signed on as members of a new political party, the Mississippi Freedom Democratic party. In the fourteen months between the demonstrations in Birmingham and the Senate's June 10 vote to impose cloture, a bipartisan agreement developed in support of a strong bill. Kennedy had been martyred in November 1963; President

Lyndon Johnson exhorted congressional leaders to keep up the fight. He was in frequent telephone communication with Senator Hubert Humphrey (D-Minnesota), floor manager for the bill. The central strategy of the opposition, led by Senator Richard Russell (D-Georgia), was reliance on a filibuster. Never before in history had cloture been invoked to prevent a filibuster on a civil rights bill, but this time the leaders of the filibuster were overpowered.[47]

The act contained new provisions to help guarantee to blacks the right to vote; to protect their access to public accommodations such as hotels, motels, restaurants, and places of amusement; to authorize the federal government to sue to desegregate public facilities and schools; to extend the life of the Civil Rights Commission for four years and enlarge its powers; to require most companies and labor unions to grant equal employment opportunity; to establish a new Community Relations Service to deal with racism; to authorize the Justice Department to enter into pending civil rights cases; and to cut off federal funds to state and private organizations and agencies if they engaged in discriminatory practices. This last provision, Title VI, gave the federal government new teeth, particularly at a time of increasing reliance on federal tax dollars in both the public and private sectors of the economy.

The bill not only put the Civil Rights Commission on a solid footing, it established a five-member Equal Employment Opportunity Commission with powers to prevent and eliminate discrimination in employment based on race, color, sex, religion, or national origin by employers, employment agencies, or labor unions. In addition to the Equal Employment Opportunity Commission and the U.S. Commission on Civil Rights, several other federal agencies were empowered to engineer the breakup of caste pluralism. The Community Relations Service was established by the Civil Rights Act of 1964 as a unit of the U.S. Department of Commerce to help communities resolve disputes arising from discriminatory practices.

The 1964 act gave the Justice Department new responsibilities to initiate suits to desegregate governmentally owned or operated facilities and public schools, upon complaint of individuals who themselves are unable to sue. Justice also was empowered to initiate suits to end discrimination in public accommodations or in employment, where such discrimination is part of a pattern or practice, and to intervene in private lawsuits involving discrimination in places of public accommodation and in employment or in suits alleging denial of equal protection of the laws.

The U.S. Office of Education—later to become a department—was charged by the act to conduct a survey on availability of equal educational opportunity and to provide technical and financial assistance to school boards in carrying out plans for the desegregation of public schools and for assisting in the resolution of problems connected to desegregation. The office would also be responsible for assuring nondiscrimination in education programs receiving federal aid, including aid to colleges and universities, elementary and secondary schools, and libraries. The U.S. Department of Health and Human Services (then the Department of Health, Education and Welfare) was given responsibility under Title VI for assuring nondiscrimination in federally assisted health and welfare departments, health clinics, and community mental health centers.

The symbolic heart of the 1964 act was Title II, which dealt with public accommodations. If blacks could eat at restaurants with whites, stay over-night at hotels and motels, visit theaters and stadiums, and fill up their tanks at gasoline stations, the obvious displays of caste would be elimi-nated. Within a year, the impact of the law was striking. Early compliance took place in more than a dozen cities, but by March 1964 the Justice Department had received more than six hundred complaints of violation of Title II. A series of lawsuits toppled the pattern of segregation in public accommodations. Agreement on obedience to the Civil Rights Act now extended to key figures who had opposed it earlier, such as Senators Richard B. Russell (D-Georgia) and Allen J. Ellender (D-Louisiana), who urged local communities to obey the law, and to businessmen and local mayors and other officials, who wanted to avoid sit-ins.[48] It would take decades for the vestiges of discrimination to be eradicated in hundreds of thousands of public accommodations, but it was plain even by the end of 1965 that long-entrenched public symbols of caste were being broken.

The volunteers in Mississippi kept organizing Freedom Schools during the day and political rallies at night following passage of the Civil Rights Act. Called vicious names by whites throughout the South, including the chairman of the House of Representatives Rules Committee, Howard W. Smith (D-Virginia), who had tried unsuccessfully to bottle up the Civil Rights Bill and who had labeled them "beatniks, misfits and agitators" working with the "aid of the Communists," the young men and women from CORE and SNCC persisted.[49] "This is our country, too," declared one young man for CORE.

The patriotic theme was picked up by the delegates of the Mississippi Freedom Democratic party, sixty-four blacks and four whites who were elected to attend the Democratic national convention in Atlanta, where they hoped to unseat the regular, all-white Democratic slate. "Is this America? . . . where we have to sleep with our telephones off the hook?" asked Fannie Lou Hamer, a former sharecropper from Sunflower City and vice chairman of the new party.[50]

The delegates of the Mississippi Freedom Democratic party appealed to the convention and to the American television audience that they and not the so-called regular delegates be seated, since only they had been elected in an open system. The nation saw Miss Hamer and others plead for the most elemental right of all in a representative government, the right to participate in the choice of one's representatives. President Johnson pressed convention managers to work out a compromise. The details, developed under the leadership of Senator Humphrey and his protégé, Minnesota's Attorney General Walter Mondale, called for two seats to go to the Mississippi Freedom Democrats. In return, the regulars would pledge to support the ticket and agree to bar any delegate in the future who supported racial discrimination. The Freedom Democrats denounced the compromise, and all but four of the regulars walked out.

The Battle of Selma

In the summer of 1964, violent race riots erupted in several northern cities. In early December, King received the Nobel Peace Prize in Norway. As the end of 1964 approached, SNCC was running out of money in its voter registration drive in Selma, Alabama, and once more local activists turned to King for leadership. The black citizens of Selma—more than half of the citizens of the city were black but less than one percent of them were registered—heard President Johnson speak on January 4, 1965, pleading for the removal of every obstacle to voting, and decided to escalate their protest. One hundred and five local teachers marched to the courthouse to protest the arrest of one of their leaders. Sheriff Jim Clark used a swagger stick to push away the teachers on the courthouse steps. The teachers then marched up again only to be beaten back. One SCLC leader, the Reverend C. T. Vivian, confronted the sheriff, likened Clark to Hitler, and asserted that the right to vote in Selma was a national problem. Clark struck Vivian with his police stick; TV also recorded the next confrontation between the two, when Vivian said to the sheriff he should go ahead and arrest the protesters, "We're willing to be beaten for democracy."[51]

Following the shooting by Alabama state troopers of a young black man who had been trying to protect his mother on a nighttime march in Marion, Alabama, the SCLC proposed to mobilize the anger of Selma's blacks by conducting a march from that city to Montgomery, the capital, fifty-four miles away, to focus the nation's attention on the denial of the most elementary right of representative democracy. When six hundred persons, led by King and Lewis, marched from Brown Chapel Church to the Edmund Pettus Bridge, they were met by state troopers who had been ordered by Governor George Wallace to stop them. With Jim Clark's posse on the sidelines, the marchers were attacked with tear gas and dispersed on what would be termed "bloody Sunday" by network evening news.

When King asked for marchers from all over the country, they came by the thousands, including 450 white ministers, priests and rabbis. The march, having been banned by a federal judge, was delayed several days, giving whites as well as blacks—labor leaders, church leaders, and politicians from all over the country—time to join the swelling ranks of the protesters. When two thousand crossed the bridge on March 9, they were ordered once again by state troopers to go back. After a hurried prayer meeting, King decided to turn back rather than risk violence and a possible public relations setback by defying the court order forbidding the march.

Most blacks and whites who had come from the North decided to stick it out until King was ready to march. A white Unitarian minister, the Reverend James Reeb, who had been out to dinner with two white colleagues, was called aside by a gang of toughs who screamed at them, "Hey, you niggers!" Reeb was beaten so severely that he died two days later. Demonstrators came to Selma from all over the country in greater numbers. The killing of Reeb underscored the moral and religious nature of the fight. One young black volunteer, Jimmy Webb, led a group past a police barricade of Brown Chapel down the street, where he confronted the police with the rhetoric of the civic culture and the civil religion on television, much as King might have done. He asked an official about to arrest him and his group, "Do you believe in equal justice for all?", then asked the police if they would pray together with his group. Denied that, he asked for permission to go to the courthouse to kneel and pray. The Selma police agreed to none of his requests and answered none of his questions.

None of Lyndon Johnson's biographers have noted any particular reaction by him to the confrontation in Selma, but one can imagine his fury as he turned to the three network nightly news programs. He was being openly challenged as president by county sheriffs, courthouse politicians, and Alabama state troopers. President Johnson appeared on television to ask for a comprehensive voting rights bill. Of the demonstrators in Selma, he said in his Texas hill country accent, "Their cause must be our cause, too . . . all of us must overcome this crippling legacy of bigotry and injustice and we shall overcome."

Watching Johnson's speech on television with Shuttlesworth and other comrades, King cried. In Montgomery, SNCC workers were still being beaten. James Forman, tired of waiting, asserted, "If we can't sit at the table, let's knock the fuckin' legs off." Then, looking up and realizing that there were young and older women in the audience, he quickly said, "Excuse me." But King's decision not to challenge the Alabama troopers was rewarded when federal judge Frank Johnson ruled that the civil rights leader and his supporters had a right to march; Lyndon Johnson feder-alized the Alabama National Guard to protect the marchers.

When 3,200 people gathered at Brown Chapel Church sixty-two days after the Selma campaign began, King exclaimed, "Now is the time to make justice a reality." After five days of marching, 25,000 blacks and whites came into Montgomery to sit and sprawl on the grounds and steps of the state capitol, where they listened to King call for a society "that can live with itself," one in which a man is not judged as a black or white man, "but man as man." There would be more casualties that night. One white woman, Viola Liuzzo, a housewife from Michigan, was shot and killed while transporting blacks in her car. Observing blacks and whites mingling on the front of the state capitol, John Lewis was awed by the moment. "You saw the power of the most powerful nation on earth," he said, referring not to the National Guard but to the moral suasion of 25,000 Americans united behind the civic culture's ideal of equal rights.

The Voting Rights Act of 1965

Most African-Americans still could not vote in most jurisdictions in the South. In Dallas County, Alabama, where the Selma campaign began on January 18 and more than 50 percent of the voting age population were black, only 2 percent of blacks were registered to vote, compared to 60 percent of whites.[52] Without the right to vote, citizenship meant little in a democracy. Despite efforts in 1870, 1957, and 1960 and the 1964 Civil Rights Act, Congress had been unable to effectuate the promise of the Fifteenth Amendment to guarantee the right to vote to all citizens. State and local officials had become extremely sophisticated in effectively ex-cluding African-Americans from political participation in many areas;[53] some jurisdictions still used "literacy tests" as a prerequisite to registra-tion, manipulating them to see that most blacks failed while most whites passed. Sometimes persons attempting to register were required to be accompanied by two persons already registered. Since whites would not accompany blacks to register, the African-American voter was effectively excluded in many jurisdictions.[54] As a result, extremely low numbers of blacks registered and voted, and few held office.

When President Eisenhower had sought to strengthen voting rights legislation in 1956 and 1960 and President Kennedy, in 1963, those who opposed comprehensive change asked that local officials, subject to ju-dicial direction, be permitted to solve the problem without federal inter-vention. But after Selma it became clear that local officials would not do the job and that federal courts without federal legislation and enforcement at the ready could not guarantee this most fundamental right. After Selma, the pressure was irresistible, and the Voting Rights Act of 1965 passed on August 6. It specified that local jurisdictions could no longer use literacy tests or other devices that had given registrars discretion to keep so-called "undesirable" citizens away from the polls. Such time-honored devices as a test to demonstrate the ability to read or write or understand any matter or to prove good moral character would hence-forth be against federal law, since they had invariably been used to deny the rights of citizens.[55]

The act gave private parties as well as the attorney general of the United States the right to file suit to enforce these guarantees. Special provisions were aimed at jurisdictions that had a prima facie record of discrimina-tions, particularly the South, although some jurisdictions outside the South were also covered. One of the most important provisions of the act gave the Justice Department the right to pre-clear any proposed change in the nature and boundaries of electoral districts to make certain they did not discriminate against blacks.

The Voting Rights Act represented the clear assertion of federal au-thority over states' rights in protecting the civil rights of individuals. That authority was backed by the ability of the federal government to use military force quickly to enforce court orders. On six separate occasions in the course of the civil rights revolution, the executive used physical force to make such orders stick: in 1957 with federalization of the Arkansas National Guard and dispatch of paratroopers by President Eisenhower to restore peace and escort black children to and from Little Rock High School; in 1961 when President Kennedy sent U.S. marshals to restore order in Montgomery to protect the freedom riders; in 1962 when he dispatched 16,000 federal troops to Mississippi to protect U.S. marshals and demonstrators at the University of Mississippi to enforce Meredith's right to admission; in 1963 when he federalized the Alabama National Guard to confront Wallace's resistance to integration of the University of Alabama; in 1964 when the federal government claimed jurisdiction in investigating the murder of Schwerner, Goodman, and Chaney; and in 1965 when President Johnson ordered the Alabama National Guard into federal service to protect the marchers from Selma to Montgomery.

Before the assertion of federal power in the 1960s, southern states harassed and even prosecuted the NAACP and other civil rights organi-zations. In 1956, Alabama had persuaded a state court to restrain the NAACP on the ground that it had never properly registered in the state, since it was incorporated elsewhere. When the organization refused to release its membership list, it was fined $100,000. The U.S. Supreme Court ruled in 1958 that the NAACP was within its rights of free asso-ciation in withholding the names (*NAACP* v. *Alabama,* 357 U.S. 449), distinguishing it from a 1928 case in which the Court upheld a New York state law requiring the Ku Klux Klan to submit its membership list on the ground that the Klan was pursuing illegal activities while the NAACP activities were legal (*Bryant* v. *Zimmerman,* 278 U.S. 63). But Alabama resisted through a variety of legal stratagems for eight years after the Alabama court had first temporarily banned the association, forcing the Court to order the Alabama Supreme Court to direct the lower state court to void the injunction against the NAACP and to take steps to permit it to operate in the state. In 1966, after three presidents had made clear their willingness to use military force to enforce the civil rights of blacks, the Court warned that if the state court did not act, the NAACP could apply for relief to the Court itself; and under that threat, Alabama complied.[56]

The Voting Rights Act was a major blow to the structure of caste. It produced astounding results quickly. Although the Civil Rights Commission reported in successive studies that there were many continuing examples of intimidation and coercion at the polls, there was an immediate, enormous rise in registration, in voting, and in officeholding by blacks throughout the South and the country. By 1974, ten years after passage of the act, 964 blacks had been elected to public office in the six states covered under the pre-clearance provisions of the act—states that had had a strong record of discrimination—plus North Carolina (Texas was not covered at the time). In the next five years, the number of African-Americans holding elective office almost doubled in most of those states.[57] In states covered under the pre-clearance provisions of the act, the number of blacks increased in each type of office. In South Carolina, the number of black county and city school board members rose from twenty-four to fifty-six. In Mississippi, the number on the county governing boards rose from eight to twenty-seven, and the number on county and city local school boards rose from twenty-seven to fifty-eight. Between 1974 and 1980, the number of African-American mayors in Louisiana tripled, from four to twelve.[58] The legal structure of caste had been substantially unraveled by 1965, but the revolution continued as blacks went on to attack the social and psychological stigma of racial caste.

Chapter Nine

"THEY NEVER DID REALLY SEE *ME*"
The Assertion of Black Ethnic Identity

AT THE height of the black renaissance in Harlem in the 1920s, the poet Countee Cullen recalled in "Incident" the memory of an eight-year-old black boy.

Now, I was eight and very small,
And he was no whit bigger,
And so I smiled but he poked out
His tongue and called me "nigger."

Cullen, poised, urbane, a man with many white as well as black friends, concluded the poem:

I saw the whole of Baltimore
From May until December;
Of all the things that happened there,
That's all that I remember.[1]

Cullen knew what all educated African-Americans knew—that whites had invented a name to keep all blacks in a position of caste. "Nigger" was their word of disrespect, contempt, and fear. It was a caste word. When Malcolm X, the most brilliant and articulate of all separatist leaders in the 1960s, spoke to a campus audience at a large university, he was heckled by hostile questions from a black intellectual who opposed Malcolm's separatist ideas. Malcolm questioned the man: "Do you know what they call a Negro scholar? Ph.D.? Professor?" "No," the man said, and Malcolm answered his own question: "They call him a nigger."[2] For Malcolm, revolution meant discarding the identity that a white racist society had imposed on African-Americans even more than it meant civil rights legislation. What, he seemed to be asking, will be the good of new laws? With or without laws, whites would continue to assault and destroy the dignity of blacks through racism unless blacks repudiated white society by creating an identity and institutions of their own. Before blacks could achieve the self-respect that was a precondition for power, they had to cast off the racist values and white names they had taken for their own.

Malcolm argued that white immigrants did not have to struggle to become Americans. "Those Hunkies that just got off the boat," he said, "they're already Americans; Polacks are already American; Italian refugees are already Americans. Everything that came out of Europe, every blue-eyed thing, is already an American . . . being born here in America doesn't make you an American . . . they don't have to pass civil-rights legislation to make a Polack an American."[3] By emphasizing race exclusively, Malcolm ignored the resistance of nativist Americans to newcomers, such as Irish Catholics and Jews. By stressing the importance of blacks discovering a new identity as African-Americans, he understood intuitively that one great advantage all immigrants—not just the Europeans—had over Negroes in being accepted as Americans was pride in their ancestral cultures. To be an ethnic-American meant three things: confronting other Americans with pride in one's past; confronting the polity with claims made in the name of the group; and embracing the symbols, institutions, and history of the American civic culture. Malcolm X wanted blacks to do the first two of these; Martin Luther King called for all three.

The issue of group pride had long plagued African-American leaders in the United States. Frederick Douglass had urged blacks to follow the example of modern Jews in Europe and America, who, by emphasizing group solidarity and pride, improved their status.[4] Booker T. Washington also pointed to the example of the Jews, to their unity, pride, and love of their own people that would, "as the years go on," make them "more and more influential in this country."[5] Only a few days before he was killed, Malcolm X told an interviewer that, unlike "the Negro . . . the Jew never lost his pride in being a Jew . . . his sense of his own value gave him the courage to fight back."[6] King also frequently compared the situation of blacks to that of Jews, arguing that blacks could learn from the Jewish combination of ethnic traditions with social and political action.[7]

How could blacks achieve the unity and pride of Jews, who for two thousand years had been held together by a sacred book and dozens of rituals, ceremonies, and customs revolving around the yearly calendar and the life cycle? To achieve such unity and pride it was necessary, Malcolm sometimes said, for blacks to accept the fact that they were not Americans; only whites were Americans, no matter what the laws said. That was a message most blacks did not want to hear. Malcolm was popular because he gave vent to the frustration, anger, and hatred blacks felt against whites, not because he repudiated American identity.

Most blacks wanted the ethnic-American identity that had been achieved by immigrants and their children. Most immigrants had been torn between two identities, but they, and especially their children, were able to combine identities by becoming ethnic-Americans. For African-Americans, the struggle between a black identity, disparaged by whites, and an American identity, holding out the promise of freedom and opportunity, was a torment. Almost fifty years after the Civil War, W. E. B. Du Bois wrote, "One feels his two-ness—an American Negro—two souls, two thoughts, two unreconciled strivings, two warring ideals in one dark body whose dogged strength alone keeps it from being torn asunder." Of the black man, he said, "He simply wishes to make it possible for a man to be both a Negro and an American without being cursed and spit upon."[8]

Martin Luther King, Jr.'s answer to that question was to try to convert whites through the Christian message of love and the Gandhian tactic of nonviolent resistance to oppression. King, no less than Malcolm X, knew that blacks had been robbed of self-esteem in a culture that not only exploited but systematically degraded them. But he and hundreds of other African-American leaders preached that self-worth would come out of a religious commitment to respect the inherent dignity of all men and women. When King preached love and nonviolence, hundreds of thousands of blacks, possessed of love for Jesus, followed him. But large numbers of other blacks, particularly those in the urban ghettoes, where more than half of America's 21.5 million blacks lived by 1965, felt hatred for whites. King and his colleagues sought integration in all aspects of American society. Certain other blacks, fearing and hating whites, wanted and expected nothing from a corrupt, racist white society, and they listened to Malcolm X.

Those tendencies—toward forgiveness of whites and integration with them versus hatred for whites and the impulse for separatism—have always been at war within black America and even within the same families and individuals. In pursuing integration, King represented the thinking of most black leaders throughout history. Douglass wanted the Fourth of July to be his. Du Bois wanted first-class citizenship. Langston Hughes wrote that blacks, too, "sing America." The black novelist Richard Wright, writing on the eve of the Second World War, asserted, "what we want, what we represent, what we endure, is what America is . . . we want what others have, the right to share in the upward march of American life."[9]

Yet, the everyday life of blacks in 1965—notwithstanding the Civil Rights Act and the Voting Rights Act—commonly meant menial jobs or unemployment, police brutality, slum housing, disease, high infant mortality, early death of adults, and crime. The pent-up rage felt by many blacks, especially young adults, erupted in riots in many U.S. cities in 1965, 1966, and 1967. Earlier acts of violence against whites, beginning with the great slave revolts of Gabriel Prosser, Denmark Vesey, and Nat Turner in the early nineteenth century, had failed, but they gave many blacks a feeling of controlling their own destiny, of power, even pride. Violence in the late 1960s' urban riots, unlike the slave revolts, did not lead to more repression, but to thoughtful reflection by white and black leaders about the corrosive despair of black Americans.

Part of that despair had to do with the confusion that blacks felt about what Du Bois called their "two-ness." King told blacks to claim their rights as Americans. Malcolm X, in the tradition of Marcus Garvey, told blacks to feel pride in themselves as blacks. By emphasizing that blacks had to discover and take pride in their own identity rather than beg to be admitted to the society of whites, Malcolm touched deep and pervasive feelings. But by rejecting integration as a goal, he was out of touch with the views of a majority of blacks, according to the Louis Harris–*Newsweek* poll of 1963. By a seven-to-one margin, blacks favored integrating the schools, and three out of four said they would prefer jobs in an integrated rather than a separated workplace.[10] Only 8 percent of African-American leaders and 6 percent of the rank and file approved of the Black Muslims.[11] The reasons they gave included: "we are Americans"; "created equal to whites"; "should be part of U.S."; "fighting to be part of U.S."; "Negroes fought for, worked, helped build country."[12] So convinced were blacks of their future in America that 91 percent of black leaders and 81 percent of all blacks said the U.S. was worth fighting for.[13] In any case, a physical return to Africa was out of the question. As the African-American journalist and author Louis E. Lomax wrote in 1962, "whatever else the Negro is, he is American. Whatever he is to become—integrated, unintegrated or disintegrated—he will become it in America."[14] But Lomax did not address the issue of "whatever else the Negro is." That, to Malcolm X, was the important question.

Most African-Americans shared an ethnic identity, forged almost entirely by their experience in the U.S. and nourished by the church, soul food, black English, folk tales, music, the Gospels, the blues, and the common memory of survival in white America. But neither whites nor blacks acknowledged the ethnic character of the African-American experience. Blacks and whites usually thought of blacks in terms of race only. Ethnicity implied a continuing cultural history linked to pre-American ancestors. It also usually implied positive, triumphant ancestral memories. The Jews, oppressed in medieval Christian Europe, read in their religious services not just about a loving God but of a great ancestral tribe that had given birth to the very ideas of monotheism and social justice. The Chinese, excluded from political power and even from owning land in many countries of Southeast Asia, felt superior to their oppressors, in part because of a heritage they could recapture, like the Jews, in the writings of their forefathers. African-Americans had to forge their ethnic identity almost entirely out of their experience in the U.S. Lomax, writing about "the emerging tribe," said in 1962 that it pained him "to recall just how close we southern Negroes were to becoming a first-rate culture group."[15] But there was a fatal flaw, he said. "We had come together as a tribe for negative, not positive reasons; we were bound together by the animus of the white man, not by historical customs and traditions such as those that have fashioned the world's peoples into culture groups."[16]

Du Bois had written in 1903 of African connections to slavery, including the African priest or medicine man as a basis for the religious consciousness and styles of slaves.[17] The white anthropologist Melville J. Herskovits had shown in 1941 that many aspects of African culture survived the middle passage of slaves and the breaking up of slave families. Some of them informed Afro-American dancing, patterns of speech and vocabulary, and other aspects of behavior. Herskovits presented intriguing evidence to challenge the assumption that the Negro is without a knowable, continuing past. It was not just pigmentation, or slavery, or caste that gave Negroes their cultural identity but African traditions, too. "To rephrase the matter," he concluded, "it is seen that the African past is no more to be thought of as having been thrown away by those of African descent than it is to assume that the traits that distinguish Italians or Germans or old Americans or Jews or Irish or Mexicans or Swedes from the entire population of which they form a part can be understood in their present forms without a reference to a preceding cultural heritage."[18] Later, in 1977, the historian Lawrence W. Levine, through an ingenious use of historical folklore, showed how the first African captives kept alive into the twentieth century important elements of African consciousness and styles in speech, humor, music, games, and storytelling.[19]

Both Herskovits and Levine seemed to be saying that blacks were like immigrant groups in that they carried forward into their life in the U.S. important ways of thinking, feeling, and acting from their ancestral cultures. Their arguments not only contradicted the conventional notion that blacks had no cultural consciousness that predated their experience in America but served a political purpose. As Herskovits wrote that to "the extent to which the past of a people is regarded as praiseworthy, their own self-esteem will be high and the opinion of others will be favorable."[20]

Levine's work was particularly convincing, but there were three limitations to the analysis that Du Bois, Herskovits, and Levine probably would have acknowledged. First, African-Americans had many tribal pasts, and it was virtually impossible to identify one's own particular historical roots. After exhaustive genealogical examination, Alex Haley went back to West Africa to claim his roots in the 1970s, but not many blacks could make the same journey, physically, intellectually, or emotionally. Second, how were they to symbolize their past? What flags, anthems, religions, heroes, and heroines were they to claim in asserting their ethnic identity? Third, there was no way to evade the fact of slavery. Except for immigrants from the Caribbean and a smaller number from

Africa and the Cape Verde islands, blacks had not chosen to come to the U.S. Although the slaves and their descendants had learned to survive, showing enormous courage and resiliency, and went far beyond survival to make extraordinary contributions to various aspects of American life, it was extremely difficult to escape the stigma of inferiority that the system of caste had imposed.

Herskovits had written that whites had assaulted pride in blacks partly by forcing them to think of Africans as savages. Malcolm X wrote in his autobiography that he never thought as a youngster about the black people in Africa. "My image of Africa, at that time, was of naked savages, cannibals, monkeys and tigers and steaming jungles."[21] Malcolm's father was a follower of Marcus Garvey, whose message of black racial pride and even superiority had led Malcolm ultimately to reject Harlem's world of prostitutes, numbers runners, and dope peddlers to follow Elijah Muhammad, leader of the Black Muslims. After Malcolm became a Muslim, he discarded the surname of his father, Little, given perhaps to his ancestor by a white slave master, and chose instead the name Malcolm X, with "X" symbolizing the true African family name that he could never know. Some European immigrants had been given simplified names by immigration officers. Others, and probably even more of their children, Anglicized their names to become acceptable to those they saw as the dominant insiders. But the vast majority kept the names of their forebears, proud to be Grabowskis, Cohens, O'Rourkes, Takashimis, and Castillos. In casting off the names slave owners had given them, converts to Islam like Malcolm asserted an identity independent of that forced on them by whites.

When Malcolm was a young boy in a detention home, the white husband and wife who were responsible for him talked "about anything and everything with me standing right there hearing them, the same way people would talk freely in front of a pet canary." They would use the word "nigger" a hundred times a day and speak about him—their mascot—as though he were not there. Malcolm the invisible mascot. "It just never dawned upon them that I could understand, that I wasn't a pet, but a human being . . . they never did really see *me*."[22]

In 1937, it was probably the rare white person who could see blacks as individual human beings. Whites had been nurtured on stereotypes of blacks in all aspects of popular culture—minstrel shows, comic strips, vaudeville, and movies. The stereotype of Sambo—the servile Negro as an object of laughter—persisted from the colonial era through the minstrel shows of the nineteenth century until the 1960s.[23] If not shown as Sambo, blacks were depicted as loyal Toms, faithful mammies, grinning coons, wide-eyed pickaninnies, or savage brutes.[24]

The most widely known caricature of blacks as frightening, grotesque brutes appeared in Thomas Dixon's 1905 best-selling novel *The Clansman,* which in 1915 was made into *The Birth of a Nation,* the greatest attraction of the silent-picture era.[25] It lost its number-one box office rating in 1939 to *Gone With the Wind,* whose blacks were inept and ignorant except for Mammy and Pork, who remained faithful to their owners throughout the war.

Richard Wright wrote in *Black Boy* of 1937 of working as a bellboy in a Memphis whorehouse. He grew used to seeing white prostitutes naked, sitting on their beds. "It was presumed that we black boys took their nakedness for granted, that it startled us no more than a blue vase or a red rug. Our presence awoke in them no sense of shame whatever, for we blacks were not considered human anyway."[26] Later, Ralph Ellison would entitle his paradigmatic novel about blacks in America *Invisible Man.*[27] James Baldwin, who had already written a series of essays to which he gave the title *Nobody Knows My Name,* went to live in Europe during the 1950s. In America, he said, "the individual must fight for his identity."[28] The only thing that blacks "held in common was their precarious, their unutterably painful relation to the white world." They needed "to remake the world in their own image, and no longer be controlled by the vision of the world, and of themselves, held by other people."[29]

Writing about ethnic identity, Baldwin listed almost all of the ethnic groups and the Indians, who joined the American "melting pot . . . but without any intention of being melted." Of the immigrants, he said, "they were here because they wanted to leave wherever they had been and they were here to make their lives, and achieve their futures, and to establish a new identity."[30] As he saw the process of Americanization, "it was their necessity to make themselves over in the image of their new and unformed country."[31] Baldwin underestimated the power of ethnic identity, believing that status became a kind of substitute for identity in the U.S. Ethnicity, he asserted, quickly gave way to status.

Actually, ethnicity did not always give way to status. Many Jews and Catholics complained that ethnicity was a block to status no matter how rich or successful one had become. For members of the Amish community or Hasidic Jews, status outside the group was unimportant. Baldwin appeared to project his own feelings as a black man when he wrote, "the one thing that all Americans have in common is that they have no other identity apart from the identity which is being achieved on this continent."[32] That was not true for the Chinese-Americans who burned incense for their dead parents, for Jewish-Americans who said *kaddish* for theirs, for Japanese-Americans who continued an exquisitely patterned tradition of gift exchange into the third and fourth generation, for Filipino-Americans who celebrated José Rizal's birthday or Filipino Independence Day.

Baldwin was right in seeing how much status meant to many of the new ethnics and that status provided for many an identity in relation to other Americans. But most immigrants and their descendants also became ethnic-Americans as a way of achieving a new identity in the U.S. They linked their Americanness to displays of old-country cultural and religious symbols, rituals, and customs, and also by making claims on the polity as ethnic-Americans. There were exceptions, of course. Not every Acadian who went to Louisiana became a Cajun. Not every Norwegian immigrant joined a Norwegian-speaking church. Not every Sicilian continued to observe the saints' days. But most did; only African-Americans, among the non-English groups, had to create their identity so heavily on the basis of their North American experience.

The appeal of Marcus Garvey, who created the only mass movement among American blacks prior to the civil rights movement, was the promise to blacks that they could claim their own identity. As the African-American sociologist Horace R. Cayton pointed out, "the Garveyites were going to have Black Cross nurses rather than White Cross or Red Cross nurses, a Black House rather than a White House, a Black Star steamship line rather than a White Star line," fulfilling the hunger in the hearts of black Americans to tear off the identity of "Negro" and "nigger" that had been imposed on them and to establish their own identity.[33] Cayton wrote that there was something "ludicrous" about it, but acknowledged that blacks should call themselves by whatever name *they* and not others chose.

The Black Debate Over What to Call Themselves

The debate among African-Americans as to what they should call themselves had been going on for over a hundred years. The term "Negro" was often used, as in the National Negro Convention movement in the 1830s and 1840s, which attacked the idea of colonization and asserted the rights of blacks as Americans. Some black nationalists who helped establish the American Colonization Society to promote migration to Africa also created the African Civilization Society, which had as its objective the building up of the civilization of Africa and of the descendants of African ancestors in any portion of the globe. Just before the Civil War, several blacks began to use the term "Anglo-African" as a way to signify their link to the history and culture of Europe and of Africa.[34]

More common was the term "Afro-American." But toward the end of the nineteenth century, the National Federation of Afro-American Women changed its name to the National Association of Colored Women. The hyphenated name was too cumbersome, argued some of the women. Others may not have liked the name "Afro-American" because of the picture commonly held by Americans of Africans as savages. One woman objected to the change, saying she was as much entitled to the name "Afro-American" as the French are to "Franco-American" or the English to "Anglo-American."[35] More than one hundred years later, Martin Luther King, Jr., resurrected the term. "The American Negro," he wrote, "is neither totally African nor totally western. He is Afro-American, a true hybrid combination of two cultures."[36]

The term "Afro-American" had fallen into disuse by the early part of the twentieth century. "Negro" and "colored" were the terms that were used almost universally, except for the derogatory "nigger." The founders of the NAACP appear to have had no major problem with the term "colored." Garvey called his organization The United Negro Improvement Association. To W. E. B. Du Bois, what blacks were called was a nonissue. A high school sophomore, Roland A. Barton, wrote him with the hope "by the time I become a man, that this word, 'Negro,' will be abolished." He thought "Negro" or "nigger" was "a white man's word to make us feel inferior." Du Bois wrote back, "The feeling of inferiority is in you, not in any name. . . . A Negro by any other name would be just as black and just as white . . . it is not the Name—it's the Thing that counts. Come on, kid, let's go get the Thing!"[37] Etymologically and phonetically, Du Bois wrote, "Negro" is much better and more logical than "'African' or 'colored' or any of the various hyphenated circumlocutions."[38] But young Barton sensed something that Malcolm X and others would emphasize in the mid-1960s.

Malcolm, who used the terms "Negro" and "black" (and sometimes Afro-American) interchangeably until his death in February 1965, chose his own name twice.[39] As minister of the Nation of Islam in the last year of his life, he chose the name El-Hajj Malik El-Shabazz and founded the Organization of Afro-American Unity. By joining the Nation of Islam, he rejected the white man's religion, too. Members of the Nation of Islam rejected integration as a trick used by whites and misinformed blacks. The white man was the enemy. If one recognized the enemy, it would be possible to disentangle one's identity from the image imposed by him. "Know thyself and be yourself," said Malcolm, contributing that psychological truth to the religion of Islam.[40] In his autobiography, Malcolm maintained, "*no one* will know *who* we are until *we* know who we are!"[41]

By preaching equal rights through racial integration, King sought the only realistic political goal for black Americans. By urging blacks to confront whites with an identity and name of their own choosing, Malcolm X wanted them to do essentially what immigrants had always done on the road to full participation in the American civic culture—to assert their claim as ethnic-Americans. "We don't believe in begging the white man, we believe in doing things for ourselves . . . we're not begging, we're demanding, we're fighting," said Malcolm.[42] Militant immigrant-ethnic activist leaders had done that since German-Americans demanded that their children be taught in German in public schools and Irish-Americans fought against Protestant influence in New York's common schools. By 1970, only a few years after Malcolm's death, the term "black" had virtually replaced "Negro" in the press, television, and even in scholarly books.[43]

Malcolm found his principal audience in the urban ghettoes of the North and among blacks in high schools, colleges, and universities. An outstanding basketball player in New York City named Ferdinand Lewis Alcindor, Jr., learned about a grandfather who migrated from Trinidad to New York and who was supposed to have spoken Yoruba, a Nigerian language. While a basketball star at UCLA in 1966, he read *The Autobiography of Malcolm X*, one year after Malcolm's death. Hurt and confused by prejudice, he wrote that "Malcolm X became my star to follow, and I've followed that star ever since."[44] Lew Alcindor, who described his growing preoccupation with black pride and power, became a Muslim and one of the all-time stars of the National Basketball League as Kareem Abdul Jabbar.

Thousands of other black Americans, often the first in their families to go to college, also were reading Malcolm X in the late 1960s, as they tried to resolve confusion about their identity. It was at the elite colleges particularly that young black men and women insisted on being called "black," and where dashikis and cornrow hairdos became proud affirmations of an ethnic identity. At Brandeis University, Professor Pauli Murray, a longtime black activist in the civil rights movement, a lawyer and poet and highly regarded teacher, looked at her new young black charges, a large proportion of whom were badly prepared for the demands of her course, and wondered why they insisted on being called black. Like Du Bois, Murray was comfortable with the term "Negro." She had been born in an era when "colored" and the lower-case "negro" were commonly used. "Negro" with a small "n" meant to her the status of a thing and not a person, and she had fought all of her adult life to get newspapers, magazines, and publishers to use the word in its capitalized form.[45] She did not like the term "black," partly because it was usually printed in lower case but also because it was allied with the ideology of separatism. The word seemed to polarize relations between blacks and whites, something she had always fought against.

When in 1968 black students took over the building in which her office was located and renamed it "Malcolm X University," she was outraged. A student told her half jokingly that they just might burn down her office. She sympathized with the black mother who came to get her son, pounded on the doors, and shouted, "Come out! I've sweated to get you to college, and I don't believe in this black power business!"[46] Murray worried that the students may have acted out of deep frustration over being unable to compete with better-prepared whites at a university with tough standards. She saw in their self-imposed segregation "a symptom of a deep-seated fear of failure in an open, competitive society, a drawing back from the stringent demands of equality at a high academic level, a self-deception that would lead ultimately to isolation and abandonment to the mediocrity of a second class citizenship which was now partially self-induced."[47]

Years after the takeover of the building at Brandeis and after she had become the first black female Episcopalian priest in the U.S., Pauli Murray reflected on the struggle of her black students to overcome their sense of powerlessness through a militant and somewhat superficial set of demands, and she concluded that "notwithstanding excesses that were destined to fail, the more enduring result of the black consciousness movement was the transformation of a people robbed of a prideful past." In the movement for black power that had outraged her at the time, she saw the attempt to retrieve a communal history. It was "the affirmation of a positive identity after centuries of denigration."[48] She still believed in integration because it promised freedom for blacks and a stronger and freer America. But "during the black student rebellion at Brandeis," she wrote, "I was too threatened to appreciate the necessary intervening stage of a newly raised ethnic consciousness."[49]

The Black Power Movement and Urban Riots

Nowhere was the sense of black powerlessness felt more keenly than in the urban ghettoes of the North. Malcolm had warned that the most dangerous and threatening black man in the United States was sealed up by northern whites in black ghettoes; and it was in the northern ghettoes that violence erupted soon after Malcolm's assassination on February 21, 1965, by followers of Elijah Muhammad, whom Malcolm had recently rejected as a spiritual leader.

The black actor Ossie Davis called Malcolm "our living black manhood! This was his meaning to his people."[50] It was to the manhood of blacks in the urban ghettoes that Malcolm spoke, especially after his death. But the stridency with which many young men of the ghetto proclaimed their manhood indicated just how shaky was their self-esteem. Black youths who called each other "man" were still called "boy" by whites and faced a bleak routine of no jobs, bad jobs, dope, numbers, and violence, contrasted with what seemed the empty promise of judicial and legislative actions and the allure of America's wealth portrayed on television. Passage of the Voting Rights Act in July meant next to nothing in the ghetto.

The blacks there did not know Hubert Humphrey, George McGovern, or other champions of civil rights legislation. They knew Mr. Charlie, Whitey, The Man, and the honkies.

The first major riot of 1965 came in Watts, a black section of Los Angeles. The Watts riot, like many of the others, began with an incident between white law enforcement officers and blacks. In an area of almost fifty square miles, buildings were looted and burned and fire trucks were stoned and shot at by snipers. National Guard troops were ordered into the area. Some rioters were killed when flushed out of looted buildings, and others were caught in exchanges of fire between police and snipers. After four days, thirty-four persons had been killed, a deputy sheriff, a policeman, a fireman, and thirty-one blacks; more than a thousand, mostly black, reported injuries. Almost four thousand local blacks were arrested, more than five hundred of them juveniles. Many retail businesses had been ravaged.

The scene in Watts was repeated in almost five dozen cities between 1964 and 1968, the worst period being the first nine months of 1967, when forty-one riots led President Johnson to appoint a National Advisory Commission on Civil Disorders, chaired by the governor of Illinois, Otto Kerner. In announcing the commission, the president spoke of "ignorance, discrimination, slums, poverty, disease," and "not enough jobs."[51] The commission found that the rioters were not just rootless, unemployed youths or radicals. According to the Kerner Commission's findings, most of those arrested actually had better employment records than non-rioters, though in Newark, where one of the worst outbreaks occurred, a larger proportion of those accused of rioting were unemployed at the time or had been unemployed the previous year than of those not accused.[52]

One twenty-four-year-old black father in Watts told an investigator from a state commission, "Man, you walk the streets all day and half the night, then you got to go home and tell your wife and kids you can't find a job. On your way home . . . some cop want to crack your skull or put you in jail for vagrancy . . . man, they can go to hell. . . . I've had it with equality and all these lies about opportunity."[53] A commission set up to investigate the causes specifically of the Watts riot found a huge gap between the aspirations and achievements of blacks. "To those who have come with high hopes and great expectations and see the success of others so close at hand, failure brings a special measure of frustration and disappointment," the commission concluded.[54] The rioters wanted jobs, and they wanted to be heard. "All we wants is that we get our story told, and get it told right! What we do last night, maybe it wasn't right. But ain't nobody come down here and listened to us before!" said a black woman in Watts.[55] "It was a revolt. Every man wants to be a man; nobody has a right to deprive them of that," said a thirty-year-old Watts tavern owner.[56] When Martin Luther King, Jr., and Bayard Rustin were told by one of the Watts rioters that blacks had won a victory, Rustin asked what he meant. The young man answered, "they finally listened to the manifesto." What was the manifesto? The man pulled out a matchbox, lit a single match, and said, "Daddy, that was our manifesto." Rustin replied, "But you haven't told me how you won." The young man countered, "We asked them to come and talk with us. They didn't come. We tried to get some war on poverty (money). It didn't come. But after our manifesto, Daddy, the mayor, the governor, you, Dr. King, everybody came."[57]

Within six months of the fires and the looting, researchers carried out eighty-eight studies of Watts. In 1968 alone, $200 million in government and private funds was allocated to Watts, up from $5 million in 1965. More than three hundred organizations, including many small community-based groups, engaged in a war on poverty and racial tension.[58] It would become clear that the problems were deeper and more complex than optimistic urban planners and antipoverty fighters believed. But to be listened to was to have some slight measure of power. By 1967, the term "black power" had become commonplace, frequently replacing the civil rights movement's "We Shall Overcome" as the rallying cry of black protesters. It was first prominently used by Stokely Carmichael, then chairman of the Student Nonviolent Coordinating Committee during a civil rights march protesting the shooting of James Meredith. But after Watts and the riots of 1967, it was heard often.

Linked to the slogan of black power was the movement for black pride. Malcolm X was dead, assassinated, but his message of pride was being preached by young black militants. "Say it loud—I'm black and I'm proud," sang the popular James Brown. "It's time to stop being ashamed of being black," said Carmichael.[59] Jesse Jackson, one of the new young black leaders, went into the Chicago schools in the early 1970s and, in the call-and-response familiar to black churchgoers, asked the students to repeat after him: "I may have lost hope . . . but I am . . . somebody . . . I am . . . black . . . beautiful . . . proud . . . I must be respected."[60]

Speaking in Harlem as director of the Black Arts Repertory Theater, LeRoi Jones rejected those who called themselves "negroes." "Everybody knows what 'Negroes' are: straight-jacketed lazy clowns, whose only joy is carrying out the white man's will . . . you know who you are . . . if you want a world where you can all be beautiful human beings, we must throw down our differences and come together as black people."[61] The insistence of Jones's plea, "We *must* unify. We *must* have unity,"[62] exposed the underlying disunity many blacks felt. The urging of black nationalist Maulana Ron Karenga to "think black, talk black, act black, create black, buy black, vote black and live black" spoke to the same psychological yearnings addressed earlier by Malcolm X, but the rhetoric did not disguise the difficulty that separatist leaders had in articulating an effective political program.

The call for black pride and power sometimes was accompanied, as in the rhetoric of Malcolm X, by references to the African roots of black Americans. Malcolm had spoken of a cultural, psychological, and philosophical migration to Africa, a restoring of the ancestral bond, to "give us the spiritual strength and the incentive to strengthen our political and social and economic position right here in America."[63] That was a difficult journey to make.

The world contained many cultures in which large numbers of blacks lived, and the term "black culture" was not easy to define. When used by civil rights activists such as Floyd McKissick of the Congress of Racial Equality it was intended to impart to blacks a sense of their own ethnic identity based on their experience in the U.S., where most blacks had developed a culture of their own—patterns of speech, food, music, and religious expression—which was linked (not always explicitly) to their African past as Herskovits had maintained and Levine would argue later. Others made explicit use of African culture like the creation of a holiday called Kawanza in 1966 by Karenga. Kawanza, which lasts seven days from December 26 to the first of the new year, coinciding with the Christmas season, was celebrated by blacks in several cities at festivities that included African songs and chants and teaching children about African traditions.[64]

By the late 1960s, blacks were doing what ethnic groups had always done in the process of ethnic-Americanization, reconfiguring their own group identity, expressing pride in their own cultural roots, mobilizing their economic and political interests, and confronting the polity as a whole with an insistence on their rights in the name of the larger myths, symbols, and ideals of the American nation. As was true of other ethnic groups, black leaders were divided on a continuum between strong militancy and flexible, moderate approaches to coalitions with others, and it would not be clear for some years which side had won.

One effort to combine black pride and power came in the founding of the militant Black Panther Party in 1966 by two young activists, Huey P. Newton and Bobby Seale. In 1964 and 1965, Newton had spent eight months in jail as a result of an assault charge stemming from an argument over the terms "Negro" and "black." Bobby Seale had been dishonorably discharged from the Army in 1958 after going AWOL. Newton and Seale had a program and they organized a party. The first point of the Black Panthers' ten-point program issued in October 1966 summed up the essence of the marriage between black pride and black power: "We want to determine the destiny of our black community," it said. The program called for exemption of all black men from military service, release of all black men (women were omitted) held in federal, state, county, and city prisons and jails, and trials for black people conducted by black judges and juries only. It also urged the United Nations to supervise a plebiscite to allow American blacks to determine their national future.[65] To these far-reaching and impossible objectives, the Panthers linked a more practical program in black communities reminiscent of the ascetic self-discipline practiced by the Black Muslims. Party members who took narcotics were expelled. Drunkenness was prohibited. Panthers were to speak politely, pay fairly for what they purchased, return everything they borrowed, refrain from taking liberties with women.[66]

Although Black Panthers said they would not use violence, they talked constantly of the violent revolution to come, and they frequently carried weapons. In 1966, they marched in and out of the California state capitol in Sacramento in uniforms with their guns at the ready. The anger and fury of blacks was focused in the rhetoric of the Black Panthers. "Off the pig," they said. "Death to the fascist pig."

By 1970, Seale and Newton were disillusioned with the tactics of their own movement. Newton acknowledged that it had been a mistake to call the church irrelevant and that it was crazy to think the Black Panther party could overthrow even the police force, let alone the entire government.[67]

After several Panthers had been killed by police and hundreds sent to prison, the leaders adopted an approach similar to that of some immigrant-ethnic political leaders of an earlier time; they sought control of local schools and of the police and attempted to provide elemental benefits for their constituencies. They organized a free breakfast program for children, free medical clinics, and a free legal assistance program. They endorsed candidates and ran for office themselves, and in 1972 were among the many black supporters of the presidential candidacy of Representative Shirley Chisholm, a moderate West Indian–born black congresswoman from New York. Bobby Seale ran second in a contest for mayor of Oakland, and Elaine Brown, another Black Panther leader, was elected to the Oakland city council in 1973.

Martin Luther King, Jr., did not live to see the transformation of the Black Panthers. In the early months of 1968, he was dispirited by the enormous problems of poverty, bad education, poor housing, and prejudice that still faced most blacks in the nation, and was frustrated by the problems of trying to organize blacks and bring about change in urban ghettoes of the North. In April 1968, he was murdered by an assassin in

Memphis. Grief and despair overcame American blacks, and a wave of rioting erupted in Washington, D.C., Atlanta, and dozens of other cities.

The National Commission on Racial Disorders reporting in 1968 warned that the United States was headed toward becoming two societies—one black and one white. Actually, it had long been two societies, based on color. In the 1960s, some blacks had begun to make substantial progress in breaking out of the lowest categories of jobs to which they had been relegated by the system of caste; in the 1970s more blacks were graduated from college and were elected to state and city government positions than in all of preceding American history. Blacks mired in poverty in the ghettoes of the North and South found the American dream as implausible as ever. So did many poor whites, who by 1985 made up 69 percent of those who lived below the poverty line, up from 66 percent in 1979; 31 percent of these poor were blacks, but blacks as a whole were only 12 percent of the population. Problems associated with poverty, undereducation, illiteracy, disease, and early mortality were disproportionately high among blacks. The problems of the persistently black poor seemed intractable. By the 1970s, the official legal system of caste had been destroyed, and with its destruction more opportunity was open for blacks than ever before. The civic culture, in which African-Americans played an increasingly significant role, had been renewed and reinvigorated by their participation, although much of the black underclass remained strangers to the civic culture.

Chapter Ten

"WE WANT FULL PARTICIPATION"
African-Americans and Coalition Politics

IN 1953, when West Indian–born Julian E. Jack was elected president of the borough of Manhattan, he became the highest-ranking African-American elected official in the nation. In 1984, a *New York Times*/CBS survey of black registered voters showed that 72 percent believed the Democratic party would nominate a black person for president within thirty years.[1] In 1988, South Carolina–born Jesse Jackson, candidate for the Democratic nomination for president, won the second-largest number of delegates to his party's convention, essentially ending an intense twenty-year debate by blacks over two fundamentally different approaches to American politics, the first separatism, the second integration and the building of coalitions.

That debate was intense in 1967 when SNCC leader Stokely Carmichael and political scientist Charles V. Hamilton challenged the strategy of coalition politics advocated by Bayard Rustin, principal organizer of the 1967 March on Washington.[2] Arguing that interests of blacks were fundamentally different from those of liberal, labor, and other reform groups, Carmichael and Hamilton urged "the total revamping of the society."[3] Liberal whites, they insisted, were tainted by racism. A liberal white "cannot ultimately escape the overpowering influence—on himself and on black people—of his whiteness in a racist society."[4] It was self-defeating, they argued, to work with whites in running schools for black children or welfare programs for black welfare mothers. "Any federal program conceived with black people in mind is doomed if blacks do not control it."

To such leaders as Rustin, as well as Martin Luther King, Jr., the thinking of Carmichael and Hamilton was self-defeating. What good would it do to control an impoverished school district? What good would it do to stigmatize only blacks as welfare recipients when most persons on welfare were white? What harm could come from making deals with representatives of other groups to achieve urgent goals? King wrote in 1967, "It is a myth to believe that the Irish, the Italians, the Jews—the ethnic groups that Black Power advocates cite as justification for their views—rose to power through separatism. It is true that they stuck together. But their group unity was always enlarged by joining in alliances with other groups."[5]

To some extent, advocates of separatism and coalition were talking past each other. In practical terms, the Black Power strategy could only be effective in small localities where blacks constituted an overwhelming majority of voters. Otherwise, a predominantly black neighborhood could try either to secede from a city government and establish its own systems of taxation, police, and other services, or make deals with other groups within the city. The first course, insisted Rustin and other advocates of coalition, was a prescription for permanent ghettoization and disaster. Community control would be used to prevent blacks from gaining power: "Blacks will have the ghetto, with its drug addiction, soaring crime rate, high unemployment, and deplorable housing. Whites will keep the suburbs, where job opportunities are expanding, the air is unpolluted, housing is decent, and school provides superior education." Only the federal government had the resources and broad legislative power to deal with the problems of housing, medical care, and unemployment in the black communities.[6]

Many young black militants, especially in Ivy League colleges, rejected the advice of Rustin and King. The rage they felt toward whites inhibited any impulse toward cooperation. In the spring of 1969, one hundred students at Cornell University, many of them armed, seized the student union building. The leaders would hear no talk of coalition or compromise with whites. One, who later became a vice president of the John Hancock Mutual Life Insurance Company, spoke to a mass rally: "In the past, it has been the black people who have done all the dying. Now the time has come when the pigs are going to die too."[7] Another leader remembered fifteen years later, after he had become an ordained Baptist minister, that all blacks at Cornell had advocated separation. For him, the worst moment had come when they began to throw bricks at the library. He recalled in 1984 that the students had been frustrated, frightened, and pessimistic, but not without hope. "They were crying out to American society, 'We want full participation.'"[8] At Cornell, full participation had much less to do with decision-making and governance than with the struggle for identity. Victory meant courses in African-American studies, and a residence house for black women.

The power to affect the fundamental allocation of resources began at the voting booth. To Malcolm X "the polls are one place where every black man could fight the black man's cause with dignity, and with the power and the tools that the white man understands, and respects, and fears." He said once, "Why, if the Mississippi black man voted in a bloc,

Eastland [James Eastland, the segregationist Democratic senator from Mississippi] would pretend to be more liberal than Jacob Javits [the liberal Republican senator from New York]—or Eastland would not survive in his office."[9]

By 1982, Eastland was dead. But in 1970, George C. Wallace of Alabama, once a national symbol of resistance to civil rights (he won ten million votes running for president in 1968, campaigning against the Civil Rights Act), was chosen as governor of Alabama with the overwhelming support of black voters. In his inaugural speech of 1971, Wallace said, "Alabama belongs to all of us—black and white, young and old, rich and poor alike."[10] By 1982, Alabama had the highest percentage of elected African-American officials in the South and blacks held 24.5 percent of all civil service jobs in the state (compared to 2 percent in 1970). In 1983 as governor, Wallace repaid African-American voters for their support with appointments to state office and with pressure to name blacks to key committees. To make it easier for blacks to register and vote, he endorsed a plan to more than double the number of black voting registrars in Alabama's counties. The once defiant segregationist had succumbed to black power at the ballot box.[11]

In 1986, the black vote was critical to the election of four southern Democratic senators and enlarged the margin of victory of Democratic senatorial candidates in several other states.[12] In three southern states, senators won with a minority of white support and about 90 percent of the black vote. On a key vote in the Senate, one southern senator told Senator Richard C. Shelby of Alabama, a freshman conservative Democrat who had voted in the House against extending the Voting Rights Act and establishing Martin Luther King, Jr.'s birthday as a national holiday, that he would have to vote on the liberal side "because you're not going to turn your back on ninety-one percent of the black voters in Alabama who got you here."[13] With rare exceptions, the sixteen Democratic senators from the South were there because of solid support of black voters.[14]

Black Elected Officials and Coalition Politics

Blacks once in office discovered (what most of them already knew) that power could not be translated into programs without building coalitions, whether they had been elected to statewide or congressional office or to the mayoralty of heavily black cities. The numbers of elected African-Americans more than quadrupled from 1,469 to 6,424 between 1970 and 1986.[15]

Many black politicians of the 1960s, 1970s, and 1980s began their careers with a narrow ethnic agenda and rapidly expanded their concerns. An early example was Leroy Johnson, a black southern politician who as a teacher in Atlanta schools in 1954, was asked by the Negro Voters' League to conduct clinics on the use of voting machines. In 1957, Atlanta's liberal white mayor, William B. Hartsfield, appointed Johnson (with a newly minted law degree) to the staff of the Fulton County (Atlanta) prosecutor; he was the first African-American in the Southeast to hold such a position. When the U.S. Supreme Court declared Georgia's notorious county unit system unconstitutional in 1962, Johnson took one of the newly created seats to represent a district with 70,000 blacks (of a total population of 90,000), the first black elected to the Georgia assembly in ninety-two years and the first elected to a southern legislature since Reconstruction. Johnson quickly became a consummate coalition politician, helping whites and blacks obtain zoning changes, liquor licenses, and jobs. In 1971, after five terms in office, during which Johnson cultivated white members of the state senate and white judges, his substantial organization helped elect a white liberal, Sam Masell, mayor of Atlanta. Johnson was now in a position to win appointments and other benefits for blacks.[16]

Gordon Lindsay, who grew up in the cotton fields of Mississippi and later worked as a janitor in Los Angeles, was elected the first black on the city council of Los Angeles (not long after, Los Angeles had a black mayor and three black councilmen). In a heavily black district (about 50 percent) that had few street lights, few parks, and virtually no street cleaning, Lindsay, like Polish, Irish, and Italian political leaders of earlier times, made sure that proper street lights were installed ("I learned how to get a street-lighting assessment district") and streets repaired and swept every week ("I learned that gas tax money was available for that purpose"). Lindsay often made as many as ten appearances in his district every weekend. "After all, these people put me here—and they keep me here. It's my job to take care of their needs and see that their interests are represented." Lindsay insisted, "I'm not a *black* Councilman . . . we don't operate on the Council as blacks. I don't have any more dealings with the black Councilmen than I do with the others."[17]

There was no more effective practitioner of coalition politics in California in the 1970s and 1980s than Willie L. Brown, Jr., a black Democrat who became speaker of the California assembly, the second-most-important elected position in the state. First elected to the legislature in 1965, Brown was chosen speaker with the help of Republicans, to whom he promised committee appointments and staff. By 1981, Brown argued that the politics of race was over and that black and white politicians should back away from such controversial issues as busing. "Winning is absolutely everything in politics," he said. "We have no impact on policies, you can deliver nothing, unless you can produce a win." Like many other ethnic-group leaders in American history, Brown had started as a militant advocate of ethnic causes, gained power, and learned that winning office was only the first step to real power; one had to bargain and negotiate with representatives of other constituencies. The big cities, the states, the nation, were too diverse to permit monoethnic-group advocates to succeed in electoral politics. Lindsay and Brown each had his own style. Lindsay was a down-home, transplanted poor boy from the South with a just-plain-folks manner. Brown was a fast-talking San Francisco lawyer, a young black urban professional with a flair for rap. Both struck chords of memory and sensibility with their black constituents.[18]

In Mississippi, a state with virtually no tradition of white liberalism on racial questions, by 1980 many small towns in the northwest delta area had governments led by the same blacks who were once refused the right to vote. Charles Evers, in his third term as the first African-American mayor of Fayette, remembered segregationist Senator Theodore G. Bilbo pointing his finger at Evers (then a small boy) and his brother Medgar while talking to his constituents. "If you white folks don't wake up," he said, according to Evers, "these two little niggers right here are going to be representing you in the legislature some day." By 1980, the Mississippi legislature had the second-largest number (seventeen) of blacks in the nation (Georgia with twenty-three was first). Among the black freshman legislators was pharmacist Aaron Henry, a hero of the civil rights movement, who once had been force-fed laxatives in a solitary confinement cell that had no toilet. Another was Fred Banks, a civil rights lawyer once called a "chimpanzee" by a white judge because he protested a courtroom mural that depicted blacks as cotton-chopping slaves. A third was Henry J. Kirksey, who had filed a suit under the Voting Rights Act to force reapportionment fourteen years earlier; a federal court order resulted, requiring single-member legislative districts to overcome the old gerrymandered system which submerged heavily black precincts in larger white precincts to keep blacks from election.[19]

Black politicians running statewide or in large cities had to win white votes to be elected. In 1984, Judge Robert Benham of the Georgia Court of Appeals became the first post-Reconstructionist African-American elected to state office in Georgia.[20] The next year L. Douglas Wilder, elected lieutenant governor of Virginia, became the first to win a major statewide office in the Old Commonwealth since Reconstruction, winning 46 percent of white votes.[21] There were still only five blacks holding statewide elected offices in the U.S.: secretary of state in Michigan, state treasurer in Connecticut, and Roland W. Burris, state comptroller in Illinois, also chosen in 1985 as vice chairman of the national democratic party. Burris, elected repeatedly with substantial white support, urged black politicians to understand that they would enhance the power of blacks by building coalitions.[22]

For black mayors of large cities where the African-American population was relatively small, including Los Angeles, where only 17 percent were black in 1986,[23] such advice was unnecessary. Even mayors of predominantly black cities learned that blacks needed the cooperation of whites in their cities, in the state capitals, and in Washington. On June 16, 1970, Newark became the fourth major American city to elect an African-American as its mayor. Kenneth A. Gibson, a thirty-eight-year-old civil engineer, said on election night: "Robert Treat, the man who founded Newark 300 years ago, never realized that someday Newark would have *soul* . . . this will be an administration of all the people—black, white, Puerto Rican, and all colors."[24] Among the many problems Gibson faced in a city approximately 61 percent black and 11 percent Puerto Rican was an unemployment rate of 14 percent, the highest crime rate of any city, the highest percentage of substandard housing, the highest rates of venereal disease, and an empty treasury.[25] Separatist politics was not an option. Community control by itself had little meaning. Although he was under pressure to name a black police commissioner, Gibson appointed as chief a white man who had been in the department since 1947 and had done an excellent job leading a special gambling squad. Black militants on the city council were furious with Gibson's choice, but Gibson, like other effective big city mayors, threatened and cajoled his opponents until he prevailed.[26]

Gibson served as mayor until 1985, when he lost an attempt to become governor of New Jersey. That year, twenty-eight blacks were serving as mayors of cities with populations above fifty thousand; the best known, Chicago's Harold Washington, was elected in 1983 in a city with a 40 percent black population. Washington, realizing he needed white votes, went to Polish communities to remind them of his support for Solidarity Day and to Jewish neighborhoods to speak about his support of Israel. In Asian communities, "I told them my purpose is to help them preserve their culture in a city where all cultures must be respected."[27] He told the multiethnic audience it was wrong to stereotype: "as a black person I assure you that we resent it. I am certain that other ethnic groups resent it too." He pointed out that "to live peacefully in a multi-ethnic society, one must give and take." The job of a modern executive, he said, was "to bring diverse people together around issues of common concern." Respect for different ethnic cultures was necessary "so long as that culture conforms to the common good as expressed in our own sovereign laws."[28] Washington won about 17 or 18 percent of the white vote (almost 40 percent of the votes of whites who called themselves liberal). The city had been so torn apart by race for so long over explosive issues of housing, schooling, crime, and power at City Hall that Washington found it virtually impossible to organize the city council, whose members took sides almost entirely on the basis of race.[29]

In the 1987 campaign, Washington found that his early cultivation of whites resulted in increased support. One Polish-American publication endorsed the mayor, and a Greek-American reelection committee was formed to support him. The vestiges of the Irish-American machine that had controlled Chicago politics for so long resisted him, but Asian-American newcomers raised more than $100,000 to support his campaign, and Hispanics and liberal whites volunteered to canvass, stuff envelopes, and make phone calls. The racial polarization of the 1983 campaign was not repeated. In every city where blacks were elected as mayors, from Birmingham and Atlanta to Newark and Chicago, African-American politicians built coalitions with whites. Mayor Tom Bradley in Los Angeles was reelected repeatedly against white candidates by winning more than 40 percent of the white votes. And David N. Dinkins became the first black mayor of New York in 1989 against a strong white candidate by winning 30 percent of the white votes.

Like the Germans, Irish, and other ethnic politicians before them, African-American elected officials moved from the ethnic base that propelled them into leadership toward coalition politics as they assumed wider responsibilities. Shirley Chisholm, who won an upset victory in a New York City congressional district 92 percent black and Puerto Rican, found that on congressional committees where she usually was the only black there was no alternative to working with whites. Chisholm, who in 1972 became the first black woman from a major party to campaign for a presidential nomination, answered Black Power critics in an autobiography: "I'm fighting within the system. There is no other place to fight . . . at least I can shake up powerful people." A self-proclaimed "militant," Chisholm worked to apply pressure to the federal machinery. An advocate of coalition politics, she insisted "that black Americans can no longer look upon our struggle for full participation within . . . American society as one that is isolated."[30]

By 1988, there were twenty-three members of the congressional Black Caucus, five of whom headed key committees of the House of Representatives.[31] Representative William Gray (D-Pennsylvania) managed in 1983 to gain an amendment to the annual appropriations bill of the Agency for International Development to channel at least 10 percent of its development assistance fund to support international efforts to minority businesses, historically black colleges and universities, and minority-controlled volunteer organizations.[32] As chairman of the Budget Committee of the House, Gray was in a good position to negotiate favors, but he knew that his power rested on his ability to transcend racial politics: "There is no title here called 'Black America Budget Chairman.' There is no title here called 'Black Caucus Budget Chairman.'" It's called 'House Budget Committee Chairman.' I happen to be black."[33]

Not one of the twenty-three blacks elected to Congress in 1986 emphasized race in their campaigns. John Lewis had organized the Mississippi Freedom Summer in 1964 and, at twenty-five, had helped to lead the march from Selma to Montgomery after being beaten severely by Alabama state troopers. Although he had been arrested forty times, Lewis disagreed with the separatist militancy of the late 1960s and was ousted as leader of the Student Nonviolent Coordinating Committee. In 1986, he defeated the popular African-American State Senator Julian Bond, another supporter of coalition, in a runoff primary for the Democratic nomination in Georgia's fifth district; he won 80 percent of the white vote in the runoff, and 47 percent of the white vote in the general election, beating his Republican opponent.[34]

Jesse Jackson's Two Rainbows

Another leader of the civil rights revolution, Jesse Jackson, often flirted with separatist politics. One of a dozen lieutenants of Martin Luther King, Jr., at the time of his death, Jackson had grown up in Greenville, South Carolina, where he watched the police round up unemployed blacks, jail them for vagrancy, then, after putting them in ankle chains, send them to clean the gutters. When Jackson began to think of running for president in the early 1980s, black separatist rhetoric was still in vogue, and there were renewed calls for a black political party. Malcolm X's Organization of African Unity had fallen apart after his assassination, and because Jesse Jackson had advocated a national black party in the early 1970s, he was a potential leader of a separatist movement. But when one thousand blacks from twenty-five states attended a convention in Philadelphia in November 1980 to establish the National Black Independent Political Party, Jackson was not there.[35] Nor did he participate in a black convention in Brooklyn that year, when more than one thousand delegates from thirty-four states formed the National Black United Front.[36] Their objective was to supplant black elected officials and the leaders of mainline black organizations, criticized by one delegate as having "sold out to whites and who function to keep community leaders from developing."[37]

Both separatist organizations died quickly. Jackson chose the route of coalition politics, but though his 1984 presidential campaign rhetoric spoke of a "Rainbow Coalition," he rarely reached out to white voters. Instead, he welcomed the highly visible support of the most militant Black Muslim, the openly anti-Semitic Reverend Louis Farrakhan, who provided Jackson with personal bodyguards during the early stages of his campaign. Jackson appeared publicly with his arms around Farrakhan, even though Farrakhan often had said that "white people are devils." Only after tremendous pressure was mounted in the press following an offhand remark by Jackson taken as anti-Semitic by many non-Jews as well as Jews did he cut loose from Farrakhan's explicit support in the campaign (without repudiating his friendship).

Jackson himself never used anything like the rhetoric of Farrakhan or other black racists, and on occasions in the 1984 campaign he tried to transcend narrow racial politics. In many of his 1984 speeches to multi-ethnic audiences, he spoke of 23,000,000 whites in poverty as well as of the 11,000,000 poor who were black and brown: "When a baby cries at midnight because it has no supper, that baby doesn't cry in black or white or brown or male or female. That baby cries in *pain*."[38]

No matter how often Jackson repeated the theme of the Rainbow Coalition, "brown, black and white, we're all precious in God's sight!" many experienced black politicians and most black primary voters evidently believed that the route to black power was through the coalition of liberal, labor and other political groups which was represented by the candidacy of former Vice President Walter Mondale. They were opposed to a candidate whose assertion that all persons are precious to God was tainted by his association with the hate-filled Farrakhan.

Although three-quarters of the African-Americans who voted in the Democratic presidential primaries voted for Jackson, a national public opinion poll showed that black Democrats preferred Vice President Walter Mondale over Jackson as the party's nominee by a margin of five to three.[39] A majority of the congressional Black Caucus said they understood the negative reaction of Jews and other whites to Jackson's rhetoric and toleration of Farrakhan, and the black mayors of many cities, including Atlanta, Los Angeles, Detroit, and Birmingham, supported Mondale.[40]

By 1988, Jackson used the term "Rainbow" much less frequently but consistently demonstrated that he meant to include many shades of white as well as brown and black. More elected black Democratic leaders supported him in the primaries than four years before. Determined to run a mainstream campaign, he spoke to white and black groups throughout the country in 1986, emphasizing his new approach to coalition politics. To the National Rainbow Coalition, at its first national convention in Washington, D.C., in April 1986, including hundreds of whites, Jackson spoke of "a new coalition," including farmers, union labor members, teachers, and others. Throughout the campaign he also emphasized the tremendous strides he thought had been made in race relations since the civil rights revolution.[41]

The new Jackson approach to coalition brought him a substantial increase in support among whites and blacks. A Joint Center for Political

Studies/Gallup National Survey in 1986 showed Jackson as the first choice for president of 48 percent of black respondents and 1 percent of white. By the fall of 1987, a new survey showed that he was the choice of 67 percent of the blacks, 9 percent of whites. In many of the 1988 primaries and caucuses, in a field that included a half dozen white candidates, he won more white votes than black.[42] On March 8, 1988, when twelve southern states held primaries, Jackson tripled his white backing, winning 10 percent of the white vote across the South and in some states receiving more white votes than major white candidates.[43] "I understand the need, given how broad our party is, to find common ground," he said. That ground, he said, was the "point where the maximum number of interests merge and form a coalition that can equal victory."[44] When a reporter asked a Polish boilermaker in Milwaukee whether he could be comfortable voting for a black man, he responded, "What difference is it, a Greek [Dukakis] or a colored guy?"[45] Black mayors of major cities who had opposed Jackson in 1984 saw new realism in his candidacy. Coleman Young of Detroit, who supported Dukakis in 1988 (and Mondale in 1984), acknowledged that Jackson was more than just a symbolic candidate precisely because he reached out to win support from white voters.[46]

Jackson quickly agreed to the recommendation of the Democratic National Committee to abide by its rules for choosing delegates and not to seek the nomination by running against the party itself should he fail to win its endorsement. He reached out not just to farmers and other disaffected economic groups, but also to Jews, granting interviews to a number of Jewish publications and speaking in conciliatory terms to Jewish audiences. Louis Farrakhan was nowhere to be seen in his campaign, and Jackson repeatedly emphasized that the major national issue was no longer racism but poverty, unemployment, and ill health; these conditions affected more white voters than blacks.[47]

The Surge of Black Political Participation

An important result of Jackson's candidacies was the tremendous growth in the participation of African-Americans in politics in the 1980s. Mainly because of Jackson, the turnout in black precincts more than doubled in the New York State 1984 primary over 1980, and in all other states for which data was reported, it increased by between 14 and 87 percent. The New York Times estimated that 3.05 million blacks voted in the Democratic primaries, 18 percent of the 16.94 million Democratic voters.[48] A national survey in fall 1984 found that 62 percent of the blacks, compared to 44 percent of the whites, said their interest in politics had increased over 1980. More blacks than whites said they helped to register voters

(30 percent against 9 percent), attended rallies (30 percent against 17 percent), and distributed campaign literature (17 percent against 8 percent).[49]

In 1968, the national black voter registration rate had been 9.2 percentage points below that of whites and the turnout 11.5 percent less than for whites. But in 1984, the year of Jackson's first run for the presidency, black registration was only 3 points below that of whites and black voter turnout only 5.6 points less than whites'. Given the high correlation between low voter turnout and problems associated with poverty, such as illness, lack of day care for children, and a low sense of political efficacy, the narrowing of the gap was extraordinary and probably could be attributed mainly to the visibility of black mayors and congressmen and especially of Jackson, who provided leadership for numerous voter registration drives. In 1984, the average rates of increase in registration and voting turnout of African-Americans were more than three times greater than corresponding rates for whites, and by 1986, for the first time, the percentage of young blacks who voted moved ahead of the percentage of young whites.[50] But the major significance of Jackson's candidacy was not his ability to mobilize black votes, but that he was able to win many white votes. The favorable reception by so many whites signified the vast distance that Americans had traveled in race relations in just a quarter of a century. Considering that Jackson had never been elected or appointed to any office and that his views on a number of issues tended to be more radical than most Americans', his success was all the more remarkable.

Perhaps as important was the growing number of African-Americans serving as administrators and judges in city, state, and federal government. When in 1987 a forty-one-year-old black man who had begun his life working by pumping gas at his grandfather's service station in rural middle Georgia was appointed city manager of Dallas, that choice symbolized as much as anything could the transformation of politics in cities long dominated by conservative white businessmen. Richard Knight, Jr., who had been an administrator in three southern cities before coming to Dallas, knew that efficient city management was neither black nor white.[51] By 1986, blacks filled 824 local judgeships, up from 58 in 1961 and 214 in 1970. Probably there was no greater symbolism of the triumph of the civic culture than the visibility of African-American judges, one of whom, former NAACP chief counsel Thurgood Marshall, had been appointed in 1967 to the U.S. Supreme Court by President Lyndon B. Johnson after service as U.S. solicitor general. Only thirty years earlier, Franklin D. Roosevelt had appointed William H. Hastie, of the Virgin Islands, the first black federal district court judge in U.S. history. By 1986, eleven blacks were serving on the U.S. Court of Appeals and forty-one as U.S. district court judges.[52]

There was no shortage of symbols in this large-scale entry of African-Americans into government and politics. When Jesse Jackson chose a headquarters for his Iowa campaign office in the primary of 1988, he picked the small (2,500) town of Greenfield, an all-white community that in the 1920s had been a center of Klan activities. When the city officials of Montgomery, Alabama, had to pick a name for an avenue in that state capital in 1987, they called it Rosa L. Parks Avenue, after the black woman arrested in 1955 for daring to sit toward the middle of a bus. When reporters interviewed George Wallace that year about his defiant stand against integrating the schools, he urged them to put that question behind them. "Let's talk about my honorary degree from Tuskegee Institute," he said.[53]

Symbolism did not bring jobs, better health, or more police protection to black communities. Nor did efforts at coalition-building by leaders always translate into effective cooperation at the grass roots. In the New York state legislature, black and Puerto Rican caucuses frequently worked together, but at the local level there were many obstacles to Hispanic-black cooperation. Exit polls of primary and caucus voters in the 1984 election showed that Jackson won only 22 percent of the Hispanic vote in New York, 18 percent in California, and 7 percent in Texas.[54] As racial tension built in neighborhoods over issues of housing and education, for example, in New York City and Boston, it became particularly difficult to build effective coalitions. In New York City, few African-Americans were elected or appointed as high officials, and it was little comfort to black politicians in New York that in 1986 a black man, Alan Wheat, was elected to Congress as a Democrat in Kansas City, Missouri, from a district that was 70 percent white.[55] But in 1989 New York's choice of David Dinkins as mayor signified a strong breakthrough in interracial coalition politics.

Politics was more fluid in places like Kansas City than in the cities of the East and Midwest, where white ethnic groups defended their power as long as possible, resenting and holding off the newest groups. That had been the way in ethnic politics ever since the late nineteenth century. Although the Irish made up a majority of Boston voters by the 1860s, it took twenty-five years to elect an Irish mayor, and in Cincinnati it took at least thirty years to elect a German mayor. One study of ten cities in California showed that the incorporation of blacks into the power structure of those cities was achieved only when African-American and white leaders formed a liberal electoral alliance soon after the large-scale entry of blacks into politics.[56]

Boston, with its century-long tradition of working-class bigotry against blacks as competitors for jobs and housing, was even more inhospitable to coalition-building than New York. Yet, even in Boston, where white resistance to busing and integrated housing was probably as high as in any northern city in the 1970s, black voters repudiated a 1986 referendum asking if they wanted to establish a municipal government made up of minority neighborhoods. The new municipality, Mandela, named after the then imprisoned South African leader of the African National Congress, would have been 90 percent minority (overwhelmingly black) on 25 percent of the city's existing land area. Black leaders were sharply divided in a bitter campaign, but the voters rejected the proposal by three to one. Such a city already existed in East St. Louis, Illinois, where the population of 55,000 was more than 95 percent black in 1986 and where the problems of malnourishment, bad education, and poor housing had not diminished. It also existed in the smaller municipality of Mound Bayou, an all-black town founded by former slaves in 1887 on land that once belonged to Jefferson Davis. Although the town of 3,000 kept getting federal money and foundation support in the 1970s, Mound Bayou went bankrupt in 1981.[57]

By voting against separatism, the black voters of Boston were to some extent expressing confidence in the white mayor, Ray Flynn, who had opposed the effort to create Mandela and who won increasing acceptance among blacks for his strong actions against racial violence. Under his administration, the number of racial incidents dropped sharply, the Boston business community took several measures toward aiding minorities, the School Committee hired a black man to head the school system, and a Boston job residency requirement was adopted mandating that at least 25 percent of the workers on any construction project that used city funds be black, Hispanic, or Asian (38 percent of the city's residents were minorities, 25 percent black). At City Hall, 40 percent of the new personnel hired by Flynn in the months following his election were members of minority groups. Several blacks were elected to the state legislature in the 1980s and two served on the city council, one of whom was the first African-American president of that body in the history of Boston.[58]

The End of Black Separatism as a Political Movement

In 1966, one year after passage of the Voting Rights Act, one of the country's leading white historians of slavery, Eugene D. Genovese, had written that the best hope for blacks to overcome the effects of decades of repression would be in "the rise of specifically black cities, counties and districts, with high-quality black schools, well paid teachers, . . . political leaders, churches and community centers." By seeking local and regional autonomy, blacks would be able to "uproot the slave tradition once and for all," and "act as a powerful lever for structural reform of the American economy and society."[59] Genovese urged black separatism as a strategy to transform the American capitalist system into one that would bring socialist justice. Many others took that position in 1966 before the Voting Rights Act had a chance to work. Twenty years later, the vision that black separatism would lead to black power was rarely advanced and had virtually no support among blacks running for office. But Harold Cruse, one of the nation's leading black intellectuals, continued to call for a black political party, in 1987. Arguing that economic self-sufficiency should be the primary goal for blacks, Cruse advocated a new racial pluralism in the U.S. based on the discredited doctrine of separate but equal.[60]

The ideal of a separate black nation or black state or city had never been appealing to large numbers of blacks. Even at the height of black militancy, only 5 percent of a sample of black respondents interviewed in a study for the Kerner Commission said there should be a separate black nation in the U.S.[61] The vast majority of African-Americans preferred inclusion in the American civic culture, with its emphasis on voluntary pluralism. Poverty kept hundreds of thousands of blacks (and whites, too) from effective participation in the American civic culture, but within the framework of voluntary pluralism, a number of African-Americans were able to start businesses, banks, community development corporations, after-school classes in African-American heritage and history, and to otherwise be ethnic-American. It was possible to have African-American churches, soul food restaurants, and poetry and song emanating from the unique experience of African-Americans. It was also possible to have black politicians who, expressing the sensibilities and claims of other blacks, practiced coalition politics in their behalf and, by so doing, enlarged the scope not just of their own political interests but of many of those with whom they negotiated and bargained. Whatever one called the process—cooptation, inclusion, integration, acculturation (and it was all of those things)—the end result was a stronger nation.

Electoral success for African-Americans remained elusive in many jurisdictions. Few blacks were elected in some southern counties, even though a majority of the population was black. Power remained largely in the hands of middle-class, conservative whites in many places where blacks were numerous in the 1980s.[62] But in 1989, there were significant breakthroughs for coalition-building African-American politicians in predominantly white districts. In addition to the election of David Dinkins as mayor of New York (where blacks made up only 25 percent of the electorate), African-Americans were elected mayor in Seattle (10 percent black) and New Haven (35 percent black). In New Haven, John Daniels won 69 percent of the vote, including Irish, Jewish, Yankee, and some

Italian voters. In Seattle, Norman Rice, a three-term city councilman, won 58 percent of the vote, defeating an opponent who built his campaign on a ballot measure to end busing for school integration.

The most important election in 1989 took place in Virginia, the heart of the old Confederacy and of massive resistance to desegregation in the 1960s, where Lieutenant Governor L. Douglas Wilder, whose grandparents had been born into slavery, succeeded to the governorship in a state where fewer than one of six voters was black. Wilder, who became the first elected black governor in U.S. history, had begun his career as an ethnic politician, an exponent of the politics of protest. As a state senator in the 1970s, he championed civil rights and other issues of particular importance to blacks. Seeking statewide office in the 1980s, he was obliged to cultivate the support of white voters by broadening his positions on the issues. "I believe in coalition politics," he declared when he announced his candidacy for lieutenant governor in 1984. Five years later, in winning the governorship, he succeeded where few would have thought it possible.

Daniels, Rice, Dinkins, and Wilder not only illustrated the importance of coalition-building, they also became examples of Tocqueville's maxim that participation in American politics encouraged patriotic feeling. Dinkins called his victory "another milestone on freedom's road" and "a victory not just for African-Americans but for . . . all Americans." Wilder, who won with 40 percent of the white vote, exclaimed in his victory speech, "As a boy, when I would read about an Abraham Lincoln or a Thomas Jefferson or about a George Mason, when I would read that all men are created equal and that they are endowed by their creator with certain inalienable rights . . . I knew it meant me." Eleanor Holmes Norton, the former chairman of the Equal Opportunity Employment Commission, called the 1989 election of black candidates in predominantly white districts "a new chapter in American democracy."[63]

The call for racial pluralism by Harold Cruse was not taken up by any of the blacks running for high political office in the U.S., even by congressmen from overwhelmingly black districts who had learned how to master the system. One of them, Representative Louis Stokes (D-Ohio), a veteran of nineteen years in Congress, serving as chairman of the extremely sensitive Permanent Select Committee on Intelligence of the House of Representatives, was a member of the select committee to investigate the covert arms transactions with Iran. Stokes told Colonel Oliver North about his own mother, a woman with an eighth-grade education who had been a domestic worker but who raised one son to become the first black mayor of a major American city (Carl Stokes, Cleveland) and the other to become a congressman. "Only in America, Colonel North, only in America," exclaimed Louis Stokes extolling the American dream before a TV audience. "If any class of Americans understand and appreciate the rule of law, the judicial process, and Constitutional law, it is those who have had to use that process to come from a status of nonpersons in American law to a status of equality under the law." Stokes, who had fought in the Second World War in a segregated Army, reminded North that the rule of law that holds the nation together would not tolerate government officials who lied to and deceived the American public with patriotism as their defense.[64]

Chapter Eleven

"WE HAVE TO BE PART OF THE POLITICAL SYSTEM"
Redefining Tribal Pluralism

"THE civil rights movement taught us not to be afraid," said John
Echo Hawk, great-grandson of a Pawnee warrior, in 1986.[1] Indians
had a tradition of resistance to whites from the seventeenth century through the nineteenth, but in the late 1940s and 1950s, Indians were
generally dispirited. Although the Indian Reorganization Act of 1934 had
signaled recognition by Congress of the failure of assimilationist policies,
John Collier resigned as Commissioner of the Bureau of Indian Affairs
in frustration in 1945 because such policies were gaining favor again in
Congress.

The new assimilationism called for termination by the federal government of tribal status of several tribes; transfer of federal responsibility
and jurisdiction over Indians to state governments; and physical relocation from reservations to urban areas. At the heart of the policy were two
powerful forces as old as the republic: greed and ideology. Some whites
desired land, timber, and other resources that were under Indian control.
Many other whites simply could not understand why Indians should have
group rights and not have to compete as individual citizens.

Following passage by Congress of a 1953 resolution declaring a policy
to free Indians from federal supervision and control, statutes from 1954
to 1962 authorized termination of more than one hundred tribes, bands,
or Indian *rancherias*. Although most of those affected were small groups
on the West Coast, two sizable tribes, the Klamaths in Oregon and the
Menominees in Wisconsin, also were terminated. (Both reservations contained important timberlands.) Twelve thousand individual Indians lost
tribal affiliations and their special political relationship with the United
States, and two and one half million acres of Indian lands were removed
from protected status.[2]

A small group of Native Americans created the National Congress of
American Indians in 1944 as a mechanism for bringing tribes together to
plan political strategy to assert Indian rights. American rhetoric against
racism in the Second World War emboldened Indian veterans, and two
went to court in 1948 to challenge Arizona and New Mexico for still

denying Indians the right to vote, in the face of 1924 Congressional legislation that declared all Indians born in the U.S. to be citizens, completing a process that had begun when all those who accepted allotments were made citizens.

In the past, Indian protest had been expressed largely outside American politics through armed resistance and messianic religious movements. In 1870, a Paiute named Wovoka who announced that he was an incarnation of the messiah preached that dancing could bring back the dead, the buffalo, and the whole way of life of the Paiutes. The messianic movement grew throughout the Great Basin and the plains, with more than a half dozen Indian tribes, including the Oglala Sioux, and Cheyenne, participating in the ghost dance religion.[3]

By the 1950s, the days of the ghost dance were over, and, in addition, it was no longer possible to fight the U.S. Cavalry. There had been virtually no Indian involvement in American politics outside Oklahoma until the successful battle for the right to vote in Arizona and New Mexico in 1948. In 1960, presidential candidate John F. Kennedy repeatedly promised that "there would be protection of the Indian land base." "Indians," he said, "have heard fine words and promises long enough. They are right in asking for deeds."[4] But deeds were not substantial in the early 1960s, despite the efforts of the new secretary of the interior, Stewart L. Udall, and Indian commissioner Philleo Nash. Congress did increase loan authorizations for Native Americans but appropriated only $4 million to assist them in purchasing land. Industrial plants were built on reservations, but their total worth was less than $100 million as late as 1968.[5]

More influential than Kennedy's rhetoric in stimulating activism was the accelerated movement for civil rights by blacks in the late 1950s. Four hundred and twenty Indians from sixty-seven tribes meeting in June 1961 at the University of Chicago issued a "Declaration of Indian Purpose" and a series of recommendations to strengthen the rights of Indian tribes.[6] It was the first major political initiative on behalf of tribal rights since Cherokee leaders lobbied Congress and appealed to the American public and the federal courts to resist President Andrew Jackson's decision to push the tribes of the Southeast to the West out of whites' way.

Facilitating Indian Power: The Economic Opportunity Act of 1964

In 1964, a major breakthrough in federal policy gave impetus to new Indian initiatives. Under the Economic Opportunity Act (1964), Indians were asked for the first time to work out plans for programs to be administered by the reservations themselves. With the appropriation of federal money to establish programs directed by Indians under the Office of

Economic Opportunity, they began to demand comparable responsibility and power on programs administered by other government agencies, including those funded by the U.S. Bureau of Indian Affairs.

The inclusion of Indians in the Economic Opportunity Act was partly the result of new Indian political activism. While the legislation was still being written and debated, Native Americans convened an American Indian conference on poverty in Washington in May 1964 to lobby members of the House and Senate and of the administration. Youthful advocates of "Red Power" demanded their right to be heard by older delegates. Speaking for the National Indian Youth Council, its president asserted that "the Indian cannot be pushed into the mainstream of American life." Explicitly rejecting assimilation as a goal, he argued that no federal policy would work unless Indians were involved in shaping it and that "Indian tribes need greater political power to act."[7]

Community Action Programs on the reservations under the Office of Economic Opportunity introduced new organizations and programs that transferred decision making from the Bureau of Indian Affairs to the tribes themselves, sometimes challenging tribal councils that had become appendages of the bureau. By the end of the 1960s, there were more than 60 locally organized Community Action Programs involving 105 reservations in 17 states and operating various economic and social enterprises. There were more whites involved in these programs (proposal writers, supervisors, and evaluators) than Indians, but by the mid-1960s, more Indians were engaged in the American political system than earlier.[8] Although the OEO and its community action committees were abolished during the early 1970s, they had provided a training ground for political activity.

Indians began to assert power on a variety of fronts. In the fall of 1964, two young Navajos were elected to the state legislature in New Mexico for the first time. Two years later, the Indians sent another tribal member to the New Mexico state senate, and in Arizona the first Navajo was elected to the state legislature. Altogether, fifteen Indians were seated in six western state legislatures; others took office as judges and county officials.[9]

The civil disobedience strategy of the black revolution was copied, as young Indians threw themselves in front of bulldozers being used to build dams on reservation land, conducted "fish-ins" to publicize the right of Puget Sound Indians to protect their treaty rights to hunt and fish, and joined Martin Luther King's poor people's march on Washington. The National Indian Youth Council (1961) provided a vehicle for militant young Indians to express outrage against the oppression Indians had suffered. Other new Indian organizations emerged, and major national newspapers and magazines began to feature Indian protest stories.[10]

The Indian activist buzzwords were "sovereign rights" and "self-determination." The founding resolution of the National Indian Youth Council called for recognition of "the sovereign rights of all Indians."[11] After a series of violent conflicts between Indian fishermen and whites in Washington, one young Indian PFC in the U.S. Army renounced his uniform, swearing that his "first allegiance" was "to Indian people and the sovereign rights of our many Tribes." But Indians had to work out their relationship to the polity as a whole by redefining tribalism in a way that acknowledged their status as Americans as well as Indians.[12]

When the rebellion of blacks erupted in the urban riots of 1965, some Indians called for violent action to press the Indian cause. An editorial in the journal of the National Congress of American Indians urged that Watts be reenacted in cities wherever large numbers of Indians lived.[13] Massive violence by urban Indians never took place, however, and armed resistance on reservations was impractical in an age of tanks and paratroopers. Using other techniques of protest, learned from the black revolution, Indians began to make their cause known through television news. Support spread among young people on college campuses, who sang Indian protest songs made popular by Johnny Cash, a descendant of Cherokees, by Floyd Westerman, a Sioux, and by Buffy St.-Marie, a Cree.

Representing almost half a million Indians in the cities, urban Indian leaders established activist organizations, which joined a nationwide federation called the American Indians Movement, to protest and lobby on fishing, water, and land rights guaranteed through treaties. On November 28, 1969, a landing party of seventy-eight Indians, calling themselves Indians of all tribes, occupied abandoned Alcatraz island in San Francisco Bay to protest the situation of Indians generally and the alleged failure of whites to acknowledge their obligations under treaties. Tens of thousands of Indians throughout the country were inspired by the action of Indian college students. Indians from reservations and other urban areas joined the occupation. Although some whites reacted with hostility, others in San Francisco sent medical supplies and food, and tourists came by to offer encouragement.[14]

Partly as a result of political activity, Indians began to win friends. Senator George McGovern (D-South Dakota), a member of the Senate Indian Affairs Subcommittee, who had benefited from Indian votes, urged the federal government to make self-determination the major goal of Indian policy.[15] Indians lobbied to support a resolution toward that end introduced by McGovern, and as a result President Johnson established two task forces to study Indian affairs and make recommendations to the White House, the essence of which was that Indians should be involved in the development and management of any program affecting Indian education, training, employment, or economic development. In response, Johnson on March 6, 1968, proposed a new goal for Indian programs that would, in McGovern's language, stress "self-determination" and end "paternalism."[16] Johnson also created a National Council on Economic Opportunity for Indians in March 1968 (an action ratified by Congress two years later), consisting of the vice president, six cabinet officials, the director of the Office of Economic Opportunity, and six Indians (increased in 1970 to eight).

The Indian members demanded the phasing out of Bureau of Indian Affairs boarding schools then attended by forty thousand Indian children. To replace them, they urged construction of a network of community schools under tribal control. Senators Robert Kennedy (D-New York) and Edward Kennedy (D-Massachusetts), successive chairmen of a special Senate subcommittee on Indian education, agreed. In the fall of 1969, the committee, calling national policies to educate American Indians a failure, offered sixty separate recommendations toward "increased Indian participation and control of their own education programs."[17] With this turning point in congressional attitudes toward assimilation—a recognition that it had failed to integrate Indians effectively into the larger American society—it became possible for executive initiatives to result in a fundamental change in policy.

New Indian Policy Calling for Self-Determination

Indians, who insisted on redefinition of tribal pluralism, met a sympathetic response from the new president, Richard M. Nixon. Calling for "self-determination without termination" in a speech on July 8, 1970, Nixon acknowledged the bankruptcy of termination and other attempts at assimilation. "The special relationship between Indians and the federal government," he said, echoing the Northwest Ordinance and decisions made by John Marshall in previous centuries, "is the result . . . of solemn obligations which have been entered into by the United States Government."[18] Nixon pointed out that of the Department of the Interior's programs directly serving Indians, only 1.5 percent were under Indian control. Only 2.4 percent of Indian health programs funded through the Department of Health, Education, and Welfare were run by Indians.[19]

The legislation Nixon proposed would empower a tribe or group of tribes or any other Indian community to take over control or operation of federally funded and administered programs in Interior and HEW. Where a federal department or agency disagreed, "the final determination should rest with the Indian community," Nixon asserted. Requesting more money for Indian health, direct control over schools attended by

Indians, and economic development, he urged that Congress create the position of Assistant Secretary of the Interior for Indian and Territorial Affairs to focus on the new effort to redirect Indian policy.

Nixon's position reflected a growing willingness in the early 1970s to respond to the deeply felt and justified grievances of minorities, including Indians. National Indian organizations, such as the National Congress of American Indians, the Native American Rights fund, the National Indian Youth Council, the Institute for the Development of Indian Law, and the American Indian Law Center, had been pressing the case for self-determination. Articles, essays, and books had been appearing regularly implying or advocating the cause of a redefinition of tribal sovereignty.[20] Two years after the Nixon speech, Congress passed the Indian Education Act of 1972, creating the Office of Indian Education and the National Council on Indian Education to further bilingual and bicultural education programs, teacher training, and early childhood education. With the passage of the Indian Self-Determination and Educational Assistance Act in 1975, local Indian communities gained more responsibility for and control over the education of their children.[21]

The act was the centerpiece of several measures aimed at redefining the structure of tribal pluralism. Native Americans continued to suffer more than any group the many ills associated with poverty, but at least the symbols and the rhetoric had changed, and a framework was evolving to provide a measure of self-determination for Indian tribes much greater than had existed for more than 150 years. In 1975, Congress created the American Indian Policy Review Commission, a joint commission with three U.S. senators, four members of the House of Representatives, and five Indian members representing major tribes and Indians as a whole. For the first time, Congress had created a body to review and recommend policies regarding Indians that had Indian members, a staff primarily of Indians, and thirty-one of thirty-three task forces chaired by Indians.

When the commission issued its report on May 17, 1977, the mood of Alcatraz and the other demonstrations of 1969 and 1970 was absent. Indian commissioners acknowledged the role they played in the first "exhaustive analysis of the relationship between the United States and native American governments and peoples" in U.S. history. "It is a reflection," they said, "of the progressive spirit of fairness predominant in the American society that Congress could commission a study of this kind, wherein Indian members have participated equally with the Congressional members in formulating comprehensive recommendations designed to shape a promising future for federal-Indian relations."[22]

Only the vice chairman, Representative Lloyd Meeds (D-Washington), disagreed with the fundamental premise that American Indian tribes are sovereign bodies with power to govern their internal affairs. To Meeds, the argument over sovereignty was more than theoretical. Indians, he argued, are subject to the power of the states in which they live, and Indian tribal self-government exists only because Congress has, to a large extent, insulated reservation Indians from state governmental power. Because Congress had decided that some American Indians should be allowed to make their own laws and be ruled by them "does not mean that it allows American Indian tribes to govern their reservations in the same way a state governs within its boundaries."[23]

Meeds was correct. The U.S. Supreme Court had repeatedly upheld the power of the state to impose its law on non-Indians within reservations. The very fact that Congress passed an Indian Self-Determination Act meant that Congress could repeal it. But, in practice, the government was working with Indians to redefine a complex new system of tribal pluralism. By 1977, there were more than four hundred tribes, but only 289 were serviced by the Bureau of Indian Affairs.[24] Of 133 nonrecognized Indian communities, with a population of 112,000, at least twenty-nine had U.S. treaty rights derived from obligations the nation had assumed from colonial powers or from treaties it negotiated with their ancestors. More than one-half of all Indians did not live on reservations; many were not subject to tribal jurisdiction; others did not belong to tribes at all.

The new system of tribal pluralism recommended by all of the commissioners except Meeds did not rest on an actual transfer of sovereignty to Indian tribes but on a respect for history, including treaties, and on the cultural integrity of contemporary Indian tribal life. Several recommendations of the commission could not be fulfilled for political reasons, such as one to transfer large portions of the states of California, Oregon, Nebraska, North Dakota, South Dakota, and Oklahoma to Indian tribes, and others could not be enacted for budgetary and administrative reasons, including extension of a vast panoply of special government services to Indians who live in cities far from reservations. But the spirit of the recommendations was generally accepted in Congress, which already had passed in 1976 the Indian Health Care Improvement Act, aimed at improving delivery of health care on reservations and training Indian professionals in modern medicine. In 1978 it passed the Indian Civil Welfare Act, granting authority to tribal courts over child custody and related cases. In the same year, Congress passed the Native American Religious Freedom Act, which obliged federal agencies to refrain from any action or policy that would interfere with the practice of traditional Indian religion.

The Native American Religious Freedom Act reflected an important premise of the new tribal pluralism: respect for the cultural integrity of Indians. By the late 1970s, it had become commonplace in legislation to insist, as in the Indian Education Act, that programs "be developed and conducted with the cooperation of tribes, parents and students, so that the Indian future in education can be determined in full conjunction with Indian desires and decisions." A 1976 pamphlet from the Office of Indian Education, explaining the goals and operations of the act, asserted that, "as the original inhabitants of this land, the Indian people have a special relationship with the United States government, which has responsibility for, and a legal and moral commitment to the protection of Indian-owned natural resources." The pamphlet boasted that the "long history of injustice, exploitation and broken promises is changing. Thanks to the passage of the Indian Education Act and other recent legislation, the pace of change is undergoing a dramatic acceleration."[25]

The newly defined relationship of the U.S. to American Indians in the 1980s consisted of five parts:

First, as reflected in the Religious Freedom Act, special respect was given through legislation for traditional Indian religious and cultural practices;

Second, the federal government recognized that Indian tribes have some of the attributes of nations that enable them to exercise government powers different from and sometimes superseding those of the states with respect to their own members;

Third, treaties signed by Indians with the U.S. government were to be given great respect. (For example, federal courts have ruled that where there are ambiguities in treaties, they are to be construed in favor of the Indian claimants);

Fourth, the federal government acknowledged a special trust responsibility to Indians to implement economic and social programs to protect their lands and to promote their well-being;

Fifth, Indians born in the U.S. or who are naturalized are entitled to all of the fundamental constitutional protections of American citizens, as reflected in the Indian Civil Rights Act of 1968, which imposes on the tribal governments specific and slightly modified individual rights derived from the First, Fourth, Fifth, Sixth, Eighth, and Fourteenth Amendments to the U.S. Constitution.[26]

In addition to these five factors, Indian members of recognized tribes were covered by affirmative action programs stemming from executive orders and regulations made pursuant to the Civil Rights Act of 1964 and other federal and state legislation.

The relationship of tribal Indians to the polity as a whole was unique. In some states Indians were permitted to engage in certain traditional religious practices such as the smoking of peyote without being liable to arrest for violating state laws, although it was constitutional for states to restrict such activity. No other ethnic groups in the U.S. except tribal

Indians were protected by treaty obligations. Only Indians (and Alaskan natives and Hawaiians) received special benefits targeted for specific ethnic groups by legislation on land use, health, housing, and education. Only Indians could determine whether adoption by a non-Indian family of an Indian child was valid through their own tribal courts, and Indian tribes were the only corporate entities with immunity against suits by their own members.

Litigating and Negotiating the Boundaries of Tribal Pluralism

Since the parameters of tribal pluralism were complex, they required frequent litigation and negotiation. Tribal courts were limited in their civil jurisdiction to two situations: first, when the defendant was a member of a tribe, and second, when the dispute was between a tribe member and a nonmember and both parties agreed to go before a tribal court. If an accident occurred on a reservation, the situation was complicated. If both plaintiff and defendant belonged to the tribe, or if plaintiff was a non-Indian and defendant a tribe member, the tribal court had jurisdiction. If both plaintiff and defendant were non-Indian, the state court had jurisdiction. But if plaintiff was a tribe member and defendant a non-Indian, it was unclear as to which court had jurisdiction.[27]

Litigation was common in the 1970s and 1980s over the assertion by Indians of treaty rights that ran afoul of the environmental, hunting, fishing, and other laws and regulations of states. Changes in administration policy toward specific Indian tribes frequently led to litigation, as when the Internal Revenue Service attempted unsuccessfully to get the Lummi Indians in the extreme northwest tip of Washington State to pay federal taxes on their income from salmon fishing in Puget Sound, a policy that reversed that of previous administrations and which the Lummis contended would effectively destroy their 1858 treaty with the U.S. government and might lead to the loss of their 12,500-acre reservation. The Lummis were joined in their opposition to the IRS by the secretary of the interior, Donald Hodel, who warned that the attempt to tax the Lummis was not only in violation of treaty law but a departure from administration policy. Like other Americans, Indians paid federal and state taxes on income earned off reservations, and on-reservation income was taxed if it was derived from sources not connected to the land. The exemption for land-based income made Indian resources particularly attractive to developers, who could avoid such taxes as the oil-windfall tax and coal-severance tax by entering into joint ventures with Indians.[28]

Non-Indian citizens often resented exemptions or special protections under treaties at least a century old. When the Chippewa Indians sold about one-third of what would become Wisconsin for a nickel an acre in

1837, the treaty sanctioning the sale contained a provision guaranteeing unrestricted hunting and fishing for the Chippewa on their former land, rights that were upheld in a federal court in 1987. Angry whites, upset because of effects of the treaty, hurled stones at Indians who were spearing for fish on lakes in Minocqua, Wisconsin. A group of high school students composed and circulated an obscene, derogatory poem about Indians. In the town of Star Lake, a boat landing dock where Indians speared fish was sprinkled with roofing nails.[29]

The resistance of whites to claims based on treaties made long ago probably was reinforced by Indians' new assertiveness. When the Passamaquoddy tribe petitioned the Department of the Interior in February 1972 to initiate a land claim on its behalf based on its interpretation of a treaty of 1794, claiming 10 to 12.5 million acres of the state, an area covering half of Maine and populated by more than 350,000 non-Indians, there was a reaction of outrage in newspaper editorials and by Maine's top governmental and civic leaders. "There is simply no equitable way of forcing a return of land which has been settled, developed and improved in good faith by Maine people for two centuries," said two of Maine's U.S. legislators, Democratic Senator William Hathaway and Republican Representative William S. Cohen.[30]

From a judicial point of view, the issue was the interpretation of the relationship of the Passamaquoddy to the federal government. The tribe had given up its land in a 1794 treaty with the state of Maine, but such treaties were not valid because the Indian Trade and Intercourse Act, passed in the first American Congress, more commonly known as the Non-Intercourse Act of 1790, prohibited states from making any agreement with Indian nations that took from them title or claim to land. Since every court that had examined the purpose of the act agreed that Congress intended to protect the lands of Indian tribes against unfair arrangements made by states or local governments, the Passamaquoddy believed they should get their land back.[31] But the issue as to whether or not the Passamaquoddy were a tribe had to be settled first, since the U.S. Bureau of Indian Affairs had not previously recognized them as such.

The issue of tribal status was critical, not just to get the land back but because tribe members become eligible for health benefits, grants to attend college, special subsidies for new housing for low-income families, and other entitlements. After the Passamaquoddy and the Penobscots gained status as federal tribes in 1978, long and difficult negotiations led to a basic agreement with both tribes, signed into law in October 1980. Both were accorded the status of state municipalities with exclusive jurisdiction over internal tribal matters, minor criminal offenses involving Indians, small claims, civil matters, and issues of domestic relations. Maine retained extensive jurisdiction over Indian lands, but $81.5 million was deposited into the tribe's joint account for the acquisition of 300,000 acres of land; a trust fund of $27 million was established to be administered for their benefit.[32]

Within a few years, other New England Indian tribes were recognized and were able to win thousands of acres of federal land and millions of dollars in benefits, including the Wampanoag Indians, whom the BIA found to have had a continuous political existence as a community in the Gay Head area on the island of Martha's Vineyard in Massachusetts. The ruling, part of a proposed settlement by which the state and federal governments provided money for the tribe to buy 175 acres from non-Indian land owners and acquire another 240 acres of undevelopable town land, meant entry into the new system of tribal pluralism for three hundred members of the tribe (about half of the total) who lived at Gay Head.[33]

It became common in the 1970s and 1980s for settlements to be negotiated. The best known, the Alaska Native Claims Settlement Act of 1971, passed by Congress with the approval of Alaskan natives (about half of whom are Eskimo, one-third Indian, and the rest Aleut), became one of the most novel social and economic experiments in American history. Alaskan natives turned their backs on a tribal reservation status and trust relationship with the government. Instead, they accepted $962.5 million and forty-four million acres of land and gave up all claims to any other land in Alaska and special rights to hunt and fish on it. Having rejected governance by tribal council or by the Bureau of Indian Affairs, they created corporations operating for profit to manage and invest the proceeds of their claims, with every native becoming a shareholder.

The new arrangements led native Alaskans to manage multimillion-dollar corporations, buy hotels and fish canneries, and contract with multinational oil companies while simultaneously trying to preserve age-old cultures. Thirteen regional corporations and more than two hundred smaller ones were established to exploit the oil, mineral, and game lands they had won under the settlement. Changes in the life-style of villagers were immense in the late 1980s, and it was uncertain whether the subsistence hunting and fishing activities that had been the focal point of native family and community life would survive.[34]

The redefining of tribal pluralism sometimes took place through joint ventures or partnerships. In 1983, the Crow Indians in Montana entered into agreement with the Buffalo Exploration Company to form the Raven Oil Company with a management committee of four Crow members and three non-Indians from Buffalo. Crow leaders recognized that they needed outside help. Although their reservation in Montana sat on top of huge coal reserves, the tribe was extremely poor. Of the 1,347 households on the Crow reservation in Bighorn and Yellowstone counties, encompassing 2,280,000 acres, 70 percent were below the federal poverty level in 1982. The Indian unemployment rate on the reservation in 1983 (almost half of the population was non-Indian) was 69 percent. Since most of the tribe's operating revenue came from the use of natural resources, with the biggest source of income from mineral leases, permits, and royalties, it was extremely important to the Crow that they negotiate a good arrangement with a competent outside group.[35]

Agreements such as the one that led to the creation of the Raven Oil Company resulted mainly from the willingness of Crow leaders to participate in the American economic and political system. Meetings were held by tribal officials throughout 1983 and 1984 with representatives of the Buffalo Exploration Company and with the staffs of the U.S. senators from Montana, three members of the U.S. House of Representatives, officials of the Bureau of Indian Affairs' Office of Energy and Mineral Resources, the assistant secretary for Indian affairs of the Department of the Interior, and the deputy undersecretary of the department.[36] Approval had to be given not just by the Crow tribal council but by the Crow membership, which voted in secret ballot, and then finally by the Bureau of Indian Affairs and the Interior Department's assistant secretary for Indian affairs.

An unusual example of the changed attitude of Indians toward partnerships with whites came in the announcement of a plan by the Navajo nation, the largest of all Indian tribes, to collaborate with the designer Oleg Cassini in building a world-class luxury resort on the Navajo reservation. Cassini, the son of immigrants from Italy and Russia, had long wanted to be involved in the creation of products based on Navajo culture, but the tribe's leaders had resisted suggestions that they work together until 1987. In praising the new plan, Peter MacDonald, the Navajo tribal chairman, told the National Press Club in Washington that the tourist resort, which would be based "on authentic designs," would help to relieve the Navajos of their dependence on the federal government. Seeking economic strength, the Navajos sought wider participation in the American marketplace.[37]

Participating in the Political System

Under the new tribal pluralism, a growing number of Indians began to participate in and acculturate to both the American marketplace economy and the American political system. In 1975, representatives of twenty-five western tribes formed the Council of Energy Resources Tribes in order to assist native Americans in energy management. The council came into being because tribal leaders were angry about leases the Bureau of Indian Affairs had negotiated for their coal, uranium, oil, and water resources. CERT's initial funding came from the U.S. Department of Energy and three other federal agencies in the form of a $2.2-million seed grant. At its annual meeting in 1979, the Indian organization received a $24-million aid package and announced six major new energy projects on Indian land "to help America get back on its energy feet again."[38]

That announced goal probably seemed startling to Indian traditionalists. Tocqueville's notion that participation in politics in America leads to or reinforces national patriotism appeared to work somewhat for Indians, too. The process of ethnic-Americanization was taking place for them in the 1980s even though their relationship to the polity as a whole was quite different from that of any other ethnic group. Participation meant forming organizations with other Indian groups and developing an identity that transcended tribal identities, but it also meant taking a more active role in the American electoral process in order to promote policies favorable to Indian tribal interests.

By the mid-1980s, organizing for political action became a principal topic of consideration for Indians. At the 1984 annual meeting of the National Congress for American Indians in Spokane, Washington, workshops were held on voter registration and political action. With nearly fifty thousand members, the NCAI had become a political force. Its main targets were the eligible Indian voters in five states: Alaska (Indians, Eskimos, and Aleuts made up more than 12 percent of all voters); New Mexico (6.6 percent); and Arizona, Oklahoma, and South Dakota (with 4.8 percent each).[39]

In 1966, only fifteen Indians held state legislative office; by 1985 thirty-five did (thirty-three from districts with Indian populations of 65 percent or more). To elect more leaders, Indian advocacy groups challenged apportionment arrangements that tended to dilute concentrations of Indian voters. Typical was the case in Bighorn County in Montana, where a federal judge ruled that the at-large system for choosing the Bighorn County Commissioner's three members was in violation of the 1965 Voting Rights Act as amended in 1982, because it diluted the Indian vote in the county.[40] Indians stepped up lobbying activity in Washington, too, and because of their extensive involvement in litigation or negotiation with the federal government about water, mineral, or land rights, by 1980 more than two dozen Indian tribes had hired prestigious law firms in the nation's capital to represent them.[41]

Learning to use the American justice system with increasing effectiveness, tribes began to hire more Indian attorneys as counsel. Indians also made more extensive use of the Legal Services Corporation, an agency that evolved from the first legal aid programs funded by the Office of Economic Opportunity under the Economic Opportunity Act of 1964 to provide legal assistance to low-income Americans.[42] The Native American

Rights Fund, founded in 1970, was the oldest and largest national Indian-interest law firm. Begun with a Ford Foundation grant, it was handling about two hundred cases a year in the 1980s, providing representation to some ninety tribes and other Indian clients. Solely dependent upon grants, contracts, and donations from foundations and private individuals, the NARF, having developed an Indian law library, was able to provide special expertise to reservation attorneys.[43] In 1985, its attorneys successfully argued the case of the Oneida nation before the U.S. Supreme Court; the Court ruled that New York State's acquisition of 146,000 acres of Oneida land had violated federal law and policy since it took place after passage of the Non-Intercourse Act of 1790. Earlier, the Court had cleared the way for the final disposition of the case by a 1974 ruling that the Non-Intercourse Act applied to the original thirteen states, thereby opening up the federal courts to the Oneidas as well as to other Indians attempting to recover land in those states.[44]

The New Tribal Pluralism and the Issue of Sovereignty

The new tribal pluralism did not make the Indian tribes sovereign in the ordinary meaning of that word. Tribal councils were not free to select their legal representatives without approval by the secretary of the interior and the commissioner of Indian affairs, according to a law that has been upheld by a federal court.[45] The agreement creating the Raven Company could not have been made without the approval of the Department of the Interior and the cooperation of elected U.S. officials. When Congress extended protection to many traditional Indian religious practices (the same protection was given to Alaskan natives and Hawaiians) and guaranteed Indians access to religious sites that otherwise would be subject to state action, the state could still exercise compelling interests, based on constitutional principles, to override religious claims. For example, in 1980, the U.S. Court of Appeals for the 10th Circuit ruled against a group of Navajo medicine men who wanted to have exclusive use of the Rainbow Bridge area in Utah as a sacred shrine for their tribe and to remove a boating dock used by tourists, stating that such an action would be a violation of the First Amendment's establishment clause because Rainbow Bridge would then become a government-managed shrine.[46]

That the ultimate power to determine the boundaries of tribal pluralism remained in Washington was made clear in the mid-1980s when the federal government intervened in a dispute between the Hopi and the Navajo tribes. Hopis had lived in relative isolation for thousands of years in what became Arizona. In the nineteenth century, Navajo herdsmen began migrating into Hopi land, particularly after the U.S. Cavalry waged all-out war on the Navajo in New Mexico. Gradually, the more numerous and more powerful Navajo settled millions of acres of desert, and the Hopi mesas became surrounded by the Navajos. By the 1980s, Navajos overwhelmingly outnumbered Hopis in the area by more than 10 to 1.

For a while, they cooperated with each other, with the Navajo taught by the Hopi how to farm in the desert and the Navajo providing a buffer against invasion from prospectors and other whites, but conflict between the two groups intensified after energy companies discovered large deposits of coal, oil, and uranium under the shared land. After the conflict worsened in the early 1980s, the federal government decided to try to end it by creating a 2.5-million-acre rectangle, with Hopi mesas at its center, as Hopi territory, necessitating relocation of ten thousand Navajo. A five-strand barbed-wire fence was strung 340 miles across the desert. Militant Navajos and their supporters were so angry that they tore down about two thousand feet of fence in July 1986. Many carried signs saying "The Creator is the Only One Who Can Relocate Us" and chanted the American Indian Movement's anthem, "Black Goat," while about seventy-five crossed the fence line to trespass on land Congress had designated as Hopi.

At the same time, another group of two hundred Navajos, led by a color guard of decorated veterans of the armed services, marched to the boundary of the disputed area, where they stood holding flags of the Navajo Nation and the United States. They recited the U.S. Pledge of Allegiance. The Navajo moderates wanted to negotiate to stop the relocation, but the Hopis wanted to negotiate to effect it. Some Indians on both sides called for the government to get out of the situation altogether and let the traditional elders resolve the dispute, but the government had entered the dispute to begin with because the Hopis had asked them to and it could not let the conflict become violent.[47]

Even the question who is an Indian was decided for certain purposes by the federal government. The issue of who belongs to a tribe was usually decided by the tribes themselves, with approximately half requiring one-quarter or more Indian blood for membership, although many others recognized persons with an eighth, a sixteenth, or even less Indian blood. But the federal government could alter the definition, as when the Reagan administration proposed in 1986 that free Indian health service care be given only to those with at least one-quarter Indian blood if they lived as a member of a federally recognized tribe or were eligible to be a member, and lived on or near a reservation; or, if not a member of a tribe or eligible for membership, to persons who lived on or near a reservation and had one-half Indian blood. But the proposed regulations were withdrawn, leaving intact a rule that a person need only belong to an Indian community (not defined) and live on or near a reservation, without having to meet any blood requirement.[48]

Although the new tribal pluralism did not mean the end of government interference in Indian affairs, it did signify a commitment by the government as a matter of policy that interference would at least in some measure be based upon the respect promised in the words of the Northwest Ordinance in the eighteenth century and in a series of Court decisions protecting Indian rights dating back to the 1830s. The decision to approve the Raven Company agreement angered a minority of the Crow. The decision to settle boundary disputes between the Hopi and the Navajo infuriated many of the Navajo. But neither decision was motivated or determined by the avarice of white Americans, as in the past. As Vine Deloria, Jr., a Sioux Indian, lawyer, and intellectual leader of those fighting for Indian cultural integrity in the 1970s and 1980s, had asserted in 1969, "Any cooperative movement must come to terms with tribalism in the Indian context before it will gain Indian support . . . Indians will not revert to their old position on the totem pole."[49]

The Self-Determination Act of 1975 did not create sovereign entities within the U.S. called Indian tribes. But it did call for "maximum Indian participation in the direction of educational as well as other federal services to Indian communities," and for "an orderly transition from Federal domination of programs for and services to Indians to effective and meaningful [Indian] participation in those programs and services."[50] Many Indians and non-Indians believed that the Self-Determination Act did not go far enough. In 1987, Interior Secretary Hodel argued before Congress that the Bureau of Indian Affairs still retained too much paternalistic power and that responsibility for developing and managing programs for Indians should be dispersed among the nation's over four hundred Indian tribes (several more had been recognized by the bureau in the 1980s).[51]

The 1980 census showed that only a little more than one-third of the 1.4 million Native Americans (including about 60,000 Eskimos and Aleuts) lived on reservations, tribal lands, or other identified Native American areas, the largest and most populous being the Navajo reservation, with 105,000 Indians in Arizona, New Mexico, and Utah. Economic conditions on most reservations were still bleak by the end of the 1980s, and not much better for urban Indians. Some progress had been made. The Indian infant mortality rate dropped from 62.7 deaths per thousand births in 1955 to 13.1 per thousand twenty years later. Public hygiene and better nutrition undoubtedly played important roles in reducing Indian infant mortality, but the Indian Health Care Improvement Act of 1976 also helped by increasing funds for Indian health and allowing tribes to operate some reservation health facilities themselves.

American Indians still were among the poorest and the unhealthiest of all Americans, particularly on the reservations, where the median family income was less than two-thirds of that of Indians living away from the reservations. Forty-one percent of American Indians living on reservations were below the poverty level, according to a report made by a presidential commission on Indian reservation economies in 1984, compared to 12 percent for the total U.S. population. The proportion of families maintained by a woman without a husband present was 50 percent higher than for the nation as a whole, and 37 percent of Indian deaths occurred among people under forty-five, compared to 12 percent for the entire population. The death rates from liver disease and cirrhosis were more than four times that of the nation as a whole; the tuberculosis death rate was seven times as high; diabetes, pneumonia, homicide, and suicide were much more common; and the death rate from accidents was more than three times what it was for the nation. With the expiration of the Indian Health Service Improvement Act in 1984 under the Reagan administration, a variety of social services were reduced. And for all of the progressive legislation and court decisions of the 1970s and 1980s, the standard of living of Indians lagged far behind that of the vast majority of Americans. The poorest Indians, like the persistently poor blacks and Puerto Ricans, lived in an ethno-underclass whose boundaries were defined by class, ethnicity, and race, and within which they were largely unconnected to mainstream institutions and opportunities.

Being Indian and American

Well into the 1980s, many traditionalist Indians who refused to be called either Indian or American and who saw their identities firmly rooted in ancestral tribal cultures, languages, and rituals, were prepared to suffer economic privation to maintain their tribal integrity. On the Rosebud Sioux Reservation in South Dakota, where a majority of workers were unemployed, the tribe refused to take the $105 million awarded to it in compensation in 1980 after a long legal battle rather than acknowledge the sovereignty of the U.S. government over the sacred Black Hills, which included the busts of four presidents at Mount Rushmore. To the Sioux Indians of Rosebud, Washington, Jefferson, Lincoln, and Theodore Roosevelt were hardly heroes. Washington had looked the other way while Indian land was stolen; Jefferson had called for removal of Indians from their homelands; Lincoln had authorized raids against them; and Theodore Roosevelt once mused that he sometimes agreed that the only good Indian was a dead one. Poverty, demoralization, alcoholism, and other diseases were common at Rosebud, but so was tribal pride.[52]

Yet, by the late 1980s militant traditionalists were heard from much less often than ten or fifteen years before. The alternative to traditionalism was no longer assimilation but a variation of the process of ethnic-Americanization commonly experienced by immigrants and their children. One could be a Seminole and an American, too. As one Hopi tribal council member said in 1986, "we believe in traditional ways but we also believe we have to function in the modern world." "To do that," she said, "we have to be part of the political system. If not, the Congress and other outsiders will determine our future."[53]

To traditionalist Indians there were dangers in becoming a part of the political system, producing fears probably not unlike those felt by Orthodox Jews in Europe at the turn of the century who were afraid to emigrate to the U.S. because their children might lose their Jewish ways, thereby betraying ancestors who struggled so long against oppression. When Lyndon Johnson asserted on March 6, 1968, that Indians should have "an opportunity to remain in their homelands, if they choose, without surrendering their dignity," but that they should also have "an opportunity to move to the towns and cities of America," he meant that Indians could be true to their ancestral cultures and be respected as Americans.[54]

Johnson's formulation—one of a long series of speeches by great white fathers—was not acceptable to the traditionalist Indians, but a growing number of Indians who did not reject tradition were ready to expand Indian participation in American political life, believing, as some Orthodox Jews came to believe, that it might be possible to keep their traditions and participate in the American political system, too. Was it possible to be both an Indian and an American, to become a hyphenated American, a Navajo-American? What did that mean, given the special claim of Indian tribes to group rights? What did it mean to be a Crow-American in what Deloria called "the context of Indian tribal history"?

One answer came from a man who became the first Indian to direct the school for Indian children at Rough Rock on the Navajo reservation in Arizona. Testifying before a special subcommittee on education of the U.S. Senate in December 1967 about the transfer of control of the 250-pupil school from the Bureau of Indian Affairs into the hands of a board of education elected by the Rough Rock Indian community, with full authority over hiring and firing, curriculum, and expenditures, he described a curriculum of instruction in the Navajo language and Navajo history and legends, along with the teaching of English and American history. In times past, he said, the United States would try to force Indian children to choose between being an American and being an Indian. At Rough Rock, he boasted, "Indian children are deliberately and consciously taught in the school to be proud of being both Indian and American."[55]

For an increasing number of Indians in the 1980s, tribal pluralism was becoming a kind of voluntary cultural pluralism combined with those special characteristics Indians on reservations possessed as members of internal, domestic nations within the larger nation. The new tribal pluralism meant they could be participants in the civic culture, too, if they chose, in ways which they now felt were not incompatible with their tribal loyalties. The process of ethnic-Americanization for Native Americans was under way, but it was different from that of immigrant-ethnic groups and of African-Americans, since it had to be accommodated to their unique history and the special claims that derived from that history. It was also affected by a legacy that left Native Americans, more than any other group, estranged from the dominant culture and suffering from the many disabilities of persistent poverty.

Chapter Twelve

"AMERICA IS IN THE HEART"
Asian Sojourners No Longer

To MAKE the point that the Japanese should not be expected to assimilate to American ways and to become loyal Americans, one of the most powerful men in Hawaii, Walter Dillingham, asked a U.S. congressional committee in 1921:

Supposing, for the sake of an example, that the Japanese on one of our mandated islands in the Pacific should develop the island by bringing in a great number of American citizens, and finally they had a situation where 110,000 red blooded American citizens were on the island where there were 18,000 pure-blooded Japanese. How would I feel having a college classmate visit me, to usher him from the boat to the house, kick off sandals and toss a kimona and say, "This is my home. My wife and I came here from America fifteen years ago, and we have made our home here and have entered into the spirit of the life. I want you to meet my boy." In comes a fine, upstanding boy, fifteen years of age. I say, "He is going to the University of Japan. He reads, writes and speaks Japanese better than he does English, and if we ever have a rumpus with Uncle Sam, that boy is true blue; he is going to fight for the Empire." Now just imagine pointing with pride to your son and you realize what you're asking of the Japanese in Hawaii.[1]

Like many leaders of his generation, Dillingham assumed that racial and cultural homogeneity were prerequisites for American unity just as they were in Japan. If he had taken the trouble to visit McKinley High School in Honolulu (often called "Tokyo High"), he might have seen the children of the issei reciting the Gettysburg Address by heart. Japanese-American youngsters spoke of "our Pilgrim forefathers" just as easily as Mary Antin and her Jewish-American classmates did in New York.[2] He also would have seen youngsters practicing democracy through their extensive student government and learning about it in a required full year of American history and government and one semester in American politics.[3]

Twenty years later, the imperial government of Japan discovered through a secret agent in Hawaii that the graduates of McKinley had become thoroughgoing Americans. When the agent tried to ascertain the political sympathies of the nisei in the islands in August 1941, "he discovered they were fanatically loyal to the United States."[4] Only a few months before the attack on Pearl Harbor, the Japanese-American Citizens' League endorsed a special pledge of allegiance to the United States: "I believe in her institutions, ideas and traditions; I glory in her heritage; I boast of her history; I trust in her future. She has granted me liberties and opportunities such as no individual enjoys in this world today. She has given me an education befitting kings. She has entrusted me with the responsibilities of the franchise. She has permitted me to build a home, to earn a livelihood, to worship, think, speak and act as I please—as a free man equal to every other man."[5]

When the attack on Pearl Harbor came, one of the first reactions of the president of the JACL was to send a telegram to President Roosevelt pledging, "we are ready and prepared to expend every effort to repel this invasion together with our fellow Americans."[6] But the American government, public opinion, and, as it turned out, the U.S. Supreme Court, were not ready to accept that pledge of loyalty at face value.

Loyalty and Fear: Japanese-Americans in the Second World War

The system of sojourner pluralism for Asian immigrants was based on the premise that they were not fit to become members of the American polity. Rationalized by racism, the system had accustomed whites to think of Asians, including Asian-American children of immigrants, as outsiders. Although many nisei, citizens because they were born in the U.S., were ready to fight, and hundreds were already serving in the armed forces, the American selective service system classified all nisei as aliens not subject to military service. American Legion Post 97 in Portland, Oregon, calling for removal of all Japanese origin persons to relocation camps, expressed the feeling of many Caucasians when it asserted that "this is no time for namby-pamby pussyfooting . . . not the time for consideration of minute Constitutional rights."[7] Issei especially were terrified. Many burned innocuous letters and photographs and other things that might show they loved Japan.

The head of the Western Defense Command, Lieutenant General John L. DeWitt, urged that Japanese aliens fourteen years of age or older be removed to the interior, exclaiming, "I don't want any of them here . . . it makes no difference whether he is an American citizen, he is still a Japanese. American citizenship does not necessarily determine loyalty."[8] Although there were actually more Italian and German aliens than Japanese living in areas DeWitt considered critical to the national defense, the secretary of war, Henry Stimson, on the advice of military authorities and politicians on the West Coast, ordered the evacuation of both issei and nisei, but not of Italian or German aliens.

Two years later, after ample demonstrations of Japanese-American loyalty to the U.S., DeWitt still justified the relocation in racial terms: "A Jap's a Jap . . . it makes no difference whether he is an American citizen; . . . he is still a Japanese, and you can't change him by giving him a piece of paper," he asserted.[9] Although Stimson did not indulge in racist rhetoric, he later justified his action on two grounds. Japanese raids on the West Coast seemed probable in the first months of the war, and it would have been foolish to take chances that they might receive help from persons of Japanese origin. In addition, such persons were themselves at risk from vigilante action and it would be better to put them out of harm's way.[10] The mayor of Fresno had said, "We don't know what the hoodlum elements might do."[11] By September 1, 1942, more than 110,000 West Coast Japanese, 64 percent of whom were American citizens, were transported to temporary assembly centers and then moved to permanent camps in remote interior regions of the West and in Arkansas.

Although Hawaii had a much larger population (160,000) of Japanese aliens and Japanese-Americans, no massive relocation was ordered there. Buddhist churches and Japanese-language schools were closed in 1941, individuals accused of cooperating with Japan were detained, 981 of whom (mostly aliens) eventually were moved to mainland relocation centers. Not a single act of sabotage or espionage took place in Hawaii throughout the war, and before the war was over more than one-third of all the territory's Japanese-American males of military age had enlisted to fight for the United States.

Having gone to American schools, the nisei leaders knew how to organize; they spoke English, and were aware of their rights as American citizens. To rebut the mounting hysteria against the Japanese, Mike Masaoka, head of the Japanese-American Citizens League, proposed that a suicide squad of nisei volunteers be organized to fight the Japanese. Military officials answered that it was not American policy to put segregated units, except for Negroes, into the field, and that they did not like the idea of suicide squads.[12] Early policy also called for the rejection of nisei volunteers generally and even the dismissal of nisei from the army, but it did not take long for some key officials in the administration to realize that they had made a terrible mistake in instructing draft boards to reject the nisei and in discharging Japanese-Americans from the army solely because of their ethnicity.

The man chosen to head the War Relocation Authority and who supervised the organization of the relocation camps, Milton Eisenhower, wrote to President Franklin Roosevelt in June 1942 of the "essential Americanism of a great majority of the evacuees, including the *issei*."[13] Seven months later, the president approved the recommendation of Secretary of War Stimson to form a nisei combat team. Roosevelt anchored his approval in a ringing affirmation of the civic culture: "The principle on which this country was founded and by which it has always been governed is that Americanism is a matter of the mind and heart; Americanism is not, and never was, a matter of race or ancestry." That Roosevelt could assert the principle of equal rights regardless of race or ancestry in the face of his own executive order that incarcerated American citizens strictly on the basis of race and ancestry was testimony to the deep ambivalence Americans had always shown toward different-looking and -sounding newcomers. The principle of equal rights had enormous symbolic power throughout American history, but it had to contend with the charter-member idea of American identity based on race and religion. "A good American," wrote the president, "is one who is loyal to this country and to our creed of liberty and democracy."[14]

Japanese-Americans, including some *kibei* (those who had spent part of their school years in Japan), were already part of the army's Japanese-language training program in San Francisco; some would later serve in the Pacific as highly valued translators and interpreters.[15] The bulk of nisei enlistees from Hawaii and the mainland joined the 442nd Regimental Combat Team. Many enlistees from Hawaii were already in the 100th Infantry Battalion, one of the three battalions of the 442nd. No other American units would see more dangerous combat service in Europe, and none would be more heavily decorated for heroic duty. The 442nd, after serving with distinction in seven major campaigns and suffering 9,487 casualties, including 600 dead, received more than 18,000 individual decorations, including 52 Distinguished Service Crosses and one Congressional Medal of Honor.[16] In the Pacific theater, nearly four thousand nisei had become attached to the Allied Translator and Interpreter Section, serving with units throughout the Pacific, many of whom were killed and others decorated.[17] Government officials acknowledged that had it not been for their participation the war would have lasted much longer with many more American casualties. Altogether, about 33,300 Japanese-Americans served in the armed forces, approximately half coming from Hawaii.

Not all Japanese-Americans rushed to support the American side, but the demonstration of loyalty by the nisei and even the overwhelming majority of the issei probably had no parallel. Certainly no single event in U.S. history testified to the power of the American civic culture as much as the response of the Japanese-Americans to the war, a response that once again demonstrated a recurring fact in American history: those whom insiders tried to exclude from membership tended to value American freedoms even more than those who took them for granted.

Sandals and kimonos obviously had nothing to do with loyalty. In fact, a great many haole armed servicemen stationed in Hawaii took to wearing sandals and kimonos, too. So strong was the loyalty of the issei and the nisei to the U.S. that by the end of the war, of the 120,000 Japanese who had been subjected to humiliating treatment in relocation centers, less than 4 percent chose to be repatriated to Japan, of whom 1,800 were youngsters under eighteen who accompanied 1,659 adult aliens back to the land of their ancestors. Of the 5,766 nisei who had renounced their citizenship earlier to protest the way they were treated, only 357 failed to ask to have it returned, and 4,978 succeeded in regaining it.[18]

But these developments came after the Supreme Court sustained as constitutional a congressional law that made it a misdemeanor for anyone to violate orders of military commanders prescribed under Roosevelt's executive order restricting the movement of nisei. A nisei Quaker university student, Gordon K. Hirabayashi, defied curfew and evacuation orders, and was arrested, tried, and sentenced to three months' imprisonment. A unanimous Court, ruling only on the curfew order, found that such a special danger existed that those responsible for our national defense had not acted unreasonably in imprisoning Hirabayashi.[19]

More than a year later, on December 18, 1944, when it was apparent that the Allies would win the war, three members of the Supreme Court had second thoughts about justifying executive action based solely on ethnicity, even in times of great peril to the nation. The Court sustained the conviction of a young shipyard welder, Fred Toyosaburo Korematsu, for remaining in a portion of a military area from which persons of Japanese ancestry had been excluded, but three justices dissented, and one of them, Robert H. Jackson, pointed out that it was "revolting among a free people who had embraced the principles set forth in the Constitution of the United States" to incarcerate any citizens on the basis of their national origin.

Jackson wrote that "all residents of this nation are kin in some way by blood or culture to a foreign land. Yet, they are primarily and necessarily a part of the new and distinct civilization of the United States. They must accordingly be treated at all times as the heirs of the American experiment and as entitled to all the rights and freedoms guaranteed by the Constitution."[20] In a companion case decided the same day, Justice William O. Douglas, writing for a unanimous Court, ordered that a young nisei woman, Mitsuye Endo, be released from the War Relocation Authority. As a loyal citizen, she should be free to come and go as she pleases regardless of her ancestry, wrote Douglas, and in language very much like that authorized by Roosevelt in his letter to Stimson almost three years earlier, he wrote for the Court that: "Loyalty is a matter of the heart and mind, not of race, creed or color."[21]

It was a principle that the nation had yet to put into practice. The U.S.

entered the war with Asian aliens still ineligible for citizenship and with Asian immigration virtually barred. If loyalty was a matter of the heart and not of race, why should such tight restrictions on membership be placed against Asians?

The Chinese and the Japanese Break the Barriers

The Chinese exclusion law had been on the books for sixty years, but now President Roosevelt argued that it had been a historic mistake. China was an ally, and, he concluded, the Chinese were entitled to preference over other Asians because of their contributions to the war effort.[22] Responding to lobbying by ethnic and religious groups, some of whom argued that the bill would aid the war effort against Japan by strengthening the alliance with China, Congress voted in 1943 to grant China an annual immigration quota of 105, and, much more significantly, to make Chinese immigrants eligible for naturalization, a change affecting about twenty thousand foreign-born Chinese. Another war measure, the War Brides Act of December 28, 1945, permitted Chinese and other alien wives and children of citizen-servicemen to immigrate outside of the quota.[23]

Like the nisei, Chinese-Americans responded patriotically to the war effort. Of nearly sixty thousand Chinese adult males in the U.S. (including resident aliens), more than 20 percent were drafted or enlisted in the army; a smaller number served in the navy and the air force.[24] But the tiny quota of immigrants assigned to China reflected the continuing fear of Asian immigration. When Representative Compton White (D-Idaho) warned Congress in the debate on the 1943 bill that Chinese immigration would bring down American civilization just as "cheap Asiatic people" had induced the collapse of Rome, the liberal, pro-immigration sponsor of the bill, Samuel Dickstein (D-New York), did not try to argue with him, but spoke about the need for this symbolic gesture to unify Americans of all backgrounds (including Chinese-Americans) to win the war.[25]

The same reasoning was applied to India and the Philippines, allies during the war, and in 1946 Congress voted to assign a quota of 100 to each country. The ineligibility provision, which formed the basis for discriminatory legislation in several states, now was invidious specifically with respect to the Japanese, by far the largest of all Asian population groups in the U.S. As aliens ineligible for citizenship, the issei had not been able to vote or hold public office, or even become lawyers. When one tried for citizenship in 1908 under an 1862 law that provided naturalization for an alien who had served honorably in the armed forces, his application was denied on the ground that he was not white.[26] Others tried immediately after the First World War pursuant to a statute passed in 1918 specifically extending the right of naturalization to aliens who had served in the armed forces in that war, but a Supreme Court decision in 1922 made it clear that for Asians to be eligible for naturalization they had to be included in the naturalization law.[27] One small breach in the restrictions occurred in 1930 when the Japanese-American Citizens' League succeeded in having Congress permit the naturalization of about seven hundred issei veterans who served in the armed forces during the war, but many states still had laws that precluded aliens ineligible for citizenship from owning land.[28] Intended to keep issei farmers as migrant workers, hired hands, tenant farmers, and sharecroppers, these laws were only partly effective, but symbolized the persistence of racism.

The nisei leaders of the JACL, many of whom had fought in the Second World War, were determined to end the law that made Japanese immigrants ineligible for citizenship. In 1946, they defeated a California referendum to make the existing alien land laws a part of the state constitution. Although slightly more than three out of seven voters supported the measure, their defeat indicated that racism against the Japanese was subsiding. The JACL next won an important Supreme Court case that had the effect of making the alien land law unenforceable as it related to ownership by citizen-minors of Japanese ancestry. Under the law, it was illegal for a Japanese-American minor to give title to his issei parents, and to get around the law an issei farmer would buy land in the name of his minor citizen-children, to whom he deeded the land as a gift while operating the farm as a trustee. Speaking for the Court in *Oyama* v. *California,* Chief Justic Fred Vinson supported the plaintiff's view that when the right of an American citizen to own land is in conflict with a state's policy on landholding, a citizen's rights must not be subordinated solely because of his father's country of origin.

Four justices thought Vinson did not go far enough to eliminate the racial bias inherent in the law. Holding that the California law was in clear violation of the Fourteenth Amendment and its promise of equal protection of the laws for all persons, Justice Hugo Black (with William Douglas concurring) saw the land law as an attempt to put "all Japanese aliens within its boundaries on the lowest possible economic level." The law was unconstitutional, he argued, because the main purpose of the Fourteenth Amendment was "to bar States from denying to some groups on account of their race or color, any rights, privileges, and opportunities accorded to other groups."[29] Justice Frank Murphy (with Wiley Rutledge concurring) was even more blunt. Calling the Alien Land Law "racist," he saw it as "nothing more than an outright racial discrimination."[30]

But the law itself remained intact and the bar to naturalizing Japanese was untouched. When President Truman's Presidential Committee on Civil Rights issued a report recommending naturalization legislation free of discriminatory provisions, the best Congress would do was to pass a law in 1948 to provide citizenship "irrespective of race" to aliens who had served in the American armed forces during either world war without being required to take the examinations prescribed by law.[31] Another 1948 law specified that issei were to be treated as other aliens with respect to the law permitting those who had been in the U.S. illegally continuously for seven years to remain if they could show that their deportation would result in extreme hardship.

Once again leading the lobbying effort of the JACL in Washington was Californian Mike Masaoka, now a 442nd Regiment veteran. Masaoka visited key members of Congress to plead for justice for Americans who had proved their loyalty in a war against the nation of their ancestors. Mainly as a result of his efforts, Congress passed the Evacuation Claims Act in 1948, allocating $38,000,000 to issei and nisei whose property had been confiscated during their relocation. The compensation—about ten cents for each dollar of loss suffered—was more symbolic than substantial, but it was a small victory on the road to recognizing equal rights for Japanese-Americans.[32]

The JACL also was active in persuading courts to invalidate several laws that discriminated against aliens who were ineligible for citizenship, including one struck down by the California Supreme Court. The court agreed with the views expressed earlier by four U.S. Supreme Court justices that the Alien Land Law in that state violated the Equal Protection Clause of the federal Constitution. Only six and seven years earlier, California, Oregon, and Washington had tightened enforcement of their alien land laws (as did thirteen other western states) in an effort to carve up Japanese property and to prevent returned evacuee farmers from regaining a foothold in the agricultural industry.[33] Now, in 1952, California's long history (and that of other states) of denying Japanese immigrants the right to own farmland, their own homes, business buildings, or other real property on an equal basis with other resident aliens was over.[34]

In the same year, intensive lobbying by the JACL ended the system of sojourner pluralism as it applied to the Japanese. The McCarran-Walter Act of 1952, an omnibus immigration bill that was essentially restrictive, put the issei on an equal footing with other aliens with respect to naturalization, but the immigration quotas assigned to Asian nations, now including Japanese for the first time, were minuscule. As foreign policy considerations became more important in affecting immigration and refugee policy, and as prejudice against Asians waned in the 1950s and 1960s, Congress acted on several occasions to admit a limited number of Asian refugees.

When President Dwight D. Eisenhower in 1954 asked Congress for a special refugee program, the law passed included several thousand Asians from the Far and Near East. A change in the law in 1957 permitted additional Chinese refugees to enter. And in 1960, when Congress passed the Fair Share Law to admit more European refugees, Senator Hiram Fong (R-Hawaii) prevailed upon the Senate to include 4,500 Chinese refugees in that bill. Although the House rejected that amendment, President Kennedy invoked the parole power given the executive branch of the government by the 1952 Immigration and Nationality Act to admit about 14,000 Hong Kong Chinese as refugees.[35]

The official immigration quotas were still tiny (Japan had the largest, 185), but because of the War Brides Act of 1943, the provision of the immigration and nationality statute that permitted U.S. citizens to petition for admission of their alien wives and minor children, and the use of the president's power to parole refugees, the number of Asians actually admitted was considerably higher than the quotas. Although Chinese-born aliens had a quota of only 105, an annual average of 3,500 Chinese were admitted as immigrants between 1950 and 1964, most of whom already were in the U.S. as nonimmigrants who simply adjusted their status.[36]

By 1964, the civil rights revolution had gained considerable momentum. Both the Republican and Democratic 1960 platforms urged more immigration on an equitable basis of admission. The Republicans called for doubling the number of immigrants and for a major overhaul of the national origins quota system. The Democrats urged the end of the national origins quota system altogether as "inconsistent with our belief in the rights of man." Four years later, the Democrats repeated their intention to "eliminate discrimination based upon race and place of birth" in our immigration law.[37] With Johnson's landslide election, and with a pro-immigration Congress, including two Asian-American senators from the state of Hawaii, the national origins quota system (and the strict numerical limits on immigrants from Asia) was abolished in 1965 and a method instituted to admit immigrants from the eastern hemisphere on an equal per-country basis of up to 20,000 per nation annually. Naturally, all Asian-American groups supported the new law, but not even the most optimistic of them believed that the law, which went into effect in 1968, would lead in the 1980s to nearly half of all immigrants coming from Asian countries.

Despite the end of prohibition against naturalization for Asian aliens and the striking down of discriminating state legislation, more than half of the adult Japanese-Americans, as late as 1958, could not vote for president or elect representatives to Congress because they lived in the territory of Hawaii. Opposition to statehood in the islands and on the mainland was based in part on the fact that nearly 40 percent of the islands' population was of Japanese descent.[38]

A comprehensive public opinion survey on the islands in 1958 revealed that 23 percent of the Caucasians (*haoles*) and 27 percent of ethnic Hawaiians polled strongly opposed statehood. Of the largest ethnic groups in the islands, only among the Japanese did a clear majority back immediate statehood.[39] In Congress, opposition came mainly from southern representatives like South Carolina's Strom Thurmond (then a Democrat). While assuring Congress that he meant no personal attack on the Japanese, Thurmond said he was convinced they could not adapt to American political institutions. He and other southern senators may have been less concerned about Japanese control in Hawaii than about the addition of two pro–civil rights senators to the upper chamber.[40]

Southern opposition was overcome in part because of the leadership of Senate Majority Leader Lyndon Johnson (D-Texas) and Speaker of the House Sam Rayburn (D-Texas), who worked out a strategy with the delegate from Hawaii, Democrat Jack Burns, for Republican-dominated Alaska to be admitted as a state first, thereby creating a strong argument for admission of the only remaining incorporated territory, (Democratically inclined) Hawaii. By separating the two statehood bills, they were able to divide the opponents of each and to persuade a majority to approve both. With pro-statehood momentum established by congressional action in early 1959, all that remained was for the voters of the territory to endorse the statehood bill in a June 1959 primary election. Despite ethnic tensions that complicated the statehood issue in Hawaii (hostilities against the Japanese among Hawaiians and *haoles* and also Filipinos and Portuguese), the final count was seventeen to one. Pro-statehood victories were posted in every state representative district; significant antistatehood sentiment was apparent in small Portuguese and Hawaiian precincts alone, where fear of Japanese-American control was the strongest.[41]

Asian-Americans and the Process of Ethnic-Americanization

The process of ethnic-Americanization for Asian-Americans in Hawaii had received a pronounced boost after 1958. The territorial legislature, controlled by a *haole*-dominated Republican oligarchy ever since Hawaii became a territory, was captured by the Democrats in 1954; nearly half of the seats went to Americans of Japanese ancestry. Two years later, the Democrats won again despite the landslide election of Dwight Eisenhower on the mainland. These political successes of Asian-Americans spurred a widespread voter turnout in 1958. Probably the most active group in the territory were the veterans from the 442nd Regimental Combat Team, who formed the 442nd Club. There were now several dozen nisei and other Asian-American political leaders in Hawaii, foremost among them Daniel K. Inouye, who would become the first American of Japanese ancestry elected to the House of Representatives following Hawaii's admission to statehood.

The son of Japanese immigrants, Inouye, like many other nisei, had a fierce determination to prove his Americanism. In his autobiography, Inouye described the bloody battles of the 442nd. "Our biggest single advance came on the day word reached us that President Roosevelt had died. Men just got up out of their holes and began fighting their way up [in northern Italy] . . . every *nisei* who had been invested with first class citizenship [was] . . . moving up for F.D.R. He had given us our chance and we had a lot of *aloha* for that man."[42] Some of the men who moved up and into heavy fire "fingered their *sen nimbari,* a piece of cloth with 1,000 stitches, each of which, in the Japanese tradition, protected the wearer against a thousand misfortunes." Leading his men in an attack against a machine gun nest, Inouye killed several Germans with his automatic gun, and was hit, first in the stomach and then by a grenade that nearly tore off his right arm. Forty-three years later, after a distinguished career in the U.S. House of Representatives, Senator Inouye served as co-chairman of the select committee in the Iran-Contra investigation of 1987. After listening patiently to testimony of high officials who had not shown a careful regard for the Constitution or laws of the U.S., Inouye pointed out that American constitutional government "is what gives us strength" and that "vigilance abroad does not require us to abandon our ideals or rule of law at home. On the contrary, without principles and without our ideals, we have little that is special or worthy to defend." Inouye's statement was an updated Japanese-American version of Carl Schurz's speech on "True Americanism" at Boston's Faneuil Hall. Inouye, in concluding the hearings, told his "fellow Americans" that he hoped the sessions had led to a better understanding and appreciation of "our Constitution," as he urged them to "strive harder to preserve it."[43]

There was a California equivalent to the Inouye story in the 1980s. Judge Robert M. Takasugi, a federal district court judge appointed by President Gerald Ford in 1976, presided over one of the most sensational drug trials of the decade. John Z. DeLorean, the millionaire industrialist, was on trial on charges that he conspired to distribute fifty-five pounds of cocaine. Born in 1930 in Tacoma, Washington, Takasugi had been interned as a teenager with his family in a Japanese-American relocation camp. The family business was lost and his father died in the camp. After the war, Takasugi became national legal counsel for the Japanese-American Citizens' League and the Japanese-American Welfare Rights Organization. An ethnic political activist, he recalled (after the DeLorean case) that the experience of being interned with his family "gave me an additional dimension into the rights of human beings . . . it did teach me something about due process of law."[44]

Following the European pattern of ethnic-Americanization, Asian-Americans used ethnic networking to mobilize in politics and in business. Second- and third-generation Asian-Americans formed new ethnic civic organizations in Hawaii, like the United Chinese Society and the United Japanese Society, and also were chosen for important positions as members of the university's board of regents and commander of the American Legion.[45] Like the other groups, the Filipinos formed their own Chamber of Commerce, providing opportunities for networking within the group and for representation outside it.[46] An increasing number of Asian-Americans were elected to office, especially in Hawaii, where they were more than half the voters in the 1960s. Successful businessman Hiram Fong was elected to the U.S. Senate in 1960, the first Asian-American to serve there, soon to be followed by Inouye and another nisei, Spark M. Matsunaga, a Democrat who had served earlier in the House. In the 1970s, voters in California sent a Republican nisei to the U.S. Senate and two Democrats to the House, one of whom had been a city councilman in Sacramento and the other a mayor of San Jose.

With the formal structure of sojourner pluralism at an end after elimination of the ban on naturalization for Asian immigrants and admission of Hawaii to statehood, Asian-Americans turned their energies to other issues in the late 1960s and 1970s. The political activity of younger Asian-Americans was affected by the black revolution, although to a lesser extent than American Indians or Mexican-Americans. A number of Asian-American students joined Third World liberation groups and took part, along with blacks, Chicanos, and whites, in demonstrations, sit-ins, marches, and other protests on college campuses. Asian Americans were particularly involved in student strikes in 1968 and 1969 at San Francisco State and the University of California at Berkeley, where they demanded more courses on Asian culture.[47]

In politics, however, Japanese and Chinese interests often clashed with those of black Americans. In 1967 in San Francisco, Chinatown Parent-Teacher Association leaders and several Chinese-language newspapers conducted a crusade against school busing. In 1971, the Chinese community boycotted the schools, achieving an absentee rate higher than 90 percent. It proved difficult, however, to raise money to support the network of private Chinese "freedom schools," and the boycott collapsed. The Chinese community was a close-knit, geographically concentrated one by choice for the most part.[48] But, in addition to conflicts with other

ethnic and racial groups, they disagreed on several domestic political
issues among themselves, and in the 1970s especially on U.S. foreign
policy toward China.

With vast increases in immigration from Asia from 1968 on, Chinese
communities in the United States became increasingly divided over U.S.
policy toward China, sharply disagreeing on how to relate to the Communist government in Peking, particularly when Vice Premier Deng Xiao
Ping made an official visit to the U.S. in early 1979. Over time, the
differences on foreign policy issues between the Cantonese-speaking population of America's Chinatowns and the immigrants from Taiwan in the
suburbs of American metropolitan cities weakened. The Asian-American
protest movement of the late 1960s also waned. San Francisco's Chinatown Red Guards, formed in 1968 in the image of the Black Panther Party
to deal with neglect of the Chinese elderly and unsanitary conditions in
their community, could never generate large-scale support in their essentially conservative communities. Some of the radical youth of the 1960s
and 1970s believed strongly in working to correct the great injustices of
American society, and they did so, as Carlos Bulosan had done in the
1930s, in the name of the principles of the Declaration of Independence.

The life of Bulosan, a Filipino-American, illustrates the process by
which the political struggle against injustice and on behalf of equal rights
often turned immigrants and their children into Americans. He knew
firsthand the system under which employers gave the worst jobs to the
most recent immigrant group and paid different wages for the same work
to different groups and otherwise ruthlessly exploited laborers.[49] Bulosan
had seen how the police cooperated in patterns of oppression against
dark-skinned workers. He watched organizations with patriotic names,
such as the Liberty League of California, the Daughters of the Golden
West, the Daughters of the American Revolution, work to deprive Filipinos and other Asians of their rights. Disillusioned, Bulosan considered
becoming a Communist; at another time, he became a thief. But his
principal passions were American politics and American literature, and
these stimulated him to organize the Committee for the Protection of
Filipino Rights, and to start a small school for migrant workers, where
"I traced the growth of democracy in the United States."[50] When he
lectured to Mexican and Filipino sugar beet workers in Santa Maria,
California, he told them that immigrants were Americans, too, recalling
that his brother had told him "America is in the hearts of men."[51] In the
Second World War, he joined other Filipino-Americans in pressuring
President Roosevelt to sign a special proclamation giving Filipinos the
right to join the armed forces. When, after months of illness and debility,
he finished his autobiography, he called it *America Is in the Heart,* using

words similar to those of President Roosevelt to Secretary of War Stimson, "Americanism is simply a matter of the mind and heart," and those of Justice Douglas, that "loyalty is a matter of the heart and mind."

By the 1980s, Asians constituted almost 50 percent of all immigrants to the U.S. The rates of naturalization for immigrants from Asia usually were higher than for nearly all other groups. Among Asians, Filipino immigrants were third, behind Asian Indians and Chinese in the speed with which they naturalized.[52] Bulosan, the Filipino migrant worker, much more than Dillingham, the scion of an old New England family, had proved to be a prescient interpreter of American nationalism. Those who had been excluded longest from membership in the American civic culture had rushed to embrace it once the barriers were lifted.

Chapter Thirteen

"CAN'T THEY SEE? I LOVE THIS COUNTRY..."
Mexican-Americans and the Battle Against Sojourner Pluralism

IN 1943, Ernesto Galarza had just completed his doctoral dissertation at Columbia University on Mexico's electric light and power industry. Inspired by the ideals of the American Declaration of Independence and Constitution, he had worked to end exploitation of agricultural workers. Puzzled when his opponents tried to smear him as un-American, Galarza asked, "Can't they see? I love this country in a way that people don't if they are born here."[1]

The transition to a settler mentality was harder for most Mexican nationals than for most other immigrant groups. The situation of Mexican nationals was complicated by factors that did not apply to Asians, for example: most settled in an area that once was Mexico before it became one-quarter of the land mass of the U.S.; the border areas of the Southwest had long been arenas of friction and conflict between Mexican nationals and European-Americans (called "Anglos" interchangeably here). Also, sojourner migration from Mexico, particularly after the start of the twentieth century, was much larger than that from Asia and virtually impossible to stem.

In New Mexico, where extensive land grants had been given to Mexicans by Spain, they were most likely to feel like a conquered people after the Mexican war. Unlike Texas or California, New Mexico had not attracted large numbers of Anglo migrants, and Hispanic-surnamed residents were more than 50 percent of the population until 1940. Despite the rapacious behavior of land speculators from outside the territory, rich ranchers and merchants of Mexican origin were influential in New Mexican politics even after New Mexico became a state in 1912. Between 1865 and 1912, the percentage of Mexican-Americans in the territorial house of representatives ranged from 42 to 95 percent.

The history of the conquest continued to have symbolic importance to many Mexican-Americans in New Mexico into the twentieth century, but only a small fraction of the Mexican-Americans and Mexicans in the U.S. are descendants of the approximately 75,000 Mexicanos who lived in conquered territories. The other areas once a part of Mexico—California,

Nevada, Utah, Colorado, Arizona, and Texas—were sparsely settled. Only ten thousand *Californios* (Mexicanos in California) lived in that province at the war's end. After the signing of the treaty of Guadalupe Hidalgo in 1848, American control of California came quickly. One hundred thousand Anglos arrived in 1849 alone, most of them in pursuit of gold. California was admitted as a state in 1850. Within two years, more than a quarter of a million European-Americans lived in the new state.

Texas was dominated by Anglos before the Mexican War. In 1830, the twenty thousand Anglos in Texas outnumbered Mexicans by five to one. In 1836, certain Mexicans joined Anglo-Americans in the successful Texas revolution, which led eventually to the annexation of Texas, but armed resistance to Anglo domination in the Rio Grande valley continued well into the twentieth century. Skirmishes along the border underlined the fact that it was an artificially created line cut through half of the Mexican nation.[2]

Mexicans moved easily back and forth across the border, and even those Mexicans who remained in the U.S. and their children were affected by the continuing flow of new nationals in a way that tended to reinforce their Mexican cultural consciousness and, in the case of many, to retard their full sense of being Americans. But over time many Mexican-Americans saw their interests and loyalties as increasingly American and distinct from those of immigrants.

La Raza

The historic experiences of the Californios, Tejanos, and Nuevo Mexicanos differed not only in the time and place of settlement but in the degree of interaction with local Indians and with recent immigrants from Mexico. In California alone were several groups: descendants of early Californio families; descendants of those who came during and after the Mexican Revolution, during the First World War, and in its aftermath; descendants of New Mexicans; descendants of Tejanos; *braceros* who came during the Second World War and after; and legal and illegal immigrants who came later. Yet most Mexican-Americans, like the Chinese, Japanese, and certain other immigrant nationalities, had a strong sense of cultural unity. The Mexicans encapsulated it in the term *La Raza*, or "the race": a sense of peoplehood based on a mixing of Hispanic and Mexican Indian cultures that had been shaped by a powerful founding myth and sustained by a pride in language and in cultural values and institutions. The founding myth holds that nomadic tribes originating in the land of Aztlán, in what is now the southwestern U.S., had migrated down ancient trails into the valley of Mexico in about the eleventh century A.D. The Aztecs, whose name comes from Aztlán, founded the city of Tenochtitlán among the shallow marshes on what was then a much larger Lake Texcoco. There they built a great empire extending over most of central and southern Mexico, with Tenochtitlán its capital. It was conquered after four centuries by Hernán Cortés and the Spanish, who ruled for another four centuries. Through intermarriage and miscegenation a new people, part Indian and part Spanish, was formed. The mestizo heritage, which many Mexican-Americans thought of as Indian in blood and soul and Spanish in language and civilization, gave Mexicans and, to a large extent, Mexican-Americans, their sense of peoplehood. The quintessential example of that blending of two ancient, great cultures into La Raza is in the basilica of Our Lady of Guadalupe, Mexico's most important shrine, which commemorates an appearance to an Indian named Juan Diego of the Virgin Mary in 1533 near a rocky hill. He repeated the tale of this vision to people throughout the countryside. The Virgin, who was the patron saint of Mexico, asked Diego to instruct the bishop of Mexico to build a shrine in her honor on that hill. When Diego asked for a sign to prove that she had visited him, a picture of the Virgin appeared on his cloak. Every year, on December 12, Mexicans hold their most important religious fiesta in and around that shrine.

No matter what they called themselves in the U.S.—Mexican-Americans, Chicanos, Latinos, Mexicanos, Latin American, Spanish-American, Hispanic—the majority of Mexican descent probably felt and still feel themselves to be a part of La Raza. The founding myth of Aztec civilization, the visitation to Juan Diego, the stoic and enduring values of Indian civilization, and the language, literature, and religious mysteries of Spanish culture, all bequeathed to many Mexican-Americans a sense of shared history and destiny.

The feeling of peoplehood among other major groups who came— Germans, Jews, and Japanese, to choose examples—was no less strong, mystical, or ethnocentric than the feelings encompassed by "La Raza." What made the Mexican-American experience exceptional was partly the history of the conquest and of continuing violent conflict between Mexicanos and gringos along the border, but also the vast and continuing flow back and forth across the border, and that a significant portion of those who came entered the U.S. illegally.

The Political Agenda of the 1960s and 1970s

The economic, social, demographic, and ideological changes resulting from the Second World War that made possible the revolution for civil rights and for black pride and power also led to new militant political action by Mexican-Americans. Having fought for democracy in the war and having won the largest proportion of Congressional Medal of Honors of any ethnic group, many Mexican-American GI's came home determined to end the status quo.[3] Educated under the GI Bill of Rights, many sought opportunities in nonagricultural jobs that had been unavailable to most of their fathers and mothers. They moved so quickly out of the agricultural sector that by 1960 only 14.9 percent of the Mexican labor force in California was engaged in agriculture. Altogether, only 23.4 percent, including farm laborers, were unskilled laborers; 46.3 percent were in semiskilled or skilled jobs, and 22.2 percent in entrepreneurial, professional, and other white-collar occupations.[4]

The restlessness of the returned GI's, unwilling to settle for the old ways, led to the organization of a Mexican-American veterans organization in Three Rivers, Texas, after the body of a Mexican-American GI, returned in 1947, was denied the right of burial through the local mortuary and in the local cemetery. The protest by Mexican-American veterans—telegrams and letters to Congress and the press—led to the burial of the young soldier in the national cemetery at Arlington, Virginia.

The former GI's met again to protest discrimination and poor services at a veterans' hospital in Corpus Christi, Texas, and christened their group of veterans "The American GI Forum of Texas," set up to protect the rights and promote the goals of Mexican-Americans through increased political participation. In California, Mexican-Americans began the Community Service Organization (CSO), focusing on local political action and community involvement. Mexican-Americans there also formed the Mexican-American Political Association (MAPA) in 1959 to work as a pressure group within the Democratic party. The League of United Latin American Citizens (LUAC), the oldest continuing Mexican-American political organization (founded in south Texas in 1928), became much more active. Its significance as a political force, particularly in California and Texas, was recognized in 1960 by presidential candidate John Kennedy and his brother Robert, who stimulated the formation of "Viva Kennedy" clubs throughout the Southwest to register and mobilize voters of Mexican ancestry.

The diversity of experience and interest of the Mexican-Americans inhibited the development of a political movement cutting across groups and states. Only in New Mexico was land an important issue. There, in 1963, a dynamic young Mexican-American, Reies López Tijerina, and a small group formed the Alianza Federal de Mercedes (Federal Alliance of Land Grants). A largely rural organization, the Alianza demanded the return of or compensation for millions of acres of land it claimed had been wrongfully acquired by the federal government. The Treaty of Guadalupe Hidalgo (1848) had stated that land grants given to New Mexicans by the Spanish and Mexican governments were to be "recognized in the tribunals of the United States," but those tribunals had, in fact, invalidated 94 percent of the land claims by Mexican-Americans.[5] Unable to achieve recognition for its claims, the Alianza decided to reoccupy various land grants by seizing U.S. government property, much of it national forest. Tijerina was sent to federal prison for his involvement in the burning of a sign on national forest land in 1967, and the Alianza dissipated.

Tijerina was never able to gain national attention for the land issue in New Mexico. The civil rights revolution of blacks had captured public attention nationally, and New Mexico's land issue seemed remote. Even Mexican-Americans in California, Texas, and Mexico seemed disinterested. Tijerina's approach was essentially militant, but also legalistic; it sought a disentangling of more than one hundred years of misinterpretation and misapplication of the Treaty of Guadalupe Hidalgo. But the Alianza program was virtually impossible to implement because rich landowners, joined by Anglo politicians and investors, had seen to it that approximately 70 percent of Spanish and Mexican land grants, private and communal, had changed hands by 1910.[6] In northern New Mexico, large pastures once considered free range were fenced in and Hispano herdsmen driven off. The creation of national forests in New Mexico absorbed additional lands owned by Hispano villagers in northern New Mexico, and the lands were fenced off and restricted in use. These land changes took place under color of legality, and therefore many court battles ensued; by the 1960s it was apparent that no legal basis on which to reclaim the lands would be recognized, and that it would be difficult to find individuals with standing to make that effort even if such a basis could be found.

More than 90 percent of the six million persons of Spanish origin living in the Southwest when the Alianza made its claims were immigrants or the children of nineteenth-century immigrants. Eighteenth-century land titles seemed remote.[7] While the Alianza was struggling to reclaim land for Mexican-Americans in New Mexico, another organization, the Crusade for Justice, begun in Denver in 1965 under the leadership of a boxer and politician, "Corky" Gonzales, considered appealing to the United Nations for a plebiscite in the Southwest to determine whether Mexican-Americans wanted independence from the U.S. The idea faded quickly as impractical, and the Crusade began to concentrate on community service, such as a nursery, a community center, and a school in Denver with classes from kindergarten through college. Gonzales instituted an annual Chicano youth liberation conference in 1969, and for several years, thousands of Chicano youth groups sent representatives to conferences to plan a rebirth of Chicano nationalism. With second-, third-, and fourth-generation Mexican-Americans integrated into every facet of American society, the Crusade had limited appeal and soon faded.

Another relatively short-lived organization was the Brown Berets, which was organized in Los Angeles and quickly spread throughout the Southwest. Focusing on issues of urban police brutality, the Brown Berets protested the killing of a Chicano youngster by an Anglo policeman in Albuquerque in 1967 and compelled the police department to set up a police community relations task force consisting of an Anglo, a Chicano, and a black.[8] The Brown Berets provided an outlet for young urban Mexican-Americans, some of whom had been members of youth gangs, but who now worked in community services. Another militant organization, the United Mexican-American Students, college students from middle-class backgrounds, taught pride in the pursuit of power, and at the University of New Mexico pressured the student government to "Mexicanize" the annual student festival and the administration to establish a Chicano studies program.

Land and independence became less important as unifying issues for Mexican-Americans than language and culture. From the militant Alianza, the Brown Berets, and the UMAS to the more conventional ethnic-American lobby groups such as LULAC and the GI Forum, all demanded respect for the cultural integrity of the Mexican-American people.

As was true in the black revolution, Mexican-Americans who asserted their pride in seeking power sought names that would indicate their control over their own destiny. During the war, Mexican-American young people, especially between thirteen and seventeen, felt caught between Mexican and Anglo cultures; they created a subculture that they called *pachuco,* with its own slang, clothing styles, and music.[9] But pachuco had more to do with the search for a personal adolescent identity than with naming a political movement. Young Mexican-Americans in politics increasingly began to use the term *Chicano* in the 1960s. Chicano became a useful name for the theme of cultural nationalism. Once used pejoratively by New Mexicans to refer to recently arrived immigrants from Mexico, Chicano had resurfaced, partly in rebellion against the older generation, which seemed to the young militants too submissive. Tijerina and the *Alianzistas* preferred *Indo-Hispano,* which to them emphasized the Indian background of Mexicans and provided, at least on the surface, a stronger basis for claims to land.

Indo-Hispano quickly disappeared. The term *Chicano* spread, popular with students in the Southwest in 1968 who boycotted classes and issued demands that the use of Spanish be permitted on school grounds and that courses in Mexican history and culture be included in the school curriculum. In the first major walkout, students left classes in East Los Angeles, the rapidly growing and already largest urban Mexican barrio. Students boycotted high school classes in Denver and San Antonio and, during the spring semester of 1968, college classes across California. At San Jose State College they held a special Chicano commencement. During the spring of 1969, in Kingsville, Texas, 116 Chicano students were arrested in a walkout, and on September 16 hundreds of thousands of Chicano students boycotted schools across the Southwest.[10]

Just as German immigrants had fought for the use of German as a language of instruction in the public schools in the nineteenth century, particularly in rural areas, and Native Americans the right to speak tribal tongues in government schools, so Mexican-Americans did not want their children to lose love for and command of Spanish. But a common love of culture and language did not mean agreement on the term *Chicano*. Those who spoke Spanish in New Mexico and southern Colorado, with little contact with Mexico, identified with the early Spaniards and preferred to be called Hispanos or "Spanish-Americans." A large number of Mexican ancestry preferred to be called "Mexican-American," and some wanted to be called simply "American." Later, the terms "Hispanic" and "Latino" provided more political clout, and *Chicano* had almost been abandoned by the late 1980s.[11]

The Movement for Farm Workers' Rights

For millions of Americans, the Chicano movement eventually meant a movement for farm workers' rights. Although much of the action for Chicano rights in the mid-1960s had shifted to the cities, where the vast majority of Mexican-Americans lived, the farm worker remained the symbol of exploitation by American employers of Mexican nationals and Mexican-Americans. Alien farm workers seldom were able to win major concessions from employers (see chapter 6). They constituted a large pool of workers intended to ensure a surplus for employers, what the voice of commercial farming, *The Western Grower and Shipper,* once called "an ample and fluid supply of labor."[12] The great strikes of the 1920s and 1930s usually ended in disaster, and so pitiful were the results of strikes in the 1950s that Ernesto Galarza made up his mind never to ask farm workers to strike again as long as *braceros* were available to replace them.[13]

When the *bracero* program ended in 1964, a new leader, Cesar Chavez, emerged to personify the hopes for a better life of those Mexican nationals and Mexican-Americans in agriculture. Chavez, born in 1927 into a farm family in Yuma, Arizona, grew up as a typical Mexican-American migrant farm worker. He attended about thirty schools before reaching the seventh grade, his last. Settled in San Jose, California, in 1950, he became active in the Community Service Organization and rose to the position of CSO director for California and Arizona. In 1962, he moved to Delano, California, to work in the vineyards, and there organized the National Farm Workers' Association. Chavez was sensitive to the cultural sensibilities of the workers and modeled his union along the lines of a nineteenth-century Mexican *mutualista* organization, establishing a death benefit plan, a cooperative grocery, a credit union, a medical clinic, a newspaper, and even a social protest theater group.[14]

Despite the tremendous growth and influence of industrial and craft unions nationally, agricultural labor was still extremely weak. The Fair Labor Standards Act did not apply to farm workers. There was no Agricultural Labor Recruitment Act to regulate the hiring of farm workers, or even an Agricultural Labor Relations Act to give farm workers the right to organize and bargain collectively. In May 1965, the Agricultural Workers Organizing Committee (AWOC) struck the Coachella Valley vineyards for union recognition and the same rate of pay ($1.40 per hour) that *braceros* were receiving. Although growers refused to grant the union recognition, they did agree to pay the $1.40. The Coachella strike was a prelude to the action in Delano in the San Joaquin Valley, where 1,300 Filipinos walked out of the vineyards on September 8, 1965, to protest their hourly wage of $1.20. When Mexican-Americans were hired as strikebreakers, the Filipino leadership asked Chavez to persuade members of the Mexican National Farm Workers Association to join the walkout. On September 16, Mexican Independence Day, Chavez won a unanimous strike vote.

Believing that the strike might succeed because of the end of the *bracero* program and because of the general consciousness of civil rights in the nation, Chavez adopted a strategy to dramatize the farm workers' situation by showing that their strike was part of a larger movement for human rights and social justice. To Mexican and Mexican-American workers, he evoked the Virgin of Guadalupe as the patron saint of the struggle; to non-Mexican liberal sympathizers, he used the symbols and the language of the civic culture, quickly winning the support of civil rights groups and religious organizations. When the seven Catholic bishops of California upheld the farm workers' right to organize and strike, the fire went out of the charge of communism used by some employers against the Farm Workers' Association. With endorsements from leaders such as California's Governor Edmund G. "Pat" Brown, Robert Kennedy (now a Democratic senator from New York), and the United Auto Workers' leader Walter Reuther, Chavez chose as a key tactic a national boycott of the purchase of American-grown table grapes (and later lettuce).

Growers, in response, brought in strikebreakers from Texas and Mexico, including, as usual, illegal aliens. The federal government gave aid to the growers when the Defense Department increased purchases of grapes by 350 percent after the start of the boycott.[15] Non-farm-worker families in Delano did not regard the growers as capitalistic exploiters but as providers of jobs and the source of economic prosperity, and withheld their own support. Many growers were themselves children of immigrants (and a few were immigrants) from Yugoslavia who had been able to benefit from the American dream of opportunity based on equal rights. The social life of the growers was centered around the Elks Club and the Slav Hall, but the term "Anglo" was used by strikers to embrace them all, including the Gutuniches, Raboviches, Pandols, Caritans, and Zaninoviches (twenty-three Zaninoviches were listed in the telephone book). The farm owners who attended Lions Club or Rotary International luncheons were ethnic-Americans who had made it. As a result, they and their friends and families saw Chavez and his union as radical interlopers.[16]

The strike was threatened when the Teamsters' Union began to organize farm workers, but Chavez deflected the Teamsters with an agreement that allowed the Teamsters to organize warehousemen and cannery workers but not field workers. In February 1968, Chavez began a twenty-five-day fast that rapidly gained more media attention. After it was over, Chavez toured eastern cities and college campuses to gain support for the boycott. Eventually, the tactics of the boycott, of highly dramatic marches, and of targeted strikes against large employers like Schenley and De-Georgio began to wear the growers down. Contracts were signed with several smaller grape growers, and when Chavez signed up Roberts Farms, one of the biggest California citrus and nut growers, other employers followed suit. On July 29, 1970, the five-year-old strike came to an end.

Curtailing the Flow of Illegal Aliens

Although victory of the farm workers was a blow against the system of sojourner pluralism that had been enforced for so long through the cooperation of growers and public authorities, its impact was weakened by the flow of illegal aliens from Mexico. Following Operation Wetback in 1955, the Immigration and Naturalization Service concluded that "the so-called 'wetback' problem no longer exists . . . the border has been secured."[17] The facts were just the opposite. As noted earlier, the *bracero* program encouraged rather than stopped the movement of undocumented workers across the border.[18]

Under the Immigration and Nationality Act of 1952 it became a crime willfully to import, transport, or harbor an illegal alien, but under the "Texas Proviso," which made clear that to *employ* was not to *harbor,* growers, ranchers, and other employers could continue to hire illegal aliens with impunity. During the Delano strike, when the growers had used many illegal aliens to undermine the new United Farm Workers, one Mexican-American striker said, "the Chicano is cheated out of even a dirty job on the United States side of the line by wage-depressing labor competition." The immigration laws, he said, "favor the alien."[19]

With the strike over and particularly with the end of the *bracero* program, the flow of illegal aliens accelerated rapidly. A large majority of illegal aliens apprehended were Mexicans, although probably no more than 60 percent of the total number of illegal aliens in 1980 were Mexican nationals.[20] Every time Mexico devalued the peso or the economy of the Southwest became bullish, the incentive to migrate was enhanced. By 1978, the best estimate was that the Mexican component of the undocumented/illegal alien resident population was almost certainly less than 3 million, and possibly only 1.5 to 2.5 million, but the majority of these, coming from five states in central Mexico and the border state of Chihuahua, constituted a pool of exploitable labor (probably as much as 70 percent young adult males) who worked long, hard, and cheap, in the fields, restaurants, and small factories in the Southwest and California.[21]

The most fundamental law of economics was at work: supply and demand. The demand was voracious, but because so much of the labor was illegal, employers did not have to bid up the price of the supply. Illegal aliens made their own way to the United States. They did not enter the welfare system as a general rule. The price of strawberries, lettuce, and other produce (and some clothing) was lower than it would have been without the labor of the undocumented workers.

Another reason for continuance of the system was the sympathetic attitude of many Mexican-Americans toward illegal aliens. As citizens and resident aliens, many had reasons for wanting to halt the flow of illegal sojourners because they competed for jobs and tended to depress wages and job standards for Mexican-Americans in some sectors of the economy.[22] Also, the larger the number of illegal aliens, the larger a "greaser-wetback" image was perpetuated in the minds of Anglos,[23] making Mexican-Americans more vulnerable to violations of their rights as American citizens or as permanent resident aliens during attempts to round up and deport illegal aliens such as in the 1930s and during Operation Wetback in 1954. Yet illegal aliens were, after all, part of La Raza, and Mexican-Americans had brotherly and sisterly feelings toward them. In some cases, the illegal aliens were relatives. Realizing that most illegal aliens simply wanted to work for a brief time in the U.S. to support their families back home, many Mexican-Americans sympathized with undocumented workers even though they may have resented them as competitors for jobs.

The leaders of Mexican-American advocacy groups were even more sympathetic. Public opinion polls in the 1980s showed that Mexican-Americans generally, by slight majorities, usually supported more effective enforcement to deter the entry of illegal aliens, including a law that would penalize employers who knowingly and willfully hired them. But leaders—perhaps also moved by questions of cultural dignity and pride—vigorously opposed attempts to pass such a law, fearing that employers would discriminate against all foreign-sounding and looking persons to protect themselves.

The primary attack on illegal migration came not from Mexican-Americans but from labor unions and liberal politicians. But it proved impossible to develop a strong congressional majority on employer sanctions as long as the debate over illegal migration focused on labor questions, such as: Do illegal aliens take jobs away from American workers?, how necessary are they to agricultural production in the United States?, what would happen to restaurants and other service industries if they disappeared? Agricultural and other employers and the U.S. Chamber of Commerce, who were pitted against organized labor, easily overmatched the unions on the illegal immigration issue, particularly since Mexican-American advocacy leaders and civil rights and civil liberties groups also opposed employer sanctions.

Although the political influence of organized labor was waning in the 1970s, it was still strong enough to stimulate introduction in Congress of several bills designed to curtail the flow of illegal aliens, particularly when the number apprehended at the Mexican border increased dramatically. But passage of such laws in 1971 and 1973 was stymied in the Senate, where agribusiness interests were strongly represented.[24] Because the debate focused on labor issues, no action was taken when a cabinet-level committee on illegal aliens appointed by President Gerald Ford recommended, in December 1976, a bill to impose penalties against employers who knowingly hired illegal aliens; nor was action initiated in 1977 when President Jimmy Carter submitted a message to Congress with proposed civil penalties for employment of illegal aliens. The Carter proposal also would have given permanent resident alien status to aliens who had been in the country continuously since 1970, and would have initiated a five-year temporary resident status program for aliens here continuously since January 1, 1977.

The Carter administration proposal left open the question of what would happen to temporary resident status aliens after five years, and it failed to include a provision for a reliable and universal system to identify citizens, permanent resident aliens, and others eligible to work, without which employer sanctions would be extremely difficult to enforce. Congress, still beset by too many conflicting political pressures, was deadlocked in considering the administration's bill.[25]

The 1979 Select Commission on Immigration and Refugee Policy

Democratic leaders, in particular, felt the conflicting pressures of organized labor and Mexican-American advocacy groups. By the mid-1970s, some of the same liberal politicians who ordinarily responded to labor pressure began to listen to Mexican-American leaders who argued that sanctions would lead to discrimination against Mexican-Americans and other foreigners. Needing time to build majority support or at the very least to avoid the growing counterpressures within the Democratic party on the issue, congressional leaders in 1978 persuaded the Congress and President Carter to accept the creation of the Select Commission on Immigration and Refugee Policy, to consider the illegal alien question and all other aspects of immigration and refugee policy and to make appropriate administrative and legislative recommendations to the president and to the Congress.

Senator Edward Kennedy, chairman of the Senate Committee on the Judiciary, had called for the commission to undertake "an objective and thorough study of current immigration law and practice—a review that is beyond the capacity and scope of a single agency of the Executive branch or a committee of Congress, and which must involve a broad spectrum of opinion and groups concerned with immigration reform."[26] Led by the commission's chairman, the Reverend Theodore M. Hesburgh, former chair of the Civil Rights Commission and a leader in many human rights causes, the sixteen-member commission (eight members of Congress, four from the cabinet, and four public members) reported in March 1981 to President Ronald Reagan and the Congress more than one hundred recommendations on immigration and refugee policy. Those that received most attention at first concerned illegal immigration. The commission concluded that although research on the impact of undocumented immigration on the economy was "inconclusive, there is evidence that shows that the toleration of a large-scale undocumented/illegal immigration can have pernicious effects on U.S. society." The commission found that illegal aliens often were at the mercy of unscrupulous employers and "coyotes" (smugglers) who smuggled them across the border, and they could not or would not avail themselves of the protection of U.S. labor laws. "Not only do they suffer, but so too does U.S. society."[27]

The commission somewhat refocused the debate on illegal immigration away from its economic impacts to an examination of the relationship of illegal immigration to the civic culture. It took the view that the presence of a substantial number of illegal aliens undercut the principle that all who live and work in the U.S., regardless of ethnicity, should have fundamental equal rights. The presence of a substantial number of undocumented/illegal aliens in the United States, it established, resulted not only in disregard for immigration law but in the breaking of minimum wage and occupational safety laws, and statutes against smuggling as well. Its most devastating impact, the commission speculated, could be the disregard it breeds for other U.S. laws.[28] Although the nation had long since rid itself of indentured servants and slavery and of contract labor arrangements to import foreigners to do dirty work, it should now, the commission maintained, cease the heavy reliance of American employers, particularly in the West and Southwest, on exploitable foreign labor, and curtail illegal migration. How to do that was the sticking point.

All sixteen commissioners recommended that a comprehensive program should be adopted to legalize undocumented aliens already in the country, making it possible to reduce substantially the size of an underclass unwilling to report crimes against themselves for fear of deportation. The commission also recommended an expansion in the number of visas available to spouses and minor children of permanent resident aliens, something that would increase substantially the flow of legal immigrants from Mexico; and it urged the clearing of existing backlogs of almost one million persons who had been precleared as eligible to immigrate.

These pro-immigration recommendations were not consistent with the general mood of the country in 1981. Antialien feelings had been stimulated by Iran's holding of American hostages in 1980, by Fidel Castro's expulsion of Cubans from Mariel Harbor (more than 120,000 Cubans arrived in Florida, at least 20,000 of whom were excludable under U.S. immigration laws), by the mounting cost of the resettlement of hundreds of thousands of Southeast Asian refugees, and by growing resentment against illegal aliens, often confused in the public mind with lawfully admitted immigrants.

Given its own emphasis on civil rights, the commission listened with particular care to the concerns of Mexican-American political leaders and representatives of lobby groups, who argued that the enactment of a program to enforce sanctions against employers who hire undocumented aliens would result in discrimination against Mexican-Americans and other foreigners. But after reviewing all existing research, after conducting new research, after twelve public hearings throughout the country and dozens of consultations and site visits, the commission staff found that some employers discriminated against people of foreign extraction, while others discriminated in favor of illegal aliens and against those who were eligible to work.

A majority of the commissioners concluded that a system with a clear mechanism for establishing eligibility to work that required no discretionary judgments by employers probably would reduce already existing discrimination and the likelihood of employer discrimination in the future. Continuing to do nothing, the staff of the commission argued, could lead to more discrimination and to severe measures like the roundups of the 1930s and 1950s that violated the civil rights of many Mexican-Americans.[29] Since each of several alternative methods for identifying persons eligible to work considered by the commission gave employers an absolute right of defense against charges of knowingly hiring an illegal alien if they asked for, noted, and recorded the authorized identification presented to them by prospective employees, there should be no additional incentive for employers to turn away persons with foreign-sounding names or those who looked or talked as though they might be illegal aliens because of an employer sanctions law. Discrimination would be reduced once employers were educated as to how the law worked.

Although opinion polls showed that the American public generally believed that too many immigrants (legal and illegal) were entering the U.S., the commission helped to deflect xenophobic concerns about the inability of immigrants to adapt to American society. Editorials in major newspapers applauded the commission's conclusion that lawful immigration was useful in every important respect and should be increased, and that employer sanctions were likely to be more protective of civil rights and more efficient in curtailing illegal immigration than conventional enforcement methods.[30] Congress would prove willing, as the commission recommended, to keep the front door wide open (the commission wanted to open it even wider) while taking steps to close the back door. Mexican-American group leaders, however, continued to believe that employer sanctions would lead to discrimination, and the U.S. Commission on Civil Rights had issued a report in October 1980 in which three of its five members agreed with them.[31]

The Immigration Reform and Control Act of 1986

When the issue came before the Congress again, it became clear that Mexican-American leaders, many of whose constituents had a stake in curtailing illegal migration, still were almost unanimously opposed to employer sanctions. But the most effective political opposition came from employer groups, particularly growers in the West and Southwest, who relied on illegal aliens. Their position was that if the government was to take action to cut back on illegal migration, it should also reinvent some version of the *bracero* program. In either case, the employers wanted to be in a position to turn the spigot on or off to regulate the flow of workers from Mexico. Key congressional leaders, for example, Senator Alan Simpson (R-Wyoming), who had replaced Edward Kennedy as chair of the Judiciary Subcommittee on Immigration; Representative Peter Rodino (D-New Jersey); and Kennedy himself (D-Massachusetts), all of whom had served on the Select Commission on Immigration and Refugee Policy, opposed a large-scale temporary worker program. Under Simpson's leadership the Senate twice (1982 and 1984), and the House once (1984), passed legislation consistent in large measure with the approach of the select commission toward illegal immigration. Nevertheless, differences between the House Democratic leadership and the Republican White House over funding the legalization program kept the two bodies from agreeing on final passage.

Five and a half years after the select commission made its report, President Reagan signed the Immigration Reform and Control Act of November 6, 1986. Its legislative history had provided a classic example of pluralistic democratic pressure groups at work. In the end, the growers were able to persuade Congress to enact a special agricultural worker program; but this time they were obliged to accept one fundamentally different from the *bracero* programs that preceded it; the new program provided for legalization of special agricultural workers free to work anywhere, even outside agriculture, and eligible to become resident aliens and also citizens.[32] Congress explicitly rejected the idea that there should be a large body of foreign workers—either through illegal migration or through some variation of the guest workers or *bracero* program—confined by law to an essentially inferior status because they are aliens. The old idea of hiring foreigners to do work others do not want to do while denying them the opportunity for membership in the polity had been abandoned as a matter of national policy.

Congress calmed the tremendous anxieties of growers of perishable commodities that in the event of effective employer sanctions their labor supply would dry up and their businesses be jeopardized, but it insisted on a price consistent with the principles of the civic culture. By insisting that alien agricultural workers not be given a *bracero*-like status but a temporary status with a choice of permanent residency and citizenship, Congress had seen to it that such workers could decide themselves whether to remain as sojourners or to become settlers. They were free to join labor unions, petition for redress of grievances, and otherwise participate in American life, whichever choice they made.

The principles of the civic culture also enabled many congresspersons to see the program to legalize illegal aliens (often called "amnesty") as in the American national interest. The law provided that illegal aliens who entered the U.S. illegally before January 1, 1982, had, in effect, become members of American society, with a right to choose permanent residency and citizenship. To deal with the possibility that employer sanctions would result in discrimination against foreign-sounding or -looking resident aliens and citizens, Congress established new civil rights protections for all Americans by broadening the antidiscrimination provisions of the Civil Rights Act of 1964 to prohibit employment discrimination based on citizenship status or national origin.[33]

Passage of the Immigration Reform and Control Act of 1986 did not, however, end coercive sojourner pluralism. The legalization plan did not reach a substantial number of illegal aliens working in the U.S. who arrived after January 1982 and who would be buried in an underclass based on illegal alienage if they remained. Some eligible aliens did not apply for legalization because they were uncertain they could produce the documents needed to make their case. Others were discouraged because they thought family members who were not eligible would be detected and deported, an eventuality that did develop in rare cases. But when the period for legalization ended, 1,760,000 (more than three-quarters of them Mexican nationals) had their initial applications for legalization approved. An additional 1,300,000 were initially accepted under a special legalization program for those who had worked in agriculture under slightly more restricted terms. Within a decade, most of these aliens who had formerly lived outside the law would be eligible for citizenship. A busboy working in a Boston restaurant said, "I feel great that I have some rights now, to be here, to be free and to be accepted."[34] In New York, a man of sixty-one shouted out, "Free at last!"[35]

The principal impact of the legislation was felt in the Southwest and West, where a large majority of all newly legalized aliens lived. Sojourner pluralism had not been eliminated, but large steps had been taken to reduce it. By 1989, the prediction of widespread discrimination from employer sanctions was disputed (there clearly had been some increase). Employers generally complied with the law, and the number of illegal aliens apprehended at the border had diminished, although it would take years for the employee eligibility system to be made substantially effective.[36] The select commission had urged reliability as well as universality in choosing a method to identify persons eligible to work, and most commissioners wanted to use a new counterfeit-resistant Social Security card as a means of identification. Congress decided to require a combination of existing identifiers, responding to the fear that a reliable system of identifying those eligible to work in the U.S. might lead to an abuse of civil liberties, a decision which left open large opportunities for fraud.

Employer sanctions could never eliminate the flow of illegal migration, given the powerful attraction of jobs for underemployed and unemployed Mexicans and others and given the historic pattern of circular migration that had become so entrenched over the decades. As long as the laws of economics continued—as long as a tremendous demand of employers for low-cost labor and a desperate need among Mexicans and others for remunerative work continued—illegal migration and the old system of sojourner pluralism would continue. It would take time for the law to modify sharply entrenched patterns of migration; but having abandoned the policy in which the nation virtually sanctioned importation of exploitable migratory labor from Mexico to do nasty jobs in the West and Southwest, it was unlikely that it would ever go back to it. The new civil rights protections for a system of employee eligibility probably would be improved over time to enhance its reliability and relative effectiveness, with the flow of illegal migration to the U.S. diminished and more manageable than it had been before.

The Fear of Mexican-American Separatism

Several generations of Mexican-Americans had proved their adaptability to American life and their loyalty to American institutions. Yet, the volume of Mexican immigration to the U.S. in the 1970s and 1980s, legal and illegal, had raised fears among scholars, journalists, and the public generally that immigration from Mexico would lead to a new bilingual, bicultural nation and to a movement for political separatism comparable to that by the Quebecois in Canada. Such views were stimulated in the late 1960s and early 1970s by the militant rhetoric of the Brown Berets and the Alianza, but it was the sheer volume of Latino (especially Mexican) migration to the U.S. that appeared the principal stimulus for alarm.

The Hispanic population grew between 1970 and 1980 by 61 percent to 14.6 million, compared to a 9 percent growth in the non-Hispanic population, and in the 1980s the Hispanic population continued to grow at a rate at least five times that of non-Hispanics. Because of immigration and the relatively high birthrate of Hispanic immigrants, the U.S. Census Bureau predicted that the Latino population would double to 36.5 million by the year 2020.[37] The numbers alone would be disquieting to persons with xenophobic feelings, but many other Americans were concerned about cultural and possibly political separatism. In a 1980 article in *Foreign Affairs*, Michael Teitelbaum, a leading student of immigration, pointed out that a minority of radical Chicano political leaders "openly refused to recognize the legitimacy of the United States-Mexican border" and that Mexican and other Hispanic leaders appeared to resist acculturation in their vigorous advocacy of "their common language as a symbol of common pride and a force for ethnic unity and power."[38] Senator Simpson, a key figure on the select commission on Immigration and Refugee Policy wrote in supplementary comments to the final report of the select commission that he was concerned about U.S. government policies "which seem actually to promote linguistic and cultural separatism"; he concluded that "if linguistic and cultural separatism rises above a certain level, the unity and political stability of the nation will in time be seriously eroded."[39] The ex-governor of Colorado and a colleague warned of an impending "immigration time bomb."[40]

Those skeptical of the ability of Mexican immigrants to integrate into American society often pointed to their low rates of naturalization. The 1980 census showed that of the almost 2.2 million people born in Mexico and living in the U.S., about 76 percent were not citizens. Many were newcomers. Still, naturalization rates for Mexicans tended to be among the lowest of all immigrant groups, largely because of proximity to the mother country (as was also true of French Canadians), but also because of other factors, such as fear of the U.S. Immigration and Naturalization Service, lack of information, problems in meeting language and civics requirements, and a general lack of a sense of political efficacy and of trust in political institutions first learned in Mexico.[41] Although the Mexican propensity to naturalize was less than for other Latin American immigrant groups, the advantages to naturalization became more apparent with the passage of time to those who remained in the U.S., as did their commitment to a fuller participation in American political life. By 1980, 49 percent of those Mexican immigrants who entered prior to 1959 (and remained) had been naturalized.[42]

The relatively low naturalization rate of Mexican immigrants did not keep the children and grandchildren of those who remained from becoming as fully acculturated to the American civic culture as other ethnic-Americans. Generalizations to the contrary about Mexican-Americans were sometimes based on surveys that failed to distinguish between the behavior of immigrants and that of Mexican-Americans born in the U.S. or even between the behavior of immigrants who had been in the country a comparatively short time and of those who had settled for a longer period.

Surveys conducted by the market research firm of Yankelovich, Clancy and Shulman in 1981 and 1984, which reinforced fears that Hispanics (especially Mexicans) tended to resist Americanization more than others, failed to make important distinctions within the population of Latinos surveyed. Of those who had been born in Spanish-speaking countries, only one in five had been in the U.S. as long as twenty years, meaning that less than half of the sample were either first-generation Americans or long-term settlers. Without disaggregating the responses of the entire group, it was not possible to learn about the pace of acculturation, and hence it was misleading for the authors to conclude, as they did, that "Hispanics share unique characteristics that distinguish them from the Anglo mainstream population."[43] It was a generalization one could make about Armenians, Jews, and most other ethnic groups in the U.S. The critical question was whether or not Mexican-origin Americans—first and second generation born in the United States—identified as Americans with the American civic culture, and the answer was unequivocally yes.

When a 1978 study compared the political opinions and attitudes of children who had been born in Mexico or whose parents (either or both) had been born there with those of children whose parents had been born in the U.S., a pronounced shift appeared toward identifying as Americans in the second group. For example, 73 percent of children (age nine to fourteen) identified themselves as American and Mexican-American rather than as Chicano and Mexican. Only 20 percent of newcomer children chose a comparable identification. Of all the age groups in the study, it was the second generation born in the U.S. who had the most positive identification with American institutions and a strong degree of trust in them.[44]

Increasing Success of Mexican-Americans in Politics

The political socialization of naturalized Mexican-Americans may have been slow and uneven compared to such settler groups as the Germans, the Irish, or the Jews, but it was also slow and uneven for other sojourner populations, among them the Greeks, Turks, Poles, Portuguese, and French-Canadians.[45] Yet, in the thirty years between 1957 and 1989, considerable growth occurred in Mexican-American and other Hispanic-American participation in national politics. The first election of a Mexican-American to Congress came in 1957, when the conservative and cautious Joseph Montoya was elected a representative from New Mexico (he became a senator in 1964). Four others were elected in the 1960s, three of them Democrats—Henry B. Gonzalez from Texas in 1961; Edward R. Roybal from California in 1962; Elio ("Kika") De la Garza from Texas in 1964—and one a Republican, Manuel Lujan from New Mexico, elected in 1968 to replace Montoya.

Roybal's entry into politics was reminiscent of that of European-American ethnic politicians in the nineteenth and early twentieth centuries. When Roybal, a veteran of the Second World War, campaigned in 1946 for the Los Angeles city council with the help of the new Community Service Organization, he argued for better streets, more parks and playgrounds, and for an end to police harassment of Mexican-Americans in East Los Angeles. He lost that first race, but he won in 1949, with a much stronger turnout from Mexican-American voters, becoming the first Mexican-American on the city council since 1881.[46]

Also similar to the behavior of the Irish and the Germans in the nineteenth century was the proliferation of ethnic slates that campaigned in support of a relatively narrow ethnic political agenda. The Political Association of Spanish-Speaking People (PASO), which grew out of the Viva Kennedy clubs, elected its slate to take control of the city council in Crystal City, Texas, in 1963, despite the opposition of the powerfully entrenched Anglo group that had run the city since its founding in 1906 and that now employed the usual tricks of political manipulation and control. A middle-class Mexican-American was co-opted by the Anglos to run on their slate. The big Del Monte packing plant suddenly ordered overtime production on election day. Texas Rangers were brought in to patrol the city on election day, with the intention of intimidating Mexican-American voters.

Because of the inexperience of the newly elected officials and the egocentric behavior of one of them, the PASO slate was defeated at the next election, but the victory at Crystal City had awakened Mexican-Americans throughout south Texas to the possibilities of political power.[47] Protesting against discrimination in the schools in Crystal City, over half of the school enrollment boycotted classes before Christmas 1969, and, through the strike, compelled the board of education to establish bilingual and bicultural programs, to end all discriminatory practices, and to hold an assembly period each September 16, the Mexican national holiday.[48]

Encouraged by the student strike, José Angel Gutierrez returned to his home in Crystal City at the end of his tenure as president of the Mexican-American Youth Organization (MAYO), to establish a new party, La Raza Unida. In 1970, the party achieved majorities of three to two on the city council and four to three on the school board. One commentator observed that "the stereotype of a fatalistic Juan Tortilla, a loyal servant happiest when he is stooped in the fields picking spinach, has been shattered for both Anglos and Chicanos."[49]

With the advent of President Johnson's War on Poverty, Mexican-Americans turned increasingly to community-based political activities. Rather than propose slates of candidates, as was done in Crystal City, where about 85 percent of the population was Mexican or Mexican-American, activists organized grass-roots political groups, one of which, the Communities Organized for Public Service (COPS), was set up with the help of private foundation funds to improve community facilities and employment opportunities for Mexican-Americans in San Antonio, Houston, and El Paso.[50]

Mexican-Americans sought political influence in state governments as well, and by 1967 more than six hundred state legislators of Mexican ancestry were serving in the Southwest.[51] In 1974, Mexican-Americans were elected as governor in two states: Raúl Hector Castro in Arizona and Jerry Apodaca in New Mexico. The election of Tony Anaya as governor of New Mexico in 1982 symbolized the transformation in the base of Mexican-American political power in that state. Many persons of Mexican ancestry had held office in New Mexico ever since the state's incorporation in 1912. But most were descendants of well-to-do Hispano families. Governor Anaya, one of ten children whose father had been a ranch hand, had grown up in an adobe hut with mud floors and no plumbing.[52]

As Mexican-Americans enlarged their role in electoral politics, the more militant separatist groups, like Alianza, the Crusade for Justice, and the Brown Berets, lost their appeal. La Raza Unida, which was to disappear as a political party in the 1980s, played an important role in determining the outcome of several local elections in south central Texas in the early 1970s, employing the political symbols and rhetoric of the civic culture, but when the Democratic and Republican parties reacted by setting up "Hispanic" offices within their party organizations (the Democrats actually guaranteed Chicano representation in their party structure in the mid-1970s), the attractiveness of La Raza Unida diminished, just as had been true for other monoethnic parties in American history.[53]

La Raza Unida could win power in Crystal City and other localities where most voters were Mexican-American, but Mexican-American candidates running for Congress or citywide office in larger cities needed to go beyond their Mexican-American base. When La Raza Unida asked a Mexican-American, Ben Reyes, to run for the Texas state legislature on its ticket, the Houstonian chose to run as a Democrat instead and won; so did Leonel Castillo in 1972, when he was elected Houston's controller. Castillo, a former Peace Corps volunteer, later Commissioner of the Immigration and Naturalization Service, appointed by President Carter, was the son of an illegal Mexican sojourner, later a settler. Like Anaya, Roybal, Reyes, Gonzalez, and others, Castillo was proud of his ancestral heritage, and was convinced that he did not have to give up la Raza—that feeling of spiritual, emotional, and cultural kinship with others from Mexico—in order to become an active American politician. Neither did Henry Cisneros, whose election as mayor of San Antonio in 1981 capstoned earlier electoral victories of Mexican-Americans in the 1970s. After studying to become an urbanologist at Harvard and MIT, Cisneros had become assistant city manager in two cities, then had worked as a White House fellow in the Nixon administration. HEW Secretary Elliott Richardson "pointed me in the direction of a political career," Cisneros testified. He was elected in 1975 to the San Antonio city council. By going beyond his ethnic base, he received more than 40 percent of the votes in three large Anglo districts. Without ethnic politics, however, Cisneros probably would not have been elected. When the U.S. Justice Department split San Antonio's at-large electoral system into ten voting districts in 1977, Mexican-Americans became much more active politically. Cisneros undoubtedly benefited from the Southwest Voter Registration Project pushed by Mexican-American organizations.

To become mayor of the tenth largest city in the U.S. (the first Mexican-American elected mayor of any large city), Cisneros displayed the qualities of the ethnic-American political leader who reaches beyond his own group just as did Carl Schurz in Wisconsin in the 1860s, Hugh O'Brien in Boston in the 1890s, and Daniel Inouye in Hawaii in the 1960s. "I am not the classic ethnic candidate," he said soon after his election.[54] Asked in an interview in 1980 (he was still on the city council) to give his interpretation of American culture, he recited from memory lines from Archibald MacLeish's "American Letter":

> The raw earth
> The mixed bloods and the strangers,
> The different eyes, the wind,
> And the heart's change.
> These we will not leave
> Though the old calls us.
> This is our country . . .

Cisneros remarked that he could read that poem "and get a standing ovation at *Cinco de Mayo* or any other Mexican holiday. That is what people believe. Those lines tell me what we are going through is something America has lived through before."[55]

Mexican-Americans loved Cinco de Mayo day no less fervently than the Irish embraced St. Patrick's Day, the Italians Columbus Day, and the Chinese their New Year. On May 5th, Mexican-Americans celebrated the repudiation by Mexicans under the leadership of Benito Juárez of an attack by a much larger, professional French army that had sought unsuccessfully to establish a permanent French empire in Mexico City. Juárez, an Indian who had left his village as a young boy and later became the president of the republic, the most revered of Mexican leaders, was portrayed by Cisneros in a 1986 article as a hero for Mexican-Americans just as James Michael Curley had depicted as American heroes for Irish-Americans the leaders of the Irish resistance to England. Cisneros wrote of Juárez, leader of the small, underequipped citizen army that defeated the French at Puebla before they could reach Mexico City, that he "fought for the rights of individuals, for tolerance, for freedom . . . for belief in the future and for a society that offered mobility to their children."[56]

There was no reason to fear that Juárez would become a symbol of resistance of Americans of Mexican origin to complete acculturation. Only the month before Cisneros's article appeared in *Vista,* the English-language monthly for Hispanics, its readers, who were overwhelmingly second-, third-, and fourth-generation Latino-Americans, responded to a survey on historical figures they most admired. Benito Juárez came in a distant fourth to George Washington, Abraham Lincoln, and Theodore Roosevelt, with Eleanor Roosevelt and Martin Luther King, Jr., sharing fifth place.[57]

Carey McWilliams, in his pathfinding history of Mexican workers in the United States, *North from Mexico* (1949), had called Mexican-Americans a "more or less voiceless, expressionless minority."[58] By 1980, Mexican-Americans were increasingly finding their voice. Yet, the inability to understand English retarded the political participation of some of them. Even by 1982, 11 percent of all eligible Mexican-American voters spoke Spanish only.[59] In 1981, a report of the U.S. Commission on Civil Rights concluded (with one dissenting vote) that English-only registration and voting impeded the political participation of voters whose common language was not English.[60] To the Civil Rights Commission, that constituted a serious form of discrimination against language minorities.[61] Yet, Congress had already taken action in 1975 to mandate bilingual ballots in jurisdictions where more than 5 percent of the citizens of voting age were members of a designated linguistic group. The 1975 law extended protection to four groups: Alaskan natives, American Indians, Asian-Americans, and those of Spanish origin; no group was more affected than Mexican-Americans, particularly in the Southwest. The year after the bill's passage, the Justice Department civil rights division sent 116 federal observers to Texas to oversee the first mandatory use of a bilingual ballot in that state's primary election.[62]

Of far greater importance to Mexican-Americans than bilingual ballots was the law's provision that any proposed changes in electoral jurisdictions were under federal scrutiny to prevent discrimination against minorities. Most important and controversial were the 1982 amendments that made it legal for any Mexican-American plaintiff to charge discrimination if election results showed the number of Mexican-Americans elected were not proportionate to the group's population in a particular district.

In attempting to change systems of representation purportedly discriminatory against Mexican-American voters, the Mexican-American Legal Defense and Education Fund, sometimes in cooperation with the Southwest Voter Registration Project, took two approaches: the first, enforcement of provisions of the Voting Rights Act, requiring counties and other jurisdictions in southern states, including Texas, to obtain federal approval of any changes in district boundaries and in systems of representation proposed after November 1, 1972; and the second, the filing of lawsuits based on the one person–one vote principle established by the U.S. Supreme Court early in the 1960s (see chapter 23).

As a result of initiatives by MALDEF and other Mexican-American groups, political participation rose in Houston, San Antonio, Dallas, and other cities. In Dallas, where the Dallas Citizens' Council, an organization of two hundred chief executive officers, ran the city council and the school board from 1936 until the late 1970s, elections were held up for ten months in 1980 under an order to make more likely the election of Mexican-American and African-American members.[63] In San Antonio, where a conservative group of Anglos worked into the 1970s through the Good Government League to maintain control of the city, the Justice Department ordered a change from a multimember district to single-member districts. In 1977, five Hispanics, including Henry Cisneros, and one black were elected, a majority of the eleven-person city council.[64]

MALDEF was particularly pleased with the results of shifting from multimember districts to single-member districts to increase Mexican-American representation. On May 15, 1984, its president and general counsel wrote to all members of the board of MALDEF that spring elections in Texas had resulted in a large increase in the number of Mexican-American elected officials: "Ten new Hispanics [Mexican-Americans] now serve on city councils. Five more serve on school boards in Texas. All were elected from single-member districts created through MALDEF lawsuits based on Section 2 of the Voting Rights Act."[65]

Mexican-Americans and the Civic Culture

Mexican-American voter registration in Texas grew from 488,000 in 1975 to 798,000 in 1980, partly as a result of the abolition of the poll tax and the introduction of bilingual ballots, but mainly because of an increased political consciousness of second- and third-generation Mexican-Americans who did not need bilingual ballots. In the mid-1980s, when many Americans were worried about the inability of Mexican immigrants to adapt to American life, Mexican-Americans were participating more actively in the political culture than ever before. The visibility of politicians like Cisneros and Kika De la Garza, chair of the Agricultural Committee of the House of Representatives, and others had become a stimulus to political activity among Mexican-Americans generally.[66] In the 1980 Democratic primary in Texas, Mexican-Americans voted in greater percentages than the rest of the population (39 percent as against 34.9 percent for the state as a whole).[67] The political potential of Mexican-American voters in states like Texas, California, Arizona, and New Mexico was large enough to attract presidential candidates in 1984 and 1988, especially in California and Texas, the first with forty-seven and the second with twenty-nine votes in the electoral college.

Mindful of Mexican-American voters, President Reagan went to San Antonio in 1983 to eat tacos, rice, and beans, and presided over ceremonies at the White House commemorating the 162nd anniversary of Mexico's independence from Spain and inaugurating Hispanic Heritage Week.[68] The Democrats had an ever greater stake in the potential Mexican-American vote, since the vast majority of Mexican-Americans voted Democratic. All presidential candidates in the Democratic primaries in Texas and California vied with each other to win favor with Mexican-American group advocacy leaders by opposing employer sanctions and supporting bilingual education.[69]

The political importance of Mexican-Americans was reflected in the quadrupling of the number of Hispanic elected officials between 1970 and 1988 from fewer than 800 to almost 3,400.[70] Yet, with about seventeen million persons of Hispanic origin, 63 percent of them Mexican-Americans, Hispanics made up only 4 percent of the vote in the 1984 presidential election. The result was partly a reflection of low voter turnout among Puerto Ricans on the mainland, of the substantial number of illegal aliens among Hispanics, and of a continuing disinclination of resident aliens to naturalize.

The 1986 elections were a turning point in the history of Hispanics in politics generally and of Mexican-Americans specifically. In Texas, Raúl González became the first Mexican-American elected to the state supreme court; of the ten Mexican-Americans who ran for Congress, all won. (The Congressional Hispanic Caucus, organized in 1975, now had eleven members, including one Puerto Rican from New York.) González was one of two Mexican-Americans who won contested party primaries for statewide office in modern Texas history. The other, a Republican, District Judge Roy Barrera, Jr., ran unsuccessfully to unseat state Attorney General Jim Maddox, a Democrat, who received strong support from Mexican-Americans despite Barerra's ethnic credentials. To counter Barerra's ethnic appeal, Maddox had learned to speak Spanish and had won the support of almost every Mexican-American politician in the state. González, who had the advantage of running as a Democrat, had been a migrant worker who eventually earned a law degree from the University of Houston. After working in Houston's Legal Foundation, a part of Lyndon B. Johnson's Office of Economic Opportunity, he became an assistant U.S. attorney; he was later appointed to the appellate court, and then to the state supreme court before being elected to fill a new term on that court.[71]

With Mexican-Americans much more active in American politics than ever before, sixty-eight Hispanic mayors were elected in 1987, nearly all of them Mexican-American, including Denver's mayor, Federico Peña, who invited all of the others to a "mayors' summit." In November, when LULAC held its annual conference, all seven Democratic presidential candidates sought the support of the 900 convention delegates, undoubtedly aware that in the state's Democratic primary in 1986, Mexican-American voters had cast almost one out of every four votes and also that registration of Mexican-Americans in Texas was increasing faster than in any other state—from 488,200 in 1976 to more than one million in 1984. "They pay more attention to us than they ever did before," said Willie Cruz, a LULAC delegate from Galveston.[72]

Although Mexican immigrants were still slow to naturalize, those who did become citizens were as likely to vote as the rest of the population.[73] A 1983 study by the University of Texas showed that Mexican-American citizens were involved in politics to about the same degree as other Americans. Of the sample of 622 Mexican-American citizens, 72 percent were registered to vote in 1980 and 58 percent had voted; 30 percent attempted to talk others into voting a certain way; 28 percent said they had attended a political meeting. As was true of the population generally, participation and trust in American politics went up with education and income.[74] With relatively strong rates of participation for those who became citizens, the National Association of Latino Elected and Appointed Officials (NALEO) in 1984 organized the National Citizenship Project to investigate the low rates of naturalization among Mexican-Americans. Hispanic city council members from across the nation sponsored citizenship resolutions to encourage municipal support for citizenship campaigns. NALEO pointed out that many Mexican-Americans did not understand the benefits of citizenship. The Social Security Administration automatically deducted 15 percent of a noncitizen's retirement benefits if he or she retired to Mexico, and noncitizens could not work in many of the better paying defense industries or for the federal government or most police and fire departments.

Research showed that the longer Mexican-Americans lived in the U.S. and furthered their education and occupational progress, the more integrated they became into the larger society.[75] Still, anxieties about political and cultural separatism continued to surface in the face of overwhelming evidence against it. Cultural bonds between Mexican-Americans and Mexicans did not result in significant political attachments to Mexico. Careful students of the subject reported that in 1980 "there is no evidence of their knowledge about or support for Mexican social and political systems."[76] Mexican-American leaders concentrated overwhelmingly on domestic issues such as jobs, education, and crime, not on problems of Mexico. They appealed to an electorate of first-generation and second-generation Mexican-Americans born in the U.S., well over 90 percent of whom were proficient in English (the second generation tended to speak English only). One survey of Mexican-American voters in East Los Angeles and San Antonio in 1983 showed that they put more stock in a candidate's party affiliation than in his or her ethnic identity. When asked to name the most trusted source of local news, respondents at all educational levels mentioned English-language television most frequently.[77] Although Mexican-Americans tended to be Democratic, they were far from monolithic in their approach to parties and issues, tending to vary their positions depending on income and education, as was true for most Americans.[78]

Mexican sojourners who became settlers and their children and grandchildren behaved in much the same ways as European immigrants and their descendants. The Mexican-American English-language magazine *Vista* featured stories on economic networking and political activism in the tradition of all major ethnic-American groups. In 1988, its second year, *Vista* was delivered to nearly 1,250,000 households in twenty-eight cities. In its first anniversary issue there were articles on the Hispanic Association on Corporate Responsibility (HACER), whose goal was to make business enterprises more aware of the Hispanic market; an advertisement from the U.S. Hispanic Chamber of Commerce featuring a large picture of Henry Cisneros with the caption "The American Dream: Now a Perfectly Realistic Goal for You"; and a report of a study from the National Council of La Raza, emphasizing the importance of learning how to speak English proficiently in order to take full part in American society.[79]

MALDEF and LULAC consistently employed the rhetoric of the civic culture as they pressed Mexican-Americans (and other Hispanics) to participate more actively in it. The Latino magazine *Nuestro,* which approved of efforts toward Americanization, praised MALDEF for showing Mexican-Americans in the Southwest, who had previously viewed the law distrustfully, "that the legal system could work for them and not just against them."[80] The founding leader of MALDEF, Vilma Martinez, and her successor, Antonia Hernandez, also used the rhetoric of American civic traditions and rights in their advocacy of Mexican-American causes.

Hernandez, whose U.S. citizen father had been deported to Mexico in the 1930s during the mistaken expulsion of many Mexican-Americans, testified on accepting the position of president and general counsel of MALDEF that "I had a lump in my throat when I took the oath of U.S. citizenship. . . . Because I wasn't born into the opportunities that this country has to offer, I don't take the rights and privileges for granted." She became an attorney in a legal aid office in Los Angeles and later a staff counsel to the U.S. Senate Judiciary Committee, chaired by Senator Edward Kennedy. In 1986, Hernandez explained, "Hispanics are no different from any other immigrants who came before us, be they English, German or Italian. The things we want are no different than what others sought."[81] Two years later, Hernandez reported to the MALDEF board and membership that it was gratifying to see the attention the Judiciary Committee showed to the testimony she and others representing the group had given. We have been "given the opportunity to make our voices heard," she said.[82] MALDEF continued to press vigorously on such issues as bilingual education, immigration, and voting rights.

LULAC had filed a lawsuit instrumental in getting Mexican-Americans into the segregated Orange County, California, public schools in the 1940s and had won lawsuits in the 1950s to gain Mexican-Americans access to juries in Texas; it had pushed hard on immigration and education issues in the 1970s and early 1980s. By the mid-1980s, it gave more attention to economic issues. "It's time for Hispanics to make the system work for us, instead of trying to go against the system," said its new president, Oscar Moran, after announcing an agreement with the Adolf Coors company in which the brewer agreed to economic affirmative action measures in Hispanic communities.[83]

Militant advocacy had not gone completely out of style, as indicated by the occasional rhetoric of MALDEF and groups such as the newly formed National Hispanic Leadership Conference, but by the end of the 1980s there was abundant evidence that Mexican-Americans were participating extensively in mainstream American politics. In every city and state where they became active in electoral politics, Mexican-Americans extended their political agenda beyond their first concerns, and elected representatives who entered coalitions with others. Alfredo Gutierrez, who began his political career working with *Chicanos por la Causa* and was subsequently elected to the state legislature from a heavily Mexican-American district, broadened the scope of his political agenda and became majority leader of the Arizona Senate in the 1970s. Raúl Castro, elected as Arizona's first Mexican-American governor in 1974, appealed, as every governor must, to a broad range of interests extending far beyond those that initially propelled him into politics.

Coalition-building did not necessarily lead to political power, as a 1984 study by three political scientists showed.[84] But it did tend to make Mexican-Americans more aware of the history and interests they shared with representatives of other groups, as when New York's Governor Mario Cuomo visited San Antonio in 1986 to speak at a fund-raising dinner honoring Representative Henry González and told the substantially Mexican-American audience, "I don't think the view of America from South Jamaica in Queens is much different from San Antonio's West Side. There was the same aching to belong in both places." He reminded the Mexican-Americans that Italian-American children also felt estranged from the dominant culture, as they tried to learn to speak English while struggling to have their own backgrounds recognized as worthwhile. He knew, he said, how hard it must have been for González to go to school "where the language was not the language of his home," because the words at school sounded different from those he had heard on the Italian streets of South Jamaica, "where passion and pride and powerlessness all lived together and people talked with their hands and their hearts."[85] Actually, the Mexican-American experience was different from that of Italian-Americans—the proximity to the ancestral homeland, the pervasiveness of Mexican culture on the border, the history of conquest, and the legal claims that derived from the Treaty of Guadalupe Hidalgo. But Cuomo's main point was correct. The anxieties of most Mexican-American youngsters—their ambivalence and high hopes as ethnic-Americans—were like those Cuomo recalled from his boyhood in Queens.

First, survival, and then, success and power were the goals pursued by the children of immigrants, success in the marketplace and power in the political system that gave Americans a sense of shared identity beyond ethnicity. By the mid-1980s, the civil rights revolution had invited Mexican-Americans to participate in the pursuit of power on a totally new basis. The old disincentives of racial prejudice, job discrimination, monolingual ballots, gerrymandered districts, and political intimidation—while not entirely gone—were largely in the past, and with their removal, the fears that Mexican-Americans would present a threat to the unity of the United States by creating another Quebec were virtually buried.

The analogy between Quebec and a hypothetical Mexican-American separatist movement was never really sound, but with the increasing large-scale participation of Mexican-Americans in the civic culture, it became absurd. Many other factors—the roles played by language, historical memory, geographic mobility, the Catholic Church, and the founding myths of the two nations—made a Mexican-American Quebecois movement impossible. Although Mexican-American leaders did raise the preservation of language as a rallying cry for ethnic mobilization, none did so in opposition to acquisition of English. In sharp contrast to the French-speaking children of Quebec, the vast majority of Mexican-Americans went to schools in which English was the major language of instruction and saw movies and watched television programs primarily in English. The French-Canadians of Quebec themselves were not simply pro-French language, but anti-English. But, although Mexico lost more than half of its national territory to the U.S. after the Texas insurrection and the Mexican War, Mexican-Americans of the 1980s had no historic memory anything as fierce as the French Canadian memory of the loss that followed the defeat of French armies by the British on the Plains of Abraham in 1763. In the 1980s, the auto license plate of Quebec bore the admonition, in French, *je souviens* (I remember).

Unlike French Canadians, Mexican-Americans did not constitute a majority in any state or region of the U.S. Moreover, they showed the typical migratory proclivities of Americans in the 1980s, spreading to states throughout the country, and more recently, moving from rural to urban areas and to the suburbs of major cities (see chapter 16).

A major difference affecting the relationship of Mexican-Americans to the polity as a whole, compared to the French Canadians of Canada, was the role of the church, a key force in stimulating nationalism in Quebec after 1837. Unlike the Catholic church in Mexico, which historically has been on the defensive in an officially anticlerical nation, the church in Quebec tried to keep French Canadians from migrating to the U.S.[86] Unlike the Quebec church, the Catholic church in the U.S. did not negotiate with the national government to maintain the economic status quo. To the contrary, in the 1970s and 1980s it had become active in promoting economic reform and social justice and was a dynamic force for integrating Mexican immigrants and their descendants into American life through instruction and preparation for citizenship, classes in English, and youth activities, such as those promoted by the Catholic Youth Organization.[87]

In their acceptance of cultural diversity, the Americanizing bishops of the 1980s differed from those of the 1890s who repudiated efforts by German-American Catholics, under the leadership of the German nobleman Peter Paul Cahensly, to establish distinctive parishes, congregations, and missions for each separate group of immigrants. When more than two hundred participants at the first Hispanic pastoral encounter met nearly ninety years after Cahensly made his effort, they found a sympathetic reception from the American bishops. The bishops received seventy-eight recommendations calling for respect for the linguistic and cultural integrity of communities at the local parish level, and emphasized that such parishes would enhance American values rather than separate from them. German Catholics who followed Cahensly emphasized the separation and preservation of immigrant communities but Mexican-Americans and other Hispanics spoke of pluralism within the framework of larger American values. "'E pluribus unum' and 'In God We Trust' mark the spirit of the people of the United States of America and of the Church of Christ," asserted delegates to the Hispanic Pastoral Encounter. "The strength of the unity of our country and our church is proportionate to the respect for individual persons, families and ethnic groups that compose them."[88]

The most important contrast between Canada and the United States in this regard derived from the founding myths of the two countries. For Canada, the central myth is based on the idea of two nations forming a federal union, each with separate cultures, languages, and religions, each nation a founding or charter member and each culture separate but equal. The implicit contract at the heart of the confederation guaranteed to the

Catholic church within Quebec control of a regionally concentrated, French-speaking Catholic population. The founding myth of the United States is that the United States is a home for all who seek equal rights as individuals.

The process by which the civic culture incorporated Mexican-Americans took many forms. Official recognition by presidents and governors of such holidays as *Cinco de Mayo* and Hispanic Heritage Week, the appointments of explicitly Mexican-American politicians to high positions, and the naming of streets and buildings after Mexican-American leaders all drew Mexican-Americans closer to the civic culture. When two Texas Democratic members of Congress, Representative Solomon T. Ortíz and Senator Lloyd Bentsen introduced legislation to rename a U.S. post office building in Corpus Christi the Dr. Hector Peréz García Post Office Building, they pointed to his six battle stars won during the Second World War, to his accomplishments as a physician and surgeon, and to his record as adviser and official representative to Presidents Kennedy, Johnson, and Carter. But García, who had received a Medal of Freedom from President Reagan, was best known among Mexican-Americans for his work as founder of the American GI Forum, the first significant Mexican-American activist group to emerge after the war to fight for their civil rights.[89]

By naming public buildings, Mexican-Americans claimed their share in the story of the making of the American nation, just as other immigrant-ethnic groups had done before them. In 1986, the principal of the Buena Vista Elementary School in San Antonio led a campaign to rename the school for Torribio Losoya, one of seven Mexican-Texans who died defending the Alamo in 1836 against the Mexican army of Santa Anna. The school principal wanted Losoya to be acknowledged as an American hero alongside Sam Bowie, Davy Crockett, and other defenders of the fort.[90]

By the 1980s, it was clear that the system worked to make immigrants and their children into Americans, not by disparaging or ignoring their ethnicity, as is done in some European countries, but by giving positive recognition to it. Typical was the volume published by the U.S. Department of Defense in 1983, *Hispanics in America's Defense*; it began with a letter from Secretary of Defense Caspar W. Weinberger paying tribute to the Hispanic men and women who fought in the armed forces. "The Hispanic community has given us generals, admirals, philosophers, statesmen, musicians, athletes and Nobel-prize winning scientists," he wrote. "Hispanic-Americans have contributed gallantly to the defense of our Nation, and thirty-seven have received the highest decoration our country can bestow—the Medal of Honor."[91]

Three years later, a Mexican-American woman who served as Deputy Assistant Secretary of the Air Force for Civilian Personnel Policy, Stella Guerra, told of attending political rallies with her father when she was very young: "He helped me become more aware of discrimination and to recognize that there was much to be done if we were ever going to overcome it." In explaining why she was dubious of the idea that young children from Spanish-speaking homes should be taught exclusively in Spanish, she said that although "we should never lose our ethnic identity, . . . we are Americans first."[92]

When Ms. Laura Martinez Herring of El Paso, who had just been named Miss U.S.A. (1985), was asked to be a featured speaker at a naturalization ceremony for people from thirty nations, Ms. Martinez, who had become a naturalized citizen at 14, reminded the about-to-become citizens (her mother included) that "becoming a U.S. citizen does not mean you may not take pride in your culture or be proud of your roots or love your people. . . . It simply means that you are now loyal to this wonderful country that is full of opportunities and you will support the Constitution." Her mother added that her citizenship meant she could "get involved now more with patriotic feelings. . . . I can vote and I can participate actively."[93]

The full story of immigrant acculturation can never ignore the maltreatment of immigrants and the bitterness they often felt against those who exploited and harassed them. Strangers and afraid, many immigrants, especially sojourners, took no part in American politics. Some immigrants, and even their children, remained parochial politicians, focusing on their own special interests over all others. But the process of political acculturation described by Alexis de Tocqueville and John Stuart Mill, as applied to Americans generally in the early nineteenth century, was valid for Mexican-Americans, just as it had been for others. Politics was the school of Americanization, said Tocqueville and Mill, an activity that, at least in the United States, often encouraged participants to widen their horizons. Without a system of corporate, pluralistic representation based on ethnicity or religion, ethnic group leaders were obliged to participate in coalitions with others whose points of view and interests also demanded attention. The view expressed by Tocqueville and Mill was too simple in the light of contemporary special interest group politics, and probably was overly romantic even in the early nineteenth century. Yet, that view was confirmed repeatedly by Mexican-Americans and others, as reflected in the remark of Andy Hernández, successor to Willie Velásquez as head of the Southwest Voter Registration and Education Project. When asked about his philosophy of politics, Hernández replied, "Politics is not just about who gets what, but about what values and principles we hold in order to create a greater public good."[94]

Mexican settlers and especially their children discovered that their participation in American political life, as for other immigrant-ethnic groups, encouraged them to espouse a wider patriotism as advocates of opportunity and civil rights for all. The literature of the children of immigrants is replete with broken dreams, alienation from their parents, and a sense of lost roots. But it does not include a lapse in patriotic loyalty to the American ideals of opportunity, freedom, and equality, ideals with special meaning for the children of immigrants. Witness not only the extraordinary record of Japanese-Americans in the 442nd Regimental Combat Team in World War II, but also Sergeant Jimmy Lopez, one of the American hostages held by Iran in 1980, who wrote on the wall of the room where he was imprisoned, "Viva el rojo, blanco e asul!" (Long live the red, white and blue).[95]

The power of the civic culture to compel the loyalty of ethnic-Americans was never better illustrated than in the story of Guy Gabaldón, a Mexican-American who won the Silver Star in the Second World War. Raised in East Los Angeles by a Japanese-American family who taught him to speak Japanese fluently, he received the medal for persuading more than one thousand Japanese soldiers to surrender during the battle for the island of Saipan.[96]

Part Four

THE AMERICAN KALEIDOSCOPE
The Ethnic Landscape, 1970–1989

America is coming to be, not a nationality but a transnationality,
a weaving back and forth, with the other lands, of many threads of
all sizes and colors.

—RANDOLPH S. BOURNE

Whenever large numbers of new kinds of immigrants arrived, anxieties were raised about the strangers' ways and whether or not Americans could preserve their unity as a nation. After passage of the 1965 amendments to the Immigration and Nationality Act and of the Refugee Act of 1980, the U.S. once again became a country of large-scale immigration, numbering almost 600,000 annually by the late 1980s plus those admitted under the 1986 immigration act (492,000 in 1989). Now anxieties about American unity were reinforced by the new ethnic pride and power movements of the 1960s and 1970s and by racially and ethnically conscious affirmative action policies.

A consequence was the "hugger-mugger," about which Harold Isaacs wrote to me in 1981—ethnic groups competing and grabbing for power, a cacophony of voices claiming benefits to compensate for the suffering of their ancestors, a proliferation of spoken foreign languages. Isaacs wondered whether the disorder he observed foretold the breaking up of a sense of shared responsibility as Americans.

Isaacs was right in thinking that the patterns of ethnicity in the U.S. had in certain ways changed: African-Americans and, to some extent, Indians were behaving more like ethnic groups than ever before; immigrants were coming in large numbers from Asia and from Latin America; all ethnic groups, including African-Americans, were becoming much more widely distributed throughout the nation; the expression of ethnic pride and the mobilization of ethnic interests were finding many more outlets; and the pace of interaction among members of different ethnic groups was accelerating, making it easier to cross ethnic boundaries, generating both friendships and conflict. The changed patterns were significant, but they did not lead to the kind of ethnic disharmony afflicting so much of the world.

The new immigrants were following the same path of ethnic-Americanization the old immigrants had followed, perhaps at a faster rate. Ethnic and racial conflict remained a serious problem, but with the acceptance and often celebration of ethnic diversity as an essential ingredient of American national identity, the *unum* was strengthened, even as the *pluribus* became more visible and noisier than ever.

Chapter Fourteen

THE BLOOD OF ALL NATIONS
The Sources of Ethnicity Become Global

IMAGINE Michel Guillaume Jean de Crèvecoeur, Ralph Waldo Emerson, Herman Melville, and Israel Zangwill, the four best known apostles of the ideal of the melting pot, at the opening ceremonies of the world summer Olympics in Los Angeles in 1984.

Crèvecoeur, a French Catholic immigrant farmer, described eighteenth-century Americans as a "promiscuous breed," arisen from "a mixture of English, Scotch, Irish, French, Dutch, Germans and Swedes."[1] His was a Eurocentric view. Emerson, the scion of nine Yankee ministers, and a minister himself before leaving his Boston pulpit, predicted that "the energy of Irish, Germans, Swedes, Poles, and Cossacks, and all the European tribes,—and of the Africans, and of the Polynesians—will construct a new race, a new religion, a new state."[2]

Herman Melville, who lived as a child in polyglot New York City and as an adolescent in multiethnic Albany, served in the Pacific with a multiethnic crew on a whaler for nearly four years. Melville, his perception perhaps enriched by his diverse experiences, said of Americans that "our blood is as the blood of the Amazon, made up of a thousand noble currents all pouring into one. We are not a nation so much as a world."[3]

In the early twentieth century, Israel Zangwill, the Jewish immigrant and playwright, in an extravagant image wrote that America is "God's crucible, the great melting pot." Of New York, he exclaimed, "Ah, what a stirring and seething! Celt and Latin, Slav and Teuton, Greek and Syrian—black and yellow . . . what is the glory of Rome and Jerusalem, where all nations and races come to worship and look back compared with the glory of America, where all races and nations come to labor and look forward!"[4]

All nations and races were coming to the United States by the early 1980s. In 1984, most of them could be found in Los Angeles' Olympic Stadium, where the mayor, himself a descendant of African slaves, opened the ceremony, and where American Indians represented the United States in the world Olympic march. Chinese-Americans cheered the Stars and Stripes and the Chinese flag for the People's Republic of China. Irish-Americans, Italian-Americans, Korean-Americans, and at least forty other ethnic groups huzzahed for the teams of their ancestral homelands, as well as for the Americans. The wildest prophecies of Emerson, Melville, and Zangwill had come true. Buddhists, Sikhs, Taoists, and Hindus—no less American than their blue-eyed and blond neighbors—cheered the victories of American athletes.

Not a Melting Pot, a Kaleidoscope

Los Angeles was not the melting pot of Crèvecoeur or Zangwill ("melt" was the verb they preferred) or the "smelting pot" of Emerson, or the "one federated whole" of Melville. But what was it? The marvelously graphic metaphor of the melting pot was only partly true. Intermarriage in the U.S. between persons of vastly different ancestral backgrounds was widespread, as Zangwill had hoped and predicted. All the concepts associated with the melting pot—mainstreaming, acculturating, assimilating, absorbing, adapting, integrating—accurately described the dynamics of the lives of many immigrants and most of their children. But "melting pot" was not and never had been the best metaphor to describe the dynamics of ethnic diversity and acculturation, certainly not for Indians or blacks, not even for immigrants and their children.

No metaphor can capture completely the complexity of ethnic dynamics in the U.S. "Melting pot" ignores the persistence and reconfiguration of ethnicity over the generations. "Mosaic," much more apt for pluralistic societies such as Kenya or India, is too static a metaphor; it fails to take into account the easy penetration of many ethnic boundaries. Nor is "salad bowl" appropriate; the ingredients of a salad bowl are mixed but do not change. "Rainbow" is a tantalizing metaphor, but rainbows disappear. "Symphony," like "rainbow," implies near perfect harmony; both fail to take into account the variety and range of ethnic conflict in the United States.

The most accurately descriptive metaphor, the one that best explains the dynamics of ethnicity, is "kaleidoscope." American ethnicity is kaleidoscopic, i.e., "complex and varied, changing form, pattern, color . . . continually shifting from one set of relations to another; rapidly changing."[5] When a kaleidoscope is in motion, the parts give the appearance of rapid change and extensive variety in color and shape and in their interrelationships. The viewer sees an endless variety of variegated patterns, just as takes place on the American ethnic landscape. The passing of Jews, Irish, Catholics and even light-skinned African-Americans into working and middle-class white Protestant society was fairly common in the eighteenth and nineteenth century. Some groups, such as the Huguenots, virtually disappeared. Others, most notably the Mormons, came upon the scene in a flash of history and gained additional adherents over time. Most immigrants and their offspring, identifying both with their countries of ancestry and with the U.S., created ethnic schools, newspapers, fire companies, fraternal associations, credit unions, businesses, and labor unions. By 1990, the patterns of ethnicity were more kaleidoscopic than ever, both in variety and interaction and in the spread of diversity to every section of the nation.

Of the nearly four million free non-Indian inhabitants counted by the first American census in 1790, only slightly more than 35 percent were not of English stock; the largest were German (9 percent), Irish (9 percent), Scottish (8 percent), Dutch (3 percent), French (less than 2 percent), and Swedish (less than 1 percent). In 1776, when the Great Seal of the Continental Congress was designed, John Adams, Benjamin Franklin, and Thomas Jefferson initially proposed that it include "the arms of the several nations from where America has been peopled, as English, Scotch, Irish, Dutch, German . . . ," but the idea was not adopted.[6]

When John Jay asserted in the Federalist Papers that Americans were "a people descended from the same ancestors," Jay, like other nationalist leaders, exaggerated the homogeneity of the American people to make his case for a unified national government. Madison's two famous Federalist essays on diversity never even mentioned immigrants or nationality.[7] But there were already large concentrations of Scotch-Irish in the Cumberland Valley of Pennsylvania and all along the Carolina piedmont; of Germans in Lancaster County, Pennsylvania, in the Mohawk and Schoharie regions of New York, and in all of the counties of the Shenandoah Valley; and of Dutch along the Hudson River—the second most populous group in New Jersey. Swedes lived in substantial numbers in Newcastle County, Delaware, and a large settlement of French immigrants at New Bordeaux, South Carolina. There were Welsh in Swansea, Massachusetts, and about eight hundred Minorcans, Greeks and Italians in the territory of East Florida.[8] Still, more than two-thirds of white Americans were of English background, and religious diversity, like ethnic variety, was limited—the proportion of Catholics in the population in 1790 was smaller than that of Muslims and Buddhists today.

In the nineteenth century, with the immigration of the Irish, and later of Germans and Scandinavians, the emancipation of blacks from slavery, and the growth of the cities, ethnicity in the U.S. became more kaleidoscopic. The great immigration from southern and eastern Europe at the turn of the century and the movement of blacks from the South to northern cities during the Second World War increased the variety, scope, and pace of movement in the kaleidoscope, but far less than the kaleidoscopic activity following the war. The old kaleidoscope of relatively limited variety became an even more diverse one in the 1970s, after the Immigration Act of 1965 went into effect in 1968.

From 1820 to 1960, 82 percent of all legal immigrants came from Europe, but between 1975 and 1979, only 15 percent originated in Europe, 41 percent from Latin America, 35 percent from Asia. By the mid-1980s, Asia had become the largest source of immigration. By 1987, Asians accounted for 43 percent of immigration, persons from Latin America and Caribbean nations 41 percent, and Europeans only 10 percent.[9]

Loosened Restrictions Since 1965

The civil rights revolution of the 1960s had put a spotlight on the racist basis of U.S. selection of immigrants under terms of the 1924 Immigration Act. It was a cruel system. It kept out many Jewish refugees from Hitler in the 1930s, and Italian, Greek, and other would-be postwar immigrants from southern and eastern Europe, barred by the narrow quotas assigned to their countries. Italian-, Polish-, and Jewish-Americans lobbied hard for a change in that system. Passage of the 1965 amendments to the Immigration and Nationality Act assigned a quota of 170,000 persons to the eastern hemisphere, with a limit of 20,000 for each country. The backlog for Italy alone was 250,000, but at least Italy would have a ceiling equal to other countries with respect to numerically restricted immigration. The new law did not take into account population size or emigration demand, but it did reduce the sharp inequities, and it continued to admit immediate relatives of U.S. citizens without numerical restriction.

Theoretically, the new law of 1965 opened immigration up to the entire world, but visas were allocated in large part to immigrants who were related to a U.S. citizen or resident, and, therefore, little Asian immigration was expected. As one senator put it, "In as much as the total Asian population is only about one half of one percent of the total American population, this means that there are very few of Asian-Pacific origin in this country who are entitled to provide the specific preference priorities to family members and close relatives residing abroad." The leader of immigration reform in the House of Representatives, Emanuel Celler (D-New York), told his colleagues that "since the people of Africa and Asia have very few relatives here, comparatively few could immigrate from those countries because they have no family ties in the U.S."[10]

The western hemisphere was now assigned an immigration ceiling for the first time in U.S. history, 120,000 with no limitation per country. Concern over increased immigration from Mexico led in 1976 to the application of the 20,000-per-country ceiling to the western hemisphere, too. Two years later, a worldwide ceiling of 290,000 (270,000 in 1980, when refugees were no longer included) was imposed, keeping the 20,000-per-country limit except for immediate relatives of citizens. The new system was driven overwhelmingly by both a compassionate and selfish interest to reunite the families of U.S. citizens and resident aliens. The emphasis on family reunification was expected to increase the number of eastern and southern European immigrants substantially. Immigration from Asia was expected to continue to be small (only 5 percent between 1931 and 1960).

The results were quite different. Increasing numbers of Asians, Latin Americans, and Africans found a variety of other ways to enter the U.S. as nonimmigrants (tourists, etc.) or refugees and eventually to adjust their status to that of an immigrant, the other term in the law for permanent resident alien. In the 1980s, about half of the persons admitted as immigrants had already entered lawfully as nonimmigrant aliens or as refugees or asylees, or even in some cases as illegal aliens.[10] The new system also provided two preferences (third and sixth) for immigrants who did not come because of close relatives in the U.S. Although these preferences (for professionals of exceptional ability and for needed workers) provided for only a total of 54,000 immigrants (including immediate family) annually, their entry led to considerable family reunification immigration subsequently.[11] Once an immigrant was in the U.S., he or she was eligible to petition for immediate family members under one preference (second), and after he or she became a citizen, it became possible to petition for immediate relatives without any wait and for less close relatives under three preferences (first, fourth, and fifth).

Asians who made use of nonfamily preferences often were able to use the family preferences later. For example, 2,208 immigrants arrived from India through one of the two occupational preferences in 1982, bringing with them 1,786 spouses and children. An Indian anesthesiologist who had left his wife in India to care for their small children to come to the U.S. in 1982 would be entitled immediately as a lawful resident alien to petition under the second preference (the only one of four family preferences available to immigrants) to bring his family in as immigrants the following year. Their ability to immigrate was limited only by the ceilings set for the world and for India for second preference (assuming they passed all the other individual qualifications dealing with health, etc., covered by exclusions). At the end of 1983, his or her spouse and children could have been among the 6,034 immediate relatives of Indian U.S. resident aliens who actually immigrated that year. The spouse, in turn, after becoming a citizen in five to six years, could sponsor her or his brothers and sisters under fifth preference and bring them to the U.S. as immigrants; they in turn would then have petitioning rights.[12]

Tourism and study by foreigners in the U.S. were other ways by which aliens could establish a basis for family reunification. In the 1980s, more than 12,000,000 foreign nationals were admitted annually as nonimmigrants, mostly as tourists and students, compared to about 5,000,000 in 1975. A majority of the more than 300,000 students admitted each year (at least 1,000 from each of sixty countries by the mid-1980s) remained at least a year or two after they finished their education. Those who married American citizens immediately became eligible for immigrant status. Those who were able to gain employment considerably improved their chances of becoming resident aliens, usually through the sixth preference admitting workers in skilled or semi-skilled occupations for which laborers were in short supply.

There were few Nigerians in the U.S. in 1968 to form a basis for family reunification when the 1965 law took effect, but in the 1970s and 1980s, large numbers of Nigerians came in as students, 20,080 in 1984, and some of them eventually qualified as sixth-preference immigrants. Others married U.S. citizens or resident aliens, and, beginning in 1982, a substantial number of Nigerians who originally had entered as students adjusted their status to that of immigrant. (Only 653 Nigerians had been admitted as immigrants in 1977; 3,278 were admitted in 1987.)

Substantial numbers of Iranian, Indian, Taiwanese, and persons from the People's Republic of China followed a similar path each year. After entering as visitors or as students, they subsequently either married citizens or were able to adjust their status to immigrant through the third or sixth preference. Once immigrants, they could petition for spouses and minor children (under second preference) to join them, their admission limited only by the numerical limits set for the world and for each country. Spouses who became citizens after five years were in a position to petition for their brothers and sisters and otherwise to avail themselves of three family reunification preferences for U.S. citizens.

More than three-fourths of the nonimmigrant aliens admitted to the U.S. in each recent year arrived as tourists. Some of them became immigrants, either by marrying citizens or resident aliens or by employers' petitions for professionals or skilled workers under the third and sixth preferences. More than 5,000 Mexicans, 4,000 Filipinos, 3,000 English, 1,000 Dominicans, 1,000 Jamaicans, and 1,000 Colombians who entered the country as tourists became immigrants in most years of the 1980s. For some countries, such as Colombia, Peru, and Egypt, with no strong base for family reunification in 1968, tourism became a significant channel for eventual immigration. Of the 4,127 Peruvians and 2,800 Egyptians admitted as immigrants in 1982, one out of every four who adjusted to that status had originally entered as a tourist. For the 8,608 Colombians admitted, the ratio was one in five. As a result, Peruvians, Egyptians, and especially Colombians developed a much stronger basis for future family reunification.[13]

The marriage of American servicemen overseas to host nationals in countries such as Korea, Japan, the Philippines, Vietnam, and especially Germany provided a direct route, one outside the numerically limited preference system, for further stimulating immigration through family reunification. Until recently, there were few Koreans in the U.S. except Hawaii, but after 1976 Korea became one of the leading countries of immigration, averaging about 20,000 annually. Approximately 8,000 refugees, war brides, and orphans were admitted between 1952 and 1960, and several thousand more wives and children of American servicemen came between 1960 and 1965. In five or six years, after becoming a citizen, a Korean spouse was in a position to sponsor family reunification immigrants.

The nationals of several countries also built the basis for family reunification through refugee and asylee admissions. Under the Refugee Act of 1980 a refugee could, after one year (an asylee after two) adjust his or her status to that of immigrant (resident alien) without regard to numerical limits, and then petition for immediate family members to join her or him under the numerically restricted second preference. After a total of about six or seven years, the refugee who had become a citizen could sponsor immediate family members without having to wait because the spouses, minor children, and parents of citizens were not subject to numerical limits. They also could petition for less close relations through the three citizen family preferences.

When the immigration act was passed in 1965, it was not anticipated that such a large number of refugees would be admitted in the 1970s and 1980s, especially from Asia. The act provided for only 17,000 refugees annually. But events in Cuba and Vietnam soon made that number unrealistic. In 1966, Congress passed the Cuban Refugee Act, which led to the admission of nearly 400,000 refugees, half of the total of 800,000 Cubans who were in the U.S. by 1985. Following the Vietnam War, the U.S. passed special refugee legislation that (along with allocations made under the Refugee Act of 1980) led to the admission of more than 900,000 Southeast Asian refugees by 1990. The 1980 act was an attempt to establish a refugee policy that applied to the world and not just to persons seeking to flee communist governments, but under it large numbers of refugees were admitted from Vietnam, Cambodia, Laos, Afghanistan, and Ethiopia, many of whom later were able to petition for relatives, as resident aliens or citizens.

By 1979, enough Vietnamese refugees had converted their status from refugee to immigrant for Vietnam to have become the fifth largest country of immigration (8 percent of all immigrants). By 1982, Vietnam was first, with all but a small fraction of the more than 70,000 immigrants admitted adjusting their status from refugee.[14] Because the number of refugees went down after 1980, few adjusted their status in 1983, and by 1984 the number of immigrants from Vietnam had slipped to 37,000 (third place, behind Mexico and the Philippines); by 1987, the number of Vietnamese immigrants was down to 24,000. But the basis for family reunification, particularly through the fifth preference (brothers and sisters of U.S. citizens), had become so strong that Vietnam probably would remain an important country of family reunification immigration for years to come, even if refugee flows were to be reduced.

In a similar fashion, as the number of refugees from Laos began to build in the late 1970s, Laotians reached ninth place as a country of immigration in 1981 (2.6 percent) and moved to fourth place in 1982 (6.1 percent), as the large number of Laotian refugees admitted in 1980 adjusted their status to that of immigrant, and back to seventh in 1983. Because refugee flows from Laos continued to fall off in the 1980s, Laotians by 1987 were out of the top fifteen immigrant groups. Cambodia made tenth place in 1981 and eleventh in 1982, back to tenth in 1983, and thirteenth in 1987, but Laos and Cambodia had established a broad enough base of resident aliens and citizens for family reunification in the years ahead.

African nationals were particularly disadvantaged by the immigration law's heavy weighting in favor of family reunification, and by small refugee allocations made by the U.S. under the Refugee Act of 1980. In the 1980s, the U.S. accepted only up to 3,000 refugees from Africa annually (that quota was never filled, despite the fact that there were more refugees in Africa than on any other continent). A large majority of those accepted were Ethiopians, most of them young men. Within a year or two, many adjusted their status to immigrant. Only 384 Ethiopians were admitted as immigrants in 1977, compared to 1,810 five years later, a large majority of whom adjusted their status from that of refugee. Enough Ethiopians had become resident aliens or citizens by 1982 so that 185 could be admitted as spouses of citizens, 130 as spouses or minor children of resident aliens, and 18 as brothers and sisters of citizens. By 1985, 3,362 Ethiopian immigrants were admitted, a majority of whom had adjusted their status from that of refugee or asylee after marrying U.S. citizens. Although Ethiopian admissions fell below 3,000 in 1986 and 1987 (refugee admissions dipped in the previous years), there was a large enough Ethiopian community in the U.S. to form a basis for further family reunification immigration.[15]

Refugees from Afghanistan followed the same pattern. In 1977, only 138 immigrants were admitted from that country, but with the admission of refugees in sizable numbers, beginning in 1979, immigration went up to nearly 2,000 each year in 1981 and 1982. Because more than 4,000 refugees were admitted in 1982, the number of immigrants rose to 2,321 in 1983, and 3,222 in 1984, a significantly large enough group to begin the process of chain migration through family reunification should relatives be permitted to leave the country.[16]

Many immigrants originally entered as illegal aliens from the Caribbean, Central America, and Mexico. Jamaicans, Dominicans, Guatemalans, Salvadoreans, and Guyanans managed eventually to adjust their status to that of immigrant and then sponsor other immigrants under the preference system. Mexicans and Jamaicans provided the most numerous examples. A substantial Jamaican community existed in New York in the 1930s due to earlier immigration, but by 1968 the basis for family reunification had become thin. Then letters, visits, and stories about opportunities in the U.S. brought Jamaicans to New York and other cities as visitors or temporary workers. Some became illegal aliens by remaining after their nonimmigrant visas expired, and subsequently were able to adjust that status to immigrant (immigration from Jamaica more than doubled between 1977 and 1987, when it was 23,000). Immigration became possible through marriage to citizens or resident aliens and also when Jamaicans employed without documents returned to Jamaica and then were sponsored in the U.S. by their former employers as needed workers under the sixth preference. Some remained out of status but became parents to U.S.-citizen children, who by the 1980s were in a position to sponsor brothers and sisters born in Jamaica, some of whom were already living in the U.S. as resident aliens or as nonimmigrants with visas for a temporary stay.

Nationals from the Dominican Republic, Barbados, other Caribbean islands, and from Mexico and Central America initiated lawful migration chains in the same way. On a visit to the American consulate in Mexico on any working day it was possible to find dozens (sometimes hundreds) of Mexican nationals applying for and entitled to a visa to enter lawfully as immigrants who already had been to the U.S. as illegal migrants or legally as nonimmigrant tourists or students. With the passage of the Immigration Reform and Control Act of 1986 and the legalization of about a million and a half heretofore illegal aliens (plus the legalization of special agricultural workers), a large number of new possibilities resulted for immigration through family reunification.

Even More Diversity Than Meets the Eye

By 1976, when the nation celebrated its 200th birthday, the proportion of foreign-born was smaller than it had been in 1876 and only half of what it had been in 1920, but by 1980 there were more than twice as many nationalities in the kaleidoscope as in 1920. The percentage of persons reported by the 1980 census as speaking a language other than English at home (11 percent) was not greater than in 1910 or 1920, but the diversity of languages—from Thai to Portuguese, from Kurdish to Ibo—was much larger. No longer did two or three groups dominate the immigration flow as they did at the turn of the century, when between 1899 and 1910, Italians, Jews, and Poles accounted for 45 percent of all immigration. By the early 1980s, the top three countries (Mexico, Vietnam, and the Philippines) were responsible for less than 30 percent of the total. In 1987, the top three (Mexico, the Philippines, and Korea) accounted for 26 percent, the top five less than 36 percent. Immigrants in the 1980s came from 174 nations and colonies, 34 in Europe, 26 in North America, 20 in Central and South America, 42 in Asia and the Middle East, and 52 in Africa. As late as 1976, only four African countries accounted for more than 500 immigrants (Cape Verde, Egypt, Nigeria, and South Africa). By 1985, nine (the new ones were Ethiopia, Ghana, Kenya, Liberia, and Morocco) sent at least that many.

The terms "Hispanics," "Asians," and "blacks" disguised the extent of variety in the kaleidoscope. Eleven Spanish-speaking nations have sent more than 1,000 immigrants annually since the mid-1980s, and two others more than 500. From Asia, the variety was even greater, with twenty nations responsible for at least 1,000 immigrants each year and fifteen of those sending more than 2,000. Undocumented aliens also contributed to variety. Although Mexico was the source of probably about 50 percent of all illegal aliens in the 1980s, perhaps about 25 percent came from other countries in the Western Hemisphere and 25 percent from several outside it.[17] Dozens of countries were represented in illegal-alien detention centers. In October 1982, a reporter found twenty-two nations represented at the Immigration and Naturalization Service's Krome facility in Miami. Seventeen were from Bangladesh, two from Argentina, two from Guatemala, one from Nigeria, one from Peru, and another from Pakistan. "It's a U.N. here," said a spokeswoman for the Immigration and Naturalization Service.[18]

In 1983, the INS recorded seventy-eight different nationalities among those who had been detained at the detention center at El Paso. In the spring of the next year, I found 415 males from twenty-eight countries at that center, including a Sikh from the Punjab in India and two young Englishmen. A chef who had been cooking at the facility since it opened six years earlier told me that when he first came to work, "99 percent of the detainees were Mexicans. Now, it's about 25 to 40 percent, depending on the day." Most came across the Mexican border, others by plane with fraudulent documents; others let their visas as tourists or students lapse; an increasing number crossed the 4,000-mile border between Canada and the U.S., one of the most loosely guarded frontiers in the world—at one point of entry, Swanton, Vermont, 2,000 illegal aliens representing sixty-seven nationalities were caught in 1983.[19]

When the editors of the *Harvard Encyclopedia of American Ethnic Groups* had to decide in 1980 how many groups to include for special essays, they chose 106, readily conceding that the number could have been much larger. Although each of at least 107 American Indian nations, most with distinctive languages and cultures, consisting of almost a million and a half people, could have been the subject of an individual entry, all Native Americans were listed under one category. Denied separate articles by the limits of space, Palestinians, Jordanians, and Syrians were lumped together as Arabs. Nigerians and Malaysians, among others, were not accorded individual treatment, but were subsumed under larger categories in order to save space.[20]

A similar oversimplification was made in 1980 when the U.S. Census Bureau asked residents if they claimed a particular ethnic heritage. Fifty non-English and twenty-four non-European identifications were claimed by at least 100,000 persons, but those numbers veiled the true extent of ethnic variety. Members of different Native American tribes were classified simply as "American Indian." Some groups such as Salvadoreans and Haitians did not make the list because of an undercount of undocumented aliens. Ethiopians, Nigerians, and persons from other African countries were put together under the general category "African." Foreign nationals and Americans from the Azores and the Cape Verde islands were grouped under Portuguese, and certain ethnic-religious groups such as the Amish and the Hutterites were not listed at all.[21] One careful analysis showed that the number of ancestry groups classified for Europe alone in 1980 actually should have been increased from fifty to eighty-five.[22]

New immigrant categories particularly veiled the diversity within them. The 209 Montagnard refugees who settled in North Carolina in 1986 were vastly different from the ethnic Chinese Catholics or Buddhist Vietnamese who came from Vietnam. And even among the Montagnards, who came from the central highlands region of South Vietnam, there were persons from three different tribes.[23] The Chinese immigrants living in the Richmond and Sunset districts of San Francisco came from half a dozen different countries, and even those who came from China spoke at least five different languages. As the director of one Chinese advocacy group pointed out in 1986, "you know, the Guan Gong Hua [Cantonese] spoken by Cantonese from Vietnam isn't the same as the one spoken in Canton—or in San Francisco."[24] Indians from South Asia, spread widely throughout the country, experienced their primary identity not as Indians but as Bengali, Gujarati, Marathi, Tamil, Kiannada, Goan, and Telugu; each of them formed associations, and many their own weekly newspapers. In addition, Parsis, Sikhs, Jains, Muslims, and Hindus each had their own religious institutions and associations.[25] The Ethiopians in the San Francisco area spoke at least six languages. About half of the refugees were members of the Coptic Christian faith; others were Muslims, and some were Jewish.[26]

There always was more variety among immigrants than it appeared to native-born Americans. Italians were not Italians to themselves, but Sicilians, Calabrese, Neapolitans, and so forth. But now there were varieties within varieties from all over the world. So Eurocentric had been immigration to the United States that in its greatest decade of immigration (1901–1910), when nearly nine million immigrants entered, the continents of Asia, Africa, and South America and the peoples of Mexico, the Caribbean, and Central America accounted for slightly under 6 percent of the total.[27] By 1982, when the number of immigrants from Italy and Greece fell below 4,000 each for the first time, seven of the top ten countries providing immigrants were in Asia and the Middle East, and only one, the U.S.S.R., was in Europe (reflecting the adjustment of status of Soviet Jewish refugees to that of immigrant). The next year there was not one country from Europe among the top ten. By 1985, Mexico, the Philippines, Korea, India, and the Dominican Republic were the top five sending countries, in that order; and the Soviet Union had dropped to thirteenth. Italy had dropped to thirty-fifth, lower than Ecuador, Honduras, and Ethiopia, and Greece was even farther down the list. By 1987, when the top five were Mexico, the Philippines, Korea, Cuba, and India, only one European country was among the leading fifteen senders of immigrants (the United Kingdom was twelfth). In 1988, the leading five were Mexico, the Philippines, Haiti, Korea, and mainland China, with the U.K. twelfth (again the only European country).

It was not the new immigration system that caused large increases in immigration from the Western Hemisphere in the 1970s and 1980s. Prior to 1976, there had been no numerical restrictions on immigration from the Caribbean, Mexico, and South America. Civil wars, oppression, poverty, inflation, and closed opportunity motivated an increasing number of Latin Americans, Haitians, Dominicans, and others in the Caribbean to leave. Radio, television, and word of mouth increased awareness of the possibilities in the U.S. In 1980, the census recorded a 61 percent increase over 1970 in the proportion of persons from Spanish-speaking countries in the U.S., with the Mexican-origin populations doubling during the decade, and both the Puerto Rican and Cuban populations having grown by more than 40 percent. These gains partly reflected the fact that the Hispanic population was disproportionately of child-bearing age (63 percent of Hispanics were twenty-nine or younger in 1980, compared to 49 percent for non-Hispanics). But they were also a result of a major change in the method of designating groups in the 1980 census, which counted as Hispanic anyone who answered that they were of Mexican, Mexican-American, Chicano, Puerto Rican, Cuban, or other Spanish origin. The 1970 census had used six subjective identifiers; some persons designated as Hispanics in 1980 had been listed as "white" in 1970.[28]

For more than a decade, Mexico had been the largest immigrant-sending country, having built a broader base for family reunification than any other nation, most of which originated with lawful migration when there was no numerical limitation on immigration from countries in the Western Hemisphere. Some Mexicans remained after the end of the *bracero* program in 1965, and they and some subsequent illegal border crossers established ties sufficient to enable them to become resident aliens. By the mid-1950s, Mexico had overtaken Canada as the leading sending country in the Western Hemisphere, and by the 1970s, even after numerical limitations had been imposed on the hemisphere, Mexico accounted for 14.2 percent of all immigrants. Mexico slipped from first to second only in 1982, when a large number of Vietnamese refugees adjusted their status to that of immigrant.

By the mid-1980s, Mexicans were first again, averaging about 10 percent of all lawfully admitted immigrants, more than half of whom were the parents, spouses, and children of U.S. citizens not subject to numerical limits. Even if illegal aliens who permanently settled were estimated liberally, Mexicans did not constitute as large a portion of the flow of immigrants in the 1980s as the English did up to the 1840s, when they were responsible for considerably more than half of the total, or as the Irish did in the 1850s, or the Germans in the 1870s, or the Italians in the first two decades of the twentieth century, when each group accounted for more than two to four times the percentage of all immigrants as Mexicans did in the 1980s.

Persons of Asian background constituted an even faster growing population than Hispanics, mainly because of immigrant and refugee migrations. During the 1960s, only 362,000 persons emigrated from Asian countries, compared to 1.5 million in the 1970s. From the decade of the 1950s to the 1970s, Filipino immigration went from 19,000 to more than 350,000, Indian immigration from 2,000 to 165,000, Korean from 6,000 to nearly 270,000, Vietnamese from 3,000 to 175,000, with sharp increases for other Asian nations, too (the number of immigrants from Bangladesh, for example, grew from 532 in 1980 to 1,649 by 1987). By 1980, there were 3.5 million Asians in the country, 812,000 of whom were Chinese, 782,000 Filipinos, 716,000 Japanese, 387,000 Asian Indians, 357,000 Koreans, and 245,000 Vietnamese.[29]

Unless surprisingly large refugee migrations come from eastern Europe or Central America, immigrants from the Philippines, Mexico, India, Korea, and from mainland China will continue to constitute the leading incoming groups for at least another decade because of the large number of resident aliens and new citizens of each of those nationalities in a position to sponsor family members. Many other countries with relatively small immigration in the 1980s may begin to build toward larger flows through family reunification, among them Sri Lanka, Ghana, Kenya, Cape Verde, Libya, St. Lucia, Dominica, Tonga, Burma, Bangladesh, St. Vincent and Grenada, Bolivia, and Uruguay, which, along with New Zealand and certain European countries (Hungary, Czechoslovakia, Sweden, Belgium, and Switzerland) averaged between 500 and 1,000 immigrants annually in the 1980s.

Not only did new immigrants bring more diversity to the kaleidoscope, but so did Puerto Ricans coming to the U.S. mainland, American Indians, rapidly growing in population and moving from state to state, and especially increasingly mobile African-Americans. Puerto Ricans began coming to the mainland in large numbers after the Second World War, when low-cost air travel from San Juan to New York City promised an escape from poverty; 70,000 lived on the mainland by 1940, 300,000 by 1950, nearly 900,000 by 1960. By 1980, more than 2,000,000 Puerto Ricans lived on the mainland.[30]

Native Americans also contributed greater variety to the kaleidoscope; at least 25,000 Indians lived in each of fourteen states in all four major regions of the U.S. As a result of a sharply reduced infant mortality rate and a continuing high birthrate (plus improvements in census procedures), the American Indian population was counted at 1,366,676 in 1980, an increase of 72 percent in a decade.[31]

In the 1970s, the black population grew by 17.3 percent from 22.6 million to 26.5 million, representing 12 percent of the total population, but the numbers masked the variety of ethnic groups among blacks.[32] By 1980, blacks included fast-growing populations of Spanish-speaking persons from Cuba and the Dominican Republic, French-speaking Haitians, English-Speaking Jamaicans and other West Indians, Ethiopians, Nigerians, Ghanians, and Guyanans.[33] More than 800,000 foreign-born blacks lived in the U.S., with Jamaicans about 25 percent of the total, followed by Cubans, Puerto Ricans, Haitians, and immigrants from Trinidad-Tobago.

By the mid-1980s, it was clear that even Melville and Zangwill had understated their fantasies of a diverse nation of nations. In New York State, aliens who registered in 1989 with the U.S. Immigration and Naturalization Service listed 164 different countries and dependencies as their place of birth.[34] In one high school in Cambridge, Massachusetts, the 2,700 pupils came from sixty-three nations and spoke forty-six languages, from Flemish to Swahili.[35] The blood of almost every nation in the world, at least as nations are counted at the United Nations, had become American blood.

Chapter Fifteen

"FROM THE MOUNTAINS, TO THE PRAIRIES, TO THE OCEANS . . ."
The Spread of Ethnic Diversity

W RITING *Inside U.S.A.* in 1947, John Gunther noted that "the foreign born scarcely exist" in Oklahoma, making up just under one percent of the population of that state.[1] By the mid-1980s, more than one thousand immigrants were arriving in Oklahoma annually, and the state ranked twenty-sixth in its proportion of Asian and Pacific Island residents. Between 1970 and 1980 the number of Chinese-born in Oklahoma grew more than 230 percent to more than 25,000; the Filipino population increased over 330 percent to nearly 12,000, and the number of Koreans to 2,223 (468 percent).[2]

In Vermont, Gunther noted that "the Vermont Yankee is . . . the most impregnably Yankee of all Yankees."[3] The foreign-born made up one percent of the state's population in 1940, and only slightly more than one-tenth of one percent of Vermonters were blacks. By 1980, the number of blacks had multiplied more than ten times, though still less than one percent; and by 1989, more immigrants had been admitted to Vermont in a decade than the total number of foreign-born living there in 1940.[4]

The ethnic kaleidoscope could be seen from coast to coast, from Portland, Maine, where several Afghanistani, Korean, and Filipino families had settled, to Portland, Oregon, where much larger numbers of Koreans and Filipinos lived and worked with expanding populations of Mexicans, Vietnamese, and Soviet Jews. Immigrant-ethnic groups still tended to favor certain regions, states, and cities, but by 1980 they were much more widely dispersed than before the Second World War, when few immigrants went to the South; the vast majority of African-Americans lived in the South and in major northern cities; native American Indians were heavily concentrated in just a few states; Mexicans lived almost entirely in the Southwest or Chicago; Puerto Ricans and West Indians lived in New York City; and almost all Chinese (except for small enclaves in the rural South) lived in big-city Chinatowns, in Hawaii, and in the West.

Five principal factors accounted for the continuing nationalization of diversity after 1950: immigrants came in large numbers to the South for the first time in the twentieth century; Asians were distributed widely throughout the nation; Hispanics showed increasing internal geographic mobility; American Indians moved out of Oklahoma and a few other states to other parts of the nation; and before 1970, blacks left the South for other parts of the country in the largest internal migration the nation has known.

Immigrants Come to the South

Even in the nineteenth century, immigrant-ethnic groups were more widely distributed than in other countries of immigration such as Argentina and Brazil. The foreign stock (foreign-born or children of foreign-born) in Iowa, Nebraska, Idaho, and Washington never fell below 35 percent in the decades after the Civil War.[5] By the end of the nineteenth century, immigrants and their American-born children constituted an actual majority, not just in states east of the Mississippi but in Minnesota, the Dakotas, Montana, Arizona, Wyoming, Utah, Nevada, and California.

Rural North Dakota, where only one of every three persons was a native American of native American parentage, was the state with the highest proportion of foreign-born stock to its total population. With the passage of time and extensive intermarriage and geographic mobility, European ethnic groups spread throughout the country. Of the thirty-four European nationalities claimed as ancestry by 100,000 or more persons in the 1980 census, only seven groups were overwhelmingly concentrated in just one of the country's four major regions—the Italians, Norwegians, Portuguese, and four small groups, mostly from eastern Europe.[6]

In most of the twentieth century, the South lacked the ethnic diversity of the rest of the country because few immigrants settled in that region, except for New Orleans. At the turn of the century, more than 86 percent of the foreign-born lived in the North Atlantic and North Central states.[7] By 1980, those same states received less than 45 percent of the new immigrants, the West more than 34 percent, and the South 21 percent.[8] One factor in the flow of immigration to the South was that air transportation had opened up ports of entry all over the country. In the nineteenth and early twentieth centuries, more than half of the immigrants admitted came through the port of New York. By the 1980s, they debarked in cities in more than thirty states, nineteen of them in the South or Southwest.[9]

So sparse was immigration to the South at the turn of the century that several states recorded less than one percent of their population as foreign-born, including North Carolina and Virginia, two of the economically better off southern states.[10] In any two years in the 1980s, more immigrants came to North Carolina than the total number of foreign-born residents, including citizens, there eight decades earlier. Even within states, the distribution of new immigrants was surprisingly wide. In

North Carolina, they came not just to one or two cities, but settled throughout the state. Of the two hundred Laotians admitted in 1982, fifty-eight were in Charlotte, thirty in Winston-Salem, twenty in Greensboro, eighteen in Raleigh, and the rest elsewhere. Of the Asian Indians who settled in North Carolina, ninety-three were in Charlotte, fifteen in Raleigh, eleven in Greensboro, three in Winston-Salem, the rest in other towns and rural places.[11]

Virginia provided another example of the spread of ethnic diversity throughout the contemporary South. The leading countries of immigration to Virginia in the early 1980s were Vietnam, Cambodia, the Philippines, Laos, Korea, and India. Three of the groups—the Southeast Asians—a majority of whom were admitted initially as refugees, were distributed widely in eight cities. A large group of Vietnamese (10 percent of the total) immigrated to Arlington, Virginia, where a substantial Vietnamese community already had been established. The rest were in other cities, towns, and rural areas. Filipinos, and especially Koreans and Indians, spread throughout the state in seven cities and rural places, although each group tended to favor certain areas, as was true in every state. In Virginia, the Filipinos preferred Virginia Beach, the Koreans, Alexandria, and the Asian Indians, Richmond.[12]

The Wide Distribution of Asian Immigrants and Asian-Americans

Many Asians went to the Sun Belt in the 1960s and early 1970s, partly because of new opportunities for incoming professionals, entrepreneurs, and technical and service workers, and partly because many of the nearly three-quarters of a million Indo-Chinese refugees who came by 1985 were resettled in the South by the federal government with the cooperation of state governments, voluntary agencies, churches, and local civic groups. By 1985, about a third of the Southeast Asian refugees lived in California (259,100), with Texas (57,700) and New York (24,700) next, but there were at least 7,000 in each of the thirteen other states.[13]

Except for whites, no other general category of ethnic group was as widely dispersed in the nation as Asians, who had become a part of the kaleidoscope in places where they hardly existed before. Persons of Asian background constituted the fastest growing population in the country, 3.4 million by 1980 (a jump of 146 percent during the 1970s) and 5.1 million by 1985, due mainly to immigration and refugee migrations. (By the year 2000, that number probably would at least double.) Although three-fourths lived in seven states, five other states had at least 50,000 in 1980.[14] By that year, 19,000 Filipinos lived in Virginia; 10,000 Japanese in Colorado; 22,000 Pakistanis in Texas; and 10,000 Vietnamese in Washington.

Although California had two of the three largest Chinese communities in the nation, only about one-third of recent immigrants from Taiwan and only a little more than a third of those who originated in mainland China settled there. Half of the Chinese lived in the western states, but by 1980 there was no state with fewer than 300, and twenty-nine had more than 3,000. At least one out of every two hundred persons in Baltimore, San Antonio, Indianapolis, Cleveland, Columbus, Nashville, Kansas City, El Paso, Detroit, Dallas, Memphis, Atlanta, and Pittsburgh was Asian. One out of every hundred was Asian in New York, Philadelphia, Phoenix, New Orleans, Jacksonville, Denver, and Oklahoma City; and at least five out of every hundred persons in Los Angeles, San Diego, San Francisco (21.7 percent), San Jose, and Seattle. The 1990 census probably would show about twice as many Asians living in most of those cities as were recorded in 1980.

Asian Indians, Koreans, Filipinos, and persons from the Middle East made substantial ethnic communities in every region. About a third of the Asian Indians were in the northeast area of New York, New Jersey, and Connecticut, and another third in California, but more than one hundred were admitted as immigrants in each year in the mid and late 1980s in at least thirty American states, and by 1987 more than 1,000 Indian immigrants settled in each of seven states. Indians from Gujarat, who had entered the motel business in every state on the mainland by the mid-1980s, were especially active in California and several states in the Southeast. For them, the motel business had become what the laundry business had been for the Chinese, construction for Italians, tailoring for Jews, and greengroceries for Koreans—an opportunity for families with a small amount of capital to start a business and succeed. Known for their merchant and entrepreneurial abilities in India, the Gujarati were drawn to an enterprise that, much like the restaurant business, does not require a great deal of training and in which families can play an important role.[15]

About a quarter of a million Koreans lived in Koreatown, Los Angeles, but there was no state to which Koreans did not immigrate; and by 1987 in ten states more than 1,000 Koreans were admitted as immigrants. Once a substantial cluster of Koreans was established, as in Kansas City, where about 3,500 had settled by 1985, family reunification (mainly through fifth preference for brothers and sisters of U.S. citizens) brought others. By the year 2000 there will be substantial Korean communities in more than one state in every region of the country, as will be the case for Filipinos, too. Although California, the traditional mainland home of Filipinos, received almost half of the total Filipino immigration in the 1980s, more than 1,000 were admitted as immigrants to each of eight other states in 1987.

The spread of Asian immigrants will change the ethnic landscape not just of states with heavy immigration like California but also of such unlikely places as Iowa, where in the 1980s more immigrants were admitted from Cambodia than from Canada, more from each of the nations of Korea, India, and the Philippines than from Germany, and many more from Laos than from the United Kingdom.[16] Wherever one traveled in the United States—from Maine to Oregon, from Iowa to Virginia, or from New York to New Mexico—Asian-Americans usually were part of the American ethnic landscape. In New Mexico, for example, almost as many immigrants were admitted from Asia as from Mexico itself in some years in the 1980s.[17]

The Spread of Hispanics Throughout the U.S.

The spread of diversity—the enlarging of the kaleidoscope—was due in considerable measure to the increasing national distribution of Hispanics, most of whom were Mexicans or Mexican-Americans. Although still concentrated to some extent in the five southwestern states of Arizona, New Mexico, California, Colorado, and Texas (more than 50 percent lived in California and Texas in 1980), they became much more widely dispersed during the 1970s, and in 1980 constituted more than 5 percent of the population in the Northeast, more than 2 percent in the north central states, and almost 6 percent in the South, in addition to 14.5 percent in the West. Illinois, Michigan, Washington, Florida, Indiana, and Ohio each had more than 50,000 persons of Mexican origin by 1980 in contrast to only two states outside the Southwest in 1970. Ohio and Minnesota had as many Mexican-Americans as Colorado and Nevada, and in Chicago, Mexican-Americans had moved into second place behind Polish-Americans as the second-largest foreign-born group from the sixteenth position they had held twenty years before. By 1980, at least two out of every hundred persons in seven of the nine subregions of the country were of Spanish origin. Only in the west north central states of Minnesota, Iowa, Missouri, North Dakota, South Dakota, Nebraska, and Kansas and in the east south central states of Kentucky, Tennessee, Alabama, and Mississippi did the proportion fall to one per hundred.[18]

Although the Mexican-American population continued to grow as well as spread, its share of the total Hispanic population was reduced from 70 percent in 1950 to 60 percent in 1980 because of the influx of Puerto Ricans, Cubans, and immigrants from Central and South America, each of which group became more widely distributed geographically with the passing of time. The 1950 census had counted only 70,000 persons of Puerto Rican background on the mainland, but by 1980 there were two million. Traditionally, the population was concentrated heavily in New

York City, but between 1970 and 1980 the New York City share of the national Puerto Rican population went down from 64 to 49 percent. New Jersey increased slightly, to 12 percent, but in Florida, Pennsylvania, Connecticut, Massachusetts, Texas, Hawaii, Indiana, Michigan, and Virginia the number of Puerto Ricans living in them more than doubled, accounting for more than 21 percent of the total. Major growth occurred in California and Illinois, too, where, between them, 10 percent of the U.S. Puerto Rican population lived.[19] In some of the states of rapid growth, such as Virginia, the number was small, but by 1980 eight states had more than 75,000 Puerto Ricans.

Although Cubans accounted for only 6 percent of the Spanish-origin population in 1980, they represented higher proportions in several states—55 percent in Florida, 16 percent in New Jersey, 10 percent in Georgia, 8 percent in both Maryland and Louisiana, and 7 percent in Nevada. The most concentrated of all the Spanish-speaking groups, except for Dominicans, the Cuban population also began to spread to other states as young men and women went to college away from home, and as employment opportunities drew them from Florida, New Jersey, and other areas of high concentration.

Also contributing to the nationalization of diversity were immigrants from Spanish-speaking countries other than Mexico, Puerto Rico, or Cuba and their children. A rising portion of Spanish origin population (21 percent in 1980), they come from the Dominican Republic, El Salvador, and other countries in Central America and from Colombia and other nations in South America. A quarter of a million were in California in 1980, but no state had fewer than one thousand, and forty-four states had more than five thousand, with over 125,000 in each of seven states.[20]

The Internal Migration of African-Americans

The new kaleidoscope was affected dramatically also by the post–Second World War migrations of blacks from the South. By 1880, on the eve of the great European migration, the center of African-American population was located 10.4 miles east of Lafayette, Georgia.[21] With immigration meeting the labor needs of the industrial North, the migration of American-born blacks to the North from the South remained slight for the next several decades. The Dillingham Immigration Commission's census of the public school population in thirty-seven cities of the U.S. in 1908 found fewer than 100 blacks in each of the school systems of San Francisco, Omaha, Milwaukee, Duluth, and several other cities.[22] Chicago had fewer than 4,000, Pittsburgh fewer than 3,000, and Boston fewer than 1,500. Cleveland had less than 1,000 black students, Detroit only 517. Of all the cities above the Mason-Dixon line, only in Baltimore did Negroes (the term used by the census) constitute more than 10 percent of the school population, and only in Pittsburgh, Philadelphia, Cincinnati, and Kansas City did they make up between 5 and 10 percent.[23]

After President Roosevelt issued Executive Order 88022 establishing a Committee on Fair Employment Practices in June 1941, jobs opened up in defense industries. To meet manpower shortages in late 1942 and early 1943, the federal government sponsored programs to subsidize domestic migration of blacks to the North. By the end of the 1940s the South still had 68 percent of the nation's African-American population, but chain migrations to almost every northern city and state had begun. By 1960, the South had lost slightly more than three million blacks to interregional migration, even though Florida was a major gainer. The North had added more than one million blacks and the north central states nearly 1.4 million, according to the 1960 census. Within the South, the movement was extensive, too; by 1960, eight of the eighteen cities in the nation with more than 100,000 blacks were in the South.

In every state outside the South, the rate of growth of the African-American population between 1940 and 1970 was higher than for the population as a whole. Where blacks were still sparsely distributed, the percentage growth from 1940 had been huge, as in Iowa and North Dakota: .07 percent to 1.5 percent in Iowa and from .004 percent to .6 percent in North Dakota. Although North Dakota's black population went up more than thirty times, while the population of the state as a whole increased by less than a quarter, more significant growth took place in industrial states in every part of the country. Indiana's black population, for example, went from 3.5 percent to more than 7.5 percent between 1940 and 1980, and New Jersey's from 5.5 percent to 12.5 percent. States with the largest percentage of blacks still were in the South, but only in two, Mississippi and South Carolina, was the population more than 30 percent African-American.[24]

The Spread of American Indians

At the time of John Gunther's visit to Oklahoma in 1947, approximately one-third of all Indians—128,000 out of 342,000—lived in that state, belonging to thirty-five tribes.[25] By 1980, the state had fallen to second place in Indian population after California. The number of Indians had almost quadrupled, principally because of rising birthrates and a lowered infant mortality rate, but the proportion in Oklahoma had gone up only 24 percent. By 1980, only half of the American Indian population of over 1,300,000 lived in the western states, with 27 percent in the South, 18 percent in the Midwest, and 6 percent in the Northeast.[26] There were more than 100,000 Indians in four states, more than 20,000 in fifteen states, more than 15,000 in twenty, at least one of which could be found in each of the major regions of the country. Indians who sought higher education tended to live away from reservations, which are largely in the West and Southwest; and of those who took the College Entrance Exam in 1984, the distribution was unusually widespread, with 28.3 percent from the West; 25.0 percent from the Middle Atlantic states; 21.0 percent from the South; 10.1 percent from the Midwest; and 8.2 percent from New England.[27]

Configurations of ethnicity varied from place to place, but most of them fell into one or more of six large categories: cities that were predominantly African-American as a result of the large migrations of blacks to them and the out-migration of whites, in which blacks played an increasingly dominant political role; rural areas in the South that were heavily African-American, still affected by older patterns of caste stratification; cities and suburbs whose character and tone were being shaped by the new Third World immigration; border cities, towns, and *colonias* between Mexico and the U.S.; cities, suburbs, and rural areas still influenced to a large degree by the older nineteenth-century immigration from northern and western Europe; and emerging world cities of such multiethnic variety that no one particular ethnic cluster clearly dominated, cities in which blacks and new immigrants and older immigrant-ethnic groups interacted in a constantly moving and changing kaleidoscope.

Predominantly Black Cities

By 1980, African-Americans constituted more than 50 percent of the population in seventeen large cities, although only five of these were among the thirty biggest cities in the United States: Washington, D.C. (the fifteenth largest city, 70.3 percent black); Atlanta (twenty-ninth largest, 66.6 percent); Detroit (sixth largest, 63.1 percent); New Orleans (twenty-first largest, 55.3 percent); and Baltimore (tenth largest, 54.8 percent). Most such cities had black mayors. A growing African-American professional class dominated their city governments and school systems, even though many lived in the suburbs. In several cities, the proportion of blacks rose swiftly, as in Detroit, from 43.6 to 63.1 percent over the decade of the 1970s, as the movement of blacks into the city was accompanied by substantial white flight from it, including the out-migration of immigrants and refugees.[28]

The predominantly black cities were subject to what William Julius Wilson called the "politics of dependency."[29] Blacks gained nominal political control of these cities, but most blacks continued to feel the pains of poverty. With the loss of manufacturing and of wholesale and retail industries in these predominantly black cities and the departure of white and black middle-class families, which reduced the tax base on which to support schools and other services, city leaders had to look to state and federal governments for help. The elected and appointed officials of such cities, usually African-Americans, had to deal with a white economic power structure downtown, the leaders of banks, the most powerful corporate businesses, and civic and cultural organizations, much in the way that the Irish of Boston had dealt with the brahmins of that city. Just as Irish political leaders such as James Michael Curley and Martin Lomasaney became political brokers in providing services for and responding to the needs of what Curley used to call "the newer races" of Jews, Italians, and others, so the preponderantly black officialdom of the larger black cities increasingly faced the responsibility of governing multiethnic communities where blacks were seen as one ethnic group—the major one— among many. Washington, D.C., for example, became home to immigrants from at least forty different countries. New Orleans, which continued to showcase the traditions of the French Catholic Acadians, about 800,000 in south central and southern Louisiana in 1985, whose ancestors had been expelled more than two hundred years earlier by the British from farms in Canada's Maritime Provinces, now had growing Cambodian, Laotian, Vietnamese, Mexican, and other ethnic neighborhoods.[30] Ethnic interaction in these cities often was abrasive and sometimes violent (see chapter 24), as when blacks competed against Hispanics for services (in Newark, New Jersey, or Gary, Indiana) or against Indo-Chinese (in New Orleans).

In some substantially black cities of the Southeast, such as Richmond (51.3 percent) and Memphis (47.6 percent), the patterns of interaction in the 1980s were still essentially between black and white because immigration was not yet large enough to establish them as multiethnic cities. Blacks increasingly played a major role in the governance of such cities, in elected positions, in the civil service, and on the police and fire forces. It was mostly in some of the smaller towns and rural areas of the Southeast that the pattern of black numbers and overwhelmingly white rule continued into the 1980s.

In the small towns of the Mississippi Delta and parts of Alabama, Georgia, and the Carolinas, more than half of the students were black in the 1980s, in schools usually controlled by white superintendents and school board members whose own children frequently enrolled in segregated private schools. In Georgia, 52 of the state's 187 school districts had a majority black student population in 1986, but only four had black school superintendents, and only one school board outside Atlanta had a majority of blacks. In Mississippi, African-American students constituted more than 85 percent of the population in 29 of 154 school districts but only ten had black school superintendents.[31] The pattern was changing in the 1980s, partly because a larger number of trained African-Americans were becoming available for the jobs, and partly because of increased black economic pressure, as in Indianola, Mississippi, where the school system was 93 percent black and where the African-American community forced the resignation of the white superintendent and the selection of a black through a boycott of the schools and of white merchants.

Citizens of such towns saw the ethnic kaleidoscope on television, but they did not experience it in their everyday lives. To be black in such places was to still live in a biracial world in which whites ruled blacks. But change was coming. By 1986, there were eight black superintendents in South Carolina, five more than eight years before. Of the thirty-two mostly black school districts in Alabama, eight had black superintendents. Only little by little did the pattern of tight, white local control erode, a process made more difficult by the departure of able black leaders from rural areas to cities such as Atlanta and Birmingham, both of which had African-American mayors and blacks in other key governmental positions in the 1980s.

The New Immigrant Cities

Growing numbers of Asian and Hispanic immigrants lived in Atlanta and Birmingham and all of the major cities of the Southeast, but, except for Miami, none could be called new-immigrant cities, places whose culture, politics, and economics were shaped significantly by the growing immigrant presence. Premier among such cities was Los Angeles. Although older ethnic communities continued to be visible there in the 1980s—Poles, Armenians, Jews, and Italians—the overall character of the city, like that of many of those in the West and Southwest, had been vastly changed by the presence of Asians and Hispanics by the 1980s.[32] In 1983, 27.1 percent of the city's 2.9 million residents were foreign-born nationals, up from 14.6 percent a decade earlier. In the fifteen years between 1970 and 1985, the proportion of Hispanic people in the Los Angeles Unified School District jumped from 20 to 51 percent, and the proportion of Asians more than doubled to almost 8 percent (blacks remained at about 21 percent). In the decade of the 1970s, the Mexican-origin population went from less than one million to more than two million. The Iranian population increased tenfold from twenty thousand to two hundred thousand. The Chinese population more than tripled, Filipinos increased five times, and Koreans fifteen times, each reaching approximately 150,000. The nearby suburban town of Gardena had become heavily Japanese, and the suburb of Montebello, Mexican-American.

The Vietnamese moved across county lines to Orange County, mainly to the suburb of Westminster, while most of the Koreans lived in Los Angeles County.

Cities such as Los Angeles, particularly those with large numbers of refugees, often found their resources strained in the 1980s, especially with respect to schools and housing, problems that created friction between Asians and Hispanics and between both groups and blacks. But the capacity to deal with the demand for services was somewhat stronger than in the predominantly black cities because middle-class blacks and whites and entrepreneurial immigrants strengthened the tax base; and because the cities of new immigration adapted more easily to high-tech opportunities than some of the older immigrant industrial cities (now heavily African-American), particularly in the Middle West.

Politics increasingly reflected the multiethnic character of the cities of new immigration, also imparting a strong sense of change, as in Monterey Park, where in 1983 the city council consisted of two Hispanics, a Filipino, a Chinese, and an Anglo.[33] But partly because of low rates of naturalization, cities such as Los Angeles with a large proportion of Mexican-origin residents still were governed overwhelmingly by Anglos, and in 1986, Hispanics held only one of fifteen seats on the city council, despite having 27 percent of the city's population. It was obvious that that would change in the 1990s.

Miami was the other outstanding example of change brought by new immigration. In no other city in American history had one large immigrant ethnic group moved so swiftly into positions of economic, political, and even cultural hegemony. Until the 1960s, Miami was a small, racially segregated city, whose economy was fueled primarily by tourism from the North. By the 1980s it probably was closer to Honolulu in its heightened multiethnic consciousness than any other city in the U.S. In 1985, even expulsions from the Miami senior high schools were reported in the newspapers according to the ethnic backgrounds of the students. No city had a higher percentage of foreign-born (53.7 percent; Los Angeles was second); most were Cubans. Miami had become the center of Cuban-American life and the cultural and economic focus of the Spanish-speaking Caribbean.

So strong was the Cuban presence in Dade County (Hialeah, the second largest city in the county, with one hundred thousand people, had a Cuban mayor in the early 1980s; Miami elected a Cuban mayor in 1985) that it would be easy to miss the complexity of its ethnic kaleidoscope. Twenty-five percent black, 56 percent Hispanic, and the rest Anglo, Miami often was called a tri-ethnic city; but the Hispanics included groups of Nicaraguans, Salvadoreans, and Mexicans. More than three hundred thousand blacks were divided among at least three linguistic and several nationality groups (native-born blacks; Haitians; Dominicans; and Cuban and other Caribbean and Central American blacks).[34]

San Francisco was another city that had been transformed by new immigration, but most of the immigration to San Francisco was Asian and not Hispanic, as it was to Miami and to such a large extent to Los Angeles. Although the population of San Francisco remained fairly stable between 1940 and the late 1980s (between about 650,000 and 750,000), its composition changed dramatically. In 1940, there were over 500,000 whites and fewer than 50,000 Asians. By 1986, there were about as many Asians as whites while the African-American and Hispanic populations each were slightly more than 12 percent. As late as 1955, San Francisco had more than one hundred German associations and lodges. A large Scandinavian community, primarily of Danish, Finnish, and Norwegian background, lived in Buena Vista Hill and in the nearby blocks around Market and Duboce Streets. By 1985, expressions of German and Scandinavian ethnicity had waned. In its place was the Manila Triangle, an area heavily populated with Filipino immigrants; an entire city softball league was reserved for Samoans. There were newcomers from all over the world in San Francisco—from South America and the South Pacific, the Middle East, and even Aleuts and Eskimos—but the newcomer Asians increasingly influenced the city's ethnic landscape.[35]

The Southwest generally and the border particularly were significantly influenced by the new immigrants. Although there were Hispanic families in the Southwest, particularly in New Mexico, who traced their history in that area back to Spanish colonial times, the Southwest was sparsely populated with Hispanics until the turn of the century. Between 1910 and 1930, approximately seven hundred thousand Mexican immigrants came; a considerable number returned to Mexico during the Depression. Many hundreds of thousands more moved back and forth between the two countries (see chapters 6 and 7). A large number of immigrants arrived in the 1950s and continued throughout the next three decades, giving the border cities, towns, and *colonias* that grew up around them a distinctive border culture reinforced by the movement of many Mexicans across the border to work lawfully under a special program for temporary daily commuters.

There were four principal centers of border culture on the American side in and around the cities of El Paso, Brownsville, Laredo, and San Diego, each of which is adjacent to a Mexican city. In the most Mexican of them all, El Paso (62.5 percent Hispanic and only 3.2 percent black in 1980), Mexican-Americans dominated the politics of the city by the 1980s.

In Brownsville, where about twenty-five thousand Mexicans crossed as commuters to work each day, a third of the pupils in the American city's public schools came from the twin Mexican city of Matamoros, and the *Brownsville Herald* was published in Spanish as well as in English.[36]

Colonias grew rapidly in the 1980s in the border cities and in the rural areas around them, so that by 1980 there were an estimated 185,000 people, virtually all of them poor Americans of Mexican heritage, living in *colonias* from California to the lower Rio Grande valley in Texas. Sometimes without water or sewer services, the rural *colonias* presented serious health problems, particularly in the area around El Paso.[37] In the *barrios* of the cities and the rural *colonias,* examples of the unique border language of Spanglish could be heard often. "If your car is not at the 'jonque' (junkyard) and has a working 'mofle' (muffler), before the political "mitin' (meeting) you can always catch a bite at the 'loncharia' or 'dina.' But you'll need 'lechuga' (cash)—preferably dollars."[38]

Of all the major cities, the Mexican influence was probably greatest in San Antonio (the tenth largest city in the U.S.); in 1980 it was 53.7 percent Hispanic and 7.3 percent African-American. But San Antonio was actually more than one hundred miles from the border and not as obviously enmeshed in the border culture as the smaller cities of El Paso and Brownsville. San Diego, on the border and often the transit point for Mexicans and other Central Americans moving north to Los Angeles, was not nearly as Latino as the other border cities. It was 14.9 percent Hispanic in 1980, but also 8.9 percent black and 6.5 percent Asian. Whites dominated most aspects of city life, much as they did in Dallas and Houston. Mexican-Americans in San Diego tended to be dispersed, without politically effective spokesmen or women, although Mexican-Americans were elected to the state legislature from San Diego and to the city council. Of the approximately thirty *barrios* in San Diego County, the best known was San Ysidro, which, because it is on the Mexican border, retained a strong Mexican atmosphere, making it almost more like a suburb of the adjacent Mexican city of Tijuana than of San Diego. Perhaps because San Diego's schools were less isolated than in Los Angeles or in other heavily Hispanic cities, a growing number of Mexican-American professionals lived in San Diego; despite its proximity to Mexico, it was taking on the cosmopolitan characteristics of a world city with seven out of one hundred San Diegans of Asian background in 1980, far more than Houston's 2.1 percent, Denver's 1.4 percent, Dallas's .8 percent or Phoenix's .9 percent. When the newspaper *U.S.A. Today* printed a representative group of American youth in July 1983, they chose a fifth-grade class in San Diego of about thirty youngsters; eight were African-American, nine or ten of Asian or Latino background.[39]

Cities of Old Immigration

San Diego was not just a city of new immigration; it had become one of the largest cities in the country. In 1940 its population barely reached 200,000, many fewer than in Milwaukee, Cleveland, Boston, or Pittsburgh, which by 1980 had slipped to seventeenth, eighteenth, twentieth, and thirtieth in size among the nation's cities, far behind San Diego's eighth. These older large cities also had new immigrants in the 1980s, and most had substantial black populations, too, but their ethnic patterns were strongly influenced by the existence of well established German, Irish, Polish, Italian, Armenian, French-Canadian, Slavic, Finnish, and other white ethnic neighborhoods. Often one or two older groups continued to give a special flavor to a city's character, as German-Americans did in Milwaukee, where in the month of August in the 1980s about twenty German societies held an annual German fest. But the German-Americans of Milwaukee were well aware of the surge of other ethnic groups in the city, and the German fest actually was inaugurated in response to other ethnic festivals, such as *Festa Italiana* and *Fiesta Mexicana*. The increasing multiethnic character of Milwaukee (23.1 percent black and 4.1 percent Hispanic) was reflected in the 1980s in a weekly feature of the city's leading newspaper, *The Journal*, entitled "Accent," with stories on Polish-Americans, blacks, Puerto Ricans, other Hispanics, and Danes (about half of the population of nearby Racine was of Danish extraction), as well as Germans.[40]

The influence of the older ethnic groups in the Middle West was on the wane by 1980, although English, German, Scandinavian, and Polish names continued to be prominent among politicians and business and labor leaders. The Scandinavian influence in Minneapolis became visible in September 1982 with the opening of "Scandinavia Today," a fifteen-month celebration of Scandinavian life in the U.S. at the Hubert H. Humphrey Metrodome, attended by Vice President Bush and the Princess of Sweden. But Minneapolis–St. Paul (7.7 and 4.9 percent black respectively), like Milwaukee, continued to receive new immigrants each year from Asia, the Caribbean, and Spanish-speaking countries; a community of ten thousand H'mong tribespeople from the highlands of Laos also lived there after having been resettled as refugees.[41]

Milwaukee and Minneapolis suffered some of the growing pains of new ethnic patterns, but not nearly so much as the old immigrant cities such as Chicago and Cleveland, with large postwar migrations of blacks and the decline in American heavy industry resulting from world competition. Chicago, home of the largest Polish community in the U.S. and of other major old ethnic communities (Jews, Italians, Slavs, Czechs, Ukrainians, and Greeks), had large black (39.8 percent) and Hispanic, mostly Mexican (14.0 percent) populations in 1980, and substantial Filipino, South American, and Chinese neighborhoods.[42] In Chicago, older ethnic groups resisted the drive of new ethnic groups for power when it became the scene of constant political warfare between its black mayor and white ethnics on the city council in the mid-1980s. Blacks particularly were seen as a threat by the Polish in Gage Park, by the Irish in Brighton Park, the Italians in Cicero, and the Serbians, Rumanians, and Croatians in Heggswisch.[43] The older ethnic groups were strong in Cleveland, too— Germans, Poles, Slavs, Hungarians, Italians, Slovenes, and Croatians had their own churches and neighborhoods—and white ethnic conflict with blacks (Cleveland was 43.8 percent black in 1980) was a common occurrence. Many whites left for the suburbs, leading to a precipitous decline in Catholic-school enrollments in Slavic and Polish communities in the 1970s.[44]

Older ethnic groups had a significant impact on the pattern of ethnic interaction in the cities of the Northeast, as well. In Boston (twentieth largest city, 22.4 percent black and 6.4 percent Hispanic), Americans of Italian and especially Irish descent still dominated the political and religious life of the city—no city outside Ireland is as Irish in tone—yet Boston, too, had a multiethnic character by the 1980s. One of its radio stations rented air time to thirteen different ethnic groups,[45] and the Boston schools conducted bilingual classes in Italian, Portuguese, Cape Verdean, and French (in addition to Chinese, Spanish, and Vietnamese), reflecting the continued migration of European immigrants. Change in Boston meant conflict just as it did in Chicago, Cleveland, and other major cities of the Middle West and Northeast where large numbers of blacks settled in the 1950s and 1960s. Boston's ethnic conflict over integrated schools and forced busing probably received more attention than such conflict in any other city in the 1970s, but racial polarization there was probably less strong than in Philadelphia, where blacks made up 37.8 percent of the population in 1980. A black mayor in Philadelphia declared a state of emergency in 1985, prohibiting gatherings of four or more people in a thirty-block area, following the racially motivated murder of a black youth and a white youth (see chapters 20 and 22).[46]

World Cities

The older immigrant groups often dominated the smaller northeastern cities, reflecting their industrial character and the labor migration to them in the last one hundred years, as in such Massachusetts cities as New Bedford (Portuguese), Fitchburg (Finnish), and Watertown (Armenian). But the new immigrant groups and American-born blacks had come to those places, too, and almost everywhere the larger and middle-sized cities of the Northeast and the Midwest had begun to take on the character of world cities. By 1980, among the thirty largest cities in the United States only seven were less than 2 percent Hispanic and Asian combined, and even they were becoming more ethnically diverse. Nashville, Tennessee, while only .8 percent Hispanic and .5 percent Asian, had become home for sixty-three ethnic groups, including Kurds and Laotians.[47]

In addition to having growing Asian populations, world cities included Hispanics, blacks, and older immigrant ethnic groups. Premier among them was New York City (25.2 percent black, 19.9 percent Hispanic, and 3.3 percent Asian in 1980). By 1986, approximately 2.3 million of that city's 7 million residents had been born outside the country. In 1986 alone, 90,000 new legal immigrants came to New York from 153 countries with numbers that ranged from 16,257 from the Dominican Republic to one each from Brunei, Benin, and Western Samoa. Travelers from most parts of the globe could find a neighborhood in which to feel at home. A section of Murray Hill, once an Armenian neighborhood, was now called Little India; East Harlem had the largest Puerto Rican population outside Puerto Rico; Brighton Beach had become home to so many Soviet Jews that the police took lessons in Russian in the 1980s; the subway line from Manhattan to Flushing in Queens, where one out of every seven residents was of Asian background, was sometimes called the Orient Express. Substantial Japanese, Albanian, and West Indian neighborhoods had formed in the Bronx. Chinese, Polish, Panamanian, Haitian, Jamaican, and other West Indian communities were well established in Brooklyn. More than 150,000 Greeks lived in western Queens, making it the third largest Greek community in the world. There were remnants of Irish and Italian neighborhoods in Jackson Heights, Queens, along with newer immigrants from mainland China and South American countries.

Often thought to be different from the rest of the country, New York presented a portrait of the ethnic kaleidoscope that was becoming increasingly characteristic of many cities, a kaleidoscope in which there were many arenas of fast-paced ethnic interaction, a growing multiethnic consciousness, strong ethnic mobilization, conflict, and accommodation, and extensive crossing of ethnic boundaries through friendship and intermarriage within the framework of the rules of a general civic culture.

Chapter Sixteen

TACOS AND KIMCHEE
The Quickening Pace of Ethnic Interaction

O N THE Green Bay peninsula in Wisconsin, a visitor in the mid-
1980s would have found some families who still spoke the Wal-
loon dialect of Belgium and kept alive customs of the southern
provinces of that country, such as the "kermiss," the thanksgiving for the
harvest. In rural Wisconsin the visitor would have found many other
examples of the persistence of old immigrant ethnicity. Until recently it
was possible to hear Welsh spoken in the little town of Cambria about
thirty miles northeast of Madison. In Sheboygan County, many rural
churches still conducted services in Dutch; in Gibbsville, some Dutch-
American farmers preferred to wear wooden shoes; and in the small town
of Chut the annual Corpus Christi procession was conducted in the
Dutch Catholic manner. In the St. Croix valley, Swedish-Americans began
preparation for the Christmas season on St. Lucia's Day, December 13,
in the old Swedish style, including the hanging of sheaves of grain in the
trees for the birds and the animals. Polish-Americans read Polish-language
newspapers at Steven's Point in central Wisconsin, around Independence
in the west central section, and in the countryside around Pulaski in the
east central part of the state.

Danish, French, Italian, Belgian, Norwegian, Swiss, Polish, Dutch, Finnish, Russian, Swedish, and Welsh immigrants and their children and
grandchildren had all created distinctive rural communities in Wisconsin.
Some of the names of small towns in that state reflected their origin:
Freistadt, Luxemburg, Viroqua, Brussels, Pulaski. Until the advent of
radio, interstate highways, and central schools, such small towns and rural
ethnic enclaves had remained largely isolated. But after the Second World
War, migration to the cities increased, and if those left behind were more
isolated by the departure of younger men and women, those who left
acquired a wider multiethnic consciousness. Welsh-Americans who returned to their childhood church in Penniel, Wisconsin (twelve miles
south of Oshkosh) on the fourth Sunday of August for a Welsh songfest,
Gymanfa Ganue, went home afterward to Oshkosh, Madison, Milwaukee,
and other cities where they worked with and met socially Americans from
a variety of other backgrounds. German-Americans from Milwaukee who
spent weekends with relatives in rural towns like Watertown, where they

brushed up on their German and ate rye bread and pumpernickel, also returned home to multiethnic cities where some bought Mexican fast food and others drank Japanese beer with friends whose ancestors came from Russia, Ireland, and China.[1]

There had always been a certain amount of contact between newcomers and natives ever since the Pilgrims first landed at Cape Cod, but the frequency became greater and the pace more rapid in the 1970s and 1980s than earlier.

In the eighteenth and much of the nineteenth century, there probably had been more interaction between Indians and Euro-Americans, new immigrants and native-born, and blacks and whites in the cities than in the first half of the twentieth century, when ethnic separatism became more prevalent. The removal and diminution of the Indians, the enforcement of Jim Crow segregation laws, and the isolation of immigrants in cities, the majority of whom were unskilled and unlettered, all occurred extensively by the early 1900s. In the cities, immigrants often lived and worked in isolation from others, blacks were segregated from them and from most other whites, and Indians barely entered the consciousness of non-Indians at all.

In late-eighteenth-century Philadelphia, there had been a considerable amount of intermingling in the streets and alleys, where a mixture of languages and dialects was spoken, but by the 1840s, after the large-scale immigration of the Irish, separatism became so common that fire companies were organized along ethnic lines, with Irish Protestants belonging to one company and Irish Catholics to another. Writing about ethnicity in Philadelphia in the 1830s and 1840s, one historian observed that "the city was becoming a mosaic of subcommunities, separated from one another by barriers of class and culture and by attitudes and behavior derived from different traditions."[2] Irish units proliferated in the state militia in New York, with perhaps as many as twenty-five or thirty by 1855, and by 1860 they had an entire regiment, the 69th, which refused to turn out for a parade honoring the visiting British Prince of Wales.[3]

Following the heavy migrations of immigrants from several European countries to Philadelphia, another historian wrote of a "cultural imperative" for clustering. Writing about Polish immigrants, she said that a Pole's "status could be defined only by interacting with other Poles."[4] In Worcester, Massachusetts, most Poles lived around a Polish-speaking church and parochial school and Polish fraternal clubs. Italians and Swedes also lived in virtual ethnic enclaves. One observer noted that the boundaries of the voluntary ghetto were so exact that knowledgeable Worcesterites could name them "almost to the house number." A small

Syrian group settled on the western slope of Oak Hill close to their Syrian Orthodox church. The original Armenian colony was on another hill, where its church was erected in 1890.[5]

A similar pattern of separation occurred in many northern cities, as both immigrant and African-American populations increased. In early-nineteenth-century Baltimore, foreign-born whites and free blacks often had intermingled along the side street and alley communities of South and West Baltimore, but by the end of the century racially and ethnically segregated neighborhoods were common. "By the end of World War I, the Germans could send their children to sixteen public schools which taught all subjects in German as well as in English."[6] The pattern of ethnically segregated neighborhoods was so well established in the two decades following the turn of the twentieth century that one well-informed, sympathetic, but concerned observer noted, "We see a conglomeration of colonies and ghettoes and immigrant sections in our large cities . . . with settlement quite as un-American as anything to be found abroad."[7]

San Francisco, and to some extent New Orleans, were exceptions. In the early nineteenth century there was extensive intermingling and widespread intermarriage between blacks and Creoles in New Orleans. But even New Orleans became more segregated after incorporation of Louisiana as a state in 1812. By the mid-nineteenth century, the city was governed by three separate submunicipalities: an Anglo-Saxon sector and two Creole sectors; the division fostered linguistic and cultural segregation, with only a tiny number of English-speakers living in the downtown Creole communities.[8] By 1880, about 60 percent of San Francisco's population consisted of foreign-born or their children (the highest percentage for any American city at the time). Multinational white working-class districts characterized the city, partly because the proportion of immigrants in the city was huge and partly because the whites had a common target of prejudice in the Chinese, whose neighborhoods were segregated and whose children were excluded from public schools until 1885.[9]

More typical were the patterns of ethnic separation of newcomers from each other and from the American-born in Manchester, New Hampshire, in the 1880s, Muncie, Indiana, in the 1920s, and Newburyport, Massachusetts, in the 1930s. The clustering of ethnic groups into strongly marked enclaves was reinforced in industrial immigrant towns because the immigrants often were imported and settled by the corporations that employed them, and also because those corporations tended to keep each group employed in a different occupation and housed separately, as on the plantations in Hawaii or near the mills of Manchester. Immigrants tended to cluster along kin and ethnic lines at the work bench.[10]

Following the sharp restriction of immigration after the First World War and the movement of a large number of American blacks from the South to the northern cities, patterns of ethnic stratification and segregation tended to be reinforced (see chapter 5). Black children who played in the same park as whites in Muncie were confined to a restricted corner.[11] In Newburyport, the distance from the worst to the best sections, from River Street and Market Square to Hill Street, was less than a mile, but the social distance among the eight ethnic groups studied in the 1930s was so great that they had little to do with each other.[12]

Patterns of ethnic separation continued even for first-generation-born Americans striving for middle-class respectability in secondary and tertiary areas of settlement. The street I lived on in the Bronx was almost entirely Jewish, but there were Irish and Italian streets nearby. Irish, Italian, and Jewish children who attended the same public school during the day shared virtually nothing of their ethnic backgrounds, did not visit in each other's homes, or otherwise socialize with each other. In a pattern typical of what historian John Higham calls "pluralistic integration," children played and studied with others at school and some parents worked in integrated settings, but nearly all returned to monoethnic apartment buildings at night.[13] I do not recall any black or Asian students in my large elementary school in the 1930s, although there were a substantial number of blacks, perhaps as much as 20 percent, at DeWitt Clinton High School in the early 1940s, which I attended; its population of about eight thousand males drew boys from Manhattan as well as the Bronx, all of whom returned to their own ethnic neighborhoods after school.

Everyone took their separateness for granted, keeping ethnic pride largely to themselves. Jews lived on or close to two major thoroughfares, the Grand Concourse and Tremont Avenue, and in two sections called Hunts Point and Morris Heights. Italians lived in Melrose and the area north of Tremont Avenue. The Irish were in Mott Haven and High Bridge, and the Germans dominated Morrisania and parts of Melrose. About a fifteen-minute walk from our apartment building was Van Cortlandt Avenue, a street lined with German residences and beer halls, which had earned the nickname "Dutch Broadway," but I was unaware of it at the time and I do not think any of my friends visited it. Nor did I realize that in the Mott Haven district just south of us lived wealthy Irish physicians in town houses along Alexander Avenue, and that other Irish called it the "Irish Fifth Avenue."[14] Evidently, there was more ethnic interaction in the Mott Haven area. A historian of the Bronx has written that in St. Mary's park, the children of Jews, Germans, Italians, Greeks, Poles, Irish, and blacks played together in the streets and playgrounds, but in my large high school there was virtually no sharing of ethnic traditions—no ethnic clubs, celebrations, or inclusion of ethnicity in the curriculum.[15]

Arenas of Interaction: Multiethnic Neighborhoods and Ethnic Food

After the war, patterns of neighborhood segregation continued in the Bronx into the 1970s and 1980s, when *bodegas* replaced Jewish grocery stores and Spanish-speaking priests took over from Irish predecessors at St. Luke's and St. Jerome's. But Puerto Ricans, blacks, and whites were much more aware of each other than ethnics were in the 1930s in the Bronx. That awareness often was stimulated by sharp conflict in the lower Bronx, but the interaction could be free of conflict in many arenas of neighborhood activity, including the neighborhood playgrounds, markets, and the streets. Before the Second World War and even before the First World War, the streets of Manhattan's Lower East Side were sharply marked by ethnic boundaries, but according to one reporter in 1972, the stroller might see "an Italian religious procession on Mott Street, with nearly all onlookers Chinese, or glimpse Italian barbers shearing Asian locks. In one store, Italians are playing cards; next door, Chinese are playing Mah-Jongg."[16]

In the earlier periods, it would have been extremely rare to see anyone but a Jew eat in a kosher restaurant. In the 1980s, one could see Jewish waiters and busboys in one of the largest and most famous of the Jewish delicatessens, Katz's, serving pastrami on rye to a substantial number of blacks, Puerto Ricans, and other non-Jews. In 1983, a reporter observed that in Jackson Heights in Queens, Italian and Irish populations blended with Indians, Chinese, Ecuadorians, Peruvians, Argentines, and Colombians. "It's a neighborhood where you can buy Venezuelan corn flour, Colombian coffee beans, and Yerba tea from Argentina." On a walk along Northern Boulevard in Flushing he found a Japanese sashimi restaurant, the first meeting house in the Americas of the Society of Friends, and the Hindu Temple Society of North America, built in the two-thousand-year-old Dravidian style of India, all within a few minutes of each other.[17] Two years later, Richmond Hill, once a solidly white area in Queens, had become 22 percent Spanish-speaking with an increasing number of Asians. There, another reporter noticed white children playing ball in the streets with children from Colombia, Ecuador, Venezuela, South Korea, and Taiwan.[18]

In the 1980s, city neighborhoods often still were segregated along ethnic lines, but in many arenas the pace of ethnic interaction had quickened considerably, and there were some new patterns. Ethnic clubs and associations were still focal points for socializing. But laundromats, health clubs, day care centers, social service agencies, and restaurants in the 1980s provided settings for ethnic intercommunication that never existed in the nineteenth and early twentieth centuries. In 1874, the Germans of the neighborhood of Jamaica Plain in Boston built a *schul-verein,* a school and social club for the German immigrants who moved into Jamaica Plain to work in the breweries, shoe factories, and tool-and-die shops and who settled on streets given names such as Beethoven, Bismarck, Mozart, and Dresden. Immigrants and their children danced to music by Strauss beneath German landscape murals after finishing a dinner of roast pork or sauerbraten. By the mid-1980s, the stucco Italianate building had become a health club that offered, among other things, Afro-Caribbean aerobics, bilingual services, and day care. It was owned and run by two Boston residents, one black and one white, and its membership reflected the diversity of Jamaica Plain's population: longtime white ethnics; Hispanic residents; blacks; and upwardly mobile whites without any special ethnic identification.[19]

The proliferation of ethnic restaurants in Jamaica Plain in the 1980s reflected a nationwide pattern. Eating out did not necessarily lead to socializing or getting to know persons from different ethnic backgrounds, but it did promote multiethnic awareness. When I visited Olympic Boulevard in Koreatown, Los Angeles, in 1980, the street offered in rapid succession Kentucky Fried Chicken, a store specializing in Cantonese fried duck, another in Korean kimchee, a fourth in Mexican tostados, and a fifth in Japanese sashimi. Visiting in a Portuguese neighborhood in North Cambridge, Massachusetts, in 1986, I saw within thirty yards of each other restaurants offering Korean, Chinese, Indian, and Italian food, alongside another called the Cajun Yankee. Even in the small university city of Bloomington, Indiana, where a quarter of a century earlier eating out meant "steaks, 'taters and salad," according to the president of the Bloomington Area Restaurant Association, it had become possible to dine at Lebanese, Chinese, Korean, Ethiopian, Afghan, Yugoslav, and Mexican restaurants (in 1986, 25 percent of the food served by restaurants was non-European).[20]

The eclectic eating habits of Americans had led to some unusual combinations, particularly in cities such as New York and Los Angeles that were strongly affected by the new immigration. In a Salvadorean neighborhood in Los Angeles in 1983, a Japanese-owned restaurant called "El Libertad El Salvador" served teriyakiburgers.[21] An ice cream maker in Los Angeles offered wasabi and lime-cilantro-jalapeño ice cream.[22] Leonel Castillo, Commissioner of the Immigration and Naturalization Service during the administration of President Jimmy Carter, told me of a Korean-owned and -managed restaurant in Los Angeles that sold kosher burritos to a black clientele.

That ethnic foods became so popular was mainly the result of the increasingly accepted norm in American society that there is nothing un-

American about expressing one's ethnic culture. One was no less American for eating kimchee rather than steaks and potatoes. In previous times it was too risky to show much of one's ethnic background. The Mexican-American head of the United Farm Workers Union, Cesar Chavez, recalled in 1983 that "our identity was strong within our own group. We hid our tacos and our tortillas. Today we promote them."[23] Ethnic pride came out of the closet, and with it arrived an expanded multiethnic consciousness in many other arenas of ethnic interaction.

Arenas of Interaction: The Churches

In the nineteenth century and well into the twentieth, churches were often divided along ethnic lines. It was necessary, as H. Richard Niebuhr wrote, for immigrants "to find a center around which they could organize their values, the leadership which would hold together the scattered individuals of the race, a form of organization which would enable them to maintain and foster their solidarity. The only center which was available, as a rule, was religion."[24] Often the preacher or the priest was the only or at least the most educated person in the immigrant community. The churches represented a kind of ethnic sectarianism, as contrasted to the old country, where they embodied the principle of ecclesiastical uniformity. Synagogues, too, were organized on an ethnic basis at the turn of the century—Rumanian, Hungarian, Russian, and others.

By the 1970s and 1980s, churches generally had become more multiethnic than earlier. Churches that had been almost entirely Anglo-American, such as the Episcopal Christ Church in Waltham, Massachusetts, by the mid-1980s had a congregation of Hispanics, Asians, Haitians, black Americans, and other regulars, as well as those from the old English and Scotch-Irish groups. In the nearby Catholic church of St. Mary's, there were no blacks and probably not more than two or three Spanish-speaking members of the congregation as late as the 1960s. "Today," the priest said in 1986, "we see a lot of blacks, Spanish, Haitians . . . they sing in the choir, they get married in our church, they are a part of the church . . . the sexton is Haitian."[25]

The old national parishes of the Northeast tended to disappear. In Waltham, St. Jude's parish, once all Irish, became Irish and Italian. The Sacred Heart church, built for Italians, now included Puerto Ricans. In many cities before the 1970s and 1980s, Italians joined the Italian parish, French joined the French parish, and so on, regardless of where they lived. Once outside of church or synagogue, Catholics, Protestants, and Jews often avoided each other as much as possible. In the town of Kapaa on the island of Kauai in Hawaii, the *naichi* (inner islands) Buddhists from Japan established a church that was separate from the Okinawan Buddhists, and both groups kept to themselves. But by the 1970s, many *naichi* attended the Okinawan church and vice versa.[26]

Ethnic churches still existed and immigrant groups still established churches of their own in the 1980s, but the ecumenical movement reached out to them in a way that had not happened in earlier decades, and multiethnic churches had become more common. The ecumenical movement also led many churches to invite other groups to worship and even to conduct services inside their doors. The huge Episcopal St. John the Divine in New York City—second only in size to St. Peter's in Rome—provided hospitality for Japanese Shinto priests, rabbis, Buddhist monks, and Islamic imams in the 1980s.[27]

In the southwestern part of the country, with its large Hispanic Catholic populations, there still were hundreds of Spanish-speaking, ethnically homogeneous churches. But the pastoral plan developed by Catholic bishops of the United States for the Hispanic-American community in 1972, a community that by the 1980s represented one-quarter of the Catholics in the U.S., emphasized integration within the church and all of American society, even as it called on others to respect the linguistic and cultural expressions of Spanish-speaking people at the local parish.[28] A majority of Hispanic immigrants and their children may not have gone to church at all, and an increasing number—many more than Catholic immigrants in the past—were attending evangelical and other Protestant churches.[29]

Arenas of Interaction: The Schools

In the North, the public schools, like some neighborhoods, had always been arenas of ethnic interaction as new immigrant children poured into them; one difference was that expressions of ethnicity often were suffocated in the name of Americanization. In the South, where there was little immigration, the strict segregation of blacks and whites meant virtually no ethnic interaction in the public schools. Fewer than one out of every thousand African-American students in the South attended schools with whites in 1954. By 1972, 91.3 percent of all blacks in the South went to schools with whites in attendance. In the border states, 76.4 percent went to such schools, and in the North and West, 89.1 percent.[30] Segregation of African-Americans in public schools was still the norm in 1972, when only a small minority attended predominantly white schools: 16.5 percent in New York, 8.1 percent in Los Angeles, 6.7 percent in Philadelphia, and 1.7 percent in Chicago.[31]

The public schools of all of these cities experienced a drop in white enrollment because white middle-class families increasingly moved to the suburbs after busing was sanctioned by the Supreme Court as a remedy for de facto segregation. Between 1970 and 1972, the overall enrollment in the nation's one hundred largest school districts dropped by 280,000, while gaining 146,000 black pupils.[32] White enrollment in the public schools of Chicago dropped sharply from 46.3 percent to 24.9 percent between 1966 and 1976.[33] But with busing and other measures to integrate the schools, the segregation of blacks nationally—as measured by the percentage of African-American students enrolled in predominantly black schools—went down slightly in the late 1970s and remained fairly level into the 1980s, with an overall drop of 76.6 percent to 63.5 percent from 1968 to 1984.[34] By 1990, however, most northern school systems had become more segregated and the education of millions of black youngsters in the inner cities had become a national disgrace. (See chapters 22 and 25.)

A growing population of immigrant newcomers in the 1980s helped to diversify the school population in Chicago somewhat (by 1980, 20.4 percent of the student enrollment was Hispanic).[35] Even where schools were listed as overwhelmingly black—and therefore heavily segregated—the population sometimes was multiethnic, as in Brooklyn's Erasmus Hall High School in New York City. When it opened in 1787, its students were all Dutch. In the 1850s, its population was predominantly Irish. By the late 1920s and into the 1930s, Erasmus Hall had become almost entirely Jewish. By 1986, 90 percent of its 3,500 students were black, most from Jamaica, Haiti, Trinidad, Barbados, Panama, Guyana, and other countries in the Caribbean.[36]

Having gone from overwhelmingly European ethnic to overwhelmingly black or overwhelmingly Hispanic, the schools of most big cities were more diverse than the designations "black" or "Hispanic" implied, and more than they had been prior to the new immigration of Dominicans, Mexicans, Chinese, Jamaicans, Indians, Koreans, Haitians, and other recent immigrants. In Cleveland in 1908, there were not enough Asians, Spanish-speaking students, and Indians in the school system to bother to count, and only a sprinkling of blacks.[37] By 1985, 70 percent of Cleveland's public school students were black, but the city also was providing bilingual education for more than a dozen new immigrant groups and forty-six American Indians.[38]

When all children of Spanish-speaking origin were considered as one group, they were more likely to attend segregated schools in 1984 than in 1968 (70.6 percent compared to 54.8 percent were enrolled in predominantly Hispanic schools). (See chapters 22 and 24.) With large numbers of Spanish-speaking immigrants from Mexico, Central America, and South America moving into Spanish-speaking neighborhoods, the trend continued into the 1980s. Usually, these were schools with serious overcrowding and underfunding in the inner cities or rural *colonias*, whose students came from homes constantly pressured by the problems of the poor.

Even in integrated schools, students of the same ethnic background grouped together in the lunchrooms and in the schoolyards in the 1980s, as I saw on my visits to the Chicago, Miami, Los Angeles, and San Francisco schools in 1979 and 1980. But the atmosphere encouraging interethnic cooperation and multiethnic appreciation was vastly different by 1980 from what it had been before 1960, when students were told to hide their tacos, blintzes, and kielbasas. In the 1980s, the State of Illinois published a newsletter on ethnicity and education that focused on the importance of multiethnic appreciation, and the first black mayor of Chicago, Harold Washington, shortly after his election in 1983 emphasized that "every citizen in a multi-ethnic society has a responsibility to try and learn something about other ethnic groups."[39] In Philadelphia, a special project called "International Classroom of the University Museum" brought foreign students into schools throughout the system to talk about and show artifacts of the countries from which many of the students came. The *Philadelphia Daily News* published a curriculum in 1986 entitled "Discovering Diversity," which, in cooperation with the schools, enabled elementary school children to become more aware of the extensive variety of ethnicity in their own city.[40]

The changed approach to ethnicity in the schools encouraged ethnic interaction, as reflected in curricula and in class exercises. In a third-grade class in Denver in 1980, I saw students being taught to count to ten in three languages in addition to English. In an elementary school in Oakland in 1985, black girls shouted their jump rope numbers in Chinese. "See you mañana," shouted a student with a Vietnamese accent.[41] In P.S. 89 in Elmhurst, Queens, New York City, 1,500 students spoke thirty-eight languages. In a second-grade class, students told their classmates about themselves as part of a class lesson: "'I come from Japan . . .' 'I come from Afghanistan . . .' 'I come from China . . .'"[42] In San Francisco's Castellar Elementary School on Yale Street in Chinatown in 1981, I saw the children of Asian immigrants playing basketball with Latino and Anglo children, and talking animatedly over lunch. After graduation, a majority of them (less true for Mexicans than the others) moved on to the San Fernando Valley Junior High School, which was predominantly Anglo. The older brothers and sisters of the immigrant children probably were enrolled in Newcomer High School, where in 1980, five hundred students spoke eighty languages.

In Los Angeles, the proportion of Hispanic pupils went from 20 to 51 percent, and the proportion of Asians more than doubled to almost 8 percent in the fifteen years between 1970 and 1985 (blacks who are not Hispanic constituted 21 percent in both years). At LeConte Junior High

School in Hollywood, students from forty-three countries in addition to American blacks and whites shared in school celebration of various Oriental New Year's Days, Armenian Martyrs' Day, and Hispanic holidays.[43]

Afghan students in Alexandria, Virginia, Kurdish students in Nashville, Iranian students in Tulsa, and Korean students in Jersey City worked and played with white, black, and Hispanic students in a kaleidoscopic pattern of interaction in the U.S. public schools that no other country in the world has ever seen. The schools were ethnic battlegrounds, too, arenas of ethnic tribalism (see chapter 20) that would not be permitted at the workplace or in the armed forces; but they were, as never before, places where youngsters were exposed to others from different ethnic backgrounds with a curriculum and text that encouraged multiethnic consciousness and appreciation.

The emphasis on the compatibility of ethnicity with Americanization made psychological and cultural ethnic interaction more possible than it had been in the multiethnic schoolrooms of the 1920s and 1930s. South Boston High School, which had been overwhelmingly Irish, had a small number of white students from other ethnic backgrounds until it was transformed by court-ordered integration and the new immigration. By 1984, its students were putting out a booklet of stories and photographs called *Mosaic*; in the 1985 issue, students from a variety of backgrounds— Vietnamese, Cambodian, Irish, American Indian, Puerto Rican, native American black, Haitian, Jamaican, Sri Lankan, and others—wrote stories highly personal and revealing about their ethnic backgrounds.[44] *Mosaic* did not depict Americanism as something that overcomes ethnic backgrounds, as had much of the school literature of the 1920s and 1930s. It assumed that its multiethnic student audience (South Boston High was only about one-third white in 1985 and 41 percent black, including black immigrants) already were Americans.

Literature like *Mosaic* was reinforced by the revision of American textbooks in social studies and history, which, by emphasizing the contributions of different ethnic groups, made students more open to contemporaries from those groups. When Frances FitzGerald studied American history schoolbooks used in the twentieth century, she found that most of the texts in the 1920s praised the racist national-origins quota system in our immigration law.[45] The American Council on Education found the portrayal of minorities in texts in 1949 "distressingly inadequate, inappropriate and even damaging to intergroup relations."[46] But by the 1970s and 1980s the treatment of ethnicity in textbooks, according to Nathan Glazer and Reed Ueda, had changed "from one with a single and simple national perspective to one that incorporates a variety of group perspectives."[47] The new history presented a "new civic morality whose major ingredients are understanding, sympathy, and respect for the hu-

manity of all ethnic minorities." There were problems with the new history—the old idea of the superiority of whites may to some extent have
been replaced, according to Glazer and Ueda, with a stress on the superior
moral qualities of some minorities—but the general effect was to enhance
the multiethnic awareness of students.[48]

The suburban schools also increasingly became arenas of ethnic interaction in the 1970s and 1980s because so much of the new immigration
went to the suburbs and also because of some movement into them by
blacks, particularly to working-class suburbs. The Census Bureau reported
that from 1975 to 1985 almost half the 4.7 million Asian, Hispanic, and
non-Hispanic black immigrants settled in suburban and nonmetropolitan
areas rather than in central cities. The movement to the suburbs took
place in every region, and was particularly strong in the West and the
South.[49] Even well-to-do suburban school systems that were all-white
Euro-American only a decade before had an increasing number of Asians
and Hispanics by the 1980s. One example of increased diversity in prestigious suburbs was Weston, Massachusetts, whose median income in the
1980s was higher than that of any other town in that state. There, in
addition to Jewish students (until the 1950s, Weston managed virtually to
exclude Jews) and youngsters of Greek, Armenian, Hispanic, and French
Canadian backgrounds, there were several students with Asian names
among the 187 who graduated in 1984, including a refugee who had
escaped Vietnam only a few years earlier and the Chinese-American president of the senior class.[50]

Arenas of Interaction: Higher Education

Prestigious institutions of higher learning, formerly overwhelmingly
white and Christian, became multiethnic, too. Some groups, particularly
the Jews, made considerable use of free public education at the university
level in the 1920s and 1930s, but elite private institutions limited the number of spaces for Jews and blacks. By the early 1980s, Jews and Asians
were represented in major colleges and universities far out of proportion
to their numbers in the population as a whole. In the 1980s, Princeton
University, long thought to be a bastion of prejudice, made available a
brochure on "Jewish Life at Princeton" as an enticement to capable
youngsters to apply, and in 1987 chose a Jew as its president. Dartmouth
College, which had a quota to restrict Jewish admissions into the 1960s,
also chose a Jew as president in the same year.

Harvard-Radcliffe had on the cover of its most important recruiting
brochure in 1984 a picture of just one student—an Asian-American. More
than one of every five undergraduates at the University of California at

Berkeley (a public university) was an Asian-American (27 percent by 1988). By 1986, about one of every ten members of the entering freshman class at Harvard was Asian-American. Two years later, 15 percent of the entering class was Asian at Harvard, and 19 percent at Stanford.[51]

Blacks and Hispanics have not been nearly as prevalent as Asians in higher education, but college enrollment for Hispanics doubled from a quarter million to a half million between 1972 and 1980,[52] and the number of black students at historically white institutions increased steadily after 1954, when the U.S. Supreme Court in *Brown* v. *Board of Education* unanimously ordered states to desegregate their public education systems, until the late 1980s, when the increase stopped. By 1984, more than four of every five black students who were in college attended predominantly white colleges.[53] By 1986, minority students were 17.9 percent of the 12.5 million students enrolled in colleges.[54] More than half of the African-American, Mexican-American, and Puerto Rican students who took the college entrance exams in 1984 reported that their fathers had never gone to college, and 24.5 percent of blacks, 37.4 percent of Puerto Ricans, and 40.3 percent of Mexican-Americans said that their fathers had never been graduated from high school. Yet, fully one-third of the Asians and one-fifth of the blacks, Mexican-Americans, and Puerto Ricans optimistically said they were aiming for a Ph.D., an M.D., or other professional degree.[55]

Blacks and Hispanics tended to lead socially separate lives on predominantly white campuses, but there were many instances of individual integration into campus life. At Wellesley, African-Americans were less than 5 percent of the student population in 1986, but black women were elected president and vice president of the student body. At the University of Missouri in Columbia, a 25,000-student campus that was only 4 percent black, the homecoming king and queen that year were black.[56]

Community colleges, a postwar development, also were important, if limited, arenas of ethnic interaction in the 1970s and 1980s. Some were dominated by one group, many others were multiethnic. In California, where there were more than two hundred community college campuses in 1984, only three were more than 40 percent Hispanic, with the highest proportion at Imperial Valley College, where 59.7 percent of more than four thousand students were from Spanish-origin backgrounds. Georgia had ten community colleges that were more than 85 percent black, but there were twice as many with only between 10 and 30 percent. Similarly, in Alabama eight community colleges in 1982 were more than 90 percent black, but at twenty-five campuses blacks constituted only between 10 and 35 percent of the student body. In three of Chicago's community colleges, more than 87 percent of the students were black, but in New York City only one community college was more than 60 percent African-American; the national pattern was closer to New York's, with a preponderance of community colleges holding a widely distributed mix of students from different backgrounds.[57]

Arenas of Interaction: The Armed Services

Probably no area of American life showed so drastic a change from racial segregation to integration as the armed services between the 1950s and 1980s. Much of the change could be attributed to the growth in black enlistments after new policies of integration were made clear. Those policies extended to recruitment for cadets at West Point as well as for enlisted personnel. The United States Military Academy at West Point was once entirely white. As late as 1968, still only .7 percent of the new class of plebes at West Point was African-American, but by 1982 the academy was 7.6 percent black, 3.7 percent Hispanic, and 2.8 percent Asian.[58] By 1986, the African-American percentage of the cadet corps remained at 7 percent, the Hispanic percentage was up to 4.4, and the Asian 3.5. That year the commandant of West Point, Brigadier General Fred A. Gordon, was an African-American; he pointed out that although President Truman had ordered the army integrated in 1948, "the practical aspect of integration began in Korea in 1952." When he himself entered the Point in 1958, there was only one other black plebe, who left at the end of the first semester.[59]

In a flash of history, the Department of Defense had become the largest "equal opportunity employer" in the world, dramatically raising the proportion of African-Americans and Hispanics at every level of each of the services by 1980 over what it had been ten years earlier, making them all thoroughly integrated. In the Second World War, more than 750,000 black men and women, many of them leaving the rural South, to which they never returned, served in uniform in overwhelmingly segregated units. The armed services were integrated during the Korean War, but the proportion of blacks remained small compared to what it was to become, especially among officers. In 1971, 11.4 percent of the total enlisted personnel in the armed services were African-American, a slightly higher proportion than in the population as a whole, but only 2.3 percent of commissioned officers were black. Ten years later, 22.1 percent of enlisted men and women were black, and 5.3 percent of officers.[60] By 1983, with more than fifteen thousand African-American officers on active duty, more than eighty were of general or flag officer rank, reflecting, in part, a dramatic shift in composition of the student bodies at the service academies; by 1986, 7 percent of all army generals on active duty were African-American.

The rise in black noncommissioned officers also was considerable. In 1972, only one in twenty-five NCOs in the army was black. By 1986, the figure was one in ten. The fact that about a third of all buck sergeants and staff sergeants and about a quarter of all first sergeants, master sergeants, and sergeants major were black had a profound impact on the social and recreational life of army posts. African-American Pentecostal congregations were established on several bases, attracting some whites, and, according to one observer, they "have begun to influence the style of worship in more conventional on-post services." Disco, soul, and rap music had strong followings among white soldiers, and the favorite comedian of enlisted men in 1986 was reported to be Eddie Murphy.[61]

Arenas of Interaction: The Workplace

The greater access of African-Americans and other minorities to higher education is one of several reasons for an increase in ethnic interaction at work in the United States. In the 1970s and 1980s, corporations sent their recruiters to colleges and community colleges, seeking Hispanic, Asian, black, and white ethnic students for a work force that tended to link occupation, education, and ethnicity to each other much less than before the Second World War. One reason is that the children, grandchildren, and great-grandchildren of Mexican immigrants were increasingly employed in middle-class occupations. The proportion of Mexican-American men employed as professionals, technicians, managers, and craft workers of all those employed rose from 32 to 36 percent between 1971 and 1981.[62] African-Americans also increased their share of officials and managers in the labor market between 1970 and 1980, from 1.9 to 4.0 percent, and black professionals went from 2.3 to 4.3 percent. Some of black managers and professionals were recent black immigrants from the Caribbean, but most were native-born black Americans who had moved into middle-class occupations.[63] (See chapter 25.)

In 1910, only 1.2 percent of immigrants admitted were professional and technical workers, compared to 4.7 percent of the American population as a whole. But by 1970, the proportion of aliens admitted who were professional and technical workers was almost double that for the American work force.[64] For some sending countries, such as India and Iran, a majority of the newcomers in the 1970s and 1980s were in white-collar occupations, in contrast to immigrants in earlier periods.

In the nineteenth century, immigrants often were imported from certain towns or regions in Europe to work in specific industries. "Langshire cotton printers came to Lowell, Paisley thread spinners to Newark, German iron puddlers to Pittsburgh, Staffordshire potters to Trenton, Welsh quarrymen to Vermont villages, and Cornish tin miners to the lead mines near Galina, Illinois," where they clustered in a particular locality or ward within a town or city, "often on the same street." Poles and other East Europeans went into Pennsylvania's anthracite region, but only Welsh could be heard at miners' meetings in Ohio's Mahoning valley, Chinese were brought in to work on the railroads and in the mines, French Canadians were imported to New England factories like the Amoskeag cotton mill in New Hampshire. Thus, ethnic groups were clustered at work as well as in neighborhoods.[65] Typically, the older northwestern European groups held the better industrial and craft jobs, as in Buffalo, where Germans comprised at least 70 percent of the masons, coopers, and shoemakers and a large majority of the cabinetmakers, tailors, butchers, and ironworkers, though less than 40 percent of the city's population. Irish formed a disproportionate percentage of unskilled laborers, domestics, and sailors.[66] Filipinos, Chinese, and other persons of color, especially blacks, were generally kept in a servile labor class, and even when they held the same jobs they were paid less than southern and eastern Europeans, who were, in turn, paid less than workers from the north and west of Europe.

In the Mississippi delta, where Chinese had been imported to replace slaves after the Civil War, they were segregated somewhere between blacks and whites, although a few eventually owned grocery stores and other retail businesses. Up to 1960, ethnic boundaries in the delta were static and highly stratified, with white planters on top, whites in businesses and middle-class occupations next, Jewish merchants and Italian farmers and working-class whites following, Chinese merchants after, and then poor whites, followed by African-American teachers and businessmen. At the bottom came Mexican farm laborers and, still below them, African-American manual and farm laborers, domestics, and unemployed.[67]

In Hawaii, plantation owners tried to stratify work by ethnicity. Scotch managers were on top, Portuguese next (often as foremen), and below them Chinese, Japanese, and Filipino workers. The Japanese and Chinese were able to break out of the roles assigned to them not because they worked in multiethnic settings but by specializing in ethnic entrepreneurship of one kind or another (see chapter 7). Stratification of jobs by ethnicity and religion had been a common feature of American life for so long that it probably would have been extremely difficult for Jews in 1930 to believe a time would come in which they were not excluded from major corporations or even entire industries, or for the Irish of the 1870s to believe that some day an end would come to newspaper advertisements that warned "No Irish Need Apply."

The shift from an industrial to a service economy accelerated the pace of ethnic interaction in the workplace. Instead of private companies bringing boatloads of Poles and Slavs to coal mines or steel factories, restaurants, supermarkets, and other retail stores looked to immigrants, particularly young ones, to work in settings where they came into contact quickly with persons from other backgrounds, although that was not their employers' intention. Other employers looked for high tech personnel—engineers, anesthesiologists and other professionals—regardless of nationality background, persons who would move quickly into integrated work settings. In Orange County, California, which drew an average of 45,000 newcomers every year in the 1970s and early 1980s, the business community cooperated with the county in establishing an immigrant and refugee planning center (funded totally from private sources) as a mechanism for facilitating the entrance of immigrants and refugees into the work force.[68]

Arenas of Interaction: Labor Unions and Social Service Agencies

By the 1980s, multiethnic integrated work forces were taken for granted by many young men and women; they could not remember when persons of color were excluded as retail clerks at major department stores and were excluded from craft unions. The International Ladies' Garment Workers Union had a long tradition of hospitality to immigrants, though less so to native-born blacks; Hispanic and Asian workers made up a large portion of the ILGWU in the 1970s and 1980s. The largest Local, 23–25, the blouse and skirt and sportswear workers of the union, was administered in the mid-1980s by an executive manager–secretary who was black.[69] Unions with a history of racial segregation were obliged to integrate under court orders and consent decrees in the 1960s and 1980s, bringing blacks, old ethnic whites, and new immigrants into greater contact with each other, not just at the workbench but at the union hall, as well. (See chapter 23.)

Much more significant as arenas of ethnic interaction than labor unions in the 1970s and 1980s were governmental social service agencies or voluntary organizations that worked with government money and which, by complying with nondiscrimination rules, fostered the mixing of persons from different ethnic backgrounds. The Copernicus Foundation Center in Chicago, intended mainly as a place for Polish folk dances, lectures, art shows, and clubs, provided hospitality for organizations of Filipino- and East Indian–Americans and for the Spanish Association of the Midwest. In 1987, 35 percent of those who called the foundation for help to deal with neighborhood and family problems were not Polish or Polish-American.[70]

The phenomenon of the ethnically based social service agency providing services to others became commonplace in the 1970s and 1980s. In Newark, for example, the North Ward Educational and Cultural Center was run by an Italian-American who forged a coalition between his own ethnic community and local blacks to ameliorate ethnic tensions and to work on other issues of common interest.[71] The Hebrew Immigrant Aid Society, while still concentrating on the settlement of Jewish refugees from the Soviet Union, helped to resettle Vietnamese refugees; so did Lutheran, Catholic, and other organized volunteer agencies without any necessary connection to the nationality or religion of the newcomers. Some government guidelines in the 1980s required immigrant-ethnic organizations receiving public funds to help persons regardless of background. In New York, the Chinatown Planning Council received funds only on condition that it provide vocational training and educational services to non-Chinese, too. And the Indo-Chinese provided English-language instruction to Central Americans and Afghans.[72]

Jews were particularly active in building organizations with other ethnic groups. In 1984 they joined with Asian groups and the Greater Boston Civil Rights Coalition to work on problems of prejudice facing newcomers from Asia.[73] In Chicago, the Jewish Council for Urban Affairs began work in 1973 with a Hispanic-led Eighteenth Street Development Corporation to rehabilitate a Hispanic neighborhood.[74] The Jewish Vocational Service, which provided free job training and placement to Jews and non-Jews, including many in the African-American community, broadened its outreach to Hispanics by announcing its services in the Latino media.[75] The American Jewish Committee joined other white ethnics, black, Hispanic, and Asian leaders to create the Illinois Ethnic Consultation as a means of providing information about different ethnic groups to one another and to build coalitions on issues of common interest.

As discussed in chapter 10, coalition politics between whites and blacks became common in the 1980s, and black organizations, after a period of strong separatism in the late 1960s and early 1970s, also began to reach out to nonblacks through such mainline organizations as the Urban Coalition, the National Association for the Advancement of Colored People, the NAACP Legal Defense Fund, and the Congress of Racial Equality. With an increasingly important place as service providers in state and local governments and voluntary agencies, African-Americans were in frequent contact with poor nonblacks in the 1980s. Following passage of the Immigration Reform and Control Act of 1986, CORE became one of sixteen private groups officially designated to help the Immigration and Naturalization Service obtain applications for legalization from undocumented aliens. The INS praised CORE's black workers for doing a superb job in New York City, where the illegal aliens they served were primarily Asian and Hispanic.[76]

The American Multiethnic Consciousness

Ethnic chauvinism sometimes was encouraged by the "roots" phenomenon—digging deeply into one's past to learn more about oneself—but the new emphasis on ethnicity also opened many Americans psychologically to the people and experiences of other cultures. The influence of schools obviously was important, but the impact of television and advertising may have been even more significant in promoting a multiethnic consciousness among Americans. "All in the Family" and its successor, "Archie Bunker's Place," which together ran for twelve years between 1971 and 1983, presented a main character who, though likable in many respects, was portrayed as a buffoon and out of date when he revealed his ethnic and racial prejudices. By the 1980s, television presented a number of programs with Asians, Hispanics, and especially blacks. The first program about a black family, "The Jeffersons," begun in 1975, was followed in the 1980s by the extraordinarily popular Bill Cosby program. Other successful programs shown in the 1980s—including "The Facts of Life," "Diff 'rent Strokes," "Silver Spoons," and "Gimme a Break,"—featured blacks and interracial themes.

Dozens of African-Americans appeared as hosts and anchorpersons on regional news programs, as did many Asians and Hispanics. Bryant Gumbel became a successful anchorman on the NBC "Today" show; in 1986, Oprah Winfrey became television's most popular nationally syndicated talk show host. Whites, according to the Harvard Medical School psychiatrist Alvin Poussaint, "listened to Oprah Winfrey as an authority."[77] Whites became much more conscious of blacks also through radio and television stations with regularly scheduled programming designed to appeal to blacks. By 1980, there were 350 such radio stations and 29 television stations, from the very small WELZ in Belzoni, Mississippi, to major outlets such as WNYC-FM in New York.[78]

The impact of American ethnic black music on American music generally has long been recognized, but by the 1980s there was more conscious understanding of ethnic crossover sounds in music than ever before. The blending of jazz harmonies with Caribbean rhythms created a sound that was labeled "crossover" and whose sources combined European, African, Caribbean, and Latino qualities.[79] Americans enjoyed the new music and other aspects of popular culture such as movies about blacks and Hispanics that avoided the ridiculous caricatures and stereotyping of the past. One of the most popular films of 1987 was *La Bamba,* which in telling the story of the singer Richie Valens sympathetically portrayed the daily lives of Mexican-Americans in the late 1950s, probably the first contact some whites had ever had with Mexican-Americans.[80]

Americans also read in their newspapers or watched on television about the appointment of Hispanics, to a lesser extent Asians, and especially African-Americans to a few high places in the government, and in private organizations. In 1982, a black man was appointed to head the world's largest foundation, the Ford Foundation; the following year a black woman was elected president of the National Education Association, and in 1984 another was elected president of the Planned Parenthood Federation. That was the year that Martin Luther King, Jr.'s birthday became a national holiday. In 1985, an African-American woman was chosen as Miss America and another black woman as her runner-up. A young black naval pilot became, briefly, a national hero on television after being shot down by the Syrians over Lebanon. The first African-American astronaut went into outer space. Michael Jackson, a hero to millions of young Americans of every background, was invited to the White House, where he was honored by President Reagan for permitting one of his most popular songs to be used in the campaign against drug addiction. In 1986, Bill Cosby received an honorary degree from the University of South Carolina, along with Alex Haley, the African-American Pulitzer Prize–winning author of *Roots*; in reporting the awards, the *New York Times* mentioned their race not as an extraordinary breakthrough but as a minor matter to be noted along with facts about the other honorary degree recipients.[81] In the same year, West Point received its first black commandant; in the following year, 1987, a black lieutenant general, Colin Powell, was appointed national security adviser to President Reagan, and two years later, now a five-star general, he was chosen by President Bush and the Senate to serve as chairman of the Joint Chiefs of Staff. Also in 1989, an African-American, Ron Brown, was picked as chairman of the National Democratic party, and a young black woman won the Miss America contest (an Asian-American was runner-up).

African-, Asian-, and Hispanic-Americans appeared with increasing frequency in television and print commercials and in comic strips. Typical was the Pan-American ad called "Sextuplets!" in the black magazine for the upwardly mobile, *Black Enterprise,* showing six one-year-old children in diapers sitting in Pan American's new Clipper Class; one was black, another Asian, two blond, and two dark-haired (one was clearly intended to look Hispanic).[82] Health-Tex, maker of children's clothing, in a six-page ad in the *New York Times Magazine* in 1984 featured the Statue of Liberty and drawings of eight small children, one of whom was black, another meant to be Hispanic, a third, Asian; two were white with red hair, one was a blond, and an eighth had brown hair and uncertain ethnic identity. On the next page were two other children with black hair, three who were Anglo-looking, and two who were Asian.[83] In 1987, the chain department store Jordan Marsh included in its fall brochure models who were obviously Hispanic, Asian, and black and, in what would have been considered a serious breach of advertising etiquette only a few years earlier, showed a picture of a black girl (apparently nine or ten years old) with her hand on the knee of a young white boy of the same age sitting next to her.[84]

The new multiethnic advertising was in sharp contrast to the advertisements on trade cards in the late nineteenth century making fun of Chinese and other groups, or magazine advertisements of the earlier twentieth century depicting blacks as shuffling and subservient. As late as 1943, an advertisement in *Life* magazine for Aunt Jemima had her exclaim, "Lawsee! Folks sho' whoops . . . over Aunt Jemima pancakes."[85] The Aunt Jemima ad contrasts with those of the late 1960s and early 1970s for Levy's Jewish rye bread, one of which showed an American Indian biting into a rye bread sandwich, with the caption, "You don't have to be Jewish to love Levy's real Jewish rye." The Levy's ad aimed at selling more rye bread by tapping into the growing multiethnic consciousness of Americans. An invitation to cross boundaries was reckoned to enhance profits.[86]

Advertising reflected the diversity of a new kaleidoscope in which it was possible to combine ethnic pride and openness to the ethnicity of others. Millions of Americans still lived in ethno-cultural isolation: blacks deep in poverty in city ghettoes or in pockets of rural isolation who never saw a white person except on television; orthodox religious Americans whose lives were bound up almost totally in relationships with their own kind; Mexican immigrants, especially illegal immigrants, who never heard or spoke a word of English. Millions of Americans still harbored deep prejudice against outsiders. And the pain of newcomers often was palpable. Ignorance, fear, suspicion, and prejudice often marked contacts between persons from different backgrounds. The advertisers also ignored the continuation of racism and the severity of racial conflict in the streets, high schools, and even college campuses. Aiming to sell products, they said nothing about the pain and bitterness and isolation felt by many blacks and Indians, the Americans whose ancestors did not choose America. But none of that was new. Yet, what made the ethnic landscape distinctive in the 1980s from what it had been in the past was not racial or ethnic conflict, or the pain of the excluded. What distinguished the ethnic landscape of the 1980s from what it had been in the past was not only the quickened pace of interaction but also a growing multiethnic awareness of and respect for diversity and the relative ease with which ethnic boundaries were crossed.

Chapter Seventeen

THE KASHAYA AND THE NYINGMA
Identities and Boundaries

THERE is a large stretch of coastal land in Sonoma County, California, that belonged to the Kashaya Indians long before Russian traders came in the early nineteenth century to establish the settlement now called Fort Ross. By 1985, only about a dozen Kashaya families were left on a forty-acre reservation. On my way to it in April of that year, driving through magnificent hills in the thick, cool northern California fog along Tin Barn Road, I passed the enormous, resplendent temple of the Nyingma Buddhists, called Odiyan. The Nyingmas, under the leadership of a Tibetan monk, had obtained 650 acres on which to build their nearly completed temple of gold leaf, copper, and beautiful California woods. Behind the high, locked fence that kept visitors from entering without special permission, Odiyan would soon receive Buddhist disciples from all over the world.

Two miles farther inland along Tin Barn Road I arrived at the small Kashaya reservation, where, with the help of five young white men and one white woman who lived nearby, the Kashayas were completing a simple wooden roundhouse with an earthen floor to serve as the center for dancing, song, and worship at their annual two-day spring strawberry festival celebrating the renewal of life. The following weekend the Kashayas would welcome other Indians, white visitors, and anyone who wished to come from Odiyan. Speaking of the newcomers at Odiyan, the Kashaya spiritual leader explained that they were one more group in a line of powerful outsiders who knew how to manipulate the world, a group whose friendship might be helpful to the Indians. Determined to penetrate the high chain link fence built around Odiyan's land, he spoke of the importance to the Kashayas of sharing spiritual and healing knowledge (what the Kashayas call *weya*, or energy) with the Nyingma sect. It was their way, he explained, but to judge from their fence, the Nyingma would keep to themselves.

Six months after my visit to the Kashaya, a much larger Indian tribe, the Cherokees of Oklahoma, elected Wilma Mankiller as their principal chief, choosing a woman for the first time. Born forty years before in a small community, Rocky Mountain, Oklahoma, to a Cherokee father and a white mother, Wilma Mankiller had moved with her family to San

Francisco when she was eleven. Stirred by Indian protests against injustice, she participated in the occupation by Indians of Alcatraz Island in San Francisco Bay, and later moved back to Oklahoma to use her college and graduate school training in social work to help the tribe, whose registered number had risen in a decade from twelve thousand to sixty-seven thousand adults and children.[1] Ms. Mankiller's history illustrated a growing and distinctive pattern in the American ethnic landscape: openness to and interaction with others combined with revived ethnic consciousness and mobilization.

The Nyingma represented a common tribal pattern found elsewhere in the world, in which a strong group identity entails tight boundaries difficult to pass. There is room for the Nyingma in the U.S., as there is for the Old Order of Mennonites, the Hutterites, Hasidim, and other groups whose requirements for membership are strict, whose suspicion of the outsider is strong, and whose techniques of internal control are powerful. For most Americans, ethnic ties of loyalty and affection, widely felt and openly expressed in the 1970s and 1980s, became, as they were for the Kashaya, increasingly subjective, a matter of individual choice. The Kashaya more than the Nyingma Buddhists represented the dominant American ethnic pattern in the kaleidoscope of the 1980s: increased ethnic consciousness and visibility and, at the same time, growing interaction with outsiders and the crossing of ethnic boundaries.

Permeable Ethnic Boundaries and Intermarriage

Intermarriage was so common in the postwar era that by 1980 the vast majority of Americans had relatives, through birth or their own marriage, from at least two different ethnic backgrounds. Only one-fifth of husbands and wives born after 1950 came from the same single ethnic ancestry (outside of the South, only 15 percent). Intermarriage was extensive for descendants of all major European ancestry groups. Persons with Irish, French, or Scotch ancestry and others whose immigrant forebears were likely to have arrived before the twentieth century had the highest proportion of mixed backgrounds, but even about half of the men and women with only Italian ancestry married entirely outside that group, and 60 percent of persons with Polish ancestry were married to individuals with no Polish ancestry at all, as the pace of intermarriage increased with the passage of time. Whereas only 15.7 percent of all those identifying as Poles claimed mixed ancestry, 78 percent of those born after 1960 did so. Only 7.7 percent of the identifying Italians born before 1920 acknowledged mixed ancestry, compared to 70.3 percent of those born after 1960.

Out-marriage among newer immigrants and among blacks is less extensive, but for those groups, too, the change was in the direction of intermarriage. Intermarriage rates for Hispanics were considerably higher for those born after 1950 than for the group born in 1920 or before, with about one-third of the men and 30 percent of the women in the younger age group having intermarried.[2] The readiness to marry outside one's group was related to education, as shown in a study of 250 Chicago Hispanics (23 percent Mexicans, 36 percent Puerto Ricans, 29 percent Cubans, and 11 percent South Americans), nine out of ten of whom were born outside the U.S. More than half of the persons in the sample were teachers, who presumably have more contact with non-Hispanics than those who are less well educated. In answer to specific questions on marriage, 58 percent said they would marry someone who is not Hispanic, compared to only 23 percent who said no (19 percent did not know).[3]

Interracial married couples were still relatively rare in the U.S., but the increase between 1970 and 1980 was almost 100 percent, rising from 310,000 to 613,000. In the decade of the 1970s, when calls for black pride and power were strongest, the number of black-white married couples more than doubled, from 65,000 to 167,000.[4] Among black men born after 1950, almost 6 percent married across racial lines, compared to less than 1 percent of those born before 1920.[5]

The proportion of nisei living in predominantly Japanese-American neighborhoods went steadily down after 1915.[6] The grandchildren of issei immigrants had extensive contact with non-Japanese at the workplace, too.[7] Interaction in neighborhoods and the workplace led to extensive intermarriage for Japanese-Americans. With so much contact between Japanese and non-Japanese, it was not surprising that a study of *sansei* (U.S.-born children of nisei parents) in California in the mid-1960s found that almost 40 percent of the males in the sample were married to non-Japanese, and more than 53 percent of those who were dating someone regularly were seeing non-Japanese-American women. Seventy-five percent of the sansei men felt that intermarriage made little difference in its effect on the partners, 15 percent thought it was good, and only 10 percent thought it was bad.[8]

In Hawaii, contact between Japanese-Americans and others was so rapid that Japanese out-marriage rates rose from .2 percent between 1912 and 1916 to 43.3 percent in 1980 for women and from .5 percent to 39.4 percent for men. By the 1980s, nisei and sansei parents (first and second generation born in the U.S.) no longer thought of intermarriage as seriously troubling. When researchers listed sixty-five items as a possible source of trouble for individual respondents, the one labeled least serious was intermarriage, even less serious than something going wrong with the car.[9]

Jews also were highly integrated in the workplace and increasingly so in suburban neighborhoods. When, in a 1984 national survey, Jews were asked to identify the three people in their neighborhoods with whom they were closest, 43 percent said two out of three were not Jewish (27 percent said all three).[10] Such extensive contact led to intermarriage rates comparable to those of the sansei, but extensive intermarriage did not mean the end of ethnicity for either Japanese or Jews. The Hawaiian study showed that the sansei as much as the nisei participated in typical Japanese activities with regard to exchanging food, repayment of obligations, and other Japanese cultural practices.[11] In the California study, the ability to speak Japanese diminished considerably between the nisei and sansei generations, but the sansei were not assimilationist in their ideology. Ninety-one percent of sansei males said they would like to speak Japanese better than they did, and 83 percent thought they ought to know more about Japanese culture. Even before the surge of ethnic consciousness in the 1960s and early 1970s, at the same time that less than one-quarter of the sansei reported that their closest friends were only Japanese-Americans, a majority of the sansei wanted to retain a clear sense of their Japanese identity, and 11 percent said they read Japanese-American newspapers regularly (33 percent occasionally).[12]

Perhaps even more than Japanese, Jews showed a propensity for combining extensive intermarriage with a surge in ethnic and religious pride. The rate of Jewish intermarriage in the 1970s and 1980s probably was higher than it had been in any earlier society; yet, at the same time, American Jewish cultural and organizational life was flourishing, including a renaissance in Yiddish, which was being taught at more than a dozen American universities. Two of many anecdotes illustrating the twin phenomena of intermarriage combined with maintenance of Jewish traditions make the point. Tamar Flowing Waters, a Jewish woman married to an American Indian, was said to "faithfully attend the Synagogue."[13] A Jewish lawyer from New York married a Vietnamese immigrant woman, adopted her Amer-Asian children, and raised them as Jews.[14]

Intermarriage, a result of the tremendous emphasis given in the dominant American culture to individual choice over and against group controls, proliferated the possibilities for choosing one's ethnic identity. The subjectivity of ethnicity meant that an increasing number of Americans became free to be as ethnic or as nonethnic as they chose, and also in some cases were able to choose from among ethnic identities. There were about five thousand Cuban-Chinese in New York City and in nearby Hoboken, New Jersey, in the mid-1980s. The elders among them had an affinity for Chinese culture and Buddhism, and usually belonged to the Chinese Benevolent Association in New York's Chinatown. Their children tended to identify with Cubans, attend the Roman Catholic church, and marry outside the Asian community. One, who came to the U.S. at the age of thirteen, said, "I am Cuban, Chinese and American . . . I speak

Spanish, not much Chinese, but was raised in the Chinese way of thinking." A graduate of Bernard M. Baruch College in business administration, she worked as an administrative assistant in a Manhattan bank and
was married to an American of Italian descent.[15]

In mixed marriages, parents often celebrated two sets of ethnic or religious holidays. For example, Satu Mehta of Cambridge, Massachusetts,
whose background was Finnish Lutheran, married a Zoroastrian from
Iran, and they and their two children regularly attended the Rama
Krishna Enanta Society, a Hindu temple in Boston, in addition to celebrating Christmas, during which season she took her children to Fitchburg, Massachusetts, to buy a Christmas tree from a Finnish immigrant
farmer with whom she conversed in the language of the old country.[16]

Being able to choose from different ethnic self-identifications meant
that individuals from Barbados could decide whether to call themselves
Barbadians, West Indians, African-Americans, or blacks, or, in a few cases
depending on color, to pass as white; it was possible for a Jew to choose
to be a Hasidic Jew, a Reform Jew, or not a Jew at all; a Mexican-origin
American could label herself Hispanic, Latina, Chicana, Mexican, Mexican-American, or just plain American; a Sioux Indian from North Dakota
could call him or herself a Lakota Sioux, an Indian, or a Native American,
or could use each of these identities at different times depending upon
the setting.

Gloria Martinez, a sophisticated middle-class medical technician from
Honduras living in New York City in the 1970s, did not think of herself
as a Honduran but as a member of one of the minority groups in Honduras, the Garifuna, who originally were a combination of Carib Indians
and Africans. In Manhattan, she learned to call African-Americans
"blacks" because that was what they wanted, adding, "I hate that word.
I wish they would use 'Negro' or 'African.' That's what they are."[17] But
most black Americans probably rejected the label "Negro" because it was
imposed from the outside and thus carried with it the stigma of oppression and submission. Garifunans were not able to develop an independent
identity in the eyes of others because there were so few of them, but
Gloria Martinez discovered that she had a variety of other ethnic identities
to choose from. Having rejected "black," she said she could easily put on
a dashiki and talk "Third World, 1970s style," or a white shirt, when
"you'd think I was Negro, but in beige I can pass for Indian. Some people
even wonder if I am part Chinese."[18] "If New Yorkers hear me speak
Spanish," she said, "they assume that I am a Puerto Rican."[19]

Passing as a Puerto Rican was easy in New York City, where 25 percent
of the people spoke Spanish, and many immigrants from Central and
South America did so in the 1980s because Puerto Ricans had the advantages that went with American citizenship. Colombians, often treated

unfairly because of widespread news coverage of Colombian drug traf-
fickers, had that additional reason to pass as Puerto Ricans. Such examples
of self-designated ethnicity for personal purposes were reported frequently in the newspapers in the 1980s. One man, who acknowledged his
parents were white, called himself black when he ran for city councilman
in Stockton, California, where blacks made up 10 percent of Stockton's
169,000 residents in 1984. After his election, his opponent complained
that since he did not deny that his parents were white, it was unfair for
him to pass as a black man. But the successful candidate claimed he had
black ancestry going back many generations and that he felt culturally
and socially black. "My choice is my choice," he said.[20] His behavior was
reminiscent of that described by a scholar of third- and fourth-generation
Polish-Americans, who said they slipped their ethnicity on and off "like
Galician dancing boots," particularly if they earned their livelihoods in
jobs related to their ethnic backgrounds.[21]

The Reconfiguration of Ethnicity: Social Pressures and Individual Choice

Reconfiguration of the identities of entire groups has been a common
occurrence in American history. The pressures to reconfigure usually are
external. One identity may be seen as more desirable than another—
American Indian over black is a historic example—or subgroups may
come together to share a common identity in order to increase their
political and economic power, as Spanish-speaking groups tried to do in
the 1970s and 1980s. A good example of self-designated change in order
to improve one's image and status was the case of the Ramapo Indians,
who had inhabited the Ramapo Mountains of northern New Jersey and
southeastern New York for more than two centuries. Outsiders in the
area called them "Buckos," a pejorative term of uncertain origin, or "Jackson whites." The name "Jackson" was supposed to be either a corruption
of the word "Hessian" or the name of a man who imported English and
black prostitutes from the West Indies, women whom the British soldiers
called "Jackson's whites."

Historian David Cohen argued that there is much evidence to show
that the people who called themselves Ramapo Indians actually were
descendants of free black pioneers and Dutch settlers and not of Indians.[22]
Cohen found that the ancestors of the Ramapos were not prostitutes and
renegades but black landowners freed by the Dutch more than a century
before the American Revolution and who had been driven to the remote
hills of the Ramapo by a New Jersey law that curtailed the movement of
free blacks across county lines. Despite the fact that the group's most
common surnames are all Dutch and that their speech still is related to

an old dialect known as "Jersey Dutch," they rejected both the popular designation of whites in the surrounding areas and of historians, choosing instead to call themselves Indians. By incorporating themselves as a tribe, the 2,500 Ramapos were able to collect on a claim of $93,000 in government money, and, should they ever be recognized as a tribe by the U.S. Bureau of Indian Affairs, they would become eligible for considerably more government aid. In the meantime, school officials were sympathetic to their claim because the Ramapos brought federal money to the Mahwah school district in New Jersey to develop and implement a curriculum dealing with Native American history and culture under a program sponsored by the Bureau.

Choosing the ethnic identification of greatest advantage, as the Ramapos did, was not always possible. In the state of Hawaii, two generations of Portuguese-Americans—many originally from the Azores and Cape Verde islands—tried unsuccessfully to be called *haole* (Caucasian). But Asians, ethnic Hawaiians, and Caucasians persisted in calling them "Portuguese" or "Portugee." Important distinctions in the homelands—like those between Portugal, the Azores, or the Cape Verdes—often were blurred, partly because the distinctions were not obvious to others and partly because it was to the advantage of newcomers to submerge their old-country identities in favor of ones that gave them more influence and/or status. Nationality distinctions among Jews who thought of themselves as Rumanians, Hungarians, Poles, or Germans were erased in part because American Gentiles saw them all as Jews, but also because Jews gained greater solidarity and influence by combining forces. Italian-Americans who wore buttons that said "Kiss me, I'm Italian" in the 1980s had grandparents who called themselves Sicilians, Calabrese, or Neapolitans and who did not think of themselves as Italians at all. Filipino-Americans who called themselves "Filipinos" had parents who would have thought of themselves as Visayans, Ilocanos, or members of one of the other major ethnic-dialect groups from the Philippines.

In the first phase of immigration, old-country tensions between groups often were exacerbated, as between northern Italians and southern Italians, Ilocanos and Visayans, German Jews and eastern European Jews, Okinawans and Naichi Japanese. Japanese from the inner islands in Japan had little contact with Okinawans, and disparaged them as an inferior, more primitive group. The stereotype that each held of the other was intensified at first in Hawaii. But eventually, the old-country tensions were eroded there in the process of ethnic regrouping and ethnic-Americanization. In schools, churches, labor unions, and other American institutions, both groups in Hawaii usually were perceived as Japanese by outsiders, and after a time it became obvious that it was to the advantage of the Okinawans and the Naichi to combine forces in economics and politics as a Japanese-American ethnic group.[23]

Many new immigrant groups were in the process of refashioning their American ethnic identities in the 1980s, including blacks from the Caribbean and Africa, Asians, and Spanish-speakers from many different countries. The situation of black immigrants was particularly complex because of the diversity of cultural and linguistic backgrounds they brought to the U.S. in increasing numbers in the 1970s and 1980s. English-speaking "West Indians" from Jamaica, Trinidad, the Bahamas, Barbados, and other island countries; Spanish-speaking Cubans, Dominicans, Panamanians; Portuguese-speaking Cape Verdeans; and French-speaking Haitians arrived, along with immigrants from Africa. How they represented themselves and perhaps even how they thought of themselves was affected by the extent to which whites and native-born American blacks saw them as members of immigrant groups as opposed to being just black. Because black immigrants from the English-speaking Caribbean often were called "West Indians" by native-born American blacks and whites, Barbadian and Jamaican workers in New York City, who tended to think of themselves as Barbadian or Jamaican at home and in their neighborhoods, often used the term "West Indian" when working with whites.[24] Because whites tended to label Cubans and Puerto Ricans who were black as Cubans and Puerto Ricans, there was little reason for them to seek a common identity with native-born black Americans.[25]

The psychology of self-identification and representation to others depended on the context in which immigrant blacks found themselves. Before the 1970s, they had little incentive to merge their identities with that of native-born African-Americans. A former student of mine from the Azores reported that his parents were surprised and somewhat dismayed when, after black music became popular in the 1970s, he openly identified with native-born American blacks. With the end of the most blatant manifestations of discrimination against African-Americans and the emergence of the movement for black pride and power, the children of black immigrants found it easier and sometimes even more desirable to identify themselves with other black Americans. But every situation depended upon the context. Black Cuban-Americans in New Jersey appeared to identify themselves within a larger Cuban community. Others thought of and presented themselves as a separate ethnic group within a large black minority. Still others identified as Hispanics, part of a larger group of dark-skinned persons from the Dominican Republic, Puerto Rico, and other places in Latin America.[26]

The diversity of black newcomers might modify the traditional system of racial classification in the U.S., based solely on black and white, to one that classified native-born African-Americans as the principal one of several black ethnic groups. Ethnicity, despite its elusive character, was becoming a way by which a great many blacks identified themselves, although race was still the dominant factor, having long been imposed by whites on blacks without respect to their ancestral backgrounds. It is possible that blacks regardless of background will again identify almost entirely on the basis of race, but unlikely as long as substantial immigration from African and Caribbean countries continues.[27]

The process of identity reconfiguration for Asian immigrants also was dynamic in the 1980s. Because Laotians, Cambodians, and Vietnamese often were combined by the media and in the minds of outsiders as "Indo-Chinese," and because leaders of those groups found that cooperation and consolidation would enhance their influence, they increasingly called themselves "Indo-Chinese," even though the differences among them were as great as among Greeks, Italians, and Spaniards. Despite the sharpness of these differences and even those within each nationality group—for example, lowland and highland Laotians—the interest that all of them had in dealing with their common problems as refugees resulted in the creation of Indo-Chinese advocacy groups in the 1980s, the most important of which was the Indo-China Resource Action Center, a national nonprofit organization serving all the Indo-Chinese communities in the U.S. (see chapter 19). By 1987, the center moved toward closer cooperation with other Asian communities, including those from the subcontinent (Pakistan and India), China, Japan, Korea, and the Philippines, but the linguistic, cultural, and historical differences among Asian groups were so vast as to inhibit their ability to regroup around a larger Asian-American ethnicity even though newspapers and television and, to some extent, foundations and government granting agencies tended to push them in that direction.[28]

The fact that Mexicans, Cubans, Puerto Ricans, Dominicans, and South and Central Americans all spoke Spanish (except for Brazilians) created an important common bond which, despite formidable differences in the experiences and interests of the various groups, led increasingly to the use of the term "Hispanic" by themselves and others to describe that shared identity. It was a term first thrust onto persons from Spanish-speaking backgrounds for the convenience of others, beginning primarily in 1970, when the U.S. Census Bureau first adopted it. Teachers of Spanish tended to like it because it contributed to the growing movement for bilingual programs. And Spanish-speaking politicians and the leaders of advocacy organizations used it because it enabled them to project an image of growing power by claiming more constituents, as when the Mexican-American Legal Defense and Education Fund began to speak consistently of Hispanics in all of its literature in the 1980s. The general media relished it because it made for stories foretelling dramatic changes in American life (the "Hispanicization of America"), and newspapers, magazines, radio, and television selling to a Spanish-speaking market had a vested interest in pushing the term.

By 1980, thirty-five markets where more than 95 percent of the Spanish-speaking population was concentrated had at least one Spanish radio station (Miami had six), totaling seventy full-time stations programmed independently and locally to meet the needs of its own community. The more than sixteen Spanish-speaking television stations, thirty-one national newspapers and periodicals, and forty local and regional newspapers wanted Spanish-speaking customers, whether their backgrounds were Cuban, Mexican, Venezuelan, or Puerto Rican.[29]

Two English-only publications aimed at readers of Hispanic background rapidly increased their circulation in the 1980s. The slick bimonthly magazine *Nuestro* (founded in 1974) featured information on Americans from a variety of Spanish-speaking backgrounds, often without mentioning the nationality of the individual. Its editors frequently used the term "Latino" or "Latina" to give the background of individuals mentioned. Latino was still used, in the West particularly, but by the late 1980s, "Hispanic" had become the dominant term used by *Nuestro,* and it was the term of choice in the rapidly expanding English-language monthly *Vista,* whose backers, before launching the magazine, conducted household research in eleven cities, where they learned there was a large market of Americans of Spanish-speaking backgrounds who wanted to read about Hispanics generally in the language they knew best, English.[30]

Resistance to the term persisted even into the 1980s, according to one study of the Mexican-American electorate in San Antonio and Los Angeles, in which only 6 percent of the citizen respondents identified themselves as Hispanic, compared to 62 percent who called themselves either Mexican-American or American.[31] But the pressure to share an identity with others of Spanish-speaking background increased with stories about a Hispanic all-star baseball team, Hispanic writers and artists, the Hispanic Caucus in Congress, and Hispanic studies programs in universities. An Argentinian-American adviser to the National Conference of Catholic Bishops on Hispanic Programs wrote that it was ironic that he was now being thought of as "Hispanic." "Only in America," he said, "Could I become 'Hispanic.' Elsewhere, the gulf between a Mexican of rural origins, a Cuban of urban mercantile background, and a South American aristocrat might make it ludicrous to lump the three together. Similarly, we 'Hispanics' come in every color—black, white, brown, red. Some of us are even Oriental." Along the way to becoming an American citizen, he discovered that for all their differences, persons of Spanish-speaking background often were treated as "one indistinguishable mass" by the majority.[32]

Whether one chose to be identified as Hispanic or Argentinian or Cuban, there were many pressures in the 1970s and 1980s to identify with some ethnic category. In a survey of students at twenty community colleges from all regions of the country, one young man from Walnut Creek, California, wrote, "everybody belongs to an ethnic group."[33] He was clearly wrong, at least in terms of self-perceptions, as shown in Richard Alba's study of "Ethnic Identity Among American Whites" in the Albany-Schenectady-Troy area, where about half the population did not claim a significant ethnic identity at all.[34] But many community college students, even those who apparently did not have a strong identification with a particular nationality, mentioned color when asked about their ethnicity (there was no specific question about race, color, or religion). Whites identified themselves ethnically as "Caucasian," "Anglo-Saxon," "Anglo-Saxon white," "white Anglo-Saxon Protestant," "Anglo," and just plain "white."

Nonwhites in the survey chose from a variety of ethnic designations that would have been listed simply as "black" by the Census Bureau, including "Ibo," "Creole-black," "West African," "Afro-American," "Negro," "Baptist black American," and "colored people." Most blacks listed simply "black" in answer to the question about ethnic identification.[35] Many blacks, regardless of background, now considered themselves as an ethnic group, a result Martin Luther King, Jr., sought in an effort to mobilize them for political and economic action and to build coalitions with Jews and others. By asserting that "the American Negro is neither totally African nor totally Western" but "is Afro-American, a true hybrid combination of two cultures,"[36] King was laying claim to an ethnic-American identity and not a racial one. There was obviously a variety of sub-identifications, even among native-born black Americans. The children of Jamaicans, Antiguans, and Nigerians, as already mentioned, would not necessarily have a strong identification with the children of sharecroppers who had moved from the South to the North during or immediately after the Second World War. The children of those sharecroppers had little in common with middle-class blacks who lived on the better streets of Harlem in New York or Roxbury in Boston. But the movement for black pride cut across those differences for many blacks, the vast majority of whom were the descendants of slaves and had deep roots in the South. All, for example, could take pride in the freeing of Nelson Mandela from a South African jail in 1990.

The black revolution and the new immigration forced scholars to think about blacks in terms of ethnicity, too, as reflected in sharp changes in scholarly treatment of the subjects of ethnicity and race between the 1960s and the 1970s. In 1961, *Daedalus,* the journal of the American Academy of Arts and Sciences, devoted its spring issue to the subject of ethnic groups in American life without reference to blacks. An issue on "color and race" was published in the spring of 1967 without any discussion of ethnicity. But in the spring of 1981, *Daedalus* published an issue dealing with American Indians, blacks, Chicanos, and Puerto Ricans—all as "ethnic groups in American life."[37]

By seeking to dismantle the structure of caste pluralism, African-Americans were asserting their right to be treated as individuals and also as members of an ethnic group. By insisting on their own ethnic identity and asserting that black is beautiful, they unleashed a surge of ethnic consciousness. The search for ethnic roots became commonplace in the 1970s, made popular in part by the publication of *Roots,* dealing with one black American's quest for his ancestors in West Africa.[38] A profusion of other books by European ethnics appeared that attempted to recapture roots for different ethnic audiences.[39] In 1974, Congress passed the Ethnic Heritage Studies Program Act "to encourage greater understanding of the ethnic backgrounds and roots of all American citizens." Ethnic magazines emphasizing the search for roots appeared in the late 1970s. Two monthly Italo-American magazines, *I/Am* and *Identity,* began in late 1976. Advertisements for food with an ethnic emphasis became commonplace, and in 1977 Pan American Airlines capitalized on the roots idea with radio and television commercials encouraging Americans to visit ancestral homelands.[40]

Probably a large number of blacks and whites, perhaps even a majority, did not think much about or act on the basis of ethnicity, but those who did had an increasing number of identities to choose from. In answer to the question about ethnicity, a student from California in the community college survey called himself a "Swedish Lutheran." Another from Kansas called herself "an Italian born-again Christian." A young man in Miami said, "I'm a Spanish Catholic Cuban." "I am a Baptist black American," replied another student.[41]

Ethnic consciousness was given considerable stimulus by the decision of the federal government to assist members of designated ethnic groups in making up for the injustices of the past through affirmative action and other programs. State and local governments, and especially the federal government, stimulated ethnic consciousness and mobilization through a large panoply of programs ranging from the promotion of ethnic art and theater to the setting of goals linked to timetables for hiring members of designated ethnic groups by employers who do business with the government.

The nature of the government program could even determine shifts in ethnic boundaries. For example, a grant for West Indian culture and art could mobilize different persons than one for black culture and art generally. Funds to stimulate employment in a Puerto Rican neighborhood would intensify Puerto Rican consciousness and mobilization; money for a bilingual education program in New York would engender Hispanic consciousness and coalition building between Latino groups. In addition to affirmative action, such programs and the extension of federal funding in other areas, such as public housing, urban renewal, and refugee resettlement, had made ethnicity a more significant basis for political mobilization than it had been in earlier decades.[42]

With the designation of protected classes and the assignment of benefits on the basis of ethnicity, ethnic groups developed a strong vested interest in ethnic classification and enumeration, lobbying hard "for separate status in census reporting, for more complete enumeration of their constituencies, and for identification procedures that classify marginal cases with a favored group."[43] By 1978, ethnic enumeration was so important that the U.S. Office of Management and Budget imposed a uniform system of ethnic accounting on all federal agencies, including the Bureau of the Census. The four groups designated as protected classes were: American Indian or Alaskan native; Asian or Pacific islander; black; and Hispanic. All other persons, called "white" regardless of their actual skin color, were those who had origins in any of the original peoples of Europe, North Africa, or the Middle East. Blacks were persons who had origins, no matter how slight, in any of the black peoples of Africa, including the most recent immigrants from Nigeria or Ethiopia. In cases of doubt, the OMB advised that "the category which most closely reflects the individual's recognition in his community should be used for purposes of reporting on persons who are of mixed racial and/or ethnic origins."[44]

In the period 1790–1820, census enumeration included slaves, tribal Indians, and foreigners not naturalized, in addition to white citizens. In 1850, persons in the U.S. were counted as whites, blacks, or mulattoes, and for the first time the country of birth was recorded for free inhabitants.[45] In 1870, all inhabitants were classified as white, black, mulatto, Chinese, or Indian, and by country of birth. In 1880, the specific country of birth was recorded for each parent of the person being enumerated; in 1920, the census recorded the mother tongue of every person and his or her parents. By 1960, the census taker could list the respondent as white, Negro, American Indian, Japanese, Chinese, Filipino, Hawaiian, part Hawaiian, Aleut, Eskimo, or anything else he or she specified.[46]

In preparing for the 1980 census, the bureau formed advisory committees for the three non-Indian groups designated as protected classes by the OMB: blacks, Spanish-origin, and Asian and Pacific Islanders. The new form included nine Asian categories plus white, black or Negro, American Indian, Hawaiian, Guamanian, Samoan, Eskimo, and Aleut, with a space that made it possible for American Indians to list their tribe. The designations were not perfectly comparable—some based on race, others more on national or territorial origins—but they all were ethnic. And the system recognized that ethnicity in the U.S. had become largely subjective despite the external pressures or inducements created by government action or society to belong to one group or another. Under the system, a respondent whose father was black and whose mother was white could choose either or both racial designations. A Chinese-Hawaiian-Portuguese *haole* in Hawaii could choose to be listed as white. A dark-skinned Puerto Rican or Cuban could choose black or white or, more likely, answer another question, which asked whether the person was of Spanish-Hispanic origin or descent, and choose one of four possible designations.

The system for enumerating members of ethnic groups was criticized for asking leading questions and, because of its reliance on self-designation, its results were subject to varying interpretations.[47] But despite external pressures from government and society, Americans were moving toward an increasingly subjective system of classifying their own ethnicity as the pace of interaction and intermarriage quickened. At the same time that Americans felt more free to display their ethnic pride and mobilize their political and economic interests on the basis of ethnicity, they also became more free to borrow and blend with other ethnic groups than ever before,[48] although it is doubtful that many dark-skinned American-born black descendants of slaves felt they had that choice. Others could choose to lead substantially insulated lives, as did the Nyingma in California. But the Kashaya Indians nearby, virtually unknown, poor, and small in number, were much more representative of what ethnicity had come to mean to an increasing number of persons in the United States: openness to interaction with others across permeable ethnic boundaries; pride in one's own ethnic background; and increasing opportunities for political mobilization based on ethnicity.

Chapter Eighteen

"THE WISH OF THE FOUNDING FATHERS"
Third World Immigrants Embrace the Civic Culture

I N THE twelve cities in which the Select Commission on Immigration and Refugee Policy held public hearings in 1979–1980, a time was always set aside for unscheduled witnesses to testify before what was called the open microphone. Such witnesses would sign up during the course of the day and be taken in order from the beginning of the session. At the commission's open-microphone session in Miami on December 4, 1979, the first witness, a strong-looking, poised man of about twenty-five, approached the commissioners, including the chairman for that session, U.S. Attorney General Benjamin Civiletti, and began his testimony:

My name is Ciro Castillo. My home is in the state of Queretaro, Mexico. I come to this country seeking work in order to feed my family in Mexico, for in my town there is no work, and unemployment is as high as fifty percent. I am here today to give testimony on behalf of the thousands of undocumented Mexican farm workers here in Florida and as a member of the International Coordination Committee . . . working for the human rights of undocumented workers.

Neither the attorney general nor any of the several U.S. marshals in the back of the hall moved to interrupt Castillo's testimony, although he was, by his own admission, an illegal alien. Probably he assumed (correctly) that he would be free from arrest and deportation while testifying in the open to claim his rights as a worker. But he could not possibly have known that the argument he made would be embodied in the Immigration Reform and Control Act seven years later. Castillo told the commissioners that in order to guarantee that all workers in the United States had fundamental rights, agricultural workers should be admitted in an expanded program that gave them an opportunity not just to be temporary laborers but to become resident aliens with the right to work any place they could find jobs, a proposal embodied in modified form in the 1986 bill.[1]

Although he had not been admitted legally, Castillo could, at least for a moment, participate in the American civic culture; as an illegal alien, Castillo could not become a permanent part of it. Although he paid Social

Security and other taxes, it was unlikely that he would ever receive any benefits. He could not vote or run for office; but at least he faced the select commission without fear, unlike the unidentified Chinese illegal worker who testified in New York City with a mask over his face, describing how a Chinese tong helped him to travel from Hong Kong to enter the country unlawfully and then enlisted him as a gang member in a protection racket in Chinatown by threatening him with bodily harm and even death if he did not comply.[2]

Castillo not only testified in the open, but he already had participated in a strike and had joined a lobby group that included American citizens and resident aliens. But technically he had none of the rights of lawfully admitted immigrants, who by the 1970s and 1980s had demonstrated that they, like the immigrants of the nineteenth and early twentieth centuries and especially their children, had learned the rules of American politics and had become active participants in the civic culture. Third World immigrants no less than European immigrants before them learned that one could become an American by asserting the rights and exercising the claims protected by the Constitution of the United States.

Samuel F. B. Morse thought the Irish Catholics could never become Americanized; Henry Adams doubted that Jews were suitable material for Americanization; Walter Dillingham thought it absurd to expect Japanese to become loyal citizens; Nelson Aldrich feared that the hordes of southern and eastern Europeans, unwashed and unlettered, would undermine American institutions and principles. What would they have thought of the more exotic immigrants from the Third World in the 1970s and 1980s, the Haitians, the H'mong, the Afghans, Iranians, and the others? Many Americans in the 1970s and 1980s expressed comparable fears to the Select Commission on Immigration and Refugee Policy with respect to the newest immigrants. Wrote one woman, "the brown flood of aliens inundating our southwestern states and Florida from Mexico, Central and South America and Cuba . . . has already changed the character of the Southwest . . . not just for twenty years but forever."[3] Another woman wrote the commission, "all of these people . . . form demanding special interest groups who disrupt and exploit the natural order already established."[4]

The hostility of many native-born Americans was always part of the agony of adjustment for immigrants and refugees. Refugees particularly—often having been driven from loved ones and having few resources—felt the stress of resettlement. Immigrants and refugees were always prey to criminal elements, sometimes from within their own groups, and they frequently experienced the strain of having to learn a new language and adapt to an unfamiliar culture. Yet, the new Third World immigrants (and even the refugees) and their children adapted remarkably well to

American life, considering the burdens that many of them carried.[5] As had always been true, successful adaptation depended in part on immigrant characteristics such as individual intelligence and health, education and skills (including literacy and English-language ability), family relationships, age, settlement intentions (sojourner vs. settler), cultural familiarity, and whether or not they had experienced recent psychological or physical trauma as refugees. Compared to the immigrants who came between 1880 and 1915, the lawfully admitted immigrant newcomers of the 1970s and 1980s had several advantages in being able to adjust to American life, including a higher proportion of persons with education, skills, and financial resources and a larger proportion of persons who came to be reunified with close family members already here and were certain that they wanted to settle in the new country.

External factors affecting the adjustment of newcomers were important, too. Some immigrants and refugees arrived at times of economic boom, others, recession. Welfare and social service support systems varied (high in California and low in Louisiana, for example). Cubans fleeing Cuba in 1980 were given authority to work; Haitians escaping Haiti were not. But the individual characteristics of immigrants and refugees probably were the most important group of factors affecting acculturation. For example, Asian Indians who came were a highly educated group, with a high school completion rate of 94 percent in 1986, compared to 76 percent for Vietnamese-Americans, undoubtedly accounting for the fact that Asian Indians had a median income only slightly lower than that for Japanese-Americans and higher than for native-born whites.[6] Cuban-Americans showed earnings just 8 percent below the national median, compared to Mexican-Americans, who were 15 percent lower, mainly because a high proportion of the Cuban immigrants were professionals and an unusually high proportion of Mexicans were relatively less skilled sojourners.[7] That Vietnamese earnings were 35 percent below the national median, compared to Filipino and Korean earnings, which were 19 and 3 percent greater respectively, was primarily due to the fact that they arrived as refugees, lacking the skills and resources of recent Filipino and Korean immigrants, and also because of their growing dependence on California's welfare system.[8]

Ethnic-Americanization: Religious, Fraternal and Economic Associations

Although there was considerable variation in the ability of different groups to adapt economically and socially, the process of ethnic-Americanization was the same for all of them, as it basically had been for the voluntary immigrants who preceded them. That process went through three stages at a different pace for various groups and for the individuals within each group, phases that often overlapped but led invariably to participation by large numbers of immigrants (and especially their children) in American civic life as ethnic-Americans.

The process of ethnicization to ethnic-Americanization followed the path of first forming associations for religious and fraternal solidarity and then organizing for economic success and political power. Just as had been true among earlier immigrants, religious immigrants in the 1970s and 1980s rapidly formed churches (Copts in Jersey City; Vietnamese Buddhists in Irving, Texas; Gujarati Swaminarayans in Glen Ellen, Illinois) and mosques (as Muslim immigrants from more than half a dozen countries did in several dozen large and small cities).[9]

The new immigrants also followed the pattern of the older groups in creating fraternal and mutual assistance organizations such as burial societies, family and neighborhood associations, and others with sundry welfare functions. By 1981, the Indo-Chinese had established more than five hundred such organizations.[10] In forming associations, immigrants were conforming to the propensity of earlier groups of ethnic-Americans to express their sensibilities, protect their interests, or promote some public good through organized activity. Among New York City policemen, for example, Polish-Americans formed the Pulaski Association, Germans the Steuben Association (both were named after foreign heroes who fought on the American side in the Revolutionary War), blacks the Guardians' Association, and Irish Americans an Emerald Society. Newcomers on the police force from Spanish-speaking countries established a Hispanic Society, and Asian-American policemen the Asian Jade Association (created in 1980). Such fraternal groups did not prevent policemen from all the different ethnic backgrounds from cooperating in an integrated police force on the job. Even in their leisure time, the policemen worked through an interethnic organization called "Brotherhood-in-Action" to perform a variety of social service projects, including one for the development of better understanding and appreciation of ethnic diversity in New York.[11]

Churches, religious organizations, fraternal associations, radio stations, and newspapers all helped newcomers in the 1970s and 1980s to keep in touch with each other and to cope with the loneliness, vulnerability, and fear that immigrants often experienced.[12] For example, Haitians in New York City had established a network of churches and fraternal organizations by the mid-1980s. On Saturday evenings, some immigrants gathered in the homes of voodoo priests to perform religious ceremonies. There were "Haitian Hours" on four radio stations in New York, and every week a Haitian-American-owned newspaper told of Haitian political meetings and cultural events in the city.[13]

In typically American fashion, immigrants also formed groups to utilize the economic opportunities that had brought most of them to the U.S. The new immigrant-ethnic groups established credit organizations, small banks, and other businesses. By 1983, the Koreans of southern California listed in a special telephone directory more than six thousand Korean-American businesses, banks, and trading companies, as well as 67 Korean-American Christian churches and 134 nonprofit associations.[14] In 1984, the Indo-Chinese in the Washington, D.C., area published an Indo-Chinese business directory that listed twenty-eight Indo-Chinese dentists and doctors and, among other things, eighteen auto repair shops, thirteen jewelers, and ten beauty salons run by refugees or immigrants from Vietnam, Cambodia, or Laos.[15]

The earliest waves of Cuban refugees followed the established ethnic-American pattern of creating banks and chambers of commerce in south Florida, but even less-affluent immigrants and refugees such as the Haitians used ethnicity as a strategy to get jobs and provide credit. Usually a relative or a friend would help a recent immigrant to locate a job, go with him for the job interview, and serve as a reference. Haitian-American ministers and priests put newcomers in touch with job seekers, and immigrants used car pools to get to work. Haitian entrepreneurs quickly sprang up to serve Haitian markets, and by 1978 the Haitian-American business directory in New York listed the names and addresses of about two hundred Haitian-American businesses, which provided employment not just for members of the owners' families but also for new Haitian immigrants who were unrelated.[16]

Ethnic-Americanization and Ethnic Politics

Churches, mosques, Hindu temples, burial societies, and mutual assistance and fraternal organizations sprang up almost unnoticed by native-born Americans as expressions of voluntary pluralism. Mobilization for ethnic power was more noticeable and more threatening, as it had always been. The calls for Catholic power in the 1840s upset Protestants, and the Black Power movement of the 1960s caused great anxiety among whites. But political mobilization by newcomer ethnic groups had always been a critical element of ethnic-Americanization, for it was through participation in American politics that immigrants and African-Americans were able to claim their share in the American patrimony and to appropriate the rhetoric and symbols of the civic culture.[17]

The lobbying of the Germans for language schools throughout the Midwest and of the Irish to have Protestant Bible reading excluded from New York schools, activities described in chapters 1 and 2, were comparable to those undertaken by many groups. In the early nineteenth century, Jews fought to have state constitutions changed to eliminate the Christian oath as prerequisite for holding office and to have state aid for parochial education applied to their schools.[18] Foreign policy lobbying by ethnic groups was almost as old as the republic, too, and particularly prominent in the earlier part of the twentieth century up through the Second World War.[19] Now, the newcomers joined the Greeks, Jews, Poles, and Irish in exercising their First Amendment rights to petition and lobby their government.

Let Americans discern a problem, Tocqueville wrote, and immediately they will spring into action to form a group to do something about it. Soon after their arrival in the 1970s and 1980s, immigrants and refugees began to behave like Americans in Tocquevillian fashion. At the public hearings held by the Select Commission on Immigration and Refugee Policy, Indo-Chinese, Caribbean, Middle Eastern, and African nationals and ethnic Americans were represented by dozens of newly organized political action groups, such as the Haitian Defense Committee of Boston, the Colorado Alliance of Pacific Asian-Americans, and the Chicago Task Force for the Defense of Filipino Immigrants. The largest number of such organizations were found in new-immigrant cities such as Los Angeles and world cities such as New York, but they surfaced along with African-American and American Indian advocacy groups in almost every middle-sized and large city, usually organized around issues of health, education, community development, and civil rights.[20]

Newcomers rapidly caught on to the fact that public expressions of ethnicity through group action were legitimate in the U.S. Although resident aliens were no longer permitted to vote, as they had been in many states in the early twentieth century, their political activity was encouraged by corporations and foundations much more than ever before. Corporations taught civics lessons because it was good business, as in the case of McDonald's Congressional Summer Internship Program begun in 1986, sponsored jointly by the fast-food firm and the congressional Hispanic caucus and which paid Hispanic high school students $1,000 a month while serving in congresspersons' offices in Washington. Only a few years before the Ford Foundation sponsored a Hispanic Leadership Opportunity Program (with cooperation of the congressional Hispanic caucus) for Hispanic college graduates and graduate students to work in congressional committees and other government-related positions. The Ford Foundation had been sponsoring its own school of civic education by giving substantial grants to Mexican-American community and political activists since the 1960s, providing initial funding for community development corporations such as Phoenix's *Chicanos Por La Causa,* which worked to improve housing, education, and economic conditions in Phoenix. Such organizations usually had a short life, but they became the training ground for young Mexican-Americans who would enter politics and become civic leaders in the 1970s and 1980s.

Newcomer immigrants followed the patterns of older groups also in mobilizing their claims and defending their interests. The Arab-American Anti-Discrimination Committee (ADC) and the National Association of Arab-Americans (ADA) both were modeled after similar Jewish groups to defend and lobby for Arab-American interests. From an original membership of four hundred in 1980, the ADA had nine thousand members in forty-four regional chapters in seventeen states with a staff of thirty-five by 1984. In that year, it claimed a role in the defeat of pro-Israeli Congressman Clarence Long (D-Maryland), and in Detroit, Pittsburgh, San Francisco, and other urban centers with large Arab-American populations it helped to raise hundreds of thousands of dollars to canvass neighborhoods and register voters on behalf of Jesse Jackson, perceived as the only presidential candidate sympathetic to the cause of Palestinian statehood and to problems of discrimination against Arabs and Arab-Americans in the U.S. "We have the same problems Jews had seventy years ago. They were viewed as sinister and [as] outsiders," a spokesman for the ADA said. "The more involved we become, the less [being] Arab becomes something to be concerned about, and people will view us as a legitimate ethnic group like Poles, Italians and Jews."[21]

Arab-Americans were not yet recognized as a legitimate ethnic group by all politicians, some of whom refused to take contributions or to accept explicit support from them. That was changing by the mid-1980s, too. When the Arab-American Institute was formed in 1984 specifically to encourage registration and political activity by Arab-Americans, it was addressed by Republican presidential candidate Senator Robert Dole (R-Kansas), who spoke again to the group two years later. "Whoever is going to be President of the United States has an obligation to talk to all Americans," said Dole. The executive director of the Arab-American Institute commented, "We are an ethnic group . . . I don't know of any politician who would refuse to talk to a Japanese group."[22]

Spokespersons for the newcomer ethnic-immigrant lobby groups did not speak with one voice any more than did the German-American, Irish-American, or Italian-American leaders in the nineteenth and early part of the twentieth century. Arab-Americans came from many different countries, worshiped in several religious communities, were in different stages of acculturation, and were far from unanimous on policy questions, even concerning the Middle East. Disagreements about old-country politics appeared among Koreans, Nicaraguans, Cubans, and other new immigrant-ethnic groups. Tens of thousands of Koreans and Korean-Americans protested in San Francisco in June 1987 against the South Korean government; other Koreans, a minority, supported the government.[23]

As historian John Bodnar has shown, the major old immigrant-ethnic groups were divided by class, generation, region, and ideology.[24] They were split not just over old-country politics, but also in facing problems of adjustment. Asian Indians provided a typical example of intragroup conflict regarding the role of Indians in American society during the 1970s and 1980s. From the beginning of the century through 1950, only a few thousand Asian Indians had been permitted to immigrate. But, largely because of the 1965 amendments to the Immigration and Nationality Act that ended the discriminatory national-origins quota system, the U.S. census counted 361,544 Asian Indians in 1980. One advocacy group, the Association of Indians in America (AIA), successfully lobbied to have the 1980 census add the classification "Asian Indians" in order to require all government agencies to classify Indians in the "Asian or Pacific Island" category rather than as "Caucasian/white."

The AIA believed that gaining minority-group status would win benefits for Asian Indians in employment, housing, education, and with respect to loans and health services. But another group, the Indian League of America, based in Chicago, opposed the drive toward minority status, believing that such a designation would provoke hostility from whites, blacks, and Hispanics against Asian Indians, who, among all immigrant groups, were the most highly educated and skilled. The AIA won a victory when the U.S. Small Business Administration concluded that Asian Indians were a "socially disadvantaged minority group" and would be eligible for the agency's program to promote minority entrepreneurship.[25]

In the 1970s and 1980s, the policy process openly encouraged ethnic lobbying more than it ever had before. The Dillingham immigration commission did not even solicit views from representatives of immigrant-ethnic groups in 1907–1910. But the Select Commission on Immigration and Refugee Policy encouraged such groups to prepare research and give testimony, as evidenced by Ciro Castillo's appearance in Miami. The Federation of Indian Associations, for example, which heretofore had existed primarily to coordinate the activities of some two dozen Asian Indian cultural organizations, was stimulated to make a study and to report to the select commission on the visa problems encountered by applicants of Indian origin in American consulates in India.[26]

When the select commission held its open-microphone session in San Francisco, it heard from representatives of many small new Filipino-American groups who saw an opportunity to petition their government. A representative of the Bay Area Task Force for the Defense of Filipino

Immigrant Rights told the commission that elderly Filipino immigrants had not been receiving their Social Security benefits; the spokeswoman for the Filipino Community Incorporated of Santa Clara County informed the commission that raids by the Immigration and Naturalization Service in public schools, intended to apprehend the children of illegal aliens, resulted in the arrest of citizen children; a representative of the Hawaii Task Force for the Defense of Filipino Rights complained of exploitation of Filipino agricultural workers brought to the U.S. under a special temporary-worker program; the man who represented the Filipino People's Far West Convention reported that the organization would be holding its tenth convention in San Francisco to continue to confront "the injustices and inequities that affect our people's daily lives"; a woman testifying for the Union of Democratic Filipinos urged Americans not to become xenophobic in bad economic times; and another representing Filipino Immigrant Services urged the commission to refute the notion that immigrants were the cause of high unemployment.[27]

The Filipina-American head of the National Women's Political Caucus, who spoke not for Filipino but for women's causes, said in 1987 that she sometimes feels that "America is just one big podium."[28] Introduced to politics as a college student in 1968 when she passed out campaign leaflets for one of the presidential candidates, she told of becoming involved in different organizations, sometimes wearing her "Asian hat" and sometimes a "woman's hat." There were more podiums, platforms, and other policy forums that gave sanction to the advocacy of immigrant-ethnic interests than ever before. Citizen advisory groups that included representatives of ethnic groups became commonplace in the 1980s. When the Los Angeles school system set up a course outline in citizenship for adult education, its advisory committee was not limited to experts, but included Hispanic and Asian community representatives.[29] Almost every major city and state had a mayor's or governor's office concerned with immigrant affairs, the existence of which encouraged the formation of immigrant and refugee advocacy groups and their participation in the policy process.[30]

Many of the state advisory committees to the U.S. Commission on Civil Rights reached out to newcomers to encourage them to express their concerns and advance their interests. When the New York State advisory committee decided in 1978 to study the situation of Asian-Americans in New York, they elicited testimony from representatives of Chinese, Japanese, Filipino, and Korean organizations on a range of issues not addressed by the organizations themselves before the hearings. The Korean Pharmaceutical Association in America lobbied against stringent requirements in New York that prevented licensing of pharmacists who had been graduated from foreign schools. The head of the Korean Nurses'

Association protested to the commission that foreign nurse graduates who were qualified as registered nurses had difficulty finding employment because hospitals in New York required two years of experience in the U.S. These policy forums nurtured advocacy groups, such as the Asian-American Postal Employees, the Philippine Democratic Club, the Asian-American Women's Caucus, and the Japanese-American Help for the Aging, all of which sent representatives to testify.[31]

No sizable new immigrant group failed to be drawn to American politics, in a process that European immigrants, Mexicans, and Chinese had followed in prior decades. Organizations to defend one's rights and express interests invariably were followed by campaigns for citizenship, as with Colombian-Americans, who in New York created the Colombian-American National Coalition, first to dispel negative feelings toward Colombian nationals because of the linkage of drug traffic to Colombia, and then to persuade Colombian immigrants to apply for citizenship.[32] At the same time as they conducted naturalization campaigns, ethnic-group leaders moved into wider arenas of politics to work with others. In New York, where the coalition of Grenadian and Vincentian activists supported Mayor Koch's reelection in 1985, a Vincentian-American became president of the board of a city-funded day care center, and Grenadian-Americans were rewarded with appointments to community school boards.[33]

Cuban-Americans and the Civic Culture

Even refugee groups, such as the Cubans, Haitians, and Indo-Chinese, who, much more than immigrants, tended to be preoccupied with old-country politics, moved with remarkable ease to participate in American politics. Once it became clear to Cubans that they were not going to return quickly to their homeland, they established themselves in Miami particularly, but also in Jersey City and other places, became citizens, and participated actively in civic and political life. As Cuban-American businesses prospered—all Hispanic-owned businesses in Dade County grew from 3,447 to 24,898 between 1969 and 1982—Cuban-Americans also began to enter politics.[34] One Cuban-American was elected to the Florida state legislature in 1981. Six years later, there were seven Cuban-Americans in the legislature, and Cuban-Americans helped to elect Florida's first governor of Spanish descent, Bob Martínez. Unlike most ethnic-American political leaders, Martínez had not begun his career in politics as an advocate of a parochial ethnic interest; but, regardless of the point of departure, all ethnic-American leaders—including those who led refugee groups—learned the skills of negotiation, bargaining, compromise, and coalition in American politics.[35]

Like many other refugee groups, Cubans faced problems of conflict over foreign policy issues—in their case, toward Fidel Castro—and toward their own approach to acculturation in the United States. One group of Cubans emerged in the 1970s, an association of business people, bankers, students, workers, and clergy, who were anxious to open up a dialogue with Premier Castro in order to increase tourism and to permit additional immigration from Cuba to the U.S. But after the Mariel sealift in 1980, when the American people were angered by Castro's decision to load mentally ill and criminal Cubans on boats with other Cubans seeking to escape as refugees, militant anti-Communist forces among Cubans and Cuban-Americans in Florida achieved dominance in the Cuban-American community.

The course of acculturation for Cubans generally followed a path of what Alejandro Portes called "from political exiles to ethnic minority."[36] While 60.6 percent of the Cuban refugees and immigrants in 1973 said they would return to Cuba if Castro fell, only 22.6 percent agreed by 1979. By 1979, 95.9 percent planned to remain permanently, compared to only 53.7 percent six years earlier.[37] Permanent settlement meant that Cuban candidates in local elections, unusual before 1980, became increasingly common thereafter, and a formerly isolated group was transformed "into another ethnic minority, with goals and interests dependent on its position within American society."[38]

What the stance of that community should be was hotly debated in the *Miami Herald* in 1988. With the election in 1987 of Xavier Suarez, the first Cuban-American mayor of Miami, it became clear that Cuban-Americans had achieved a degree of political as well as economic and cultural hegemony in that south Florida city with unparalleled swiftness. But an article by Cuban-American columnist Guillarmo Martínez, commenting on a poll that showed that barely one percent of non-Cubans regarded the migration of Cuban-Americans to Florida as positive, forced a period of intense introspection among Cuban-American leaders. The negative results probably were linked to recent riots by Cuban *Marielitos* in federal penitentiaries protesting a decision of the federal government to deport some who had been forced out by Castro, because they were ineligible for refugee or immigrant status in the U.S. The negative poll results also reflected resentment by non-Cubans because of the rapid economic and political success of the Cuban immigrants.[39] Despite that resentment, the first Cuban-American was elected to Congress from Miami in 1989 with substantial non-Cuban backing.

Hostility toward an achieving minority has been commonplace in history. The Ibos in West Africa, the Palestinian Arabs in the Middle East, the Chinese in Southeast Asia, the Japanese on the West Coast of the U.S., and the Jews everywhere had been targets of resentment by others.

But the Cubans were answering the central issue—whether or not they were too parochial—by their own behavior, as increasing numbers learned to speak English, participated in communitywide civic organizations, and otherwise became ethnic-Americans.

Haitian-Americans and the Civic Culture

Given the relatively high level of education and skills of the pre-Mariel Cuban-American community, it was not surprising that they were able to achieve considerable political success by the late 1980s. But the Haitians who arrived in south Florida in 1980 and subsequent years were mostly poor and uneducated. In flight from repression and poverty in their homeland, they were not even granted the status of political refugees accorded routinely to the Cubans (before Mariel), to the Vietnamese, and to others fleeing Communist countries.

A smaller group of better-educated Haitian-Americans in New York had begun to participate in politics in the wake of the civil rights movement in the late 1960s and early 1970s. A Haitian-American political organization was established, a small number of Haitian-Americans ran for local office, and one of them was appointed chairman of the Election Committee on the Nationalities for Percy E. Sutton, candidate for re-election as borough president of Manhattan.[40] The arrival of Haitians fleeing poverty and oppression in the late 1970s and early 1980s stimulated a renewal of political activity by the Haitian-Americans who preceded them, but the poor Haitians who came to south Florida in the early 1980s lacked the skill and education associated with success in politics. Of 499 adult Haitians studied in south Florida in 1983 and 1984, none of whom had been in the U.S. for more than three years, 44 percent still had no knowledge of English and 63 percent held unskilled or semiskilled jobs.[41]

Although Haitians had tremendous difficulties in finding employment and despite the fact that they were excluded from the legal protection and economic support given other refugee groups under the Refugee Act of 1980, 68 percent reported that they planned to become American citizens.[42] Despite their lack of education and relative poverty, many of the refugees, aided by the local Catholic archdiocese and a coalition of Protestant churches called the Christian Community Service Agency, became involved in advocacy politics. In 1973, the CCSA established the Haitian Refugee Center to provide social services, whose Office of Community Relations for Haitian Refugees became the political arm of a growing coalition of Haitian refugees and of church and legal aid activists. The HRC quickly learned how to lobby in American politics, boasting that "our January 1977 Vigil Activities in Washington demonstrated that we could get National News Media; that we had the support of at least twenty-five Congressional offices; and that we had the beginnings of a tri-partite network: refugees/resident Haitians/U.S. supporters."[43]

The Haitian coalition, led by the Haitian Refugee Center's director, the Rev. Gérard Jean-Juste, urged that Haitians be released from detention centers and given refugee or asylee status. Demonstrations by Haitians in Miami were joined by representatives of the NAACP and the Union of American Hebrew Congregations, as the Haitians learned to participate in coalition politics.[44] In 1981, some ten thousand Haitian-Americans, Haitian immigrants, refugees, and others came to Washington to demand the release of Haitian asylum seekers from immigration detention centers.[45]

The focus of Haitian-American political organizations turned away from local issues with the diminution of federally funded community corporations and especially because of increased attention to the political situation in Haiti. In order to force the resignation of Haiti's president for life, Jean-Claude "Baby Doc" Duvalier, tens of thousands of Haitians picketed and marched in protest demonstrations in New York City.[46] Although the demonstrations revolved around foreign policy issues, they were comparable to those organized by Archbishop John Hughes in protesting discrimination against Catholics in the public schools more than 140 years earlier in that both demonstrations became occasions for organizing immigrants as ethnic-Americans in a common political cause.

Relatively weak and small in numbers, Haitian-Americans saw within a relatively short time the effect of their lobbying on American public opinion about the Duvalier regime, when Duvalier fled Haiti on February 7, 1986, after a year of demonstrations in Haiti and the U.S. They also saw, in November 1986, the passage of the Immigration Reform and Control Act, which gave permanent resident-alien status to the post-1980 Haitian asylum seekers. There were many reasons why the Haitian-Americans had not yet become a more significant political force in either New York or Miami. The upper- and middle-class Haitian community was extremely small; the vast majority of Haitians were poor and spoke English badly if at all; most had not yet become citizens; their overall numbers were relatively small; and their political energies and interests were still focused mainly on the homeland. But given these factors, the extent and effectiveness of their mobilization was remarkable, and the process of ethnic-Americanization was well under way for the Haitians.

Indo-Chinese-Americans and the Civic Culture

The potential for mobilizing political power was much greater for the Indo-Chinese than for the Haitians, partly because they were more numerous. By 1985, the Population Reference Bureau estimated that there were 634,200 Vietnamese, 218,400 Laotians, and 160,800 Cambodians in the U.S.[47] The Indo-Chinese were introduced quickly to contact with the government because federal and state officials administered refugee resettlement programs for them in cooperation with voluntary agencies. The more highly educated and skilled of the Vietnamese refugees, particularly those who came before 1975, including a disproportionate number of ethnic Chinese, followed the common immigrant-ethnic pattern of economic networking and began to achieve a degree of success in small businesses—fishing, agriculture, and retailing—in California, Texas, and Virginia. The outstanding example occurred in Westminster, California, where there were more than two hundred Vietnamese-owned businesses by 1984 (serving Orange County's estimated 77,000 to 90,000 Vietnamese) compared to only three in 1978.[48] Despite the economic activity of the Vietnamese in what was called "Little Saigon" in Westminster, there was considerable unemployment and welfare dependency among Southeast Asian refugees in the 1980s, particularly in California, where more than one-third of the Indo-Chinese refugees lived.[49]

The severe economic struggle of the refugees and their children undoubtedly retarded political incorporation to some extent. Like other immigrant-ethnic groups, the Indo-Chinese were a highly diverse group, whose interests varied greatly in terms of nationality, language, and religion, as well as occupation and education. The H'mong and other hill tribes from the Laotian highlands had little in common with French-educated professionals from Saigon. Divisions existed even within a relatively homogenous community, as in San Jose, California, where a majority of the Vietnamese Catholics urged the bishop to give them a parish just for Vietnamese, as national parishes had been established for Poles, Germans, and Italians.[50]

Despite these differences, their lack of language skills, and relative poverty, the Indo-Chinese began to naturalize in increasing numbers as they realized they would not be able to return to their homelands. Once naturalized, they felt empowered in American politics. One Vietnamese woman, recently sworn in as a citizen in Houston, exclaimed to her social worker that now she received letters from her congressman. Before, "no one paid attention."[51] As more of them became involved in politics, they saw the advantage of reconfiguring their identity, learning to mobilize as Indo-Chinese and not just as Laotians, Cambodians, and Vietnamese. As one of the Vietnamese leaders in California, Vu Duc Vuong, a senior consultant to the California state legislature's Joint Committee on Refugee Settlement and Immigration, said, "with a thousand Indo-Chinese votes you can swing the vote, at the local level." "The sooner we understand the system and participate, the better," said Rosa Kwong, an aide to California Assemblyman Art Agnos, who began to realize in the early 1980s the potential power of the Indo-Chinese vote in Orange County.

When Agnos ran for mayor of San Francisco in 1988, refugee citizens distributed signs and campaign literature, raised funds, and voted for him. One Vietnamese leader, another longtime Agnos supporter, said, "A successful candidate needs two basic things, money and votes. We intend to provide both." As a result, he and his colleagues conducted the first registration campaign for Vietnamese voters in the Tenderloin area of San Francisco, where about 15,000 Southeast Asian refugees lived. Following Agnos's election, one of the Vietnamese leaders, the executive director of the Mutual Assistance Association Council, was appointed by Agnos to the Commission for Community Development, where he helped to select community organizations for funding from a federal block grant.[52]

Under the leadership of Lee Xuan Khoa, the Vietnamese decided to form a national lobby with the other Indo-Chinese groups, and they established the Indochina Resource Action Center. By June 1986, the IRAC held its first national Indo-Chinese community leadership convention with three hundred participants from thirty-seven states, most of whom came at their own expense. They listened to Senator Mark O. Hatfield (R-Oregon) exhorting them to become more active in politics. "This is a call," he said, "for active, participating citizenship; help bring the pressure to bear on your government . . . become citizens, write your representatives, get involved."[53]

At the state level, Indochina refugees formed mutual assistance associations, usually with the help of outside funding, which mushroomed in states throughout the country in the mid-1980s, and which also became involved in political action. The Brown County H'mong Association of Green Bay, Wisconsin, received funding from eleven different sources between 1983 and 1986, including money from the Office of Refugee Relief made available through the Office of the Coordinator of Refugee Affairs in Wisconsin.[54] A founding member of the Wisconsin United Coalition of Mutual Assistance Associations (nine other MAAs were included), the H'mong Association had grown into a multiservice agency with nine paid staff and four full-time volunteers, who operated a H'mong center for community meetings, English language instruction, and other community activities for the eleven hundred H'mong refugee residents of Brown County.

The Laotian highland H'mong, who had come from a preliterate culture, participated in coalition politics elsewhere, too. In the southern

Minnesota city of Rochester, with a population of 60,000, including 2,000 Southeast Asians, the Indo-Chinese formed a multiethnic mutual assistance association in 1983 to represent the Vietnamese, Cambodians, and Laotians. Meeting ten times in five months, they created a board in 1984 composed of nine Cambodians, six Vietnamese, and three Lao/ H'mong, with a rotating board chairmanship among the three groups on an annual basis. In 1986, they joined with sixty other organizations to form the Minnesota Refugee Advocacy Coalition, which held an evening open forum attended by staff members for both senators and five representatives from Minnesota in order to make their case for expeditious refugee admissions.[55]

In Orange County, California, a Cambodian refugee ran for election to the Long Beach city council in 1986, finishing a close fourth in a field of nine candidates. Although only about 15 percent of the Indo-Chinese in southern California had become citizens, they formed an organization of Indo-Chinese-Americans which walked door to door and registered new citizens as voters. Evaluating his loss, the candidate concluded there had been too little follow-up. "That's a lesson we learned the hard way. Now we have first hand knowledge and we know what to do next time."[56]

Commenting on the election in Long Beach, Vu Duc Vuong, who had become executive director of the Center for Southeast Asian Refugee Resettlement in San Francisco and head of the Vietnamese-American Democratic Club, predicted there would be many Indo-Chinese running for office in subsequent years. Applauding the burgeoning of political clubs and citizen/voter leagues within the refugee community, he said, "The only decisive show of strength is the actual votes."[57] Praising Southeast Asians for their economic success and the accomplishments of their children at school, Vu Duc argued that there was another level of integration that must be achieved. Probably unaware that he was paraphrasing Tocqueville, he wrote in *The Bridge,* the organ of the Indochina Resource Action Center, that political action based on self-interest is good for society as a whole. Through participation, Indochina refugees and their children would be able to pay the U.S. back.[58]

A major opportunity for political action in the Indo-Chinese community came in 1987. Following the June 1986 Indo-Chinese Community Leadership Convention, the IRAC board, working together with Indo-Chinese MAAs, sent a fact-finding team to the Southeast Asian refugee camps in February 1987. Following an intensive briefing of 350 congressional staffers and 120 journalists with prior Indo-China experience, the IRAC team held a press conference in the capital on March 2 to publicize the tremendous difficulties that refugees, particularly the H'mong/highlanders and Cambodians, were having in the refugee camps in Thailand. As a result of their efforts, Hatfield and six other senators together with

Congressman Chester G. Atkins (D-Massachusetts) and six other members of the House, introduced legislation with four objectives: to shift the responsibility for Indo-Chinese refugee processing from the Immigration and Naturalization Service to the State Department; to increase slightly the number of refugees to be admitted under U.S. programs; to set aside slots for those who had been in camps for at least three years; and to provide additional money for financial assistance to protect and educate refugees in Thailand.

The IRAC contacted Indo-Chinese leaders and other supporters all over the country with an action alert bulletin urging them to write and call congressmen to ask them to co-sponsor the Hatfield-Atkins bill. Laotian and Cambodian mutual assistance associations, which were expected to celebrate their New Year during the congressional recess, were encouraged to invite their representatives and senators to the festivities. "If they agree to come, make sure they get a chance to speak and give them an award; even if they send a staffer, make sure to give public acknowledgment of their commitment and support," advised the IRAC action alert bulletin.[59] Recipients of the message (it was sent to fifteen hundred refugee mutual assistance associations and other self-help groups) were told not only to thank senators and representatives who already supported the bill, but to remind them that "you and other members of the Indo-Chinese-American community are (or will soon become) voting citizens." Advice also was given to contact the media and church groups and any organization that might be interested in supporting the measure. A sample letter to a congressman was enclosed. After a summer of lobbying activity, the Hatfield-Atkins Bill passed the Senate. Senator Hatfield acknowledged the help given by the Indochina Resource Action Center, saying it played a "critical role in assuring the consideration and passage of the historic bill."[60]

The IRAC was learning that success in American politics depended upon coalition building. To win votes on one issue, it was sometimes necessary to become informed and committed with respect to issues that concerned others. Its newsletters increasingly emphasized the importance of reaching out to non-Indo-Chinese refugee groups and their advocates, and in 1987 the IRAC endorsed a bill in the House of Representatives to protect Salvadorans (and Nicaraguans, too) from deportation by granting them Extended Voluntary Departure status (considered a temporary refuge status as opposed to refugee or asylum status, which implies permanency by making the newcomers eligible for citizenship after six years). The following year, the IRAC joined the American Jewish Committee in protesting a cut in the already announced allocation of refugees from Southeast Asia for fiscal year 1989.

Politics was a never-ending educational process which, as it had done for immigrant-ethnic groups before, spurred the Americanization of the Indo-Chinese community. In cities with a large number of Vietnamese, such as San Jose, where the city's population was 10 percent Vietnamese by 1985, the local community supported 320 Vietnamese-owned businesses, two daily Vietnamese language newspapers, a dozen weekly and monthly publications, four weekly news-oriented television programs, and a daily television newscast in Vietnamese, the community was becoming increasingly organized in politics.

Divided by class, religion, and in other ways, Vietnamese leaders had different opinions with respect to U.S. policy toward the old country and on a range of domestic policy questions, too. But in San Jose, where they were most effectively organized for political action (10,000 registered voters out of a total Vietnamese population of 75,000), the head of the newly formed Vietnamese Voters Registration Project pointed out that their political energy could no longer be focused on old-country politics but now must be directed "toward effective fights in Congress, to deal with issues involving the Hatfield bill, the Refugee Reauthorization Act, or the repatriation of refugees now in Hong Kong." San Jose attorney Tiep Nguyen, who was active in local Republican politics, emphasized that it was important for the community to look even beyond issues relative strictly to refugees. "We now look at ourselves as an integral part of American society . . . our concerns are not that different than that of the man next door—housing, education, taxes. . . ."[61]

As the most numerous, best educated, and most financially resourceful of the Indo-Chinese groups, the Vietnamese showed the highest propensity to participate in various aspects of American life. But the refugees from the mountains of Laos, the H'mong, the preliterate tribespeople who had fought alongside the Americans in the Vietnam War, showed the most surprising example of a Third World refugee group's reaction to the American civic culture. In Dixon, Illinois, a H'mong refugee, Nyia Yang, and twenty other families discovered that to obtain a loan from the Small Business Administration and contracts to make T-shirts for the U.S. government in a small shirt-manufacturing company they had started, it was necessary for the company's directors to become U.S. citizens. By 1985, the firm embarked on a campaign to make all of its workers citizens. While sewing and folding shirts, they listened to a taped voice piped over the factory's public address system, preparing them for their naturalization interviews. "Who was the first President of the United States?"[62] Carl Schurz, Mary Antin, Carlos Bulosan, and tens of thousands of other self-consciously Americanizing immigrants would have answered, "George Washington, our forefather," which is almost like the answer given me by a third-grade Vietnamese youngster in the Cheltingham School in Denver in 1980, a boy who had been in the U.S. only six months.

It was the month of February, and pictures of George Washington and Abraham Lincoln were on the wall. After visiting with the third-grade class, which included students from at least a half dozen nationalities, and listening to them learn to count to ten in three languages, I asked one of the blond, blue-eyed Anglo youngsters to identify the picture of the man with the white hair on the wall. "Who was that," I asked. "George Washington," came the quick reply. "What did he do?" I queried. Came the tentative answer, "I don't know. He died." I next approached the Vietnamese youngster, a refugee in his Cub Scout uniform, and asked him the same questions. His reply, in the tradition of Mary Antin, "He was the father of our country," came as no shock to the other children or teachers standing close by. His claim to membership in the American polity was taken as a matter of fact, a situation that probably could not have occurred in any other country in the world.

When the wife of the governor of Massachusetts, Kitty Dukakis, and Congressman Atkins were hosts at a reception on July 1, 1986, for one hundred immigrants who were to be sworn in as citizens at the State House the next day, they listened to a speech from Giao Valentino, a Vietnamese immigrant who worked in the legal department of the International Institute of Boston, a voluntary organization focused on assisting immigrants and refugees. Speaking in the tradition of Carl Schurz, only about a mile from Faneuil Hall, Valentino urged the immigrants to remember that citizenship would give them greater opportunities and protection under the laws, but that it also entailed responsibilities, the most important of which was to "uphold the ideals of the Constitution." Extolling the founding myth, Valentino reminded them that only if they participated actively in government could they carry forward "the wish of the Founding Fathers who wrote the Constitution and who wanted this country to be an asylum for all those seeking freedom from persecution, without regard to their country of origin and race."[63] Valentino may not have been perfectly correct historically. The founding fathers knew little of what is now called the Third World and expected no immigrants from it; but their founding myth of the U.S. as an asylum for foreigners seeking freedom and opportunity now included all countries and peoples, who, like the European immigrants, embraced the American political culture as ethnic-Americans.

Chapter Nineteen

"ALL THESE . . . ARE THE LIFE BLOOD OF AMERICA"
Celebrating Diversity

MILLIONS of Americans and foreign nationals visiting the U.S.A. Exhibition at the Epcot Center in Disney World in the 1970s and 1980s saw a multimedia show, including figures from American history, in which one of the two narrators, Mark Twain, (the other was Benjamin Franklin) exclaimed, "We built America out of different races and the process made us Americans." The Pilgrims, who came to America to enforce religious conformity on their children, were portrayed as dedicated to religious freedom. Frederick Douglass, a former slave, who spoke frequently and with bitter fury against slavery and caste, is shown as a man of great optimism and hope. Chief Joseph, who lamented the destruction of his people, the Nez Percé, by American intruders, is quoted, misleadingly, as speaking of "one government for all."

The idea behind the exhibition was not to give an authentic American history lesson, but to help Americans leave the exhibit feeling uplifted and united. The search for themes to unite Americans was understandable and even useful at a time when immigrants and refugees were arriving from all over the world in large numbers and when blacks and Native Americans were asserting rights long denied them. Designers of shows such as the U.S.A. Exhibition at Disney World, politicians and movie makers, comic strip writers, and leaders in all aspects of American public and popular culture celebrated the diverse racial, religious, and nationality backgrounds of Americans, almost as if orchestrated by an unseen conductor. As articulated by them, ethnic diversity was a unique and unifying American characteristic. Ethnic diversity itself had become a shared core value.

The first president to speak of diversity as a core American value was Franklin D. Roosevelt, who talked of it frequently during the presidential campaign of 1940 as the United States moved closer to participation in the war. Unlike his cousin Theodore, or Woodrow Wilson, who had attacked the concept of hyphenated Americanism during the First World War, Roosevelt acknowledged and even celebrated the ethnic diversity of Americans. Concerned that racial and ethnic prejudice threatened American unity and productivity, Roosevelt told an audience in Boston, "We are Anglo-Saxon and Latin, we are Irish and Teuton and Jewish and Scandinavian. . . . We belong to many races and colors and creeds—we are Americans." In Brooklyn he repeated, "We are a nation of many nationalities, many races, many religions—bound together by a single unity, the unity of freedom and equality," concluding his remarks with a plea to forestall those who sought to set nationalities, races, and religions against one another. During the war, he reminded Americans that among those fighting and dying were "the Murphys and the Kellys, the Smiths and the Joneses, the Cohens, the Carusos, the Kowalskis, the Schultzes, the Olsens, the Swobodas, and—right in with all the rest of them—the Cabots and the Lowells." "All these," he said, "and others like them are the life blood of America."[1]

Roosevelt was not just courting the votes of ethnics, appearing at ethnic celebrations and praising one group or another, as other presidents had done; he was celebrating ethnic diversity as a distinctive feature of American nationality. It was one reason why Jews, believing that Roosevelt welcomed them fully as Americans, rewarded him so handsomely with their votes.[2] Roosevelt and his wife, Eleanor, overcame the anti-Semitism of their class and family background, but a great many Americans still thought of the United States as a Christian nation. Throughout most of American history, leading spokesmen for the republic wrote and spoke easily of America as a "Christian nation." Daniel Webster, while unsuccessful in contesting the right of a Philadelphia philanthropist to establish a secular orphanage in 1844, exclaimed, "Christianity, genial, tolerant Christianity, Christianity . . . is the law of the land."[3] Fifty-two years later in 1896, the U.S. Congress, in passing a resolution to protest the massacres by Turks of Armenians, said, "Whereas the American people, in common with all Christian people everywhere, have beheld with horror the recent appalling outrages and massacres. . . ," appearing to take it for granted that American and Christian identity were one.[4] Thirty-four years later, in 1930, a majority of the Supreme Court justices, in upholding the right of the U.S. to deny naturalization to a Canadian alien who would not promise in advance to bear arms in defense of the U.S., proclaimed, somewhat irrelevantly, "We are a Christian people."[5]

By the time of Roosevelt's presidency, all of the Ivy League colleges, conscious of their roles as guardians of character and quality of American life, had established quotas to keep Jewish students from crowding their classrooms, and discrimination against Jews remained an aspect of admissions policies at Ivy League schools until the late 1950s and early 1960s.[6] Jews also were limited in obtaining faculty appointments in many colleges and universities, particularly in such fields as American history and American literature. In defending Dartmouth's discriminatory admissions policies, its president acknowledged that Dartmouth had become a secular school, but it was, after all, a "Christian college founded for the Christianization of its students."[7]

But the tribal character of the Ivies was radically transformed in the 1970s and 1980s. Dartmouth, the last of the holdouts for quotas, became one of the first of the prestigious New England schools to appoint a Jew as president. Princeton, long believed to be the least hospitable and most anti-Semitic of the Ivy League colleges, by 1987 was one of three universities in the entire nation that operated its own kosher kitchen. At a school where exclusive Christian eating clubs once dominated campus social life, there were now a Jewish quarterly newspaper, a Jewish theater project, Yiddish film festivals, and a Hebrew choir.[8]

By the 1980s, despite the persistence of anti-Semitism, Jews did stand "on the same eminence as other sects," as Jacob De La Motta had boasted inaccurately in 1820, and it became common for politicians and civic leaders to speak of the Judeo-Christian foundations of American nationhood. But even that conception was doomed because of the changing religious composition of the American population. A growing number of Muslims, Hindus, Buddhists, and Sikhs were joining the armed forces and a number soon would be running for elective office. (The armed services appointed its first Buddhist chaplain in 1987.) The post-1965 immigration combined with repeated decisions by the Supreme Court strengthening First Amendment protections for freedom of religion made certain that the American sense of shared identity—the feeling of we-ness as a nation—would one day no longer be linked exclusively to the Judeo-Christian tradition.

What was true for religion was also true for nationality. The idea that American identity was determined by its predominantly Anglo-Saxon origins (discounting Indians and blacks) breathed its last in the eloquent but failed efforts by Senator Sam J. Ervin, Jr. (D-North Carolina) to maintain the national-origins quota system prior to passage of the 1965 amendments to the Immigration and Nationality Act. Ervin thought his argument that preference be given to applicants for immigration with a closer kinship with those who had made the seminal historical contributions to the nation was plausible. "Do you not believe that it is much easier to assimilate into our nation people who bear a likeness to those who are here?" he asked. "Do you not believe it is much easier to assimilate into this nation people who have, more or less, similar ideas in respect to government and in respect to philosophy?"[9]

The facts of American life had passed that argument by. The descendants of Greeks, Italians, Jews, Japanese, and others who testified against the national origins quota system were living refutations of Ervin's position. These hyphenated Americans had not made the nation into a polyglot culture or a society without a core of national identity. When

Anthony J. Celebrezze, Secretary of the Department of Health, Education and Welfare, testified on behalf of the 1965 amendments, he did so as the seventeenth immigrant to have been a member of a presidential cabinet. Ervin's argument collapsed under the weight of history. The children of the "Palatine boors," as Franklin had called them, had become Americans easily, and so had the children of the "Hunkies," "Dagos," "Kikes," "Frogs," "Chinks," "Greasers," and all those other immigrants whose parents had been viewed suspiciously as outsiders and unfit for membership.

In 1965, the most powerful positions in the American government were still held by white Anglo-Saxon Protestants, including President Lyndon Johnson and Secretary of State Dean Rusk (who was said by an assistant to have sympathized with Ervin's general view but testified against it), but most of them now repudiated the charter member idea of American identity.[10] Johnson, who as a senator had voted for the 1952 McCarran-Walter Act, which ratified the national-origins quota system for allocating visas, as president pressed hard for a new system that would make no discrimination on the basis of nationality. Rusk, testifying at Johnson's direction, told Ervin that immigration policy should not ask of a man "whether he came from Britain or Ethiopia, but what can he contribute here, and whether he would make a good citizen."[11]

Back in the 1930s and 1940s, most Americans preferred the charter member approach to immigration policy. Not only were Americans generally against admitting immigrants and refugees in the 1930s and 1940s, but they had strong nationality preferences concerning those to be admitted.[12] By 1965, as the civil rights revolution entered high gear, the national-origins system increasingly was in disfavor among Americans. When the Gallup Poll asked Americans if they would favor changing the immigration law "so that people would be admitted on the basis of their occupational skills rather than on the basis of the country they came from," 51 percent favored such a change, with only 30 percent against it.[13]

Opposition to large-scale immigration in the postwar period probably derived much more from concerns about economics and demography than nationality. In May 1980, only one year before the Select Commission on Immigration and Refugee Policy sent its recommendations to Congress and the president calling for an increase in immigration, 66 percent of the American people said immigration should be halted "until the unemployment rate in the United States drops" rather than "permit persons who leave other countries because of their political oppression to come and live in the United States," but national-origins criteria were no longer the overriding consideration in their opposition to expanded immigration.[14]

When respondents in one 1984 survey were asked whether "a man from

Taiwan who wants to come to the United States to be with his daughter, who immigrated here ten years ago," should be admitted, only 16 percent said no, compared to 75 percent who said yes. When the sample was asked if "a Jew from the Soviet Union facing persecution because he is Jewish should be admitted," only 14 percent said no and 79 percent yes. Sixty-six percent believed that "a man from El Salvador who comes from a town in which many people were killed by fighters from both sides of that country's civil war and who fears that if he is forced to return he will be in great danger" should be admitted, while only 24 percent said no. Most surprising of all, while 52 percent said they would admit a man from England "who wants to start a new life for himself in this country," even more, 57 percent, said they would admit a man from Mexico with the same intention.[15] An immigration policy that had once been governed to a large extent by considerations of color, nationality, and religion (in September 1944, 46 percent of the Americans answering a Gallup survey said that Jews should be stopped from coming to the U.S. altogether, with 8 percent undecided) had been transformed to one virtually free of considerations of color, nationality, or religion.

As an increasing number of African and especially Latin and Asian immigrants became citizens, and as their children were born in the U.S., Euro-Americans generally became accustomed to the multiethnic character of their nation. In Iowa, whose only president, Herbert Hoover, had attacked New York's Mayor Fiorello LaGuardia and other Italo-Americans as outsiders, a higher proportion of Southeast Asian refugees was settled in relationship to the population than in any other state. Iowa's Anglo-Saxon governor pointed out that what he called our formerly "homogeneous communities . . . are now the beneficiaries of contributions the refugees are making as productive members of our society."[16]

From a world perspective, an extraordinary paradox developed in American society in the 1970s and 1980s. In dozens of nations throughout the world—from Burundi and Ethiopia to England and the Soviet Union—ethnic diversity was perceived as a threat to national unity. But in the United States, ethnic diversity was celebrated as a feature of American national unity. It was done not just at Disney World and in the comics, but in museums, textbooks, and other educational settings. Diversity was celebrated increasingly on such annual national holidays as Independence Day and Thanksgiving, and also in a series of special holidays and events, massive cultural displays such as the centennial of the Statue of Liberty, the bicentennial of the Constitution, and the restoration of Ellis Island. And unity through ethnic diversity was trumpeted by leaders of both political parties.

Ethnicity was now so central to the American story—to the way Americans looked at themselves and presented themselves to the world—that after *Time* magazine ran an Independence Day story in 1983 celebrating ethnic diversity in Los Angeles, it did not publish a single letter to the editor that warned against the dangers of such diversity. Of the five letters printed about the article, two came from Korean-Americans and one from a Mexican-American congressman, each emphasizing the positive aspects of diversity. Another was from a Protestant minister in a small town in Illinois who wrote that "America has grown by accepting and appreciating the gifts and contributions of all our minorities and ethnic groups." The fifth was from a second-grade teacher in La Habra, California, who boasted of her multiethnic class, with children from Jordan, Egypt, Mexico, Peru, Cuba, the Philippines, Korea, Thailand, and Lebanon. Proudly she wrote, "I have Irish and Polish and English-Americans, a first generation Italian, and a child from Sri Lanka . . . America is blessed by these immigrants. We can learn so much from them."[17]

On the mall in the nation's capital on July 4, 1983, the National Symphony, conducted by a Russian refugee, Mstislav Rostropovich, featured the distinctive American music of Jewish-American composers George Gershwin and Aaron Copland, arias from *Porgy and Bess* sung by the great American black singer Leontyne Price and "A Lincoln Portrait" narrated by the black American baseball player Willie Stargell. Newcomer Americans from at least two dozen Asian, African, and Latin American countries tapped and drummed to "The Stars and Stripes Forever," composed by the Portuguese-American John Philip Sousa.[18]

The Fourth of July, with its emphasis on the war for national independence and personal freedom, is the quintessential holiday of the civic culture. Thanksgiving, which became the premier holiday of the civil religion, offered another opportunity for the celebration of ethnic diversity. The theme of Thanksgiving, proclaimed by George Washington in 1789 and again by President Lincoln in 1863 as a national holiday, memorializing the 1621 feast of thanks given by the Pilgrims (who did not call themselves Pilgrims or wear tall hats or black suits with wide collars or eat turkey) at Plymouth, had been turned into more or less a religious appreciation of the benefits of freedom and opportunity in the United States. But in the 1970s and 1980s, Thanksgiving became another occasion for the celebration of ethnic diversity. In 1976, the *New York Times* told of an Italian family who ate a Thanksgiving dinner as they imagined Columbus might have had. A Russian-American family featured a Russian dessert made from cranberries; a Chinese-American family ate Peking Duck instead of turkey; and an Austrian-American family feasted on braised turkey and white beans.[19] A *Boston Globe* story in 1985 told of Cambodians, Vietnamese, and Laotians celebrating Thanksgiving at a feast sponsored by the Jewish Vocational Service. There, the refugee families ate fiery Nuk Chau sauce and Cha Gio egg rolls along with their roast turkey, cranberry sauce, and pumpkin pie. At the end of the day, a Cambodian refugee remarked, "It is good to learn of this Thanksgiving Day. When we hear of all the many immigrants who came before us we do not feel so much alone."[20]

By 1986, a writer for the *New York Times* concluded that "as an American holiday, Thanksgiving's universality must lie in its ability to welcome succeeding generations of immigrants to these shores." She wrote of Haitians, Barbadians, Jamaicans, Panamanians, and Trinidadians sitting down with family members for dinners that merged the culinary traditions of their homeland cultures with those of the more traditional Thanksgiving. "For me," reported one second-generation American of West Indian background, "Thanksgiving is a mixing of the black-American traditions with the Caribbean."[21]

Celebrating Diversity: Special Events of the 1980s

The centennial celebration of the Statue of Liberty and the bicentennial of the Constitution became occasions for renewed emphasis on the myth of asylum and ethnic diversity. John Higham observed that when Emma Lazarus's poem "The New Colossus" was inscribed on a bronze tablet attached to the interior wall of the statue's pedestal in 1903, "the event passed without ceremony or public notice. In fact, the poem rested there for another thirty years without attracting any publicity at all."[22] According to Higham, the statue had virtually no mythic power even into the 1930s, when, if people thought of it at all, most of them probably did so in terms of the traditional symbol of Franco-American friendship and liberty. But by 1941, the *New York Times* called it "our number one symbol."[23] What Higham called the Statue of Liberty "boom" continued during the Second World War, but it is doubtful if even Higham could have anticipated the powerful and widespread uses to which this mythic symbol would be put in the 1970s and 1980s, particularly at the time of the celebration of its centennial, when diversity was celebrated as the principal expression of liberty. On the eve of the statue's centennial, eighty Americans from forty-two ethnic groups were honored with the Ellis Island medal of honor for what news anchorman Tom Brokaw, the host for the occasion, called their dedication "to the American way of life while preserving the values or tenets of a particular heritage group." One of the speakers, Senator Daniel Patrick Moynihan (D-New York), called the event "an unabashed celebration of ethnicity."[24]

Liberty weekend began officially on the evening of July 3 with the chief justice of the Supreme Court, Warren Burger, swearing in fifteen thousand new citizens at five different locations (at least forty-four other naturalization ceremonies were held in cities throughout the nation), followed by President Reagan awarding a new Medal of Liberty to twelve naturalized citizens who had made outstanding contributions in their chosen fields and to the U.S. Nine of the twelve had come from Europe, the traditional source of American immigration (only three were Third World immigrants, from Panama, China, and Costa Rica). But the celebration was enthusiastically embraced by Third World immigrants, as well as Euro-Americans. One Vietnamese refugee ecstatically displayed a T-shirt with Miss Liberty's face in the center and the legend "Forever."[25] And while fireworks were going off in New York City's harbor on July Fourth to honor Miss Liberty, Hispanic members of Local 23–25 of the Blouse, Skirt and Sportswear Workers of the International Ladies' Garment Workers' Union in New York sponsored a "dance for liberty" featuring two live bands. The Chinese members of Local 23–25 held a "Chinatown Liberty Fair"; Jewish-Americans and Italo-Americans held their own special celebrations.[26]

Shortly before relighting the Statue of Liberty, Ronald Reagan reported on the observations of one of the French workers who had come to work on the restoration. The Frenchman told newspapers that for the first time "they worked in proximity with Americans of Jewish, black, Italian, Irish, Russian, Polish and Indian backgrounds," and were fascinated to see different ethnic-Americans working so well together. Reagan advanced the familiar theme of asylum. He said he thought "God has his reasons for placing this land here between two great oceans." And of the immigrants who came, he said that "whatever corner of the world they came from there would be in their hearts a fervent love of freedom."[27] Reagan did not neglect the Third World immigrants, either. A cover story appeared under his name in the June 29, 1986, issue of *Parade* magazine, a few days before the celebration, in which the president stressed the advances Americans had made in overcoming bigotry against blacks and Jews and others. A photograph showed him with four children on the lawn at the back of the White House, one white, one black, another Asian, and a fourth almost certainly Hispanic who sat on his lap.[28]

Like most other chiefs of state after Roosevelt, Reagan often emphasized the theme of diversity as central to American identity. Harry Truman, in opposing the national origins quota system for admitting immigrants, stressed the contributions of diverse ethnic groups to American strength, as did Lyndon Johnson, when he signed the 1965 law abolishing the system. John F. Kennedy, the grandson of immigrants, wrote a book on immigrants and often spoke about the United States as a nation of immigrants. Lyndon Johnson, more than any other president in history, emphasized the common American identity of blacks and whites. Jimmy Carter, who had hung a picture of Martin Luther King, Jr., at the governor's mansion in Georgia during his tenure there, appointed more blacks, Hispanics, and Asian-Americans than any president before him. He routinely issued proclamations—as did his successors—extolling immigrant-ethnic groups, as when he proclaimed the celebration of Asian-Pacific Heritage Week in 1980, stressing that America's strength is in "the richness of its cultural diversity," and that "the strong and varied traditions of their Asian and Pacific homelands . . . greatly enriched our cultural heritage and institutions."[29]

Even before he was elected, President Reagan explained to the Spanish International Television Network that Americans were special because they "came from every corner of the world." As a consequence, he said, "We've all kept our pride . . . whether it was our parents or grandparents or great-grandparents who came from somewhere else . . . we've kept alive the culture. . . . I've been to many ethnic festivals recently—Ukrainian, Lithuanian, Polish—and seen how they've kept alive the customs of the country, and yet they are Americans."[30]

In his speech accepting the Republican nomination on July 17, 1980, Reagan stressed the theme of asylum in words he wrote himself: "Can we doubt that only a Divine Providence placed this land, this island of freedom here as a refuge for all those people in the world who yearn to breathe freely: Jews and Christians enduring persecution behind the Iron Curtain, the boat people of Southeast Asia, of Cuba and Haiti, victims of drought and famine in Africa."[31] In his acceptance speech four years later, Reagan spoke of the "golden door" that continued to welcome the way to new immigrants from all over the world. Speaking about the athletes representing 140 countries at the Olympic Games, he praised the U.S. as "the one country in the world whose people carry the bloodlines of all of those 140 countries and more." Telling about the journey of the Olympic torch in the spring and summer immediately past, he spoke of a Vietnamese immigrant in San Francisco holding his son on his shoulders and dodging reporters and policemen "to cheer a nineteen year old black man pushing an eighty-eight year old white woman in a wheelchair as she carried the torch." "My friends," said Reagan, "that's America."[32]

Reagan's White House utilized many opportunities for identifying the president as someone who welcomed ethnic diversity in American life, giving sanction for the acceptance of persons who used to be considered outsiders by the chief of state. On one occasion, the president telephoned to congratulate a young Vietnamese girl in Honolulu who wrote a prize-winning essay on the meaning of liberty for the centennial, and another time, when a twelve-year-old Cambodian girl came in second in a spelling bee in Chattanooga after stumbling on the word "enchilada," she also received a call from Reagan, who said that the fifth-grader was an example of "what's right with our society."[33]

The theme of diversity as central to American identity was reflected in the Vietnam War Memorial statues of 1984 depicting three soldiers, a white, a black, and a Hispanic, and in historical museums throughout the country. In an exhibit at the Smithsonian Institution in the 1980s, entitled "A Nation of Nations," previous ways of defining American identity by excluding or repressing diversity were offered as examples to be scorned as un-American and as events that happened a long time ago. Its theme, the triumph of cultural diversity, presented immigrants from every continent as contributors to and shapers of American life. In one film, which ran continuously, the title boasted, *Direct from Europe, Africa and Asia in Its Second Smash Century: Presenting American Entertainment.*

Celebrations of diversity took place in dozens of local museums and fairs, too. Patriotic ethnic fairs were held in American cities in the late nineteenth and early twentieth centuries. In Worcester, for example, French Canadians celebrated St. Jean Baptiste Day, Swedes held a fair on Midsummer Day, and the Irish frequently held community fairs, but none of these were held as part of a multiethnic celebration, or advertised as open to outsiders, as was commonly done in the 1980s in every big and middle-sized city in the North and increasingly in the South, too.[34] In many of the early fairs, an attempt was made to link love of one's ethnic group with loyalty to the United States. By the 1980s, it was the theme of ethnic diversity itself that was tied to American patriotic sentiments, as in Fall River, Massachusetts, where the flags of the ancestral homelands of that city's ethnic groups flew in front of City Hall.[35]

Reinforcing the Unum: Immigrants Teach the Nation

Immigrants invariably were displayed in the news media in the 1980s as exemplars of the American dream of freedom and opportunity for all. Occasional articles would appear on Jamaican drug gangs or the Chinese Mafia, but the dominant emphasis was on freedom received and freedom cherished; opportunity seized and achievements won in art, literature, and business. A widely used advertisement for the *Wall Street Journal* in 1986 showed a picture of immigrants debarking at Ellis Island with the headline "They Didn't Bring Riches. They Brought Something Better." In a widely distributed comic strip, "Fun Facts with Nikki, Todd and Randy," the three youngsters debated whether or not they should buy only American cars, as Todd, the young black boy, suggested. Randy, the Asian youngster, demurred, reminding the blond girl, Nikki, that her great-grandfather came from Ireland and Todd that his great-great-grandfather came from Africa. "And my parents came here from Cambodia . . . so in a way, aren't we all imports?" asked Randy.[36]

Stories became commonplace about immigrant valedictorians recently off the boat from Vietnam or other countries. One such appeared in June 1983 about Hoan Binh La, who was a Vietnamese refugee (ethnically Chinese). Penniless and friendless, she was malnourished when she arrived in the U.S. because she had eaten only coconut and food scraps for almost a year. But three years later in 1983, she delivered the valedictory speech to her Madison Park High School graduating class in Boston after achieving straight A's in all of her classes. "The world is offering us a challenge," she said in her address. "Nothing is so difficult that we cannot face it."[37]

When Carlos Bulosan wrote in his 1943 autobiography that "from the first Adams to the last Filipino, native born or alien, educated or illiterate—*We are America!*," it is unlikely that a majority of Americans were ready for his message.[38] When Mary Antin wrote in her autobiography that she loved her county just as much as George Washington did, polemics were written against her by Henry Pratt Fairchild and others for daring to make such a claim.[39] But when Ted Morgan, a French-born naturalized American citizen (1977) wrote that "the true American . . . is the immigrant, for he is an American by choice," he expressed nothing novel or daring but something that had become almost a cliché in the news media.

Immigrants in the 1980s often were portrayed by conservative columnists as confirming and reinvigorating American values. Columnist George F. Will wrote that he was convinced that "the newest citizens have the clearest idea of what we are celebrating when we raise a red, white and blue ruckus on the Fourth of July."[40] Another conservative, Jeane Kirkpatrick, ambassador to the United Nations under President Reagan, wrote in 1986 that "only those who do not understand America believe that families that have been here for ten generations are more American than the tens of thousands of new citizens naturalized last year. And only those who do not understand America think it is 'un-American' for Cuban-Americans to have a special interest in Cuba, or black Americans to have a special interest in Africa, or Polish-Americans in Poland, or Jews in Israel." The values of the republic, she wrote, receive "continual renewal by new citizens, who bring to us a special personal sense of the importance of freedom." She cited one Vietnamese refugee who arrived in 1979 after suffering for two years in Vietnam prisons: "Perhaps it is the immigrants' function from generation to generation to remind them [Americans] of what a treasure it is they own."[41]

One distinctively American cultural display, the mass naturalization ceremony, gave journalists and headline writers sentimental material for patriotic stories.[42] Headlines in newspapers about such ceremonies became opportunities for teaching about the civic culture, not just to the immigrants but to native-born Americans too: "Miss Liberty to Embrace New Citizens"; "A Cheerful Celebration of the Good-Hearted American Idyll"; "New U.S. Citizen's Heart Beats 'Because It's American'"; "My Life Is Complete—And This Is the Land That Made it All Possible"; "America Gave me a Home—A Chance to Be Somebody"; "New Citizens: A Sense of Belonging Spiced with Opportunity"; "Red, White and Blue Rose is an All-American Beauty at 83"; "They Wore U.S. Flag on Their Hearts"; "127 New Americans Proudly Step Forward"; and "Smiles Light up the Dark: 2500 Gain Citizenship."[43] The celebratory headlines obscured the fact that immigrants often chose to become Americans for more selfish reasons than to affirm the values of the American Constitution. They naturalized to have petitioning rights to be reunified with their relatives, to be able to hold a job that required government clearance, or to receive the protection that a U.S. passport gave them when traveling abroad.

But the expressions of new citizens were touchingly patriotic. "Now my heart will start beating again because it's an American heart," said an eighty-year-old Latvian, who collapsed with heart trouble but refused to be taken to the hospital until he could take his oath as an American citizen.[44] Said another newly naturalized immigrant, "I have a big American flag on my heart. Today all our dreams have come true." The American Legion president in Boston who witnessed that swearing in told a reporter, "I wish more people who were citizens from birth would come here just to experience the feeling."[45]

Often the newcomers expressed an appreciation to America for allowing them to retain a love for their homeland, even though to be naturalized they had to renounce political allegiance to it.[46] One newly naturalized immigrant from Vietnam, who used to call her son "you American" with a touch of envy, said she looked back to American history to make her realize that it was possible to become a loyal American and still love Vietnamese culture. "I feel I have something new to give to this country. There were the Irish, the Germans, Italians, Chinese and Cubans, and now the Vietnamese."[47]

At a mass ceremony in which 2,500 immigrants gained citizenship in Honolulu in 1983, the invocation was delivered by the Reverend Abraham Akaka, the state's best-known native Hawaiian minister, who urged the newcomers from dozens of different countries to make their new country a better place. A Chinese-American U.S. district judge, Harold Fong, urged the immigrants to remember that citizenship carried responsibilities.[48] An archetypal speech was given by U.S. District Judge Joseph Young in Baltimore, who told immigrants from several dozen countries about rights and privileges. "Those of us who were born in the United States have always had these rights, and have sometimes failed to appreciate them; those of you who come from countries where they are denied can remind the rest of us of how important they are." The new citizens, he said, have "the duty to help maintain and advance the principles and ideals upon which our republic was founded and built."[49] High U.S. officials praised the new citizens as teachers of American ideals, as when President Reagan in 1984 told 1,548 of them from 82 countries that the immigrants proved that American values were still powerful. Native-born Americans, he said, "have wondered if our nation still has meaning. But then we see you today and it's an affirmation."[50] At another naturalization ceremony, Secretary of State George Shultz emphasized that such occasions "serve to highlight our great heritage."[51]

The mass naturalization ceremonies, the celebrations on July Fourth and Thanksgiving, and especially the celebration of the centennial of the Statue of Liberty, which one reporter called "a convocation of a common secular faith," constituted a triumph of at least the rhetoric of the civic culture and the civil religion. That particular reporter, who saw subway passengers spontaneously burst into patriotic song on Liberty Weekend, concluded that "the Indian news dealer, the Haitian cabbie, the Greek cook—with their energy and their dreams, they nourish and redeem a nation's soul."[52] There were many important social critics who doubted that the nation's soul had been redeemed—believing that the covenant demanded by the civil religion to sacrifice for the ideals of freedom and equality had been abandoned by most Americans in Ronald Reagan's glossy America—but most reporters and politicians knew by the mid-1980s that the rewriting of history to make cultural diversity a part of the American founding myth and the glorification of diversity to help unify the country sold papers and was good politics, too.[53]

Chapter Twenty

XENOPHOBIA, RACISM, AND BIGOTRY
Conflict in the Kaleidoscope

ETHNIC conflict, bigotry, and violence were also part of the ethnic landscape in the 1970s and 1980s. Conflict and violence had declined since the 1960s, when riots erupted in a number of cities, but the patterns of xenophobia, racism and anti-Semitism, and ethnic conflict over territory, jobs, and power continued. And the acceleration of contacts between members of different ethnic groups in a variety of settings brought conflict into the open in some places, such as elite colleges, where it had scarcely appeared before.

Hostility Toward Immigrants

Every previous period of large-scale immigration had resulted in an upsurge of xenophobia; earlier immigrants and refugees had been harassed and even attacked more frequently than in the 1970s and 1980s. But fear and dislike of newcomer immigrants still led to attacks in many cities against Cubans, Haitians, Asian Indians, Vietnamese, Mexicans, and Puerto Ricans. The scope and intensity of the hostility depended upon the size of the target group, the suddenness with which they arrived in the community, and the economic context. In 1984, when the federal government decided to allow 100,000 Cuban refugees to seek permanent residency, two Miami radio talk show hosts initiated a postcard campaign to the White House; switchboards were jammed, with 95 percent of the callers protesting allowing the "Marielitos" to stay.[1]

In Jersey City, where a substantial number of Asian Indians settled over a short period of time in 1987, Indian women wearing traditional saris became targets of harassment by native-born whites and blacks (and some Hispanic youths). "We will go to any extreme to get Indians to move out of Jersey City," wrote one correspondent to the *Jersey Journal*; the 9,000 members of the Indian community stayed indoors after dark and avoided walking alone on the streets. One young white boy said, "It's white people against the Hindus," and an Indian woman wondered, "Why they kill us? . . . We are Americans, too."[2] Korean merchants in Washington and New York, Cambodians in several cities in Massachusetts, H'mong in Philadelphia, and Vietnamese in Florida, Texas, and California also encountered incidents of violence. One Justice Department official called violence against Asians "the fastest growing area of discrimination" in the country.[3] So common and severe were episodes of harassment and violence against Asians, whether U.S. citizens or not, that the Civil Rights Commission in 1984 investigated such incidents in eight states and in the District of Columbia, and not surprisingly found them to be on the rise as more Asians came to the U.S.

Native-born blacks in Los Angeles charged that the new immigrants were discriminating against them; they complained that Korean store owners treated them rudely, would not hire them, and made money from the African-American community without putting anything back.[4] In Philadelphia in 1984, hundreds of the 5,000 H'mong refugees who had resettled in a poor, mostly black neighborhood fled when local residents responded with hostility, including muggings and pistol whippings, apparently the work of about twenty teen-agers. Many adult blacks resented the refugees for what they perceived to be special favors doled out by the government. As was also true for many whites, their perceptions were based on badly distorted information, but their resentment was no less intense, as they fought over jobs, housing, and other goods in scarce supply.[5] The H'mong encountered trouble wherever they went, even in Minneapolis, where their resettlement was probably more successful than elsewhere.

Probably the most persistent conflict between blacks and immigrants occurred in Miami, scene of four major riots, one as late as 1989. Although the uprisings were usually precipitated by a conflict with the police, an important underlying cause was resentment toward newcomers from Cuba and Central America. Even the 50,000 Haitians who came between 1975 and 1982 were a target.[6] In one survey, almost as many Haitians said they thought black Americans were prejudiced against them as white (39 and 41.4 percent).[7] But the primary targets were the Cubans, much more numerous than any other group, some wealthy, many politically influential. When Nicaraguans began to arrive in large numbers in 1988 and 1989, many in the Cuban community offered assistance. Nicaraguans who claimed asylum received work authorization, and many found jobs even though they spoke no English, deepening the resentment of blacks, whose own unemployment rose between 1981 and 1987 from 9 percent to 10.4 percent. Hispanic unemployment went down from 8.7 to 5.8 percent.[8]

Sometimes conflict between blacks and recent immigrant-ethnic groups focused explicitly in competition over highly visible public jobs. In 1984, three Cuban members of the Miami city commission voted to fire the black city manager over the votes of the two blacks on the commission.[9] Aware of the resentment of many blacks toward the police, the new white city manager appointed a black man as police chief, assigning a white, a

Puerto Rican, and a Cuban as assistant chiefs.[10] In the same year, the African-American and Hispanic communities in Chicago fought over the Board of Education's firing of the black superintendent of schools; the board was chaired by a Hispanic. Hispanic activists protested that the superintendent had failed to correct overcrowded conditions in Hispanic districts and to stanch the high dropout rate in predominantly Hispanic schools. Some blacks saw the move as an attempt to crowd them out of positions of power only recently won in that city.[11]

Tension between blacks and Puerto Ricans in New York flared periodically.[12] But whites resented Hispanics, too, not just because of competition for territory, jobs, housing, and political preferment, but because of differences in language and culture. Neighborhood violence erupted between young Puerto Ricans and French Canadians in Lawrence, Massachusetts, in August 1984, in a dispute over a broken windshield. It was a symptom of long-standing feelings of antagonism between the two groups based in part on French Canadians' suspicion that Hispanics (mostly Puerto Ricans and Dominicans) were receiving favored treatment.[13] Tension in the area had been building for months; the police captain, who put down the violence with 154 state and local police officers, had anticipated a riot.[14]

Linguistic politics was a surrogate for many other issues, and surfaced wherever a large number of Hispanics lived. (See chapter 24.) "It isn't our town anymore . . . it isn't an American city anymore," said one white in Monterey Park, California, a town of 60,000 that in the late 1980s had become three-fourths Asian and Hispanic. Mexican-Americans resented the Asians' success, and many whites, seeing street signs in foreign languages, viewed the Mexicans, Vietnamese, and Chinese as outsiders taking over the city.[15]

With so much movement of population in the major cities, turf fights between different ethnic groups and even within ethnic groups were common. Some of the tensions of suburban Monterey Park surfaced in nearby Los Angeles when in 1986 the Justice Department filed a suit to overturn a 1982 redistricting plan on the grounds that it deprived Hispanic residents of adequate representation on the city council. A revised plan, backed by Hispanics, aroused the resentment of Chinese residents, since it appeared to eliminate the only Chinese member.[16] In Cambridge, Massachusetts, when the school committee voted to name a Hispanic woman assistant principal of an elementary school where nearly half the children were of Portuguese heritage, the Portuguese community protested because one of their own had not been appointed.[17] When the Chinese expanded into neighborhoods on the Lower East Side of New York City in the early 1970s, Italians organized the Little Restoration Association (LIRA) to resist the change.[18] American-born Chinese labeled Chinese from Hong Kong "*jook kok*" (bamboo stalks closed at one end with the roots intact, presumably seen as rigid and old-fashioned), while young immigrants from Hong Kong and Taiwan retaliated with the epithet "*jook sing*" (a bamboo stalk empty at both ends, presumably lacking in content). Italian-Americans took to calling recently arrived Italians "guineas," an epithet used in earlier decades against their own families.[19] Albanian immigrants, some alleged to carry weapons, frightened Italian and Irish residents in the North Bronx. Greeks and Turks clashed over the proclamation of a Turkish national day. Hindus and Sikhs fought about Sikh nationalism. But such conflicts did not threaten the nation's self-confidence as did persistent clashes between blacks and whites.

Blacks Versus Whites

"Racism is still with us, North and South," acknowledged President Reagan in 1987, referring to a racial attack in Queens, New York City, and to racial confrontations in rural Georgia.[20] White ethnic groups particularly felt besieged when black children moved into white neighborhood schools and black families began to live closer to or within predominantly white neighborhoods. Jonathan Rieder studied the reaction of Jewish and Italian families to what they saw as an invasion by blacks in the Canarsie section of Brooklyn in the 1970s, and J. Anthony Lukas described the anxieties of Irish and black families as integration of the Boston public schools proceeded under a federal court order.[21]

But the course of violent conflict over school integration generally changed from the 1960s and 1970s into the 1980s from group action to individual acts of violence. Residents of South Boston expressed a deep sense of loss when blacks were bused to "their" high school in the mid-1980s, but the militant protests, stone-throwing, and assaults against blacks that had been common in South Boston in the 1970s were not repeated.[22] White protests against housing integration continued. In the mid-1980s, poor whites in Philadelphia felt trapped by incoming blacks, just as some blacks resented the resettlement of the H'mong in their own neighborhoods.[23] Whites in Dearborn, Michigan, were so fearful of an invasion of recreation areas by Detroit blacks that in 1985 a referendum was passed barring nonresidents from using all but three of the city's forty parks.[24]

In Yonkers, New York, a court order that called for housing blacks and others in white ethnic neighborhoods in the 1980s led to furious white protest rallies.[25] White families in Yonkers and other cities were frightened that integrated or predominantly black public housing in their neighborhoods would reduce property values. They saw such court-ordered solutions to housing problems for minorities as providing a special benefit that had not been given to the Irish or the Italians, greatly underestimating the extent to which access to housing and other benefits in the free market were available to whites and not to blacks.[26] In the Belmont section of the Bronx in 1986, a white resident complained that when Belmont had been an Italian neighborhood, nothing bad happened. "Then these other elements—and you know who I mean—move in and suddenly there's crime, dope and trouble." Only a week before, eight white youths armed with baseball bats beat two Puerto Ricans who had wandered into a park in Belmont, and only two days before, a group of Hispanic and black youths retaliated by beating two Yugoslav brothers who had come to Belmont to attend a wedding reception. The Italian-, Yugoslav-, and Albanian-Americans of Belmont were reported to have accepted African-American and Hispanic newcomers who bought homes and operated businesses in their neighborhood, blaming the crime and drugs on blacks and Hispanics who did not live there. The reporter found that black and Hispanic adults with a stake in the community went unmolested; youngsters from outside the neighborhood were harassed and attacked.[27]

In Queens in mid-December 1987, in a section called Howard Beach, a young black man was struck and killed by a car after a band of white teen-agers chased him onto a highway. "In South Africa, our people are massacred by white racism, and it is the same here in New York City, too," exclaimed the executive director of the United Church of Christ's Commission on Racial Justice.[28] Angry protesters, defying a judicial order, blocked traffic on the Brooklyn Bridge and stopped service on eight subway lines by pulling emergency cords, holding doors open, and leaping onto tracks at key stations.[29] Blacks saw the Howard Beach incident as linked to the deaths of other blacks, including one said to have been beaten by police. Three white teen-agers in the Howard Beach case were found guilty of manslaughter, but the episode set off several vigilante actions by young black men against whites and whites against blacks.[30]

A second act of racial violence by white teen-agers in New York further exacerbated racial tensions there. A sixteen-year-old black youth in the predominantly Italian-American Bensonhurst section of Brooklyn was surrounded and shot to death by one of a gang of white teen-agers who mistakenly thought he was headed for a birthday party at the invitation of an Italian-American girl in their neighborhood (actually, he was there to answer an advertisement for the sale of an automobile). Seven whites were arrested, one of whom was charged with the killing. The murder in Bensonhurst led to protest demonstrations by blacks (and ugly counter-demonstrations) and to weeks of meetings and discussions in New York about the meaning of acts obviously motivated by bigotry and how to prevent them. Some black leaders saw in the murder an expression of

pervasive racism among whites in Bensonhurst. Many whites acknowledged the existence of racism, but others called the violence a tragic
aberration and defended the general desire of Italian-Americans to maintain their ethnic neighborhoods without interference from any outside
ethnic group, regardless of race.[31]

Racial and ethnic violence in the streets usually was committed by teen-
agers or young adults. In Staten Island in New York City, thirty white
teen-agers shattered windows on a bus, terrifying African-American and
white student riders, in revenge against a black youngster said to have
snatched a gold chain from one of their friends.[32] Big-city high schools
also were often centers of racial-ethnic tension. At Christopher Columbus
High School in the Bronx, blacks would begin punching if they thought
a white stepped on their sneakers, whites if they thought a black brushed
up against their car. Racism was contained at the school, according to
the assistant principal, through "civility," but in the cafeteria the Arthur
Avenue Italians sat apart from the Morris Park Italians, the Hispanics and
the Parkchester blacks apart from each other. Behind them were the Cambodians, and in another area the West Indian blacks. "I don't think there's
really any hatred," said one of the youngsters, a daughter of Italian immigrants. "It's just that people stay within their own groups—blacks with
blacks, Italians with Italians, Spanish with the Spanish."[33]

Racism at the college level was less violent, but many news stories in
the 1980s described racial incidents at both public and private institutions
as different as the University of Michigan, the University of Texas, Amherst, Dartmouth, Brown, and the Citadel in Charleston, South Carolina,
where in 1986 five white cadets clad in white sheets and hoods invaded a
black cadet's room at night shouting racial obscenities and burned a paper
cross.[34] Racial slurs and jokes, hazing, spraying of racial slogans, and even
physical attacks caused a flurry of investigations and reports, and the
introduction of special training programs and curricula to deal with racial-
ethnic tensions.

Changing Anti-Semitism

Anti-Semitic incidents also were reported at high schools and colleges
in the 1970s and 1980s, despite the fact that the three major historical
manifestations of anti-Semitism were in sharp decline by the end of the
1980s. The populist anti-Semitism that earlier found a home in hate
groups such as the Ku Klux Klan and primarily in the rural Midwest and
South had eroded. The old turf battles between other ethnics and Jews
in the major cities, which saw Jewish gangs pitted against other ethnic
gangs, were over. And the genteel anti-Semitism of the Anglo-Protestant
establishment, while still apparent in acts of social discrimination, no

longer seemed to keep Jews from positions at universities or major corporations or the State Department (anti-Semitism at State was probably one cause of the government's refusal to admit thousands of refugees from Hitler's Germany).[35]

Apart from the anti-Semitism of hate groups, including militant armed extremists, visible public expressions of anti-Semitism usually occurred among high-school-age students and, to some extent, among black nationalist leaders. Teachers of a national curriculum dealing with the Holocaust reported that urban high school students often expressed age-old canards against Jews, most of which reflected envy and resentment, such as "The Jews have all the connections." Some teachers reported that Christian anti-Semitism was still strong. "I believe the Jews do drink the blood of Christians," said one youngster. Another, "The Jews are Christ-killers."[36] Acts of vandalism against synagogues and other Jewish institutions, which reportedly increased in the early 1980s, declined for a period, and then increased again in the late 1980s. They were blamed on young people, especially a group of neo-Nazis who called themselves "skinheads" and were reported in 1989 to have about two thousand members, mostly in California with smaller groups in several other states. In a typical incident, swastikas would be painted on a building or on sacred objects, or a Torah (the Jewish Old Testament) would be destroyed. Slogans like "Death to the Jews" would be written on walls. Violent personal attacks on Jews also were on the rise in the late 1980s.[37]

The phenomenon of black anti-Semitism, possibly with its roots, in part, in Christian anti-Semitism, was complicated by the fact that Jews, who had played a major part in the civil rights movement, sometimes expressed skepticism about and even opposition to forms of affirmative action many saw as quotas. Black anti-Semitism also had something to do with the fact that blacks often moved into neighborhoods earlier occupied by Jews where Jewish storekeepers and landlords continued to do business and were seen by some blacks as exploiters. It was ironic that black hostility toward Jews should rise at the very time that older forms of anti-Semitism were in decline nationally, since in earlier decades Jews had been perceived by blacks as more friendly to their cause than other whites. Now, blacks sometimes resented the presumption by Jews that they were more liberal than other whites. Although Jews had long been used to the role of scapegoat for the frustrations of many poor whites, both in Europe and in the U.S., the rise of anti-Semitism among blacks alarmed many black and Jewish leaders.

The episodes of racial, religious, or ethnic conflict in the 1970s and 1980s nonetheless were considerably diminished over previous decades. The ethnic gang fights in New York in the early and mid-nineteenth century had been more vicious and had involved many more persons than those of the 1980s.[38] The sporadic cross-burnings of the Klan in the 1980s could not be compared to the reign of terror through the former states of the Confederacy in the late 1860s and 1870s, when one commanding general of federal troops in Texas reported, "Murders of Negroes are so common as to render it impossible to keep accurate accounts of them."[39] The scale and intensity of acts of anti-Semitism by vandals in the 1980s were far less severe than in the 1930s, when, in New York City, hundreds of signs appeared in shop windows carrying the message, "Don't buy from Jews."[40] And in the 1980s, virtually no anti-Catholic violence was reported, a sign of the end to the oldest and most pervasive of all American prejudices next to racism against blacks and bigotry toward Indians.

The scale of discrimination and open ethnic conflict was down in large measure because the context of American social and political life had changed. In the nineteenth century, politicians had often openly stimulated ethnic conflict, as when Fernando Wood, campaigning in 1861 for reelection as mayor of New York, accused the Republicans of spending Irish-American and German-American blood in war only to bring black laborers into the North "to steal the work and bread of the honest Irish and Germans." No such appeal to ethnic and racial prejudice could be made by an important city official in the 1970s and 1980s.[41] In the late nineteenth century, Italian fishermen who came into the port of Boston after dark remained on board until morning rather than run the risk of being beaten up by Irish street gangs; the Boston police force would not have tolerated such a state of affairs in the 1980s.[42] In Worcester, the charge in 1886 that a wire company was hiring Swedes to replace Irishmen because Protestants were preferred to Catholics would, a hundred years later, be subject to investigation by several government agencies and in violation of several state and federal laws.[43]

In the early nineteenth century, Protestants in Jersey City—anti-Catholic and nativistic—kept control of all aspects of city government as long as they could by merging church and state through the schools and voluntary societies in ways that would have been impossible in the 1980s.[44] By the 1970s and 1980s, U.S. Supreme Court decisions had outlawed older systems of gerrymandering that permitted dominant ethnic groups to freeze out newcomers, as they did in Boston, where not until 1939 was an Italian elected to the city council.[45] Free blacks in the antebellum North were the principal victims of violent rampages in dozens of cities, as in Philadelphia in the 1830s and 1840s, where blacks were killed, beaten, and run out of town, and Negro churches, schools, homes, and even an orphanage were set on fire in a half dozen race riots, or in Cincinnati in 1862, when Irish dock workers conducted a two-day riot that destroyed black homes in retaliation against attempts of black laborers to underbid them for jobs.[46]

Acts of violence against blacks in the 1980s invariably brought swift official disapproval and often punishment. The civil rights revolution had built a structure of laws, executive and judicial enforcement agencies, and mediative arrangements to punish and prevent such actions. Potential for xenophobic and racial violence still existed, and there was always the danger that in a future time of severe recession more Americans would start blaming immigrants, Jews or dark-skinned people generally for their economic woes. But in the newly strengthened American civic culture an elaborate structure existed to protect the civil rights of members of the *pluribus*. The civic culture had become more inclusive and stronger in the struggle to make Americans safe in their diversity.

Part Five

PLURALISM, PUBLIC POLICY, AND THE CIVIC CULTURE, 1970-1989

There is an inexhaustible power . . . in that system of government, which makes the protection of individual rights a matter of common interest.

—CARL SCHURZ

All men are equal in rights, but they are not equal in power; the weak cannot protect themselves against the strong. The institution of civil society is for the purpose of making an equalization of powers that shall guarantee the equality of rights.

—THOMAS PAINE

When, in 1987, Soviet leader Mikhail S. Gorbachev suggested to a group of American congressmen visiting Moscow that the U.S. should set up autonomous regions for its large racial and religious minorities in order to have a truly pluralistic society, Representative Len Aspin (D-Wisconsin) pointed out that Gorbachev did not understand how the American system worked. Gorbachev was thinking in terms of group rights, and that was alien, Aspin said, to the American system.[1]

As the ninth decade of the twentieth century closed, a complex institutional structure existed, born of the civil rights movement of the 1950s and 1960s, and designed to protect and advance the rights of blacks and of all other Americans. There were laws against acts of discrimination and against bigotry-motivated crimes, and new agencies and systems to enforce those laws. There was a new and powerful etiquette of public discourse concerning race, religion, and ethnicity. Hundreds of private and public agencies had been set up to bring about better understanding and appreciation of persons of diverse ethnic backgrounds through school curricula, training sessions, and workshops for community leaders.

The institutionalization and socialization of civil rights did not eliminate bigotry or discrimination, but it did check their ugliest manifestations. By 1989, the agreement on civil rights and pluralism was so widespread that virtually no dissent existed over the fundamentals of public policy concerning the protection of individual rights. Nor was there any substantial movement against the continued admission of more than 700,000 immigrants and refugees annually, most of them neither white nor Protestant nor European.

The principal differences of view that did flourish on public policy on civil rights concerned the appropriateness of race-conscious remedies. The central question was: When is it legally and constitutionally permissible to count by race in order to achieve equal rights for African-Americans and members of other designated minority groups, and by what methods? Sharp disagreement arose over mandatory busing, racial quotas in housing, redistricting to promote ethnic representation, and numerical goals linked to timetables for blacks and others in employment and higher education.

All sides generally agreed that public policy should seek equal opportunity without regard to race, national origin, religion, gender, or physical handicap. Almost everyone approved of Martin Luther King's wish that his children be judged by their character and not by the color of their skin. Civic leaders and public officials accepted the dictum of Supreme Court Justice John Marshall Harlan that the Constitution is color-blind and should not recognize any permanent entitlement based on one's race, ethnicity, or religion.

There was nevertheless widespread understanding that temporarily, in some settings, and for some purposes it was necessary to have race- or ethnic-conscious remedies in order to advance the rights of African-Americans and others. Advocates of race-conscious remedies did not argue their position in terms of group rights, acknowledging that while individual rights could give rise to group claims, it was not permissible under the Constitution to advance those claims as a matter of right for any group except Native American Indians (and, in more limited ways, ethnic Hawaiians, Aleuts, and Eskimos). While the *unum* had the responsibility to prevent and prosecute violations of individual rights, the *pluribus* had the responsibility to base group claims on individual rights.

Conflicts over language policy revealed the special nature of the relationship in the U.S. between the *pluribus* and the *unum,* compared to countries like Canada and Belgium. Canada had two official languages, and Belgium, official language regions with linguistic borders, but Americans took for granted that English was the language of public business, while acknowledging the right of individuals to express themselves in other languages in private relationships. In the debate about language policy, most advocates of bilingual education, bilingual ballots, and bilingual services justified their position in terms of individual rights, and none of the opponents of bilingualism denied the right of individuals to speak whatever languages they chose among friends and family or in religious worship. Advocates of bilingualism asked not to be disqualified from the right to participate fully in American society because of language disability; their opponents worried that bilingual programs would move the society toward recognizing language-group entitlements, placing some groups on a different footing from others, and undermining both the principle of equal rights for all individuals and the common language of the civic culture.

That these problems of public policy were complex and controversial, leading to impassioned conflict in many instances, did not obscure the fact that the civic culture, based on the principle of individual rights, was stronger and more inclusive than it had ever been, or the fact that voluntary pluralism was thriving. Yet, the legacies of the coercive systems of racial caste pluralism, sojourner pluralism, and of predatory pluralism were manifest not just in lingering, sometimes subtle, discrimination, but in the disproportionate poverty of persons of color, particularly African-Americans, Puerto Ricans, and Native Americans. Those who lived in persistent poverty were the new outsiders, ethnic underclasses whose problems were largely unresponsive to the race-conscious public policies that had helped many better-educated, already more mobile persons of color achieve the benefits of participation in the American civic culture.

Americans managed traditional problems of membership better than any other large multiethnic nation. They expanded immigration from all over the world with relative ease at a time when most other nations were becoming more restrictionist. They made more fluid the boundaries between aliens and citizens. They reduced the barriers of color for those in the working and middle classes. But they struggled with the problems of native-born American citizens of color who were chronically poor—the ethnic underclass—with only meager success.

Chapter Twenty-One

"EQUAL AND EXACT JUSTICE"
The Civil Rights Compact

THE myth of equal rights always had a powerful grip on the consciousness of Americans. But the gap between myth and reality had been enormous. Until the 1970s and 1980s, public officials had spoken with great passion about equal rights for all without awareness that the rhetoric had no meaning for millions of Americans, as when Theodore Roosevelt, then a U.S. civil service commissioner, exclaimed in Boston in 1893 that "we Americans give to men of all races equal and exact justice."[1] Roosevelt was indifferent to justice for Indians and either did not know or ignored the fact that, as he spoke, Texas Rangers roamed the Texas-Mexican border, harassing Mexicans and Mexican-Americans with virtually no restraint from courts of law, or that in the year before he spoke, 154 American blacks had been lynched, and that, in 1891, eleven Italians awaiting trial in New Orleans had been taken from jail by a vengeful mob and hanged.

For more than seventy years after Roosevelt's panegyric to his fellow Americans, no national civil rights agreement existed on the importance of equal and exact justice for all. But after the civil rights revolution of the 1960s and the decades of the 1970s and 1980s, a national compact manifested itself in a variety of ways, the most important of which was a structure of legislation, court decisions, and executive action against discrimination on the basis of race, ethnicity, or religion.

The Pennsylvania idea of voluntary pluralism had been based on the implicit premise that individuals would be protected by civil authorities against discrimination, but that premise was not institutionalized effectively in the U.S. until the 1970s and 1980s. To effectuate the premise, more than fifty federal statutes were passed, most enacted after 1964, to constitute the basic legal structure of civil rights, along with hundreds of state and local laws.

The principal enforcement agencies created in the federal government were the Civil Rights Division of the Departments of Justice, the Equal Employment Opportunity Commission, the Federal Contract Compliance Office of the Department of Labor, the Civil Rights Divisions of the Departments of Health and Human Services and of Education, the

Office of Special Counsel in the Justice Department set up to enforce the antidiscrimination provisions of the Immigration Reform and Control Act of 1986, and the antidiscrimination enforcement mechanisms established in amendments to the Fair Housing Act in 1988.

To watch over the area of civil rights, the Civil Rights Commission was created in 1957 as a temporary and independent body within the executive branch. Although it had no enforcement power, in 1960 it was granted the authority to administer oaths and take sworn testimony, and in 1964, under the Civil Rights Act, it gained investigatory responsibility through subpoena power. In addition to the Civil Rights Commission, with its fifty-one advisory committees (the states and the District of Columbia), there grew up a panoply of private civil rights organizations to perform watchdog functions, the major one of which was the Leadership Conference on Civil Rights, an umbrella organization for 180 civil rights groups.

The Civil Rights Compact and the Reagan Administration

By the time of the Reagan administration, 1981–1988, a formidable civil rights lobby accused Reagan's Civil Rights Division of the Justice Department of trying to slow progress on civil rights. Spokesmen for the White House and Justice protested their ardent support for civil rights, even as they criticized several race-conscious remedies adopted by previous administrations and by the courts to affirm equal opportunity. Specifically, the Reagan administration argued that it should be necessary to show intent to discriminate before applying to an institution, government agency, or business a remedial plan that included counting by race. The administration opposed forced busing to integrate public schools and fought racial ceilings to integrate public housing, arguing that such measures severely limited freedom of choice in violation of the principle of equal rights itself. It also opposed most efforts to redraw electoral districts that aimed to elect someone from a particular racial or ethnic group (blacks and Hispanics) and resisted most efforts to set numerical goals and timetables in employment and contracting, stating that these amounted to quotas, which could lead to reverse discrimination against individual white males.

In its 1987 report *Enforcing the Law,* the Civil Rights Division claimed success in pursuing antidiscrimination cases on which there was evidence of intentional discrimination, pointing out that it had filed double the number of such employment discrimination cases from 1983 through 1986 than during a comparable four-year period in the Carter administration, and that it had entered into a slightly larger number of employment consent decrees.[2]

Given its view that counting by race led to constitutionally impermissible quotas and reverse discrimination, the Reagan administration depicted itself as a champion of civil rights. It measured its own success in protecting individual rights not just by its effectiveness in litigating against discrimination (where intent could be shown or inferred) but by its ability to retard the use of numerical goals and timetables or comparable race-conscious remedies. The Civil Rights Division itself boasted of its success in developing alternatives to mandatory busing to achieve public school integration and in establishing affirmative action remedies in employment that emphasized recruitment and training rather than numerical goals to be achieved by a certain time.[3]

Most civil rights activists for their part saw these moves as flagrant attempts to erode vigorous earlier strategies to protect civil rights that had involved counting by race. They pointed to regulations proposed by the administration shortly after it took office in 1981 that would have exempted at least two-thirds of all federal contractors from taking account of race in hiring; limited back pay remedies only to identified victims of discrimination; and disallowed statistical results as a standard for determining classwide remedies for discrimination in programs enforced by the Office of Federal Contract Compliance. Strong opposition in Congress (from seventy senators and more than two hundred representatives) forced withdrawal of the proposed regulations, but Congress was unable to prevent slackening in the pace of enforcement by the OFCC or by the Equal Employment Opportunity Commission.[4]

The Reagan administration also attempted to have its view on remedies prevail by an overhaul of the Civil Rights Commission and by the appointment of federal judges. Determined that the Civil Rights Commission should reflect his views on affirmative action remedies, Reagan fired three commissioners, appointing in their place persons who shared his opposition to forced busing and counting by race. But Congress, a majority of whose members disagreed with the administration on appropriate civil rights remedies, fought back by limiting the budget and the activities of the commission. By 1989, with a sharply limited budget, the commission avoided the more contentious issues about remedies and concentrated on investigations and hearings that put the spotlight on continuing, blatant patterns of discrimination.

Congress also rebuffed Reagan in his attempt in 1986 to nominate the assistant attorney general for civil rights, William Bradford Reynolds, to be associate attorney general. The nomination of Reynolds, who, more than any other individual, was associated with the Reagan approach to civil rights remedies—opposition to forced busing, numerical goals, timetables, and a statistical standard for proof of discrimination—was defeated by the civil rights lobby, led by the thirty-seven-year-old Leadership Conference on Civil Rights. The conference also won a victory it regarded as crucial when the Senate rejected Reagan's nomination of Circuit Court Judge Robert Bork to the Supreme Court.

In 1987, the year celebrating the bicentennial of the Constitution, the Bork nomination became an occasion for a major public seminar via televised hearings on the meaning of the Constitution, in general, and civil rights and liberties, in particular. Of the nearly two thousand members of the legal and academic professions who wrote to oppose Bork's appointment, including thirty-two law school deans and seventy-one professors of constitutional law, a large majority focused on what they perceived to be Bork's constricted interpretation of civil rights under the Fourteenth Amendment and the Civil Rights Act of 1964, and on what they said was his narrow view of First Amendment protections of individual free speech and his failure to find in the Constitution a generalized right of privacy. Much of the debate surrounding Bork constituted a national referendum on the history of civil rights legislation and its implementation, since Bork had originally opposed the public accommodations provisions of the Civil Rights Act of 1964 and had raised objections to Title VII, which prohibited employment discrimination. Bork had also expressed negative views about busing to achieve desegregation and skepticism that numerical goals and timetables could be kept from becoming quotas.

As the debate about Bork developed, it became clear that his views on contemporary issues were less a problem than the suspicion by Congress that his nomination was an attempt by the Reagan administration to slow progress in civil rights. However much Bork's views may have been exaggerated and even distorted by opponents to his nomination, the Senate did not want even to appear to retreat from the major achievements of the civil rights revolution and turned back his nomination following a bipartisan nine-to-five negative vote in the Judiciary Committee.[5]

What seemed most worrisome to editorial writers and key members of Congress about Bork, who no one accused of personal bigotry, was that his view of U.S. Supreme Court decisions, in the words of the *New York Times*, "is almost always the same—unfavorable to minorities." Of all the testimony given against Bork, probably the most effective came from black men and women who expressed their fears that a man who had opposed civil rights legislation, and who had criticized the Court decisions banning enforcement of restrictive covenants, eliminating poll taxes, and banning school segregation in Washington, D.C., would threaten their hard-won struggle for equal rights.[6]

Stressing how difficult it was for him to oppose the nomination of a man "of powerful intellect whom I respect and like," Republican Senator Arlen Spector (Pennsylvania) emphasized as his reason for doing so the importance of protecting "individual and minority rights . . . fundamental values rooted in the tradition of our people."[7] Spector's vote to block the Bork nomination and those of all of the southern Democrats on the Judiciary Committee, demonstrated how deep and widespread was the national agreement on civil rights. Bork was stopped not because he lacked qualifications or even because his contemporary views were inconsistent with a reasonable rationale for civil rights enforcement, but because he had too often been on the wrong side in opposing major civil rights advances.

The Civil Rights Compact and the Courts

The Supreme Court also generally disagreed with the Reagan administration's approach on controversial antidiscrimination enforcement issues, with some exceptions. The first concerned the Court's 1984 decision in the Grove City College case, when it ruled that the prohibition in Title IX of the education amendments of 1972 against federal funding of sex discrimination extended only to the specific program or activity receiving the funds, and not to the entire recipient institution. Congress overrode the decision by passing the Civil Rights Restoration Act of 1987 by an overwhelming bipartisan vote over a presidential veto. Another major exception (see chapter 22) was the decision by a federal district court judge that attempts by private landlords to limit the number of blacks in federally assisted housing violated the Fair Housing Act, even when the intent of the landlord was to maintain racial integration.[8] Other exceptions, discussed below and in chapter 23, came in 1989 after Reagan had left office, when a new Supreme Court majority seemed willing to move toward the positions espoused by the Reagan administration.

On other key controversial issues, the Court tended to oppose positions taken by the Reagan administration. On the question of numerical goals, it usually approved counting-by-race measures (see chapter 23). On another controversial issue—whether or not statistics can be used as proof of discrimination—the Court decided that a former bank employee, a black woman from Fort Worth, should not have been kept from using statistics about employment patterns as the basis for her charges against the bank of discrimination.[9] The Court remained sympathetic to the use of statistics by individual plaintiffs seeking to prove discrimination against them even as late as 1989, when it held that in such cases employers had the legal burden of proving that a refusal to hire or promote the individual plaintiff was based on legitimate and not discriminatory grounds.[10] But in another case in 1989, the Court ruled that when the plaintiff was a category of workers (blacks, Hispanics, etc.) the burden of proof is on the plaintiff to prove that the employer actually practiced discrimination and not a policy that could be justified as necessary to the employer's business. The decision appeared to reverse a 1971 ruling that employers had the responsibility to justify policies that resulted in a statistical imbalance of minorities or women among their employees, and it was attacked by civil rights activists as a major breach in civil rights protections.[11] It clearly indicated that the Court, now more conservative than earlier in the 1980s, was moving away from group entitlements based on statistical patterns even as it continued to make it easy for individuals charging discrimination to back those charges by using statistics.

In other areas of civil rights, the Court broke new ground in expanding protection against discrimination. The Court overruled a 1965 decision that blacks could be excluded from a jury on the speculation that they would be more sympathetic to black defendants. The new ruling, which made impermissible any challenge of a prospective black juror on the ground that he or she was black, was praised by the Court's only black justice, Thurgood Marshall, as "an historic step."[12] The Court also substantially enlarged the scope of civil rights protections when it ruled in 1987 that an 1866 civil rights statute prohibiting discrimination in the making of private and public contracts applied to discrimination based upon one's ancestry or ethnicity as well as discrimination based on race. It was a significant advance in civil rights, because the 1866 law permitted compensatory and punitive damages not available under Title VII of the Civil Rights Act, and covered employers with fewer than fifteen employees.[13] Representatives of several ethnic groups applauded the decision because many of their constituents now had a legal remedy against discrimination not available before. Hispanic-Americans were particularly grateful because, having been classified usually as Caucasians, they had not been covered by the 1866 law and now had become the most likely beneficiaries of the Court's decision.[14] But in 1989, a more conservative Court somewhat narrowed the ability of blacks and members of other minority groups to use the Civil Rights Act of 1866 when it ruled in a five-to-four vote that lawsuits under the act could be brought only in connection with hiring and not over alleged racial mistreatment on the job. It also ruled five to four that the law could not be used to bring damage suits against local governments for the alleged costs of racial discrimination.[15]

Despite these limits on the 1866 law, the basic structure of civil rights protections remained substantially intact, even in the hands of a court majority that civil rights advocates attacked. For example, the same Court ruled unanimously in 1989 that cities can be sued for damages if the failure to give police officers or other employees adequate training resulted in violation of an individual's constitutional rights. The trend line in the 1989 cases was clear, however. The Court was inching away from justifying group entitlements while holding fast to the principle of individual rights. But it had not yet thwarted the major race-conscious remedies taken by legislatures and lower courts to assure the rights of blacks and members of other groups identified as needing special protection.

The Civil Rights Compact and the Congress

The civil rights compact was consistently and forcefully expressed in Congress in the 1980s in a sharp reversal of the slow, almost nonexistent pace of action by the Congress from the end of Reconstruction until the 1960s. Bipartisan majorities in Congress took a number of initiatives, often against the opposition of the administration, to translate civil rights into public policy at home and abroad. The Congress passed the Civil Rights Restoration Act of 1987 over President Reagan's veto, and successfully resisted Reagan's attempt to change the Civil Rights Commission's approach to race-conscious remedies. It also stopped the substantial revision of regulations governing enforcement by the Office of Federal Contract Compliance, and blocked the nomination of judicial and other appointees thought insufficiently committed to civil rights.

Probably the most important symbolic act was its passage of legislation in 1984 by overwhelming majorities in both houses, against President Reagan's initial wishes, to make Martin Luther King, Jr.'s birthday a national holiday. Congress also initiated and passed three major civil rights laws, signed, in the first two instances, by a reluctant president. Perhaps its most far-reaching and potentially controversial action came in 1982, with amendments to the Voting Rights Act that made it lawful to judge the discriminatory effects of electoral systems by finding that blacks and Hispanics were not getting elected from areas where substantial numbers of them lived. By this action, Congress decided that equal access to the polls was not enough to guarantee voting power for minorities, but that it also was necessary to oblige communities to change electoral districts to make it more likely that blacks and/or Hispanics would be elected.

Four years later, Congress passed new antidiscrimination provisions in the Immigration Reform and Control Act in response to fears of Hispanics and others that employers would shy away from hiring foreign-sounding or -looking persons lest they be illegal aliens, since under the IRCA, employers who willfully and knowingly hired such aliens were subject to penalties. For the first time, Congress made it clear that it was illegal to refuse to hire a person because of the applicant's alien status. The new law covered all employers, making its coverage more extensive than that of the Civil Rights Act (Title VII), which applied only to employers of fifteen or more.

The third important piece of civil rights legislation was passed by Congress in 1988 through amendments to the 1968 Fair Housing Law, strengthening the federal government's authority to act in housing discrimination cases. The 1968 law, which made it illegal to discriminate in the sale or rental of public or private housing on the basis of race, color, sex, religion, or national origin, had been much less effective than had been hoped by its sponsors (see chapter 22). In an important expansion of civil rights, the new bill gave power to administrative law judges to investigate charges of housing discrimination brought either by an individual or by the secretary of housing and urban development on behalf of an individual; it also provided for large fines for guilty builders, real estate agents, and landlords.[16]

The new civil rights agreement of Americans had an enormous impact on immigration, refugee, and foreign policies in the 1970s and 1980s. In 1974, Congress expressed its disapproval of the denial of basic rights to Soviet Jews, who not only were systematically persecuted but also were prevented from emigrating; Congress barred trade benefits, including export-import bank credits and nondiscriminatory tariffs on imports, to any Communist country that restricted emigration. Soon after, Congress linked human rights to other issues in international affairs when, in 1977, it upgraded the status of the Human Rights Office of the State Department, giving its director the rank of assistant secretary. And, in 1985, Congress, over Reagan's veto, applied strong sanctions against South Africa for its violation of the human rights of blacks. Senator Ernest F. Hollings (D-South Carolina), reflecting the views of many congressmen that apartheid was an American civil rights issue, remarked that "whether it works or not is not the issue at all. We're trying our own case as a people."[17]

The Civil Rights Compact and Bigotry-Motivated Crimes

Whatever differences President Reagan had with Congress over affirmative action remedies and other aspects of civil rights enforcement, they were united in seeking effective legislation and enforcement against crimes motivated by ethnic, racial or religious bigotry, a resolve reflected in a number of ways, one of which was the vigorous prosecution by the Justice Department in the 1980s of Nazi war persecutors who had somehow entered the country under fraud. In 1978, Congress excluded anyone otherwise qualified for admission who had engaged in persecution as a Nazi or had cooperated with Nazis in persecutions. In part, Congress was making up for the nation's past shortcomings in admitting refugees from Nazi persecution. Anti-Semitism in refugee policy had persisted as late as 1948, when discrimination against Jews was implicitly incorporated into the Displaced Persons Act.[18] One of the principal Justice Department investigators of former Nazis said, "We are proceeding against [former Nazi persecutors] . . . not because of what they might do in the future but because to look the other way would be necessarily to forgive what they did in the past."[19] By 1981, the Office of Special Investigations, established to track down former Nazis in the U.S., had eighteen cases in litigation and more than two hundred under active investigation. By July 1983, it had investigated seven hundred cases and prosecuted thirty-two.[20] By 1987, twenty former Nazis had been stripped of their American citizenship and thirteen had been deported. In the most controversial case, Attorney General Edwin Meese, who had been strongly criticized by civil rights groups for his insensitivity to human rights, overrode right-wing opinion and deported Karl Linnis, a former concentration camp commander, to the Soviet Union, where he was under a death sentence for killing innocent Jews.[21]

The Reagan Civil Rights Division of the Justice Department also gave priority to cases of racial violence, achieving success against Ku Klux Klan members in several states. In the five-year period between 1983 and 1987, the department prosecuted 115 defendants, 64 of whom were members of the Klan, compared to a total of 69 defendants in the previous five-year period, 46 of whom were Klan members.[22]

By the end of the decade, the federal government had provided to victims of racially and religiously motivated violence a variety of federal criminal and civil remedies.[23] There also were a vast number of state and local laws aimed at preventing and punishing hate-motivated crimes.[24] A common approach was to enact statutes imposing penalties for certain criminal actions when motivated by religious or racial hatred.[25] Forty states provided for criminal punishment for such crimes although they failed to empower victims to obtain compensation from the offender in a civil suit for damages.[26] The lack of uniformity of state laws meant that the desecration of a synagogue in one state might be covered only by laws against abuse of property and trespassing, whereas in another state the penalties were heightened if a determination was made that the crime had been motivated by religious bigotry. But the general trend in the states in the late 1980s was to tighten laws and increase penalties for crimes tinged by racial and religious hatred, with most state legislation aimed at paramilitary hate groups.[27]

In 1984, an Alabama circuit court judge broke precedent in that state by overruling a jury and sentencing a convicted member of the Ku Klux Klan to death in the electric chair for killing a black man.[28] In 1985, a leader of the Confederate Knights of the Klan in Raleigh, North Carolina, agreed, after a $1 million lawsuit had been filed against the group, that the Knights would not march in black neighborhoods and would not harass blacks.[29] In 1986, a U.S. District Court jury convicted the North

Carolina Klan leader and his organization, the White Patriot Party, of operating a paramilitary organization in violation of an earlier court injunction, and for breaking two state laws prohibiting secret military or political organizations.[30] The following year, an all-white jury in Mobile, Alabama, found two Klan members guilty of murdering a young black man seven years earlier and, concluding that the United Klans of America was civilly liable under a Reconstruction statute for the young man's death, ordered the defendants to pay his mother $7 million in damages. As a result, the building that housed former headquarters of the UKA, held in the name of the Anglo-Saxon Club, Inc., was turned over to her.[31]

In 1986, the secretary of defense issued a directive calling on military commanders to curtail membership of GI's in hate groups such as the Klan, an order that appeared likely to hold despite the opposition on constitutional grounds of the American Civil Liberties Union.[32] Continuing its crackdown against criminal activity in the white supremacist movement the following year, the Justice Department indicted fifteen white supremacists on charges ranging from civil rights violations to sedition in an effort to break the backs of the organized hate groups. So successful were those efforts that the Anti-Defamation League of B'nai B'rith reported that the Ku Klux Klan, neo-Nazis, and similar groups had been seriously weakened by government prosecutions and that total Klan membership had fallen to fewer than 5,500 (from its postwar peak of 55,000 in 1967).[33]

Not only had the law shifted to protect blacks against Klansmen, but African-Americans themselves were now involved in making the law and enforcing it. In the summer of 1987 in Greensboro, North Carolina, a black state official who as a child had watched the Klan in fear from a distance helped provide security for about 150 Klan marchers. The African-American official, a supervisor at the state Bureau of Investigation, said, "When I took the oath of office, I said I'd uphold the rights of everyone, no matter what I think of their beliefs." Six hundred anti-Klan citizens held their own rally the day before. Most Greensboro residents ignored the Klan march. Klansmen were no longer everyone's uncle, brother, or father. In what used to be Klan country, they were now seen as outside of the American mainstream.[34]

The hate groups were not finished as the decade ended, but the law was arrayed against them and they no longer had even slight support among officials at any level of government. When 150 white supremacists of the Aryan Nation Congress, the umbrella organization for all of the major hate groups, met in Hayden Lake, Idaho, in 1986, Governor John Evans joined human rights advocates ten miles away to denounce racism and prejudice at a "Good Neighbor Day" meeting organized by a local task force on human relations. Acknowledging 170 resolutions denouncing the hate groups from officials and local governments in Idaho, Wyoming, Montana, and Oregon, Evans warned against "the passive bigotry of failing to respond and object to the violence and intimidation of the hate groups."[35]

The problem of bigotry-motivated crime in the big cities, especially in the North, was not so much an issue of controlling or dismantling the Klan and other organized hate groups as it was of preventing spontaneous neighborhood violence. Although most such violence was committed by persons who did not belong to any organized hate group, those convicted of such crimes often met with stiff penalties, just as if they had been members of the Klan. When two black men in 1984 in Cambridge, Massachusetts, were physically attacked without provocation by men who shouted racial slurs as they were walking near their homes, the attorneys for the youngest of the assailants (aged seventeen) pleaded that he had been a hyperactive child and a special-needs student who found it hard to adapt to newcomers moving into his neighborhood. The judge sentenced him to a ten-year term in prison, of which he suspended five years, but his nineteen-year-old partner, for whom no such mitigating circumstances were advanced, was sentenced to ten years with no suspended time.[36]

When a white man in Philadelphia was convicted in 1986 of spray painting the words "we don't want no niggers KKK" on the front of a brick row house a black family wished to purchase, the judge repudiated the defense attorney's argument that the man should be treated leniently because he was a stable and loving father of three children, one of whom suffered from muscular dystrophy. "Your client should have thought of that when he was writing those obscenities," the municipal court judge told the lawyer, after finding the defendant guilty of ethnic intimidation, criminal mischief, and defacement of property. The sentence: a maximum penalty of a year in jail and a $2,500 fine. In another Philadelphia case, a young white man who had set fire to a house that had been purchased by blacks (and abandoned because of white hostility) was sentenced to five years in prison and his two white accomplices to three years each. "What they did was despicable," said the judge. "To terrorize: that was the whole purpose of this action."[37]

A factor in preventing bigotry-motivated crimes in major cities in the 1980s was new training programs for police officers, who in the ghettoes still often were considered more a cause of racial brutality than agents for preventing it. Despite that perception, the police in the 1980s were taking a more active role in the prevention and enforcement of bigotry-motivated crimes. The FBI conducted a national program to train more than one thousand police officers a year at its National Academy in Virginia in the area of civil rights.[38] Many cities developed special units within their police departments to deal with civil rights violations. In Boston, the police department's Community Disorders Unit, established in 1978, was made responsible for handling all racially motivated crime in the city. Officers assigned to the unit initiated community meetings, held training sessions for law enforcement employees, gave lectures in Boston schools, and worked closely with the Greater Boston Civil Rights Coalition, made up of thirty-five community groups. Its success could perhaps be measured by the fact that the number of racially, ethnically, or religiously motivated crimes it tracked went down from at least six hundred in the late 1970s to below two hundred annually after 1983.[39]

New systems for collecting data on incidents of hate violence gave federal and state governments another tool for fighting bigotry-motivated crimes. In 1987, Pennsylvania became the second state (joining Maryland) to require state and local police agencies to maintain such records. In 1988, Congress passed a federal Hate Crimes Statistics Act in an effort to provide a comprehensive crime-reporting system at the federal, state, and local government levels that specifically identified racially or religiously motivated crimes. By 1989, few parts of the country were not covered by such reporting systems and by laws against bigotry-motivated violence, and few cities were governed by mayors who did not act swiftly to condemn such crimes and vigorously criticize their perpetrators.[40]

Many big-city mayors in the 1980s were African-American, but a number of white mayors also denounced, prevented, and punished racial violence. In Boston in 1984, Mayor Raymond Flynn ordered the payment of more than $844,000 to the widow of a black man shot nine years earlier by two white police officers; he publicly apologized to the family for the city's failure to act earlier.[41] When a group of white teen-agers chased three black men in a predominantly white neighborhood in Howard Beach in Queens, in 1987, and beat them with baseball bats and sticks, Mayor Edward Koch, whose relations with African-American leaders in the city had been acrimonious, immediately compared the killing of one who in an effort to escape had been hit by an automobile to "the kind of lynching party that took place in the Deep South."[42] "We have had 1800 murders a year in this city," Koch said, "but this was the worst murder, I believe, that has taken place in the modern era."[43]

The Civil Rights Compact: Education and Mediation

New laws, vigorous prosecution, and tough sentences helped to reduce racial crimes in the 1980s. So did special citizens' committees (often working with local police) and hundreds of educational organizations and human relations councils. Before the civil rights revolution, the only major national organizations with the primary educational goal of reducing racial and religious tension and violence were the National Conference of Christians and Jews and the Anti-Defamation League of B'nai B'rith. By 1980, the NCCJ, organized in 1928, had seventy-eight offices in seventy-two cities. It assisted communities to develop voluntary programs of compliance for court-ordered desegregation, to hold conferences to promote understanding between Hispanics and non-Hispanics, and to develop activities in interreligious understanding for schools, churches, and synagogues.[44] The Anti-Defamation League, which up to the 1950s had focused on defending Jews against anti-Semitism, expanded its educational efforts in the 1970s and 1980s to deal with the broader issue of preventing and ameliorating ethnic conflict.[45]

In the 1970s and 1980s, several other private organizations were established to protect civil rights and pluralism. The Institute for Group Pluralism of the American Jewish Committee published literature, conducted workshops, and worked with government agencies to combat prejudice and develop effective programs to prevent racial, ethnic, and religious violence. Other new organizations—the Center for Democratic Renewal, the National Institute Against Prejudice and Violence, the Southern Poverty Law Center, and the Facing History and Ourselves Foundation— developed their own approaches to the objective proclaimed by the executive director of the National Conference of Christians and Jews in 1987, "to eradicate racial, religious and ethnic prejudices and discriminations."[46]

In addition to these private organizations, dozens of governmental agencies were established to deal with problems of ethnic and racial conflict. The state advisory committees of the U.S. Commission on Civil Rights frequently held meetings spotlighting problems of bigotry and discrimination. The Justice Department's Community Relations Service and its regional offices investigated bigotry-driven violence and published reports highlighting the issues. Statewide human relations councils held hearings and made recommendations for training law enforcement officers and for educational programs in the public schools.[47] Local human relations groups appeared throughout the country, often as a result of the leadership of ministers, priests, and rabbis, as when in 1979 fifty religious and civic leaders in Little Rock, site of the first great resistance to school desegregation twenty-two years earlier, formed a committee to make that city "a model to the entire country" for good race relations.[48]

Local groups, federal and state agencies, and private organizations to deal with problems of ethnic conflict came together in almost every state in the 1980s, as in Woodburn, Oregon, after the murder of an undocumented Mexican worker by a police sergeant in 1983, when a citizens' review commission was established with four Hispanics among its twelve members to hear citizen complaints about violence against Hispanics.

Working with city officials, police officers were taught basic Spanish so they could communicate better with the local population. Another group, the Community United for Justice, met with city officials and the U.S. Department of Justice Community Relations Service before and after the establishment of the citizens' review commission to help pick a new city administrator; one was chosen because of his presumed ability to work with members of different ethnic groups.[49]

Incidents of bigotry, sometimes violent, continued to occur in all of the major cities through the decade, but the public agreement against racial and ethnic bigotry was stronger than it had ever been in American history. In the racially mixed city of New Orleans, recently arrived immigrants and refugees were given a pamphlet published by the National Council of Jewish Women and Associated Catholic Charities. After extolling racial peace, the pamphlet told the newcomers, "We do not mean to imply, however, that there are no racial tensions or problems in New Orleans. As in any locale where people of differing racial and cultural backgrounds live together, tensions inevitably exist." The booklet explained to the refugees that they should not be surprised or disturbed to see people of different races in their neighborhoods. "It is important for all Americans to contribute to harmonious race relations," the booklet went on, praising the diversity that Americans had come to see as a distinctive feature of their national identity.[50]

Pluralism and the Etiquette of Public Discourse in the Civic Culture

The emerging majority on civil rights and pluralism of the 1970s and 1980s reflected in the New Orleans orientation booklet for refugees and immigrants was manifest nationally in the public disapproval of racial, religious, or ethnic slurs or innuendos, especially by public officials, candidates, and those in private institutions with a visible responsibility to the public. Before the civil rights revolution, candidates in the South often vied with each other to smear their opponents as "nigger-lovers." Anti-Catholic pronouncements and literature were a staple of Republican attacks on Alfred E. Smith in the 1928 presidential election campaign. Anti-Semitism in public discourse such as expressed by a half dozen senators and representatives in the 1930s and 1940s often passed without reprimand from colleagues or the press then, but by the 1970s, candidates for high office and public officials could not disparage or even tolerate the disparagement of any ethnic or religious group without suffering severe and widespread public condemnation.

Politicians with multiethnic constituencies had emphasized the importance of ethnic peace in earlier decades. Franklin D. Roosevelt, stressing that "we are a nation of many nationalities, many races, many religions—bound together by a single unity, the unity of freedom and equality," lectured that "whoever seeks to set one nationality against another, seeks to degrade all nationalities. Whoever seeks to set one race against another seeks to enslave all races. Whoever seeks to set one religion against another, seeks to destroy all religion."[51] James Michael Curley, mayor of Boston, denounced ethnic prejudice as he sought the votes of Jews and Italians, realizing that it would take more than Irish votes to keep him in office. When a city planning board blamed slum housing in East Boston on the Jews living there, Curley denounced the report as a "flagrant insult" and ordered the city printer to delete the derogatory remarks.[52] The citizens of Hawaii, aware of the dangers of ethnic conflict, learned early in the postwar era to keep racial animosity below the surface by developing a strong taboo against remarks that disparaged ethnic groups. When a newly appointed liquor commissioner, responding to the arrest of a Filipino for assault with a weapon in a Honolulu bar in 1959, remarked to the press that Filipinos were troublemakers, the governor immediately withdrew the appointee's renomination papers.[53] Such remarks violated the standard for acceptable public discourse in the Aloha State.

But not until the 1970s and 1980s did the etiquette of public discourse established in Hawaiian politics become standard for national politics in the U.S. The issue surfaced most prominently in the Republican party at the national level, partly because the party controlled the presidency in the 1980s and partly because right-wing extremists who attacked blacks and Jews were more likely to be Republicans than Democrats. When the Ku Klux Klan endorsed Ronald Reagan's quest for the presidency in 1980, he repudiated the endorsement. When they did it again in 1984, Reagan wrote a letter to the Civil Rights Commission saying, "If anything, my feelings on this subject have only grown stronger," and he denounced "the politics of racial hatred and religious bigotry practiced by the Klan."[54]

President Reagan accepted a series of resignations from federal officials who broke the rules of etiquette in public discourse concerning race or ethnicity. In 1983, Interior Secretary James Watt, after pointing to high rates of alcoholism and other problems among Indians on reservations, was bombarded with criticism that forced him to make an explicit apology before Indian leaders.[55] Seven months later, Watt, speaking of his appointments to a minor commission, said that he had chosen "every kind of mix you can have. I have a black, I have a woman, two Jews, and a cripple," and although he apologized and explicitly repudiated the idea that he was insulting any group, he was fired for insensitivity after key Republican senators called for his resignation.[56]

Republican senators and congressmen also urged Reagan to force the resignation of his appointee to the chairmanship of the Copyright Tribunal for having co-authored a book that disparaged black Americans.[57] President Reagan was again embarrassed after he nominated for the Board for International Broadcasting a man who had been director of a foundation that funded research purporting to show that blacks are genetically less intelligent than whites; when it became apparent that a majority of the Senate Foreign Relations Committee opposed the nomination, the man withdrew his name from consideration.[58]

When the Senate Judiciary Committee rejected Reagan's nomination of Jeffrey B. Sessions III to be a federal district judge in Alabama, it was partly because he had once said he thought members of the Ku Klux Klan "were OK until I found out they smoked pot," and also because he once had labeled the NAACP Legal Defense Fund and the National Council of Churches as "un-American."[59] Vice President George Bush, campaigning for the presidency in 1988, also backed away from associates who had been known to express bigotry. When it came out that several prominent Bush supporters had been connected with pro-Nazi and anti-Semitic activities, he dropped them from their campaign positions.[60]

Expressions of prejudice or bigotry were much more likely to surface in local politics than in national politics, where by the 1988 election the unwritten rules concerning public discourse on race, ethnicity, and religion had been firmly established. But even in city elections it had become commonplace for candidates for citywide office to disassociate themselves from extreme statements that might exacerbate racial, religious, or ethnic tensions. Chicago, notorious for such campaigning, established a Committee on Decent Unbiased Campaign Tactics in 1983 to whose platform the mayoral candidates subscribed.[61] In 1985, the four major candidates for mayor in Philadelphia agreed to a fair election campaign code issued by a nonpartisan fellowship commission.[62]

The principal objective of formal codes of etiquette such as the one in Philadelphia was to keep candidates from pandering to or inciting racial prejudice. In every major city, racial tension was close to the surface, often revolving around black complaints of harsh treatment by police and other local officials. When the white police chief of Los Angeles suggested that some blacks might be more susceptible than "normal people" to injury caused by officers applying a choke hold that constricts the flow of blood in the carotid arteries to the brain, the chief, besieged with protests from black organizations and other civil rights and antidefamation groups, was obliged to apologize and to explain that he did not mean to exclude blacks or Latinos from his categorization of "normal people."[63] When the chief of police (a Chinese-American) in a predominantly white suburb of New Orleans announced that he had ordered his officers to stop blacks routinely in white neighborhoods, he was forced to make a public apology and rescind the order. Following a wave of protest by black leaders and civil libertarians, he expressed his continuing commitment "to the civil rights of everyone."[64]

In 1987, the police commissioner of New York City (a black man) took the unusual step of issuing an order promising swift punishment for police department personnel who made racial or ethnic slurs.[65] But the question of what constituted a racial or ethnic slur was not always clear; witness the reaction of black Americans to the criticism made by the white police commissioner in Boston in 1985 of one of his black deputy super-intendents for being "inappropriate and inaccurate" when the officer la-beled a certain heavily black section of the city unsafe because of infestation with drug dealers and other criminals. The commissioner thought that even a black police officer should not issue what to him sounded like a slur against the blacks of that neighborhood. But many black citizens agreed with the characterization of the neighborhood as "unsafe" and were more concerned that the commissioner might not appreciate just how bad the situation was.[66]

When the campaign manager of the Republican candidate for governor in California in 1982 expressed the view that up to 5 percent of white voters would conceal racial prejudice when asked by poll takers if they would support a black candidate for governor, he was asked to resign, even though almost every knowledgeable politician in California probably would have agreed with his assessment.[67] Any comment that might be interpreted as racist was suspect in the new etiquette of public discourse, whether it was meant to be pejorative or not.

Blatantly bigoted speech was less common than the more ambiguous kind. There was no ambiguity when members of a fraternity and a so-rority at the University of Southern California chanted anti-Semitic slo-gans and painted "Jew Week" on a sidewalk outside a predominantly Jewish fraternity, leading to suspension of the offending groups.[68] But when a member of the board of trustees at Wellesley College in Massa-chusetts was asked about her business experiences and commented that she had trouble keeping black assembly line workers from going "back to the streets to earn more money" selling drugs, the campus erupted with criticism and she was forced to resign from the board.[69]

The prohibition on remarks that could be interpreted as racist extended to utterances by private persons whose activities were of considerable interest to the public. In 1987 and 1988, two prominent sports personalities were fired because of remarks with racist implications, even though it was generally acknowledged that neither person was bigoted. When the vice president of the Los Angeles Dodgers suggested that black baseball play-ers were not appointed as field managers or general managers because "they may not have some of the necessities," he apologized and resigned in the face of widespread protests.[70] The following year, a prominent commentator on sporting events suggested that blacks in general were more athletically gifted than whites partly because of breeding that had taken place during slavery, thus violating the rules of etiquette in public discourse by suggesting that there were inherent physiological differences between whites and blacks.[71]

Racist remarks by blacks against whites also were criticized, although not as swiftly or decisively punished. When an affirmative action manual issued to train New York State employees of the state insurance fund characterized all white Americans as racist, it was withdrawn as an embarrassment to the agency.[72] And when a manual used to train thousands of new teachers in the New York City public schools said that all whites are racists, even if unaware of their racism, because they benefit from a white racist society, the chairman of the state assembly's panel on human rights sharply criticized the manual.[73] But the affirmative action officer who prepared the first manual was not removed from her job, only reprimanded, and those responsible for the second manual were not criticized officially.[74] And the leaders of the state legislature's black and Puerto Rican caucus strongly defended state affirmative action materials that called all whites racists, saying the materials were useful in provoking discussion.[75]

The etiquette of public discourse with respect to remarks that disparaged racial or religious groups was less stringent for blacks making remarks about whites. When a prominent black minister in Brooklyn, the Reverend Al Sharpton, publicly compared the state attorney general, Robert Abrams, to Adolf Hitler, despite Abrams's long record of devotion to civil rights, the chairman of the New York State black and Puerto Rican legislative caucus criticized Sharpton for going too far. But the criticism of Sharpton was highly controversial among blacks in New York City.[76] Sharpton was able to say about a white man what no white minister could publicly say about a black person in a city such as New York without bringing about nearly universal condemnation from white public officials.

Jesse Jackson, as a candidate for president in 1984, also violated the etiquette of public discourse without being widely criticized openly by other black leaders. A black journalist reported on Jackson's private anti-Semitic remarks (the candidate had called Jews by the term "Hymie" and New York City "Hymietown"). Jackson first denied having made the statements, then, in the face of published contradictory evidence, explained that he had meant those things to be heard only in private. When that explanation proved insufficient to stop criticism, he apologized. Jackson entered more serious trouble that year by failing to repudiate the support of the Reverend Louis Farrakhan, one of his earliest and strongest backers and a member of his early campaign entourage, who had called

Judaism a "dirty religion." Dozens of white leaders called Farrakhan's remarks outside the bounds of acceptable political rhetoric. The U.S. Senate voted unanimously to condemn "anti-Jewish and racist sentiments such as those reportedly being made by Louis Farrakhan," and the leadership of the Senate was instructed to communicate with the chairmen of the Democratic and Republican parties to request that they repudiate in writing these sentiments of hatred made by Farrakhan. One senator after another, many from states with a small number of Jewish voters, denounced those remarks as violating the fundamental principles of pluralism in the United States.[77]

While Jackson did not repudiate Farrakhan, he did denounce anti-Semitism in his speech to the Democratic convention in 1984. After the convention, the Democratic National Committee unanimously passed a resolution reaffirming its "adherence to pluralistic principles" and repudiated and disassociated itself completely "from people who promote all forms of hatred, bigotry, racism and anti-Semitism."[78] That Jackson escaped from universal condemnation and was able to run much more effectively for president in 1988 than four years earlier was due partly to the fact that an easier standard concerning public discourse was applied to him than to white candidates. If the head of the Irish Independent Republican Army had been a good friend of John F. Kennedy and had supplied campaign bodyguards for him in the early primaries in 1960, and had made derogatory remarks about "Prots" and called Protestantism a "dirty religion," Kennedy would have been driven from public life. If in 1976 Jimmy Carter had chosen members of the Ku Klux Klan as his bodyguards and had been introduced frequently by the Imperial Wizard at campaign stops, Carter could never have survived the early primaries. That so few black leaders criticized Jackson for failing to repudiate Farrakhan indicated something of Jackson's practical difficulty in doing so.[79]

By the end of the decade, the civic culture's etiquette for public discourse on race and religion appeared to be widely accepted as an important method of protecting voluntary pluralism.[80] Racism and religious bigotry had become ineffective in elections for high office. Successful southern white senatorial and gubernatorial candidates had totally abandoned racist rhetoric by the early 1980s, and in 1986, when 234 extremist candidates, a large number of whom were anti-Semitic, ran in state primaries, only thirteen made it to the November elections, and all were defeated.[81] The strong standards set by public officials and candidates against any suspicion of racism in public discourse extended even to speech by foreign leaders about Americans. When in September 1986 Prime Minister Yashuhiro Nakasone of Japan told a meeting in his country that the United States would not be able to do as well as Japan in meeting the demands of a highly technological society because it had "a considerable number of blacks, Puerto Ricans and Mexicans," the reaction from Democrats and Republicans in Congress was swift. Senator John Heinz (R-Pennsylvania) insisted that Nakasone "publicly repudiate and completely disassociate himself from any form of bigotry." Following a public apology by the Japanese ambassador delivered to members of Congress and administration officials, the State Department officially declared that "the Japanese are well aware that we consider our racial and ethnic diversity to be a source of strength and vitality in our society."[82]

Expiating Past Bigotry: Symbolic Gestures

The new majority on civil rights and voluntary pluralism could not make up for past bigotry, oppression, and discrimination based on race, ethnicity, or religion. Completely making up for the past in any tangible way, or even through symbolic acts, was impossible to accomplish with respect to Jews who remembered the turning back of relatives in refugee boats, or blacks whose ancestors had been lynched, or Native American Indians or ethnic Hawaiians whose ancestors had suffered cultural and physical aggression and whose descendants in the 1980s still felt dispossessed from their land.[83] It was impossible to undo entirely the punishing effects of predatory pluralism, caste pluralism, or sojourner pluralism, but Americans were proving that it was possible to organize their society in an effort to prevent a repetition of the injustices of the past. And in one case it was possible for the national government to take a specific symbolic action to make up for one of the most singular examples of the violation of the rights of Americans, when Congress in 1988 passed a law signed by the president authorizing tax-free payments of $20,000 to descendants of those Japanese-Americans interned in concentration camps during the Second World War.

By the 1980s, an increasing number of Americans were aware of the great wrong done to American citizens of Japanese ancestry and their parents under President Roosevelt's executive order that led to the removal and replacement of 120,000 in camps.[84] Although the litigation of individual cases for nisei brought a redress of injustice to a few of them, the episode remained unacknowledged until Congress in 1980 established a bipartisan commission on wartime location and internment of civilians and directed it to recommend appropriate remedies.[85] Issuing its unanimous report in 1983, the commission concluded that "nations that forget or ignore injustices are more likely to repeat them" and recommended that Congress pass a joint resolution recognizing the grave injustice committed against Japanese-Americans and that Congress appropriate money to establish a special foundation for educational and humanitarian purposes related to the wartime events, although "no fund would be sufficient to make whole again the lives damaged by the exclusion and detention."[86]

Eight members of the nine-person commission recommended that Congress establish a fund to provide a one-time per capita compensatory payment of $20,000 to each of the 60,000 surviving persons excluded from their places of residence under the executive order.[87] Robert Matsui, a nisei U.S. representative from California, who was ten months old when his parents were forced to leave their California home with him to move to an internment camp, told the panel as he wiped away tears from his eyes that the bill was needed so "Americans can look back and say, 'We were wrong.'" Legislation embodying the recommendation passed in 1988. Although Congress delayed appropriating money to implement it, action taken in 1989 appeared to assure that payments would begin no later than 1991.[88] Millions of Americans seemed to acknowledge that those who spoke and acted for the nation on Japanese internment during the war violated the basic principles of the civic culture. Having made that acknowledgment and symbolic acts of contrition, Americans were evolving an institutional structure, supported by cultural norms, in an extraordinary effort to build a decent multiethnic society.

Racism, anti-Semitism, and ethnic conflict were still part of the American ethnic landscape. Many blacks and some whites believed that racism was spreading and that the civil rights compact was eroding as the 1980s came to a close. They saw dangerous signals in a sudden increase in reported bigotry-motivated crimes. Some believed that decisions taken by the Supreme Court to trim aspects of affirmative action reflected a more general racism in society.[89] Racism was palpable in the actions of such groups as the skinheads, in the ugly language of callers to television and radio talk shows, and even in the actions of some police officers. But the charge of racism was sometimes misplaced, as when students in New York City called a teacher a racist when he taught them about tyrannical leaders in African countries, or when those who disagreed with aspects of affirmative action were called racist, or in the accusations of racism against colleges and universities for failing to hire a certain proportion of minority professors. There were obvious dangers to the civil rights compact when the charge of racism was hurled loosely. Name-calling made friends into bystanders and bystanders into enemies. And those who made such accusations were themselves distracted from solving real problems that may have had little or nothing to do with racism.[90] Although racism persisted, it was clear by 1990 that bigotry was not practiced on anywhere near the scale that it had been in previous generations, and, most important, it was now discouraged and punished much more often than in the past by laws, programs, and public opinion.

Chapter Twenty-Two

"TO GET BEYOND RACISM"
Integrating Education and Housing

I N JUNE 1958, an African-American woman named Virginia Mildred Jeeter and a white man, Richard Loving, married in the District of Columbia and returned to their home in Virginia, where they were indicted for violating that state's ban on interracial marriages. Nine years later, the U.S. Supreme Court reversed their convictions. In ruling the Virginia Racial Integration Act of 1924 unconstitutional, the Court re-iterated its view that the clear and central purpose of the Fourteenth Amendment was to eliminate all official sources of discrimination in the states.[1]

The Court did not rule that all racial classifications violated the Four-teenth Amendment. Action by states to penalize miscegenation—in-tended to stigmatize blacks and keep them in a caste status—was obviously invidious. But what about action undertaken not to injure Af-rican-Americans or other ethnic groups, but to remedy past injustice? If race-conscious measures could be justified by a compelling public purpose such as equal educational opportunity for blacks, it usually was sanctioned by the courts in the 1970s and 1980s under the general principle enunci-ated by Justice Harry Blackmun: "In order to get beyond racism we must first take account of race. There is no other way. . . . In order to treat persons equally, we must treat them differently."[2]

The Debate Over Counting by Race

That proposition was based on the premise that membership in a group—black, Hispanic, Asian or Pacific Islander, or American Indian—resulted, by virtue of a pervasive pattern of past discrimination, in an inequality of powers that neutral or color-blind, ethnic-blind laws were insufficient to correct. It was not enough, according to that premise, that every adult should have the right to be free from explicit discrimination and protected against bigotry-motivated crimes; it was necessary to affirm their equality through the active intervention of government and of all institutions with a broad public purpose, in order to reverse the condi-tions that public and private oppression had worked to create. Blackmun and all others who supported race-conscious remedies in principle did not maintain that membership in a particular group entitled one to rights not possessed by others, but that counting by race was necessary to achieve rights for blacks equal to those of others.[3]

Those who opposed counting by race—so many blacks in this school, that housing project, that city council, that telephone company or medical school—argued that while the presumption of inequality by reason of color or membership in an ethnic group based on past discrimination might be justified for many individuals, the remedy of counting by race ignored the great differences in ability and advantage that existed within every group, and inevitably led to interventions that gave preference to or favored treatment to individuals solely because of their race or ethnicity, thereby vitiating the Fourteenth Amendment's insistence on "equal protection of the laws" regardless of race or ethnicity.[4] They pointed to a long and odious history of counting by race or religion principally to keep African-Americans and Jews in their place, which finally led the U.S. Supreme Court to declare that race when used for any public policy purpose is a suspect classification.[5]

Advocates of race-conscious remedies countered by arguing that such classifications were suspect when they were intended to discriminate or limit the rights of African-Americans and members of other minority groups, not when they were intended to fulfill rights previously denied. It was exactly because both sides argued on the basis of the fundamental principle of individual rights that actual cases were so difficult and that it fell to the courts to decide when, if ever, public policy could require or encourage counting by race and ethnicity, for what purpose, with what methods, and for how long. The unifying principle of equal rights was accepted by nearly everyone; it was the application that was in dispute because of a genuine dilemma: pervasive racial discrimination could not be entirely reversed by new antidiscrimination laws, even by their vigorous enforcement. It was too subtle and powerful a systemic force; yet, counting by race implied group entitlements that could lead to invidious discrimination against individuals not included among the designated beneficiary groups.

The vast majority of affirmative action programs in the 1970s and 1980s were noncontroversial, accepted by most Americans as legitimate attempts to promote equality of opportunity, especially for blacks. The range of affirmative action activities in the private sector was enormous. Foundations, especially the Ford Foundation, the world's largest, stimulated a variety of programs to recruit, train, and reward blacks and Hispanics. In 1984, it announced plans for a 60-percent increase in support of Hispanic programs, totaling $16 million, and representing 11 percent of the foundation's budget for its national programs.[6] The Robert Wood Johnson Foundation (second largest in the world) ran a minority medical faculty development program during the 1980s; it offered four-year, post-doctoral research fellowships to minority persons who had demonstrated superior academic and clinical skills and were committed to careers in academic medicine and biomedical research.[7] In one program announced in 1987, the Associated Medical Schools of New York organized a program to increase minority-group representation among medical students being trained in hospitals in that state.[8]

Colleges and universities organized a great variety of affirmative action programs that did not necessarily call for a statistical measure of success. Many of them initiated upward-bound programs in the 1970s, mainly to help designated minority students make a transition from high school to college. In the 1980s, the board of governors of the state system of higher education in Pennsylvania authorized state universities to waive tuition payments for one percent of their full-time undergraduates, with the principal goal of bringing more African-Americans and Hispanics to college.[9] The Massachusetts Institute of Technology carried a program throughout the 1970s into the 1980s known as MITES, the Minority Introduction to Engineering and Science program, which by the mid-1980s had grown to more than fifty students each year, who received six weeks of rigorous academic training featuring the sciences.[10] In a new approach to attracting faculty members from minority groups, Columbia University announced a program in 1987 that would begin paying off the undergraduate loan debts of its minority-group graduates who went on to earn Ph.D.'s.[11]

Newspapers stimulated recruitment and networking for minority students, as in February 1984 when five organized a conference open to all minority students from eastern colleges and universities to interview persons for entry-level newsroom positions as reporters, photographers, copy editors, and news assistants. "We're doing this because we recognize a dearth of minority representation in the news room," said one of the sponsors of the conference.[12] Some major corporations made affirmative action in recruitment and training a central part of their operations. The Ford Motor Company created a Minority Dealer Operations and Training Department, which by the 1980s concentrated not just on how to recruit and train minority dealers but also on how to retain them. Three years later, Ford organized a Minority Supplier Development Department in an effort to increase the number of minority suppliers doing business with the automotive company. The Coca-Cola Corporation established a $1.8-million minority capital fund to help finance new businesses and planned to spend $14 million with minority vendors.[13]

In 1984, the Adolph Coors Breweries inaugurated a plan to begin twenty black distributorships within a year (only one out of five hundred existed at the time) and to invest at least 8 percent of its pension funds in black-owned businesses and financial institutions.[14] The Equitable Life Assurance Society boasted in 1983 that it had sought out minority men and women to fill vital positions for years and had spent in excess of $22 million purchasing products and services from minority-owned firms while maintaining accounts in several minority-owned banks.[15]

Many corporate affirmative action plans were stimulated by pressure from blacks themselves. The agreement Coors signed with the National Black Economic Coalition in Denver in 1984 was reached after local chapters of the NAACP had launched a boycott.[16] Agreements with Coca-Cola, Kentucky Fried Chicken, Seven-Up, and the Burger King Corporation to enhance business opportunities for blacks were made with the civil rights lobby PUSH.[17] African-American organizations also participated in special affirmative action programs that did not entail statistical measures of success. The first major one was the recruiting and training program of the A. Philip Randolph Institute in the 1970s, which placed some 18,000 qualified minority-group members as apprentices in the building trades, thousands of whom became journeymen.[18] Black executives and professionals in Detroit gave a series of seminars in the 1980s to prepare high school students for work in a program called Efficacy Detroit.[19] In Atlanta, about 1,600 African-American doctors, lawyers, bankers, accountants, and entrepreneurs pooled their resources in an organization called Atlanta Exchange; through "Motivation Day" programs a large number of high school students were introduced to a variety of career options and to professionals who served as role models and guidance counselors.[20]

The tens of thousands of outreach programs by corporations, universities, state and local authorities, or the federal government were widely accepted by Americans in the 1980s. But four major issues were at controversy concerning the kind of affirmative action that involved counting by race: To what extent and by what methods should race be counted to bring about desegregation of public schools? To what extent and how should race be counted in attempting to integrate housing? To what extent and by what methods should electoral districts be shaped in order to encourage the election of black and Hispanic persons? And when and how should counting by race be undertaken to encourage economic gain in hiring and promoting, in the letting of contracts, and in admission to higher education.

Counting by Race and Public School Desegregation

Counting-by-race remedies to ensure equal rights for blacks began with the proposition laid down by a unanimous Supreme Court in the case of *Brown* v. *Board of Education* in 1954, when it said that the rights of black children to an equal education could be protected only if they attended integrated schools (the Court did not actually put it that way, but that was the clear inference from the decision). Given that implicit assumption, it eventually became necessary to count by race and assign students through some predetermined balance of blacks and whites in order to achieve integrated schools. The principal way to move them practically was by busing, and in a number of places where busing was adopted as a remedy to implement a counting-by-race plan, many white parents (and some African-American parents) resisted, expressing strongly held views about local control of education and the importance of neighborhood schools as extensions of family and community. Underlying those arguments of white parents was the fear that their children would lose an educational edge by attending schools with blacks that were known to be inferior, and, worse, that they would be harmed by what they saw as the values and life-styles of black children. But those feelings were on a collision course with a powerful constitutional mandate implemented by legislation and the vast power of the federal courts.

The courts had decided that segregated education denied black children an equal educational opportunity, condemning them to inferior education and limited contacts, and, since busing was the only practical way to achieve desegregation in many school jurisdictions, the Supreme Court ruled in 1971 that busing a child because of the color of his or her skin was a constitutionally permissible remedy to ensure blacks equal protection of the laws, a remedy that did not cause undue harm to whites. The decision came after the Charlotte-Mecklenburg school district in North Carolina (the city of Charlotte was part of Mecklenburg County's school district of 550 square miles) drew geographic school zones that led to substantially segregated schools because nearly all of the 29 percent of the schoolchildren in the county who were black lived in Charlotte. To overcome what it saw as a denial of equal rights for the African-American children, the Court approved a plan that called for busing about half of the children, white and black, into and out of the city, some for distances of up to fifteen miles.[21]

Charlotte-Mecklenburg had deliberately created segregated school zones; but what about school districts where de facto segregation existed but there had been no recent history of legally enforced segregation? In 1973, the Court answered that question by approving a court-ordered busing plan for Denver because the city school board had, in one portion of the city, taken steps that the district court had interpreted as segregative in intent as well as in effect.[22]

Conflicts over busing appeared in city after city, even before the Charlotte and Denver decisions, as in Boston, where a blue-ribbon commission appointed by Governor Endicott Peabody in 1964 recommended the desegregation of schools through a racial imbalance law. Under the 1965 law, schools could be deemed imbalanced if they were more than 50 percent black, as was true then of some schools in Boston, Springfield, and Cambridge. Irish and Italian middle-class families in Boston were furious. None of the thirty distinguished members of the commission sent their own children to Boston's public schools, and the upper-middle-class Irish judge who enforced the law by taking over the school system in 1974 lived in Wellesley, a handsome suburb far from the turmoil created by busing.[23]

Under the relentless pressure of court-ordered busing, city after city complied, with the result that many white parents sent their children to private schools and/or moved from the city, creating a demographic momentum that made integration more difficult, even with the use of buses, particularly since the U.S. Supreme Court had decided in a five-to-four decision in 1974 that the many suburban school systems that surrounded Detroit could not be compelled to join Detroit in a busing plan to integrate the city's schools.[24] What distinguished Charlotte and the communities around it in Mecklenburg County from Detroit and its suburbs was that Charlotte-Mecklenburg had long constituted a single school district, while Detroit and its suburbs had always been divided into independent districts. Surely zoning and other actions had been taken by the suburban communities with the intention of keeping blacks out, but those acts of discrimination would have to be handled through antidiscrimination-in-housing legislation and court orders or consent decrees to build low-cost housing for minorities in predominantly white areas, something extremely difficult to achieve.

Despite the jurisdictional problems posed in the Detroit decision and the demographic obstacles to integration created by white flight, integration increased in nearly every jurisdiction where busing was tried, according to a 1987 Civil Rights Commission study. Of the nine cities in which the typical black student went to schools with at least 50 percent whites in 1987, mandatory busing was involved in every instance. Of the twelve least-integrated school systems in the U.S. (where the typical black student attended schools in which whites constituted 20 percent or less of the population), nine did not have mandatory busing plans.[25]

Where it was constitutionally permissible to merge previously independent systems (as the Court ruled it was not in the Detroit area or other metropolitan areas in the North) because it could be demonstrated that they had a history of purposeful school segregation, extraordinary progress was made. All of the metropolitan areas with the highest levels of integration for blacks had comprehensive city-suburban busing orders, and two of the leaders in increased integration during the 1970s (Louisville, Kentucky, and Wilmington, Delaware) obeyed court orders forcing the desegregation and merger of previously independent city and suburban schools within the same counties. Delaware, Kentucky, and Florida, states that used countywide busing plans involving both central cities and suburban areas, made the most progress, and by 1980 nine-tenths of their black students were in integrated schools.[26]

In the South, where demographic and jurisdictional problems were least difficult, public schools moved from the most segregated in the country to the most integrated.[27] Where federal courts rejected city-suburban desegregation in southern metropolitan areas, as in Richmond and Atlanta, progress was slow. In Richmond, a typical black student in the 1970s attended a school almost three-fourths black; in Atlanta, where segregation actually increased during the 1970s, black students were even more segregated than in Richmond. Where jurisdictional and demographic opportunities existed, as in Florida, whose countywide districts invariably included substantial white and black populations, and where the courts imposed countywide remedies, or in Omaha, Indianapolis, Minneapolis, Denver, and Seattle, where large numbers of white children remained in the public school system, progress toward integration was considerable.

Yet, in the 1980s, nearly one-third of all black students still attended all-minority schools, and nearly three out of five attended schools in which more than half of the students were members of minority groups, principally because large northern cities had become increasingly black and Hispanic. Neither New York City, Detroit, nor Chicago had a comprehensive plan within their overwhelmingly minority central school systems, or voluntary programs for the exchange of students with suburban school districts in the 1980s; and Illinois, Michigan, and New York were the states with the highest levels of school segregation.[28]

There was considerable evidence by the 1980s that integration resulted in academic achievement by blacks and a more integrated society. Studies showed that minority students in predominantly white schools scored higher on achievement tests than those in segregated schools and generally performed better academically without risk to the academic records of white children.[29] African-American students who attended integrated elementary and secondary schools also were more likely to enroll in college than those who attended segregated schools, and integrated education had positive effects not only on college-going but on college completion, on obtaining jobs, and on the likelihood of living in integrated communities as adults.[30] Blacks from integrated schools had greater social opportunities, were more likely to work in integrated firms, to have white social contacts, and to live in integrated neighborhoods. African-Americans from integrated schools generally evaluated their white co-workers and supervisors more positively than those who had gone to segregated schools and grown up in segregated environments.[31]

It wasn't mere mixing of blacks, Hispanics, and whites that improved the quality of education for these students, but rather that expectations and also programs and quality of teaching experience were higher in schools attended by large numbers of white children. But some blacks who had fought for busing changed their minds, as in the case of Charles Evers, the former mayor of Fayette, Mississippi, who said in 1978 that the goal of quality education had not been achieved in Fayette. "They've bused every black kid out of our neighborhood, fifteen and ten and thirty miles away to predominantly white neighborhoods . . . they closed down the black schools. We didn't want that. We lost our identity."[32] Some black and white parents and their children complained about busing, because of the long bus rides, and also because it was difficult for parents to come to schools to meet with teachers.

Although the proportion of Americans who believed that white and black children should attend school together increased steadily and substantially in the 1970s, busing remained unpopular, and in 1981, President Reagan's secretary of education, Terrel H. Bell, announced that he would not actively press lawsuits to desegregate public schools through the use of busing. When Senators Jesse Helms (R-North Carolina) and Strom Thurmond (R-South Carolina) and others pushed legislation to deprive the federal courts entirely of their authority to issue school desegregation orders, Congress compromised by passing a resolution in 1982 opposing busing and urging other remedies to bring about integration. But between 1981 and 1988, public opinion shifted toward increased support of busing, and by 1986, 66 percent of the blacks, 58 percent of the Hispanics, and 36 percent of the whites in one survey supported it. Among those under thirty, a majority, including whites, agreed with mandatory busing to achieve integration.[33]

In the 1980s, busing was relied upon less often than in the 1970s as a remedy to desegregate schools. In Nashville in 1980, a federal court judge decided that it would be all right if black children attended neighborhood schools through the fourth grade—something the African-American plaintiff parents wanted—but he also ordered more extensive integration at the high school level through a new program to include magnet schools.[34] Plans for desegregation increasingly included what two scholars called "a bewildering diversity of arrangements, *ad hoc* in nature, varying enormously both in content and in implementation."[35] While some jurisdictions had seen continued efforts to implement an extensive busing plan combined with a redrawing of district lines, other systems, such as Milwaukee, Detroit, Chicago, New York, and Cincinnati, experimented with magnet schools to attract whites and blacks.[36]

Responding to a court desegregation order providing that minority enrollments in at least 75 percent of the schools must not fall below 25 percent and must not exceed 60 percent, Milwaukee discovered that it was not possible to achieve perfect compliance even with magnet schools accepting voluntary transfers (by 1984, one high school had a student body more than 90 percent African-American). Milwaukee tried a variety of strategies to meet the court's standard, including special partnerships between the University of Wisconsin and high schools that featured a pre-college center to bring minority high school sophomores and juniors interested in math and science to the university campus for a seven-week summer program taught by college professors, and also specific relationships between university faculties and staffs and particular high schools, an approach replicated elsewhere.[37]

By 1987, it had become clear that Milwaukee could not desegregate its schools effectively without help from the suburbs. Joining with the NAACP, Milwaukee filed suit against twenty-four suburbs, charging that racial segregation existed in the city's schools as a result of action taken by them and the state. The Milwaukee school board argued that as long as 52 percent of Milwaukee's public school students were black, it would be virtually impossible to achieve effective desegregation without extensive mandatory interdistrict busing of whites and blacks, an expensive and unpopular remedy. By charging that the state had failed to enforce fair-housing laws and had repealed a school consolidation measure aimed at greater integration, it hoped that the courts would find the state and the suburbs responsible for segregation in Milwaukee.[38]

White flight and the growth of black and Hispanic populations in many cities forced them to look to remedies that relied upon parental choice to achieve integration. The system of what was called "controlled choice," pioneered in Cambridge, Massachusetts, in 1982, began to be copied in the late 1980s in other school systems, including Little Rock. Under the Cambridge plan, individual school attendance boundaries were dismantled and parents were permitted to choose from any of the city's thirteen grammar schools and rank them from one to three. The ranking was required because Cambridge, committed to having the schools' racial enrollments close to the city's racial composition (53 percent white and 47 percent minority in 1987), could not guarantee the parents' first choice. So successful was the program that the number of whites attending public schools actually rose, and by the eighth grade, minority students were outperforming white students in math and reading in 60 percent of the schools.[39]

The success of Cambridge was unusual in northern cities and attributable in part to the fact that a substantial population of the city's white youngsters went to public schools. In some cities it was almost impossible to avoid segregation, as in Washington, D.C., where more than 80 percent of all the students went to schools that were 99 to 100 percent minority. But in many school districts, such as Chicago, Dade County, Houston, Los Angeles, San Diego, and even New York and Philadelphia, white students who left the schools between 1968 and 1986 were replaced more by Hispanic (and to a lesser extent Asian) students than by blacks. While these schools were not becoming integrated in the sense that they had achieved some balance between white and black students, they were becoming more multicultural.[40]

The decline in the white student population in many of those cities meant that busing had become outdated as a remedy in some. In Boston in 1972, when African-American parents brought suit charging that the school committee discriminated against their children, the system had 96,000 students, of whom 60 percent were white. By 1989, the number of pupils was down to 57,000, only 24 percent of whom were white. Busing thus often meant moving black children from an almost-all-black school across the city to attend a school with a minority of white children, leading the mayor, the school committee, and other leaders of the city to advocate a new student assignment plan based on qualified free choice of schools by parents.[41] Across the country in Los Angeles, civil rights officials decided in 1988 to drop a twenty-five-year-old desegregation suit, recognizing that the busing remedies sought in the past would not work in a district where the proportion of white students had dropped from 65 to 17 percent. The nation's largest desegregation suit, filed in 1963, led to three years of mandatory, court-ordered busing ending in 1981, but by 1988, when the school population was 56.8 percent Hispanic, 17.7 percent black, and 17 percent white with the rest Asians and American Indians, busing was no longer seen as a significant way to improve and integrate the schools where 70 percent of the black students were enrolled with 90 to 100 percent of African-Americans and other minorities.[42]

Because of jurisdictional and demographic problems, only a little more than one-third of all minority students in the nation (mainly African-American) went to schools that were less than 50 percent minority in population. More than half of all black, Hispanic, and Asian students attended schools with more than 90 percent minority population. The demographic and jurisdictional limits on achieving desegregation in the public schools were even more severe for Hispanic children than for

African-Americans. In 1970, Hispanic students made up about one-twentieth of all students in the country; by 1980, one-twelfth. Still concentrated in several states (the West had 44 percent of the nation's Hispanic students in 1980, although only 19 percent of all students), the typical Hispanic student attended a school that was more segregated than that of the typical black student.

The percentage of Hispanic students attending predominantly minority schools actually went up nationally (but not in every city) between 1968 and 1980 and continued to rise in the following decade.[43] With large increases in Hispanic population, due to immigration and relatively high birth rates, and with the school policy of concentrating bilingual programs, and hence, Hispanic students, in certain schools, the typical Hispanic student by 1980 was in a school two-thirds minority, compared to 1970, when he or she was likely to be in a school one-half white.[44]

The effects of resegregation or the failure to desegregate because of demographic and jurisdictional limits would not have been so harmful for African-American and Hispanic students if there had been a major equalization of resources and standards between poor and well-to-do school districts in the 1980s. But just the opposite was true. In late 1988, a special task force on the education of children and youth appointed by the New York State education commissioner portrayed "two unequal educational systems," which tended to create and perpetuate "a permanent underclass in New York." While acknowledging that other factors contributed to the creation of such schools, the report suggested that race was a basic cause. One task force member, the superintendent of schools in Buffalo, pointed out that where a school system was made up predominantly of minority students, there tended to be a drop in support for those schools. Commenting on a situation in which 77 percent of the state's African-American and Hispanic students were enrolled in city schools, the report pointed out that in New York City three out of four blacks and four out of five Hispanics failed to complete high school within four years.[45]

The evidence was strong that the resegregation of northern schools led to the same kinds of neglect of minority students that had been pervasive in segregated southern school systems prior to the implementation of desegregation orders in the 1960s and 1970s. Overwhelmingly black schools invariably were neglected, compared to those that had achieved some degree of integration or were mainly white. A dramatic example existed in the Bronx in the 1980s at Public School No. 24, in the middle-class neighborhood of Riverdale, where special programs were offered and computers were easily available. Only a few miles away at Public School No. 79 in the Fordham area of the Bronx, where most of the black and Puerto Rican students came from poor families, there were twice as many pupils for each computer terminal. The children of inner cities and in poor school districts everywhere would continue to be deprived of equal educational opportunities as long as state systems for financing public schools relied overwhelmingly on local tax revenues whether or not they became integrated. School financing systems were attacked in several state courts in the late 1980s, and a few notable battles for equal opportunity were won, but as the decade came to a close there remained glaring disparities between rich and poor school districts throughout the nation.[46]

Segregation of African-American and Hispanic students was likely to continue in many jurisdictions well into the twenty-first century. Desegregation had achieved many of its goals where it could be implemented, but new educational strategies and resources were needed to deal with the reality of segregation where it existed, to prevent the corrosive effects on poor black and Hispanic children who attended segregated schools. The terrible fights of the 1960s and 1970s over forced busing were over as the 1980s came to a close. Many more African-American students went to school in integrated settings than when *Brown* was decided in 1954 (primarily in the South), but there had been little progress in the integration of black students with whites in urban districts since the mid-1970s. Where segregation persisted or reemerged, it appeared to be as harmful as it was in the past for African-American and Hispanic students. Varied educational programs were badly needed for urban schools, but it was unlikely that even with imaginative, innovative programs, the schools of most cities would become more integrated unless patterns in housing changed substantially.

Counting by Race and Integrating Housing

The largest single obstacle to desegregation in the public schools was the continuation of segregated housing. In the 1980s, equal rights in housing remained the most elusive of civil rights. Despite extensive legislation and regulations aimed at integrating housing, most American communities remained segregated by the end of the 1980s.

The effort to protect the civil rights of blacks and other minorities with respect to housing began in 1962 with Executive Order 11063 by President John F. Kennedy, which stipulated that discrimination based on race, color, creed, or national origin was to be prohibited in any property or facility owned or operated by the federal government or which benefited from federal money, an order that covered less than one percent of the nation's housing. The big breakthroughs in antidiscrimination legislation came with the passage of Title VI of the Civil Rights Act of 1964 and especially in 1968 with the passage of Title VIII (the Fair Housing Act), covering more than 80 percent of the nation's housing, including all segments of the real estate industry.[47]

That the enforcement mechanisms of the FHA were weak—relying on conciliation and mediation—reflected the deep and pervasive resistance by whites to integrating housing. Many white Americans opposed integrated housing even more than integrated schooling, partly because of racism but also because they believed that neighborhoods were an extension of ethnic and family values, to be guarded from intrusion by outsiders, and because they were fearful that if blacks moved into white neighborhoods, it would reduce the worth of their own property.[48] Housing policies were caught in a conflict between two significant values of the civic culture—integration and voluntary pluralism—a conflict reflected in the policies of the Department of Housing and Urban Development in the 1970s and 1980s. At the same time that several of its programs were aimed at mixing income levels and racial groups to break up black ghetto areas, the department's Office of Neighborhood Self Help tried to assist ethnic groups in preserving their neighborhoods.[49]

The self-segregation of immigrant communities (and later ethnic groups) went back to the seventeenth and eighteenth centuries, ever since Huguenots, Mennonites, and others created their own communities, apart from others, to sustain and nourish the religions and cultures they brought with them from the old countries. Scotch-Irish and Germans sometimes lived in communities as completely isolated from each other as they were from English settlements. Later, those who lived in ethnically homogeneous neighborhoods in the big cities did so in large measure to be with their own kind. Streets and neighborhoods developed an ethnic character, with social life revolving around the stoops and courtyards of apartment buildings. Neighborhood clubhouses and stores were places to gain information on anything from apartments to credit to job opportunities.[50] But the Post–Second World War migration of blacks and Hispanics to the cities, the breaking up of the old neighborhoods through urban renewal, and the building of the interstate highway system combined with the civil rights revolution to break up old patterns of segregated ethnic neighborhoods. Despite these changes, white ethnics who continued to live in cities—Italians, Greeks, Poles, Slavs—were reluctant to permit inroads against the ethnic solidarity they valued. Thus the voluntary isolation of white ethnic groups led to the compulsory isolation of blacks in urban ghettoes, with little individual freedom of choice to move out.

Some third- and fourth-generation white ethnics chose to move to the suburbs, partly because of federal housing policies but also because of the loss of manufacturing jobs in the cities. Loans at 4.5 percent in the 1950s for single-family housing on quarter-acre lots with picket fences in the suburbs basically were for whites only. Just at the time when blacks were moving into the cities and whites moving out, manufacturing jobs also left the cities. In New York City alone, some 600,000 manufacturing jobs were taken from the labor market during the 1960s. Some of the older ethnic neighborhoods held on, but as conditions in the inner city, now associated with drugs and crime, deteriorated further, more whites moved away.[51] Heroin addiction rose dramatically in the Bronx in the 1960s, particularly in the South Bronx. Reported assaults in the Bronx rose from 998 in 1960 to 4,256 in 1969. By the late 1970s, vacant buildings were common in the South Bronx, many looking as though they had been bombed in a terrible war. Muggers and street gangs roamed the neighborhoods.[52]

Although resistance to integration resulted in part from the desire to maintain ethnic neighborhoods and from the fear of contamination by the poor, particularly the poor outsider, there was ample evidence that the outsiders least wanted were blacks. The National Association of Real Estate Boards actually advised its members to be on guard against "a colored man of means" who thought that his children "were entitled to live among whites," comparing such a man to a gangster who wanted to hide his activities by living in a better neighborhood. Although the NAREB modified its advice in 1950, it still warned realtors not to introduce anyone into a neighborhood who would reduce property values. In 1963, only one year before passage of the Civil Rights Act, it advised realtors to help clients who wished to discriminate, rather than continue the past practice of simply telling Negroes they were not wanted.[53]

A variety of devices were effective in keeping blacks segregated. Zoning codes often determined the cost of housing and sometimes prohibited the building of federally subsidized housing or even privately developed multifamily units in certain neighborhoods. African-Americans seeking to rent or purchase housing were steered by realtors to racially changing or deteriorating neighborhoods. Real estate agents engaged in block-busting by selling a house to an African-American family and passing the word around the neighborhood to encourage whites to sell their property before its value declined precipitously. Banks and mortgage companies engaged in redlining by refusing to make loans for housing in black areas of cities, requiring stricter lending terms for low-income housing, and rejecting applicants for loans on houses over a certain age, all practices designed both to make it difficult for blacks to sell their homes and to keep them confined to certain areas.[54]

Overcoming these practices under the Fair Housing Act required the cooperation of realtors, private insurance agencies, and mortgage lenders, the very people who had often practiced discrimination. Even after passage of the act, it was impossible to keep real estate agents from steering blacks away from certain neighborhoods, or to keep banks and mortgage companies from denying mortgages or stipulating unfavorable terms for blacks who sought to move into middle- and upper-income communities. In many cases, African-Americans who did manage to move into an all-white neighborhood—having passed the realtors and the banks—met with intimidation and harassment by their neighbors.[55]

So pervasive was resistance to integrated housing that seven years after passage of the act, when the Department of Housing and Urban Development worked out a voluntary affirmative marketing agreement with the National Association of Realtors which stipulated several requirements for all developers seeking federal mortgage insurance,[56] the realtors, afraid that white homeowners would not use the service of brokers who had signed the voluntary agreement, required that the names of their firms be kept secret. So weak was enforcement of the agreement that ten years later HUD officials conceded that two hundred of the six hundred community housing resource boards (volunteer community groups) established to implement the agreement were inoperative.[57]

Although considerable progress was made in desegregating schools in the 1970s because of mandatory busing, there was virtually none to report in the area of housing, where it was not possible to bar subtle forms of discrimination or, where blacks moved into white areas, to force whites to continue to live in those neighborhoods. Ten years after passage of the Fair Housing Act, the National Committee Against Discrimination in Housing conducted a series of tests nationally in which teams of black and white couples with identical financial backgrounds posed as prospective home buyers or apartment renters before the same realtors and apartment or condominium owners. The black couples encountered discrimination in 48 percent of their attempts to purchase homes, and even more frequent discrimination in rental situations.[58] A study based on the 1980 census demonstrated that in metropolitan areas the segregation index—the percentage of population that lived in all-black or all-white neighborhoods—went down in only three of the fifteen most segregated cities between 1970 and 1980, all of them in the South, and even there by only about 10 percent. In Cleveland, the segregation index actually went up from 90 to 91 percent.[59]

Resistance to integrated housing remained massive in the 1980s, even in public housing. After studying nearly fifty cities around the nation for over a year, the *Dallas Morning News* in February 1985 published an eight-part series entitled "Separate and Unequal," pointing out that not one of the cities had a fully integrated federal housing project.[60] Private housing was even more difficult to integrate, and although there was a 40 percent increase in the black suburban population between 1970 and 1980, it was concentrated in relatively few suburban communities that ringed the major cities of the Northeast. Many suburbs, such as Mount Vernon, New York, which were once all-white, became largely African-American. Even in suburbs that were substantially integrated, such as Montclair, New Jersey, and New Rochelle, New York, housing was segregated into white and black neighborhoods.[61] Suburban low-income projects built with the promise of helping poor blacks leave the central cities nearly always were occupied by whites.[62]

Despite obstacles to enforcing equal opportunity in housing, strong enforcement efforts—including the threat of penalties—sometimes helped blacks and members of other minority groups achieve greater access to a broader and better range of housing in cities and suburbs. Fair-housing advocates and individual plaintiffs used court orders based on constitutional protections or various statutes to force communities to build affordable low-cost housing in middle-class neighborhoods and to oblige localities to build integrated public housing. Controlled tenancy policies aimed at keeping a balance of ethnic and racial groups in public housing or publicly assisted private housing were occasionally successful. And a few communities were ingenious in providing incentives for developers and owners and managers of housing stock to promote integration.

Success stories in the 1980s, exemplary but rare, began to point the way toward new housing integration strategies. Federal orders to integrate the public housing of major cities and their suburbs resulted in increased integration of public housing during the 1980s in Massachusetts, where the state government's commission against discrimination and Office of Communities and Development also applied pressure on cities and towns to provide greater access to blacks, Hispanics, and Asians. After state officials in 1987 ordered local authorities to advertise for minority applicants to increase their numbers in public housing, several communities reported significant increases in the number of blacks and other minorities. In Ipswich, the 113 state-approved family units occupied by members of minority groups rose in one year from 5 percent to the 13 percent mix that state authorities had suggested as a norm for metropolitan Boston.[63]

It was even possible to achieve progress against enormous opposition in building public housing when the federal government, local housing authorities, and other city officials cooperated in a carefully implemented plan. One of the best examples was in the Forest Hills section of Queens, when residents in that largely middle-class neighborhood demonstrated, threatening to block construction with their bodies when it was first announced that public housing would be built in their neighborhood. Eventually, an agreement was negotiated to reduce the number of apartments to be built and include a senior center, nursery, and after-school center open to everyone, including those who lived in private housing nearby. Through a careful selection process, which eliminated any potential tenant likely to be disruptive, the Forest Hills public housing units were substantially integrated by 1988 (65 percent white, 14.4 percent black, and the rest Hispanic and Asian).[64]

Sometimes extraordinary measures were required to gain the compliance of local governments, as in the Yonkers case. The Justice Department sued the board of education, the City of Yonkers, and the Yonkers Community Development Agency in 1980, charging that the city racially discriminated in education and public housing. On November 20, 1985, Federal District Court Judge Leonard B. Sand held that Yonkers officials were liable for the perpetuation of segregated schools, partly because they deliberately placed all subsidized housing projects in minority neighborhoods.[65] After extensive negotiations, the city council, in January 1988, approved a consent decree to build public housing, but eight months later it rejected a zoning amendment that was needed to build the eight hundred units, leading Judge Sand to hold in contempt of court the council members who voted against the amendment and to make them liable along with the city to extremely heavy fines (the councilmen were fined $500 a day, and the city's fines doubled daily, starting at $100). After a panel of the federal court of appeals upheld the contempt ruling and the fines, two councilmen reversed themselves and approved the zoning amendment.[66] When faced with the choice of desegregating the city or dismantling the government, the council decided to comply with the law.

The case in Yonkers was initiated through a U.S. government lawsuit, but increasingly in the 1980s, favorable decisions against discrimination were achieved in the courts as a result of the action of private plaintiffs, often working in cooperation with private centers concerned with open housing, which in some cases were given standing to bring suits and recover damages.[67] Private, nonprofit fair-housing organizations received complaints, attempted conciliation, and referred cases to public agencies for enforcement, in addition to bringing action themselves.[68]

Some communities developed ingenious approaches to integrating housing without pressure from court orders or consent decrees. One of the most original took place in Oak Park, Illinois, where the governing body of that middle-class suburb approved a 1984 plan to give $400,000 in subsidies and grants to building owners who entered into a five-year agreement with the village to permit the Oak Park Housing Center, a nonprofit agency set up to provide housing counseling to facilitate racial integration, to act as a rental agent. Under the plan, the center found African-American tenants for buildings that were predominantly white and whites for housing that had been predominantly black. Landlords who participated were eligible to receive matching grants of up to $1,000 per unit to improve interiors and larger matching grants for exterior innovations. Another Oak Park program was based on a 1978 equity insurance plan to guarantee property owners the value of their homes if racial change should cause prices to fall precipitously. As a result, Oak Park not only ensured that its community would be integrated but property values actually increased.[69]

Counting by race in Oak Park was implicit. When counting by race was explicit, everyone involved faced an extremely difficult question: Should integration be achieved at the price of individual discrimination? Although quotas in housing, even for the purpose of achieving integration, were condemned by the Reagan administration, several public housing projects employed them, with the permission of the Department of Housing and Urban Development. Various discriminatory strategies were employed to entice whites into integrated or predominantly African-American projects, such as allowing them to have pets or installing air conditioners.[70] The key to maintaining integration in public housing in several instances was the use of quotas, even when they were obvious, as in Boston, where development managers in the 1980s had huge boards with boxes representing the apartments, each marked by a color symbolizing the race or ethnicity of the tenant family.[71] In no other area of public policy as in public housing was integration so dependent on quotas. Even with ingenious incentives, it was difficult to prevent "tipping" (white flight) from integrated public housing without counting by race. "Buddy systems" (help to a family moving in from a family of another race already there) or other kinds of "welcoming committees" were helpful, but the most successful public housing authorities practiced some form of skipping over African-American or Hispanic applicants in favor of whites in order to maintain racial balance.[72]

The constitutionality of such arrangements in public housing had not been decided by the Supreme Court (Boston operated under a consent decree), but from the point of view of blacks or Hispanics seeking public housing who were kept on waiting lists longer than whites in order to develop a predetermined balance of groups, such distinctions clearly were invidious.[73] In 1988, the Court let stand a federal district court ruling that systems of "controlled tenancy" used by private developers and managers, even when they received public assistance, was in violation of the Fair Housing Act. The decision involved Starrett City, in Brooklyn, the largest and most successfully integrated of the federally subsidized middle-income housing programs in the country (more than 20,000 people and 5,881 families lived in 46 buildings by 1987). It depended on a policy of controlled tenancy in which integration was maintained by limiting African-American and Hispanic tenants to about 40 percent of the total. That clear policy of limiting tenancy by race led five black rental applicants who had been denied housing to file a class action discrimination suit in 1979, which was settled when Starrett agreed to rent an additional 3 percent of its apartments to minorities by 1989. But the Reagan administration intervened to charge Starrett with discrimination in violation of the Fair Housing Act, showing that by the summer of 1981, minorities constituted three-quarters of Starrett's waiting list, and that black families had to wait much longer than white families for apartments. The Starrett system to maintain integration (prevent tipping) by giving preferential treatment to whites was supported by blacks who already lived in the housing complex. Everyone involved in the case acknowledged that Starrett was a remarkable integration success story. No one disputed the good will of the people behind it. But Starrett lost the case when the judge decided that even though the managers and landlords "were not motivated by racial animus," they clearly engaged in discrimination under the law.[74]

As the 1980s came to a close, there was probably no area of life so basic to the dignity of human beings in which discrimination was as widely practiced as in housing. That basically was the conclusion of the congressional committees that held hearings on the enforcement of the Fair Housing Act. With the passage of amendments that would allow HUD to bring cases of alleged discrimination before an administrative law judge and for the Justice Department to seek substantial civil monetary penalties against violators, it was almost certain that there would be more success in enforcing the act in the 1990s than in the previous two decades. Already, Americans were beginning to show a variety of innovative approaches to housing that were likely to encourage integration. One approach was to scatter new dwellings for the use of families with low and moderate incomes throughout a community rather than concentrate them in high-rise buildings. Sometimes that strategy was adopted under a local ordinance, as in Rockville, Maryland, where builders were required to locate 12 percent of all such new dwellings in cluster housing throughout the city. Other times, private developers undertook the approach on their own.

In San Francisco, a nonprofit developer built more than 3,000 units of housing between 1983 and 1988, including more than 1,300 low- and moderate-income units, distributed in relatively small clusters. The results were likely to be successful when cities offered incentives, as in Richmond, which provided tax-exempt bond financing for developers on condition that they build 20 percent of their units for low- and moderate-income inhabitants, which they did in clusters of eight to twelve units. Like many other cities, Richmond also inaugurated a program to repair houses scattered throughout middle-class neighborhoods for rent or sale to people of low or moderate income.[75]

The dilemmas of counting by race in housing were greater than in any other area of public policy. Even if counting by race—controlled tenancy—became more common in public housing, Americans would have to invent other methods of achieving integration in private housing, even when publicly assisted. But the obstacles were formidable, partly because racial discrimination in housing was much harder to detect than in any other field. Yet, without progress toward integration in housing, there would not be much more progress in integrating schools. As the 1980s came to a close, it became apparent that progress in both areas depended to a considerable degree on the economic success of African-Americans and Hispanics. Economic opportunity was the key to a more integrated society, and it was in that area that counting-by-race remedies were most widely and effectively employed.

Chapter Twenty-Three

"TO GET BEYOND RACISM"
Political Access and Economic Opportunity

S EGREGATION in schools and housing were signs of caste; denial of the right to vote and of economic opportunity constituted the basis of caste. Votes and jobs were at the heart of a better life for African-Americans. Without them, decent schools, housing, and access to good public accommodations would be out of reach, whatever the laws said about segregation.

As discussed in chapter 10, the Voting Rights Act of 1965 had spectacular success in destroying grandfather clauses, literacy tests, poll taxes, and other devices long used to keep African-Americans from voting. So extraordinary was the success of the Voting Rights Act that by 1981–1982, the spread between black and white registration in Georgia was only 2.8 percent, in South Carolina 3.2 percent, in Virginia 7.2 percent, and in Mississippi 9.4 percent.[1]

So successful was the act in enfranchising African-Americans in the early 1970s that Mexican-Americans, who were not covered (as noted, classified as white by the Census Bureau, except in 1930), and who had sometimes been kept from the polls in Texas and other areas of the Southwest by intimidation, argued that they, too, needed special protection. As a result of a strong lobbying effort by the Leadership Conference on Civil Rights and allied groups, Congress passed amendments to the Voting Rights Act in 1975 extending coverage to counties throughout the nation where more than 5 percent of the voting-age population constituted a language minority group, where only English ballots had been used, and where the voter turnout had been under 50 percent in the previous presidential election. The underlying premise was that in such jurisdictions members of non-English-speaking groups (mainly Mexican-Americans) had suffered discrimination. As a result, Texas, Arizona, and Alaska and several counties in California and in other states were brought under the provisions of the act.[2]

Counting by Race and Equal Rights in Politics

Leaders of both African- and Mexican-American groups argued that access to the polling booth did not translate into power unless members of minority groups could ensure election of persons of their own kind. Once again the Leadership Conference on Civil Rights mobilized a strong lobbying effort in Congress; in 1982 additional amendments to the Voting Rights Act were passed that made it possible for black or other minority plaintiffs to challenge any jurisdiction for engaging in electoral discrimination if election results showed that the number of blacks, Mexican-Americans, or other minorities elected were not commensurate with the overall population proportions in a city, county, or other jurisdiction.

Congress validated a system of counting by race on the basis of a radically new theory of representation, that electoral districts should be designed or redesigned in order to promote the election of persons from designated minority groups. It would no longer be necessary for plaintiffs to prove discriminatory intent on the part of those who had designed the electoral districts, as the U.S. Supreme Court had decided in a 1980 case; it would be enough to show that African- or Mexican-Americans were not getting elected.[3]

The intent standard, by which plaintiffs were required to prove that an at-large election system had been adopted or maintained for a racially discriminatory purpose, was not controversial, but had not been easy to demonstrate.[4] The effects test was much easier to utilize since it was based on statistics. With blacks holding only 1.2 percent of the elective offices in the U.S. and constituting 10.5 percent of the voting-age population in 1985, hundreds of jurisdictions were vulnerable to challenge under the effects test.[5]

Even before the 1982 amendments, the Court had ruled in 1975 that in drawing up a reapportionment plan a state might count by race to ensure that African-Americans and other nonwhites had majorities in certain legislative districts. The Voting Rights Act of 1965 called for clearance by the U.S. attorney general of any plan to redistrict jurisdictions covered by the act. When New York State was obliged to redraw its state legislative districts, the attorney general raised questions about the plan submitted as insufficient to guarantee equal voting rights for blacks, whereupon the state redrew the district lines on the premise that a 65 percent nonwhite population would be needed to obtain the approval of the attorney general as a sufficient number likely to promote the election of a black in two state senate districts and two state assembly districts in Brooklyn. The Hasidic Jews who lived in the area challenged the constitutionality of the state's action, arguing that racial gerrymandering diluted their voting strength by taking them out of a single assembly district and a single state senate district where their voting power had been considerable and distributing them in two districts. But the Supreme Court validated the redistricting plan and the Voting Rights Act as constitutional.[6]

With passage of the 1982 amendments clearing up any ambiguity as to the appropriateness of counting by race in order to encourage the election of blacks and Hispanics, Justice Department attorneys routinely checked redistricting plans to make certain they were likely to result in the election of blacks or Hispanics, wherever possible. The new premise was that fairly drawn plans were those that gave blacks safe seats in proportion to the African-American population, to the degree possible.[7] By the mid-1980s, black plaintiffs were winning voting rights cases outside the South, primarily by calling for replacement of multimember districts by single-member districts in jurisdictions where African-Americans constituted a substantial minority of voters.

Although minority plaintiffs almost always won their cases, the actual electoral results still depended on the organization, energy, and appeal of black candidates and on their ability to mobilize supporters. In addition, even safe seats for black and Hispanic representatives, councilmen, or commissioners did not necessarily mean more power for African-American and Hispanic voters. Abigail Thernstrom, in an extensive analysis of the effects of the Voting Rights Act, quoted a black politician in Anniston, Alabama, that for thirty years the minority vote had been the deciding factor in at-large elections. By gerrymandering districts to win two safe seats for blacks, she argued, African-Americans were likely to give up some influence on the outcome of citywide issues. An African-American judge in Norfolk, Virginia, asked, "How does it help the black community to limit itself to two predominantly black wards and be of no consequence in the rest of the community?"[8]

Some African-Americans began to wonder whether a 65 percent black majority district constituted a waste of black votes in certain situations. In creating a 65 percent black majority in Georgia's Fifth District to elect a black candidate (the percentage commonly used by courts in reapportionment cases), the neighboring Fourth District saw its African-American voting population reduced from 28 to 13 percent, resulting in the defeat of a moderate Democrat by an extreme right-wing Republican. A political scientist from Howard University, Robert Smith, pointed out that it was difficult to see how the outcome served the interests of the black community of Georgia. "It's the responsibility of the black political leadership to register its constituency and mobilize them to turn out. The Court should not do this work for them, because to do so may retard the long-term political development of the black community."[9] In some cases, redistricting could mean elimination of white liberals with seniority on key legislative committees who had strongly supported the interests of African-Americans.

That Hispanics or blacks did not necessarily have to elect one of their own kind to be adequately represented was reflected in actual voting behavior of Hispanics and blacks in many elections, as Thernstrom pointed out.[10] In 1987, the Mexican-American Legal Defense and Education Fund asserted that the inability of Hispanics to win elections to a Colorado county commission even though the county was 41 percent Hispanic (not registered voters but total population) was proof of discrimination against them. MALDEF also argued that failure to elect Hispanics meant that they were inadequately represented in Saguache County. The judge disagreed, stating that since most of the plaintiffs were Democrats and that the three Anglos elected to the commission in the previous ten years also were Democrats, the right of Mexican-Americans to influence decision-making in the county had not been injured.

MALDEF complained that the needs of Hispanics could not be met by elected officials who were non-Hispanic simply because they shared a common political affiliation with Hispanic voters. Such an assumption, said MALDEF, ignored "the differences in issues and problems which confront Hispanics in this country."[11] But it could have been argued, at least as logically, that the needs of Hispanics were not being met simply by the election of Hispanics, since that would ignore the tremendous differences in issues and problems among Hispanic voters, a position implicit in the decision of the federal district court judge.

The replacement of multimember districts with single-member districts might, in the short run, give blacks and Hispanics a greater opportunity to elect more of their own kind, but over time, changing demography, the mobility of blacks to other areas, or an increase in the number of blacks in the city or county as a whole might turn a new single-member district arrangement into one that encouraged whites, with a small voting population concentrated in a few districts, to vote along racial lines. In 1987, a group of seven whites and four African-Americans challenged the multimember system for electing city councillors in Birmingham, Alabama. Because the mayor and six of the nine city council members were black, even though blacks made up only 55 percent of the registered voters, the white plaintiffs (with the agreement of some black plaintiffs) challenged the system as denying them a voice.[12]

The principle that ethnic groups should be represented by their own kind in legislative bodies quite logically would apply to other groups and to appointive bodies, too. Ethnic appointments, even to judicial bodies, have been commonplace in American history, but as a matter of custom and not law. Justice Benjamin Cardozo, the first Jew appointed to the Supreme Court, was replaced by another Jew, Louis D. Brandeis, who was replaced by still another Jew, Felix Frankfurter, and then by Arthur Goldberg and Abe Fortas. But after Fortas resigned, President Nixon did not replace him with a Jew. Justice Thurgood Marshall was chosen by President Lyndon Johnson as the first African-American Supreme Court justice. These were matters of leadership responding to political pressures and perceived inequities. Congress had no intention of establishing by law an African-American or a Jewish or a female seat on the Supreme Court, although legislatures occasionally made provision for minority seating on lesser boards and commissions.[13]

Congress and the courts wanted to compensate for historic state and local practices that often had the effect of discouraging or preventing the political participation of blacks. To do that, they sharply modified the constitutional principle enunciated by the U.S. Supreme Court in 1964 in *Anderson* v. *Martin* that a state may not encourage its citizens to vote for a candidate solely on account of race. Black appellants in East Baton Rouge, Louisiana, had sought election to the school board of their parish in the 1962 Democratic primary election. A Louisiana statute required that in all primary, general, or special elections, nomination papers and ballots must designate the race of candidates for elective office. The law was intended to discriminate against black candidates, in clear violation of the Equal Protection Clause of the Fourteenth Amendment. The Court pointed out that such a statute, by encouraging voters to discriminate on the grounds of race, was unconstitutional, and that it was likely to arouse racial hostility and resentment by those who did not feel they were the beneficiaries of the law. The Court warned against a law "which may decisively influence the citizen to cast his ballot along racial lines." In a system that encourages counting by race, it pointed out that when blacks predominated in a district, they would be favored by a racial designation on the ballot; when whites were in a large majority, they would be favored. "The vice lies . . . in the placing of the power of the state behind a racial classification that induces racial prejudice at the polls."[14]

Eighteen years later, the 1982 amendments did just that. The changing of district lines now was done to encourage voters presumed to have been discriminated against in the electoral process to vote for their own kind. What made the 1962 Baton Rouge system of designating candidates by color illegitimate was the intention of the authorities to help whites avoid voting for blacks. What legitimized the 1982 amendments to the Voting Rights Act was the intention of Congress to elect blacks and Hispanics because the system itself had so long discouraged, even prevented, their election. The case for counting by race in order to elect blacks and Hispanics rested on the proposition that blacks, Mexican-Americans, and Puerto Ricans should be encouraged to participate in elections by assurances that their votes could now lead to election of members of their own group, and that this, in turn, would stimulate political interest and participation. The axiom that participation itself leads to patriotism had been demonstrated throughout American history, and it was reasonable to argue that counting by race was necessary as a temporary spur to greater confidence on the part of blacks and Hispanics in the civic culture itself.

The legal director of the Southwest Voter Registration Education Project pointed out in San Antonio in 1982 that "the fact that we now have more minorities in the city government has created a more positive attitude and increased political participation by the community as a whole."[15]

Clearly, greater participation by African-Americans, Puerto Ricans, and others long excluded or discouraged from politics was and is desirable from a civic culture perspective. The goal was to redress the balance. The implication was that the 1982 amendments would be temporary since permanent racial voting, white, black, or Hispanic, would tend to undermine the civic culture's requirement that citizens vote with concern for the individual rights of all Americans, regardless of race or ethnicity. Of course, that ideal is rarely achieved; nor is special-interest politics limited to racial and ethnic groups. But an American political system with representation based largely on race and ethnicity would be dangerously divisive. It would be particularly harmful to the civic culture to encourage immigrants and their children coming from dozens of countries to think that they could not achieve fair representation unless they could elect one of their own kind. No theory of past compensation or present inequities could justify the 1982 amendments when applied to Hispanic, West Indian, or African immigrants, who make up an increasing proportion of the persons covered by them. To restore the principle that the state should not encourage ethnic voting, Congress would have to return to the standards set by the U.S. Supreme Court in 1980, under which it would be necessary to prove discriminatory intent in order to rationalize the redrawing of district lines to encourage the election of a black or other designated minority group member.

Counting by Race and Making a Living

In some respects, the ability to make a living is the most important civil right of all. Even one's ability to vote, and especially to gain access to good schools and housing, depends upon economic circumstances. By law, polling booths and absentee ballots are now available to all. In reality, sickness, disability, bad education, and other factors associated with poverty have been barriers to registration and voting, and being poor almost always has prohibited the acquisition of decent housing and usually of a good education.

When eight freed African-Americans in Georgia (seven were ministers) were asked by General William T. Sherman and Secretary Edwin M. Stanton in 1864 what it was they wanted most, they thought of economic opportunity. "The best way we can take care of ourselves is to have land, and turn it and till it by our own labor," they told Sherman and Stanton. Acting on his own and illegally, General Sherman set up a system to provide up to forty acres of tillable ground for freed Negro heads of families in localities selected for that purpose, making it clear that no white person should be permitted to reside on such land. Under this major act of affirmative action, 40,000 freedmen received land, but the amnesty granted to southerners by President Andrew Johnson in May 1865 restored all rights of property (except slaves themselves) to those who had participated in the rebellion, whereupon more than 38,000 freed blacks were obliged by the end of 1868 to give up the land they had begun to cultivate. Other efforts to give special economic assistance to freed men and women were substantially over by the end of Reconstruction.[16]

Caste rested on the proposition that blacks were fit only for the most menial jobs. Even by 1960, centuries of caste discrimination and years of insufficient schooling and habits of prejudice kept blacks in those jobs (see chapter 5). The first major legislative step to end economic inequality was passage of Title VII of the Civil Rights Act of 1964 prohibiting discrimination. But the customs of generations could not be overcome by antidiscrimination statutes only, and in 1976 the U.S. Department of Labor stipulated regulations pursuant to executive orders issued by President Lyndon Johnson which not only prohibited federal contractors from discriminating but mandated that "the contractor will take affirmative action to ensure that applicants are employed, and that employees are treated during employment, without regard to their race, color, religion, sex or national origin." Counting by race was mandated when the department said an acceptable affirmative action program must include an analysis of underutilization of minority groups and women in the employ of the contractor and the specification of goals and timetables "to increase materially the utilization of minorities and women, at all levels, and in all segments of his work force where deficiencies exist."[17] Counting by race remedies became commonplace in the 1970s and 1980s; they went further than Title VII, which had stipulated that nothing should be interpreted to require any employer "to grant preferential treatment to any individual or to any group because of the race, color, religion, sex or national origin of such individual or group on account of an imbalance" in an employer's work force.[18] Counting by race, it was decided, did not necessarily constitute illegitimate preferential treatment when undertaken in behalf of those who were members of groups that had long suffered discrimination.

The Railroad Rehabilitation Regulation Reform Act of 1976 included a goal to assign 15 percent of the $6.4 billion authorized for railroad rehabilitation contracts to minority-run enterprises. The following year, the Public Works Employment Act provided that state or local governments use 10 percent of the federal funds allocated to them for public works contracts to procure services or supplies from businesses owned or controlled by Negroes, Spanish-speakers, Orientals, Indians, Eskimos, and Aleuts.[19] With passage of the Surface Transportation and Uniform Reallocation Act of 1987, women were designated, along with blacks, Hispanics, Asians and American Indians, as contractors eligible to receive a portion of the quota of 10 percent of the contracts for federally aided road projects, an innovation to which many leaders of racial and ethnic minority groups reacted angrily.[20]

By 1980, numerical goals and timetables for hiring and promotion in employment and admissions to institutions of higher education and set-asides or goals in contracting constituted major national strategies for promoting equal economic opportunity for African-Americans and other groups. These remedies, involving counting by race, had become controversial, particularly for those who saw them as leading to quotas and reverse discrimination; and by the end of the 1980s, Americans were still divided on the question as to whether it should be permissible to count by race in order to overcome the consequences of three hundred years of racism in employment, higher education, and contracting.

Many Americans made a distinction between quotas, which they saw as rigid requirements, and goals, which obligated employers to a good-faith effort to meet numerical targets. Federal regulations urged "results-oriented procedures" and emphasized the concept of "under-utilization," which was defined as "having fewer minorities or women in a particular job classification than would reasonably be expected by their availability." But the regulations also stated that "goals may not be rigid and inflexible quotas which must be met, but must be targets reasonably attainable by means of applying every good-faith effort to make all aspects of the entire affirmative-action program work."[21]

Those 1971 guidelines presented a problem in enforcement and litigation. To help blacks (and Hispanics and other designated minorities) achieve equality of economic opportunity, employers were obliged to set numerical goals and work toward them in good faith. But how were enforcers to test good faith conclusively unless employers made substantial progress toward meeting those goals? How could employers avoid costly investigations and litigation unless they treated numerical goals as if they were quotas? How, if employers treated numerical goals as quotas, could they possibly avoid giving preferences to minority members and perhaps discriminating against those who were not members of the designated beneficiary groups under their affirmative action plans? How, if employers felt the pressure to hire and promote on the basis of race in order to meet targets they treated as hard and fast, could they avoid violating the Civil Rights Act of 1964, which barred preferential treatment, and—if state and local employers—the Fourteenth Amendment's insistence that no person be denied equal protection of the laws?

The Supreme Court on Counting by Race

These were questions that faced the U.S. Supreme Court throughout the 1970s and 1980s. It was in the cases concerning economic opportunity that counting-by-race remedies raised the most complicated dilemmas for public policy from the different perspectives of the civic culture. In education, the Court decided there was no legal or constitutional barrier to mandatory busing; in housing, it let stand a lower court's decision that quotas in private stock housing, even if federally assisted, were in violation of the law; no constitutional barrier had been set against the 1982 amendments that mandated reconfiguration of political jurisdictions to encourage the election of black and Hispanic representatives. Busing, housing, and voting cases often were contentious, but they did not produce the volume of philosophical speculation and reasoning by the Supreme Court that recurred in cases dealing with economic opportunity.

The philosophical and constitutional questions revolving around counting by race to achieve economic opportunity were first raised in an opinion by Justice William O. Douglas in 1974 in *DeFunis* v. *Odegaard* which had no effect in the law since a majority of the Court declared the case moot.[22] Marco DeFunis, a Phi Beta Kappa graduate of the University of Washington, sued the university's law school on the ground that he had been unconstitutionally denied admission when the law school set aside thirty-seven places for black, Chicano, American Indian, and Filipino applicants without giving him a chance to compete for those slots. Of the thirty-seven students admitted under that set-aside or quota, thirty-six had composite score averages below that achieved by DeFunis (forty-eight nonminority applicants who were accepted, twenty-three of them returning veterans, also had averages below DeFunis's).[23]

Justice Douglas, in a twelve-page opinion, more an essay than a "legal opinion," touched on the principal philosophical questions that would confront the Court in subsequent cases. He first issued the ritual assertion that racial classifications are highly suspect and that enforcement of proportional representation by the state is constitutionally impermissible, pointing out that there are no group rights in the U.S., only individual rights. "The Equal Protection Clause commands the elimination of racial barriers, not their creation in order to satisfy our theory as to how society ought to be organized." Douglas also pointed to the danger of lowering standards to fulfill a numerical goal: "a segregated admissions process creates suggestions of stigma and caste no less than a segregated classroom . . . that is a stamp of inferiority that a state is not permitted to place on any lawyer . . . any state-sponsored preference to one race over another in that competition is in my view 'invidious' and 'violative of the Equal Protection Clause.'"[24]

Douglas also wondered about the dangers and impracticability of picking some groups to be counted by race and not others. The University of Washington, he noticed, counted Filipinos but not Chinese or Japanese. Another school might limit its program to blacks, or to blacks and Chicanos. He wondered what the Court would do when a rejected applicant of Japanese ancestry brought suit to require the University of Washington to include his group, one that certainly had a history of discrimination against it in the state of Washington. Could the Court attempt to assess how grievously each group had suffered from discrimination and allocate proportions accordingly?

Douglas did not, however, conclude that the specific procedure of the University of Washington law school that excluded DeFunis violated the Equal Protection Clause of the Fourteenth Amendment. More facts were needed about how the system worked. He speculated that existing tests, especially the Legal Scholastic Aptitude Tests (LSATs), were so culturally biased as to be totally inadequate for judging the quality and character of applicants of the Yakimas, Muckleshoots, or Nez Percé in the state of Washington: "At least as respects Indians, Blacks, and Chicanos—as well as those from Asian cultures—I think a separate classification of these applicants is warranted, lest race be a subtle force in eliminating minority members because of cultural differences." Douglas acknowledged that a program that considered race as one of several factors in choosing law schools students might be desirable. "Such a program might be less convenient administratively than simply sorting students by race, but we have never held administrative convenience to justify racial discrimination."[25]

When Counting by Race Is Permissible

Douglas was thinking out loud about the dilemmas of counting by race from the perspectives of the civic culture: how can public policy assure genuine equality of opportunity by setting up a system of group entitlements without leading to invidious discrimination against individuals? Over the course of the next fifteen years, the Supreme Court elaborated on the themes discussed by Douglas in ten major cases. Only in four of them did the Court find that counting-by-race remedies were invidious, causing impermissible injury to the white males involved. In the other six cases, majorities of the Court decided that race- (and gender-) conscious remedies were valid under the law and the Constitution to assist persons identified as belonging to groups that had long suffered discrimination.

The first of those six was decided in 1979 when the Court approved a voluntary agreement between the Kaiser Aluminum and Chemical Corporation in Gramercy, Louisiana, and the United Steelworkers of America, in which trainees for a job training program were selected on two separate tracks (on the basis of seniority in each). Half of the openings were reserved for blacks so that the proportion of black craft workers, then 2 percent, could be raised to the proportion of blacks in the area labor force, about 39 percent. A white worker, Brian Weber, sued on the ground that he had not been selected for training although he had more seniority than blacks who were accepted. In a five to two decision (two justices not participating) the Court ruled that the 1964 Civil Rights Act had not been intended to prohibit voluntary, private efforts to end the effects of severe racial discrimination in cases like this where there had been a clear pattern and practice of excluding blacks from craft jobs for decades. Not only was counting by race justified by history and by compelling need, the Court decided, but no obvious and substantial injury had been done to Weber or other whites, since the Kaiser program did not prevent them from advancing (it may have postponed advancement), and since no whites had been discharged to make room for blacks.[26]

Two years later, in *Fullilove* v. *Klutznick,* the Court approved as constitutional a provision of the Public Works Employment Act of 1977 that state and local governments set aside 10 percent of federal funds for public works to procure services or supplies from businesses owned or controlled by persons from minority groups. Three justices thought the set-asides were unconstitutional quotas, leading to a kind of proportional distribution of shares that severely injured the rights of individuals, but three other justices found that taking account of race in this instance was permissible because of the strong interest Congress had in overcoming the effects of discrimination in an industry where it had been substantial. Three others gave this particular program a cautious endorsement. Counting by race was permissible, they reasoned, since Congress limited the scope of its program to favor businesses that had been disadvantaged by discrimination and did not impose a great burden on innocent persons. (There was ample opportunity for white-owned businesses to bid for contracts.)[27]

In 1986, the Court upheld counting by race in two additional important cases. In *Sheet Metal Workers* v. *EEOC,* it approved by a vote of five to four a lower court order requiring a New York City sheet metal workers' union to meet a 29 percent minority membership goal by 1987. Twenty-two years earlier, the New York State Commission for Human Rights had determined that the local had systematically excluded blacks from its apprenticeship program in violation of state law. The union, joined by the Reagan administration, argued that the district court could award preferential relief only to actual victims of unlawful discrimination. The 29 percent minority membership goal—which obviously benefited persons not themselves the victims of such discrimination—did not, insisted the union and the Reagan administration, meet the standard for racial remedies set down in the Civil Rights Act.

Justice William Brennan, writing for the Court, disagreed, pointing out that the Civil Rights Act did not require a union to admit "unqualified" individuals to membership. Counting by race could not be invoked simply to create a balanced work force regardless of qualifications—a kind of proportional representation—declared Brennan. But the Civil Rights Act, by vesting courts "with broad discretion to award 'appropriate' equitable relief to remedy unlawful discrimination, gave them the power to grant relief even to persons who were not themselves the actual victims of discrimination," where the facts of a case justified it.

Justice Brennan did not make crystal clear the criteria which must be present to justify such relief, but there appear to have been three of them: There must be a history of strong, systematic discrimination to be overcome; a remedy must not lead to proportional representation without regard to qualifications of the individual seeking relief; and it must not do palpable injury to innocent persons. On the last point, Brennan concluded that the district court's orders in this case "will have only a marginal impact on the interests of white workers." Justices Byron White and William Rehnquist disagreed, finding that the plan in this case actually constituted proportional representation. It called for "not just a minority membership goal but a strict racial quota that the union was required to attain," maintained White. Rehnquist held fast to the position that only an actual victim of a particular employer's racial discrimination was entitled to benefit from a race-conscious remedy under the Civil Rights Act.[28]

In the second 1986 case, *Firefighters* v. *Cleveland,* the Court held, six to three, that lower federal courts had broad discretion to approve agreements in which employers consented to settle discrimination suits by establishing goals and timetables for minority group members, even though white employees objected. In this case, the city of Cleveland had agreed to settle a job-discrimination suit by black and Hispanic firefighters by temporarily promoting black and Hispanic workers on one list ahead of whites on another list even though the whites might have more seniority and better test scores.

In *Weber,* the Court had approved a purely private contractual agreement to establish race-conscious goals and timetables. In the sheet metal workers' case, the Court found that a court order to the same purpose was permissible under certain circumstances. And in the Cleveland case, Justice Brennan wrote for the majority that a consent decree also had legitimacy and did not violate Title VII of the Civil Rights Act or the Fourteenth Amendment when the race-conscious remedy was reasonable. To the majority, a properly designed remedy to overcome the effects of racial discrimination against blacks was permissible even if it negatively affected innocent persons, as long as the damage was slight—i.e., waiting a little longer to be hired or promoted, as opposed to being laid off or denied admission to a medical school.[29]

To Justice White, in the minority, the Cleveland plan permitted a "kind of leapfrogging" (minorities over senior and better-qualified whites). It was not permissible under Title VII because, he reasoned, "None of the racially preferred blacks in the present case was shown to have been a victim of discriminatory promotion practices: and none of the whites denied promotion was shown to have been responsible or in any way implicated in the discriminatory practices recited in the decree." To Justice Rehnquist, the Civil Rights Act clearly was intended to protect innocent nonminority employees "from the evil of court-sanctioned racial quotas" or from discrimination just as surely as it was intended to prevent discrimination against blacks.[30]

Counting-by-race remedies were approved by the Court in two additional significant 1987 cases. In one, *U.S.* v. *Paradise,* the Court upheld a one-black-for-one-white promotion plan imposed on the Alabama Department of Public Safety by a federal district court after a finding of persistent discrimination by the state of Alabama in hiring and promoting state highway patrolmen. In making its decision, the Court reasoned that the remedy in this case was flexible, temporary, and applicable only if qualified blacks were available.[31] The district court had found that in the thirty-seven year history of the patrol there had never been an African-American trooper and that the only blacks ever employed by the department were non-merit-system laborers. The order to hire one black trooper for each white, a plan approved by the Fifth Circuit Court of Appeals, was to hold until the force became 25 percent black. Once again, a slim majority found that it was permissible to oblige employers to count by race in order to achieve a compelling public purpose, especially when employers had a history of discrimination.

The second major case in 1987, *Johnson* v. *Santa Clara,* dealt with race indirectly, although involving a challenge by a white male to a voluntary affirmative action plan implemented by a public agency. The plaintiff, Paul Johnson, complained that a white woman had been promoted to a road dispatcher position, even though she had placed behind him on an oral examination and he had been recommended for the job by the examining board. The defendant, the Transportation Agency of Santa Clara County, California, made the appointment according to the plan, which called for the work force in all major job classifications to approximate the distribution of women, minorities, and handicapped persons in the county labor market. Johnson claimed that the agency's promotion of the woman over him violated Title VII's prohibition against sex discrimination (he did not claim a violation of his right to equal protection of the laws under the Fourteenth Amendment). The district court had found that Johnson was the better-qualified applicant, and that he had not been promoted only because he was male. The judge reasoned that the affirmative action plan did not meet the standards established by the Supreme Court in *Weber,* but the U.S. court of appeals reversed and was sustained by the Supreme Court by a vote of six to three. The Court held that the plan represented a flexible, case-by-case approach to bringing about improvement in the representation of minorities and women in the agency. (None of the 238 skilled craft positions in the agency had ever been held by a woman.)[32]

A minority of the justices in these cases consistently held that numerical goals and timetables—counting by race—should be permitted only to eliminate actual or apparent discrimination or, at least, the lingering effects of discrimination, and that in no case should explicit injury be done to an innocent person. A majority of the Court held that counting by race was permissible when it did not lead to a fixed system of proportional representation based on race and when injury to innocent persons was remote or slight. The Santa Clara case went beyond any of those that preceded it by validating a race-conscious (or gender-conscious) remedy premised solely on statistical imbalance, with the intention of attaining rough or approximate proportionality. The Alabama state trooper case went further than earlier decisions by permitting judges to order employers to use strict racial quotas temporarily in promotions as well as hiring to counter severe past discrimination against blacks.

When Counting by Race Is Impermissible

An examination of the four major cases in the 1970s and 1980s in which the Court found that counting by race was impermissible shows how the Court has sought to balance the degree and the nature of the discrimination to be rectified and the appropriateness of the plan aimed at rectifying it against the nature and degree of the injury imposed on innocent individuals. In those cases, beginning with the most famous of them, *Regents of the University of California* v. *Bakke* (1978), the Supreme Court said that the injury to innocent white persons was too severe to justify the race-counting remedy put forth by the defendants.

A white student, Allan Bakke, challenged an admissions program at the University of California Medical School at Davis that denied him admission while setting aside sixteen places for minority students against whom he was not allowed to compete. Agreeing with four other justices to constitute a majority of five to four, Justice Lewis Powell found that by reserving sixteen of one hundred openings *exclusively* for qualified minorities, the medical school at Davis had set up a program that discriminated against Bakke in violation of his Fourteenth Amendment rights and the protection against reverse discrimination covered by Title IV of the Civil Rights Act. Powell appeared to be saying that states' race-conscious remedies that did not set up explicit quotas that demonstrably hurt innocent persons would pass the constitutional test and also be acceptable under the Civil Rights Act. Race could be taken into consideration; but it could not be the sole criterion for selecting applicants in this case, even though they met some minimum standard of qualification, because the injury to Bakke was so severe.[33]

Six years later (1984), in *Firefighters* v. *Stotts,* a six-to-three majority struck down a court order that had stopped the layoff of black firefighters hired under a court-approved affirmative action plan. The city of Memphis had entered into an agreement to remedy its fire department's hiring and promotion practices with respect to blacks. When a budgetary cutback required a layoff of personnel, the newly hired black firemen were laid off under the seniority provisions of the union contract. Writing for the majority, Justice Byron White argued that the only way that Title VII permitted courts to order counting by race to keep recently hired blacks and to lay off longtime white employees would be if blacks were "actual victims of illegal discrimination." Here, the injury to innocent white parties—losing their jobs—was too severe to justify counting by race.[34]

In 1986, the same year when the Court upheld counting-by-race remedies in cases involving the Sheet Metal Workers of New York and the firefighters of Cleveland, it ruled five to four that a Jackson, Michigan, school board policy of laying off white teachers before minority-group teachers with less seniority was unconstitutional. In effect, the Court seems to be saying that it was one thing to give a qualified person a job or a promotion in order to advance the cause of racial justice, and to make someone else wait a little while longer on the reasonable assumption that there will be other jobs and opportunities for promotion, but it is quite another matter to take a job away from someone with seniority— and perhaps superior qualifications—in order to apply a broad social remedy, as was the situation in Jackson. The Court ruled that the layoff provision had been too broadly drawn in an attempt to benefit newly hired blacks who were not themselves the direct victims of discrimination, and it had too severe an impact on innocent whites.[35]

The insistence by the Court that counting-by-race remedies be justified by a clear case-related history of discrimination was reiterated in 1989 when, in *Croson* v. *Virginia,* it overturned a Richmond ordinance that required prime contractors to whom the city awarded construction contracts to subcontract at least 30 percent of the dollar amount of the contract to one or more minority-owned and -controlled (51 percent) business enterprises. A white-owned mechanical plumbing and heating contractor, J. A. Croson, challenged the law after it lost a bid to supply toilets for the city jail when it was unable to certify that it would use minority-owned contractors for 30 percent of the $126,000 contract and was denied its request for a waiver of the 30 percent requirement.

The Court's decision, written by Justice Sandra Day O'Connor, did not constitute a full-scale assault on counting by race. It let stand the congressional set-aside program already approved by the Court; its ruling that the Richmond ordinance violated the equal protection clause of the Fourteenth Amendment had no bearing on private affirmative action programs. According to the majority of six justices, several things were wrong with the program. First, the city had never rationalized its ordinance by presenting evidence of discrimination in the Richmond construction industry; second, there was no evidence or even a presumption of discrimination against nonblack minorities—Spanish-speaking, Orientals, Indians, Eskimos, or Aleuts—who were listed specifically as beneficiaries of the program; third, even if one quite reasonably presumed that there had been a history of discrimination against black subcontractors in Richmond, the plan was loosely open to businesses from anyplace outside the Richmond area; fourth, the set-aside in question constituted a rigid quota and not a target or a goal that allowed for flexibility; and fifth, the Court noted that since blacks comprised approximately 50 percent of the population of the city and that five of nine seats on the city council were held by African-Americans, it was especially incumbent on city officials to go beyond making "an amorphous claim" of past discrimination in a particular industry when establishing "an unyielding racial quota." State and local governments, wrote O'Connor, should not be given a license to create a system of racial preferences based on assumptions about how many subcontractors had actually suffered discrimination without educing considerable evidence to support those statistical claims. It was not enough that Richmond had good intentions. The city had to back them up with a much more tightly drawn law and historical context to pass the "strict scrutiny" that the Court now said must be given to any state or local racial or ethnic classification.

The decision in the Richmond case probably left intact a majority of the minority set-aside contracting programs of 190 cities and 36 states, nearly all of which called for flexible targets much closer to the federal government's goal of 10 percent than Richmond's 30 percent. But each city and state would now have to pass the Court's strict scrutiny by linking its program to a history of discrimination against African-Americans or some other designated beneficiary group.

Even that standard was not applied rigorously enough for one of the majority, Justice Antonin Scalia, who, in a concurring opinion, insisted that to establish any racial classification violated the Fourteenth Amendment's equal protection clause no matter how benign the intention, unless it was done specifically to undo a system of unlawful discrimination already in place. The three dissenters in the Richmond case, Justices Marshall, Brennan, and Blackmun, all of whom had dissented in the Bakke case, thought it wrong to apply strict scrutiny at all to racially conscious remedies designated to overcome the legacy of caste. States and localities should be given a large space in designing counting-by-race programs to overcome the effects of historical discrimination, they reasoned, and the fact that less than one percent of the dollars spent by Richmond in construction went to minority-owned firms prior to the introduction of its set-aside program was ample evidence of those effects.

The dissenters spoke to a practical problem. It was particularly difficult for new minority subcontractors to raise the capital to meet bonding requirements imposed by law on them. Although that was true for any new contractor without resources—white, black, Hispanic, or Asian—African-Americans, unless they inherited wealth from their families or other businesses, were disproportionately poor, and it was harder for most of them than for most whites to enter the construction or other businesses. It could also be assumed, although not necessarily proved, that racial prejudice induced negative expectations by whites who were responsible for awarding contracts, and discouraged entrepreneurial efforts by blacks.

Although the majority of the Court may have recognized those realities, it said in the Richmond case, as it did in *Bakke,* that race-conscious remedies must be tailored carefully not only to avoid trampling on the individual rights of any person because of his or her color, but also to establish a clear connecting link between the special claim of discrimination and the remedy proposed to correct it. Justice O'Connor recognized the tension between the Fourteenth Amendment's guarantee of equal treatment to all citizens and the legitimate use of race-based measures to overcome the continuing effects of discrimination, but the Court had shown that there was no easy constitutional calculus by which to judge the cases that came before it.[36]

Shifting majorities had ruled that reasonable numerical goals were permissible when used to overcome a history of blatant discrimination against blacks, the effects of which were widespread and distinctive, even though they benefited African-American or other individuals who had not themselves felt discrimination directly. The implementation of such goals should not, according to the Court, result in rigid quotas or cause obvious and/or substantial injury to innocent persons. If they do, they constitute a kind of classification by race that is impermissible, and, when authorized by state or local governments, they violate the Fourteenth Amendment standard that no state deprive any person who lives and works legally in the U.S. of equal protection of the laws.[37]

The Results of Counting by Race

The main goal of counting-by-race remedies in the field of economic opportunity is to assure that African-Americans can overcome the persistent effects of racism. But many opponents of goals and timetables opposed them not just as a matter of principle but because, they argued, such measures had done little or no good to improve economic opportunity for African-Americans. Economist Thomas Sowell, for example, while acknowledging that blacks with more education and more job experience "have been advancing economically, both absolutely and relative to their white counterparts," doubted that government-imposed goals and timetables have had anything to do with those gains.[38]

Most economic progress for blacks between 1960 and 1990 took place in the 1960s, before the initiation of goals and timetables by the federal government at the end of 1971. The percentage of blacks among all workers employed in government rose from 13.3 to 21.4 between 1960 and 1970 due to strong affirmative action recruitment efforts prior to the imposition of civil service regulations calling for numerical goals linked to timetables.[39] The 1960s also were a time of active recruitment by many colleges of African-Americans, whose enrollment in all colleges and universities went from 340,000 to 814,000 between 1966 and 1974, for the most part without the pressure of federal government guidelines calling for numerical goals.[40] There was also a dramatic change in the recruiting approach of corporations to black colleges between 1960 and 1970. In 1960, Tuskegee and Hampton were the only black colleges where a substantial number of corporations interviewed job candidates among graduating seniors. By 1970, all of the major black universities and colleges were visited by corporate recruiters. The average number of visits increased from 4 to 297 in the decade.[41] These efforts—some of which involved voluntary counting by race—probably accounted for some of the gains made by blacks in the 1970s. The most spectacular gain, perhaps, was the increase in the annual income of college-educated black males relative to their white counterparts, which went from 74 to 98 percent between 1967 and 1978.[42]

The evidence, if inconclusive, suggests that the use of goals and timetables before *and* after 1970 probably helped to speed the integration of blacks into dominant American institutions such as labor unions, police and fire departments, and white-collar positions, and that integration with whites reduced racism and gave millions of African-Americans more hope. One study showed that blacks increased their participation rates in five white-collar categories examined during the 1970s, when counting by race in employment became fairly common.[43] Another study showed a greater relative increase in black male employment in establishments under Office of Federal Contract Compliance rules (affirmative action obligations) than in noncontractor establishments between 1974 and 1980, regardless of establishment size, industry growth, region, occupational structure, corporate structure, and past employment share, and that the positive impact was relatively greater in the more highly skilled occupations.[44] The percentage of African-Americans holding jobs as managers and officials almost doubled between 1972 and 1982, rising from 2.4 to 4.2 percent.[45]

Although it is impossible to prove that some of these gains resulted specifically from the numerical goals–timetables approach, that seems a reasonable inference. For example, in the Philadelphia construction industry, where the concept of numerical goals and timetables was first applied, the percentage of minority construction workers rose from 1 to 12 between 1969 and 1981.[46] In the public sector, the gains of African-American executives were particularly strong after the Civil Service Commission instituted goals linked to strict timetables in 1971, setting targets for occupations and grade levels where minority employment was found to be disproportionately low in relation to the potential supply of qualified minority group members in the work force.

Voluntary programs, consent decrees, and compliance orders setting numerical goals contributed to a large increase of African-American public employees at every level of government. The number of black police officers nationwide, for example, increased from 24,000 to 43,000 between 1970 and 1980.[47] The conservative white Republican mayor of Indianapolis, William Hudnut, who in 1986 resisted an attempt by the Justice Department to have that city (and fifty other jurisdictions) abandon the numerical goals–timetables approach, argued that counting by race was responsible for the increase in the percentage of black firefighters in Indianapolis from 7.9 in 1975 to 13.3 in 1985, and of black police officers from 9.8 to 14.0. Hudnut maintained that minorities and women "will be excluded just by the very nature of the system itself whereby for so long practically one hundred percent of the jobs went to white males without the imposition of numerical goals."[48] The habits of racial discrimination could not be broken, he maintained, without race-conscious remedies.

It also seems highly probable that goals linked to timetables helped to double the percentage of black officers in the U.S. armed services between 1971 and 1981 from 2.3 to 5.5, and played a major role in stimulating the increase in the proportion of blacks in the National Guard from 1 to 17 percent between 1971 and 1980, and of black officers in the National Guard from 2.5 to 8 percent between 1978 and 1980.[49] It is not as likely that numerical goals and timetables were major factors in the increase in black enrollments at elite colleges and universities and in professional schools as in police or fire departments, but counting-by-race programs probably were significantly responsible for the increase in African-American enrollment in law schools between 1969 and 1979, when the percentage went up from 3.0 to 4.2, and in medical schools, where black enrollment rose from 2.7 percent in 1968 to 5.7 in 1980.[50]

Five or six years after most affirmative action numerical goal programs were instituted, the Louis Harris organization, in a 1978 survey commissioned by the National Conference of Christians and Jews, asked blacks and whites a series of questions about racial attitudes and behaviors identical to those asked in a 1963 Harris poll. The most impressive finding was that whites who worked directly with blacks were significantly freer of prejudice than those who did not. Overall, the percentage of whites who indicated strong personal antagonism to having black neighbors dropped from 47 to 14 between 1963 and 1978, and the percentage of those who said they were either already living in proximity to black neighbors or would have no objection to doing so rose from 36 to 60.[51]

The growth in the integration of blacks and whites, attributable at least in part to counting by race, may also be responsible for increasing the confidence of blacks in their own country, taking them further from the anguished doubts of W. E. B. Du Bois and closer to the optimism of Martin Luther King, Jr. Surveys in the 1980s showed that an increasing number of blacks shared King's belief that the dream of a land of opportunity for all regardless of skin color could become a reality. In 1969, the National Advisory Commission on Civil Disorders (the Kerner Commission) warned that the nation was splitting in two, blacks and whites.[52] But by 1984 a CBS News poll of registered voters reported that 39 percent of black respondents said they believed "most whites want racial equality," and 72 percent said they believed "Democrats will nominate a black for President within thirty years."[53] In a 1985 survey by the Center for Media and Public Affairs, 66 percent of rank-and-file African-Americans polled believed that blacks were making progress and not going backward (61 percent of black leaders said backward).[54]

Counting by Race and the Civic Culture

By 1989, there was sufficient evidence to conclude that counting by race had helped to produce a more integrated work force and better access for blacks to housing, education, and political power, and that the United States was a more strongly unified nation than it had been before such race-conscious remedies were adopted. The evidence that race relations improved during the period of counting by race rather than becoming worse, as many opponents of affirmative action had predicted, was abundant. But the problems raised by counting by race were as severe in 1989 as they were in 1971.

A majority of Americans consistently disagreed with the Supreme Court that counting by race (or gender) was a legitimate method of preventing discrimination or making up for past discrimination. The Democratic platform in 1984 endorsed numerical goals, timetables, and other verifiable measurements for demonstrating equality of opportunity for blacks, but a majority of Democrats (and every other major population group except blacks) disapproved of the decision in the Santa Clara case that employers might promote women and minorities ahead of better qualified men and whites to achieve a more equitable distribution of minorities and women in the work force.[55]

Despite their opposition to counting by race, a large majority of the American people approved of softer forms of affirmative action by 1988. In 1978, only 36 percent of Americans agreed with the statement that "if there are no affirmative action programs helping women and minorities in employment and education, then these groups will continue to fail to get their share of jobs and higher education, thereby continuing past discrimination in the future." But ten years later, 71 percent agreed and only 27 percent disagreed. Three out of four Americans in the late 1980s approved of federal laws requiring affirmative action programs in employment and education, "provided there are no rigid quotas," and four out of five believed that it made sense "to give special training and advice to women and minorities so they can perform better on the job (as long as there were no 'rigid quotas')."[56] Overall, the results showed that Americans had moved substantially toward pro–affirmative action policies in the 1970s and 1980s, as long as they did not involve counting by race to achieve a numerical goal according to a fixed timetable (a quota).

There were many reasons to oppose counting by race from a civic culture perspective. One of them, that counting by race was an invitation to fraud, was especially applicable in the awards of contracts to minority designated firms. Several cases emerged in which a member of the entitled group was used as a front for a white male contractor or owner of a business, particularly under state programs. In New York State, an investigation found that dozens of construction companies engaged in such fraud.[57] In 1985, the Federal Highway Administration's monitoring of contracts in the six-state New England region found that twenty of the forty-two firms reviewed had "ineligible or questionable" certification as being legitimately owned by members of minority groups or women.[58] So widespread was the abuse nationally that the U.S. Civil Rights Commission in 1986 called for a suspension of federal programs that reserved money or contracts for businesses owned by blacks, Hispanics, or women. The commission concluded that the programs, under which federal agencies awarded more than $5 billion in 1985, with at least sixteen states setting numerical goals for the purchase of goods and services, was marked by "rampant corruption."[59]

Although Congress did not act on the proposal for a moratorium in the set-aside programs, two federal court decisions raised questions about such programs in trying to help the companies of blacks and other designated groups. In 1987, before the 1989 Court decision in the Richmond case, the U.S. Circuit Court of Appeals in San Francisco struck down an ordinance that conferred a 10 percent set-aside and a 5 percent bidding preference for minority-owned business on the ground that such preferences were not justified by findings of past discrimination. In the same year, a federal district court judge decided that a set-aside program established by Fulton County, Georgia, was unconstitutional when applied in a situation where there had been no previous record of discrimination.[60] One of the most bizarre examples of abuse came in 1988, when it was revealed that two men were suspended from the Boston fire department for having pretended they were black in order to benefit from a 1974 court order to desegregate the fire department and a second court order in 1982 requiring that the percentage of minority members on the force be maintained despite layoffs due to budgetary stringency. Since the results of these court orders led to an integrated fire-fighting force in fourteen years, the defenders of the program argued that unusual instances of fraud should not tarnish a strategy whose overall results had been effective.[61]

The ease with which fraud infiltrated set-aside programs may have been one reason for their apparent vulnerability before the courts in the late 1980s. An egregious example of fraud occurred after the Wedtech Corporation, a South Bronx military contractor founded by a businessman born in Puerto Rico, was awarded $250 million in military contracts under the set-aside program of the Small Business Act (1968), which authorized that government procurement contracts be set aside for companies owned and controlled by women and members of minority groups without competitive bidding. Wedtech became the subject of five state and federal criminal investigations tracking allegations that its executives bribed federal officials and conspired to obtain contracts through fraud and misrepresentation.[62] The Wedtech fraud could easily have occurred without a set-aside program, and defenders of such programs pointed out that even spectacular examples of abuse ought not obscure the many successes they produced. The programs, used by more than four thousand minority-owned businesses since it started, continued to receive support from the Reagan administration and leading members of Congress.[63] As was true with respect to counting by race in employment, the programs were justified on balance as a way to achieve genuine equality of opportunity for many African-Americans and others designated as disadvantaged who otherwise would not have been able to succeed.

Although fraud undermined confidence in set-aside programs, there was a more serious theoretical problem from the perspective of the civic culture with respect to all of the equal opportunity programs that linked numerical goals to timetables. It was the suspicion that such programs in many cases tended toward a kind of proportional representation that reflected demographics but not the varying interests and talents of different population groups. Proportionality made some sense in fire departments and police departments. But, as Frederick Douglass had pointed out in another context in an earlier time, employment in most occupations cannot be fixed by proportional representation for ethnic groups in defiance of the unequal distribution of experiences, interests, and talents found among members of them. In answering a letter from another black leader, Martin Delany, who had argued that blacks should be appointed to government departments according to their population, Douglass wrote, "Upon your statistical principle, the colored people of the United States . . . should constitute one-eighth of the poets, statesmen, scholars, authors, and philosophers of the country." Calling such a system absurd, he wondered why it would be applied to Negroes only and not to Germans, Irish, and other nationalities. "Now, my old friend, there is no man in the United States who knows better than you do that equality of numbers has nothing to do with equality of attainments."[64]

Carried to its logical conclusion, proportional representation in occupations seemed absurd. One Chinese-American assistant professor of history complained that racism channeled Chinese into science and engineering (Asian-Americans provided 6.6 percent of American scientists with doctorates in 1985). The logic for that position would have been to establish numerical goals for Asian-Americans in graduate programs in the humanities, for Polish-Americans as theoretical mathematicians, and Jewish-Americans as veterinarians, all occupations in which those groups were underrepresented, or put limitations on the number of Chinese-Americans who might be admitted to graduate programs in science and engineering in order to admit more Hispanics and blacks.[65]

One did not have to be a student of cultural anthropology to know that there were differences in aptitude, inclination, curiosity, and achievement based upon different cultural traditions and values as well as historical experience. The fact that Norwegian-Americans dominated the tugboat business in New York and that Jews were disproportionately represented as professors in the social sciences and medicine and that

Chinese-Americans succeeded far out of proportion to their numbers in engineering and applied mathematics had little to do with racism but resulted from a combination of cultural and other factors. Defenders of counting by race did not advocate strict proportional representation, but argued that without goals and timetables, employers would slip into well-established habits of racism that denied blacks and other designated minorities genuine equality of opportunity. Remedies were not aimed at overcoming the different proclivities of members of one group or another for certain occupations growing out of cultural traditions and values, but at breaking up patterns of exclusion established by historical oppression and discrimination.

The most difficult issue revolved around the possibility that the use of group statistics might lead to discrimination against white males, denying them equal protection of the law. Reverse discrimination, or what Nathan Glazer called "affirmative discrimination," resulted when someone was not hired or promoted or was laid off solely because of group characteristics. Essentially, critics of counting by race charged that such an action violated the core principle of the civic culture—reward for individual merit, ability, or achievement without regard to group characteristics. Plaintiffs in litigation charging reverse discrimination did not quarrel with the objectives of affirmative action, but claimed that, as individuals, they were unfairly victimized by it. Bryan Weber was not convinced by any theory of social justice or argument about the national interest. It did not matter to him personally that white males for centuries had received preferential treatment in hiring for all kinds of jobs, an advantage based on skin color and not merit. Because of his having to wait longer for admission to an apprentice program, he and his family were hurt, at least to some degree. It was little compensation to him that the Supreme Court ruled that its decision was limited to voluntary, private affirmative action programs undertaken to correct long-standing racial imbalances. When it ruled that the program did not unnecessarily trammel the interests of white employees, Weber's grievance probably was not assuaged at all.

The question of affirmative discrimination was sharpened when individuals were passed over because of group characteristics even though they scored comparatively well on competitive tests. It must have given little comfort to Paul Johnson in the Santa Clara Transportation case to learn that he did not get the job because of his gender and skin color despite his superior test scores. Society clearly had made it difficult, indeed impossible, for women to take skilled craft positions in the Santa Clara Transportation Agency before the adoption of the affirmative action plan. But to Johnson, who was not promoted despite his seniority, his superior experience as a road dispatcher, and his higher score on an examination, the fact that the affirmative action plan did not involve hard and fast quotas and had been adopted voluntarily probably made little personal difference. The Court's view that the Santa Clara plan was not unduly burdensome to white males in general probably seemed irrelevant to him as an individual.[66]

Another serious problem with counting by race was the perception, primarily among whites, that it rewarded blacks who were not qualified for the positions they held. From this point of view, counting by race would lead to a debasing tokenism against which many blacks and Hispanics complained. Harvard's professor of political economy Glen C. Loury wrote about his experience as an African-American professional whose achievements were diminished because of the perception that his success was due to affirmative action.[67] The Mexican-American writer Richard Rodriguez described his history as both beneficiary and victim of affirmative action. As someone who was recruited, promoted, and rewarded for being a Hispanic, he also was aware of being pigeonholed, suspected, and disparaged because of the assumption that he had been rewarded beyond his abilities.[68]

No one argued that merit ought to be disregarded in hiring, promotion, and layoffs or in the letting of contracts. The arguments in *Weber, Johnson,* and many other cases rested on the conviction that numerical goals should reward only those who were qualified, although in some cases they might be marginally less qualified than white males. Those who advocated the use of numerical goals and timetables did so on the quite reasonable premise that broad, sweeping measures had to be undertaken in order to overcome the legacy of slavery and caste and make equality of opportunity a reality for African-Americans. Most of them also assumed that such programs, by helping to produce a more integrated work force and better access for African-Americans to housing, education, and political power, would make the nation stronger and more unified.[69]

As the decade of the 1980s closed, race-conscious remedies were still established as law and widely in practice. More than 60 percent of firms in the U.S. employing more than one thousand persons used written affirmative action plans that incorporated goals and timetables (more than 50 percent for those that employed fewer than one thousand). The overturn of the Richmond set-aside program in 1989 forced states and localities to reshape their plans more carefully in order to show how they were intended to overcome a pattern of discrimination and also to avoid the appearance of hard and fast quotas. From the point of view of most businesses, the Santa Clara decision was much more important than the Richmond case, and it constituted a signal that appropriately designed programs would pass under the Civil Rights Act and the Constitution, a sign that most of them welcomed.[70]

Although quotas were not accepted by the courts or by public opinion, most Americans supported affirmative action programs that brought qualified African-Americans and others to skilled jobs and professions who would not have obtained them otherwise because of racism. Possibly one reason for the building of confidence in such programs was that the Supreme Court turned down those plans that, it said, did establish quotas and/or resulted in a denial of equal protection of the laws to individual whites, as in the California medical school program, the Richmond set-asides, the Memphis fire-fighter layoff plan, and the Jackson, Michigan, school board program to lay off white teachers.

The civic culture had little meaning, given the history of American slavery and caste, unless Americans made broad attempts, however imperfect, to overcome the effects of that history. But its basic premise—a guarantee of equal rights to all, including poor and otherwise disadvantaged whites—would be vitiated by programs that denied those rights to anyone because of skin color, gender, religion, or ethnicity. Thus, affirmative action programs often had to rely on statistics, but heavy reliance on them was suspect and worthy of strict scrutiny from a constitutional point of view. Should public opinion perceive counting-by-race remedies as undermining the civic culture's promise of reward for merit (including achievement, experience, and other factors) regardless of color or creed, the confidence of whites and many blacks in the essential fairness of such programs would be undermined.

Counting by Race and the Problem of Standards

Perhaps no factor undermines confidence in counting-by-race remedies as much as the charge that they undermine standards. The question of standards cannot be avoided in any discussion of affirmative action. Blacks as well as whites—and most people—want to be assured that those in positions of responsibility are qualified.[71] The issue is difficult partly because it is not always easy to determine what constitutes qualification for many positions. Tests, which are not necessarily related to performance, are not the only way to measure qualifications. Yet, as imperfect as they are, they are a better alternative to filling positions or making promotions than nepotism, racism, or sexism. The assault on racism in the U.S. led, in many cases, to a redesigning of tests to eliminate racial bias in them. New York City provided an example of how tests could be improved to bring more qualified nonwhite teachers into the classroom without jeopardizing standards. In 1969, only 1 percent of the licensed public school principals in the city's schools were African-Americans, and only one principal was Hispanic (even though a large majority of the student body was nonwhite or Hispanic). Selection policies were changed under a court order to combine state certification in school administration with on-the-job evaluations instead of written examinations. As a consequence, the proportion of African-American principals rose to 19.9 percent. The court then authorized New York City to reinstate the qualifying examinations, which were changed by the city's board of examiners to ensure that all questions were job-related. The combination of tests with other affirmative action strategies resulted in the appointment of many capable black and Hispanic principals.[72]

How far could one go in throwing out tests in order to achieve numerical goals? In 1981, the Texas legislature required students to pass a test of twelfth-grade reading, writing, and arithmetic skills as a condition of admission to a state-approved teacher-education program. Only 34 percent of the Latinos and 23 percent of the blacks who took the exam passed, compared to 73 percent of the whites. U.S. District Judge William W. Justice, who ruled the test discriminatory, concluded reasonably that the failure of the minority groups was a result, at least in part, of past discrimination in the Texas elementary and secondary system. Yet, the Texas education department believed just as reasonably that those who teach children arithmetic and writing in high school ought themselves to be able to perform at the twelfth-grade level. The Texas state director of the League of United Latin American Citizens was correct when he asserted that "not everyone is capable of taking tests"; but abandonment of tests means the utilization of some other method of selection to determine qualifications.[73]

The federal government and black, Hispanic, and women's groups in New York City charged in 1981 that police department examinations for officers who aspired to become sergeants discriminated against minority-group members. A new test sought to minimize the importance of reading and writing abilities by relying on videotaped scenes of police officers responding to various emergencies, but candidates still had to show that they understood such words as "relevant," "disposition," "unsubstantiated," "tactfully," and "interested party." The results were disappointing for black and Hispanic candidates, who did not do nearly as well as the white police officers tested. The Guardians Association, representing black police officers, called the exam "racially biased," and an attorney with the Puerto Rican Legal Defense Fund charged that although he had not seen the exam, he believed it probably was "culturally biased." But the consultants who designed the test in order to eliminate bias from it and from the police department argued that requiring mastery of basic, standard English to function as a police sergeant in New York City was reasonable and not racially or culturally biased at all.[74]

The question of tests gained increasing attention from African-American educators and social scientists in the 1980s. In one study, concerned about the high rate of attrition of African-Americans training to be pilots and navigators in the armed forces, the author concluded that one factor that bears on performance in flight training is a candidate's academic background, and that those who graduate from college with less than a strong proficiency in verbal and quantitative skills would probably have difficulty keeping up with the rigorous curriculum and rapid pace of flight training, "whether they are blacks or whites."[75]

The NAACP and others were rightly concerned that the use of tests was often insufficient for evaluating merit in the competition for jobs or promotion. One researcher reported that "although teacher competency tests are meant to screen out incompetent teachers, studies have not found any consistent relationship between scores on the teacher tests and measures of performances in the classroom."[76] But the fact that tests are not perfect in determining qualification in many cases could not lead to their abandonment. From a civil culture perspective, the historic methods of selective recruitment still prevalent in many situations—favoritism for relatives, friends, whites, males, and political allies—were not preferable over constant efforts to improve tests and better preparation for all Americans to pass them.[77]

Many African-Americans passed tests outstandingly—as did Lieutenant Robert O. Goodman, one of 260 blacks among 18,000 Navy fliers in 1984, who gained national attention that year when his plane was shot down over Lebanon. In Indianapolis, twenty-two-year-old Darryl A. Hayden topped all 1,250 black and white applicants in the 1985 exam for fire fighters.[78] The setting of numerical goals by the U.S. Navy and the Indianapolis fire department probably led to vigorous recruitment among blacks. But neither Goodman nor Hayden would have been heard from had they not performed exceptionally well on reasonable tests related to the work they were expected to do.

Most jobs are more like Hayden's than Goodman's. They do not require a strict set of objective testing criteria to determine merit. There was no sense in assigning points to an African-American candidate for pilot of an F-16 in an effort to fulfill an affirmative action goal. Affirmative action for black navy fliers, as for ballet dancers, was necessarily limited to special recruitment and training efforts. But affirmative action for fire fighters, machinists, computer operators, and candidates for dental school included numerical goals and permitted race to be counted as one of many factors in attempting to meet them, along with insisting on basic qualifications.

Some African-American educators and parents welcomed the opportunity for black youngsters to have the chance to measure their own progress through performance on exams. In Massachusetts in 1985, for example, black students showed much more improvement in all basic skills than white children in the same schools and at the same grade levels. At the national level, black students' aptitude test scores on the SATs went up seven points between 1982–83 and 1983–84, while the increase for all groups together was only four points. (The gap was still close to 100 points between blacks and all students: 91 on the verbal, 98 on the math.)[79] Standardized aptitude tests can help identify capable black and other minority group students who have not performed particularly well in high school. In San Antonio and its suburbs, where the schools have a large Mexican-American enrollment, high school juniors were encouraged to take the Preliminary Scholastic Aptitude Test (PSAT) without having to pay the regular fee. The program identified and counseled students with relatively high aptitude and low achievement, and encouraged them to go on to college.[80]

Who Should Be the Beneficiaries of Affirmative Action?

The inclusion of Asians, Pacific Islanders, Puerto Ricans, and other Hispanics as groups to be counted toward meeting numerical goals may have complicated and weakened the nation's efforts to deal with what continued to be its most fundamental problem: the consequences for native-born black Americans of three hundred years of racism. The Thirteenth, Fourteenth, and Fifteenth Amendments, which provide the constitutional basis for strong affirmative action measures, were meant to deal only with blacks: the Civil Rights Act of 1964, which is the progenitor of other contemporary civil rights legislation and regulations authorizing affirmative action, also was intended to remedy the effects of enslavement and subsequent segregation of black Americans.

There was confusion as to which theory—restitution for past discrimination, remedy for present inequities, or the need to develop role models—justified the inclusion of nonblacks in counting-by-race programs, as in the Richmond set-aside case. Japanese-Americans, who suffered discrimination, particularly on the West Coast, were included in the protected class of Asians, although by 1980 they had the highest median family income of any ethnic group in California. In Hawaii, where Japanese-Americans dominated political life by the 1970s, Democratic party leaders had to make a special effort to include at least sixteen Caucasians in Hawaii's delegation to the Democratic national convention in 1974 to meet the party's affirmative action goals. In New Mexico, light-skinned Mexican-Americans whose families had been successful *rancheros* for many years were also included. Counted among the Hispanics were German-Chileans, Judeo-Argentines, and U.S. citizens from twenty Latin American republics, Spain, and Puerto Rico, regardless of their economic circumstances and educational backgrounds.

Never before in the history of the U.S. did immigration bring such a high proportion of well-educated professional and technical workers as in the 1970s and 1980s. Yet, more than 75 percent of the immigrants fit into one or more of the designated beneficiary classes (gender and Asian, black and Hispanic). In Miami, Cuban-Americans probably achieved political, economic, and cultural success more quickly than any immigrant group in any other city in U.S. history. Yet, they were included in the beneficiary class of Hispanics under most affirmative action programs. In the country generally, Asian immigrants and their children in the aggregate were doing well economically, although many of them, particularly refugees, were below the poverty line. But even the most educated and successful could be counted in trying to fill numerical goals according to a timetable.[81] A Peruvian of middle-class background who emigrated originally from Italy could be the beneficiary of affirmative action, but a poor Italian immigrant who came directly to the U.S. could not. One example of how problematic classifying by race can become took place in 1979 when the Small Business Administration was asked by the Hasidim of Brooklyn to designate Hasidic Jewish-Americans as a minority group. The SBA determined that the Hasidic Jews were a socially and economically disadvantaged group who met all of the criteria necessary to be designated as a group under the agency's affirmative action programs. The only thing that kept the Hasidim from making the list is that they are a religious group, and ultimately the SBA decided that it might violate the Constitution's insistence on neutrality toward religion if they were included.[82]

Arguments to include ethnic groups other than blacks in affirmative action programs rested on the proposition that all persons of color historically were the victims of discrimination. Against that premise was the argument that the children of Asian and Hispanic immigrants had choices available to them which did not exist for African-Americans (see chapter 7). Despite constraints of poverty and prejudice, the law did not pervasively and systematically enforce discrimination against any group of American-born children except blacks. Even the Chinese, harassed by legislation aimed specifically at them, were able to make choices denied to most blacks. The descendants of Mexicans who lived in what became U.S. territory following the Texas annexation and the Mexican War could claim a legacy of colonization, but their numbers were a small fraction of the Mexican immigrants and their descendants who came subsequent to those events. In most states, brown-skinned Mexicans could eat in restaurants for whites only. Mexicans and Asians could ride in whites-only streetcars and trains in the South and attend first-class theaters, while well-educated, prominent African-Americans could not.[83] Immigrants and their children usually could intermarry with whites; African-Americans were barred from intermarriage by statute in most states, even when they were of the lightest color.

The historic experience of African-Americans also could be distinguished from other groups covered by affirmative action plans—native American Indians and other indigenous peoples, Puerto Ricans, and women. The issue of numerical goals and timetables under the Civil Rights Act and subsequent executive orders was virtually irrelevant with respect to Indians, Hawaiians, Aleuts, and Eskimos. Recognition of Indians as a special beneficiary class preceded those executive orders. For example, in 1974 the Supreme Court ruled that Congress did not intend the antidiscrimination provisions of the Equal Opportunity Act of 1972 to repeal a provision of the Indian Reorganization Act of 1934 that specifically stipulated employment preferences for qualified Indians in the Bureau of Indian Affairs.[84] The preferences, like other special benefits conferred on Indians with respect to religious practices, land, education, housing, employment, and health care, were granted to Indians as members of "quasi-sovereign tribes," and not because they had been kept in certain kinds of jobs as a result of caste, although in the twentieth century there was considerable job discrimination against them (see chapter 11).

Like Native Americans, Puerto Ricans had been colonized by white Americans, but they have voted repeatedly for commonwealth status in Puerto Rico (most federal benefits without federal taxation) and ever since 1916 have been citizens, free to live anywhere in the continental United States. Although not subject to the coercive restraints of formal systems of sojourner pluralism, as were Asians and Mexican-Americans, they also suffered from discrimination and from the liabilities of being sojourners. By the 1980s, they constituted the most economically disadvantaged of all minority groups except for Native Americans (see chapter 25). But counting-by-race remedies probably did little to help the poorest Puerto Ricans, even though the argument that they were useful in eroding past habits of prejudice and discrimination probably was as valid for Puerto Ricans as for African-Americans.

The anomalies presented in counting by gender began to make gender-based goals and timetables controversial in the 1980s. Not only were some young white females advantaged by family wealth and education, but a large number of them were favored compared to blacks; immigrant women actually achieved earnings equal to those of native-born women sooner than immigrant men did relative to U.S.-born males.[85] Counting by gender in higher education became a moot issue, for the most part, by the middle of the 1980s, when at least a quarter of those entering prestigious medical, law, and business schools were women. But work-role stereotyping by gender was still widespread, and affirmative action pressures probably helped to reduce it. The number of women coal miners increased significantly after a complaint was filed with the Office of Federal Contract Compliance Programs in 1978, and the coal industry was targeted for careful inspection of its employment practices. In 1975, there had been no female coal miners in the U.S., but by 1980, 3,295 women were coal miners, and 8.7 percent of all coal miners hired that year were women.[86] Most women probably were much less concerned with counting-by-gender remedies to prevent discrimination in employment than with their need for more support as principal care givers for the young and the old. More and better day care facilities and better pay for professional care givers; paid leaves for parents after giving birth and to care for hospitalized children; stronger nutritional, health, and income supports for women, children, and families; and more flextime and part-time employment for women (and men) all demanded urgent attention.[87]

The question of who should benefit by statistically based affirmative action programs was further complicated by the relative economic success of black immigrants to the United States.[88] But for all the ambiguities involved in the administration and enforcement of affirmative action programs, no popular political movement developed in the U.S. in the 1980s to restrict such programs to American-born blacks. As the 1980s closed, public opinion seemed generally satisfied that the struggle to eliminate racism, sexism, and prejudice against the handicapped in economic matters had been aided by race-, gender-, and handicap-conscious remedies. By making the rights of blacks the common concern of all, the civic culture had been strengthened. No political group called for permanent group entitlements. Those members of the Supreme Court who had been strongest in their advocacy of temporary group entitlements in the 1980s—Justices Marshall, Brennan, and Blackmun—never wavered in maintaining that group-conscious measures based on race, ethnicity, or gender should be considered as temporary remedies to protect the individual rights of those affected by America's history of exclusion and discrimination based on color and gender. In the Bakke case, which ruled against quotas, Brennan argued in his dissent that human equality is linked "with the proposition that differences in color or creed, birth or status, are neither significant nor relevant to the way in which such persons are treated." Justice Marshall, in his dissent, repeating Martin Luther King, Jr., said that he wanted to live in a society "in which the color of a person's skin will not determine the opportunities available to him or her," and Justice Blackmun called for a society in which "persons will be regarded as persons," without regard to color or ethnicity. The protection of individual and not group rights was the basis for their positions and of the civic culture.

It was also Blackmun who said, with the agreement of nearly all his colleagues at some point, that in order to get beyond race it may be necessary to take race into account. That is the justification for counting by race. But by the late 1980s, it had become clear, as William Julius Wilson pointed out in 1981, that affirmative action programs, "which have benefited the more educated and trained blacks, are not designed to deal with the unique problems of the black poor—problems that have devastatingly affected the makeup of underclass families."[89] Richard Rodriguez also was concerned that Mexican-Americans who worked as menial laborers were not helped by affirmative action.[90] One scholar speculated that statistically based remedies had a negative effect on the development of "highly targeted, color-blind programs designed to increase human capital and provide positive economic incentives for employers to incorporate minorities within the primary labor market."[91] The increasing irrelevance of counting-by-race remedies to the problems of the ethno-underclass did not make the problems obsolete, as tens of thousands of African-Americans could testify, but there was increasing evidence that the strongest and most pervasive barriers to economic opportunity in the U.S. were based at least as much on class as on race or ethnicity. Counting-by-race remedies probably would fade from the American ethnic landscape over time. Some will succeed to the point of being unnecessary. Those that include blatant quotas or clearly invade individual rights will be ended or changed. Continued large-scale immigration may force the modification of some programs. And the need to establish national priorities to deal with the many problems of ethno-underclasses (see chapter 25) will cause a shift in attention away from counting-by-race remedies by advocates of social justice to remedies that address the pressing needs of the persistently poor.

Chapter Twenty-Four

RESPECTING DIVERSITY, PROMOTING UNITY
The Language Issue

T HE NEW federal Constitution said nothing about language, but
Noah Webster, creator and conservator of American English, wrote
in 1789 that "our political harmony is therefore concerned in a
uniformity of language."[1] Webster was partly right. English became the
public language of almost all citizens, but non-English-speaking immigrants, and sometimes their children and grandchildren, too, maintained
their ancestral languages in family, church, and neighborhood.

Non-English-speakers from Europe typically established parochial schools
and churches in which German, Swedish, Norwegian, and other languages were spoken, periodically arousing anxieties among English-
speaking Americans that German immigrants did not want to belong to
the American nation. An editorial in the *North American Review* urged
the Germans to speak the language their neighbors could understand,
"the language in which the laws of the land . . . are made and administered."[2] As German immigration increased in response to an open immigration policy in the 1830s and 1840s, midwestern states began to
accommodate the needs of the newcomers. Several legislatures passed
laws permitting German to be taught in public schools in districts where
large German populations resided.[3] Only Pennsylvania permitted establishment of German schools with all instruction in German. In Wisconsin,
instruction was sometimes conducted either exclusively in German or in
both German and English in newly created school districts with large
German populations.[4]

Not until the nineteenth century were laws enacted to ensure the pri-
macy of English. In 1882, the federal government passed the Pendleton
Act establishing the civil service merit system; it limited federal government employment to citizens who could pass an examination in English.
That stipulation spread quickly to cover jobs in local governments.[5] In
1906, congressional amendments to the Naturalization Act were passed
to require petitioners for citizenship to be able to speak English.[6] Many
state and local legislators became concerned about the persistent use of
foreign languages. Both Wisconsin and the city of Chicago in 1899 banned
instruction in parochial as well as in public elementary schools in any

language other than English.[7] English literacy tests as a requirement for suffrage passed in one state after another. In the South, the intention was principally to keep blacks from voting. In the North and West, the restriction was aimed at non-English-speakers from Europe. A law passed in 1918 in New York State, where the largest number of immigrants lived and worked, required the establishment of night schools and employer-maintained schools with compulsory attendance of every employed minor sixteen to twenty-one who did not speak, read, or write English in order to correct those deficiencies. Much of the antiforeign feeling let loose during the First World War focused on the language question. But an editorial in the *Syracuse Herald* explained the purpose of the new law as one to "stimulate the taking out of citizenship papers, and to aid in other ways the assimilation of immigrants." Comparable laws were passed in dozens of other states, some providing evening education, others a comprehensive Americanization program.[8]

To former president Theodore Roosevelt, English was such a critical precondition of membership in the polity that he would require every immigrant to learn English, with instruction free. "If after five years he has not learned it," said Roosevelt, "let him be returned to the country from which he came."[9] Roosevelt's view was extreme for the time, but most Americans probably believed that instruction in the public schools should be in English only, since by 1923 thirty-four states required it for all elementary schools.[10]

As noted in chapter 3, the Supreme Court overturned statutes that prohibited the teaching of non-English languages as second and third languages;[11] it did not approve of the prohibition of Japanese or any other private foreign language schools.[12] But it upheld English literacy tests as a condition for voting, even after the Second World War, as long as such tests had no discriminatory intent.[13] The naturalization requirement of an ability to speak English was strengthened in 1950 by Congress with additional requirements to read and write as well as speak "words in ordinary usage in the English language."[14]

In the 1960s, the policy emphasis shifted from concern with the requirements of the *unum* to the rights of members of the *pluribus,* with the focus on the educational rights of children and the voting rights of adults. In 1964, the Civil Rights Act prohibited denial of access to education on the basis of a student's limited English proficiency. Four years later, Congress passed amendments to the Elementary and Secondary Education Act (the Bilingual Education Act) to provide short-term help to school districts with high concentrations of students from low-income homes who had limited English-speaking ability. Then, in 1974, the Supreme Court ruled in *Lao* v. *Nichols* that English-limited children who were being taught in English must be given special help to guarantee their equality under the law with students who spoke English as a first language.[15] Under the impetus of congressional and judicial action, more than twenty states passed bilingual education acts, and the Office of Civil Rights of the Department of Health, Education and Welfare was established to implement Title VI of the Civil Rights Act. It directed that any school district in which children were effectively excluded from participation in the educational program because of English language deficiency must take affirmative measures to rectify the deficiency.[16] To protect the voting rights of African-Americans, the English literacy requirements in state laws were suspended by the Voting Rights Act of 1965 and banned altogether ten years later. The 1975 act also required bilingual ballots if more than 5 percent of the voters of a district constituted a language minority and if the illiteracy rate of such persons was higher than the national rate.[17]

By 1975, the essential constitutional and legal requirements of language policy were clear. English could continue to be required for civil service examinations and for naturalization. They dealt with critical aspects of the civic culture—requirements for membership and national public service. The right to maintain one's ancestral language in essentially private, associational activities, including the right to establish foreign-language schools and to conduct worship services in non-English languages, was completely protected. Now, the right of English-limited children to equal educational opportunity and of English-limited voters to equal access to the voting booth were protected by the law.[18]

Linguistic Nationalism Versus Linguistic Pluralism

Negative reaction to the growth of bilingual education and services and to the use of bilingual ballots grew swiftly in the late 1970s and the 1980s. Much of it focused on opposition to the use of Spanish in areas where large numbers of Hispanic immigrants and refugees lived. One way employed to discourage the use of foreign languages in public settings was to pass ordinances and laws establishing English as the official U.S. language. Beginning with Dade County, Florida, where an English-only ordinance was adopted in 1980, many jurisdictions legislated comparable measures. In part, the English-only movement reflected a fear that "the common tie of society," as John Locke called language, would be broken. Typical of the concerns was that of journalist Theodore H. White, who wrote in 1982 that he was particularly worried about immigration from Mexico and what he thought was the demand that many Hispanics made to have the U.S. officially acknowledge itself to be a bicultural, bilingual nation. "The Hispanics demand that the United States become a bilingual country," he wrote, "with all children entitled to be taught in the language of their heritage, at public expense." Deploring that hundreds of communities were obliged to print their ballots in foreign languages as well as in English, he expressed fear for the survival of American national unity under the impact of Hispanic immigration.[19] Two years later, historian John Lukacs echoed this concern that "the very essence of American nationality was being diluted—culturally, and not merely racially."[20]

It was not just disunity that worried White and Lukacs. Their writing revealed a fear of dispossession, an anxiety that the immigrants would Hispanicize them, just as Benjamin Franklin had worried in his own time that immigrants would "Germanize us" and Henry Adams, Henry Pratt Fairchild, and others had feared dispossession by Jews, Italians, and Poles at the turn of the century. The concerns of White and Lukacs were expressed most often in cities with high concentrations of Hispanic immigrants, such as Miami and Los Angeles. One woman who moved from St. Louis to Los Angeles in 1982 complained to a reporter that "no one speaks English," and "it bothers me. I feel it's not my country any more."[21] The resentment against non-English-speakers in the 1980s was fueled by the children and grandchildren of immigrants from Europe and Asia who recalled that no one used to receive special help through bilingual programs. One Italian-American wrote angrily that "no one taught me in my own language. I had to learn [English] the hard way. . . . This is an English speaking country; if the parents want their kids to speak Spanish, they should teach them at home."[22]

Such concerns combined to produce the U.S. English movement, a lobbying group organized in the early 1980s to press for a constitutional amendment to declare English the official American language. The movement was headed not by an Anglo-American, as Americanization organizations in the early part of the century had been, but by the Canadian-born son of Japanese immigrants, a semanticist and former U.S. senator, S. I. Hayakawa, who wanted all newcomers to learn English "as my parents did."[23] For Hayakawa, the new movement was necessary to prevent a division of the nation along language lines such as had occurred in Canada, the land of his birth, and in several other countries. English, he argued, was more critical as a means of unifying Americans than it had ever been now that immigrants were coming from all over the world, speaking dozens of languages. As he put it, the U.S. offered the newcomers "the opportunity to participate fully in our society . . . the key to that participation is taking the time to speak with us."[24]

English was a sign of belonging. Now that the civic culture had prevailed as the central, organizing principle of American national unity— now that the old Massachusetts charter-member idea of American membership had been finished—English was more important than it had ever been. Although the bilingual movement was sponsored overwhelmingly by Hispanics (mainly Mexican-Americans), the English-only movement opposed the use of any foreign language in public settings. In the summer of 1986, the city council of Monterey Park, California, passed a resolution urging that English be made the official language; in that city, Asians outnumbered Hispanics (40 percent and 35 percent of the population, respectively). In Philadelphia, the city decided to remove Korean-language street signs from a district in which many Koreans lived and worked and that had been paid for by the Korean community, following objections by non-Koreans and acts of vandalism that had damaged the signs.[25]

In 1988, voters in Arizona, Colorado, and Florida passed official English-only referenda, bringing to seventeen the states that designated English as the only official language.[26] The texts of such laws usually were vague and subject to interpretation. (In California, for example, part of the statute read, "The legislature shall make no law which diminishes or ignores the role of English as the common language of the state of California.") These laws had little effect on bilingual education programs or special services, including bilingual ballots, but newcomer immigrant-ethnic groups, especially Mexican-Americans, nevertheless tended to consider the English-only movement as a symbolic attack on their ancestral cultures.[27] They feared that, should it prevail, their children would be deprived of their ancestral languages and cultures and perhaps be alienated from their parents.

For many Hispanics, the language issue had become a struggle not only for specific rights, but for a symbolic affirmation of the worth of their culture. Like immigrants before them, the newcomers wanted to prevent the alienation of their children from the culture and language of their grandparents, even as they became Americans. A Scandinavian immigrant in the Midwest in 1898 expressed the anxiety typical of many immigrants: "The question no longer is: How shall we learn English so that we may take part in the social life of America and partake of her benefits; the question is: How can we preserve the language of our ancestors here, in a strange environment, and pass on to our descendants the treasures which it contains?"[28] The worry of Hispanic immigrants that their grandchildren would speak no Spanish at all was justified by history and contemporary research; a Rand Corporation study in 1985 found that more than 95 percent of first-generation Mexican-Americans born in the U.S. became proficient in English, and more than half of the second generation spoke no Spanish at all.[29]

Actually, the possibilities for maintaining cultural continuity were large, if that was what families chose to do. There was a harshness in the English-only movement that seemed to many Latinos to constitute a repetition of the assault on old-country traditions often made before in American history. But the linguistic xenophobia of times past had sharply diminished in the 1970s and 1980s. It was unthinkable that a congressman would call for legislation to forbid the use of U.S. mails under second-class mailing privileges to papers printed in non-English languages, as was proposed repeatedly in the 1940s.[30] No longer did teachers punish children for using the language of their non-English-speaking immigrant parents in the school yard, as they used to do routinely. No teacher would, as earlier, make Puerto Rican children write over and over in class, "I must not speak Spanish."[31] But those memories were fresh to many Latinos, who were afraid that the English-only language laws adopted in seventeen states and the various constitutional amendments proposed to make English the official language would diminish health, legal, welfare, bilingual education, and other services to non-English speakers.

Opposition to the English-only movement did not mean opposition to English. "We have to learn to speak English, but not at the expense of Spanish," said the Puerto Rican vice president of New York City's board of education in 1985.[32] "Fluency in English is necessary to advance socially, economically and politically here," said a Cuban-American leader. "To make English the official language is redundant. We know, and respect, that it is the language of the United States," said another.[33] Indeed, English was even more necessary for success in the 1970s and 1980s than in earlier times because it had become the lingua franca of the modern commercial world, dominating international exchange in commerce, aviation, shipping, tourism, diplomacy, science, technology, and even popular culture. In Hong Kong, nine of every ten secondary school students chose English because it had become the key to jobs in an economy dependent on international trade. In France, where every student in state secondary schools was required to take four years of English or German, 83 percent in 1984 chose English. Even in the Soviet Union, more than half of the secondary school students studied English, and in China the English-language telecast by the BBC was seen by more than 100,000,000 Chinese in the mid-1980s.[34]

English was the ticket to success in the U.S., perhaps even more for Latinos than Asians. Ninety-two percent of Mexican-origin Americans and 90.2 percent of Puerto Ricans who took the SATs for college entrance in 1984 said English was their best language (only 71.7 percent of Asian-American students said English was their best language).[35] One study concluded that Puerto Rican men with fluency in English may have raised their wages by as much as 20 percent, Cubans and Central and South Americans from 12 to 14 percent, and Mexican-Americans from 4 to 6 percent. It was estimated that the average wage offered to Mexican-American males would go up 16 percent if their education levels could be raised an average of three grades, something that would require effectiveness in English.[36]

The educational issue was not whether the children and grandchildren of immigrants would learn English; it was how well they would learn English to be able to participate in public life. Richard Rodriguez wrote of listening to the sounds of the gringo as a youngster and being frightened when he participated in public life; he felt safe only at home. He would have been much less nervous if his teachers had addressed him in Spanish. But he had to learn "the language of public society," to have a public identity and no longer feel an outsider in the public world. When he entered school he knew only about fifty English words and felt like an alien. By the time he was seven, "I came to believe what had been technically true since my birth: I was an American citizen," because he understood and could speak English. Once he spoke English, his father stopped using the word gringo with bitterness and disgust. Young Rodriguez had become a bridge between the private and the public worlds of his family.[37] His family continued to use Spanish among themselves and with friends and when they prayed in their particular Spanish way.[38] And Rodriguez also understood that the decision to belong to the culture of one's ancestors by learning and using their language was a familial and personal one, protected but not assured by the civic culture. That was up to the individual and the family.

The history of immigrants revealed how difficult it had been to preserve the language of the past. After-school private lessons in Hebrew, Chinese, Japanese, and other languages were arranged by immigrant parents and sometimes by their children for the second generation born in America. Religious communities such as the Hutterites and the Amish kept the language of their forefathers without government help and against hostile pressures from the outside. Even in the 1980s, the Amish of Pennsylvania conducted their daily lives mostly in the vernacular of Pennsylvania Dutch, a dialect of the German language, the familiar tongue of children at home and in other informal conversations. They also spoke some High German in religious services (the language taught by lay teachers on winter Saturday afternoons) and English, which the children learned in school. An Amish child entering school frequently had no English vocabulary, but readily learned the second language and soon spoke it without noticeable accent. Later, as adults, the Amish would use it when they went to town or had to speak with an English-speaking salesman.[39]

The Civic Culture and Bilingual Education

The situation of the Amish reflected the fundamentals of language policy prior to the Civil Rights Act of 1964, the Bilingual Education Act of 1968, and the Supreme Court's decision in *Lao* v. *Nichols* in 1974. The state was not permitted to interfere in the use of other languages in essentially private relationships. It could not keep parents from establishing schools to teach other languages. Nor could it keep local school districts from teaching foreign languages. In these matters, ethnic and religious groups (the *pluribus*) could count on the protection of the civic culture (the *unum*). The legislation of the 1960s and *Lao* v. *Nichols* answered another question: Youngsters with limited proficiency in English had a right to special educational assistance to help them learn English. The Court decided in *Lao* v. *Nichols* that the failure of the San Francisco school system to provide special English-language instruction to the approximately 1,800 students of Chinese ancestry who did not speak English violated civil rights statutes by denying them equal opportunity to participate in the public educational program. This was precisely the point made by the Chinese parents in their complaint. The Court, concluding that "students who do not understand English are effectively foreclosed from any meaningful education," ordered the San Francisco school district to take steps to give those parents and children appropriate relief.[40]

In permitting bilingual instruction under the Bilingual Education Act of 1968, the Congress had returned to the policies of several states in the nineteenth century, but now it did so with federal money generating new cadres of bilingual-education teachers and supervisors and materials for them to teach. The central purpose of bilingual education—to develop competence in English—was set forth repeatedly in national and state legislation and regulations. Consider the language of the 1975 Bilingual Education Statute in Wisconsin: "It is the policy of this state that fundamental courses may be taught in the pupil's non-English language to support the understanding of concepts, while the ultimate objective shall be to provide a proficiency in those courses in the English language *in order that the pupil will be able to participate fully in a society whose language is English* [Italics mine]."[41] By 1983, twelve states and one U.S. territory mandated bilingual education and twelve others permitted it. West Virginia was the only state that expressly prohibited teaching regular subjects in a language other than English; in that state, only 4.2 percent of the students were estimated to be from a minority language population.[42]

The 1980 census revealed that 17 percent of the school-age population were minority-language children, with 1.6 million in California, one million in New York, and 900,000 in Texas. Thirteen other states had at least 100,000 minority-language children, and the number grew as a result of immigration in the 1980s. Since more than 50 percent of all minority-language children were in Spanish-speaking families (5.7 million Latinos under eighteen), nearly all of the spokespersons and most of the teachers and language materials served Hispanic populations (at least 75 percent of the programs were in Spanish).[43] Federal courts frequently required cities and school districts to develop remedial educational programs, including bilingual education, in order to rectify violations of the Civil Rights Act of 1964 or the Equal Educational Opportunities Act of 1974.[44] Two principal concerns were raised. The first was that programs aimed at improving English language competence might turn into programs to preserve foreign languages and cultures, even though only transitional programs were allowed under the Bilingual Education Act. The second, strictly pedagogic, was that bilingual programs might be less effective than other approaches in helping students with limited English proficiency. In addressing the first issue, one student of bilingual programs, Noel Epstein, in 1977 asked: "Is the *national government* responsible for financing and promoting attachments to ethnic languages and cultures?"[45]

From a civic culture perspective, the question was important. The civic culture had a responsibility to help prepare students to participate in public life and the wider marketplace, and its schools had a responsibility to teach the language of the civic culture by the methods that worked best. The schools also had a responsibility to respect the cultural backgrounds of the children they taught, but they had no obligation to maintain those cultures and their languages. If bilingual education programs helped students learn English more effectively than other methods, educators could justify the temporary separation of students on the basis of language on the theory that the effective acquisition of English by the limited-English-speakers would strengthen the civic culture in the end. But some immigrant parents were dubious when programs separated the non-English-speaking students from the English-speakers. One of them, the president of the Arlington, Virginia, Vietnamese Parents Association, argued in 1984 that since America "is a multicultural society . . . I don't want to see each language group build its own empire—Spanish, Italian, Vietnamese. We have to agree that English is the one common language. Each group can use their own language at home; it's the difference between inside and outside the family."[46]

By the late 1980s, the issue of bilingual education had become less ideological and more pedagogic, but the debate over the effectiveness of various methods used to teach English to students with limited proficiency was not informed by research findings that clearly compelled the use of one approach over the others. A major research study in 1978 had been inconclusive about the effectiveness of different approaches to teaching limited-English students, and subsequent studies and reviews of research in the early 1980s and in 1987 did not produce conclusive evidence of relative effectiveness either.[47] The authors of a major 1980 study concluded that federal policy should not endorse bilingualism as the only approach to helping limited-English students. The Department of Education in the Reagan administration agreed. It argued that other methods which did not use native languages showed more promise. The opinion was rebutted by a General Accounting Office review in 1987, in which eight of ten experts concluded that the results supported the law's requirement that native languages be used to the extent necessary to learn English. But that formulation begged the pedagogic question as to which methods worked best and were most cost effective. Even supporters of bilingual programs acknowledged that there was considerable variation in their quality.[48]

Yet, educators with a strong professional stake in bilingual education resisted moves by the Reagan administration to allow for more experimentation with other than bilingual approaches to helping English-deficient students. By 1986, the pressure on states to adopt bilingual programs was great. Only 4 percent of the monies authorized by Congress in 1984 legislation to help such students (around $140 million a year in the mid and late 1980s) were available for programs not taught in the students' native languages. Lacking flexibility in developing programs to help limited-English students, many of the 15,500 school districts in the country felt compelled to choose the bilingual approach. As a result, Congress in 1988 amended the Bilingual Education Act to authorize up to 25 percent of federal funds to be spent on alternative programs. (The Reagan administration wanted to remove the cap altogether.)[49] Considerable experimentation with alternative programs had already taken place. A growing number of educators and parents argued for programs in English as a second language, in which students usually received extra instruction in English beyond the regular classes taught in English. In New York City, the most successful high school in teaching English to English-limited students, International High School in Queens, sending 85 percent of its graduates to four-year colleges, taught English as a second language in connection with instruction in its regular subjects, and eschewed bilingual methods altogether. The results were particularly remarkable because the only students admitted to it had to have resided in the U.S. for less than four years and had to have failed the English language requirement for high school attendance.[50] Other educators preferred some form of immersion, in which all instruction took place in English with teachers trained to be able to respond to some extent in the students' home language. An immersion approach differed from traditional bilingual education in that the foreign language was rarely or never used by the teacher except when taught as a subject. All other instruction was given entirely in English.[51]

Some immigrant parents insisted that their children be taught exclusively in English. In Los Angeles, one principal reported that the parents of all but three of her Ethiopian students had asked that their children be taught only in English, a method educators called "submersion."[52] This method had been used in American schools with earlier generations, but it now appeared to be in violation of federal policy unless it could be justified as another way of providing special help to English-limited students. The city of El Paso turned to immersion for high school students with such effectiveness that Latino groups who had opposed immersion programs changed their minds.[53] As the 1980 decade ended, there was greater experimentation in language instruction than ever before. In Martin Luther King, Jr., High School in New York City, nineteen students from Cambodia, Haiti, Afghanistan, Mali, Uruguay, and Yemen studied Emily Dickinson using no language other than English. In the same school, twenty-two students from the Dominican Republic, some in the country only three weeks, used Spanish to ask questions and talk among themselves, while the teacher drilled them and answered their questions in English.[54]

There were certain practical limits on bilingualism, given the increased rate of immigration in the late 1980s and the variety of languages to be accommodated. Of the students taking bilingual education classes funded by the federal government in 1988, the proportion who used a language other than Spanish had risen to 34 percent, making it extremely costly and sometimes impossible to service the students who were entitled by law to receive special assistance. There had always been a greater demand for bilingual teachers than could be met, but by the fall of 1986, New York City, with the school system less than three weeks from opening, found that it could not fill two-thirds of the 665 new bilingual teaching jobs that had been authorized. About 40 percent of the students with limited English who were entitled to bilingual education, or other help, did not receive it even twelve years after a consent decree had been signed by the New York board of education stipulating that such children receive a full bilingual program.[55]

Although the demand for Spanish-speaking teachers was greater than for any other language, schools were particularly hard-pressed, for example, to find Cambodian teachers, and it was difficult to find or create textbooks in Khmer, Cambodian, and several other languages.[56] In the Los Angeles schools in 1987, more than 150,000 non-English-speaking students spoke seventy-seven languages, leading the teachers' union to vote to abolish the transitional program. Many teachers reported that they thought methods other than bilingual education would be more helpful in guaranteeing equal educational opportunity for those deficient in English.[57] Teachers all over the country were concerned, as were parents, that by failing to teach the children English, they would be preparing them badly for work in a high-tech, information society. "At the turn of the century, you could drop out of school at fourteen and it didn't matter," remarked an official of the National Association of Latino Elected and Appointed Officials in 1987. "In today's technological society, English is a must."[58] It was also a must, according to Hayakawa, because immigrants now came from all over the world and it was the one language by which Americans could signal to each other that they cared about the common good.[59]

The Language Problem in Justice, Safety, Health, and Welfare

Nothing comparable to the Bilingual Education Act existed for such other services as health care, welfare, safety, and justice. The fear that such other services would be curtailed or inhibited by the English-only movement appeared justified for a brief time after passage of the English-only ordinance in Dade County in 1980. Jackson Memorial Hospital, for example, stopped providing prenatal care, postoperative instructions, and billing information in Spanish for Spanish-speaking patients; bus signs in Spanish and other languages besides English were removed from the streets. But in 1983, the Dade County Commission passed a health and safety exemption, and Spanish bus signs were restored when it became clear that they were desirable for everyone's safety.[60]

The issue of language services was not ideological; it was practical. It did not flow from constitutional rights; it stemmed from a reasonable expectation that since the U.S. maintained a substantial level of immigration, the civic culture was obligated through the federal government and the states to develop what the Democratic party platform in 1984 called "language barrier-free social and health services."[61] Awareness of the need for such services or of the government's obligation to provide them had been much lower in earlier periods of high immigration. Edith Abbott reported a case at the turn of the century of a sixteen-year-old Polish youth who had been arrested for stealing coal from the New York Central Railroad. When the interpreter, thought to be competent in Polish and Lithuanian, was asked to translate a key passage from a relevant document, he mangled the English.[62]

In the 1980s, the shortage of good interpreters was even more acute because of the greater variety of languages spoken by immigrants. Without legal standards for interpreters, many non-English-speakers could be denied their constitutional right to a fair trial, for example. The federal court system developed a rigorous test for Spanish interpreters, demanding of a candidate precise knowledge both of Spanish and English. Few states adopted such standards for state courts.[63] In world cities such as New York, the problems were especially severe because of the demand for interpreters in a great variety of languages, including Yoruba, Farsi, Bengali, and Punjabi.[64]

Passage of English-only legislation would not obviate the need for interpreters, nor would it make less important the hiring of police and fire officers and telephone receptionists able to handle emergency calls. Nor would such laws vitiate the practical value of bilingual signs at major intersections and highway exits on transportation lines frequented by large numbers of Spanish or Chinese immigrants. Nor would they elim-inate the need to develop vital health services—particularly dealing with AIDS and other public health problems—for language minority com-munities.

When the first National Conference on Asian-American Mental Health was held in 1972, it was funded by the National Institute of Mental Health on the sound premise that special strategies and programs were needed to reach Asian communities with respect to their mental health needs. New outreach programs offered bilingual services that sometimes were provided by community residents themselves.[65] In health matters partic-ularly, as in education and in providing justice, the civic culture owed language services to those who needed them, limited only by cost relative to other priorities and by the means to pay for them. It was not simply a matter of hospitality or even of individual rights, but also of providing for the general welfare of all Americans.

The Importance of English in the Civic Culture

The anxieties that lay behind the English-only movement focused over-whelmingly on Latinos because of a perception that they presented a more serious threat than other immigrant groups to the dominance of English. Despite new factors promoting language maintenance such as Spanish-language cable television and radio, English in television and movies, in schooling, in jobs, and in politics drew American-born Latinos and many immigrants into the orbit of prevailing cultural norms. To obtain signif-icant power in cultural and intellectual fields, it was desirable to attend graduate schools, where the only language of instruction was English. To gain economic power, except in markets in ethnic enclaves, it was imper-ative to deal with persons who spoke English. Within large corporations, mobility up the ladder usually involved physical mobility and contact with English-speakers from various backgrounds. To succeed in politics, at least at a level beyond the barrios, it was necessary to make deals and compromises in the English language. The *pluribus* needed English more than ever, and, as Hayakawa argued, so did the *unum*. Now with immigrants coming from more than 150 nations, it was vital that Americans share a common language in their public affairs, a premise that was accepted in establishing the English language requirement for naturalization and public employment in the Immigration Reform and Control Act of 1986, which provided that those newly legalized aliens who wished to become permanent-resident aliens must pass a basic English and civics test, or, as interpreted by the Immigration and Naturalization Service, be enrolled in a sixty-hour course in a school certified by the INS.

One member of the Select Commission on Immigration and Refugee Policy, Cruz Reynoso, the first Mexican-American appointee to the California Supreme Court, argued in 1980 against efforts to strengthen the English language requirement for naturalization, maintaining that English language skills for citizenship should not be required any more than a religious test.[66] But Reynoso passed over the difference between religion, which is essentially a private matter protected by the civic culture, and language, which is both private and public. One does not have to be religious to be a good citizen in a republic that separates church and state, but it is necessary to participate in the affairs of government to be an effective citizen, and that is difficult in the U.S. without a basic knowledge of English. Research showed that Spanish monolinguals, regardless of age, were less interested in politics and generally more alienated from the political system than bilinguals and English-only speakers.[67]

Many of those who emphasized the importance of English, such as S. I. Hayakawa, were not antiimmigrant or antiforeign. They spoke from a civic culture perspective that stressed the importance of America's common political tradition. The Declaration of Independence and Lincoln's Gettysburg Address undoubtedly can be understood in dozens of languages, but the meaning of the principles embodied in them evolved over time because of the ability of Americans to talk about them with each other. Since good citizenship required an understanding of those principles and a growing ability to understand and act on public issues, the English language requirement for naturalization and for civil service examinations seemed reasonable from a civic culture perspective.[68] Many who agreed with that point of view did not believe that an amendment to the Constitution to make English the official language was needed to strengthen the requirement for naturalization, and by 1989 the official English language constitutional amendment movement appeared to be waning. The controversy over bilingual ballots had subsided, too. The California Supreme Court had ruled that English may not be a requirement for otherwise qualified voters who speak Spanish, but if the naturalization requirement for English was effective, non-English election ballots would not be necessary as a practical matter except for elderly citizens, who were exempt from the English-language naturalization test.[69] To help relate the English-language naturalization requirement directly to preparation for voting, the Immigration and Naturalization Service could require that the naturalization test include voting in English in a mock election. Referenda issues could be printed in the foreign-language press or distributed in pamphlets in non-English languages by proponents, opponents, and the state itself, as was commonly done in jurisdictions that did not require bilingual ballots.

The ballot and naturalization issues were remote from the central question of language policy—how to keep English-limited youngsters in school. The high early dropout rate among Puerto Ricans and Mexican-Americans (see chapter 25) created a class of persons identified by ethnicity and language deficiency who were doomed to function outside of the dominant, primary labor markets and the civic culture. By the mid-1980s, approximately 40 percent of Hispanic youth dropped out of high school by the fall of their sophomore year, and 50 percent failed to complete it.[70]

The dropout situation was particularly severe for Mexican-American and Puerto Rican youngsters, partly because of the sojourner characteristics of Mexican and Puerto Rican families, but also as a result of the increased segregation of schools attended by Puerto Rican and Mexican-American students and the disproportionate amount of poverty afflicting both groups, especially Puerto Ricans.[71] Dropping out of school could easily doom one to illiteracy as an adult. Indeed, the highest rates of adult illiteracy were among those whose native language was not English.[72] Those Latino students who remained in high school in their senior year actually had slightly better grades in English than did black students.[73] Puerto Rican and Mexican-American high school graduates who took SATs did slightly better than blacks on the verbal test, although less well than Asian-Americans.[74] Keeping Latino students in school long enough that they could do well in English and other subjects became a major challenge to American teachers and school administrators in the 1980s. The personal loss to individual dropouts was severe; the cost to society was large.

The answer to the dropout rate, as of poor school performance, probably lay in large part in reducing poverty. By 1984, four out of ten Puerto Rican–American families and one out of four Mexican-American families lived below the poverty level, compared to 13 percent for Cuban-Americans and 11 percent for non-Hispanics.[75] Hispanic schoolchildren generally, and poor children particularly, were far more likely to attend segregated schools than they were twenty years before, settings in which it was less likely that they would acquire effective use of English. The answer to reducing poverty, in the long run, depended in part on reducing the dropout rate. But that was especially difficult in the areas most afflicted by poverty. Of the thirty-six schools listed as overcrowded by the Chicago school board in 1987, thirty-three were in Hispanic neighborhoods.[76] There were effective programs to help keep Mexican-Americans and Puerto Rican–Americans in school, but children in families living below the poverty level found it difficult to remain in school.[77] Americans needed a comprehensive, multifaceted plan, of which training in the English language was only a part, to reverse the problems of Hispanic ethnounderclasses.

Chapter Twenty-Five

QUESTIONS OF MEMBERSHIP
Who Are the Outsiders?

A LL countries that accept immigration decide the degree to which newcomers are accorded membership in the polity. After the Second World War, U.S. barriers that had been set earlier against Asians and Latinos (compared to Europeans) were substantially removed, making the American approach to immigration and naturalization increasingly more uniform. The tendency to reduce the differences in the nature of the welcome accorded different kinds of newcomers was matched by a tendency to reduce differences in rights and privileges between naturalized and native-born citizens, between citizens and permanent-resident aliens, and, to some extent, between illegal aliens and resident aliens.

The 1986 decision of Congress to legalize what turned out to be three million undocumented aliens was so at variance with the past experience of the aliens that when the Immigration and Naturalization Service began a vigorous campaign in 1987 to reach those eligible for legalization, it was difficult for many of them to believe that they could apply without risking apprehension and deportation. To overcome those fears, the INS used Mexican street bands and free food and drinks to encourage illegal aliens to come to special mobile vans for legalization applications. INS regional offices held amnesty fairs, town meetings, and open houses, sponsored booths and floats at ethnic festivals, and enlisted the Boy Scouts to reach out to eligible aliens. One legalization officer wrote a song, "Amnestia," to be played on Spanish-language radio stations along the Rio Grande, and in the southern region, aliens were targeted with amnesty flyers stuffed with 580,000 packages of tortillas.[1]

The INS's approach to legalization signified the acceptance by Congress of the 1981 recommendations of the Select Commission on Immigration and Refugee Policy that the front door to lawful immigration should be kept open even as the government tried to close the back door to illegal aliens in the future by penalizing employers who knowingly and willfully hired them. Although much of the media attention to the Immigration Reform and Control Act of 1986 centered on the employer sanctions provision to deter illegal migration, several other measures in the act, especially those concerning the legalization of illegal aliens, were strongly pro-immigration. In addition to its comprehensive legalization program (1.77 million applicants), Congress also passed a special legalization program for illegal aliens who had worked in agriculture for ninety days in the previous year and for another group who could persuade the INS that they had worked for ninety days in three successive previous years (1.3 million additional applicants). These special agricultural workers represented a concession to the old immigration tradition of the Southwest and California, in which low-cost workers were supplied to employers with the help of the government. But the program also signaled a fundamental departure from that tradition by specifying that the workers would not be confined to agriculture or to any section of the country and that they could become eligible for permanent residency.

In addition to these major increases in lawful immigration, Congress in 1986 took other steps to open the front door: it increased the immigration ceilings for colonies and dependencies from 500 to 6,000; adjusted the status of nearly 100,000 special entrants who came from Cuba and Haiti in the early 1980s to that of permanent resident alien; and added 5,000 immigrants annually for two years to be chosen from nationals of thirty-six countries with low rates of immigration attributed to the 1965 amendments' emphasis on family reunification. The last provision was extended to bring 15,000 additional immigrants in 1989 and in 1990; and in 1988, Congress increased immigration once more by providing 10,000 additional visas annually for 1990 and 1991 for would-be immigrants from 162 countries to be chosen by lottery.

The results of the select commission's recommendations in 1981 were directly the opposite of those made by the Dillingham Commission (1907–1911). Then, the country had been alerted to the alleged dangers of large-scale immigration, with a special warning against those who came from eastern and southern Europe. Now, Congress accepted the select commission's recommendation that immigration at somewhat higher levels than the already post–Second World War high was good for the nation as long as it was legal; in 1989, the Senate voted to admit an additional 50,000 immigrants annually independent of family relations.

U.S. Immigration Policy in Contrast with Other Western Nations

Of all the Western nations, only Canada thought in terms of expanding general immigration in the late 1980s (West Germany wanted more Germans and Israel more Jews). Canada decided in 1988 to accept about 160,000 in 1989, 40,000 more than the previous year. But Canada in 1988 decided against an amnesty program to confer legal resident status on 85,000 people who claimed to be refugees and who were living in the country on temporary permits.[2] In other Western nations, opposition to immigration intensified in the late 1980s. Having sought foreign workers from the Middle East and North Africa after the Second World War to do jobs their own people would not do, several European democracies now tried to figure out how to get those guest workers and their families to return home. Opposition to immigrants and immigration in Australia tended to focus on Asian refugees.[3] Even in Sweden, which by 1985 counted 430,000 foreigners, mostly Finns, among its 8.2 million inhabitants, there was growing concern about the non-Nordic nationals who wished to settle there. Other Scandinavians could immigrate freely, but non-Nordic nationals had to possess both residence and work permits before being allowed to enter the country.[4]

The European nations had a particular problem in that most foreigners who came to their countries in the 1980s were not traditional immigrants attempting to settle in a new land for good. Either they were illegal aliens seeking work or persons claiming asylee status, most of whom were fleeing poverty, civil war, discrimination, or some combination of them. As the number of asylum seekers increased substantially in the 1980s, European governments began to curtail sharply the proportion of applications approved in an effort to stem the tide. In Sweden and Denmark, known for a liberal attitude toward refugees, denial rates for those seeking asylum from Lebanon, Sri Lanka, Iran, and other Third World countries were stimulated by xenophobic feelings.

The fear that asylum claims could become a back door to immigration extended to the U.S., too, where, in the 1980s, the Coast Guard intercepted more than 18,000 Haitian asylum seekers on the seas before they ever reached the U.S. (only six were given asylum) and where the INS adopted streamlined procedures to process asylum claims of persons from Central America, granting approval only in rare cases when a well-founded fear of persecution was proved to the agency's and the State Department's satisfaction. Stern measures were taken to dissuade asylum seekers in the U.S., including detention while claims were being processed, but in Europe, where, except for France, there had been no long tradition of immigration, such measures were part of a growing sentiment against immigration generally. U.S. asylum policy was criticized for its uneven application, because, as with respect to refugee policy, admissions often were made in response to considerations of foreign policy. But compared to European countries, there was relatively less xenophobia against immigrants generally, and the U.S. actually increased the number of refugees it accepted each year in 1988, 1989, and 1990, while other Western countries became more restrictive.[5]

The fact that most of the people of the world on the move—immigrants, refugees, or asylees—were of dark color raised questions of racism in all of the Western countries, including Great Britain, which faced serious questions with the end of the Empire: To what extent should former British subjects be given an opportunity to emigrate to Great Britain? With what rights and privileges? Who should be eligible for citizenship? Many of the distinctions made in answering those questions in the 1970s and 1980s reflected racial concerns. English law gave an automatic right of residence to all citizens of the Channel Isles, the Isle of Man, the Falkland Islands, and Gibraltar, nearly all of whom were white, but told one and a half million Chinese and other "British overseas citizens" who chose British citizenship when Great Britain granted independence to the East African colonies and Malaysia after the war that they were specifically excluded from passing citizenship on to their children even if the children were born in Britain. Thus, Great Britain ended a seven-century-old legal tradition by which any child born in Britain was automatically eligible for citizenship. British law also told more than three million people who lived in the British colonies of Hong Kong, Bermuda, Belize, and the British Virgin Islands that they had no automatic right of residence in Great Britain but had to apply just as if they were immigrants.[6] France, despite its tradition of immigration, was more xenophobic than the U.S. Although the percentage of foreigners in both countries was approximately the same in 1988 (about 8 percent in France and about 7 percent in the U.S.), attacks against foreigners (primarily Arabs from North Africa) increased in France, in contrast to the American celebration of diversity.[7]

The fact that Europe generally tightened its rules for admission for immigration as well as refugees and asylees in the 1980s at the same time that the U.S. had become more open to more diverse immigration could be explained mainly by the impact of the civil rights revolution, which led to the conclusion that it is wrong not only to abridge fundamental rights by race, religion, or nationality, but also wrong to base immigration policy on those considerations.

Whereas Europeans generally asked about foreigners in their countries, How can we get these outsiders to go home? or, failing that, How can we keep them outside the polity a while longer even as they work among us?, the U.S. approached newcomers—including those illegal aliens granted amnesty—by asking, What measures should be taken to help these newcomers become Americanized?

Blurring Distinctions Between Aliens and Citizens: Making Membership More Inclusive

In addition to expanding immigration, Congress and the Courts in the 1970s and 1980s tended to make the rights of all who lived and worked in the U.S. more uniform. In 1967, less than two years after passage of the liberalized Immigration Act of 1965, the Supreme Court decided that Congress lacked the constitutional power to pass laws depriving an American citizen of his or her nationality without consent, even when the person involved was a naturalized citizen who had voted in foreign elections. The decision made it clear that citizenship and allegiance were voluntary. Writing for the majority, Justice Hugo Black held that a naturalized citizen, no less than one born in the U.S., had "a Constitutional right to remain a citizen in a free country unless he voluntarily relinquishes that citizenship."[8] The gap between naturalized and American-born citizens was narrowed further in February 1988 when a federal district court judge ruled that two naturalized American citizens of Vietnamese birth had the same rights as other Americans to security clearances that gave them access to government secrets, affecting an estimated 23,600 naturalized citizens who were employees of the Defense Department or employed by contractors working for it.[9]

Aliens still did not have the same rights as naturalized citizens (they were subject to deportation on several grounds, for example), but the clear trend in the 1970s and 1980s was to reverse the laws derogating alien rights which had been passed in reaction to the large immigration at the turn of the century. Aiming principally to limit eastern and southern European immigrants, many states had passed ordinances in the 1890s denying immigrant resident aliens licenses to operate certain kinds of businesses. Virtually all states had excluded resident aliens from dentistry, medicine, engineering, optometry, the law, and other professions; those with the largest number of aliens tended to have the most severe restrictions.[10] Some states even had denied resident aliens the opportunity to work as undertakers or barbers or pool hall operators. A Cincinnati law that prohibited aliens from owning and operating pool rooms had been upheld by the U.S. Supreme Court, which found reasonable the premise of the law—that citizen proprietors were not as likely as aliens to allow the pool rooms to become social nuisances. In Rhode Island in 1924, a state court upheld a law which denied permission for aliens to drive motorbuses because, the court reasoned, "aliens as a class are naturally less interested in the state, the safety of its citizens, and the public welfare."[11]

By 1971, just as immigration from non-European countries began to increase substantially, the Court ruled most of these restrictions invalid. The key case involved a law that made welfare payments available only to citizens or long-term resident aliens. Such a law, said the Court, was in conflict with the Fourteenth Amendment's equal protection clause, since there was no compelling public interest in limiting welfare payments to citizens.[12] The ruling had vast implications for the rights of resident aliens. States could no longer discriminate to keep them from practicing law, or working as civil engineers, or attending educational institutions, or receiving major benefits, as they had in the past.[13]

The Fourteenth Amendment did not invalidate state laws that were deemed to have a political function, such as those barring aliens from voting or from being public school teachers, police officers, probation officers, and jurors. If aliens wanted to play a full role in civic life, they had to become citizens. Other distinctions between resident aliens and citizens were continued, even one that excluded aliens from Medicare supplemental insurance programs unless they had lived in the U.S. at least five years. Despite these limitations, the overall effect of judicial and legislative action in the 1970s and 1980s was to narrow the gap between citizen and alien rights, especially after passage of the Immigration Reform and Control Act of 1986, which prohibited discrimination against aliens in employment and created the Office of Special Counsel to receive complaints by aliens and to make independent investigations of possible discrimination against persons on the basis of alienage.[14]

Some distinctions in rights and privileges still were made between different categories of aliens. Resident aliens, for example, were the only group of aliens allocated an immigrant preference to enable them to petition for their immediate relatives to become permanent resident aliens, too. Those aliens granted refugee or asylee status were eligible for a full range of federally funded services, and, after one year for refugees and two for asylees, they could adjust their status to that of permanent resident. Those who were permitted to stay in the country through a procedure that granted them what was called extended voluntary departure—substantially, a temporary stay of refuge—or who were given special entrant status or were paroled into the U.S. by the attorney general were eligible for work permits and Supplemental Security Income (SSI) and sometimes for Aid to Families with Dependent Children (AFDC) and Medicare, but asylum applicants (applications pending) ordinarily had no access to any of these programs and sometimes were denied authorization to work.

Congress and the courts also expanded the civil rights of nonimmigrant aliens in the 1980s. Legislation was passed in December 1987 (subject to renewal) to prevent the deportation of nonimmigrant aliens on the basis of their belief or associations, although the executive branch retained the ability to deport (or exclude) aliens on foreign policy grounds. In December of 1988, a federal district court judge ruled as unconstitutional key parts of the Immigration and Nationality Act of 1952 (the McCarran-Walter Act) as depriving resident aliens of rights to free speech. Seven Palestinians had been arrested and ordered deported by the INS for allegedly supporting a radical Palestinian terrorist group. The 1952 law was ruled unconstitutional because the free speech of aliens was protected by the Constitution equally with the free speech of citizens. Also ruled as invalid was the portion of the otherwise liberalizing 1987 law which specified that members of the Palestinian Liberation Organization could be deported for their views.[15]

The sharpest distinctions with respect to rights were between those who were in the country illegally and lawfully admitted aliens. But even illegal aliens, and especially their children, had some rights. In 1982, the Supreme Court ruled that the Equal Protection Clause of the Fourteenth Amendment prevented the state of Texas from denying to undocumented school-age children the same free public education it provided to children who were citizens or legally admitted aliens.[16] Texas had benefited from the labor of illegal aliens, yet it had authorized individual school districts either to prohibit undocumented alien children from attending public schools or to accomplish the same goal by charging them tuition. The Court held that the protection of the Fourteenth Amendment "extends to anyone, citizen or stranger, who is subject to the laws of the state," and it emphasized that undocumented children should not be made victims of the illegal behavior of their parents or of the inability of the U.S. to effectively enforce its immigration law.

In speaking for the majority of the Court, Justice William Brennan exposed the fundamental hypocrisy of a policy that exempted employers of illegal aliens from any penalty (changed in 1986) while denying the children of such alien workers the most elemental right of a public education. "This situation," wrote Brennan, "raises the specter of a permanent caste of undocumented resident aliens [sic], encouraged by some to remain here as a source of cheap labor, but nevertheless denied the benefits our society makes available to citizens and lawful residents," which was precisely the point of sojourner pluralism as applied to many Mexican workers throughout most of the twentieth century.[17]

The Fourteenth Amendment conferred additional rights on illegal aliens. The undocumented worker who established the necessary domicile could pursue remedies available under workers' compensation laws in the event of injury in the course of employment. The tendency in the 1980s was to expand slightly the due process rights of illegal aliens confronted with deportation. In 1987, the Court ruled that because of the basic constitutional requirement of due process an illegal alien reentering the country after being deported could not be prosecuted for illegal reentry if he or she could show that the original deportation order had been invalid.[18] Three years earlier, the Court had ruled that it was an unfair labor practice for an employer to report illegal aliens to the Immigration and Naturalization Service in retaliation against the aliens' efforts to organize a union, since under then existing law it was not illegal to hire an undocumented alien.[19] And, in 1987, the Eleventh Circuit of the Court of Appeals ruled that undocumented aliens were entitled to the minimum wage and over-time pay guaranteed by federal law under the Fair Labor Standards Act of 1938.[20] In another case, a federal district court ruled in 1986 that federal authorities had acted improperly in prohibiting Medicaid assistance for illegal aliens because the 1966 statute authorizing Medicaid contained "no express restrictions on alien eligibility."[21]

No constitutional rights to Medicaid or most other benefits for illegal aliens had been established, and under the Immigration Reform and Control Act of 1986, benefits were sharply limited for the aliens legalized under the two broad amnesty programs. But the tendency to weaken distinctions between different categories of aliens, including illegal aliens, and citizens was manifest in a variety of state and local actions and even in decisions by the INS. In 1988, the INS ruled that undocumented alien children who could not meet the residency requirement were not disqualified from becoming legal residents under the legalization program of the Immigration Reform and Control Act under certain circumstances.[22] Some scholars and advocates of immigration believed that the tendency to blur distinctions in rights and privileges between aliens, particularly illegal aliens, and U.S. citizens demeaned the value of membership in the American polity,[23] but in fact most illegal aliens continued to live to a large extent outside of the protections afforded resident aliens and citizens. Those caught at the border were turned around without any hearing, and although the courts expanded due process remedies in some respects for illegal aliens, they narrowed them in others. The rights of illegal aliens, and of resident aliens, and sometimes citizens, too, were infringed by INS practices on occasion in raids in neighborhoods and places of employment.[24]

It was precisely the vulnerability of the underclass of illegal aliens who had been in the U.S. for a relatively long period that, in large part, had led Congress to enact the legalization programs of the 1986 law. Illegal aliens who applied for legalization were well aware that they were moving out of an underclass status into something much closer to full membership in American life. "This means I won't have to live like a second class person," said a legalization applicant from El Salvador who had been in the U.S. for eight years. "Now I will no longer be at a lower level than other people. I can do what I want."[25] "This is our country now," said a Nicaraguan illegal alien as he applied for legalization on the first day of the program.[26] A thirty-five-year-old Brazilian man who had been trained as an engineer but worked as a busboy exclaimed, "I feel great that I have some rights now, to be here, to be free and to be accepted."[27]

Probably more than any other country in history, the United States no longer defined outsiders by reason of nationality or even because of alien status. Yet, as Americans expanded legal immigration and made more inclusive the boundaries of membership regardless of nationality and alien status, some Americans, mostly citizens by birth, lived increasingly outside of and alienated from mainstream economic and political institutions as members of an ethno-underclass.

The problems of those in an ethno-underclass—the chronically poor native-born blacks, Indians, Puerto Ricans, and Mexican-Americans—persisted despite the triumph of the civic culture. Although those problems were related to historic systems of coercive pluralism, they were severe in the 1980s, even after the dismantling of caste pluralism, the radical transformation of predatory pluralism, and inroads that had been made against sojourner pluralism. Except for illegal aliens, members of an ethno-underclass were not outsiders by reason of status, as were Asian immigrant settlers through nearly all of American history. They did not suffer segregation or discrimination by sanction of law, as had been true of African-Americans until the civil rights revolution. They were not manipulated by employers with the cooperation of the state, as temporary workers to be discarded when no longer needed and kept distant from membership in the political community, as were large numbers of lawfully admitted Asians and Mexicans for many decades. Nor were they physically uprooted, attacked, and colonized, as Indians had been for most of American history.

Yet, they were outsiders—outside of any meaningful participation in the national American community—even though their position as outsiders had not been fixed by law or government policy. For these poor and black or Hispanic or Indian outsiders, the American founding myth of freedom and opportunity and the civil rights revolution had little meaning. Unlike upwardly mobile blacks, Hispanics, and Asian-Americans, they were unlikely to vote or participate in other civic activities. Their life choices and chances were to a large extent circumscribed by seemingly impermeable boundaries of class reinforced by race or ethnicity.

The New Black Middle Class

The rise of a new black middle class following the civil rights revolution served to dramatize the apparently worsening situation of African-Americans who lived in those urban census tracts (usually comprising 2,000 to 5,000 persons) characterized by unemployment, low labor force participation, children in poverty, and crime. Blacks in the high-rise public housing projects of urban ghettoes were constantly reminded on television of the success of members of the black middle class, whose lives were as remote from their own as those of successful whites. Some middle-class African-Americans came to the ghetto as teachers, as social workers, civil servants, and even as policemen and firemen, but they generally lived elsewhere, away from broken bottles, graffiti, rusted automobiles, and abandoned apartment buildings. Other middle-class blacks, unlike the earlier African-American middle class of undertakers, insurance agents, teachers, and preachers, worked in mainstream and integrated markets and institutions, leaving the ghetto behind altogether.

Nothing measured the demise of caste between 1940 and 1970 so much as the escape of large numbers of blacks from the dirtiest, most menial occupations. In 1940, only 1.8 percent of all blacks did professional or technical work, a proportion that rose to 7 percent thirty years later; the percentage of black clerical and sales personnel went from 2.2 to 10.2 percent, and operatives from 12.7 to 29.4 percent.[28] By the mid-1980s, 6 percent of all managerial and professional positions in the U.S. were held by blacks, and nearly 8 percent of all technical, sales, and administrative positions. In some occupations, such as engineering, the proportion of African-Americans remained quite low, but in others, such as mathematical and computer scientist and computer systems analyst, it was relatively high (6.2 percent in 1983). Blacks made up over 18 percent of social workers, 14 percent of educational and vocational counselors, and 11 percent of administrators in education and related fields.[29]

The rise in the occupational status of middle-class African-Americans reflected breakthroughs in higher education. In 1960, there were only a quarter of a million blacks in college; by 1970, a half million; and by 1980, more than one million. In 1959, black males with a B.A. degree achieved only 59 percent of the income of white college graduates, but by 1979 they earned 84 percent, and by 1980 blacks with graduate degrees earned about the same amount as their white counterparts. Principally as a result of more education, black male wages increased faster than white between 1940 and 1980. In 1940, the typical black male worker earned only 43 percent as much as his white counterpart; by 1980, the figure was 73 percent. In 1940, the typical black male earned around $4,500 (in 1984 dollars); a black male similarly employed in 1980 earned almost $19,000.[30] Black women with higher education were more able to take advantage of the dismantling of caste than black men. Those women who obtained college degrees were slightly more likely than white women of comparable education to be in the top occupational categories in 1980, while black men were at a slight disadvantage.[31]

The declining significance of race in employment and income patterns was revealed most clearly in the data concerning black married-couple families in which the wife worked outside the home. By 1986, those families had the highest median income of all African-American families ($31,949), an income 82 percent of that for white married-couple families. Keeping dollars constant, 21.2 percent of black families earned more than

$35,000 in 1986, compared to 15.7 percent in 1970. There was even a slight expansion of relatively wealthy African-American families in the 1980s, with 8.8 percent earning more than $50,000 in 1986, compared to 8.6 percent in 1980.[32]

Identification with the middle class, considered nearly a betrayal of African-American aspirations at elite colleges in the 1960s, was accepted by the 1980s as a mark of inclusion and fulfillment. Magazines such as *Black Enterprise, Jet,* and *Ebony* chronicled the success of middle-class blacks, as black newspapers had done for the old middle class before the Second World War; articles now were more likely to be about portfolio management than cotillion balls. Most militant young blacks at predominantly white elite universities in the late 1960s would have scorned the notion that personal satisfaction came from membership in a fitness club or ownership of a town house. But, in 1984, *Black Enterprise* ran an article entitled "Are You a BUPPY?" which described a category of college-educated young black urban professionals with disposable income. After detailing the sociology of the BUPPY, the author concluded that "aspiring for the finer things in life is wonderful. We need more folks that know that squash is not just a vegetable. Like a renovated Harlem brownstone, the phenomenon of the BUPPY is solid, classic, and much appreciated by everyone."[33]

The Black Urban Underclass

Despite the gains of better-educated blacks, those with a high school education or less were sharply disadvantaged with respect to occupational status and income compared to whites; by 1980, 31 percent of all blacks lived in poverty, nearly three times the proportion for whites. The extremely poor were becoming more numerous, too. By 1986, 14 percent of all black families received an income of less than $5,000, compared to 9.6 percent in 1970, and slightly more than 30 percent earned less than $10,000, compared to 26.8 percent (keeping dollars constant).[34] Perhaps a million and a half African-Americans lived in census tracts where large numbers of men no longer even looked for work, let alone voted or otherwise participated in American civic life, and where women struggled to raise children without much help from the biological fathers of those children. By 1985, 13 percent of all black men aged thirty-four to forty-four were not participating in the labor force at all, compared to only 5 percent for white men.[35]

The problems of family and community associated with high rates of unemployment and nonparticipation in the labor force for black males were described and analyzed by psychologist Kenneth B. Clark in 1964 in his book *Dark Ghetto.* In the same year, Daniel P. Moynihan, then U.S.

assistant secretary of labor, wrote a report in which he noted that almost 25 percent of African-American families were headed by women, one-third of all black children were not living with both parents, one black baby in four was born out of wedlock, and all of those factors were linked to high male unemployment. He saw the strains on black families as the fundamental obstacle to breaking the cycle of poverty and deprivation into which so many African-American children were born.[36]

Neither Clark nor Moynihan used the term "underclass," but by the mid-1980s it was commonly employed by social analysts—black and white—to characterize a cluster of behaviors: unemployment and low labor force participation by males; high rates of drug abuse and other crimes by men and women; high welfare dependency; high dropout rates from school; a high percentage of babies born with precariously low weight; a disproportionate number of single parents and teen-age mothers leading to a high percentage of female-headed households; and a distrust of mainstream institutions, including the police and elected officials.

In his threshold 1980 book, *The Declining Significance of Race*, William Julius Wilson emphasized the growing importance of class and particularly of lower-class poverty among African-Americans. He pointed out the growing disparity in life chances between those youngsters growing up in an expanding African-American middle class and those in the underclass, particularly in single-parent female-headed households, and predicted that their numbers would grow in the 1980s, even as other blacks moved into the new middle class.[37] The number had been growing already. When Clark and Moynihan issued their warnings, 25 percent of all African-American households were headed by women and 25 percent of all black babies were born to mothers not married. When Wilson wrote in 1980, the percentages were up to 40 and 50 percent.[38] The population of black female-headed households increased in the 1970s by about 92,000 a year, a pace of increase that would have alarmed Moynihan and Clark, but the number kept going up in the 1980s, averaging over 150,000 annually. By 1984, 50.2 percent of all black children, the vast majority of whom were in poverty, lived in female-headed households, compared with only 14.3 percent of white children.[39]

Single-parent, female-headed households were poor partly because women were limited in the numbers of hours they could work; many gave birth when they were young and dropped out of school, which kept them from the skills and education necessary to get good jobs. African-Americans were ingenious in inventing support systems, including extended families made up of aunts, cousins, grandmothers, and neighbors, but the problems were overwhelming: taking care of the children when ill; going to school to talk to teachers; taking children to the hospital when there was an accident; talking to the police; getting proper nutrition for infants; keeping children away from the drug dealers and homicidal young male gangs who roamed the streets. Help in caring for children in extreme poverty did not often come from biological fathers, partly because many were seen by African-American mothers as unreliable partners, men who could cause trouble at the worst, or, at the least, deprive them of a reliable income, as insufficient as it was, from federal programs such as Aid to Families with Dependent Children.

The black underclass included not just women and children in such households or men who were unemployed or not seeking work, but also the low-status dishwasher, hospital orderly, or janitor, who, according to Wilson, did not attach themselves permanently to a specific job because they knew that such jobs, the most menial, would always be available. Many blacks were attracted to illegal activities that produced much more income than the lowest-level jobs available to those with meager skills and education.[40] It was a phenomenon of young black male life in the ghettoes about which Elliot Liebow wrote in *Talley's Corner* in 1967— young men who just hung out, picked up low-level jobs from time to time, ran numbers, and competed in macho games. By 1980 the behavioral patterns—especially drug use and dealing—were much more prevalent than they had been when Liebow wrote.[41]

In 1981, Wilson made a sharper distinction between what he called the "underclass" and the "lower class." In underclass families, he wrote, "the head of the household is, almost invariably, a woman," but the underclass also included a large number of adult males with no fixed address, many of whom had been unemployed for a long time and others who had dropped out of the labor market.[42] Wilson accepted the conventional explanation that the loss of manufacturing jobs in the cities reduced opportunities for good employment for males, but he challenged two major assumptions of civil rights leaders. He argued that numerical goals and timetables were virtually irrelevant to the problems of the underclass, and that the welfare system, by denying welfare to families with a man in the house (and other practices) had actually weakened the family role of the poor black male.[43]

Family was a focal point of a series of three conferences of some thirty black scholars in 1981, 1982, and 1983, leading to the publication by the Joint Center for Political Studies, the major think tank concerned with African-American affairs, of a pamphlet entitled *A Policy Framework for Racial Justice*. Pointing out that until the 1960s, 75 percent of African-American families included both husband and wife, its authors emphasized the impact of the migration of blacks from rural areas in the South to large cities in the North, where they were unable to find or hold jobs, leading to "the recent rise in female-headed households." Black births to single mothers were not confined to a single region in 1979, the year for which the scholars reported data: Arkansas (54 percent); Indiana (57 percent); Wisconsin (63 percent); and New Jersey (60 percent).[44] The authors pointed out that many teen-age mothers were unprepared for motherhood, that their education was incomplete, that they were unable to enter the job market with any skills, and that their children were growing up without consistent, constructive male models. Almost thirty years after Clark and Moynihan had made similar pleas, they argued that "a major national goal for this decade should be to arrest the proliferation of disadvantaged female-headed black families." Estimating that if the increase in female-headed households had not occurred during the 1970s, overall black family income would have increased by 11.3 percent instead of decreasing by 5 percent, they concluded that "black husband-wife families provide the foundation for a permanent black middle class."[45]

The "policy framework" issued by the Joint Center for Political Studies established a new context for discussing the question of the African-American poor. Some African-American scholars, such as Thomas Sowell and Glenn C. Loury, went further than Wilson in deemphasizing the connection between racism and the problems of the black poor. Black leaders, wrote Loury, a professor of economics and Afro-American studies at Harvard University, should stop externalizing the causes of out-of-wedlock births among young black women. To tell young blacks in the ghetto that racism was responsible for poverty in their lives would be, according to Loury, to take away their single most important tool for change, belief in themselves.[46] But Loury was no more clear than anyone else as to how to get such young men, who never held a job or did well in school, to believe in themselves; and the proportion of black males under twenty-four who had never held a job increased from 9.9 percent in 1966 to 23.3 percent in 1977, and became worse in the early 1980s.[47]

By 1985, when half of all black children under six lived in poverty, African-American leaders put questions of poverty and family high on their agenda for action. Civil rights legislation could not break the links between bad education (more than 50 percent of America's black youngsters were in the twelve largest inner-city school systems), segregated housing, unemployment, bad health, and female-headed single-parent households. Several studies and articles recited the increasingly familiar problems of the black underclass, particularly after the Census Bureau announced in 1984 that 59.2 percent of black families with children had only one parent present, up sharply from 51.9 percent in 1980 and 35.7 percent in 1970.[48]

Robert L. Woodson, an African-American leader in the housing field, asked for an end to dependence on government, maintaining that two-worker black households were undermined by the welfare system.[49]

Andrew F. Brimmer, an African-American economist and former member of the Federal Reserve Board, wrote in 1985 that the black community itself should "campaign to reduce the extremely high birth rate among unmarried black teenage girls."[50] In the same year, the president of the National Council of Negro Women wrote in *Ebony* magazine of the need to deal with the crisis of teen-age pregnancy, which "contributes tragically to the steady erosion of our great historical asset, the strong two-parent family, with its extended branches enfolding, protecting and strengthening each newcomer."[51] The following year (August 1986), *Ebony* devoted an entire issue to "the crisis of the black family," focusing on teenage pregnancy, female-headed households, and children at risk.

The emphasis on self-help to strengthen black families, achieve excellence in schools, and compete effectively in employment was repeated when the Committee on Policy for Racial Justice met again in 1986 and issued a new report under the title *Black Initiative and Governmental Responsibility*.[52] Although "governmental responsibility" received equal billing with "black initiative," the report did not refer to affirmative action or counting by race, but focused instead on welfare reform, employment and job training, educational innovation, and comprehensive child development programs.[53] In the foreword, Eddie M. Williams, president of the Joint Center for Political Studies, quoted Frederick Douglass, Martin Luther King, Jr., and W. E. B. Du Bois on the importance of the black community taking measures to help itself.[54] Recognizing that "the very success of our civil rights movement . . . has created a gap in socioeconomic status between those blacks who were in the best position to seize new opportunities and those who were not, facilitating physical and economic separation," the report called for community initiatives to bring well-to-do blacks into the lives of the isolated ghetto poor.[55]

The theme of self-help held an honorable, if controversial, place in the history of African-Americans, as Williams pointed out, one that had become identified primarily with Booker T. Washington. Yet, it was Du Bois who, in his study of blacks in Philadelphia in the 1890s, came closest to anticipating the analysis made by African-Americans in the 1980s. "Against prejudice, injustice and wrong the Negro ought to protest energetically and continuously," wrote Du Bois, "but he must never forget that he protests because those things hinder his own efforts, and that those efforts are the key to his future."[56] Du Bois decried the neglect of children in the ghetto, the extent of crime there, and emphasized the importance of good jobs in solving many of its problems. The prolific African-American scholar wrote at a time of caste, when even educated Philadelphia blacks were compelled to work as chambermaids and bootblacks. By the 1980s, caste had been removed. But the problems described by Du Bois for Philadelphia's blacks ninety years earlier were much worse for the 1.6 million Americans (overwhelmingly black and Hispanic) who lived in the poorest census tracts of the inner city.[57]

The ghetto ethno-underclass, where dropping out of high school, participation in the illicit economy, male unemployment and female welfare dependency, drug use, and violent crime were common, resulted from generations of segregation and isolation from mainstream American institutions, breeding a deep sense of psychological isolation from well-to-do whites and African-Americans, whose values, attitudes, and life-styles sometimes seemed almost foreign to many in the underclass. The legacy of caste was palpable in such ghetto areas, where for many who belonged to it the black ethno-underclass was not just a statistical category but a way of life isolated from the main economic institutions of American society and its political culture.[58]

The Puerto Rican Underclass

Of all the Hispanic groups, Puerto Ricans, who became U.S. citizens in 1917 with an unrestricted right of movement between the island and the mainland, were afflicted disproportionately with the problems characteristic of an ethno-underclass in the 1970s and 1980s. The number of Puerto Ricans on the mainland was relatively small before the Second World War (in 1940, only about 70,000), but after the war, economic expansion in the U.S., quick and relatively inexpensive airplane travel, and a growing consciousness of opportunities on the mainland led to a large migration from the island; 900,000 lived on the mainland in 1960. Ten years later, there were about 1.4 million, 2 million by 1980, and 2.6 million in 1985.

The situation of the extremely poor in Puerto Rico and their sense of hopelessness was described by anthropologist Oscar Lewis in 1967.[59] The "culture of poverty," as Lewis called it, in the slum shantytowns of the island did not yield many migrants to the mainland because their inhabitants rarely could produce the money and initiative to make the trip. But some Puerto Ricans from rural backwaters who came to New York and Chicago, while materially better off than they had been in Puerto Rico, became part of an urban ethno-underclass whose members, to judge by three key measures—welfare payments per capita, school dropouts, single-parent female-headed households—actually were worse off than mainland-born blacks and non–Puerto Rican Hispanics.

In their 1964 book about ethnicity in New York City, Nathan Glazer and Daniel P. Moynihan noted that Puerto Rican median family income in the city was considerably lower and unemployment higher than that of blacks.[60] Puerto Rican families suffered from the stress of migration to and from the island. In East Harlem and the South Bronx, where most of New York's Puerto Ricans lived, children were frequently taken out of school for months at a time to return with their families to Puerto Rico. On the mainland, where women often could earn at least as much money as men, stress on marriages intensified as males found their *machismo* under attack and often suffered a loss in self-esteem. Women who were discouraged with marriage had the alternative of welfare, as they also did in Puerto Rico, but in the cities of the Northeast they could reject their husbands without experiencing daily sharp and nearly universal disapproval from their extended families and communities. The task of child rearing for single mothers became especially severe, particularly for those who worked away from home, but also because uncles, aunts, and grandparents often remained behind in Puerto Rico.

The fact that so many Puerto Ricans were sojourners caused the children to have a particularly difficult time with language at school. As early as 1958, the New York City board of education, pointing out that one-tenth of the children in the schools were Puerto Rican, commented that their "lack of ability to speak or understand English represented a considerable handicap to learning."[61] Movement back and forth, language problems, and family stress all contributed to a high dropout rate in New York City (and other cities in the Northeast and Midwest), but even though Puerto Rican youngsters presumably left school to find jobs, unemployment rates were consistently highest among Puerto Rican teenagers compared to all other groups, sometimes over 50 percent.[62]

As was true for blacks, the census tracts with large numbers of unemployed Puerto Rican males also had large numbers of female-headed households living in poverty. Nationally, the 1980 census revealed that 35.3 percent of Puerto Rican households were headed by women, compared to 16.4 percent for Mexicans and 14.9 percent for Cubans: it was in the Northeast particularly (New York and New Jersey) that unemployment rates and other characteristics of the underclass were strongest (among Puerto Ricans in New York and New Jersey, poverty afflicted almost four out of ten families during the 1980s).[63]

California, only fifth in Puerto Rican population among the states in 1980 (93,038), presented a demographic profile in sharp contrast to New York, New Jersey, and Illinois. In California, the Puerto Rican population was much older; a much higher proportion of the adults had completed high school; and a third of the Puerto Ricans were monolingual English speakers (contrasted to about one out of ten in the states where Puerto Ricans were most numerous). Puerto Ricans there had relatively high rates of employment, lower rates of poverty, and, not unexpectedly, a higher proportion of children in two-parent households than in the northeastern states.[64]

Only in California were Puerto Ricans likely to be better off than

Mexicans. In California, the proportion of Hispanic households with income under $20,000 in the 1980s was much higher than for African-Americans (40 percent to 27 percent), attributable to a considerable extent to the large number of Mexican sojourners and especially illegal aliens who came to Los Angeles, San Diego, and other areas of the state. But even the barrios of the cities of California were not characterized by the alienation from mainstream jobs and institutions of the poorest black and Puerto Rican ghettoes in the Northeast. (One survey showed that 78 percent of the Hispanics of Los Angeles believed the city offered a good living to willing workers, the same percentage as whites.)[65]

Except in California, Puerto Ricans were much more likely to live in an underclass than were Mexicans and Mexican-Americans. In 1980, the relative percentage of Puerto Rican female-headed households (35.3 percent) compared to Mexican and Mexican-American female-headed households (16.4 percent) correlated closely with the percentage of all families in the two groups living below the poverty level (39.4 percent for Puerto Ricans, 20.6 percent for Mexicans). Household composition was a key factor—whether a cause, an effect, or both—in determining whether children in Hispanic families would be raised in poverty. When married Puerto Rican and Mexican couples with children were compared, the poverty gap almost disappeared ($14,855 median income for Mexicans, $13,428 for Puerto Ricans).[66] By 1987, the difference in median income for Puerto Ricans and Mexicans for all households was between $23,300 for Mexicans and $15,000 for Puerto Ricans, mainly because 48 percent of all Puerto Rican families were then headed by single parents, compared to 24 percent for Mexicans and Mexican-Americans.[67]

Those Mexican nationals who were illegal aliens, like Salvadoreans, Dominicans, and others who were undocumented, were likely to be part of that kind of underclass determined by legal status.[68] Confined to temporary or unstable jobs, often exploited by employers, and usually unable to avail themselves of the protection or benefits of the civic culture, most of them probably found it even more difficult to live and work in the U.S. than illegal aliens had before the passage of employer sanctions in 1986. But undocumented aliens were less likely to live in a culture dominated by unemployment and absence from the work force than the poorest African-Americans and Puerto Ricans of the cities or Indians on reservations, since the primary reason illegal aliens remained in the U.S. was that they were able to find work. Nor were they as likely to live in the drug-infested public housing characteristic of black and Puerto Rican ghettoes in several major cities.

Who Are the Outsiders?

The most serious problems in American society in the 1980s were not, as in nearly all other multiethnic nations, those of racial, religious, and nationality conflict. No nation in history had proven as successful as the United States in managing ethnic diversity. No nation before had ever made diversity itself a source of national identity and unity. No nation in history had so eroded the distinction between naturalized and native-born citizens or had made it so easy for aliens from vastly different cultures to become citizens.

Yet, no nation's families seemed to suffer from as much stress. Nowhere else was such a burden put on children because of broken families. And never before was extreme poverty, and all of the problems connected with it, so clearly linked to household composition. (Although only 13 percent of U.S. families were headed by women in 1980, such families constituted 70 percent of the underclass.)⁶⁹ Most Americans who lived in poverty were white; a majority of high school dropouts were white. To be poor and white in the 1980s was to be excluded from many aspects of American life. To be black and poor, or Hispanic and poor, or Indian and poor was to be marked as an outsider by both ethnicity and class; but class boundaries, reinforced by race, probably were the most difficult to cross.

Well-to-do Americans of all colors and backgrounds increasingly were welcomed almost anywhere in the United States in the 1980s, but the poorest Americans, particularly those of color, were seen not just as afflicted with problems but as the bearers of trouble. The underclass was not a new concept; it certainly was not a new phenomenon. In the middle decades of the nineteenth century, Irish immigrants—with high rates of crime, disease, and family separation—constituted a kind of underclass, too. Now, when the completion of high school at least was necessary to hold a good job, the problems of the persistently poor seemed more intractable than in previous eras.

Crèvecoeur and Tocqueville, Grund, and other foreign observers of nineteenth-century America wrote and spoke about the integrative and co-optive power of American capitalism and politics. The history of the absorption and integration of immigrants into mainstream institutions in the U.S., including those from the Third World—despite the hardships and even the agony of many immigrants—justified their optimism. The immigrants and their children became Americans by seizing economic opportunity and, as Lincoln emphasized (echoing Tocqueville) by claiming their rights. The civic culture, by protecting those rights—permitting and even encouraging voluntary pluralism—won their loyalty. That process worked increasingly in the 1970s and 1980s for many African-Americans, Puerto Ricans, and even some Indians, who, among all Americans perhaps had the least reason to give their loyalty. But to most Americans living in an ethno-underclass, the civic culture and economic opportunity (outside of illicit activities) had little meaning. A 1985 article in the NAACP's national magazine, *The Crisis,* in emphasizing the importance of blacks becoming entrepreneurs, captioned the picture accompanying the article: "To Seek Opportunity Is to Be American . . ."[70] But blacks in the underclass found it extremely difficult to save and invest like capitalists (except in an underground economy) because their lack of education and other problems associated with poverty seemed to put good jobs out of reach; often they did not have enough hope to lobby or petition their government, or even to vote.

The courageous fight of blacks, Hispanics, Asians, Indians, and whites to end the worst features of the old systems of coercive pluralism had succeeded. Because of their successful struggle, the United States had become a more just nation. But the race-conscious and language remedies fostered by the civil rights movement were less pertinent to solving or even alleviating the problems of the persistent poor than programs that helped young children in poverty, regardless of color or ethnicity. A major study issued in 1989 by the National Academy of Sciences, *A Common Destiny: Blacks and American Society,* made it clear that the environment of poverty itself is the major factor connected to such problems as infant mortality or dropping out of high school.[71] The bad news in the 1980s was that the problems of the ethno-underclass worsened. The good news was that although scholars disagreed on the causes of poverty, several programs were effective in dealing with some of its worst consequences.[72] Until Americans developed the will and skill to apply such programs widely, children born into the ethno-underclass would be likely to remain substantially outside of the civic culture.

Because the civic culture is the common culture of Americans, patriotism consists primarily in acting on its basic principle of equal rights. Belief in that principle led African-Americans and their allies to overthrow caste, forced the U.S. to reshape its relationship to Native Americans, eliminated racial and ethnic considerations from U.S. immigration policy, and expanded the rights of aliens. By 1990, the biggest domestic challenge to those who believed in equal rights lay in enhancing opportunity for those children born into the underclass.

Notes

Part 1. The Civic Culture and Voluntary Pluralism

1. Uri Ra'anan, ed., *Ethnic Resurgence in Modern Democratic States: A Multidisciplinary Approach to Human Resources and Concepts* (New York: Pergamon Press, 1980). This is a collection of articles on various multiethnic nations.
2. Alexis de Tocqueville, *Democracy in America,* The Henry Reeve text as revised by Francis Bowen, 2 vols. (New York: Vintage Books, 1945), 1:251–253.
3. Ibid., 2:124.
4. Ibid., p. 125.
5. Ibid., p. 127.
6. Ibid., p. 126.
7. Ibid., p. 270.
8. John Stuart Mill, "On Tocqueville," in Mortimer J. Adler, Otto Bird, and Robert M. Hutchins, eds., *The Great Ideas Today, 1964* (Chicago: William Benton, Publisher. Encyclopedia Britannica, Inc., 1964), p. 479.
9. John Stuart Mill, "On the Extension of the Suffrage," in Robert M. Hutchins, ed., *Great Books of the Western World* (Chicago: William Benton, Publisher. Encyclopedia Britannica, Inc., 1952), 43:381.
10. Ibid., p. 382.
11. Gabriel A. Almond and Sidney Verba, *The Civic Culture Revisited* (Boston: Little, Brown, 1980), p. 4. Their first description and analysis of the subject appeared in *The Civic Culture* (Princeton, N.J.: Princeton University Press, 1963).
12. Almond and Verba, *Civic Culture Revisited,* p. 179.
13. Washington is quoted in Henry Steele Commager, ed., *Living Ideas in America* (New York: Harper & Brothers, 1951), p. 145.

1. "True Americanism": The Foundations of the Civic Culture

1. Morris U. Schappes, ed., *A Documentary History of the Jews in the United States, 1654–1875* (New York: Schocken Books, 1971), pp. 150–157.
2. Lawrence H. Fuchs, *The Political Behavior of American Jews* (Glencoe, Ill.: The Free Press, 1956). See pp. 25–30 for early Jewish activity in American politics.
3. Darrett B. Ruthman, *Winthrop's Boston: The Portrait of a Puritan Town, 1630–1649* (Chapel Hill: University of North Carolina Press, 1965), p. 136.
4. Martin E. Marty, *Pilgrims in Their Own Land: Five Hundred Years of Religion in America* (New York: Penguin Books, 1984), p. 84.
5. Ibid., p. 86.
6. Maldwyn Allen Jones, *American Immigration* (Chicago: University of Chicago Press, 1960), p. 20.
7. *On Common Ground; The Boston Jewish Experience, 1649–1980* (Boston: The American Jewish Historical Society, 1981).
8. Lee M. Friedman, *Judah Monis,* pamphlet (Baltimore, 1914).

9. *On Common Ground.*
10. Harry Smith and J. Hugo Talsch, *Moses Michael Hays: Merchant, Citizen, Free-mason, 1739–1805,* pamphlet (Boston: 1937).
11. Bernard Bailyn, *The Peopling of British North America* (New York: Alfred A. Knopf, 1986), p. 100.
12. Edmund S. Morgan, *American Slavery, American Freedom: The Ordeal of Colonial Virginia* (New York: W. W. Norton & Company, 1975), p. 216.
13. Ibid., p. 217.
14. Ibid., p. 297.
15. Bailyn, *Peopling of British North America,* p. 101.
16. Ibid., p. 331.
17. Ibid., p. 335.
18. Ibid., p. 344.
19. Jones, *American Immigration,* p. 47.
20. Susan S. Forbes and Peter Lemos, "A History of American Language Policy," *Papers on U.S. Immigration History: U.S. Immigration Policy and the National Interest,* Appendix A to the Staff Report of the Select Commission on Immigration and Refugee Policy (Washington, D.C.: 1981), p. 24.
21. James H. Kettner, *The Development of American Citizenship, 1608–1870* (Chapel Hill: University of North Carolina Press, 1978), p. 110.
22. Forbes and Lemos, "American Language Policy," p. 29.
23. Ibid., p. 27.
24. Marty, *Pilgrims in Their Own land,* pp. 115–156.
25. Bailyn, *Peopling of British North America,* p. 85.
26. Maxine Seller, *To Seek America: A History of Ethnic Life in the United States* (New York: James S. Ozer, 1977), p. 15.
27. Bernard Mayo, ed., *Jefferson Himself: The Personal Narrative of a Many-Sided American* (Boston: Houghton Mifflin, 1942), pp. 70, 72.
28. Merrill D. Peterson, ed., *The Portable Thomas Jefferson* (New York: Penguin Books, 1977), p. 125.
29. Kettner, *Development of American Citizenship,* p. 214.
30. Ibid., p. 216.
31. Ibid., p. 215.
32. Ibid., p. 214.
33. Ibid., p. 216.
34. Ibid., p. 27.
35. Ibid., p. 228.
36. Ibid., p. 26.
37. Benjamin R. Ringer, *We, The People, and Others* (New York: Tavistock Publications, 1983), pp. 109, 110.
38. Kettner, *Development of American Citizenship,* p. 237.
39. Ibid., p. 238.
40. Ringer, *We, The People, and Others,* pp. 110, 111.
41. Kettner, *Development of American Citizenship,* p. 240.
42. Ringer, *We, The People, and Others,* pp. 112–115.
43. Kettner, *Development of American Citizenship,* p. 242.
44. Howard W. Preston, ed., *Documents Illustrative of American History, 1606–1863, with Introduction and References* (New York: P. T. Putnam's Sons, 1886), p. 278.
45. The Federalist position is quoted in Henry Steele Commager, ed., *Documents of American History* (New York: Appleton-Century-Crofts, 1963), p. 210.
46. Alexander Hamilton, James Madison, and John Jay, *The Federalist,* ed. Edward Mead Earle (New York: Modern Library, 1937), p. 9. Although descendants of

the English dominated the free white population at the beginning of the republic, the first census of 1790 showed that the English and their descendants constituted just under half the total population of 3,929,000. Twenty percent were from Africa. Almost a third were of Scotch-Irish, German, Scottish, French, Irish, Swiss, Spanish, Dutch, and other backgrounds.

47. More than 50,000 immigrants arrived annually beginning in 1832, the year of Tocqueville's visit, except for 1835 and 1838, and in the 1840s a total of 1,713,251 immigrants arrived, a large majority either Irish or German. Between 1831 and 1840, Ireland led in the number of immigrants with 207,381, Germany was second with 152,454, and the United Kingdom was third with 75,810. Between 1841 and 1850, Ireland went up to 780,719; Germany, 434,624; and the U.K., 267,044. Between 1851 and 1860, the numbers were: Germany 951,666; Ireland, 914,119; and the U.K., 423,974. Between 1821 and 1830, there had been only 6,761 immigrants from Germany, a smaller number than from France. *1985 Statistical Yearbook of the Immigration and Naturalization Service,* U.S. Department of Justice, Immigration and Naturalization Service (Washington, D.C.: U.S. Government Printing Office, 1946), p. 2.

48. John A. Hostetler, *Hutterite Society* (Baltimore: Johns Hopkins University Press, 1974).

49. John A. Hostetler, *Amish Society* (Baltimore: Johns Hopkins University Press, 1968).

50. Kathleen Neils Conzen, "Germans," in Stephan Thernstrom, ed., *Harvard Encyclopedia of American Ethnic Groups* (Cambridge: Harvard University Press, 1980), p. 410.

51. Arthur Mann, *The One and the Many: Reflections on the American Identity* (Chicago: University of Chicago Press, 1979), p. 61.

52. Alexis de Tocqueville, *Democracy in America,* The Henry Reeve text as revised by Francis Bowen, 2 vols. (New York: Vintage Books, 1945), 1:259.

53. Ibid., p. 83.

54. Conzen, "Germans," p. 412. In 1850, the percentage of German-born of all foreign-born varied by regions. It was highest in the east north central states (39.1 percent) and middle Atlantic states (36.0 percent).

55. Ibid., p. 406.

56. Francis Joseph Grund, *The Americans in Their Moral, Social, and Political Relations* (Boston: March, Capen and Lyon, 1837).

57. Ibid., p. 68.

58. Ibid., pp. 212, 213.

59. Ibid., p. 74.

60. Conzen, "Germans," p. 417. By 1850, there were substantial numbers of German-born in several cities: New York (56,141), Cincinnati (33,374), Philadelphia (23,020), St. Louis (22,571), and Baltimore (19,274), with growing communities in Chicago, New Orleans, Buffalo, and Milwaukee.

61. Ibid., p. 418.

62. Hector St. Jean de Crèvecoeur, *Letters from an American Farmer and Sketches of Eighteenth-Century America* (New York: New American Library, Signet Edition, 1963), p. 64.

63. Michael Kraus, *Immigration and the American Mosaic* (Princeton, N.J.: D. Van Nostrand Company, 1966), p. 120.

64. Ibid.

65. Ibid., p. 122.

66. Ibid.

67. Ibid., p. 123.

68. Ibid., p. 128.
69. Ibid., p. 121.
70. Charlotte Erickson, *Invisible Immigrants: The Adaptation of English and Scottish Immigrants in Nineteenth Century America* (Coral Gables: University of Miami Press, 1972), pp. 117, 118.
71. Grund, *The Americans,* p. 69.
72. Ibid., pp. 413–415.
73. Ibid., pp. 156, 157.
74. Ibid., pp. 209–210.
75. Ibid., p. 148.
76. Moses Rischin, *Immigration and the American Tradition* (Indianapolis: Bobbs-Merrill, 1966), p. 47.
77. Dale T. Knobel, "To Be an American: Ethnicity, Fraternity and the Improved Order of Redmen," *Journal of American History,* 4 (Fall 1984):65.
78. Ibid., pp. 66–67.
79. Ibid., pp. 73–75.
80. Victor R. Greene, *American Immigrant Leaders, 1800–1910: Marginality and Identity* (Baltimore: Johns Hopkins University Press, 1987), p. 47.
81. Ibid., p. 50.
82. Ibid., p. 54.
83. Ibid., p. 58.
84. Conzen, "Germans," p. 420. According to Conzen, four of five children of German stock were in public schools by 1880, compared to 1860, when only one of five went to public schools, the increase resulting from the introduction of bilingualism in the St. Louis schools. One estimate for 1886 holds that about 430,000 children nationwide were in schools with German instruction, 35 percent of them public schools.
85. David A. Gerber, "Language Maintenance, Ethnic Group Formation, and Public Schools: Changing Patterns of German Concern, Buffalo, 1837–1874," *Journal of American Ethnic History,* Fall 1984.
86. Grund, *The Americans,* p. 216.
87. Ibid., p. 69.
88. Quoted in Henry Steele Commager, ed., *America in Perspective* (New York: New American Library, 1947), p. 143.
89. Ibid.
90. Quoted in Jerry Eastland and William J. Bennett, eds., *Counting by Race: Equality from the Founding Fathers to Bakke and Weber* (New York: Basic Books, 1979), p. 53.
91. Rischin, *Immigration and the American Tradition,* p. 124.
92. Ibid., p. 129.
93. Willi Paul Adams, "Ethnic Leadership Among German-Americans: Report on a Research Project in Progress," unpublished paper delivered at the Woodrow Wilson International Center for Scholars, September 8, 1981. Of the forty-three German-born elected to Congress, almost all had occupied public offices in their community or state before they went to Washington. Seventeen had been members of their state House of Representatives, eight had been state senators, six had been mayors, six postmasters, six members of the board of education, five members of the city council, two governor or lieutenant governor of their state, and one each a U.S. marshal, a state treasurer, a judge, and a coroner.
94. Ibid., p. 16.

95. Ibid., p. 18.
96. Grund, *The Americans,* pp. 109, 150.
97. Ibid., p. 71.
98. Ibid., pp. 107, 108.
99. The term "civic religion" came into prominence as a result of an article by Robert N. Bellah, "Civil Religion in America," *Daedalus,* "Religion in America," Winter 1967. It was first used by Rousseau in *The Social Contract.* Rousseau's civil religion was a vaguely formulated idea; it included an inhibition on religious intolerance. According to Bellah, all of the major biblical archetypes and symbols lay behind the civil religion of the U.S.: the Exodus, chosen people, promised land, new Jerusalem, sacrificial death and rebirth. The Americans evolved their own prophets, martyrs, sacred events and places, rituals, and symbols. Key elements in the civil religion, in addition to an inhibition on sectarian intolerance, are a general belief in God, convictions that the creation of the U.S. was providential and that the American people have covenanted with God to promote liberty and opportunity for all. In the same year as Bellah's article, I developed the idea of the American "culture religion," in *John F. Kennedy and American Catholicism* (New York: Meredith Press, 1967). I emphasized the same components as Bellah, whose term "civil religion" is better than "culture religion" because it is more precise. It is the religion that sanctifies the myths, institutions, symbols, rituals, and beliefs of Americans concerning principles of free government. Catherine Albanese, in *Sons of the Fathers: The Civil Religion and the American Revolution* (Philadelphia: Temple University Press, 1976), elaborated on Bellah's initial thesis with respect to the origins of the civil religion in the American Revolution. The concept has undergone controversy in recent years (George Armstrong Kelly, *Politics and Religious Consciousness in America,* [New Brunswick, N.J.: Transaction Books, 1984]), and even Bellah has argued that the American people have failed to live up to their part of the covenant in *The Broken Covenant: American Civil Religion in Time of Trial* (New York: Seabury Press, 1975).
100. Rischin, *Immigration and the American Tradition,* p. 44.
101. Frank G. Franklin, *Legislative History of Naturalization* (New York: Arno Press, 1969), p. 97.
102. Ibid., p. 43.
103. Yehoshua Arieli, *Individualism and Nationalism in American Ideology* (Baltimore: Penguin Books, 1966), p. 49. Arieli brilliantly demonstrated the relationship of the ideal of individual freedom to the development of patriotic nationalism in the U.S.
104. Fuchs, *Kennedy and American Catholicism,* p. 15.
105. Schappes, *A Documentary History of the Jews,* p. 83.
106. Fuchs, *Kennedy and American Catholicism,* p. 18.
107. Ibid.
108. Ibid., p. 25.
109. Barry Schwartz, "The Jewish Prayer for the Government in America," *American Jewish History,* March 1987, p. 336.
110. Roy Rosenzweig, *Eight Hours for What We Will: Workers and Leisure in an Industrial City, 1870–1920* (New York: Cambridge University Press, 1983), p. 82.
111. Mann, *The One and the Many,* p. 64.
112. Grund, *The Americans,* p. 165.
113. Crèvecoeur, *Letters from an American Farmer,* p. 70. It was Crèvecoeur's observation that religious freedom served to unify Americans rather than disturb them. See p. 323.

114. Mayo, *Jefferson Himself*, p. 81.
115. Grund, *The Americans*, p. 158.
116. Tocqueville, *Democracy in America*, 2, pp. 391, 392.
117. Grund, *The Americans*, p. 374.

2. *"Reinforcements to Republicanism":*
Irish Catholic Response to the Civic Culture

1. Lawrence H. Fuchs, *John F. Kennedy and American Catholicism* (New York: Meredith Press, 1967), pp. 179–181.
2. Ray Allen Billington, *The Protestant Crusade 1800–1860: A Study of the Origins of American Nativism* (New York: Rinehart & Co., Inc., 1938). See pp. 11–13 for anti-Catholic legislation and other actions in the colonies in the period just before the Revolution.
3. Fuchs, *Kennedy and American Catholicism*, pp. 35–36.
4. Billington, *Protestant Crusade*, p. 18.
5. Hector St. Jean de Crèvecoeur, *Letters from an American Farmer* (New York: New American Library, Signet Edition, 1963), pp. 68, 69.
6. Fuchs, *Kennedy and American Catholicism*, pp. 36, 37.
7. James Hennessey, S.J., *American Catholics: A History of the Roman Catholic Community in the United States* (New York: Oxford University Press, 1981), p. 73.
8. Kirk H. Porter and Donald Bruce Johnson, eds., *National Party Platforms, 1840–1868*, rev. ed. (Urbana: University of Illinois Press, 1970), pp. 2, 3, 11, 17.
9. *New England Magazine*, 7 (December 1834): 471–77.
10. *National Intelligencer*, July 6, 1844, from U.S. Congress, "Foreign Paupers and Naturalization Laws: Report of the Select Committee," House Report 1040, 25th Cong., 2nd Session, 1838, p. 111.
11. Dale T. Knobel, *Paddy and the Republic: Ethnicity and Nationality in Antebellum America* (Middletown, Conn.: Wesleyan University Press, 1985), p. 71.
12. Moses Rischin, *Immigration and the American Tradition* (Indianapolis: Bobbs-Merrill, 1966), p. 74.
13. Ibid., p. 75.
14. Speech by Louis C. Levin, quoted in Ira M. Leonard and Robert D. Parmet, *American Nativism, 1830–1860* (New York: D. Van Nostrand Reinhold Co., 1971), pp. 132–133. The American Republican Association asked for a residency period of twenty-one years before granting newcomers the vote and proposed that only native-born Americans be appointed to office. The Irish, according to the American Party, were strangers to the "moderation and self-control of American republicanism." See John Hancock Lee, *The Origin and Purposes of the American Party in Politics: Embracing a Complete History of the Philadelphia Riots in May and July, 1844, with a Full Description of the Great American Procession of July 4, and a Refutation of the Arguments Founded on the Charges and Religious Proscriptions and Secret Combinations* (Philadelphia: Elliott and Gihon, 1855), p. 21.
15. Rischin, *Immigration and the American Tradition*, p. 68.
16. Billington, *Protestant Crusade*, pp. 300–303.
17. Ibid., pp. 131–132.
18. Ibid., p. 380.
19. Ibid., pp. 383–386.
20. Jean Baker, *Ambivalent Americans: The Know-Nothing Party in Maryland* (Baltimore: Johns Hopkins University Press, 1977), p. 77.
21. Billington, *Protestant Crusade*, p. 388.

22. Ibid.
23. Porter and Johnson, *National Party Platforms*, 1:24–25.
24. Fuchs, *Kennedy and American Catholicism*, p. 57.
25. Dennis Clark, "The Irish Catholics," in Randall M. Miller and Thomas E. Marzik, eds., *Immigrants and Religion in Urban America* (Philadelphia: Temple University Press, 1977), p. 49.
26. Patrick J. Blessing, "Irish," *Harvard Encyclopedia of American Ethnic Groups,* ed. Stephan Thernstrom (Cambridge: Harvard University Press, 1980), pp. 143–144, 151.
27. Diane Ravitch, *The Great School Wars: New York City, 1805–1973* (New York: Basic Books, 1974), p. 67.
28. Ibid., p. 68.
29. Ibid., pp. 150–153.
30. Fuchs, *Kennedy and American Catholicism*, p. 53.
31. Kirby A. Miller, *Emigrants and Exiles: Ireland and the Irish Exodus to North America* (New York: Oxford University Press, 1985), p. 329.
32. Oscar Handlin, *Boston's Immigrants: 1790–1880* (New York: Atheneum, 1972).
33. Ibid., p. 19.
34. Ibid., pp. 23–25.
35. Ibid., pp. 54–116 for social and economic conditions of the Irish and their impact on the city.
36. Dennis P. Ryan, *Beyond the Ballot Box: A Social History of the Boston Irish, 1848–1917* (Rutherford, N.J.: Fairleigh Dickinson University Press, 1983), p. 50.
37. Thomas H. O'Connor, *Bibles, Brahmins and Bosses: A Short History of Boston* (Boston: Boston Public Library, 1976), p. 93.
38. Ryan, *Beyond the Ballot Box,* p. 50.
39. Blessing, "Irish," p. 531.
40. Jeremiah O'Donovan, *Irish Immigration in the United States: Immigrant Interviews* (New York: Arno Press and The New York Times, 1966), p. 241.
41. Robert Francis Hueston, "The Catholic Press and Nativism, 1840–1860," (Ph.D. diss., University of Notre Dame, 1972). See chapters 5, 6, and 7. Also see William Leonard Joyce, *Editors and Ethnicity: A History of the Irish-American Press* (New York: Arno Press, 1976). The editors, like the politicians, married what Joyce calls "Constitutional nationalism" (p. 184) with Irish-American culture, helping the Irish to adopt an identity that was both Irish and American.
42. Victor Greene, *American Immigrant Leaders, 1800–1910: Marginality and Identity* (Baltimore: Johns Hopkins University Press, 1987), pp. 33–36.
43. Ibid., p. 36.
44. Ibid., p. 38.
45. Ibid., p. 38.
46. Ibid., p. 93.
47. Doris Kearns Goodwin, *The Fitzgeralds and the Kennedys* (New York: Simon & Schuster, 1987). The material on John Fitzgerald is in chapters 4, 5, and 6.
48. Ibid., p. 112.
49. Ibid., p. 13.
50. James Michael Curley, *I'd Do It Again: A Record of All My Uproarious Years* (Englewood Cliffs, N.J.: (Prentice-Hall, 1957).
51. James Michael Curley, speech to visitors to Boston, undated, audio tape in author's files.
52. Curley, *I'd Do It Again*, pp. 207, 208.
53. Hueston, "The Catholic Press and Nativism," p. 309.
54. Ibid., pp. 315–318.

55. Thomas N. Brown, *Irish-American Nationalism: 1870–1890* (Philadelphia: J. B. Lippincott, 1966).
56. The above and the following discussion can be found in Fuchs, *Kennedy and American Catholicism*, pp. 94–116.
57. Ibid., p. 180.
58. Ibid., pp. 240, 241.
59. Curley, *I'd Do It Again*, p. 359.
60. William J. Galush, "Faith and Fatherland: Dimensions of Polish-American Ethno-Religion, 1875–1975," in Miller and Marzik, eds., *Immigrants and Religion*, p. 84.
61. J. P. Dolan, "Philadelphia and the German Catholic Community," in Miller and Marzik, eds., *Immigrants and Religion*, pp. 69, 70.
62. Ibid., p. 59.
63. John Lukacs, *Outgrowing Democracy: The History of the United States in the Twentieth Century* (New York: Doubleday & Co., 1984), p. 350.
64. *New York Times*, September 16, 1986, p. B2.
65. Hueston, "The Catholic Press and Nativism," pp. 247, 248.

3. More Slovenian and More American: How the Hyphen Unites

1. David B. Little, *America's First Centennial Celebration* (Boston: Houghton Mifflin Company, 1974), p. 56.
2. Kirk H. Porter and Donald Bruce Johnson, eds., *National Party Platforms, 1840–1868* (Urbana: University of Illinois Press, 1970), pp. 35, 40.
3. *1985 Statistical Yearbook of the Immigration and Naturalization Service*, U.S. Department of Justice, Immigration and Naturalization Service (Washington, D.C.: U.S. Government Printing Office, 1986). When this book went to press, the Statistical Yearbooks for 1986, 1987, and 1988 had been published. They will be used subsequently. For historical statistics, the 1985 yearbook will be used unless otherwise indicated.
4. *Immigration Policy and the National Interest*, Staff Report of the Select Commission on Immigration and Refugee Policy, Supplement to the Final Report and Recommendations of the Select Commission, April 30, 1981, p. 28.
5. Ibid., p. 230. Reporting of immigration via U.S. land borders with Mexico and Canada was not fully established until 1908.
6. Woodrow Wilson, *A History of the American People*, 5 vols. (New York: Harper & Brothers, 1901), 5:212–214.
7. Thomas Bailey Aldrich, "Unguarded Gates," *Atlantic Monthly*, April 1892, p. 57. Aldrich was editor of this Boston-based magazine.
8. Nathaniel Shaler, *The Neighbor: The Natural History of Human Contacts* (Boston: Houghton Mifflin Company, 1904), p. 65.
9. Ibid., pp. 124, 125.
10. Ibid., p. 328.
11. John Higham, *Strangers in the Land: Patterns of American Nativism, 1860–1925* (New York: Atheneum, 1963), p. 123. Higham's book is the classic interpretation of the rise and fall of confidence of Anglo-Americans in their ability to absorb immigrants, leading to the culmination of restrictionist thinking in passage of laws by Congress in the 1920s sharply curtailing immigration.
12. Ellwood P. Cubberly, a major spokesman for the restrictionists, is quoted in Lawrence A. Cremin, *The Transformation of the School: Progressives in American Education, 1876–1957* (New York: Alfred A. Knopf, 1961, Vintage Books Edition, 1964), pp. 67, 68.

13. E. P. Hutchinson, *Legislative History of American Immigration Policy, 1798–1965* (Philadelphia: University of Pennsylvania Press, 1981), pp. 77–155.
14. Porter and Johnson, *National Party Platforms,* p. 187.
15. Ibid., pp. 195–196.
16. Ibid., pp. 202–203.
17. Higham, *Strangers in the Land,* p. 203. The literacy test actually was not terribly stringent. It called for adult immigrants to read a simple passage in some language and exempted anyone who was a member of the immediate family of an admissible alien and all aliens who could prove they were fleeing from religious persecution.
18. Ibid., pp. 291, 292; Kenneth T. Jackson, *The Ku Klux Klan in the City, 1915–1930* (New York: Oxford University Press, 1967), p. 201.
19. Julius Drachsler, *Democracy and Assimilation,* (New York: Macmillan, 1920), p. 194.
20. Madison Grant, "America for the Americans," *The Forum,* December 1925, p. 351.
21. Johnson is quoted in Roger Daniels, "American Refugee Policy in Historical Perspective," in J. C. Jackman and Carla Borden, eds., *The Muses Flee Hitler: Cultural Transfer and Adaptation, 1930–1945* (Washington, D.C., Smithsonian Institution Press, 1983), p. 65.21.
22. Henry Pratt Fairchild, *The Melting Pot Mistake* (Boston: Little, Brown and Company, 1926), p. 245.
23. Higham, *Strangers in the Land,* p. 243.
24. *Americanization Bulletin* 1 (October 15, 1918): 1 (Washington, D.C.: U.S. Department of Interior).
25. Edward George Hartmann, *The Movement to Americanize the Immigrant* (New York: Columbia University Press, 1948), p. 38.
26. Ibid., p. 42.
27. Ibid., p. 51.
28. Ibid., pp. 45–48.
29. Herbert Gutman, *Work, Culture and Society in Industrializing America* (New York: Random House, 1976), p. 6.
30. Hartmann, *Movement to Americanize,* pp. 102–109.
31. Ibid., pp. 235–253.
32. Elisabeth C. Barney Buel, compiler, *Manual of the United States: For the Information of Immigrants and Foreigners,* 5th edition (Washington, D.C.: The National Society of the Daughters of the American Revolution, 1928).
33. Address by Mrs. George Maynard Minor, Waterford, Connecticut, 1920, ibid., pp. 12, 13.
34. Ibid., p. 15.
35. Ibid., p. 17.
36. Ibid., p. 26.
37. Hjalmar Hjorth Boyesen, "The Immigrant's Unhappy Predicament," in Moses Rischin, ed., *Immigration and the American Tradition* (Indianapolis: Bobbs-Merrill, 1966), p. 299.
38. Charles F. Heartman, *The Necessity of Prohibiting German Newspapers, from a Different Point of View,* pamphlet, 1918.
39. Gustavus Ohlinger, *True and Faithful Allegiance* (New York: Macmillan Company, 1916), pp. 68–70.
40. Ibid., pp. 119, 120.
41. Hartmann, *Movement to Americanize,* p. 256.
42. Ibid., p. 257.
43. Lawrence H. Fuchs, *The Political Behavior of American Jews* (Glencoe, Ill.: The Free Press, 1956), p. 51.

44. Hartmann, *Movement to Americanize*, p. III.
45. Lawrence McGuffin, *Waltham Book of American Citizenship*, Waltham Evening Schools, published for the adult education classes (Waltham, Mass., 1929), p. 4.
46. Ibid., p. 9.
47. Hoover is quoted in E. D. Baltzell, *The Protestant Establishment: Aristocracy and Caste in America* (New York: Vintage Books, 1965), p. 30.
48. Lincoln is quoted in Jerry Eastland and William J. Bennett, *Counting by Race: Equality from the Founding Fathers to Bakke and Weber* (New York: Basic Books, 1979), p. 53.
49. Adams is quoted in Philip Perlmutter, "Ethnicity, Education and Prejudice: The Teaching of Contempt," *Ethnicity*, 8 (1981): 58.
50. Mary Antin, *The Promised Land* (Boston: Houghton Mifflin and Company, 1912), p. 225.
51. Ibid., p. 341.
52. The exchange between Abrams and Judge Clayton is quoted in Richard Polenberg, "Progressivism and Anarchism: Judge Henry D. Clayton and the Abrams Trial," *Law and History Review*, 4 (Fall 1985): 397.
53. Ibid., p. 402.
54. Ibid., p. 405.
55. Ibid., p. 407.
56. Randolph S. Bourne, "Trans-National America," *Atlantic Monthly*, July 1916, p. 88.
57. Higham, *Strangers in the Land*, chapter 10, "The Tribal Twenties," pp. 264–299.
58. Ibid., p. 264.
59. William Addison Blakely, ed., *American State Papers on Freedom and Religion* (Washington, D.C.: published for the Religious Liberty Association by the *Review and Herald*, 1943), p. 630. See *Meyer v. State of Nebraska*, Supreme Court of the U.S., 262 U.S. 390 (1923), pp. 401–403.
60. Blakely, ibid., p. 624. See *Pierce, Governor of Oregon, et al. v. The Society of Sisters*, 268 U.S. 510 (1925).
61. *Farrington, Governor of Hawaii, et al. v. Tokushige et al.*, 284 U.S. 298 (1926).
62. Jacob A. Riis, *The Making of an American* (New York: Macmillan Company, 1960).
63. Louis Adamic, *My America, 1928–1938* (New York: Harper Brothers, 1938), pp. 126–127.
64. Ibid., pp. 128.
65. Fairchild, *Melting Pot Mistake*, p. 172.
66. Ibid., p. 173.
67. Rudolph J. Vecoli, "Cult and Occult in Italian-American Culture: The Persistence of a Religious Heritage," in *Immigrants and Religion in Urban America*, ed. Randall M. Miller and Thomas D. Marzik (Philadelphia: Temple University Press, 1977), chapter 2.
68. William J. Galush, "Faith and Fatherland: Dimensions of Polish-American Ethno-Religion, 1875–1975," in Miller and Marzik, ibid., pp. 91ff.
69. Roy Rosenzweig, *Eight Hours for What We Will: Workers and Leisure in an Industrial City, 1870–1920* (New York: Cambridge University Press, 1983), p. 77.
70. Ibid., p. 85.
71. Ibid., pp. 84, 85.
72. Dennis Patrick Ryan, *Beyond the Ballot Box: A Social History of the Boston Irish, 1848–1917* (Rutherford, N.J.: Fairleigh Dickinson University Press, 1983), pp. 137–138.

73. Robert Park and Herbert Miller, *Old World Traits Transplanted* (New York: Harper and Brothers, 1921).
74. Horace M. Kallen, "Democracy vs. the Melting Pot: A Study in American Nationality," *The Nation*, 100 (February 25, 1915): 218–220.
75. The education of Horace Kallen on this point by John Dewey and Kallen's change are described in a pamphlet by Moses Rischin, *The Jews and Pluralism: Toward an American Freedom Symphony*, The Institute of Human Relations Press of the American Jewish Committee, March 1980, pp. 15, 16.

Part 2. Outside the Civic Culture: The Coercive Pluralisms

1. W. E. B. Du Bois, *The Souls of Black Folk* (New York: Fawcett Publications, Inc., 1961), p. 22.

4. "Go Back to the Country from Whence You Came": Predatory Pluralism and the Native American Response

1. Jack D. Forbes, ed., *The Indian in America's Past* (Englewood Cliffs, N.J.: Prentice-Hall, Inc., 1974), p. 59.
2. Wilcombe Washburn, *Red Man's Land/White Man's Law: A Study of the Past and Present Status of the American Indian* (New York: Charles Scribner's Sons, 1971), Document 51.
3. Forbes, *The Indian in America's Past*, p. 100. For a broad understanding of American policy toward Indians, see also Angie Debo, *A History of the Indians in the United States* (Norman: University of Oklahoma Press, 1970); Brian W. Dippie, *The Vanishing American: White Attitudes and U.S. Indian Policy* (Middletown, Conn.: Wesleyan University Press, 1982); and Vine DeLoria, Jr., and Clifford M. Lytle, *American Indians, American Justice* (Austin: University of Texas Press, 1983).
4. Forbes, *The Indian in America's Past*, p. 100.
5. Ibid., p. 101.
6. Ibid.
7. Ibid., p. 102.
8. Jackson is quoted in Roy Pearce, *The Savages of America* (Baltimore: Johns Hopkins University Press, 1953), p. 57.
9. For a discussion of these cases and their aftermath, see Debo, *History of the Indians*, pp. 105–107.
10. The Norwegian settler is quoted in Edward Ifkovic, ed., *American Letter, Immigrant and Ethnic Writing* (Englewood Cliffs, N.J.: Prentice-Hall, Inc., 1975), pp. 173, 174.
11. Speech at the conclusion of Black Hawk's War, 1832, in Forbes, *The Indian in America's Past*, p. 64.
12. Leonard A. Carlson, *Indians, Bureaucrats and Land: The Dawes Act and the Decline of Indian Farming* (Westport, Conn.: Greenwood Press, 1981), p. 7.
13. Roosevelt's letter is cited in Louis H. Carlson and George A. Colburn, *In Their Place: White America Defines Her Minorities, 1850–1950* (New York: John Wiley and Sons, Inc., 1972), p. 16.
14. Dippie, *Vanishing American*, p. 204.
15. Debo, *History of the Indians*, pp. 339–342.
16. U.S. Statutes at Large, 67:B132, August 1, 1953.

5. "This Fourth of July is Yours": African-Americans and Caste Pluralism

1. Frederick A. Douglass, "What to the Slave is the Fourth of July?" West Indian Emancipation Speech of August 1853, quoted in Arnold Adolph, ed., *Black on Black* (New York: Macmillan Company, 1968), p. 2.
2. This brief history relies heavily on superb surveys, including John Hope Franklin, *From Slavery to Freedom: A History of Negro Americans,* 2nd ed. (New York: Alfred A. Knopf, 1964), and August Meyer and Elliott Rudwick, *From Plantation to Ghetto: An Interpretive History of American Negroes,* 3rd ed. (New York: Hill and Wang, 1976).
3. Andrew T. Mellon, *Early American Views on Negro Slavery,* with an introduction by Richard B. Morris (New York: Bergman, 1969), p. 84.
4. Ibid., p. 12.
5. Terry Eastland and William J. Bennett, *Counting by Race: Equality from the Founding Fathers to Bakke and Weber* (New York: Basic Books, 1979), pp. 37, 49.
6. Mellon, *Early American Views on Negro Slavery,* p. 63.
7. Ibid., pp. 65, 66.
8. Ibid., p. 71.
9. Ibid., pp. 80, 81.
10. Alexander Hamilton, John Jay, and James Madison, *The Federalist Papers,* with an introduction by Edward Mead Earle (New York: Random House Modern Library, 1937), p. 272.
11. *Federalist Papers,* ibid., p. 273.
12. Mellon, *Early American Views on Negro Slavery,* p. 163.
13. Ibid., pp. 106–110.
14. Ibid., p. 112.
15. Ibid., p. 117.
16. Material on the system of slavery and the lives of slaves comes from Frederick Douglass, *My Bondage and My Freedom* (New York: Miller, Orton and Mulligan, 1855); Charles Ball, *Slavery in the United States: A Narrative of the Life and Adventure of Charles Ball, a Black Man* (New York: John S. Taylor, 1837); Solomon Northrup, *Twelve Years a Slave* (Auburn, New York: Derby & Miller, 1853); *The Unwritten History of Slavery: Autobiographical Accounts of Negro Ex-Slaves* (Nashville, Tenn.: Fisk University, Social Science Institute, Social Science Documents No. 1, 1945); B. A. Botkin, ed., *Lay My Burden Down: A Folk History of Slavery* (Chicago: University of Chicago Press, 1945); John Harris, *Voices from Slavery* (New York: Tower Publications, Inc., 1971); Julius Lester, *To Be a Slave* (New York: Dell Publishing Co., Inc., 1968); and John F. Bayliss, *Black Slave Narratives* (London: Collier-Macmillan Ltd., 1970).
17. Franklin, *From Slavery to Freedom,* pp. 208–211.
18. Ibid., p. 264.
19. Ibid., p. 216.
20. Don E. Fehrenbacher, *Slavery, Law and Politics: The Dred Scott Case in Historical Perspective* (New York: Oxford University Press, 1981), pp. 31–33.
21. Ibid.
22. Alexis de Tocqueville, *Democracy in America,* The Henry Reeve text as revised by Francis Bowen, 2 vols. (New York: Vintage Books, 1945), 1:271.22.
23. *Scott* v. *Sanford,* 393 U.S. 1957 (1862), p. 403. The development of exclusionary land policies and the prohibition on blacks serving in the post office is discussed in Leon F. Litwack, "The Federal Government and the Free Negro, 1790–1860," *Journal of Negro History,* October 1958, pp. 261–278.
24. James H. Kettner, *The Development of American Citizenship, 1608–1870,* published

for the Institute of Early American History and Culture, Williamsburg, Va. (Chapel Hill: University of North Carolina Press, 1978), p. 328.

25. Richard C. Wade, *Slavery in the Cities: The South, 1820–1860* (London: Oxford University Press, 1964), p. 107.
26. Ibid., p. 273.
27. Ira Berlin, *Slaves Without Masters: The Free Negro in the Ante Bellum South* (New York: Vintage Books, 1976), p. iii.
28. Ibid., p. 215.
29. Franklin, *From Slavery to Freedom*, p. 220.
30. V. Jacques Voegeli, *Free But Not Equal: The Midwest and the Negro During the Civil War* (Chicago: University of Chicago Press, 1967), pp. 165–172.
31. *The Congressional Globe,* 39th Congress, 1st Session, 1866, p. 880.
32. Ibid., p. 2538.
33. Ibid., pp. 695–696.
34. Ibid., p. 983.
35. *United States* v. *Cruikshank* 92 U.S. 542 (1876).
36. *Civil Rights Cases* 109 U.S. III (1883).
37. *Plessy* v. *Ferguson* 163 U.S. 537 (1895).
38. Ibid., p. 476.
39. C. Vann Woodward, *The Strange Career of Jim Crow* (New York: Oxford University Press, 1965).
40. C. Vann Woodward, *Origins of the New South, 1877–1913* (Baton Rouge: Louisiana State University Press, 1971), p. 180. Woodward called the lien system "a curse to the soil." Under it, the farmer who needed tools borrowed from the merchant and found that his bill was larger than his profit.
41. Charles L. Flynn, Jr., *White Land, Black Labor: Caste and Class in Late Nineteenth-Century Georgia* (Baton Rouge: Louisiana State University Press, 1983), pp. 182, 183.
42. Ibid., pp. 181, 182.
43. Franklin, *From Slavery to Freedom*, pp. 231, 232.
44. Ibid., p. 337.
45. Ibid., p. 467.
46. Ibid., pp. 471–478.
47. Finley Peter Dunne, *The World of Mr. Dooley,* with an introduction by Louis Filler (New York: Collier Books, 1962), p. 100.
48. Woodward, *Strange Career of Jim Crow,* pp. 94–95.
49. Melvin Steinfield, *Cracks in the Melting Pot: Racism and Discrimination in American History* (Beverly Hills, Calif.: Glencoe Press, 1970), p. 243.
50. Ibid., p. 253. The quotation is from Kathleen Wolgemuth, "Woodrow Wilson and Federal Segregation," first published in *Journal of Negro History,* April 1959.
51. Stanley Lieberson, *A Piece of the Pie: Blacks and White Immigrants Since 1880* (Berkeley: University of California Press, 1980), p. 235.
52. Ibid., pp. 236–237.
53. Ibid., p. 238.
54. Gunnar Myrdal, *An American Dilemma: The Negro Problem in Modern Democracy,* 2 vols. (New York: Harper and Brothers, 1944), 1:292.
55. Dennis C. Dickerson, *Out of the Crucible: Black Steelworkers in Western Pennsylvania, 1875–1980* (Albany: State University of New York Press, 1986). Also, Sterling D. Spiro and Abram L. Harris, *The Black Worker* (New York: Atheneum, 1968, originally published by Columbia University Press, 1931).
56. August Meier and Elliott Rudwick, *Black Detroit and the Rise of the U.A.W.* (New York: Oxford University Press, 1981).

57. Spiro and Harris, *The Black Worker,* p. 79.

58. Ibid., p. 113.

59. Herbert Hill, "Race, Ethnicity and Organized Labor: The Opposition to Affirmative Action," *New Politics,* Winter 1987, p. 46.59.

60. Spiro and Harris, *The Black Worker,* p. 169.

61. Ibid., p. 341.

62. Hill, "Race, Ethnicity and Organized Labor," p. 47. For Hill's criticism of the ILGWU, see ibid., p. 54. On organized labor and blacks, see Julius Jacobson, ed., *The Negro and the American Labor Movement* (Garden City, N.Y.: Doubleday and Company, 1968).

63. John Bodnar, *Immigration and Industrialization: Ethnicity in an American Mill Town, 1870–1940* (Pittsburgh: University of Pittsburgh Press, 1977), p. 135. For a superb study of the rejection of blacks in this period, see William H. Harris, *The Harder We Run: Black Workers Since the Civil War* (New York: Oxford University Press, 1982).

64. St. Clair Drake and Horace R. Cayton, *Black Metropolis: A Study of Negro Life in a Northern City,* 2 vols. (New York: Harper and Row, revised and enlarged edition, 1945).

65. Ibid., 1:267.

66. Ibid., pp. 271, 272.

67. Ibid., pp. 219, 220.

68. Ibid., p. 222.

69. Langston Hughes and Arna Bontemps, eds., *The Poetry of the Negro, 1746–1949* (Garden City, N.Y.: Doubleday and Company, 1949), p. 107.

70. Robert S. Lynd and Helen Merrell Lynd, *Middletown: A Study in American Culture* (New York: Harcourt, Brace & World, 1929), p. 479.

71. Robert S. Lynd and Helen Merrell Lynd, *Middletown in Transition: A Study in Cultural Conflicts* (New York: Harcourt, Brace & World, 1947), p. 463.

72. Arnold R. Hirsch, *Making the Second Ghetto: Race and Housing in Chicago, 1940–1960* (Cambridge: Cambridge University Press, 1983); Gilbert Osofsky, *Harlem: The Making of a Ghetto, 1890–1930* (New York: Harper & Row, 1963); Joe William Trotter, Jr., *Black Milwaukee: The Making of an Industrial Proletariat, 1915–1945* (Urbana: University of Illinois Press, 1985); Alan H. Spear, *Black Chicago: The Making of a Negro Ghetto, 1890–1920* (Chicago: University of Chicago Press, 1967); Kenneth Kusmer, *A Ghetto Takes Shape: Black Cleveland, 1870–1930* (Urbana: University of Illinois Press, 1976).

73. Eugene S. Uyeki, "Ethnic and Race Segregation, Cleveland, 1910–1970," *Ethnicity,* December 1980, p. 398.

74. Gilbert Osofsky, in preface to Arthur F. Raper's *Preface to Peasantry* (New York: Atheneum, 1968), p. viii.

75. Raper, *Preface to Peasantry,* p. 301.

76. Ibid.

77. Ibid., pp. 165, 166.

78. John Dollard, *Caste and Class in a Southern Town* (Garden City, N.Y.: Doubleday and Company, 1937, 1957 Doubleday Anchor Edition), p. 3.

79. Ibid., 217.

80. Ibid., p. 129.

81. Ibid., p. 201.

82. Ibid., pp. 189–194, 197–198, 203–204.

83. Hortense Powdermaker, *After Freedom* (New York: Atheneum, 1967, originally Viking Press, 1939).

84. Ibid., p. 65.

85. Ibid., p. 45.
86. Myrdal, *An American Dilemma* 1:xxix. Also see 2:chapter 31, "Caste and Class."
87. Ibid., 2:667.
88. Ibid., p. 669.
89. Ibid., p. 685.
90. Ibid., p. 305.
91. Hughes and Bontemps, *Poetry of the Negro,* p. 97, for "I, Too, Sing America," and pp. 106–108 for "Let America Be America Again."
92. Philip S. Foner, ed., *We, the Other People: Alternative Declarations of Independence by Labor Groups, Farmers, Woman's Rights Advocates, Socialists and Blacks, 1829–1975* (Urbana: University of Illinois Press, 1976), p. 15.
93. Langston Hughest and Milton Meltzer, *A Pictorial History of the Negro in America* (New York: Crown Publishers, Inc., 1963), p. 258.
94. Meyer Weinberg, ed., *W. E. B. Du Bois: A Leader* (New York: Harper & Row, Inc., 1970), pp. 4, 5.
95. W. E. B. Du Bois, *The Souls of Black Folk* (Greenwich, Conn.: Fawcett Publications, Inc., 1961), pp. 189–190. More on the odyssey of Du Bois can be found in Elliott M. Rudwick, *W. E. B. Du Bois: Propagandist of the Negro Protest* (New York: Atheneum Edition, 1972, originally published in 1960 by the University of Pennsylvania Press).
96. A. Jacques Garvey, *Garvey and Garveyism* (Kingston, Jamaica: United Printers, 1963); Albert B. Cleage, Jr., *The Black Messiah* (New York: Sheed and Ward, 1968); and Edmond David Cronin, *Black Moses: The Story of Marcus Garvey and the Universal Negro Improvement Association* (Madison: University of Wisconsin Press, 1964).
97. Harold R. Isaacs, *The New World of Negro Americans* (New York: John Day Co., Inc., 1963), p. 140.
98. Myrdal, *An American Dilemma,* 2:chapter 34, "Accommodating Leadership."
99. Ibid., 2:757.
100. Harold F. Gosnell, *Negro Politicians: The Rise of Negro Politics in Chicago* (Chicago: University of Chicago Press, 1935), Chapter 8.
101. Ibid., pp. 238, 239.
102. Ibid., pp. 371, 373.
103. Franklin, *From Slavery to Freedom,* pp. 512–515.
104. Ibid., pp. 520, 521. For more on the situation of blacks during the New Deal, see Harvard Sitkoff, *A New Deal for Blacks: The Emergence of Civil Rights as a National Issue: The Depression Decade* (New York: Oxford University Press, 1978), pp. 41–46. The key figures around Roosevelt, with the exception of Mrs. Eleanor Roosevelt and Secretary of Interior Harold Ickes, generally accepted the situation of caste, including his top political advisers, Louis Howe and James A. Farley, and his White House confidants, press secretary Stephen Early and appointments secretary Marvin MacIntyre. Even Henry Wallace, the liberal secretary of agriculture, did not want to antagonize southerners on race questions. And Congress was dominated by southern Democrats.
105. Franklin, *From Slavery to Freedom,* chapter 26, "A Harlem Renaissance."
106. Myrdal, *An American Dilemma,* 2:chapter 24, "Inequality of Justice," and 2:chapter 26, "Courts, Sentences and Prisons."
107. Ibid., 1:chapter 13, "Seeking Jobs Outside of Agriculture"; 1:chapter 16, "Income, Consumption and Housing"; 1:chapter 17, "Mechanics of Economic Discrimination"; and 1:chapter 18, "Pre-War Labor Markets Controls and Their Consequences to the Negro."

6. "I Go Sad and Heavy Hearted":
Sojourner Pluralism for Asians and Mexicans

1. The ballad "An Emigrant's Farewell" is quoted in Lawrence Cardoso, *Mexican Emigration to the United States, 1897–1931: Socio-Economic Patterns* (Tucson: University of Arizona Press, 1980), pp. 76, 77.
2. The story of the colonization of northern Mexico by the U.S. and the subsequent resistance of Mexicans and Mexican-Americans is told by Robert J. Rosenbaum, *Mexicano Resistance in the Southwest: "The Sacred Right of Self Preservation"* (Austin: University of Texas Press, 1981). Also see Alfredo Mirandé, *Gringo Justice* (Notre Dame, Ind.: University of Notre Dame Press, 1987). On immigration before the Second World War, see Cardoso, *Mexican Emigration*, ibid.
3. *New York Times*, February 24, 1987, p. A12.
4. Benjamin B. Ringer, *We, the People, and Others: Duality and America's Treatment of Its Racial Minorities* (New York: Tavistock, 1983), p. 628.
5. Kirk H. Porter and Donald Bruce Johnson, eds., *National Party Platforms, 1840–1968* (Urbana: University of Illinois Press, 1970), p. 67.
6. Stuart Creighton Miller, *The Unwelcome Immigrant: The American Image of the Chinese, 1785–1882* (Berkeley: University of California Press, 1969).
7. Ibid., p. 166.
8. Ibid., p. 168.
9. Ibid., p. 170.
10. F. P. Thompson, State Superintendent of Public Printing, *Chinese Immigration: The Social, Moral and Political Effect of Chinese Immigration.* Testimony taken before a committee of the Senate of the State of California (Sacramento: State Printing Office, 1876), p. 60.
11. Ibid., p. 45.
12. Ringer, *We, the People*, p. 582.
13. Hubert Howe Bancroft, *Popular Tribunals*, 2 vols. (San Francisco: The History Company Publishers, 1887), 1:612.
14. Ibid., p. 643.
15. Ibid., 2:717–718.
16. Chester Lloyd Jones, "The Legislative History of Exclusion Legislation," in Emory R. Johnson, ed., *Chinese and Japanese in America, the Annals of the American Academy of Political and Social Science*, 34 (September 1909), p. 135.
17. Vincent G. Nee and Brett DeBarry Nee, *Longtime Californ'* (New York: Pantheon, 1972), p. 54.
18. Vincenza Scarpaci, *The Portrait of the Italians in America* (New York: Charles Scribner's Sons, 1983), pp. 121, 122.
19. Concerning the behavior of U.S. marshals' intimidation of Chinese, see *Chinese Exclusion. Testimony taken before the Committee on Immigration, United States Senate, on Senate Bill 2960 and Certain Other Bills Before the Committee Providing for the Exclusion of Chinese Laborers*, U.S. Senate, 57th Congress, 1st Session, Report 776, Part Two (Washington, D.C.: U.S. Government Printing Office, 1902), p. 46. With respect to the systematic intimidation of Asian workers in Hawaii by the police and justice system, see Lawrence H. Fuchs, *Hawaii Pono* (New York: Harcourt, 1961), chapters 8 and 9, "No Concessions Whatsoever" and "Merchant Street versus the Voice of Labor."
20. Ringer, *We, the People*, p. 592.
21. Royal D. Mead, "The Sugar Industry in Hawaii," *San Francisco Chronicle*, July 18, 1910.

22. H. A. Millis, *The Japanese Problem in the United States* (New York: The Macmillan Company, 1915), pp. 273–274.

23. Harry H. L. Kitano and Roger Daniels, *Asian-Americans: Emerging Minorities* (Englewood Cliffs, N.J.: Prentice-Hall, 1988), pp. 24, 80. For a good review of the early Chinese and Filipino experiences, see H. M. Lai, "Chinese," and H. Brett Melendy, "Filipinos," in Stephan Thernstrom, ed., *Harvard Encyclopedia of American Ethnic Groups* (Cambridge: Harvard University Press, 1980).

24. Millis, *The Japanese Problem*, p. 316.

25. Harry H. L. Kitano, "Japanese," in Thernstrom, *Harvard Encyclopedia of American Ethnic Groups*, pp. 61–71.

26. Roger Daniels, *The Politics of Prejudice: The Anti-Japanese Movement in California and the Struggle for Japanese Exclusion* (Berkeley: University of California Press, 1962), p. 79.

27. John E. Reinecke, *Feigned Ethnicity: Hawaii's Attempt to Obtain Chinese Contract Labor, 1921–1923* (San Francisco: Chinese Materials Center, 1979). A masterful account of how sojourner pluralism operated in Hawaii. The oligarchy in the islands did not have the clout of leaders in California with Congress. When a representative of the oligarchy, part-Hawaiian John Wise, testified before Congress, he acknowledged, to the dismay of several Congressmen, that if a Chinese worker married an American woman and had a child in the islands, it was his view that the father should be deported after his five-year contract had been completed. Also see Fuchs, *Hawaii Pono*, p. 229.

28. Hearings before the U.S. Senate Committee on Immigration on S-2576, "A Bill to Limit the Immigration of Aliens into the United States and for Other Purposes," 68th Congress, 1st Session (Washington, D.C.: U.S. Government Printing Office, 1924), p. 62.

29. Ibid., p. 48.

30. Fuchs, *Hawaii Pono*, p. 235.

31. Cardoso, *Mexican Emigration*, p. 22.

32. Stan Steiner, *La Raza: The Mexican-American* (New York: Harper and Row, 1969), p. 126.

33. Gloria Bonilla Santiago, "Puerto Rico Migrant Farmworkers: An Untold Story," *Migration World* 14 (1986): 14–18.

34. Armando B. Rendon, *Chicano Manifesto* (New York: Collier Books, 1971), pp. 20, 27.

35. Douglas S. Massey, "Do Undocumented Migrants Earn Lower Wages than Legal Immigrants? New Evidence from Mexico," *International Migration Review* 21 (Summer 1987): 268. Massey also suggested that employers might have discriminated as much against documented as undocumented Mexican migrants because they tended to think of all of them as illegal and exploitable.

36. Cardoso, *Mexican Emigration*, p. 34.

37. Ibid.

38. Ibid., p. 32.

39. Henry C. Kaiser, "Mexican-American Labor before World War II," *Journal of Mexican-American History* 2 (1972): 130.

40. Cardoso, *Mexican Emigration*, pp. 85, 86.

41. Arnoldo De Leon, *They Called Them Greasers: Anglo Attitudes Toward Mexicans in Texas, 1821–1900* (Austin: University of Texas Press, 1983), pp. 101–105.

42. Mario Barrera, *Race and Class in the Southwest: A Theory of Racial Inequality* (Notre Dame, Ind.: University of Notre Dame Press, 1979), pp. 125–127.

43. Julian Samora, *Los Mojados: The Wetback Story* (Notre Dame, Ind.: University of Notre Dame Press, 1971).

44. Ernesto Galarza, *Barrio Boy* (Notre Dame, Ind.: University of Notre Dame Press, 1961), p. 263.
45. Evan Anders, *Boss Rule in South Texas: The Progressive Era* (Austin: University of Texas Press, 1982), p. 7.
46. Ibid., pp. 14, 15, 283. Wells was able to get Mexican residents to vote who never intended to become citizens, including some who lived south of the Rio Grande most of the time. He was at the center of south Texas politics for four decades between the 1880s and up to the 1920s. It was only when thousands of Anglo settlers were attracted into the valley through development schemes, some sponsored by Wells, that the politics of Cameron County changed. But in Duvall County, the family of Archie Parr, its major boss, retained control until 1975 and even into the 1980s through a combination of paternalism, intimidation, and corruption fostered by the southwestern pattern of Mexican sojourner pluralism.
47. For another brief history of the *bracero* program, in addition to Samora's *Los Mojados,* see Matt S. Meier and Feliciano Rivera, *The Chicanos: A History of Mexican-Americans* (New York: Hill and Wang, 1972), chapters 22 and 23.
48. Meier and Rivera, *The Chicanos,* p. 220.
49. Samora, *Los Mojados,* p. 52.
50. *U.S. Immigration Law and Policy: 1952–1979,* Congressional Research Service, Library of Congress, 96th Congress, 1st Session (Washington, D.C.: U.S. Government Printing Office, May 1979), p. 36.
51. Samora, *Los Mojados,* pp. 52–54.
52. Carlos E. Cortés, "Mexicans," in Thernstrom, *Harvard Encyclopedia of American Ethnic Groups,* p. 703.
53. Meier and Rivera, *The Chicanos,* p. 235.
54. Joan London and Henry Anderson, "Man of Fire: Ernesto Galarza," in Renato Rosaldo, Robert A. Calvert, and Gustav L. Seligmann, eds., *Chicano! The Evolution of a People* (Minneapolis: Winston Press, 1973), p. 280.
55. Ibid., p. 282.
56. Ibid., p. 291.
57. Vernon M. Briggs, Jr., "Foreign Labor Programs as an Alternative to Illegal Immigration: A Dissenting View," in Peter G. Brown and Henry Shue, ed., *The Border that Joins: Mexican Migrants and U.S. Responsibility* (Totowa, N.J.: Rowman and Littlefield, 1983), p. 228.
58. Philip Martin, *Illegal Immigration and the Colonization of the American Labor Market,* Center for Immigration Studies Paper No. 1 (January 1986), pp. 25, 26.
59. David North and Marion Houstoun, *The Characteristics and Role of Illegal Aliens in the U.S. Labor Market: An Exploratory Study* (Washington, D.C.: New Trans-Century, 1976).
60. Martin, *Illegal Immigration,* p. 12.
61. Jacob S. Seigal, Jeffrey S. Passal, and J. Gregory Robinson, "Preliminary Review of Existing Studies of the Number of Illegal Residents in the U.S.," working paper prepared for use of the Select Commission on Immigration and Refugee Policy, January 1980. See *U.S. Immigration Policy and the National Interest,* Staff Report of the Select Commission on Immigration and Refugee Policy, chapter 9, "Illegal Migration" (Washington, D.C.: U.S. Government Printing Office, 1981).
62. A. J. Jaffe, Ruth M. Cullen, and Thomas D. Boswell, *The Changing Demography of Spanish Americans* (New York: Academic Press, 1980), p. 122.
63. Ibid.
64. Linda Gordon, Office of Refugee Resettlement, "Asian Immigration Since World War II," unpublished paper, pp. 3, 4.

7. *"The Road of Hope": Asians and Mexicans Find Cracks in the System*

1. Lawrence H. Fuchs, *Hawaii Pono* (New York: Harcourt, 1961), chapter 3, "Success, Pake Style."

2. Sue Chen Chan, *This Bittersweet Soil: The Chinese in California Agriculture, 1860–1910* (Berkeley: University of California Press, 1986), p. 58.

3. Ibid., p. 71.

4. Victor G. Nee and Brett DeBarry Nee, *Longtime Californ'* (New York: Pantheon, 1972), pp. 75–80.

5. Chan, *This Bittersweet Soil*, p. 77.

6. Ibid., p. 403. Many of these sojourners went into agriculture in the late nineteenth century, particularly in the Sacramento–San Joaquin delta, where 95 percent of the Chinese population became farmers who played an extremely important role in the development of intensive agriculture in California.

7. Ibid., p. 406.

8. H. M. Lai, "Chinese," *Harvard Encyclopedia of American Ethnic Groups*, ed. Stephan Thernstrom (Cambridge: Harvard University Press, 1980), pp. 222–224.

9. Chan, *This Bittersweet Soil*, pp. 355–357.

10. Ibid., pp. 330, 331.

11. Ibid., p. 403.

12. Ibid., pp. 328–330.

13. Ibid., p. 331.

14. Ibid., p. 334.

15. Ibid., p. 334.

16. Ibid., p. 332.

17. *United States* v. *Ark Kim Wong*, 169 U.S. 649 (1897), and *United States* v. *Mrs. Gue Lim*, 176 U.S. 459 (1899).

18. Betty L. Sung, *The Story of the Chinese in America* (New York: Collier Books, 1967), p. 99.

19. Shih-Shan Henry Tsai, *The Chinese Experience in America* (Bloomington: Indiana University Press, 1986), p. 98.

20. Ibid., pp. 96–98.

21. Edna Bonacich and John Modell, *The Economic Basis of Ethnic Solidarity: Small Business in the Japanese-American Community* (Berkeley: University of California Press, 1980), p. 51.

22. Ibid., pp. 45–46, 48.

23. Harry H. L. Kitano, "Japanese," *Harvard Encyclopedia of American Ethnic Groups*, p. 563.

24. Ivan Light, *Ethnic Enterprise in America: Business and Welfare Among Chinese, Japanese and Blacks* (Berkeley: University of California Press, 1972).

25. Bonacich and Modell, *Economic Basis of Ethnic Solidarity*, p. 55.

26. Ibid., p. 56.

27. Fuchs, *Hawaii Pono*, p. 123. For a full account of the economic mobility of the Japanese in Hawaii, see pp. 106–137.

28. Stephan Thernstrom, *Poverty and Progress: Social Mobility in a Nineteenth Century City* (Cambridge: Harvard University Press, 1964), chapter 8. See also Stephan Thernstrom, *The Other Bostonians: Social Mobility in the American Metropolis, 1880–1970* (Cambridge: Harvard University Press, 1973).

29. Ukiko Kamura, "Social-Historical Background of Okinawans in Hawaii," in *Uchinanchu: A History of Okinawans in Hawaii*, Oral History Studies Project, United Okinawan Association of Hawaii (Honolulu: University of Hawaii Press, 1968), p. 67.

30. Dennis M. Ogawa entitled his book on the Japanese-American experience in Hawaii *Kodomo No Tame Ni: For the Sake of the Children* (Honolulu: University of Hawaii Press, 1978).

31. Chan, *This Bittersweet Soil*, p. 355.

32. Kitano, "Japanese," p. 565.

33. A. J. Jaffe, Ruth M. Cullen, and Thomas D. Boswell, *The Changing Demography of Spanish-Americans* (New York: Academic Press, 1980), p. 121.

34. Lawrence Cardoso, *Mexican Emigration to the United States, 1897–1931: Socio-Economic Patterns* (Tucson: University of Arizona Press, 1980), p. 92.

35. Ibid., p. 89.

36. Delia Flores, "My Father Crossed the Border and Gave Us a Future," *Wall Street Journal*, July 29, 1987, p. 16.

37. Jésus Luna, "Luna's Abe Lincoln Story," in Renato Rosaldo, Robert A. Calvert, and Gustave L. Seligman, eds., *Chicano: The Evolution of a People* (Minneapolis: Winston Press, 1973), pp. 347–355; quotation on p. 354.

38. Ernesto Galarza, "California, the Uncommonwealth," in ibid., p. 163.

39. Jaffe, Cullen, and Boswell, *Changing Demography of Spanish-Americans*, p. 166.

40. Ibid., pp. 165–167.

41. Leonardo F. Estrada, et al., "Chicanos in the United States: A History of Exploitation and Resistance," *Daedalus*, Spring 1981, p. 129.

42. Thomas Sowell, *Ethnic America: A History* (New York: Basic Books, 1981), p. 260.

43. Ibid.

44. Stanley Lieberson, *A Piece of the Pie: Blacks and White Immigrants Since 1880* (Berkeley: University of California Press, 1980).

45. Carlos Vélez-Ibañez, *Bonds of Mutual Trust: The Culture Systems of Rotating Credit Associations Among Urban Mexicans and Chicanos* (New Brunswick, N.J.: Rutgers University Press, 1983).

46. Arnold Schenkman, *Ambivalent Friends: Afro-Americans View the Immigrant* (Westport, Conn.: Greenwood Press, 1982), p. 156.

47. Charles Wollenberg, *All Deliberate Speed: Segregation and Exclusion in California Schools, 1855–1975* (Berkeley: University of California Press, 1976), pp. 44, 65, 66, 72.

48. Ibid., pp. 116, 117.

49. Fred R. von der Mehden, *The Ethnic Groups of Houston* (Houston: Rice University Studies, 1984), p. 55. See also Guadalupe San Miguel, Jr., *"Let Them All Take Heed": Mexican-Americans and the Campaign for Educational Equality in Texas, 1910–1981* (Austin: University of Texas Press, 1987).

50. Ibid., p. 44.

51. Matt S. Meier and Feliciano Rivera, *The Chicanos: A History of Mexican-Americans* (New York: Hill and Wang, 1972), p. 210.

52. Douglas S. Massey, "Residential Segregation of Spanish-Americans in United States Urban Areas," *Demography* 16 (1970): 553–563; Douglas S. Massey, "Effects of Socio-Economic Factors on the Residential Segregation of Blacks and Spanish-Americans in United States Urbanized Areas," *American Sociological Review* 44 (1979): 1015–1022; M. M. Lopez, "Patterns of Interethnic Residential Segregation in the Urban Southwest, 1960 and 1970," *Social Science Quarterly* 62 (1981): 50–63; K. E. Taeuber and A. F. Taeuber, "The Negro as an Immigrant Group: Recent Trends in Racial and Ethnic Segregation in Chicago," *The American Journal of Sociology* 69 (1964): 374–382; K. E. Taeuber and A. F. Taeuber, *Negroes in Cities: Residential Segregation and Neighborhood Change* (Chicago: Aldine, 1965); and K. E. Taeuber, "The Effect of Income Redistribution on Racial Residential Segregation," *Urban Affairs Quarterly* 4 (1968): 5–14.

53. Harold F. Gosnell, *The Negro Politician: The Rise of Negro Politics in Chicago* (Chicago: University of Chicago Press, 1935), p. 238.

54. Darryl Montero, *Japanese-Americans: Changing Patterns of Ethnic Affiliation over Three Generations* (Boulder, Colo.: Westview Press, 1980), pp. 36–39.

55. Virginia R. Dominguez, "The Legal Side of Blackness," paper presented at the International Conference on Immigration and the Changing Black Population in the United States, May 18–21, 1983, University of Michigan, Ann Arbor, p. 15.

56. Ibid., p. 13.

57. Sung, *Story of the Chinese in America,* pp. 48, 49.

58. Lai, "Chinese," p. 223.

59. Benjamin R. Ringer, *"We, the People" and Others: Duality and America's Treatment of Its Racial Minorities* (New York: Tavistock, 1983), p. 599.

60. Ibid., p. 98.

61. Cardoso, *Mexican Emigration,* p. 67.

62. Ibid., p. 68.

63. Francisco E. Balderrama, *In Defense of La Raza: The Los Angeles Mexican Consulate and the Mexican Community, 1929–1936* (Tucson: University of Arizona Press, 1982). Also see Cardoso, *Mexican Emigration.*

64. Malcolm X, with the assistance of Alex Haley, *The Autobiography of Malcolm X* (New York: Grove Press, Inc., 1964), pp. 35–37.

65. Katheryn L. Morgan, *Children of Strangers: The Stories of a Black Family* (Philadelphia: Temple University Press, 1980), p. 35.

66. Fuchs, *Hawaii Pono,* pp. 288, 289.

67. Richard Rodriguez, *Hunger of Memory: The Education of Richard Rodriguez* (Boston: David R. Godine, 1982), pp. 59, 60.

68. Ernesto Galarza, *Barrio Boy* (Notre Dame, Ind.: University of Notre Dame Press, 1971), p. 211.

69. Stan Steiner, *La Raza: The Mexican-Americans* (New York: Harper and Row, 1969), chapter 16.

70. Von der Mehden, *Ethnic Groups of Houston,* p. 44. The Rusk Settlement House in Houston had Mexican and Jewish clients at the same time.

71. Raymond A. Mohl, "Cultural Pluralism in Immigrant Education: The International Institutes of Boston, Philadelphia and San Francisco, 1920–1940," *Journal of American Ethnic History,* Spring 1982, pp. 44, 47–50.

72. Elizabeth C. Barney Buel, compiler, *Manual of the United States: For the Information of Immigrants and Foreigners,* 5th edition (Washington, D.C.: The National Society of the Daughters of the American Revolution, 1928).

73. Chan, *This Bittersweet Soil,* p. 333.

74. Edward D. Beechert, *Working in Hawaii: A Labor History* (Honolulu: University of Hawaii Press, 1985), p. 121.

75. Ibid., p. 122.

76. James D. Crockcroft, *Outlaws in the Promised Land: Mexican Immigrant Workers and America's Future* (New York: Globe Press, 1986), pp. 54–61.

77. Beechert, *Working in Hawaii,* pp. 220–226.

78. Mario T. García, *Desert Immigrants: The Mexicans of El Paso* (New Haven: Yale University Press, 1981), p. 226.

79. Carlos Cortés, "Mexicans," *Harvard Encyclopedia of Ethnic Groups,* p. 709.

80. James W. Loewn, *Mississippi Chinese: Between Black and White* (Cambridge: Harvard University Press, 1971), and Robert Seto Quan in collaboration with Julian B. Roebuck, *Lotus Among the Magnolias: The Mississippi Chinese* (Jackson: University Press of Mississippi, 1982).

81. Reports of the Immigration Commission, 42 vols. *Recent Immigrants in Agri-*

culture, part 24, in vol. 2 (Washington, D.C.: U.S. Government Printing Office, 1911). Reprint edition (New York: Arno Press, 1970), p. 464.

82. Arnoldo De Leon, *They Called Them Greasers: Anglo Attitudes Toward Mexicans in Texas, 1821–1900* (Austin: University of Texas Press, 1983), p. 95.

83. Gerald D. Suttles, *The Social Order of the Slum: Ethnicity and Territory in the Inner City* (Chicago: The University of Chicago Press, 1968), p. 124.

84. Ibid., p. 137.

85. Ibid., p. 165.

86. Nee and Nee, *Longtime Californ',* pp. 79, 80.

87. Rodriquez, *Hunger of Memory,* pp. 116, 119.

88. Ruben R. Alcantara, *Sakada: Filipino Adaptation in Hawaii* (Washington, D.C.: University Press of America, 1981), p. 34.

89. Barbara M. Posados, "The Hierarchy of Color and Psychological Adjustment in an Industrial Environment; Filipinos, the Pullman Company, and the Brotherhood of Sleeping Car Porters," *Labor History* 23 (Summer 1982): 350–355. There is no question that the immigrant mentality, even for dark-skinned immigrants from the West Indies or the Cape Verde islands, made it possible for some to seize control over their own lives in a way that was much more difficult for native-born African-Americans. The Cape Verdeans, most of whom are indistinguishable in color from African-Americans, provide an exemplary example of the immigrant mentality. Although imported to do the hardest and dirtiest work, whether on the cranberry bogs or in the mills of Massachusetts, and subject to persistent abuse, they began to behave like immigrant settlers, creating a variety of associations—professional, business, labor, and recreational—to gain strength in confronting the American environment. Stressing their language and cultural heritage, they identified themselves as distinct from the local black American population and began the process of ethnic-Americanization. The Dillingham Immigration Commission found them asserting their rights as they became more important in the local economy of southeastern Massachusetts. For a full discussion, see Marilyn B. Halter, "Cape Verdean–American Immigration and Patterns of Settlement, 1860–1940," Ph.D. diss., Boston University, 1986, especially pp. 161, 191–193, and 197. Also see Reports of the Immigration Commission, 42 vols. *Recent Immigrants in Industries,* part 24, in vol. 2, p. 551.

90. Carlos Bulosan, *America Is in the Heart: A Personal History* (Seattle: University of Washington Press, 1943).

91. Ibid., p. 312.

92. Arnold Shankman, *Ambivalent Friends: Afro-Americans View the Immigrant* (Westport, Conn.: Greenwood Press, 1982), p. 16.

93. Ibid., p. 72.

94. Ibid., p. 73.

Part 3. The Outsiders Move In: The Triumph of the Civic Culture

8. "Do You Understand Your Own Language?": Black Americans' Attack on Caste

1. Martin D. Kilson, "Towards Freedom: An Analysis of Slave Revolts in the United States," *Phylon* 25 (1964): 175–187.

2. Williams is quoted in Benjamin Quarles, *Black Abolitionists* (New York: Oxford University Press, 1969), p. 7.

3. Ibid., p. 8. David Walker's *Appeal to the Coloured Citizens of the World, but in Particular, and Very Expressly, to Those of the United States of America* was read by blacks, even in the South, but ignored by whites.

4. Ibid., p. 74.

5. Douglass is quoted in David Howard-Pitney, "The Jeremiads of Frederick Douglass, Booker T. Washington, and W. E. B. Du Bois and Changing Patterns of Black Messianic Rhetoric, 1841–1920," *The Journal of American Ethnic History* 6 (Fall 1986): 51.

6. Ibid., p. 58.

7. Gunnar Myrdal, *An American Dilemma: The Negro Problem and Modern Democracy*, 2 vols. (New York: Harper and Row, 1944).

8. Ibid., 2:1009.

9. *Plessy* v. *Ferguson*, 163 U.S. 537 (1896), p. 476.

10. Monroe Berger, *Equality by Statute: The Revolution in Civil Rights* (New York: Doubleday & Co., 1968), p. 86. Between 1868 and 1936, blacks won only two of fourteen cases in which they claimed the right to use the same facilities as whites in common carriers, public places, and schools or housing; they won ten of sixteen cases in which they sought federal protection of their right to vote, or of other rights deemed to be attributes of federal citizenship; they won twelve of twenty-one cases when they sought to obtain a fair trial in criminal cases; and three cases in which they sought federal protection from peonage.

11. Virginia R. Dominguez, "The Legal Side of Blackness," unpublished paper presented at the International Conference on Immigration and the Changing Black Population in the United States, May 18–21, 1983, University of Michigan, Ann Arbor, p. 3. Ten years after *An American Dilemma* was published, North Carolina, Maryland, Tennessee, and Texas still prohibited marriages between whites and "persons of Negro blood to the third generation," laws not officially repealed until 1967 in Maryland, 1969 in Texas, 1973 in North Carolina, and in the case of Tennessee's constitutional provision, until 1978. The voters of Mississippi repudiated the antimiscegenation provision of their state constitution in 1987.

12. "Whites Look at Negroes and Negro Problems," Confidential Report, Copy No. 81 of the National Opinion Research Center, University of Denver, December 1944, pp. 48, 51, and 56.

13. Ibid., p. 71. The survey was based on a cross section of the white population with proper proportions for each demographic group in each geographic section. The survey included 2,523 personal interviews.

14. John Howard Griffin, *Black Like Me* (New York: Signet, 1960), p. 96.

15. Ibid., p. 64.

16. Ruth Benedict, *Race, Science and Politics* (New York: Viking Press, 1943).

17. Earl Brown and George R. Leighton, *The Negro and the War Effort*, Public Affairs Pamphlet No. 71, 1942.

18. Ruth Benedict and Gene Weltfish, *The Races of Mankind*, Public Affairs Pamphlet No. 8, 1943.

19. Ibid., p. 46.

20. John Hope Franklin, *From Slavery to Freedom: The History of American Negroes* (New York: Alfred Knopf, 1956), p. 441.

21. William H. Harris, *The Harder We Run: Black Workers Since the Civil War* (New York: Oxford University Press, 1982), p. 114.

22. John P. Davis, "The Negro in the Armed Forces of America," in John P. Davis, ed., *The American Negro Reference Book* (Englewood Cliffs, N.J.: Prentice-Hall, 1966), pp. 630–632.

23. Ibid., p. 634.

24. Ibid., pp. 643–647.
25. Daniel M. Johnson and Rex R. Campbell, *Black Migration in America: A Social Demographic History* (Durham, N.C.: Duke University Press, 1981), p. 115.
26. Ibid., p. 129. In the nation as a whole, young white males actually moved more than black males, but much of the movement of whites was within the same metropolitan areas or suburbs within the same region.
27. Ibid., p. 130.
28. In no text is the ten years of the civil rights revolution better documented than in the six-part public broadcasting series "Eyes on the Prize: America's Civil Rights Years, 1954–1965" (Henry Hampton, producer, Blackside: 1987). This quotation comes from part one, "Awakenings, 1954–56." It is necessary to see the television series to realize the full force of King's leadership, particularly if one did not follow the civil rights struggle on television at the time. Much of this material is also available in a book written in conjunction with the series: Juan Williams, *Eyes on the Prize: America's Civil Rights Years, 1954–1965* (New York: Viking, 1987). Also see Tyler Branch, *Breaking the Waters: America in the King Years, 1954–1963* (New York: Simon and Schuster, 1988).
29. "Eyes on the Prize," part 1.
30. Ibid.
31. Adam Fairclough, *To Redeem the Soul of America: The Southern Christian Leadership Conference and Martin Luther King, Jr.* (Athens: University of Georgia Press, 1987).
32. David J. Garrow, *Bearing the Cross: Martin Luther King, Jr., and the Southern Christian Leadership Conference* (New York: William Morrow and Company, Inc., 1986).
33. Ibid., pp. 99, 100.
34. Steven Cohen, ed., *Eyes on the Prize: America's Civil Rights Years, 1954–1965, A Source Book* (Boston: Blackside, 1987). The quotation from Eisenhower is on page 10.
35. "Eyes on the Prize," part two: "Fighting Back, 1957–62."
36. "Eyes on the Prize," part three: "Ain't Scared of Your Jails, 1960–61."
37. "Eyes on the Prize," part four: "No Easy Walk, 1962–66."
38. For the 1944 data, see "Whites Look at Negroes and Negro Problems," p. 45. For the 1963 data, see William Brink and Louis Harris, *The Negro Revolution in America* (New York: Simon & Schuster, 1964), p. 148.
39. "Whites Look at Negroes and Negro Problems," p. 512 for 1944 data. For 1963 data, see Brink and Harris, p. 148.
40. "White Look at Negroes and Negro Problems," p. 55; also see Brink and Harris, p. 148.
41. Brink and Harris, p. 202.
42. Ibid., p. 203.
43. Ibid.
44. Ibid., p. 205.
45. Ibid., p. 207.
46. Ibid., pp. 220–221.
47. For a description and analysis of the legislative history of the Civil Rights Bill, see "Revolution in Civil Rights," *Congressional Quarterly Service* (Washington, D.C., 1964). Black civil rights groups, labor unions, and church and Jewish organizations lobbied Congress constantly in support of the bill. The major civil rights organizations formed a civil rights coordinating agency, the Leadership Conference, in 1949, which had gained experience mobilizing support for the relatively mild 1957 and 1960 Civil Rights Acts dealing with voting. The orga-

nization, which started with twenty participating groups, had seventy-nine by 1963 and a permanent Washington office.

48. Ibid., pp. 75–77.
49. Ibid., p. 69.
50. "Eyes on the Prize," part five, "Is This America?, 1962–64."
51. Ibid.
52. Cohen, ed., *Eyes on the Prize*, p. 54.
53. U.S. Commission on Civil Rights, *Political Participation* (1968), pp. 6, 7.
54. Washington Research Project, *The Shameful Blight: The Survival of Racial Discrimination in Voting in the South* (Washington, D.C.: 1972), p. 1.
55. "The Voting Rights Act: Unfulfilled Goals," A Report of the United States Commission on Civil Rights (Washington, D.C.: 1981), p. 5.
56. Berger, *Equality by Statute*, p. 125. Other decisions of the Supreme Court in the 1960s ruled against a segregation ordinance as violating the Equal Protection Clause of the Fourteenth Amendment (*Peterson* v. *Greenville*, 373 U.S. 244 [1963]); ruled in favor of compelling public officials to allow blacks to be seated in desegregated restaurants (*Lombard* v. *Louisiana*, 373 U.S. 267 [1963]); and ruled for the protection of the rights of blacks to nonsegregated services at lunch counters even though the assertion of their rights might provoke a riot (*Abernathy* v. *Alabama*, 380 U.S. 447 [1965]).
57. Berger, *Equality by Statute*, p. 11.
58. Ibid., p. 13.

9. *"They Never Did Really See Me": The Assertion of Black Ethnic Identity*

1. Langston Hughes and Arna Bontemps, eds., *The Poetry of the Negro, 1746–1949* (Garden City, N.Y.: Doubleday and Company, 1949), p. 128. For more on Countee Cullen and the Harlem renaissance, see Blanche Ferguson, *Countee Cullen and the Negro Renaissance* (New York: Dodd, Mead and Company, 1966).
2. Malcolm X is quoted in William H. Greer and Price M. Cobbs, *Black Rage* (New York: Bantam, 1969), pp. 140–141.
3. George Breitman, ed., *Malcolm X Speaks* (New York: Grove Press, 1965), p. 26. Malcolm returned again and again to the idea that Negroes in the U.S. would gain increased respect when they connected to their African heritage. He saw a particular opportunity in the newly won independence of many African states. "Now you don't have a Negro's chance. But with Africa getting its independence, you and I will have more of a chance. I believe in that one hundred percent." See p. 211.
4. Wilson Jeremiah Moses, *The Golden Age of Black Nationalism, 1850–1925* (Hamden, Conn.: Anchor Books, 1978), pp. 39, 40.
5. Ibid., p. 96.
6. Breitman, ed., *Malcolm X Speaks*, p. 198.
7. Martin Luther King, Jr., *Where Do We Go from Here: Chaos or Community?* (New York: Bantam Books, 1968), p. 181.
8. W. E. B. Du Bois, *The Souls of Black Folk* (New York: Fawcett Publications, Inc., 1961), p. 17. *The Souls of Black Folk* was first published by A. C. McClurg and Co. in Chicago in 1903.
9. Richard Wright, *Twelve Million Black Voices* (New York: Viking Press, 1941), in Herbert Hill, ed., *Anger and Beyond: The Negro Writer in the United States* (New York: Harper and Row, 1966), p. 49.
10. William Brink and Louis Harris, *The Negro Revolution in America* (New York: Simon and Schuster, 1964), p. 157.

11. Ibid., p. 225.
12. Ibid., p. 251.
13. Ibid., p. 199.
14. Louis E. Lomax, *The Negro Revolt* (New York: Signet, 1963), p. 264.
15. Ibid., p. 64.
16. Ibid., p. 64.
17. Du Bois, *Souls of Black Folk*, p. 144.
18. Melville J. Herskovits, *The Myth of the Negro Past* (Boston: Beacon Press, 1958), p. 299.
19. Lawrence W. Levine, *Black Culture and Black Consciousness: Afro-American Folk Thought from Slavery to Freedom* (New York: Oxford University Press, 1977).
20. Herskovits, *Myth of the Negro Past*, p. 299.
21. Malcolm X, with the assistance of Alex Haley, *The Autobiography of Malcolm X* (New York: Grove Press, Inc., 1964), p. 7.
22. Ibid., pp. 26, 27.
23. Joseph Boskin, *Sambo: The Rise and Demise of an American Jester* (New York: Oxford University Press, 1986), p. 252.
24. An extraordinarily powerful dramatization of the stereotypes appears on video in *Ethnic Notions,* produced by California Newsreel, 1987.
25. Thomas Dixon, Jr., *The Clansman* (New York: Grosset and Dunlap, 1905).
26. Richard Wright, *Black Boy* (New York: Harper and Row, 1966), p. 221.
27. Ralph Ellison, *Invisible Man* (New York: Vintage Books, 1952).
28. James Baldwin, *Nobody Knows My Name* (New York: Dell, 1961), p. 22.
29. Ibid., p. 35.
30. Ibid., p. 109.
31. Ibid., p. 110.
32. Ibid., p. 114.
33. Horace R. Cayton, "Ideological Forces in the Work of Negro Writers," in Hill, ed., *Anger and Beyond*, p. 45.
34. Moses, *Golden Age of Black Nationalism*, p. 32.
35. Ibid., p. 127.
36. King, *Where Do We Go from Here?*, p. 62.
37. Arnold Adoff, ed., *Black on Black: Commentaries by Negro Americans,* with a foreword by Roger Mae Johnson (New York: Macmillan, 1968), pp. 23–25.
38. Ibid.
39. Breitman, ed., *Malcolm X Speaks,* p. 216. Malcolm called his last formal speech "The Black Revolution and Its Effect Upon the Negroes of the Western Hemisphere."
40. From the *Los Angeles Herald Dispatch,* January 16, 1960, in Eric Lincoln, *The Black Muslims in America* (Boston: Beacon Press, 1961), p. 92.
41. Malcolm X, *Autobiography,* p. 252.
42. George Breitman, *The Last Year of Malcolm X: The Evolution of a Revolutionary* (New York: Schocken Books, 1967), p. 14.
43. From 1968 on, it was commonplace for books about African-Americans in the U.S. to use the term "black" in the title. See Stokely Carmichael and Charles V. Hamilton, *Black Power: The Politics of Liberation in America* (New York: Random House, 1967); William H. Grier and Price M. Cobbs, *Black Rage* (New York: Bantam, 1968); C. Eric Lincoln, *Is Anybody Listening to Black America?* (New York: The Seabury Press, 1968); Benjamin Quarles, *Black Abolitionists* (London: Oxford University Press, 1969); Arnold Schuchter, *White Power/Black Freedom* (Boston: Beacon Press, 1968); and August Meier and Elliott Rudwick, eds., *The Making of Black America,* 2 vols. (New York: Atheneum, 1971).

44. Kareem A. Jabbar (Lew Alcindor), "U.C.L.A. Was a Mistake," in Jay Schulman, Aubrey Shatter, and Rosalie Ehrlich, eds., *Pride and Protest: Ethnic Groups in America* (New York: Dell, 1977), p. 120.

45. Pauli Murray, *Song in a Weary Throat: An American Pilgrimage* (New York: Harper and Row, 1987), p. 404.

46. Ibid., p. 412.

47. Ibid., p. 396.

48. Ibid., p. 415.

49. Ibid.

50. *Black in White America: The Search for Unity and Equality,* developed by Education Development Center under the direction of Orlando Patterson and Lawrence H. Fuchs (New York: Collier-Macmillan, 1974), p. 156.

51. *Report of the National Advisory Commission on Civil Disorders,* with a special introduction by Tom Wicker of the *New York Times* (New York: Bantam Books, New York Times Company, 1968), p. 539.

52. Ibid., pp. 131–133. For data on Watts, see Nathan Cohen, ed., *The Los Angeles Riots* (New York: Praeger Publications, Inc., 1970), pp. 219, 221, 222.

53. Cohen, ed., *Los Angeles Riots,* p. 185.

54. "Violence in the City—An End or a Beginning? A Report by the Governor's Commission on the Los Angeles Riots" (Los Angeles: State of California, 1965), p. 4. The commission was chaired by John McCone, a distinguished banker who had served as a high official in the federal government.

55. Robert Conot, *Rivers of Blood, Years of Darkness* (New York: William Morrow and Company, 1967), p. 150.

56. Jerry Cohen and William S. Murphy, *Burn, Baby, Burn* (New York: Avon Books, 1966), pp. 183–184.

57. Shalom Endleman, ed., *Violence in the Streets* (Chicago: Quadrangle Books, Inc., 1968), p. 249.

58. *Business Week,* August 14, 1971, p. 70.

59. Dorothy Sterling, *Tear Down the Walls* (Garden City, N.Y.: Doubleday and Company, 1968), p. 226.

60. William Serrin, "Jesse Jackson: 'I Am . . . ,'" *New York Times Magazine,* July 9, 1972, p. 14. Jackson argued in 1989 that "to be called 'African-American' has cultural integrity . . . every ethnic group in this country has a reference to some land base, some historical, cultural base. African-Americans have hit that level of cultural maturity." See Joanne Ball, "Jackson, Others Urge New Name for Blacks," *Boston Sunday Globe,* January 1, 1989, p. 1. Jackson found some support in the U.S. and among African leaders for his plea, but as the 1980s closed, it remained a controversial proposal, and the term "black" was much more commonly used than "African-American." See the *New York Times,* January 12, 1989, p. A15.

61. LeRoi Jones, *Home: Social Essays* (New York: William Morrow, 1965), pp. 235–237.

62. Ibid., p. 236.

63. Breitman, ed., *Malcolm X Speaks,* p. 211.

64. *Boston Globe,* December 24, 1984, p. 317.

65. Bobby Seale, *Seize the Time* (New York: Random House, 1970), pp. 59–60.

66. Morris Freedman and Carolyn Banks, eds., *American Mix* (Philadelphia: J. B. Lippincott Company, 1972), pp. 146–147.

67. Huey P. Newton, *To Die for the People* (New York: Random House, 1972), p. 45.

10. "We Want Full Participation": African-Americans and Coalition Politics

1. *New York Times*/CBS News Poll, *New York Times,* July 10, 1984, p. A16.
2. Stokely Carmichael and Charles V. Hamilton, *Black Power: The Politics of Liberation in America* (New York: Vintage Books, 1967); Bayard Rustin, "Black Power and Coalition Politics," *Commentary,* September 1966.
3. Carmichael and Hamilton, *Black Power,* pp. 60, 61.
4. Ibid.
5. Martin Luther King, Jr., *Where Do We Go from Here: Chaos or Community?* (New York: Bantam Books, 1968), p. 58.
6. Bayard Rustin, "Community Control: Separatism Repackaged," *New York Times,* June 11, 1972, p. 9.
7. "A Look Back in Anger: Eleven Blacks Recall Their Rebellion at Cornell and How It Changed Their Lives," *Newsweek,* May 23, 1984, pp. 36–40.
8. Ibid., p. 39.
9. Malcolm X, *The Autobiography of Malcolm X* (New York: Grove Press, Inc., 1966), p. 313.
10. Neil R. Pierce and Jerry Hagstrom, *The Book of America: Inside Fifty States Today* (New York: W. W. Norton, 1983), p. 446.
11. Roy Reed, "George Wallace's Bid for the New South," *New York Times,* September 5, 1982, Section VI, p. 14. For a more detailed analysis of the transformation of Wallace and other white southern politicians, see Earl Black and Merle Black, *Politics and Society in the South* (Cambridge: Harvard University Press, 1987), p. 302.
12. Linda Williams, "1986 Elections: Major Implications for Black Politics," *Focus,* November–December 1986, p. 5.
13. Dale Russakoff, "How Judge Bork's Southern Exposure Crippled His Nomination," *Washington Post National Weekly Edition,* October 19, 1987, p. 12.
14. Jack Bass, "Bork's Worry: Southern Senators," *New York Times,* September 21, 1987, p. A19. There were dozens of examples of black voters and their representatives making bargains to elect white candidates and thereby winning a share of power, as the elected officials acknowledged. See *New York Times,* August 6, 1984, p. B28, and October 1, 1984, p. B18.
15. *Black Elected Officials: A National Roster* (Washington, D.C.: Joint Center for Political Studies, 1986), p. ix.
16. *Black in White America: The Struggle for Black Identity and Power,* developed by Education Development Center under the direction of Orlando Patterson and Lawrence H. Fuchs (New York: Collier-Macmillan, 1974), pp. 118–124.1.
17. "Getting and Using Power: Political Access Without Discrimination," *The American Experiment: E Pluribus Unum,* developed by Education Development Center, Lawrence H. Fuchs, principal scholar (Newton, Mass.: Education Development Center, Inc., 1982), p. 78.
18. David S. Broder, "Willie Brown's Winning Ways," *Washington Post,* February 22, 1981, p. C7.
19. William P. Rose, "Blacks in the Legislature: A Prophecy Comes True in Mississippi," *Washington Post* January 11, 1980, p. A10.
20. *New York Times,* August 16, 1984, p. B28.
21. *Washington Post National Weekly Edition,* August 11, 1986, p. 14; Eddie Williams, "Perspective," *Focus,* November–December 1985, p. 2.
22. Roland W. Burris, "Winning Statewide Office," *Focus,* October 1985, p. 3.
23. *Black Elected Officials,* p. 21.
24. *Black in White America,* p. 135.

25. Ibid., p. 136.
26. Ibid., p. 140.
27. *Heritage, the Newsletter of the Illinois Consultation in Ethnicity,* Summer 1983, p. 6.
28. Ibid., p. 7.
29. Thomas E. Cavanaugh, "How Washington Won Chicago," *Focus,* May 1983, pp. 3, 7, 8.
30. Shirley Chisholm, "The Politics of Coalition," *The Black Scholar,* September 1972, pp. 30–31; also see Shirley Chisholm's autobiography *Unbought and Unbossed* (New York: Avon Books, 1970), pp. 94–165.
31. The committees included the Budget Committee (William Gray, D-Pennsylvania), the House Education and Labor Committee (Augustus F. Hawkins, D-California), the Select Committee on Narcotics Abuse and Control (Charles Rangel, D-New York), and chairman of the House Intelligence Committee (Louis Stokes, D-Ohio).
32. *Black Enterprise,* August 1987, p. 24.
33. Carl Hall, "How a Philadelphia Preacher Won Converts to His Budget Gospel," *Washington Post National Weekly Edition,* June 10, 1985, p. 12. Blacks elected to the U.S. Senate and House of Representatives during Reconstruction, as Du Bois pointed out, were also able to work effectively with whites in the discharge of their responsibilities. In addition, many blacks appointed to positions of high responsibility in state government quickly mastered the arts of administration and politics. See W. E. B. Du Bois, *The Gift of Black Folk: The Negroes in the Making of America* (New York: Washington Square Press, 1970), originally published in 1924, pp. 118, 119.
34. *The Washington Report of the American Jewish Committee,* 1, no. 4 (November 17, 1986): 15; David S. Broder, "Hard-Working John Lewis, Atlanta Victory," *Boston Globe,* October 7, 1986, p. A25; *Black Elected Officials: A National Roster,* p. 19; "Political Trend Letter," *Focus,* November/December 1986, p. 2.
35. *New York Times,* November 23, 1980, p. 26.
36. Thomas A. Johnson, "New Black Rights Organization Formed by 1,000 from 34 States," *New York Times,* June 30, 1980, p. 15.
37. Ibid.
38. Myra McPherson, "Pain and Passion: The Mystique of Jesse Jackson," *Washington Post,* May 21, 1984, p. D1.
39. *New York Times,* July 10, 1984, p. A16.
40. Kitty O. Cohen, "Black-Jewish Relations in 1984: A Survey of Black U.S. Congressmen," *Patterns of Prejudice,* 19, no. 2 (1985), p. 10; William E. Schmidt, "Not All Black Mayors Hitch Fortune to Jackson's Star," *New York Times,* November 1, 1987, p. 4.
41. For Jackson's National Rainbow Coalition speech, see *Focus,* May 1986, p. 3; also see Michael Oreskes, "Jackson Sets Sights on White Vote," *New York Times,* March 2, 1988, p. D26.
42. "Political Trend Letter," *Focus,* November–December, 1987).
43. Thomas B. Edsall and Richard Morin, "Super Tuesday's Showing," *Washington Post National Weekly Edition,* March 14–20, 1988, p. 37.
44. Doug Foster, "Interview: Why Jesse Jackson Believes He Can Win," *Utne Reader: The Best of the Alternative Press,* January/February 1988, p. 108.
45. R. W. Apple, Jr., "Blue-Collar Contrast," *New York Times,* April 2, 1988, p. 9.
46. Curtis Wilkie, "Detroit's Young Softens His Opposition to Jackson," *Boston Globe,* March 24, 1988, p. 22.
47. Edward Walsh, "A Pol at the End of the Rainbow," *Washington Post National Weekly Edition,* May 4, 1987, p. 16.

48. Thomas E. Cavanaugh, *The Message of the Black Vote in the 1984 Elections* (Washington, D.C.: Joint Center for Political Studies, 1985), pp. 12–13.

49. Ibid., p. 11.

50. Eddie Williams, "A Growing Black Vote: Dr. King's Legacy," *Focus,* January 1988, p. 2; Report from the Census Bureau, "Voting by Black Youths Surged in '86," *Boston Globe,* October 7, 1987, p. 10.

51. Robert Reinhold, "Black at Helm of Dallas Symbolizes Transition from Conservative Past," *New York Times,* December 22, 1986, p. A21.

52. *Elected and Appointed Black Judges in the United States, 1986* (Washington, D.C.: The Joint Center for Political Studies and the Judicial Council of the National Bar Association, 1986), pp. 15–18.

53. Al Neuharth, "In the Heart of Dixie Image is the Issue," *U.S.A. Today,* September 4, 1987, p. 6A.

54. Robert García, "Hispanics Have to Work Closely with Blacks," *New York Times,* May 3, 1980, p. 23; Kevin Merida, "Issues Create Obstacles to Black-Hispanic Ties," *Dallas Morning News,* June 10, 1984, p. 1.

55. *New York Times,* March 31, 1987, p. B14.

56. Rufus P. Browning, Dale Rogers Marshall, and David H. Tabb, *Protest Is Not Enough: The Struggle of Blacks and Hispanics for Equality in Urban Politics* (Berkeley: University of California Press, 1986), pp. 246–249.

57. Pierce and Hagstrom, *Book of America,* pp. 476, 477.

58. Charles Kenney, "The Politics of Turmoil," *Boston Globe Magazine,* April 19, 1987, p. 18.

59. Eugene D. Genovese, "The Legacy of Slavery and the Roots of Black Nationalism," *Studies on the Left,* November–December 1966, pp. 14–26; also see Thomas Wagstaff, ed., *Black Power: The Radical Response to White America* (Beverly Hills, Calif.: Glencoe Press, 1969), p. 149.

60. Harold Cruse, *Plural but Equal: A Critical Study of Blacks and Minorities and America's Plural Society* (New York: Morrow, 1987).

61. Howard Schuman and Shirley Hatchett, *Black Racial Attitudes: Trends and Complexities* (Ann Arbor: Survey Research Center, University of Michigan, 1974), pp. 79–80.

62. Earl Black and Merle Black, *Politics and Society in the South* (Cambridge: Harvard University Press, 1987). In the most significant book ever written on southern politics, V. O. Key, Jr. had predicted that the large-scale entry of blacks into southern politics would greatly strengthen southern liberalism. See V. O. Key, Jr., *Southern Politics in State and Nation* (New York: Alfred Knopf, 1949), p. 4. As late as 1985, there were fifteen southern counties with a majority black population where the five-member county governing boards were all white, and twenty-three others where only a single black served. See Margaret Edds, *Free at Last: What Really Happened When Civil Rights Came to Southern Politics* (Bethesda, Md.: Adler and Adler, 1987).

63. Information on the New Haven election comes from Nick Ravo, "Ex-Athlete Revisits City Hall, but as Mayor," *New York Times,* November 10, 1989, p. B1; information on the Seattle election comes from Timothy Egan, "First Black Elected Mayor," *New York Times,* November 9, 1989, p. B15; Douglas Wilder's affirmation of coalition politics is in B. Drummond Ayres, Jr., "From Confrontation to Conciliation," *New York Times,* November 8, 1989, p. B10; David Dinkins's patriotic statement is in "From Protest to Politics," *New York Times,* November 9, 1989, p. 34; Wilder's testament to the Declaration of Independence is in Michael K. Frisby, "Wilder Ascribes Win to Mainstream Views," *Boston*

Globe, November 9, 1989, p. 43; Eleanor Holmes Norton made her statement on National Public Radio, November 11, 1989.

64. Statement of Louis Stokes addressing Lieutenant Colonel North before the select committee to investigate covert arms transactions with Iran, July 14, 1987, *Congressional Record,* Proceedings and Debates of the 100th Congress, First Session. Vol. 133, No. 120, July 21, 1987, p. H6408.

11. *"We Have to Be Part of the Political System": Redefining Tribal Pluralism*

1. *Denver Post Magazine,* March 9, 1986, p. 16.
2. U.S. Commission on Civil Rights. *Indian Tribes: A Continuing Quest for Survival* (Washington, D.C.: U.S. Government Printing Office, June 1981), p. 23. For a review of earlier assimilation movements, see Henry Fritz, *The Movement for Indian Assimilation, 1860–1890* (Philadelphia: University of Pennsylvania Press, 1963), and Francis Paul Prucha, *Americanizing the American Indians* (Cambridge: Harvard University Press, 1973).
3. Alice Marriott and Carol K. Rachlin, *American Epic: The Story of the American Indian* (New York: New American Library, 1969), pp. 172–176.
4. Angie Debo, *A History of the Indians of the United States* (Norman: University of Oklahoma Press, 1970), p. 312.
5. Ibid., p. 343.
6. Allen M. Josephy, Jr., *Red Power: The American Indians Fight for Freedom* (New York: American Heritage Press, 1971), pp. 49–52.
7. Ibid., pp. 67, 68.
8. Harold E. Fey and D'Arcy McNickle, *Indians and Other Americans: Two Ways of Life Meet* (New York: Harper and Row, 1970), pp. 247, 248.
9. Stan Steiner, *The New Indians* (New York: Dell, 1968), pp. 232–233.
10. Fey and McNickle, *Indians and Other Americans,* pp. 243–244.
11. Steiner, *The New Indians,* p. 303.
12. Josephy, *Red Power,* p. 93.
13. Steiner, *The New Indians,* p. 9.
14. Josephy, *Red Power,* pp. 197–201.
15. Ibid., p. 73.
16. Ibid., p. 72.
17. Ibid., pp. 170–172. Actually, only 32.7 percent of the 152,000 Indian children between six and eighteen attending school were enrolled in federal schools at the time, a percentage that fell further in subsequent years. An educational policy that would cover children in all fifty states, coming from three hundred different Indian groups, would be extremely difficult to plan and implement.
18. Ibid., p. 226.
19. Ibid., p. 227.
20. Scholarly books that empathized with the Indians appearing in the 1960s and 1970s included Wilcombe Washburn, ed., *The Indian and the White Man* (Garden City, N.Y.: Doubleday and Company, Inc., 1964), and Stuart Levine and Nancy Oestreich Luri, eds., *The American Indian Today* (Baltimore: Penguin Books, 1965). More influential were popular books written by Vine Deloria, Jr., a Standing Rock Sioux, who had been executive director of the National Congress of American Indians, *Custer Died for Your Sins: An Indian Manifesto* (New York: Avon Books, 1969), and Dee Brown, *Bury My Heart at Wounded Knee* (New York: Holt, Rinehart and Winston, 1971).
21. *U.S. Statutes at Large,* 88:2203, 1975, Title XXV, Section 450(A), pp. 1, 2.

22. *Final Report of the American Indian Policy Review Commission,* May 17, 1977, Vol. I (Washington, D.C.: U.S. Government Printing Office, 1977), p. 621.

23. Ibid., p. 574.

24. Ibid., p. 461.

25. *The Indian Education Act: Reformation and Progress,* Department of Health, Education and Welfare, Publication No. (OE) 760, 60-02403, Office of Indian Education, Washington, D.C., 1976, pp. 7, 8.

26. Morris A. Dorris, "The Grass Still Grows, the Rivers Still Flow: Contemporary Native American," *Daedalus,* Spring 1981, p. 11. The list is my own, but the article by Dorris discusses many of these developments.

27. Vine Deloria, Jr., and Clifford M. Lytle, *American Indians, American Justice* (Austin: University of Texas Press, 1983), p. 210.

28. Cass Peterson, "There's Something Fishy on the Lummi Reservation," *Washington Post National Weekly Edition,* March 31, 1986, p. B15.

29. *New York Times,* May 16, 1987, p. 8.

30. Representative William S. Cohen (R-Maine) and Senator William D. Hathaway (D-Maine) in *Indian Tribes: A Continuing Quest for Survival,* A Report of the United States Commission on Civil Rights (Washington, D.C.: U.S. Government Printing Office, June 1981), pp. 123, 124.

31. Ibid., p. 105.

32. Ibid., p. 133. Also see Margot Kemper's "Contemporary Dimensions of Group Rights: The Maine Indian Land Claim and Japanese-American Redress," Ph.D. diss., Brandeis University, April 1986.

33. "New Legislative Step Taken in Gay Head Indian Claim," *Boston Globe,* December 4, 1983, p. 63.

34. "Treaty Rights and Dual Status: Who Owes What to Native Americans?" in *The American Experiment: E Pluribus Unum,* developed by Education Development Center, Lawrence H. Fuchs, principal scholar (Newton, Mass.: Education Development Center, Inc., 1981), pp. 72–77. In addition to the Alaskan Indians and Eskimos, the small Aleut population also was involved in the settlement. Numbering between 5,000 and 7,000 individuals, about 3,000 of whom made their home on the Aleutians and the nearby Pribilof Islands, the Aleuts, the descendants of nomadic tribes that arrived about ten thousand years ago from Central Asia, are probably the oldest civilization in North America. They received one of the regional corporations, a profit-making enterprise covering a territory comprised of two hundred Aleutian islands extending 1,200 miles from the Alaskan mainland, plus two large and two small islands of the Pribilof group.

35. Bureau of Indian Affairs, Department of the Interior, *Environmental Assessment, Raven Oil Company Agreement Between the Crow Indian Tribe and Buffalo Exploration Company* (Washington, D.C.: U.S. Government Printing Office, October 1983), pp. 73–75.

36. Unpublished chronology of Raven Oil Company formation supplied to the author by Evert Mackin, president of the Buffalo Exploration Company.

37. Wayne King, "Navajos Plan Luxury Tourist Resort on Reservation," *New York Times,* October 28, 1987, p. A20.

38. "Treaty Rights and Dual Status," p. 29.

39. Susan Rasky, "Indians Begin to Weigh Their Political Potential," *New York Times,* September 16, 1984, p. E8.

40. Iver Peterson, "Indians in West Turning to Voting Rights Tool that Aided Blacks in the South," *New York Times,* July 5, 1986, p. 6. Although Indians made up 41 percent of the county's 7,300 voters, no Indian had been elected to the county

commission and only one Indian had won a seat on the six-member county school board.

41. Arthur D. Close, ed., *1980 Washington Representatives,* 4th ed. (Washington, D.C.: Columbian Books, Inc., 1980).

42. Deloria and Lytle, *American Indians, American Justice,* pp. 152–153.

43. Ibid., pp. 157–159.

44. Laurence M. Hauptman, *The Iroquois Struggle for Survival: World War II to Red Power* (Syracuse, N.Y.: Syracuse University Press, 1986), p. 202.

45. Deloria and Lytle, *American Indians, American Justice,* p. 154.

46. Ibid., p. 239.

47. *Boston Globe,* July 9, 1986, p. 4. Also see Iver Peterson, "At White Man's Deadline Hopi-Navajo Line Is Still Not Settled," *New York Times,* July 6, 1986, p. 10.

48. "U.S. Refines Its Eligibility Rules for the Indian Health Service," *New York Times,* October 4, 1987, p. 29.

49. Deloria, *Custer Died for Your Sins,* p. 195.

50. Public Law 93-638, 93rd Congress, S-1017, January 4, 1975, p. 1.

51. Wayne King, "Hodel Urging Shift in Indian Programs," *New York Times,* October 27, 1987, p. A18.

52. *Washington Post National Edition,* September 24, 1984, p. 6. The situation of many Indian tribes received a considerable amount of national attention. Not so that of another colonized people, native Hawaiians. There were few full-blooded Hawaiians left by 1989. But part-Hawaiians numbered 200,000, over 34 percent of whom lived below the poverty level. There had been no Self-Determination Act for Hawaiians as was passed for Indians. The 1921 program to facilitate Hawaiian homesteading had been badly abused. And land sacred to Hawaiians had often been put to use by non-Hawaiian commercial interests. Neither the state of Hawaii nor the U.S. government appeared ready to address the call of militant Hawaiians for a return of good land so that they could live in relationship to the federal government and the state in some kind of quasi-sovereign status comparable to recognized Indian tribes. See Viveca Novak, "Hawaii's Dirty Secret," *Common Cause,* November/December 1989, pp. 10–16, 27.

53. *Boston Sunday Globe,* July 13, 1986, p. .3.

54. Debo, *A History of the Indians of the United States,* p. 346.

55. Fey and McNickle, *Indians and Other Americans,* p. 251.

12. "America Is in the Heart": Asian Sojourners No Longer

1. Hearings before the U.S. Congress, Committee on Immigration and Naturalization, *Immigration into Hawaii,* U.S. Senate, 67th Congress, 1st Session (Washington, D.C.: U.S. Government Printing Office, 1921), p. 100.

2. Lawrence H. Fuchs, *Hawaii Pono* (New York: Harcourt Brace Jovanovich, 1963), p. 283.

3. Ibid., pp. 286, 287.

4. Bill Hosokawa, *Nisei: The Quiet Americans* (New York: William Morrow and Company, Inc., 1969), p. 216.

5. Hearings before the Committee on Governmental Affairs, U.S. Senate, 96th Congress, 2nd Session on S.17, March 18, 1980, Commission on Wartime Relocation and Internment of Civilians Act (Washington, D.C.: U.S. Government Printing Office, 1980), p. 205.

6. Hosokawa, *Nisei: The Quiet Americans,* p. 225.

7. Morton Grodzins, *Americans Betrayed: Politics and the Japanese Evacuation* (Chicago: University of Chicago Press, 1949), p. 42.

8. Ibid., p. 282.
9. Hosokawa, *Nisei: The Quiet Americans,* pp. 257, 258.
10. Ibid., p. 275.
11. Ibid., p. 232.
12. Ibid., p. 272.
13. Ibid., p. 347.
14. Ibid., p. 366.
15. Robert A. Wilson and Bill Hosokawa, *East to America: A History of the Japanese in the United States* (New York: William Morrow and Company), pp. 265, 269.
16. Ibid., p. 240.
17. Ibid., p. 241.
18. Hosokawa, *Nisei: The Quiet Americans,* p. 440.
19. Ibid., p. 366.
20. Ibid., p. 429.
21. Ibid., p. 430.
22. Shih-Shan Henry Tsai, *The Chinese Experience in America* (Bloomington: Indiana University Press, 1986), p. 115.
23. E. P. Hutchinson, *Legislative History of American Immigration Policy, 1798–1965* (Philadelphia: University of Pennsylvania Press, 1981), p. 269.
24. Tsai, *Chinese Experience,* p. 117.
25. *Congressional Record,* 78th Cong., 1st sess., June 16, 1943, pp. 5966–5967, and October 21, 1943, pp. 8625–8627.
26. Wilson and Hosokawa, *East to America,* p. 246.
27. Ibid., p. 247.
28. Ibid., p. 248.
29. *Oyama* v. *California,* 9. L. Ed 260.
30. Wilson and Hosokawa, *East to America,* p. 261.
31. Ibid., p. 259.
32. Ibid., p. 260.
33. Benjamin R. Ringer, *"We, the People" and Others* (New York: Tavistock Publications), 1983, pp. 9, 10.
34. Wilson and Hosokawa, *East to America,* p. 232. Finally, the last of the alien land laws was eliminated in 1966 when the JACL led a campaign to end it by referendum.
35. David M. Reimers, *Still the Golden Door: The Third World Comes to America* (New York: Columbia University Press, 1985), pp. 23–26.
36. Ibid., p. 27.
37. Kirk H. Porter and Donald Bruce Johnson, eds., *National Party Platforms, 1840–1968,* rev. ed. (Urbana: University of Illinois Press, 1970). See p. 577 for the Democratic platform and p. 620 for the Republican platform of 1964, and p. 652 for 1968.
38. Fear of Japanese domination was expressed openly by some opponents of statehood. See U.S. Congress, Senate Subcommittee on Public Lands, *Hearings,* Statement of Mrs. Alice Kamokila Campbell, 80th Cong., 2nd sess., January–April (Washington, D.C.: U.S. Government Printing Office, 1984), pp. 410–416.
39. Ibid., p. 412.
40. Fuchs, *Hawaii Pono,* p. 411.
41. Ibid., p. 414.
42. Daniel K. Inouye, *Journey to Washington* (Englewood Cliffs, N.J.: Prentice-Hall, 1967), pp. 146–154, for a short description of the battle.
43. *New York Times,* August 4, 1987, p. 87.

44. Judith Cummings, "DeLorean Trial Judge: Robert Mitsuhiro Takasugi," *New York Times,* June 28, 1984, p. A23.

45. Fuchs, *Hawaii Pono,* pp. 437, 438.

46. Ibid., p. 442.

47. Tsai, *Chinese Experience in America,* p. 170.

48. Ibid., p. 169.

49. Edna Bonacich, "A Theory of Ethnic Antagonism: The Split Labor Market," *American Sociological Review,* 37 (October 1972): 547–559.

50. Carlos Bulosan, *America Is in the Heart* (New York: Harcourt, Brace and Company, Inc., 1943), p. 311.

51. Ibid., p. 314.

52. Elliott R. Barkan, "Whom Shall We Integrate?: A Comparative Analysis of Immigration and Naturalization Trends of Asians Before and After the 1965 Immigration Act (1951–1978)," *Journal of American Ethnic History,* Fall 1983, p. 48.

13. "Can't They See? I Love This Country . . .":
Mexican-Americans and the Battle Against Sojourner Pluralism

1. Quoted in Joan London and Henry Anderson, "Man of Fire: Ernesto Galarza," in Renato Rosaldo, Robert A. Calvert, and Gustav L. Seligmann, eds., *Chicano: The Evolution of a People* (Minneapolis: Winston Press, 1973), p. 285.

2. For more on the situation of Mexicans and Mexican-Americans in the Southwest in the nineteenth century, see Robert J. Rosenbaum, *Mexicano Resistance in the Southwest: The Sacred Right of Self Preservation* (Austin: University of Texas Press, 1981), pp. 3–28.

3. Armando B. Rendon, *Chicano Manifesto: The History and Aspirations of the Second Largest Minority in America* (New York: Collier Books, 1971), p. 116.

4. Fernando Peñalosa, "The Changing Mexican-American in Southern California," in Rosaldo, Calvert, and Seligmann, eds., *Chicano,* p. 259.

5. Rendon, *Chicano Manifesto,* pp. 72, 73.

6. Manuel A. Machado, Jr., *Listen, Chicano! An Informal History of the Mexican-American* (Chicago: Nilson-Hall, 1978), p. 108.

7. Niles Hansen, *The Border Economy: Regional Development in the Southwest* (Austin: University of Texas Press, 1981), p. 85.

8. Richard Griego and Gilbert W. Merks, "Crisis in New Mexico," in Rosaldo, Calvert, and Seligmann, eds., *Chicano,* p. 389.

9. Machado, *Listen, Chicano!,* pp. 80, 81.

10. Rendon, *Chicano Manifesto,* p. 194.

11. For a superb article on Mexican-American identity and historiography, see Fernando Peñalosa, "Toward an Operational Definition of the Mexican-American," in Rosaldo, Calvert, and Seligmann, eds., *Chicano,* pp. 255–262.

12. Ernesto Galarza, "California, the Uncommonwealth," reprinted from *Merchants of Labor: The Mexican Bracero Society* in Rosaldo, Calvert, and Seligmann, eds., *Chicano,* p. 165.

13. London and Anderson, "Man of Fire," p. 283.

14. Matt S. Meier and Feliciano Rivera, *The Chicanos: A History of Mexican-Americans* (New York: Hill and Wang, 1972), pp. 261, 262.

15. Rendon, *Chicano Manifesto,* p. 149.

16. John Gregory Dunne, *Delano: The Story of the California Grape Strike* (New York: Farrar, Straus and Giroux, 1967), p. 10.

17. Congressional Research Service, Library of Congress, *History of the Immigration*

and Naturalization Service (Washington, D.C.: U.S. Government Printing Office, 1980), p. 66.

18. Congressional Research Service, Library of Congress, *Temporary Worker Programs: Background and Issues,* Report Prepared for the U.S. Senate, Committee on the Judiciary (Washington, D.C.: U.S. Government Printing Office, 1980), pp. 26, 27.

19. Rendon, *Chicano Manifesto,* p. 155.

20. Select Commission on Immigration and Refugee Policy, "The Half Open Door: Illegal Immigration to the United States," chapter 9 of part III, "The Rule of Law," *Immigration Policy and the National Interest. Staff Report, Supplement to the Final Report and Recommendations of the Select Commission on Immigration and Refugee Policy* (Washington, D.C.: U.S. Government Printing Office, April 30, 1981).

21. Ibid., p. 483.

22. Ibid., pp. 500–516.

23. Rendon, *Chicano Manifesto,* p. 47.

24. Select Commission on Immigration and Refugee Policy, *Immigration Policy and the National Interest,* p. 630.

25. Congressional Research Service, Library of Congress, *U.S. Immigration Law and Policy: 1952–1979* (Washington, D.C.: U.S. Government Printing Office, 1979), pp. 71–76. This report was prepared at the request of Senator Edward M. Kennedy, Chairman, Committee on the Judiciary, U.S. Senate, upon the formation of the Select Commission on Immigration and Refugee Policy.

26. Ibid., p. 68.

27. Select Commission on Immigration and Refugee Policy. *Final Report and Recommendations of the Select Commission on Immigration and Refugee Policy* (Washington, D.C.: U.S. Government Printing Office, March 1, 1981), p. 41.

28. Ibid., p. 42.

29. *Immigration Policy and the National Interest,* p. 583.

30. *Christian Science Monitor,* December 10, 1980, p. 24; *Cincinnati Enquirer,* December 29, 1980, p. A10; *Washington Post,* January 10, 1981, p. A16; *New York Times,* March 1, 1981, p. E18; *Los Angeles Times,* March 1, 1981, p. IV-4 l e; *Washington Post,* February 6, 1981, p. A14; *Boston Globe,* March 3, 1981, p. 14.

31. The Civil Rights Commission, *The Tarnished Golden Door: Civil Rights Issues in Immigration* (Washington, D.C.: U.S. Government Printing Office, September 1985), pp. 65–68.

32. See S. 1200, *Conference Report on the Immigration Reform and Control Act of 1986,* which passed as amendments to the Immigration and Nationality Act. The provisions on agricultural workers can be found in Title III, Part A, Sections 301–305, pp. 46–67 of *Immigration Reform and Control Act of 1986,* 99th Congress, 2nd Session, House of Representatives, Report 99-1000 (Washington, D.C.: U.S. Government Printing Office, October 14, 1986). The new agricultural program called for two groups of agricultural workers to be adjusted or admitted into programs that could lead to permanent residency and citizenship; seasonal agricultural workers and replenishment agricultural workers. Any alien who worked ninety days in perishable agriculture during the twelve-month period ending May 1, 1986, could apply for lawful temporary resident status as a seasonal agricultural worker and, after two years, apply to adjust his or her status to that of a lawful permanent resident. Those aliens who met the ninety-day requirement and also performed ninety days of labor in perishable agriculture during the twelve-month periods ending May 1, 1985, and May 1, 1984, were obliged to remain in temporary status for only one year before adjusting their status to that of

permanent resident, although no more than 350,000 aliens would be permitted to become temporary residents under the one-year provision. As with aliens legalized under the broader legalization program, such individuals were not eligible to receive Aid to Families with Dependent Children for five years and were granted limited access to Medicaid benefits for that period, but in other respects they could become participants in and beneficiaries of American society much as permanent residents do.

33. The new law went beyond the Civil Rights Act in its application to employers of more than three employees (the Civil Rights Act covers only employers of fifteen or more) and provided for the creation of a special counsel within the Department of Justice to be responsible for investigating charges of discrimination and to issue complaints about discrimination for prosecution before administrative law judges.

34. Doris Sue Wong, "Immigrants Feeling Good About Amnesty," *Boston Globe,* August 26, 1987, p. B1.

35. Howard W. French, "Immigrant's Family Pins Hope on Amnesty," *New York Times,* August 20, 1987, p. B1.

36. David S. North, *Immigration Reform in Its First Year* (Washington, D.C.: Center for Immigration Studies, 1987); also *Immigration Reform: Status of Implementing Employer Sanctions after One Year,* U.S. General Accounting Office, Report to the Congress (Washington, D.C.: U.S. Government Printing Office, November 1987). The GAO issued a second annual report in November 1988 showing an increase in the amount of antidiscrimination complaints reported and processed, causing the U.S. Catholic bishops to urge that employer sanctions be rescinded. Whether or not employer sanctions was working as intended—more effective and benign enforcement without substantial discrimination—was a matter of dispute, but neither the GAO nor leaders in Congress called for its repeal. See "Bishops Urge Change in Immigration Law," *Miami Herald,* November 18, 1988, p. A26. High officials in the INS in early 1989 agreed that it was necessary to maintain a strong outreach campaign to employers concerning their responsibilities under the antidiscrimination provisions of the Immigration Reform and Control Act of 1986.

37. Joan Beck, "The Hispanic Tide and the U.S.—The Pope Put It Mildly!" *Chicago Tribune,* September 17, 1987, p. 15.

38. Michael Teitelbaum, "Right Versus Right: Immigration and Refugee Policy in the United States," *Foreign Affairs* 59, no. 1 (1980): 43.

39. *Final Report and Recommendations of the Select Commission on Immigration and Refugee Policy,* pp. 412–413.

40. Richard D. Lamm and Gary Imhoff, *The Immigration Time Bomb* (New York: Dutton, 1985).

41. For a survey of the literature on Mexican naturalization in the U.S., see John A. García, "Political Integration of Mexican Immigrants: Explorations into the Naturalization Process," *International Migration Review,* Winter (1981): 608–625.

42. Edward W. Fernandez and Arthur R. Cresce, "The Hispanic Foreign Born and the Assimilation Experience," *Migration World* 14, no. 5 (1986): 8, 9. Also see an excellent review of the literature and new comparative data for the 1970s in Alejandro Portes and Rafael Mozo, "The Political Adaptation Process of Cubans and Other Ethnic Minorities in the United States: A Preliminary Analysis," *International Migration Review,* Spring 1985, 35–63. In some cities in the Southwest, the INS itself appeared to have a deterrent effect on applications because of the strictness with which it applied its tests. A 1986 study showed that in San Antonio only 46.4 percent of applicants were approved for citizenship, and in Harlingen

the rate was only 44.1 percent. These contrasted with the national average at all district offices of the INS of 71.8 percent. No one knows how many of those sent away come back later to try to naturalize. See David North, "The Long Gray Welcome: A Study of the American Naturalization Program," *International Migration Review*, Summer 1987, pp. 311–326.

43. Barbara Caplan, "Linking Cultural Characteristics to Political Opinion," in Rodolfo O. de la Garza, ed., *Ignored Voices: Public Opinion Polls and the Latino Community* (Austin: The center for Mexican-American Studies, University of Texas at Austin, 1987), p. 159.

44. James W. Lamare, "The Political Integration of Mexican-American Children: A Generational Analysis," *International Migration Review*, Spring 1982, p. 175. The author was concerned that third-generation children—children whose parents and grandparents had been born in the U.S.—were found to be less positively identified with American political institutions and more distrustful of government than those of the second generation. That result was hardly surprising, especially in 1978, when such children probably had opinions very much like those of non-Mexican-origin third-generation American youngsters, whose cynicism and disrespect for authority generally was quite high. In any case, it is the first generation born in the U.S. that usually becomes most self-consciously American. Ibid., pp. 178, 179.

45. John A. García, "The Political Integration of Mexican Immigrants: Examining Some Political Orientations," *International Migration Review*, Summer 1987, pp. 372–387.

46. Ricardo Romo, *East Los Angeles* (Austin: University of Texas Press, 1983), pp. 168, 169.

47. John Shockley, "Crystal City: Los Cinco Mexicanos," in Rosaldo, Calvert, and Seligmann, eds., *Chicano*, pp. 303–313.

48. Ibid., pp. 314–326.

49. Ibid., p. 326.

50. Niles Hansen, *The Border Economy: Regional Development in the Southwest* (Austin: University of Texas Press, 1981), p. 153. Also see Calvin Trillin, "U.S. Journal: San Antonio: Some Elements of Power," *The New Yorker*, May 2, 1977, pp. 92—97.

51. Leo Grebler, Joan W. Moore, and Ralph C. Guzman, *The Mexican-American People* (New York: The Free Press, 1970), p. 561.

52. *Boston Globe*, June 5, 1983, p. 15.

53. Rodolfo O. de la Garza, "Chicanos and U.S. Foreign Policy: The Future of Chicano-Mexican Relations," *Western Political Quarterly*, December 1980, p. 579.

54. Dan Balz, "San Antonio Gets Hispanic Mayor," *Boston Globe*, April 6, 1981, p. 3.

55. Quoted by Griffin Smith, Jr., in "The Mexican-Americans: A People on the Move," *National Geographic*, June 1980, p. 796.

56. Henry Cisneros, "The Meaning for Hispanics of Five de Mayo," *Vista*, May 3, 1986, pp. 12, 13.

57. *Vista*, April 1986, p. 18.

58. Carey McWilliams, *North from Mexico: The Spanish-Speaking People of the United States* (Philadelphia: J. B. Lippincott, 1949), p. 302.

59. Rodolfo O. de la Garza and Robert R. Brischetto, *The Mexican-American Electorate: A Demographic Profile*, Mexican-American Electorate Series, a joint publication of The Southwest Voter Registration Education Project, San Antonio, and the Hispanic Population Studies Program of the Center for Mexican-American Studies, University of Texas at Austin (Austin and San Antonio: 1982).

60. U.S. Commission on Civil Rights, *The Voting Rights Act: Unfulfilled Goals* (Washington, D.C.: U.S. Commission on Civil Rights, 1981).

61. Ibid.

62. John M. Crewdson, "U.S. to Oversee Texas Bilingual Votes," *New York Times*, May 1, 1976, p. 1, 9.

63. See Abigail M. Thernstrom, *Whose Votes Count?: Affirmative Action and Minority Voting Rights*, A Twentieth Century Fund Study (Cambridge: Harvard University Press, 1987).

64. Crewdson, "U.S. to Oversee Texas Bilingual Votes," pp. 1, 9.

65. Letter to the Board of MALDEF from Joaquin V. Avila, president and general counsel, May 15, 1984.

66. From Michal Barone, "Unequivocally American: The Politics of Two Powerful Hispanics," *Washington Post National Weekly Edition*, August 5, 1985, p. 16.

67. Wayne King, "Texas Governor is Courting Mexican-American Voters in Close Campaign," *New York Times*, October 14, 1982, p. B12.

68. Barbara Gutierrez, "Hispanic Vote: Sleeping Giant Awakening," *Miami Herald*, January 9, 1988, p. A6. Also, Don Campbell, "Trio Vie for Texans' Votes in Debate," *U.S.A. Today*, May 3, 1984, p. 3; Roberto Fabricio, "Texas Caucuses Show Power of Hispanic Issues," *Miami Herald*, May 5, 1984, p. B1; "Democratic Hopefuls Court Hispanics," *Dallas Morning News*, May 14, 1984, p. A7; Peter Grier, "U.S. Politicians Court Hispanics," *Christian Science Monitor*, May 30, 1984, p. 1; and *Washington Times*, September 12, 1983, p. 28.

69. Frank Clifford, "Mondale Barely Edges Jackson in Latino Vote," *Los Angeles Times*, May 14, 1984, p. 1.

70. Jesse Treviño, "The Political Game," *Vista*, January 15, 1989, pp. 6, 7, 13.

71. Dave McNeely, "Hispanic Power at the Polls," *Vista*, November 1, 1986, pp. 8–12.

72. *Nuestro*, April 1987, p. 4.

73. Raymond E. Wolfinger and Steven J. Rosenstone, *Who Votes?* (New Haven: Yale University Press, 1980), p. 92. Actually, the data showed that Mexican-Americans were 3 percent more likely to vote than the rest of the population, but the possibility of statistical error makes it prudent to estimate the turnout of Mexican-Americans at about that of the rest of the population. In 1988, 55 percent of all Hispanics registered to vote in the country did vote, just below the national average. See Treviño, "The Political Game," pp. 6, 7, 13.

74. Robert R. Brischetto and Rodolfo O. de la Garza, *The Mexican-American Electorate: Political Participation and Ideology*, The Mexican-American Electorate Series, Hispanic Population Studies Program Occasional Paper No. 3, a joint publication of the Southwest Voter Registration Education Project and the Hispanic Population Studies Program of the Center for Mexican-American Studies, the University of Texas at Austin (Austin and San Antonio: 1983), pp. 1, 2, 6, 14, 15, 26.74.

75. For a summary of the literature on acculturation, see R. Burdiaga Valdez, Kevin F. McCarthy, and Connie Malcolm Moreno, *An Annotated Bibliography of Sources on Mexican Immigration* (Santa Monica, Calif.: The Rand Corporation, 1987). See especially pp. 42–52.

76. de la Garza, "Chicanos and U.S. Foreign Policy," p. 574; also see Rodolfo de la Garza, "Chicano-Mexican Relations: A Framework for Research," *Social Science Quarterly*, March 1982, pp. 116–121.

77. Rodolfo O. de la Garza and Robert R. Brischetto with the assistance of David Vaughn, *The Mexican-American Electorate: Information Sources and Policy Orientations*, The Mexican-American Series, Hispanic Population Studies Program

Occasional Paper No. 2, a joint publication of the Southwest Voter Registration Education Project and the Hispanic Population Studies Program of the Center for Mexican-American Studies, the University of Texas at Austin (Austin and San Antonio: 1983), pp. 12–15.

78. Rodolfo O. de la Garza, *Ignored Voices: Public Opinion Polls and the Latino Community,* pp. 3, 6, 47, 59, 61, 68, 74, 77, 101, 103.

79. *Vista,* September 7, 1986. See particularly Renato Perez, "The Business of Hispanics: HACER and Corporate Giants Establish a Dialog for the Benefit of All," p. 10. See p. 11 for the Chamber of Commerce ad and p. 22, "Bridging the Illiteracy Barrier," for the item on *La Raza.*

80. *Nuestro,* August 1983, p. 26.

81. MALDEF, Mexican-American Legal and Education Defense Fund, Newsletter, January 1986, p. 3.

82. Ibid., p. 2.

83. Matt Moffett, "LULAC, Hispanic Advocacy Group, Turns Away from Liberal Traditions under New Leadership," *Wall Street Journal,* March 19, 1986, p. 62.

84. Rufus P. Browning, Dale Rogers Marshall, and David H. Tabb, *Protest Is Not Enough: The Struggle of Blacks and Hispanics for Equality in Urban Politics* (Berkeley: University of California Press, 1984). See chapter 6 for a summary of a study of ten cities with the largest black and Hispanic populations in northern California and of the factors that led to their political incorporation and responsiveness to their needs.

85. *Nuestro,* March 1986, p. 9.

86. Jay Monet, "French Canadian Nationalism and the Challenge of Ultramontanism," *Canadian Historical Association* (Cambridge: Harvard University Press, 1966), pp. 41–56; R. Vicero, "The Immigration of French Canadians to New England, 1840–1900," Ph.D. diss., University of Wisconsin, 1968).

87. L. H. Gann and Peter J. Duignan, "Latinos and the Catholic Church in America," *Nuestro,* May 1987, pp. 12–14.

88. Anthony M. Stevens-Arroyo, "Cahensly Revisited: The National Pastoral Encounter of America's Hispanic Catholics," *Migration World,* 15, no. 3 (1987): 18.

89. *Nuestro,* May 1987, p. 7.

90. *Vista,* April 4, 1987, p. 3.

91. Introductory letter from Caspar W. Weinberger in *Hispanics in America's Defense,* Office of Deputy Assistant Secretary of Defense for Equal Opportunity and Safety Policy.

92. Dan Allsup, "The Story of Stella," *Vista,* September 1986, p. 16.

93. John Gonzalez, "Queen for a Day: Miss U.S.A.'s Mom Becomes a Citizen," *Dallas Morning News,* October 10, 1985.

94. Treviño, "The Political Game," pp. 6, 7, 13.

95. Jimmy Lopez is quoted in Select Commission on Immigration and Refugee Policy, *U.S. Immigration Policy and the National Interest,* Staff Report, p. 157.

96. Meier and Rivera, *The Chicanos,* p. 189.

Part 4. The American Kaleidoscope:
The Ethnic Landscape, 1970–1989

14. The Blood of All Nations: The Sources of Ethnicity Become Global

1. Hector St. John Crèvecoeur, *Letters from an American Farmer,* in Moses Rischin, *Immigration and the American Tradition* (New York: Bobbs-Merrill, 1976), p. 24.

When *Letters from an American Farmer* was published, Crévecoeur used the Anglicized first name of Hector St. John.

2. Ralph Waldo Emerson, in Ralph Henry Gabriel, *The Course of American Democratic Thought* (New York: Greenwood Press, 1986), p. 46.

3. Herman Melville, *Redburn* (Boston: St. Botolph's Press, 1924), pp. 169, 170. Melville wrote: "Settled by the people of all nations, all nations may claim her for their own. You cannot spill a drop of American blood without spilling the blood of the whole world . . . our blood is as the blood of the Amazon, made up of a thousand noble currents all pouring into one. We are not a nation so much as a world . . . we are without father or mother . . . we are the heirs of all time, and with all nations we divide our inheritance. On this western hemisphere, all tribes and people are forming into one federated whole; and there is a future which shall see the estranged children of Adam restored as to the old hearthstone in Eden."

4. Israel Zangwill, *The Melting Pot: Drama in Four Acts,* new and rev. ed. (New York: Macmillan, 1922), pp. 184, 185.

5. Jess Stern, ed., *The Random House Dictionary of the English Language,* unabridged edition (New York: Random House, 1967), p. 778. *Webster's New Collegiate Dictionary* speaks of a kaleidoscope as presenting "an endless variety of patterns" and of "variegated changing patterns." (Springfield, Mass.: G. & C. Merriam & Co., 1974), p. 629.

6. Willi Paul Adams, "The Founding Fathers and the Immigrant," in *La Révolution Américaine et l'Europe* (Paris: Centre National de la Recherche Scientifique, 1979), p. 141.

7. *The Federalist, a Commentary on the Constitution of the United States, from the Original Text of Alexander Hamilton, John Jay and James Madison with an Introduction by Edward Mead Earle* (New York: The Modern Library, 1937), p. 9.

8. Lester J. Cappon, ed. in chief, *Atlas of Early American History: The Revolutionary Era, 1760–1790* (Princeton, N.J.: Princeton University Press, 1976), pp. 98, 99.

9. At the time of this writing, only summary data were available from the Immigration and Naturalization Service for immigration statistics for fiscal year 1988 (see *Advance Report,* April 1989). Complete data were available for fiscal year 1987 in unpublished, unbound, and unpaginated material. Most of the statistical data on immigration reported in this chapter come from the 1987 material, which undoubtedly will be published in bound form by the time this book is published. Data reported in subsequent pages without citation can be assumed to come from the as yet unpaginated *1988 Statistical Yearbook,* which includes data on immigration by decades and the immediate years preceding 1987. Data cited here can be checked easily by reference to the Table of Contents of the published version of the yearbook. Data cited in this and subsequent chapters from previously published *Statistical Yearbooks* from 1982 through 1986 will be included in full in the chapter notes.

10. David M. Reimers, *Still the Golden Door: The Third World Comes to America* (New York: Columbia University Press, 1985), p. 76.

11. The preference system, which had been established for the eastern hemisphere in 1965 and applied to the western hemisphere in 1976, allocated a fixed percentage of the total number of immigrants to be admitted from the world and each country. Only 20 percent of the total number of numerically restricted immigrants were allowed to enter the U.S. independent of a petition from a relative who was already a resident alien or citizen. In addition to numerically restricted immigration, the spouses, minor children, and parents (over twenty-one) of U.S. citizens and refugees were permitted to become immigrants (resident aliens),

leading to a total annual average of 565,837 immigrants between 1980 and 1985 (the number for fiscal year 1985 was 570,009) and to more than 600,000 in 1986, 1987 and 1988.

12. U.S. Immigration and Naturalization Service, *1982 Statistical Yearbook of the Immigration and Naturalization Service* (Washington, D.C.: U.S. Government Printing Office, 1984), p. 16. Also see *1983 Statistical Yearbook of the Immigration and Naturalization Service* (Washington, D.C.: U.S. Government Printing Office, 1985), p. 16. Second and fifth preference were two of six preferences coming under a worldwide system of immigration limited to 270,000 annually. The first preference admitted unmarried sons and daughters of U.S. citizens and their children (up to 20 percent, or 54,000); second preference admitted spouses and unmarried sons and daughters of permanent resident aliens (26 percent, or 70,200); third preference was for members of the professions of exceptional ability and their spouses and children (10 percent, or 27,000); fourth preference, married sons and daughters of U.S. citizens, their spouses and children (10 percent, or 27,000); fifth preference, brothers and sisters of U.S. citizens (at least twenty-one years of age) and their spouses and children (24 percent, or 64,800); and sixth preference, workers in skilled or unskilled occupations in which laborers are in short supply in the U.S., their spouses and children (10 percent, or 27,000). Numbers not used in higher preferences could be used in second, fourth, or fifth preference. Spouses, children and parents (of U.S. citizens at least twenty-one years of age) were admitted without numerical restriction, subject only to a system of thirty-three qualifying exclusions. Refugees and asylees could adjust their status to that of immigrant, and a small number of special immigrants were admitted, e.g., certain ministers of religion and certain former employees of the U.S. government abroad.

13. *1982 Statistical Yearbook of the Immigration and Naturalization Service,* Table IMM 3.2, pp. 42-45.

14. Ibid., p. 39.

15. *1985 Statistical Yearbook of the Immigration and Naturalization Service* (Washington, D.C.: U.S. Government Printing Office, 1986), p. 39.

16. Ibid., p. 38. The 1980 yearbook provided specific information on categories of adjustment from refugee status and other nonimmigrant statuses to that of immigrant.

17. Select Commission on Immigration and Refugee Policy, *Immigration Policy and the National Interest. Staff Report, Supplement to the Final Report and Recommendations of the Select Commission on Immigration and Refugee Policy* (Washington, D.C.: U.S. Government Printing Office, April 30, 1981), pp. 483, 484. Also see Jacob S. Siegel, Jeffrey S. Passel, and J. Gregory Robinson, "Preliminary Review of Existing Studies of the Number of Illegal Residents in the United States," in Select Commission on Immigration and Refugee Policy, *Appendix E to the Final Report,* pp. 19, 20.

18. *Miami Herald,* October 8, 1982, p. 10.

19. *Christian Science Monitor,* September 8, 1983, pp. B1, B3.

20. Stephan Thernstrom, ed., *Harvard Encyclopedia of American Ethnic Groups* (Cambridge: Harvard University Press, 1980).

21. U.S. Bureau of the Census, *1980 Census of Population: Supplementary Report, Ancestry of Population by State: 1980,* PC. 80-S1-10. Ancestral origins claimed by 100,000 or more Americans were: English, 49,598,035; German, 49,224,146; Irish, 40,165,702; Afro-American, 20,964,729; French, 12,892,246; Italian, 12,183,691;

Scottish, 10,048,816; Polish, 8,228,037; Mexican, 7,692,619; American Indian, 6,715,819; Dutch, 6,304,499; Swedish, 4,345,392; Norwegian, 3,453,839; Russian, 2,781,432; Spanish-Hispanic, 2,686,680; Czech, 1,892,456; Hungarian, 1,776,902; Welsh, 1,664,598; Danish, 1,518,273; Puerto Rican, 1,443,862; Portuguese, 1,024,351; Swiss, 981,543; Greek, 959,856; Austrian, 948,558; Chinese, 894,453; Filipino, 795,255; Japanese, 791,275; French Canadian, 780,488; Slovak, 776,806; Lithuanian, 742,776; Ukrainian, 730,056; Finnish, 615,872; Cuban, 597,702; Canadian, 456,212; Korean, 376,676; Belgian, 360,277; Yugoslavian, 360,174; Romanian, 315,258; Asian Indian, 311,953; Lebanese, 294,895; Jamaican, 253,268; Croatian, 252,970; Vietnamese, 215,184; Armenian, 212,621; African, 203,791; Hawaiian, 202,052; Dominican, 170,698; Colombian, 156,276; Slovene, 126,463; Iranian, 122,890; Syrian, 106,638; and Serbian, 100,941.

22. Paul Robert Magocsi, "Are the Armenians Really Russians? Or, How the U.S. Census Bureau Classifies America's Ethnic Groups," *Government Publications Review,* 14 (1967): 133–168.

23. *New York Times,* November 25, 1980, p. A14.

24. "Which Chinese?" *San Francisco Focus,* September 1986, p. 74.

25. Myron Weiner, "Asian Immigration and U.S. Foreign Policy," paper presented to the Lehrman Institute, 1987, p. 21.

26. Lesley R. Drake, "Ethiopians in California: Aspirations and Reality," *Refugees,* August 1987, p. 18.

27. When the congressionally established immigration commission known as the Dillingham Commission investigated the nationality of pupils in the public schools of thirty-six cities in 1909 (as measured by their fathers' nativity) it found sixty nationalities represented, but the number of non-Europeans was small, including only sixteen Filipinos, ten Arabs, eight Koreans, and eight West Indians. Dillingham Commission, "Abstracts of Reports of the Immigration Commission," *Reports of the Immigration Commission,* Vol. 2 (Washington, D.C.: U.S. Government Printing Office, 1911), p. 16. Reprint edition 1970 by Arno Press (New York: 1970).

28. U.S. Bureau of the Census, "Persons of Spanish Speaking Origin by State: 1980," *1980 Census of Population: Supplementary Report,* P.C. 80-5-7, pp. 1–2. Also see Cary Davis, Carl Haub, and JoAnne Willette, *U.S. Hispanics: Changing the Face of America,* Population Reference Bureau, Inc., Vol. 38, No. 3, June 1983.

29. U.S. Bureau of the Census, *1980 Census of Population: Supplementary Report, Asian and Pacific Islander Population by State: 1980,* P.C. 80-S1-12. The other Asian population comprised about 5 percent of the total Asian population by 1980, the largest groups being Laotian (47,682) and Thai (45,279).

30. U.S. Bureau of the Census, *1980 Census of Population: Supplementary Report, Persons of Spanish Origin by State: 1980,* P.C. 80-S1-7.

31. U.S. Bureau of the Census, *1980 Census of Population: Supplementary Report, American Indian Areas and Alaska Native Villages: 1980,* P.C. 80-S1-13.

32. U.S. Bureau of the Census, *America's Black Population: A Statistical View,* Special Publication AIO/Pop-83-1 (Washington, D.C.: U.S. Government Printing Office), p. 1.

33. By the 1980s, immigrants from Jamaica and the Dominican Republic were among the largest groups to immigrate annually. Immigrants from Guyana in South America and Belize in Central America constituted small but growing elements in the new kaleidoscope. Immigrants from Guyana increased from 1,148 in 1968 to 7,614 in 1979 to 10,059 in 1982 and 8,020 in 1984. An even more obscure

example: immigration from Belize went from 528 in 1973 to 1,033 in 1978 and 2,031 in 1982 to 1,492 in 1984.

34. *New York Times,* May 6, 1981, pp. A1, B4.

35. Paul Hirshson, "Cambridge's High School for All," *Boston Globe,* November 4, 1986, p. 2. The high school is Cambridge Rindge and Latin School.

15. "From the Mountains, to the Prairies, to the Oceans . . .": The Spread of Ethnic Diversity

1. John Gunther, *Inside U.S.A.* (New York: Harper and Brothers, 1947), p. 878.

2. U.S. Bureau of the Census, *1980 Census of Population: Supplementary Report, Race of the Population by State: 1980,* P.C. 80-S1-3 (Washington, D.C.: U.S. Government Printing Office), Table 7, pp. 13, 14.

3. Gunther, *Inside U.S.A.,* p. 493.

4. *1980 Census of Population: Supplementary Report,* ibid., Tables 1 and 5, pp. 6, 12.

5. For a discussion of the spread of diversity in the nineteenth century, see Arthur Mann, *The One and the Many: Reflections on the American Identity* (Chicago: University of Chicago Press, 1979), p. 77. The data on foreign stock in the Midwest come from the U.S. Bureau of Census, 11th census, 1890, Population I (Washington, D.C.: U.S. Government Printing Office) clv: clxii; clxiii; and U.S. Bureau of Census, *13th Census of the United States, 1920,* Population IV (Washington, D.C.: U.S. Government Printing Office, 1922), 2:33.

6. U.S. Bureau of the Census, *1980 Census of Population: Supplementary Report, Ancestry of the Population by State: 1980,* P.C. 80-S1-10, p. 69. Seventy percent of those claiming Slovenian ancestry were in the north central states, as were 60 percent of those identifying as Belgians. Of the rest, only the Croatians (56.5 percent North Central), Italians (56.4 percent Northeast), Norwegians (55 percent North Central), Serbs (54.2 percent North Central), Ukrainians (55.1 percent North Central), Portuguese (50.1 percent Northeast) and Slovaks (50.1 percent North Central) have concentrated in just one region.

7. Dillingham Commission, *Distribution of Immigrants, 1850–1900, Reports of the Immigration Commission,* 42 vols. (Washington, D.C.: U.S. Government Printing Office, 1911; reprint ed., New York: Arno Press, 1970), 3:64.

8. U.S. Immigration and Naturalization Service, *1982 Statistical Yearbook of the Immigration and Naturalization Service* (Washington, D.C.: U.S. Government Printing Office, 1984), pp. 65–77.

9. U.S. Immigration and Naturalization Service, *1985 Statistical Yearbook of the Immigration and Naturalization Service* (Washington, D.C.: U.S. Government Printing Office, 1986), p. 15.

10. Dillingham Commission, *Reports of the Immigration Commission,* 3:127.

11. U.S. Immigration and Naturalization Service, *1982 Statistical Yearbook,* p. 75. Of the 3,181 immigrants admitted to North Carolina in 1987, the largest numbers came from Korea (355), India (333), the Philippines (199), the United Kingdom (187), Canada (172), Vietnam (145), and Cambodia (111).

12. Ibid., p. 77. The Norfolk–Virginia Beach–Newport News combination in Virginia provided a good example of how one area becomes a target for a chain of migration from a particular country. The buildup of the Filipino community in those cities was so strong that by 1985, 489 Filipino immigrants indicated that they intended to reside in one of those cities, more than in New Orleans, Baltimore, or Philadelphia. See U.S. Immigration and Naturalization Service, *1985 Statistical Yearbook,* p. 61. By 1987, 682 Filipinos stated their intention to reside in the Norfolk–Virginia Beach–Newport News area.

13. *The Bridge,* publication of the Indo-China Resource Action Center, March 8, 1984,

p. 8. The numbers were as follows: Washington (32,700), Illinois (25,100), Pennsylvania (24,500), Minnesota (22,400), Massachusetts (17,500), Oregon (17,000), Louisiana (14,000), Wisconsin (10,000). Georgia, Iowa, Kansas, and Utah each had nearly 9,000, Missouri almost 7,000, Arizona more than 5,000, and Arkansas 3,000.

14. U.S. Bureau of the Census, *1980 Census of Population: Supplementary Report, Asian and Pacific Islander Population by State: 1980,* P.C. 80-S1-12, iv. In the nation there were 869,000 Chinese, 774,000 Filipinos, 701,000 Japanese, 362,000 Asian Indians, 355,000 Koreans, and 262,000 Vietnamese. See *1980 Census of Population,* I: Chapter B for data on distribution of Chinese and other ethnic groups by states. Also see Robert W. Gardner, Bryant Robey, and Peter C. Smith, *Asian-Americans: Growth, Change and Diversity* (Washington, D.C.: Population Reference Bureau, Inc., 1985) for post-1980 data quoted here.

15. *New York Times,* June 22, 1985, p. 52. Among Georgia's 347 Asian Indians in 1980, 200 to 250 were reported as working in the motel business. There was one Indian-run motel on nearly every exit of Interstate 75.

16. U.S. Immigration and Naturalization Service. *1982 Statistical Yearbook,* p. 73.

17. Ibid., p. 75. By 1987, immigration to New Mexico from Asian countries had slackened off. Mexico accounted for 1,491 of the 2,302 immigrants intending to reside in New Mexico.

18. U.S. Bureau of the Census, *1980 Census of Population: Supplementary Report, Persons of Spanish Origin by State: 1980,* P.C. 80-S1-7. Close to half of the nation's Hispanic population was in ten metropolitan areas, three of which are part of the Los Angeles urban complex. Part of the increase in the number of Hispanics identified in 1980 over 1970 can be attributed to a change in census procedures. In the 1970 census, persons were identified as Hispanic by their birthplace or parentage data, and only 5.2 million were counted. In 1980, the Spanish-origin question was subjective, asking persons whether they identified themselves as Hispanic.

19. Ibid., pp. 2, 13.

20. Ibid., p. 6.

21. Daniel M. Johnson and Rex R. Campbell, *Black Migration in America: A Social Demographic History* (Durham, N.C.: Duke University Press, 1981), p. 48.

22. Dillingham Commission, "The Children of Immigrants in Schools," *Reports of the Immigration Commission,* 29:11–15.

23. Ibid., pp. 19, 21.

24. See chart of population, data taken from the 1940 census, in Gunther, *Inside U.S.A.* Also see U.S. Bureau of the Census, *1980 Census of Population: Supplementary Report, Age, Sex, Race and Spanish Origin of the Population by Regions, Divisions and States: 1980,* P.C. 80-S1-10, p. 6.

25. Ibid., pp. 8, 71.

26. U.S. Bureau of the Census, *1980 Census of Population: Supplementary Report, American Indian Areas and Alaska Native Villages: 1980,* P.C. 80-S1-10, pp. v, 2.

27. Solomon Arbeiter, *Profiles: College-Bound Seniors, 1984* (New York: College Entrance Examination Board, 1984), pp. 1, 2.

28. The proportion of foreign-born in Detroit went from 7.9 to 5.7 percent between 1970 and 1980, but even in Detroit older ethnic groups remained, such as the Polish section of Chasdey in south Detroit. The early decline of the older ethnic neighborhoods in Detroit was analyzed by Olivier Zunz in *The Changing Face of Inequality: Urbanization, Industrialization and Immigrants in Detroit, 1880–1920* (Chicago: University of Chicago Press, 1982); however, Detroit remained a city with highly visible older ethnic groups into the 1970s. See Otto Feinstein, ed., *Ethnic Groups in the City* (Lexington, Mass.: D. C. Heath, Lexington Books, 1971).

Ethnic Groups in the City (Lexington, Mass.: D. C. Heath, Lexington Books, 1971).

29. William Julius Wilson, *The Declining Significance of Race: Blacks and Changing American Institutions* (Chicago: University of Chicago Press, 1978), p. 139.

30. Joseph Logsdon, "Immigration Through the Port of New Orleans," in M. Mark Stolarik, ed., *Forgotten Doors: The Other Ports of Entry to the United States* (Philadelphia: The Balch Institute Press, 1988).

31. Dudley Clenenden, "White Grip on Southern Schools: Keeping Control," *New York Times,* June 23, 1986, p. A10.

32. In 1930, nearly 43 percent of Los Angeles County's population was of foreign stock. By contrast, 75 percent of New York's population in 1930 consisted of foreigners and their children. See Elliott R. Barkan, "Immigration Through the Port of Los Angeles," in Stolarik, ed., *Forgotten Doors.*

33. "The New Ellis Island," *Time,* June 13, 1983. By 1983, the term "Anglo" essentially meant "Caucasian."

34. Little Haiti, a Miami neighborhood of about forty thousand, became nationally known in the early 1980s, partly because of the federal government's unwillingness to grant asylum en bloc to Haitians claiming it, and also because of the notoriety given to the disease AIDS, which was found to exist disproportionately among Haitians. The complexity of the situation of blacks in Miami is illustrated by the situation of Cuban blacks. See Heriberto Dixon, "The Cuban-American Counterpoint: Black Cubans in the United States," paper presented to the International Symposium on the Cultural Expression of Hispanics in the United States, sponsored by the Association for the Diffusion and Study of Latin Cultures in North America, March 12, 1986, Paris.

35. Frank Viviano and Sharon Silva, "The New San Francisco," a special report, *San Francisco Focus,* September 1986, pp. 64–75.

36. "The Border: Where Two Worlds Meet," *The Economist,* August 20, 1983, p. 29. In 1985, more than 300,000 people crossed the Mexican border legally, including lawfully admitted aliens, temporary visitors such as students and tourists, commuters from Mexico, and Americans or others coming into the U.S. from Mexico. American cities with the largest number of crossings in order of frequency were: San Diego; El Paso; Laredo, Texas; Calexico, California; Brownsville, Texas; McCallen, Texas; Nogales, Arizona; San Luis, Arizona; Eagle Pass, Texas; and Douglas, Arizona. Every one of these cities was adjacent to a sister city across the border that was larger, except for San Diego, which is larger than Tijuana.

37. Peter Applebome, "Along U.S. Border, a Third World is Reborn," *New York Times,* March 27, 1988, pp. 1, 28.

38. "The Border: Where Two Worlds Meet," *The Economist.* For a thorough analysis of the border from an economic perspective, see Niles Hansen, *The Border Economy: Regional Development in the Southwest* (Austin: University of Texas Press, 1981).

39. *U.S.A. Today,* July 11, 1983, p. 8A.

40. *Milwaukee Journal,* "Accent," August 12, 1981, p. 1. In 1986, one school in Milwaukee had students coming from homes where twenty-seven languages other than English were spoken. Conversation with superintendent of Milwaukee schools Lee R. McMurrin, July 1986.

41. For the story on "Scandinavia Today," see the *New York Times,* September 12, 1982. For information on ethnic diversity in Minneapolis, see *The Humanities and the Immigration Issue: A Report to the Mayors in Four Pilot Cities,* U.S. Conference of Mayors, Washington, D.C., 1983, pp. 17–23. Minneapolis/St. Paul has

groups of Cubans, Haitians, Ethiopians, Poles, Mexicans, Cambodians, Vietnamese, Soviet Jews, Indians, Pakistanis, Koreans, Chinese, and lowland Laotians in addition to the H'mong. German-Americans also became much more visible in 1983, when they celebrated their tricentennial in the U.S. There were more than five hundred events in forty-three states. See Ben Bradlee, Jr., "German-American Tricentennial: After Years of Low Profile, America's Largest Ethnic Group Asserting Pride," *Boston Globe,* October 30, 1983, p. A2.

42. See Peter D'A. Jones and Melvin G. Halli, eds., *Ethnic Chicago* (Chicago: University of Chicago Press, 1981) for essays on seven groups, including Japanese-Americans. More than a half dozen other sizable groups in Chicago—blacks, Poles, Norwegians, Swedes, Czechs, Austrians, Mexicans, Hungarians, and Puerto Ricans—were not even included.

43. Wilson, *Declining Significance of Race,* p. 117.

44. The persistence of ethnic neighborhoods in Cleveland is described in an unpublished manuscript by Karl Bonutti and George Prpic, "Social-Economic Studies of Selected Ethnic Neighborhoods," Cleveland Urban Observatory for the Office of Assistant Secretary for Policy Development and Research, Department of Housing and Urban Development, 1974.

45. *Boston Globe,* December 29, 1985, p. 25.

46. See J. Anthony Lucas, *On Common Ground* (Boston: Little Brown, 1985) for a sensitive account of ethnic conflict and accommodation over school integration in Boston. See *New York Times,* December 1, 1985, p. 52 for an account of racial polarization in Philadelphia.

47. The other six cities with low percentages of Hispanic and Asian populations were Baltimore, Memphis, Nashville, St. Louis, Atlanta, and Pittsburgh. *Humanities and the Immigration Issue,* pp. 33–39.

16. Tacos and Kimchee: The Quickening Pace of Ethnic Interaction

1. For a description of the rich and persistent ethnic life of rural Wisconsin, see Henry Lenzen Schmitz, "Some Do Not Melt in the Pot," manuscript, circa 1975.

2. Allen F. Davis and Mark H. Haller, eds., *Peoples of Philadelphia: A History of Ethnic Groups and Lower Class Life, 1790–1940* (Philadelphia: Temple University Press, 1973), p. 13.

3. Francis Hueston, "The Catholic Press and Nativism, 1840–1860," Ph.D. diss., University of Notre Dame, June 1972, pp. 46, 318.

4. Caroline Golub, *Immigrant Destinations* (Philadelphia: Temple University Press, 1977), p. 122.

5. Roy Rosenzweig, *Eight Hours for What We Will: Workers and Leisure in an Industrial City, 1870–1920* (New York: Cambridge University Press, 1983), p. 30.

6. Dean R. Esslinger, "Immigration Through the Port of Baltimore," in M. Mark Stolarik, ed., *Forgotten Doors: The Other Ports of Entry to the United States* (Philadelphia: The Balch Institute Press, 1988), pp. 61–64.

7. Frances A. Kellor is quoted in Henry Pratt Fairchild, *The Melting Pot Mistake* (Boston: Little Brown & Company, 1926), p. 161.

8. Joseph Logsdon, "Immigration Through the Port of New Orleans," in Stolarik, ed., *Forgotten Doors,* pp. 51–53. The relative ease with which people in New Orleans crossed ethnic boundaries even extended to dock workers in that city at the turn of the century, when the term "half and half " was given to the cooperative relationship that developed between black and white longshoremen. See Daniel Rosenberg, *New Orleans Dock Workers: Race, Labor and Unionism, 1892–1923* (Albany: State University of New York, 1988).

9. Charles Wollenberg, "Immigration Through the Port of San Francisco," in Stolarik, ed., *Forgotten Doors,* pp. 143–155.

10. Tamara K. Haraven, "Family and Work Patterns of Immigrant Laborers in a Planned Industrial Town, 1900–1930," in Richard L. Ehrlich, ed., *Immigrants in Industrial America, 1850–1920* (Charlottesville: University of Virginia Press, 1987), pp. 59, 60.

11. W. Lloyd Warner and Leo Srole, *The Social Systems of American Ethnic Groups,* Yankee City Series, vol. 3 (New Haven: Yale University Press, 1945).

12. Robert S. Lynd and Helen Merrell Lynd, *Middletown: A Study in Modern American Culture* (New York: Harcourt, Brace and World, 1929), p. 479.

13. John Higham, *Send These to Me* (New York: Atheneum, 1974), chapter 10.

14. *Devastation/Resurrection: The South Bronx* (New York: The Bronx Museum of Arts, 1979), pp. 31–35.

15. Lloyd Ultan, in collaboration with the Bronx County Historical Society, *The Beautiful Bronx (1920–1950)* (New York: Arlington House, 1979), p. 13.

16. John L. Hess, "Shifting Patterns of Immigration Add New Flavor to the City's Melting Pot," *New York Times,* September 25, 1972, p. 39.

17. Fred Feretti, "Queens at 300, Still Growing and Full of Surprises: A Guide to What's Best of the Old and New," *New York Times,* October 28, 1983, p. C22.

18. Jane Ross, "In Richmond Hill, Latins Are the Latest Immigrants to Join the Melting Pot," *New York Times,* May 17, 1985, p. 24.

19. Richard Higgins, "The Mirror of a Neighborhood," *Boston Globe,* October 7, 1987, pp. 21, 22.

20. John Maxwell Hamilton, "Ethnic Eateries: The Melting Pot's A-Boiling," *Christian Science Monitor,* April 14, 1986, p. 19.

21. "The New Ellis Island," *Time,* June 13, 1983, p. 24.

22. *San Francisco Examiner,* June 28, 1987, p. A2.

23. Thomas B. Morgan, "The Latinization of America," *Esquire,* May 1983, p. 54.

24. H. Richard Niebuhr, *The Social Sources of Denominationalism* (New York: Henry Holt & Company, 1929). Citation from Merriam Books Edition (New York, 1957), pp. 222, 223.

25. Lowell Seitel, "Christ Church in Waltham," manuscript, 1986.

26. Ukiko Kamura, "Social-Historical Background of the Okinawans in Hawaii," in *Uchinanchu: A History of Okinawans in Hawaii* (Honolulu: University of Hawaii, 1968), p. 62.

27. *Newsweek,* June 16, 1986, p. 59.

28. Anthony M. Stevens-Arroyo, "Cahensly Revisited?: The National Pastoral Encounter of America's Hispanic Catholics," *Migration World,* 15, no. 3: 16–19.

29. L. H. Gann and Peter J. Duignan, "Latinos and the Catholic Church in America," *Nuestro,* May 1987, pp. 10–13.

30. U.S. Commission on Civil Rights, *Twenty Years After Brown: The Report of the United States Commission on Civil Rights* (Washington, D.C.: U.S. Government Printing Office, June 1974), p. 50. In the 1970s, the percentage of white students in predominantly black schools, especially in the South, went up sharply in several major cities, leading to extensive contact between black and white youngsters on sports teams, marching bands, school government councils, and in other activities.

31. Ibid., p. 51.

32. Ibid., pp. 49, 50.

33. William Julius Wilson, *The Declining Significance of Race: Blacks and Changing American Institutions* (Chicago: University of Chicago Press, 1978), p. 114.

34. U.S. Department of Education, news release, *U.S. News and World Report,* August 10, 1987, p. 47.

35. Gary Orfield, *Public Desegregation in the United States, 1968–1980* (Washington, D.C.: Joint Center for Political Studies, 1983), p. 35.

36. Joe Starita, "America's Gateway is Beckoning Still: New York Immigrants are Home," *Miami Herald,* June 22, 1986, p. 1-A. The school's valedictorian in 1986 was a Guyanese and its honor society president a Haitian.

37. Dillingham Commission, "The Children of Immigrants in Schools," *Reports of the Immigration Commission,* 42 vols. (Washington, D.C.: U.S. Government Printing Office, 1911; reprint ed., New York: Arno Press, 1970), 39:19.

38. Mrs. Carmen Alicia, acting director, Bilingual/Multicultural Education Office, to Lawrence H. Fuchs, August 12, 1983, author's files.

39. *Heritage: The Newsletter of the Illinois Ethnic Consultation,* Winter 1987, p. 2.

40. *Philadelphia Daily News,* May 19, 1986, pp. S1–S10.

41. "Immigrants," *Time,* July 8, 1985, p. 29.

42. "The New Ellis Island," *Time,* June 13, 1983, p. 24.

43. *Los Angeles Times,* June 20, 1981, p. 1.

44. *Mosaic: Knowing the Light Will Come, Stories and Photographs by Students at South Boston High,* edited by Katie Singer, photography editor Judith Sedwick, June 1987.

45. Frances FitzGerald, *America Revised: History Schoolbooks in the Twentieth Century* (New York: Vintage Books, 1979), p. 79.

46. U.S. Commission on Civil Rights, *Characters in Textbooks: A Review of the Literature* (Washington, D.C.: Clearinghouse Publication 62, May 1980), p. 1.

47. Nathan Glazer and Reed Ueda, *Ethnic Groups in History Textbooks* (Washington, D.C.: Ethics and Public Policy Center, 1976), p. 57.

48. Ibid., p. 60.

49. Discussion of the suburbanization of immigration can be found in John Herbers, "Suburbs Absorb More Immigrants, Mostly the Affluent and Educated," *New York Times,* December 14, 1986, p. 4, and Mark Gibney, "Lady Liberty and Her Huddled Masses," *Christian Science Monitor,* September 30, 1986, p. 6. For a discussion of movement by refugees and immigrants to working-class suburbs, see John Herbers, "America's Newest Immigrants Choosing Suburbs over Cities," *New York Times,* March 1, 1983, p. A1. The percentage of foreign-born in Cleveland, Detroit, and Baltimore actually declined slightly in the 1970s and early 1980s, while their suburbs contained more foreigners in both numbers and percentages. There were more than twice as many people of foreign birth in Cleveland's suburbs as in the city itself by 1980, although in most areas, especially in the coastal cities, the percentage of foreign-born of the total population was greater in the central cities than in the suburbs. The Census Bureau reported a shift of blacks who lived in urbanized areas between 1970 and 1980 from the central city to the suburbs. Of such blacks, 28.2 percent lived in suburbs of urban areas in 1980, compared to 17.1 percent in 1970. See William P. O'Hare, "The Urban Commuter," *Focus,* The Joint Center for Political Studies, January 1985, p. 6.

50. Weston, Massachusetts, graduating class program, 1984. It is often from suburban schools that ethnically diverse and talented students compete in national spelling bees and science contests. The last 135 contestants in the 1986 National Spelling Bee sponsored by the Scripps Howard publishers, representing new and old ethnic groups in the U.S., came mainly from small cities and towns and from suburbs. *U.S.A. Today,* May 30, 1986, p. 6-A. The last twenty-five contestants included Scott Zimmerman from Pottsville, Pennsylvania; Derek Bruneau from

Trenton, Georgia; Christine Gonzalez from Del Rio, Texas; Kate Mikulka from Montville, New Jersey; Priya Rangaswamy from Port Jefferson Station, New York; and Babu Brahma from Clovis, California. The following dropped out in the previous round: Kim Dorazio from Audubon, Pennsylvania; Victoria Chiou from Middletown, New York; Sherine Varghese from Cleveland, Tennessee; Rageshree Ramchandran from Carmichael, California; Amit Caplish from Pond City, Florida; Natasha Filipski from Bakersfield, California; and Dona Wu from Flagstaff, Arizona.

51. Andrew Hacker, "Affirmative Action: The New Look," *The New York Review,* October 12, 1989, p. 64. At the prestige women's Wellesley College in Massachusetts, Asians made up 15 percent of entering students by 1986 (information from admissions office). Among the almost one hundred young women of Asian background entering Wellesley were eight with the name Kim and nine with Lee, indicating a high proportion of Koreans and Chinese. Their home towns showed how widely distributed were Asian-Americans: Newport Beach, California; Springfield, Massachusetts; Maryville, Tennessee; Whitestone, New York; Dryden, New York; Coshocton, Ohio; Cherry Hill, New Jersey; Irving, Texas; Highland Heights, Ohio; Tenafly, New Jersey; Saddle River, New Jersey; Flushing, New York; Cresskill, New Jersey; Baltimore, Maryland; Bridgewater, New Jersey; Northport, New York; and Pasadena, California.

52. Douglas S. Massey and Kathleen Schnabel, "Recent Trends in Hispanic Immigration to the United States," *International Migration Review* 17 (Summer 1983): 32.

53. Gaynelle Evans, "Black Students Who Attend White Colleges Face Contradictions in Their Campus Life," *The Chronicle of Higher Education,* April 30, 1986, p. 29.

54. Jean Evangelauf, "Minorities' Share of College Enrollments Edges Up, as Number of Asian and Hispanic Students Soars," *The Chronicle of Higher Education,* March 9, 1988, p. A33. The ten-year gains in college enrollment reported in 1986 for American citizens and resident aliens were: 9.2 percent for whites; 4.6 percent for blacks; 62.5 percent for Hispanic-Americans; 126.3 percent for Asian-Americans; and 18.4 percent for American Indians. The total enrollment for foreign nationals in American colleges went up 57.1 percent in the ten-year period.

55. Solomon Arbeiter, *Profiles: College-Bound Seniors, 1984* (New York: College Entrance Examination Board, 1984), pp. 3, 5. The 1974 *Webster's New Collegiate Dictionary* presented with its definition of "mortarboard" a picture of a black graduate wearing one.

56. Evans, "Black Students Who Attend White Colleges," p. 29. Also see Jacqueline Flemming, *Blacks in College: A Comparative Study of Students' Success in Black and in White Institutions* (New York: Jossey-Bass, 1989). There was enormous evidence of psychological estrangement as well as social isolation at overwhelmingly white institutions. The dropout rate at such colleges and universities was much higher for blacks than for Asians, Hispanics, or whites. Blacks commonly reported feelings of alienation.

57. *Chronicle of Higher Education,* December 5, 1984, pp. 13–24. One example of how the civil rights revolution created new arenas of interaction is that the seventeen traditionally black land-grant colleges and universities, established because the Morrill Act of 1890 required that any state that did not admit black students to its land-grant colleges must designate a second institution to carry out the land-grant mission for black citizens, now served whites as well as blacks. See Scott Jaschik, "For the Nation's Seventeen Black Land-Grant Colleges, Unique Difficulties and New Strategies," *Chronicle of Higher Education,* October 28, 1987, p. A31.

58. Charles C. Moskos, "Success Story: Blacks in the Army," *The Atlantic Monthly,* May 1986, p. 66, for information on 1968; *The Chronicle of Higher Education,* December 5, 1984, pp. 13–24, for information on 1982. In 1982, the U.S. Air Force Academy was 7.9 percent black, 4.7 percent Hispanic, 3.2 percent Asian, and 0.7 percent American Indian; the U.S. Naval Academy was 4.7 percent black, 4.4 percent Hispanic, 4.7 percent Asian, and 0.5 percent American Indian.

59. James Feron, "At West Point, Symbol of Change for the Army," *New York Times,* October 28, 1987, pp. B1, B2.

60. U.S. Department of Defense, Office of the Deputy Assistant Secretary of Defense for Equal Opportunity and Safety Policy, *Black Americans in Defense of Our Nation* (Washington, D.C.: U.S. Government Printing Office, 1983), p. 436. Black women were particularly overrepresented. By 1984, 42 percent of women in the Army were black, 24.6 percent of women Marines, 21.3 percent of women in the Air Force, and 18.9 percent of women in the Navy (*Black Enterprise,* April 1986, p. 43).

61. Moskos, "Success Story: Blacks in the Army," pp. 65–67.

62. Massey and Schnabel, "Recent Trends in Hispanic Immigration," p. 36.

63. Herbert Hammerman, "A Decade of New Opportunity: Affirmative Action in the 1970s," data from the Potomac Institute, Washington, D.C., as reported in the *Boston Globe,* March 25, 1985, p. 3.

64. Gibney, "Lady Liberty and Her Huddled Masses," p. 16.

65. Milton Cantor, "Ethnicity and the World of Work," in M. Mark Stolarik and Murray Friedman, eds., *Making It in America: The Role of Ethnicity in Business Enterprise, Education and Work Choices* (Lewisburg, Pa.: Bucknell University Press, 1986), p. 101.

66. Lawrence Glasco, "Ethnicity and Occupation in the Mid-Nineteenth Century: Irish, Germans and Native Born Whites in Buffalo, New York," in Erhlich, *Immigrants in Industrial America,* p. 155.

67. James W. Lowen, *The Mississippi Chinese: Between Black and White* (Cambridge: Harvard University Press, 1971).

68. *Christian Science Monitor,* September 14, 1982, p. 1.

69. *Local 23–25 News,* International Ladies' Garment Workers Union, 35, no. 4 (October 1986): 4.

70. *Heritage: The Newsletter of the Illinois Ethnic Consultation,* Winter 1987, p. 4.

71. Geoffrey Godsell, "One Nation Indivisible: The Last, Best Hope on Earth," *Christian Science Monitor,* January 9, 1981, p. 12.

72. Information from staff visit, Select Commission on Immigration and Refugee Policy, November 30, 1979.

73. *A.D.L. Bulletin,* published by the Anti-Defamation League of B'nai B'rith, June 1987, p. 9.

74. *Chicago Tribune Magazine,* March 16, 1986, Section 10, p. 13.

75. Ibid., p. 24.

76. George Archibald, "CORE Aids 6500 in Alien Amnesty," *Washington Times,* August 26, 1987, p. 12.

77. "TV's Disappearing Color Line," *U.S. News and World Report,* July 13, 1987, p. 56.

78. *Burrelle's Special Groups Media Directory: Special Edition* (Livingston, N.J.: Burrelle Publishers, 1980).

79. "Cultural Crossover": Breaking Barriers with New Sounds and Images," *Vista,* April 5, 1986, p. 8.

80. *U.S. News and World Report,* August 10, 1987, p. 48. In 1988, another popular movie about Mexican-Americans was released, *The Milagro Beanfield War,* about Mexican-Americans in northern New Mexico trying to reclaim their water rights

from an Anglo developer. Director Robert Redford said he took special pains to "get their culture right." (Jay Carr, "Robert Redford," *Boston Globe,* March 27, 1988, p. 86).

81. *New York Times,* May 18, 1986, p. 36.
82. *Black Enterprise,* December 1984, pp. 61–62.
83. *New York Times Magazine,* March 11, 1984, pp. 72–77. The example of multiethnic representation in comic strips appeared in the 1986 "Fun Facts," in which three children appear, Nikki (blond and blue-eyed), Todd (a black boy with curly hair), and Randy (a Chinese youngster from Cambodia), written by Gary Luciano and distributed by the *Boston Globe.*
84. Jordan Marsh fall sale, "Kids' Sale," August 20–September 5, p. 10.
85. Gail F. Stern, "Packaging: Container as Context," *Ethnic Images in Advertising,* with an introduction by Gail P. Stern (Philadelphia: The Balch Institute for Ethnic Studies and the Anti-Defamation League of B'nai B'rith, 1984), p. 21.
86. Carol Nathanson-Moog, "The Psychological Power of Ethnic Images in Advertising," *Ethnic Images in Advertising,* p. 21.

17. *The Kashaya and the Nyingma: Identities and Boundaries*

1. *New York Times,* December 15, 1985, p. 30.
2. The data on intermarriage come from Richard D. Alba, "Interethnic Marriage in the 1980 census," paper presented at meetings of the American Sociological Association, 1985, pp. 6–13.
3. Earl J. Ogletree and Vilma E. Ujlaki, "American-Hispanics in a Pluralistic Society," *Migration Today,* 13, no. 3 (1985): 32. Also see Irma D. Herrera, "Mixed Marriages: Will the Happiness Last?" *Vista,* June 7, 1986, pp. 8–10. The author writes of intermarriage resulting in many non-Hispanic spouses embracing Hispanic customs, p. 8.
4. U.S. Bureau of the Census, "National Data Book and Guide to Sources," in *Statistical Abstract of the United States* (Washington, D.C.: U.S. Government Printing Office, 1984), p. 45.
5. Alba, "Interethnic Marriage," p. 6.
6. Darrel Montero, *Japanese-Americans: Changing Patterns of Ethnic Affiliation Over Three Generations* (Boulder, Colo.: Westview Press, 1980), p. 37.
7. Edna Bonacich and John Modell, *The Economic Basis of Ethnic Solidarity: Small Business in the Japanese-American Community* (Berkeley: University of California Press, 1980), chapter 10, "Work History."
8. Ibid., p. 246.
9. These data come from Jeanette Takamura, "Trouble and the Use of Informal Support Systems: A Case of the Japanese-Americans in Hawaii," Ph.D. diss., Brandeis University, 1984. Hawaii is the best example of all states of the paradox of the increased permeability of ethnic boundaries amid the recent ethnic revival. In no other state are Americans such as the Japanese so ethnic-minded, but there probably is no other state with so much intermarriage. See Lawrence H. Fuchs, *Hawaii Pono: A Social History* (New York: Harcourt Brace Jovanovich, 1961).
10. Steven M. Cohen, *The 1984 National Survey of American Jews,* conducted for the American Jewish Committee (New York: American Jewish Committee, October 1984). The sample size in this study was 959, much larger than the subsample of Jews usually taken in national surveys.
11. Takamura, "Trouble and the Use of Informal Support Systems."
12. Bonacich and Modell, *Economic Basis of Ethnic Solidarity,* p. 246.

13. Geoffrey Wigoder, "Assessing the Future of American Jewry," *The Jerusalem Post International Edition,* May 27–June 3, 1984, p. 13.
14. CNN-TV, November 23, 1984.
15. *New York Times,* June 17, 1985, p. B8.
16. *Boston Globe,* December 24, 1984, p. 16.
17. Thomas Kessner and Betty Boyd Caroli, *Today's Immigrants, Their Stories: A New Look at the Newest Americans* (New York: Oxford University Press, 1981), p. 292.
18. Ibid., pp. 296, 297.
19. Ibid., p. 292.
20. *Boston Globe,* May 9, 1984, p. 24.
21. John J. Bukowczyk, *And My Children Did Not Know Me: A History of the Polish-Americans* (Bloomington: Indiana University Press, 1987), p. 120.
22. David Steven Cohen, *The Ramapo Mountain People* (New Brunswick, N.J.: Rutgers University Press, 1974).
23. Henry Toyama and Kiyoshi Ikeda, "The Okinawan-Naichi Relationship," in *Uchinanchu: A History of Okinawans in Hawaii* compiled by Ethnic Studies Oral History Project (Honolulu: Ethnic Studies Program, University of Hawaii, 1968). In the mid-twentieth century, Okinawans constituted 10 to 15 percent of the total Japanese population in the islands.
24. Nancy Foner, "Jamaican Journey: Race and Ethnicity Among Jamaican Migrants in New York City," paper prepared for conference on "Immigration and the Changing Black Population in the U.S.A.," University of Michigan, Center for Afro-American and African Studies, May 18–21, 1983.
25. Gloria Marshall, "Racial Classifications; Popular and Scientific," in Margaret Mead at al., eds., *Science and the Concepts of Race* (New York: Columbia University Press, 1968), pp. 152–153.
26. Heriberto Dixon, "Some Thoughts on the Social Evolution of Black Cubans in the United States," unpublished paper (July 1985), pp. 6, 7.
27. Niara Sudarkasa, "Race, Ethnicity and Identity: Some Conceptual Issues in Defining the Black Population in the United States," paper delivered to a conference on "Immigration and the Changing Black Population," Ann Arbor, Michigan, May 18–21, 1983. The special pride that each nationality group felt in its own background was a deterrent to a reconfiguration of identity based entirely on color. One teacher in the early 1980s said that at Barnard College the Haitian Club—French-speaking—would have nothing to do with the Pan-African Club, made up of black Americans; the Spanish clubs also were separate; and the Caribbean Club, which was English-speaking and black, would not even meet with the Pan-Africans to hold a party. See Kessner and Caroli, *Today's Immigrants,* p. 188. Jamaicans in New York "are eager to let whites know their nationality," which is "a source of pride and a sense of self-worth" that gives them a "feeling of superiority" to black Americans (Nancy Foner, "Race and Color: Jamaican Migrants in London and New York City," *International Migration Review,* 69, no. 4 [1985]: 724). One West Indian in Boston asked, "Why do we want to assimilate into a group that's been oppressed?" (Barry Werth, "A Different Shade of Black," *New England Monthly,* January 1987, p. 32).
28. André Nguyen Van Chau, "From Conflict to Inter-Ethnic Cooperation: Issues Confronting Asian-Americans," *The Bridge,* Summer 1987, p. 5. The news media often failed to distinguish among Asian groups. For a headline that deals only with Southeast Asians, see "Relocation Drive Upsets Many Asian Refugees," *New York Times,* April 22, 1987. An article in the *Washington Post* was headlined "Asian-Americans Outperform Others in School and Work," even though the differences in college attendance between Chinese-Americans and Filipino-Americans were

vast (*Washington Post,* October 10, 1985, p. 1). There are exceptions. A headline in the *Christian Science Monitor* featured diversity: "Asian-Americans: Soaring Minority, Diversity is the Most Striking Feature of This Prospering Group" (*Christian Science Monitor,* October 10, 1985, p. 3).

29. *Burrelle's Special Groups Media Directory,* Special Edition (Livingston, N.J.: Burrelle Publishers, 1980), pp. 1–85.

30. Circulation, audit, and distribution data statement, *Vista,* January 12, 1987.

31. Rodolfo O. de la Garza and Robert R. Brischetto, *The Mexican-American Electorate: The Demographic Profile,* Mexican-American Electorate Series, Occasional Paper No. 1, a joint publication of the Southwest Voter Registration Education Project, San Antonio, and the Hispanic Populations Studies Program of the Center for Mexican-American Studies, University of Texas, Austin (Austin and San Antonio: 1982), p. 15.

32. Cecelio J. Morales, Jr., "Only in America Can You Be Hispanic: How the D.C. Immigration Boys Keep Reinforcing Your Identity," *Washington Post,* August 2, 1981, p. C1, C5. Richard Rodriguez wrote that the term "Hispanic . . . signals a movement out of the *barrio.*" He thought it was a useful adjective for "emerging middle class . . . business executives and lawyers and doctors and writers like me." See Richard Rodriguez, "Hispanics, in Changing, Change America," *Los Angeles Times,* May 20, 1986, part 2, p. 5.

33. Catherine Cobb Morocco, *National Field Test Evaluation Report: The American Experiment: E Pluribus Unum* (Newton, Mass.: Education Development Center, 1982). The data were compiled from student answers to questions about ethnic identity and from student essays.

34. Richard D. Alba, "Ethnic Identity Among American Whites," paper presented at a meeting of the American Sociological Association in Chicago, 1987, p. 26.

35. Morocco, *National Field Test Evaluation Report.*

36. Martin Luther King, Jr., *Where Do We Go from Here: Chaos or Community?* (New York: Bantam Books, 1968), pp. 61–62.

37. "Ethnic Groups in American Life," *Daedalus,* Spring 1981; "Color and Race," *Daedalus,* Spring 1967; "American Indians, Blacks, Chicanos and Puerto Ricans," *Daedalus,* Spring 1981.

38. Alex Haley, *Roots* (New York: Doubleday and Co., Inc., 1976).

39. See for well-known examples: Michael J. Arlen, *Journey to Ararat* (New York: Farrar, Straus and Giroux, Inc., 1975); Richard Gambino, *Blood of My Blood: The Dilemma of the Italian Americans* (New York: Doubleday and Company, Inc., 1974); Irving Howe, *The World of Our Fathers* (New York: Harcourt Brace Jovanovich, 1976).

40. The search for roots also encouraged a new interest in genealogy and publication of many books. See Charles L. Blockson and Ron Fry, *Black Genealogy: How to Discover Your Own Family's Roots* (New Jersey: Prentice-Hall, Inc., 1977); Jeane Eddy Westin, *Finding Your Roots: How Every American Can Trace His Ancestors, at Home and Abroad* (New York: St. Martin's Press, Inc., 1977); and Dan Rottenberg, *Finding Our Fathers: A Guidebook to Jewish Genealogy* (New York: Random House, Inc., 1977).

41. Morocco, *National Field Test Evaluation Report.*

42. Nathan Glazer and Daniel P. Moynihan, eds., *Ethnicity* (Cambridge: Harvard University Press, 1975). Glazer and Moynihan stress the "strategic efficacy of ethnicity as a basis for asserting claims against government" (p. 10). Also see Susan Olzak, "Contemporary Ethnic Mobilization," *The Annual Review of Sociology* 9 (1983): 355–374.

43. Ira S. Lowry, "The Science and Politics of Ethnic Enumeration," unpublished paper, January 1980, p. 2.

44. Ibid., p. 15.

45. Ibid., p. 8.

46. Ibid., p. 9.

47. Ibid., p. 20.

48. Examples of ethnic borrowing and blending proliferated in the 1980s. In New York City in the 1980s, three Catholic schools marched in the annual Queens *Purim* (Jewish holiday) parade. In 1986, one Jewish parochial school decided to have a marching band of its own, and the school's headmaster commented that "bands are as American as apple pie and we want our kids to feel comfortable with their Americanism and Jewishness." *New York Times*, March 21, 1986, p. B1. Another example of how boundaries are crossed took place when Muslims (of whom there were more than two million in the U.S. in the 1980s) unable to purchase *halal* meat (killed according to proper Islamic practice) were given permission from religious leaders to buy kosher meat from Jewish delicatessens or butcher shops. See Yvonne Yazbeck Haddad and Adair T. Lummis, *Islamic Values in the United States* (New York: Oxford University Press, 1987), p. 116. Another example of boundary-crossing took place when Chinese businessmen in Flushing, Queens, paid for the community's traditional Christmas holiday lights on condition that they would remain up to welcome the dawn of the Chinese lunar New Year (*New York Times*, February 20, 1988, p. 30). Not all contacts led to cross-borrowing. For example, although physicians in St. Paul did not object when H'mong patients suffering from middle ear infections drank the H'mong shamans' herbal concoctions and the shamans agreed to let the patients take antibiotics, the drawing of blood and surgery often were resisted by the shamans. (Alan M. Kraut, "The Care of Brothers: Treating the Sick in the Immigrant Community," *American Inquiry*, 1989, p. 44.)

18. "The Wish of the Founding Fathers":
Third World Immigrants Embrace the Civic Culture

1. Testimony of Ciro Castillo before the Select Task Force on Immigration of the International Coordination Committee before the Select Commission on Immigration and Refugee Policy, Miami, December 4, 1979.

2. Testimony of unidentified Chinese illegal worker before the Select Commission on Immigration and Refugee Policy, New York City, January 21, 1980.

3. Select Commission on Immigration and Refugee Policy, *Immigration Policy and the National Interest. Staff Report, Supplement to the Final Report and Recommendations of the Select Commission on Immigration and Refugee Policy* (Washington, D.C.: U.S. Government Printing Office, April 30, 1981), p. 221. By 1985, not a single European country was among the top ten senders of immigrants to the U.S. (the top ten were, in order: Mexico, the Philippines, Korea, Vietnam, India, China, the Dominican Republic, Cuba, Jamaica, and Iran).

4. Select Commission on Immigration and Refugee Policy, *Immigration Policy and the National Interest*, p. 222.

5. For a survey of studies on adaptation, see T. A. Goodis, *Adaptation Processes of Recent Immigrants to the United States: A Review of Demographic and Social Aspects* (Washington, D.C.: The Urban Institute, 1986).

6. Social Research Services, American Council of Life Insurance, *New Immigrants/ New Minorities: Their Impact on Societal Sectors*, Trend Analysis Program, p. 19;

also see Spencer Rich, "Asian-Americans Outperform Others in School and Work," *New York Times,* October 10, 1985, p. A1.

7. Ibid., p. 5.

8. Ibid.

9. Raymond Brady Williams, "The Role of Asian Indian Religious Organizations in the Formation and Preservation of Ethnic Identity," unpublished paper, 1983, p. 6. The Swaminarayan religion is a Gujarati form of Hinduism. The Gujarati, a distinctive ethnic-Hindu group in India, had three temples in the U.S. and centers in eighteen other cities. Also see Yvonne Yazbeck Haddad and Adair T. Lummis, *Islamic Values in the United States* (New York: Oxford University Press, 1987). By 1986, there were 598 mosques/Islamic centers operating in every region of the U.S., including Alabama, Mississippi, Oklahoma, New Mexico, Washington, and West Virginia.

By establishing a social life around churches, new groups were following the pattern of Germans, Swedes, and Norwegians with Lutheran churches, the Russians and the Greeks with Orthodox churches, and Catholics in establishing parishes based on Italian, French Canadian, Irish, Polish, and other nationality backgrounds. Organized archdioceses exist for the Albanians, Bulgarians, Byelorussians, Carpatho-Rusians, Macedonians, Rumanians, Serbians, and Ukrainians. There are also parishes for small groups of Estonians and Finns. See Thomas E. Bird, "Eastern Orthodox," in Stephan Thernstrom, ed., *Harvard Encyclopedia of American Ethnic Groups* (Cambridge: Harvard University Press, 1980), pp. 302–303.

There are many other groups in which ethnicity and religion are closely connected in addition to the Eastern Orthodox, ethnic Catholics, and Jews. They include: Armenian Orthodox; Chinese Buddhists; Indian Hindus; Pakistani Muslims; Scottish Presbyterians; Mormons; Hutterites; and Amish. See Harold J. Abramson, *Ethnic Diversity in Catholic America* (New York: John Wiley, 1973). For essays on the interrelationships of ethnicity and religion (including Jews), see Randall M. Miller and Thomas D. Marzik, eds., *Immigrants and Religion in Urban America* (Notre Dame, Ind.: Notre Dame University Press, 1981).

10. *The Indo-Chinese Mutual Assistance Associations: Characteristics, Composition, Capacity-Building, Needs, and Future Directions,* Indo-Chinese Resource Action Center, March 1981.

Of the various texts on the history of immigrant-ethnic acculturation, the one that is probably richest in its descriptions of the associational life of ethnic groups is Maxine Sellers, *To Seek America: The History of Ethnic Life in the United States* (New York: Ozer, 1977). A more recent history of immigrants also emphasizes the strengths of immigrants in shaping their own lives as ethnic-Americans. See John Bodnar, *The Transplanted: A History of Immigrants in Urban America* (Bloomington: Indiana University Press, 1985).

The first major analytical study dealing with the associational and communal life of immigrant-ethnic groups was by Robert E. Park and Herbert Miller, *Old World Traits Transplanted* (New York: Harper and Brothers, 1921), especially chapter 6. There are dozens of books on particular immigrant-ethnic groups that describe and analyze associational activity. Some early examples are Theodore Saloutos, *The Greek in the United States* (Cambridge: Harvard University Press, 1964), chapter 4; and Arthur A. Goren, *New York Jews and the Quest for Community: The Kehillah Experiment, 1908–1922* (New York: Columbia University Press, 1970). Jews formed Landsmanschaften Societies of townsmen; in 1917 there were 3,600 of them in New York, with one thousand calling themselves by the name of some locality in eastern Europe (p. 20) as well as synagogues along nationality group lines.

11. Jesse Margolin, Board of Directors, Brotherhood-in-Action, Inc., to Lawrence H. Fuchs, March 31, 1981.

12. By 1976, sixty-three ethnic groups, not counting American Indians or black American presses, issued 976 newspapers and magazines either in English, a foreign language, or in two languages. Lubomyr R. Wynar, "Ethnic Newspapers and Periodicals in the United States: Present Status and Problems of Bibliographic Control," *Ethnic Forum,* Fall 1982, pp. 42–43. Of the 963 ethnic publications in 1976, 386 titles were not published in English, 246 were bilingual, and 328 were in English.

The first book about the immigrant press was by Robert E. Park, *The Immigrant Press and Its Control* (New York: Harper, 1922). The first survey of ethnic newspapers and periodicals was conducted during 1970 and 1971, resulting in the first edition of the *Encyclopedia Directory of Ethnic Newspapers and Periodicals in the United States* (Middletown, Colo.: Libraries Unlimited, 1972). Also see Edward Hunter in *Many Voices: Our Fabulous Foreign Language Press* (Norman Park, Ga.: Norman College, 1961). There are several other books dealing with the foreign language press in general and particular ethnic language presses.

13. Michael S. Laguerre, *American Odyssey: Haitians in New York City* (Ithaca, N.Y.: Cornell University Press, 1984), p. 31.

14. *The Korean Directory of Southern California* (Los Angeles: Keys Advertising and Printing Co., 1978), pp. 820–828. A disproportionate number of Korean immigrants in the U.S. are Christians; in Korea only about one-sixth of the population is Christian. Among organizations listed in the directory were self-improvement groups (the Asian-American Temperance League, the Asian-American Drug Abuse Program, the Korean Intermarriage Society); social groups (the All Korean University Alumni Association of California, the Korean Veterans Association of America, the Korean Amateur Sports Association); cultural groups (the Korean Classical Music Institute, the Korean Philharmonic Orchestra); economic groups (the Korean Petroleum Dealeers Association of California, the Korean Traders Association of America, the Korean Chamber of Commerce of Southern California, the Korean-American CPA Society); and political groups (the Korean-American Political Association of Southern California, the Korean-American Community for Equal Justice, Koreans Unity for Restoration of Human Rights, and the One Korea Movement).

15. *Indo-Chinese Business Directory in the Washington, D.C. Metropolitan Area,* Indo-China Resource Action Center, 1984.

16. Laguerre, *American Odyssey,* pp. 91–95.

17. See Lawrence H. Fuchs, ed., *American Ethnic Politics* (New York: Harper Torchbooks, 1967); Brett W. Hawkins and Robert A. Lorinskas, eds., *The Ethnic Factor in American Politics* (Columbus, Ohio: Charles Merrill, 1970); and more recently, Joseph S. Roucek and Bernard Eisenberg, eds., *America's Ethnic Politics* (Westport, Conn.: Greenwood Press, 1982). There is an excellent article on ethnic politics, "Politics," by Edward R. Kantowicz, in Thernstrom, *Harvard Encyclopedia of American Ethnic Groups,* pp. 803–813.

18. On Jewish political behavior, see Lawrence H. Fuchs, *The Political Behavior of American Jews* (Glencoe, Ill.: The Free Press, 1956). For a specific reference to these two political efforts by Jews, see Morris U. Schappes, ed., *A Documented History of Jews in the United States 1654–1875* (New York: Schocken Books, 1971), pp. 126, 210. On early Catholic political mobilization, see Lawrence H. Fuchs, *John F. Kennedy and American Catholicism* (New York: Meredith Press, 1967),

p. 53. For interpretations of ethnic politics in the nineteenth century, see Lee Benson, *The Concept of Jacksonian Democracy: New York as a Test Case* (Princeton, N.J.: Princeton University Press, 1961), and Richard Jensen, *The Winning of the Midwest: Social and Political Conflict, 1888–1896* (Chicago: University of Chicago Press, 1971). Also see Robert L. Kelley, *The Cultural Pattern in American Politics: The First Century* (New York: Alfred A. Knopf, 1979), especially pp. 107–184. John F. Stack, Jr., *International Conflict in an American City: Boston's Irish, Italians and Jews, 1935–1944* (Westport, Conn.: Greenwood Press, 1979) shows how foreign policy issues can exacerbate tensions that already exist. Ronald H. Bayor, *Neighbors in Conflict: The Irish, Germans, Jews and Italians in New York City, 1929–1941* (Baltimore: Johns Hopkins University Press, 1978), does much the same thing for New York.

19. Louis L. Gerson, *The Hyphenates in Recent American Politics and Diplomacy* (Lawrence: University of Kansas Press, 1964). Also see Lawrence H. Fuchs, "Minority Groups and Foreign Policy," *Political Science Quarterly* 74, no. 2 (1959): 161–175; and Charles N. Mathias, "Ethnic Groups and Foreign Policy," *Foreign Affairs*, 59, no. 5 (1981): 975–998.

20. On a visit to Santa Rosa, California, in September 1984, the author found, in addition to a Native American Indian health and nutrition project, an Indian education and development organization, Blacks for Community Development (with office in Petaluma), an Indo-Chinese American Council, a Filipino community center, the California Human Development Corporation (primarily a Latino community development group), and several organizations dealing with immigrant issues.

21. Joe Picherallo and Mary Thornton, "Arab-Americans Play Major Role in Jackson Drive," *Washington Post*, May 21, 1984, p. A3.

22. Wayne King, "Dole Urges Continued Contacts with Arab World," *New York Times*, March 14, 1987, p. A9. Also see Wayne King, "Arab-Americans Move Toward Political Activity," *New York Times*, August 3, 1987, p. A14.

23. L. A. Chung, "Homeland's Unrest is Stirring Up Bay Area Koreans," *San Francisco Chronicle*, June 26, 1987, p. 21.

24. Bodnar, *The Transplanted*, p. 117.

25. Robert J. Fornaro, "Asian-Indians in America: Acculturation and Minority Status," *Migration Today*, November 3, 1984, pp. 28, 29, 30.

26. Letter from Dr. Rohini Ramanathan, Federation of Indian Associations, to Lawrence H. Fuchs, September 17, 1980.

27. Select Commission on Immigration and Refugee Policy, Summary of San Francisco Regional Hearing, June 9, 1980, *Select Commission on Immigration and Refugee Policy, Second Semiannual Report to Congress*, printed for the use of the Committees on the Judiciary, House of Representatives and U.S. Senate, 96th Congress (Washington, D.C.: U.S. Government Printing Office, October 1980), p. 181.

28. Barbara Gamarekian, "Carrying Word of a Woman's Agenda," *New York Times*, November 18, 1987, p. A26.

29. *Citizenship*, Course Outline in Career and Continuing Education, Los Angeles City Schools, Division of Career and Continuing Education, Community Adult Schools, 1976 Revision, p. 2.

30. In 1986, Mayor Edward Koch of New York appointed Richard Mei, Jr., as his liaison aide to Asian-American communities. (*New York Times*, February 13, 1986, B3). In 1987, twenty-two immigration and refugee advocacy organizations formed a coalition to coordinate some of their activities (International Institute of Boston, *Newsletter*, May–June 1987, p. 4).

31. *Asian-Americans: Agenda for Action,* a conference summary report prepared by the New York State Advisory Committee to the United States Commission on Civil Rights (February 1980), p. 24.

Typical of the way in which the policy process invites ethnic advocacy groups to mobilize was the creation of a Commission on Hispanic Concerns by the mayor of New York in 1986. The commission heard public testimony from over two hundred community service organizations, political leaders, and interested individuals, who made recommendations on education, economic development, housing, language services, and other issues. See City of New York, *Report of the Mayor's Commission on Hispanic Concerns,* mimeo (New York, December 10, 1986), p. 477.

32. Hugo Sabogal, "Fighting Back: Colombians Strive to Reverse Their Tarnished Image," *Vista,* October 5, 1986, p. 8.

33. Linda Basch, "The Vincentians and Grenadians: The Role of Voluntary Associations in Immigrant Adaptation to New York City," in Nancy Foner, ed., *New Immigrants in New York* (New York: Columbia University Press, 1987), pp. 179, 180.

34. "Cuban Firms Said to Be at Turning Point," *Miami Herald,* January 11, 1988, p. 14.

35. Renato Perez, "A Governor Named Martínez," *Vista,* January 3, 1987, p. 10. A grandson of paternal grandparents from Spain, Martínez was not sure whether his maternal ancestors came from Cuba or not. But he grew up in the largely Cuban quarter of Tampa, earned a graduate degree in teaching and eventually a master's in Labor and Industrial Relations. Married to an Italian-American childhood sweetheart "from Tampa's Italian settlement," Martínez was quick to assert that he was not the Cuban-American or Hispanic-American governor. "I am first an American, second a Floridian, and I am also proud of my Spanish heritage," he said.

36. Alejandro Portes, "The Rise of Ethnicity: Determinants of Ethnic Perceptions among Cuban Exiles in Miami," *American Sociological Review* 49 (June 1984): 386.

37. Ibid., p. 387.

38. Ibid., p. 395.

39. "Cubans and the Community—From All Angles," *Miami Herald,* January 9, 1988, p. 18A. The acculturative power of American society was demonstrated by the steady integration of the Mariel refugees into Cuban-American society. The Mariel boatlift, which brought 124,779 Cubans to the U.S. from April 21 through October 26, 1980, included a disproportionate number of poor, unskilled, and ill-educated Cubans, as well as several who were excludable on grounds of health or criminality. Within several years, most of the adult refugees had accommodated themselves effectively to American life, and the children were doing particularly well. See Alejandro Portes and Juan M. Clark, "Mariel Refugees: Six Years After," summary report of a study conducted by Johns Hopkins University in collaboration with Miami-Dade Community (January 1987), pp. 1–14, and Robert F. Sanchez, "Mariel Has Libeled the Many for the Sins of the Very Few," *Miami Herald,* August 24, 1985, p. 23A.

40. Laguerre, *American Odyssey,* pp. 150–154.

41. Alex Stepick and Alejandro Portes, "Flight into Despair: Profile of Recent Haitian Refugees in South Florida," *International Migration Review,* Summer 1986, pp. 337, 341.

42. Ibid., p. 347.

43. Haitian Refugee Center, *1977 Evaluation,* mimeo, quoted in Anthony P. Maingot,

"Ethnic Bargaining and the Non-Citizen: Cubans and Haitians in Miami," manuscript, p. 39.

44. Laguerre, *American Odyssey,* p. 12.

45. Nina Glick Schiller, Marie Lucie Brutus, Carolle Charles, Adrian Dewind, Georges Fouron, and Luis Thomas, "Exile, Ethnic, Refugee: The Changing Organizational Identities of Haitian Immigrants," *Migration World,* November 1, 1987, p. 8.

46. Ibid., p. 11.

47. Harry H. L. Kitano and Roger Daniels, *Asian-Americans: Emerging Minorities* (Englewood Cliffs, N.J.: Prentice-Hall, 1988), p. 138.

48. Jeffrey Brody, "Little Saigon," *The Register,* September 25, 1984, p. E1.

49. Ibid.

50. "Vietnamese Group in Church Dispute," *New York Times,* December 26, 1986, p. A29.

51. Clara Germani, "Indo-Chinese Join American World of Politics," *Christian Science Monitor,* September 16, 1983, p. 1.

52. *Refugee Reports,* published in Washington, D.C., by U.S. Committee for Refugees, November 11, 1987, pp. 10, 11. The Laotian and Cambodian refugees did not move as quickly as the Vietnamese. With 15,000 Laotians in the San Francisco Bay area, only 1,000 had become U.S. citizens by the end of 1988. But the Laotians conducted their own voter registration drive among them. The Cambodians were most passive, possibly because of their persecution under the Khmer Rouge dictatorship in Cambodia, but some of them became active in local politics and even in the Dukakis presidential campaign. It was only a matter of time until the Laotians and the Cambodians became more active.

53. Ibid., p. 4.

54. "Brown County H'mong Association," *The Bridge,* a publication of the Indo-Chinese Resource Action Center, Washington, D.C., December 1986, p. 9.

55. *The Bridge,* September 1986, pp. 12–14, 17.

56. *The Bridge,* December 1986, p. 13.

57. Vu Duc Vuong, "The Next Frontier: Political Empowerment," *The Bridge,* December 1986, p. 18.

58. Ibid., pp. 2, 18.

59. "Action Alert to All MAAs and Community Advocates," Indochina Resource Action Center, Washington, D.C., May 4, 1987, p. 3.

60. Newsletter of the Indochina Resource Action Center, October 15, 1987. This was not the first political victory of the Indo-Chinese community. In 1985, Indo-Chinese refugee groups joined with other refugees through mutual assistance associations and as individuals to obtain a judicial emergency order restraining the Reagan administration from withholding $11.5 million of funds earmarked by Congress for the Targeted Assistance Program, which allocates funds to counties heavily impacted with refugees. The leadership of the refugee communities learned an important political lesson: power is divided among three branches of government. They were thwarted in the executive branch, found allies in Congress, and used the judicial system to assert their interests. Robert Rubin, "The Empowerment of the Refugee Community," *World Refugee Survey: 1986 in Review,* U.S. Committee for Refugees (Washington, D.C.: American Council for Nationalities Service, 1987), pp. 19–23.

61. *Refugee Reports,* November 11, 1988, pp. 11, 12. Also see John Flinn, "San Jose Vietnamese Flex Their Political Muscles," *San Francisco Examiner,* June 14, 1987, pp. B1, B7.

62. Gaynell Evans, "From English Lessons to T-Shirt Stitching," *Chronicle of Higher Education,* November 20, 1985, p. 3.
63. Newsletter, International Institute of Boston (September–October 1986), p. 4.

19. "All These . . . Are the Life Blood of America": Celebrating Diversity

1. E. Taylor Parks and Lois F. Parks, comps., *Memorable Quotations of Franklin D. Roosevelt* (New York: Thomas Y. Crowell Company, 1965), pp. 63, 64. Roosevelt's speeches were in Boston, October 30, 1940; Brooklyn, November 1, 1940; and Boston, November 4, 1944.
2. Lawrence H. Fuchs, *The Political Behavior of American Jews* (Glencoe, Ill., The Free Press, 1956).
3. *Vidal* v. *Girard's Executors,* 43 U.S. (2) How. (1844), p. 61.
4. Quotation in *U.S. Recognition of the Armenian Genocide,* Fact Sheet Number Two (Washington, D.C.: Armenian Assembly of America, 1985).
5. *U.S.* v. *Macintosh,* 283 U.S. 605 (1930).
6. Dan Oren, *Joining the Club* (New Haven: Yale University Press, 1985).
7. Martin E. Marty, *Pilgrims in Their Own Land: Five Hundred Years of Religion in America* (New York: Penguin Books, 1986), p. 393.
8. Marianne Sanua, "Stages in the Development of Jewish Life at Princeton University," *American Jewish History,* June 1987, p. 391. Princeton also appointed a Jew to be its president in 1987.
9. Ervin is quoted in Ted Morgan, *On Becoming American* (Boston: Houghton Mifflin Company, 1978), p. 104.
10. This information comes from a conversation with Abba Schwartz, former State Department official who had responsibility for the visa office in 1965 and who worked on amendments to the Immigration and Nationality Act. Schwartz told the author that Secretary of State Dean Rusk told him he was personally sympathetic to Senator Ervin's position, but he would give the testimony to reflect the president's views.
11. Morgan, *On Becoming American,* p. 104.
12. Rita J. Simon, *Public Opinion and the Immigrant: Print Media Coverage, 1880–1980* (Lexington, Mass.: Lexington Books, 1985), pp. 34–36.
13. Ibid., p. 40.
14. Ibid., p. 43.
15. *Public Attitudes on Refugees,* United States Committee for Refugees, Washington, D.C. (June 7, 1984). This national public opinion poll was conducted in 1984 by Kene, Parsons and Associates, Inc., which said it was accurate to within four to five percentage points.
16. Governor Robert D. Ray, quoted in *Refugee Reports,* U.S. Commission for Refugees, Washington, D.C., February 1985, p. 29.
17. *Time,* July 4, 1983, p. 8.
18. The author enjoyed the celebration on the mall and mixed among ethnic Americans from Asia, Latin America, and Africa.
19. *New York Times,* November 22, 1976, p. C8.
20. Colin Nickerson, *Boston Globe,* November 27, 1985, pp. 1, 8.
21. Daryl Royster Alexander, "A Spicy Blend of Caribbean and Black-American Flavors," *New York Times,* November 19, 1986, p. C1.
22. John Higham, *Send These to Me: Jews and Other Immigrants in Urban America* (New York: Atheneum, 1975), p. 81.
23. Ibid., p. 86.

24. Eleanor Blau, "Liberty Medals Celebrate Diversity," *New York Times,* October 28, 1986, p. B3.
25. Samuel G. Freedman, "For Vietnamese Refugee, a Heartfelt Celebration of Liberty," *New York Times,* July 5, 1986, p. 31.
26. *Local 23–25 News,* International Ladies' Garment Workers Union, 35, no. 3 (October 1986): 4. The restoration of Ellis Island became a major project in the 1980s. A presidential commission headed by Lee A. Iacocca, Chairman of Chrysler Corporation, conducted a public fund-raising campaign throughout the nation to renovate the facilities and create a museum where it will be theoretically possible for nearly 100 million Americans whose ancestors stopped at the island (more than twelve million between 1892 and 1954) to find out information about them.
27. *New York Times,* July 4, 1986, p. B3.
28. Ronald Reagan, "Now, More Than Ever . . . , The Meaning of Liberty," *Parade* magazine, *Boston Sunday Globe,* June 26, 1986.
29. *Federal Register,* 35, no. 42 (February 29, 1980).
30. Interview with Ronald Reagan, Spanish International Network, 1980, unpublished transcript in author's files.
31. *Congressional Quarterly,* July 19, 1980, p. 2006.
32. *Congressional Quarterly,* August 25, 1984, p. 2126.
33. *Boston Globe,* April 29, 1983, p. 7.
34. Roy Rosenzweig, *Eight Hours for What We Will: Workers and Leisure in an Industrial City, 1870–1920* (New York: Cambridge University Press, 1983), chapter 3.
35. In Philadelphia, more than forty-five ethnic communities held an annual three-day folk fair in the 1980s, which included performances by Icelandic, Albanian, Senegalese, and Thai groups. See *Folk Fair,* pamphlet (Philadelphia: The Nationalities Service Center and the Ethnic Communities of Philadelphia, 1980).

  The borough of Queens in New York City held an annual ethnic music and dance festival in which taxi drivers, plumbers, painters, and other blue-collar workers played Yugoslav accordions, Cretan rebecs, and Italian maranzannos while traditional Greek, Bulgarian, and Macedonian dances were performed in a kind of celebration of ethnic diversity that had become common in many cities. See John Pareles, "Astoria with an Ethnic Beat," *New York Times,* June 3, 1983, p. C3. Memphis began its annual ethnic heritage festival in 1982 with participation from Jewish, Greek, German, Italian, Scottish, Indian, Hispanic, Chinese, H'mong, and Laotian groups. See *Update,* Center for Southern Folklore (Memphis, December 1981).
36. *Boston Sunday Globe* comics, March 31, 1985.
37. *Boston Globe,* June 7, 1983, p. 1.
38. Carlos Bulosan, *America Is in the Heart* (New York: Harcourt, Brace and World, 1943), pp. xxiii, xxiv.
39. Mary Antin, *The Promised Land* (Boston: Houghton Mifflin, 1912), pp. 225–226.
40. George F. Will, *Newsweek,* July 18, 1980, p. 76.
41. Jeane Kirkpatrick, "We Need the Immigrants," *Washington Post,* June 30, 1986, p. A11.
42. Mass naturalization ceremonies were popular at earlier times in the twentieth century, but they became extremely common in the 1980s. Newly minted citizens usually receive a scroll with the Bill of Rights, a brochure on the Pledge of Allegiance, and a booklet of documents from America's past which lists further historic documents and artifacts at the National Archives. Between 200,000 and 250,000 immigrants each year were naturalized in the 1980s after taking an oral

exam in which every question dealt with either the Constitution or the American system of government or a few basic historical facts about them. Typical questions were: Who is President of the U.S.A.? Must the President be a citizen? What was the name of the first President? Who gives the government its power? How many Houses are there in Congress? Is Congress the lawmaking branch of our government? How many parts are there in our government? How many Justices are on the Supreme Court? Name two of the first thirteen colonies. When was the Constitution accepted by the states? What is the highest court in the country? How many states are in the Union? What is the name given the first ten amendments of the Constitution? What are some of your rights as a citizen? What system of government does the U.S.A. have?

43. "Miss Liberty to Embrace New Citizens," *New Jersey Star-Ledger,* August 30, 1984, p. 1; Samuel G. Freedman, "A Cheerful Celebration of the Good-Hearted American Idyll," *New York Times,* July 6, 1986, p. 17; "New U.S. Citizen's Heart Beats 'Because It's American,'" *Chicago Tribune,* July 31, 1985, p. 4; Louisa Morale, "My Life Is Complete—And This Is the Land That Made it All Possible," *National Enquirer,* July 12, 1981, p. 11; Mattia Benevenuto, "America Gave Me a Home—A Chance to Be Somebody," *National Enquirer,* July 12, 1983, p. 11; Judith Cummings, "New Citizens: A Sense of Belonging Spiced with Opportunity," *New York Times,* December 1, 1984, p. 8; Jane Cahoun, "Red, White and Blue Rose is an All-American Beauty at 83," *Cleveland Plain Dealer,* June 18, 1985, p. 10; Marvin Pave, "They Wore U.S. Flag on Their Hearts," *Boston Globe,* April 21, 1985, p. 29; Dan Rodricks, "126 New Americans Proudly Step Forward," *Baltimore News-American,* June 1983, p. 7; and Laurel Loo, "Smiles Light up the Dark: 2500 Gain Citizenship," *Honolulu Advertiser,* July 14, 1983, p. A3.

44. "New U.S. Citizen's Heart Beats Again," p. 4.

45. Pave, "They Wore U.S. Flag on Their Hearts," p. 29.

46. Morale, "My Life is Complete," p. 11.

47. Rich Schein, "A Special Fourth for Our New Americans," *U.S.A. Today,* July 5, 1985, p. 1.

48. Loo, "Smiles Light Up the Dark," p. A3.

49. Rodricks, "126 New Americans," p. 7.

50. Bernard Weinraub, "Reagan Sharply Contrasts His Vision with Mondale's," *New York Times,* October 2, 1984, p. A22.

51. "Miss Liberty to Embrace New Citizens," *New Jersey Star-Ledger,* August 30, 1984, p. 1.

52. Freedman, "Cheerful Celebration," p. 17.

53. When Myra A. McDaniel took the oath of office to become Texas's first black secretary of state on September 18, 1984, she spoke of Texas (the home of the Texas Rangers) as having "always been and still is a frontier of hope for people of all races and creeds" (*The Crisis,* 91, no. 10 [December 1984]: 10). The rewriting of history was not restricted to presidents.

20. *Xenophobia, Racism, and Bigotry: Conflict in the Kaleidoscope*

1. Ben Barber, "Cuban Influx Alarms Miami Whites," *U.S.A. Today,* December 6, 1984, p. 3A.

2. Michael Marriot, "In Jersey City, Indians Face Violence," *New York Times,* October 12, 1987, p. B1. Labeling was common in Jersey City, where Indians were called "dotheads." Two Indians were mugged and beaten into a coma; one of them died. Indians were particularly resented because they appeared to have achieved economic success quickly.

3. U.S. Commission on Civil Rights, *Recent Activities Against Citizens and Residents of Asian Descent* (Clearing House Publication No. 1986, Washington, D.C.: 1986). In 1985, eleven Washington stores owned by Korean merchants were firebombed. In one incident, a Korean woman was shot and killed. See Lena Williams, "A Neighborhood Divided," *New York Times,* November 24, 1986, p. B16. For descriptions of hostility toward Asians in Massachusetts, see Carol Pearson, "In Revere, a Tense Street Scene after Sentence in Racial Attack," *Boston Globe,* April 18, 1986, p. 25; and Diane E. Lewis, "Cambodian Family Sues Housing Authority in Somerville after Alleged Racial Attacks," *Boston Globe,* May 28, 1987, p. 25. The quotation is from Martin A. Walsh. See Jan Wong, "Asia Bashing," *Wall Street Journal,* November 28, 1986, p. 1.

4. Marshall Ingweson, "Korean Merchants in Watts Try to Defuse Resentment," *Los Angeles Times,* June 16, 1985, pp. 1, 11.

5. Michael Coakley, "Laotians Came for Refuge, They Got Rage," *Chicago Tribune,* October 21, 1984, p. 4. In Philadelphia, many H'mong families fled the city. Two years later, there were additional attacks by blacks against the H'mong ("Immigrants: New Victims," *Newsweek,* May 12, 1986, p. 57).

6. Edward City, "Resentment Builds as Haitians Scramble Past Ghetto Neighbors," *Washington Post,* May 16, 1987, p. A2.

7. Peter Slevin and Yves Colon, "Cloud of Despair Still Hangs over Haitians," *Miami Herald,* July 1, 1984, p. 16A.

8. Marvin Dunn, "Alliances and Conflicts Between Immigrants and Blacks in Miami," unpublished paper, 1984. See also Barry Bearak, "Miami Facing Trauma of a New Cuban Influx," *Los Angeles Times,* December 23, 1984, p. 1. So many whites felt themselves under siege that a popular bumper sticker read "Will the last American to leave Miami please take the flag?" For information on the 1989 Miami riots and comparative unemployment rates, see Jeffrey Schmalz, "Miami Mayor Apologizes to Police for Actions at Scene of Disorder," *New York Times,* January 19, 1989, p. A18, and Jeffrey Schmalz, "Dreams and Despair Collide as Miami Searches for Itself," *New York Times,* January 23, 1989, pp. A1, B8.

9. *Miami Herald,* January 11, 1985, pp. 1C, 2C.

10. *Miami Herald,* January 10, 1985, pp. 1A, 8A.

11. E. R. Shipp, "Dispute Heads Curriculum in Chicago," *New York Times,* November 1, 1984, p. A26; Pamela DeFiglio, "Hispanics Send a Message to Ruth Love," *Heritage,* newsletter of the Illinois Consultation on Ethnicity in Education, Autumn 1984, p. 1; the board that fired Ruth B. Love, the black superintendent, was divided. Three Hispanic members and three whites voted to dismiss the superintendent; four black members and one white voted to keep her (E. R. Shipp, "Chicago Divided on Move Against Schools' Chief," *New York Times,* August 9, 1984, p. A12).

12. *New York Times,* August 16, 1984, p. B3.

13. *Boston Globe,* August 12, 1984, p. 1.

14. *Boston Globe,* August 10, 1984, p. 1.

15. Nicholas Lemann, "Growing Pains," *Atlantic Monthly,* January 1988, p. 57.

16. Judith Cummings, "Los Angeles Minorities Split over Council Plan," *New York Times,* July 6, 1986, p. 22.

17. Brad Pokorny, "Concerns Expressed over Ethnic Harmony in Cambridge," *Boston Globe,* August 29, 1985, p. 33, and Paul Hirshson, "Hispanic Gets Post at Cambridge School Despite Objections from Parent Group," *Boston Globe,* September 4, 1985, p. 19.

18. Thomas Kessner and Betty Boyd Caroli, *Today's Immigrants, Their Stories: A New*

Look at the Newest Americans (New York: Oxford University Press, 1981), pp. 248, 249, 252.

19. Ibid., pp. 239, 240.

20. "Still Around: Ghosts of Lincoln and His Era," *New York Times,* February 13, 1987, p. 18. Reagan made his remarks in a Lincoln's Birthday speech to junior high school students in Washington, D.C.

21. Jonathan Rieder, *Canarsie* (Cambridge: Harvard University Press, 1985), and J. Anthony Lukas, *Common Ground* (New York: Vintage Books, 1986).

22. Betsy A. Lehman, "South Boston Residents Express Sense of Loss," *Boston Globe,* June 25, 1984, p. 7.

23. William E. Stevens, "Racial Tensions Start to Simmer Down," *New York Times,* December 1, 1985, p. 52. Philadelphia, like most cities, was highly segregated residentially, with three-quarters of Philadelphia's blacks, about 40 percent of the population, living in predominantly black neighborhoods.

24. Mireille Grangenois Gates, "They're Upset with Outsiders in Dearborn, Mich.," *U.S.A. Today,* June 16, 1986, p. 11A. When Henry Ford opened the 1,200-acre automotive manufacturing complex in Dearborn in 1920, thousands of European and Arab workers and some blacks came to work on the assembly line, but blacks were kept from settling in Dearborn.

25. Sarah Riemer, "Council Backs Housing Order in Yonkers," *New York Times,* January 29, 1988, p. B1.

26. *New York Times,* December 22, 1987, p. B7.

27. Samuel G. Freedman, "For Belmont, New Days, New Fears," *New York Times,* August 6, 1986, p. B1.

28. Steven Erlanger, "Five Hundred Mourn Man Killed in Queens," *New York Times,* December 21, 1987, p. B1.

29. Robert D. McFadden, "Racism Protest Disrupts Brooklyn Subway Service," *New York Times,* December 22, 1987, p. B1.

30. Todd S. Purdum, "Acts Reported to be Linked to Bias Rise," *New York Times,* December 25, 1987, p. B1. Racially motivated attacks against blacks in New York in 1987 went up from 68 in the previous year to 162. Such attacks against whites went from 17 to 80 (*Black Enterprise,* March 1988, p. 20).

31. Alan Weisman, "Flatbush, '60s; Bensonhurst, '89," *New York Times,* September 5, 1989, p. 19. Weisman recounts the history of white racism and anti-Semitism in Flatbush in the 1960s, arguing that such ethnically chauvinistic neighborhoods create a climate for bigotry-motivated crimes. Also see "The Nature of Racism: 2 Clergymen," *New York Times,* September 6, 1989, p. B1. A black minister and an Italian-American priest had trouble agreeing on the extent and nature of racism in Bensonhurst. Also see M. A. Farber, "In Son's Death, a Father Finds a Mission," *New York Times,* September 28, 1989, p. B1.

32. Maureen Dowd, "Racial Attacks on Students Revive Tensions on Staten Island," *New York Times,* June 21, 1985, p. B1. The sought-for alleged chief of the gang was not on the bus. These high school students sought revenge even though their school had several courses dealing with prejudice and persecution and had hired a black and a white counselor to conduct sessions with the students about racial tensions.

33. Sarah Riemer, "Learning to Live Peacefully in High School Melting Pot," *New York Times,* May 17, 1984, p. 1.

34. For a review of such incidents, see Steve Curwood, "Reports of Racism on Campus Rising, Observers Say," *Boston Sunday Globe,* December 21, 1986, p. 15. Also see "Inquiry at Citadel Says Record on Race is Good," *New York Times,* February 19, 1987, p. A20; Bonnie V. Winston, "Dukakis, Students Meet on U

Mass Violence," *Boston Globe*, February 15, 1987, p. 43; Isabel Wilkerson, "Campus Race Incidents Disquiet U of Michigan," *New York Times*, March 9, 1987, p. A12.

35. Richard D. Breitman and Alan M. Kraut, "Anti-Semitism in the State Department, 1933–1944, Four Case Studies," in David Gerber, ed., *Anti-Semitism in American History* (Urbana: University of Illinois, 1986). Of the four high State Department officials involved in administration of immigration policy, three made anti-Semitic comments fairly frequently in their diaries and even in conversation. Also see Henry L. Feingold, *The Politics of Rescue: The Roosevelt Administration and the Holocaust, 1938–1945* (New Brunswick, N.J.: Rutgers University Press, 1970), and David S. Wyman, *Paper Walls: America and the Refugee Crisis, 1938–1941* (Amherst: University of Massachusetts Press, 1968). On estimates of Ku Klux Klan membership at its peak see William Pierce Randall, *The Ku Klux Klan: A Century of Tyranny* (Philadelphia: Chilton Books, 1965), p. 194. Christian anti-Semitism was the basis for several new organized hate groups, including the Order, an offshoot of the Aryan Nation, the activist wing of the Church of Jesus Christ Christian at Hayden Lake, Idaho. Its leaders, speaking for the Christian Identity Movement, an association of churches and sects, taught that the Caucasian races are the true chosen people of God and that the Jews are impostors and offspring of Satan through the line of Cain. Wayne King, "Neo-Nazis' Dream of Racist Territory in Pacific Northwest Refuses to Die," *New York Times*, July 5, 1986, p. 10. The audience for such extremism grew smaller in the 1980s. The most popular anti-Jewish weekly tabloid, *The Spotlight,* published by one of the groups, went down in circulation from 315,000 in 1981 to 112,000 by 1987 ("The Hate Movement Today: A Chronicle of Violence and Disarray," Special Report, Anti-Defamation League (Washington, D.C., 1987), p. 2.

36. Transcript of meeting between the author and teachers of "Facing History and Ourselves," sponsored by the Facing History Foundation, February 1983.

37. *The Near East Report,* January 21, 1985, p. 12. In one high school in Port Washington, Long Island, supporters of students running for election on a Nazi party slate wrote anti-Semitic slogans on walls, lockers, and notebooks. See "Anti-Semitic Incidents in the Community," Institute for Human Relations, American Jewish Committee, 1982. In 1981, three youths from Chicago's affluent North Shore suburbs conducted an anti-Semitic mail campaign against Jewish businessmen (*Illinois Consultation on Ethnicity and Education,* October 1982, Vol. 6, No. 1). In 1988, a 34 percent rise in anti-Semitic acts was reported over the previous year by the Anti-Defamation League, the first year in six to see an increase (*A.D.L. Bulletin,* January 1989, pp. 2, 4).

38. Adrian Cook, *The Armies of the Streets: The New York City Draft Riots of 1863* (Lexington: University Press of Kentucky, 1974), p. 19.

39. *Hate Groups in America: A Record of Bigotry and Violence* (New York: Anti-Defamation League of B'nai B'rith, 1983), p. 72. Testimony was given that at least two thousand blacks had been killed, wounded, or injured in Louisiana in the few weeks preceding the presidential election of 1868.

40. Ronald Bayor, *Neighbors in Conflict: The Irish, Germans, Jews and Italians in New York City, 1929–1941* (Baltimore: Johns Hopkins University Press, 1978), p. 69.

41. Cook, *Armies of the Streets,* p. 205.

42. Dennis P. Ryan, *Beyond the Ballot Box: A Social History of the Boston Irish, 1848–1917* (Rutherford, N.J.: Fairleigh Dickinson University Press, 1983), p. 140.

43. Roy Rosenzweig, *Eight Hours for What We Will: Workers and Leisure in an Industrial City, 1870–1920* (New York: Cambridge University Press, 1983), pp. 88, 89.

44. Douglas V. Shaw, *The Making of an Immigrant City: Ethnic and Cultural Conflict in Jersey City, New Jersey, 1850–1877)* (New York: Arno Press, Inc., 1973). Although most paupers living in the almshouse in the 1850s were Irish Catholic, they were forbidden to have a priest in attendance unless Protestants could observe them.

45. John F. Stack, Jr., *International Conflict in an American City: Boston's Irish, Italians and Jews, 1935–1944* (Westport, Conn.: Greenwood Press, 1979), pp. 34, 35.

46. Theodore Hershberg, "Free Blacks in Ante-Bellum Philadelphia," in Allen F. Davis and Mark H. Haller, eds., *The Peoples of Philadelphia: A History of Ethnic Groups and Lower Class Life, 1790–1940* (Philadelphia: Temple University Press, 1973), p. 113; and Steven J. Ross, *Workers on the Edge: Work, Leisure and Politics in Industrializing Cincinnati, 1788–1898* (New York: Columbia University Press, 1985), p. 195.

Part 5. Pluralism, Public Policy, and the Civic Culture, 1970–1989

1. Bill Keller, "Gorbachev Urges Minority States," *New York Times*, April 18, 1987, p. A5. Gorbachev apparently did not understand that when Americans celebrated diversity, often calling it pluralism, they were really celebrating individual rights.

21. *"Equal and Exact Justice": The Civil Rights Compact*

1. From *An Inquiry into the Object and Purposes of the So-Called 'American Protective Association,'* pamphlet in Widener Library, Harvard University (Boston: 1893, no publisher listed), p. 11.

2. U.S. Department of Justice, Civil Rights Division, *Enforcing the Law, January 20, 1981–January 31, 1987* (Washington, D.C.: U.S. Government Printing Office, 1987). Among the more important cases, the Civil Rights Commission brought suit against all-white suburbs of Chicago and Detroit and forced them to stop maintaining residency requirements for employment that operated to exclude black applicants, and another suit against Gallup, New Mexico, which was obliged to provide $750,000 in back pay and priority job offers with retroactive seniority to 225 American Indians as compensation for discrimination, the greatest amount of back pay for American Indians in any employment discrimination case. In 1983, the division filed suit and negotiated a consent decree with the Richland Parish district in Louisiana to require that teachers be hired and assigned on a nondiscriminatory basis and that two blacks improperly passed over for principalships be promoted to principal or an equivalent position. In 1985, the division entered into a consent decree with the Phoenix high school district to require two schools to desegregate by converting into magnet schools. It also filed a successful suit in Yonkers, New York, to force desegregation of the public schools and creation of subsidized housing in predominantly white areas (pp. 1–3).

3. The Civil Rights Division was established in 1957 following enactment of the first civil rights statutes since Reconstruction. It became the main agency within the federal government responsible for enforcing federal statutes prohibiting discrimination. It greatly expanded its responsibilities with enactment of the 1964 Civil Rights Act, the Voting Rights Act of 1965, the Fair Housing Act of 1968, the Equal Credit Opportunity Act of 1974, the Equal Educational Opportunities Act of 1974, amendments to the Voting Rights Act in 1978, and the Fair Housing Act in 1988.

4. Leadership Conference Education Fund, *Civil Rights Monitor,* December 1987, pp. 10–12; *The Washington Report,* The American Jewish Committee, December

I, 1986, p. 19. Enforcement powers of the EEOC, created by the Civil Rights Act of 1964 to enforce Title VII, dealing with equal employment, were strengthened in 1972 with amendments that covered more businesses and labor organizations, state and local government employees, and employees of educational institutions. An independent general counsel appointed by the president with the advice and consent of the Senate was empowered to bring a civil action in federal court against an employer whom the EEOC had found to be discriminatory and with whom the agency had failed to secure a conciliation agreement. The act gave federal judges the power to order remedies, including back pay.

5. U.S. Senate, Committee on the Judiciary, "Nomination of Robert H. Bork to Be an Associate Justice of the United States Supreme Court," *Report of the Committee on the Judiciary* (100th Cong., 1st sess., October 13, 1987). For a view from the lobbyists, see *Civil Rights Monitor,* Leadership Conference Education Fund, October 1987; Howard Kurtz, "Civil Rights Lobby Has a New Rallying Cry: Block That Nominee," *Washington Post National Weekly Edition,* June 23, 1986, p. 11.

6. "Nomination of Robert H. Bork," pp. 36–44. Early in the Reagan administration, the EEOC decided to concentrate on providing remedies for individual victims of discrimination and no longer make large class action complaints against employers (*Chronicle of Higher Education,* February 20, 1985, p. 2).

7. "Nomination of Robert H. Bork," p. 213.

8. Ruth Marcus, "Push Comes to Shove on Grove City," *Washington Post National Weekly Edition,* March 14–20, 1988, p. 31. Prior to the Reagan veto, the House bipartisan majority was 315 to 98 and in the Senate the vote was 75 to 14 to reverse the Grove City decision.

9. Kenneth B. Noble, "The Supreme Court: A Restriction on Unions and a Defeat for the Administration," *New York Times,* June 30, 1988, p. A19.

10. *Price Waterhouse* v. *Hopkins,* No. 87-1167 (1989).

11. *Wards Cove Packing* v. *Atonio,* No. 87-1387.

12. *New York Times,* May 1, 1986, p. B8.

13. *Civil Rights Monitor,* Leadership Conference Education Fund, June/July 1987, pp. 16, 17.

14. Stuart Taylor, Jr., "High Court Turns 1866 Race-Bias Law into Broader Tool," *New York Times,* May 19, 1987, p. 1. Also see Ethan Bronner, "Justices Extend Anti-Bias Laws," *Boston Globe,* May 19, 1987, p. 1. In 1976, the Supreme Court decided that the 1886 Reconstruction-era law providing that all persons in the U.S. have the same right to make and enforce contracts as white citizens meant that plaintiffs could sue private schools and seek damages for racial discrimination in private businesses generally. When, in 1987, the Court invited arguments in a case to see whether the interpretation of the law should be reconsidered, a bipartisan group of sixty senators and forty-seven state attorney generals joined members of the House of Representatives in urging that the 1976 interpretation should stand. See Stuart Taylor, Jr., "High Court Gets an Unusual Plea Not to Reverse Key Rights Ruling," *New York Times,* June 24, 1988, p. 1. In one case involving the 1866 statute, an Iraqi-American alleged that he had been denied tenure at the college at which he taught because of his Arab ancestry. In the second case, members of a Jewish congregation whose synagogue had been sprayed with anti-Semitic slogans and symbols had been dismissed as plaintiffs by a district court in their suit to receive compensatory damages but were affirmed by the Court, who reasoned that the term "race" in 1866, as it was then used, included ethnic groups.

State courts in the 1980s actually expanded protection of individual rights beyond the requirements set by the Supreme Court in several respects, reversing a pattern that had prevailed for most of the century. Robert Pear, "State Courts Move Beyond U.S. Bench in Rights Rulings," *New York Times,* May 4, 1986, p. 1.

15. *Patterson* v. *McLean Credit Union,* No. 87-107 (1989). Also see *Jett* v. *Dallas Independent School District,* No. 87-2084 (1989), and *City of Canton* v. *Harris,* No. 86-1088 (1989).

16. Irvin Molotsky, "Senate Acts to Enforce Housing Law," *New York Times,* August 5, 1988, p. B5.

17. Adam Pertman, "Senators Say Vote Was a Matter of Rights, Not Foreign Policy," *Boston Globe,* October 3, 1985, p. 5. Beginning in 1958, Congress and other public officials proclaimed Captive Nations Week annually to call attention to the denial of human rights in Communist countries, particularly in eastern Europe. In addition, senators and representatives frequently made speeches decrying the violation of human rights abroad. See a speech by Senator William Bradley (D-New Jersey) urging his colleagues to honor Armenian Martyrs' Day (recalling the death of more than 1.5 million Armenians in the Ottoman Empire between 1915 and 1923) and a speech by Senator William O. Proxmire (D-Wisconsin) urging Congress never to forget Europe's historic persecution of the Jews. The speech by Bradley is in the *Congressional Record,* 98th Cong., 1st sess., April 28, 1983, Vol. 129, no. 56, p. 5514. The speech by Proxmire is in the *Congressional Record,* 1st sess., April 21, 1983, Vol. 129, no. 52, p. 5057.

18. William Mandell, "Nazi Persecutors in the United States: Proposed Consolidation of Denaturalization and Deportation Procedures," *Boston College International and Comparative Law Review,* Summer 1982, p. 389. For a discussion of the anti-Semitic implications of the Displaced Persons Act, see Norman L. Zucker and Naomi Flink Zucker, *The Guarded Gate: The Reality of American Refugee Policy* (New York: Harcourt Brace Jovanovich, 1987), pp. 28, 29.

19. Mandell, "Nazi Persecutors," p. 408. When the U.S. passed its Refugee Act in 1980, largely at the initiative of congressional leaders, providing for admission of refugees who had a well-founded fear of persecution should they be returned to their homeland, it excluded from admission any person who had ordered, incited, assisted, or otherwise participated in persecution on account of race, religion, nationality, membership in a particular group, or political opinion.

20. *New York Times,* July 16, 1983, p. 12.

21. *New York Times,* April 29, 1987, p. A34. Possibly the most difficult deportation case was that of Rumanian Orthodox Archbishop Valerian Trifia, who fled from the U.S. to Portugal, ending a nine-year effort by the U.S. government to strip him of citizenship even though he held an important position in Michigan as leader of the 35,000-member Rumanian Orthodox Church in the U.S. and Canada (*Miami Herald,* August 15, 1985, p. 4A). Archbiship Trifia had lied in filling out the documents that enabled him to enter in 1950 and to become a naturalized citizen in 1957, never mentioning that he had been a major figure in the violent fascist and anti-Semitic Iron Guard in Bucharest (Miles Cunningham, "Archbishop's File is Most Active for U.S. Nazi-Hunters," *New York Times,* August 29, 1983, p. 14).

22. U.S. Department of Justice, Civil Rights Division, *Enforcing the Law,* p. IIB.

23. One federal statute prohibited conspiracy to injure any citizen in the exercise of rights protected by the Constitution or the laws of the U.S. Another prohibited willful deprivation of constitutional and federal statutory rights by those acting under color of law, a provision of the federal code used to prosecute misconduct by state or local police. A third, enacted in response to violent attacks on civil rights workers in the South, prohibited intentional interference by force or threat

of force with certain rights. Four other federal statutes provided civil causes for action for victims of racially and religiously motivated violence by private citizens. Another law enacted by Congress during Reconstruction to provide redress for victims of the Ku Klux Klan imposed a civil penalty on those who conspired to deprive another person or class of persons of "the equal protection of the laws or of equal privileges and immunities under the laws." The Fair Housing Act of 1968 created a civil cause of action in favor of anyone who was coerced, threatened, intimidated, or interfered with in the exercise of rights guaranteed under the equal opportunity sections of the act. See National Institute Against Prejudice and Violence, *Striking Back at Bigotry: Remedies under Federal and State Law for Violence Motivated by Racial, Religious, and Ethnic Prejudice* (Washington, D.C., 1986), pp. 12, 18, 23, 31, 35, 36).

24. *The Washington Report,* American Jewish Committee, May 11, 1987, p. 42. By 1986, only Alaska, Iowa, Montana, New Hampshire, Utah, and Vermont had not passed legislation specifically aimed at punishing racially and religiously motivated violence. Between 1979 and 1984, three hundred members of organized hate groups were arrested for racially motivated murders, bombings, and acts of intimidation and harassment.

25. Ibid., pp. 63, 64. In Oregon, for example, a person was automatically judged guilty of intimidation in the second degree if he or she committed either criminal mischief in the third degree or harassment because of the race, color, religion, or national origin of the victim.

26. Ibid., p. 59.

27. For a catalog of state statutes as of 1986, see ibid., pp. 97–159. Between 1981 and 1988, eighteen states adopted antiparamilitary training laws to inhibit violence-prone extremist hate groups, several of which resulted in successful prosecutions. See *A.D.L. Bulletin,* Anti-Defamation League of B'nai B'rith, February 1987, pp. 15, 16. The states that had antiparamilitary training laws were Arkansas, California, Colorado, Connecticut, Florida, Georgia, Idaho, Illinois, Michigan, Missouri, Nebraska, New Jersey, North Carolina, Oregon, Pennsylvania, Rhode Island, Virginia, and West Virginia. "The Hate Movement Today: A Chronicle of Violence and Disarray," and A.D.L. special report, 1988. Connecticut's 1981 law was typical; it made it a crime to teach, train, or take instruction in the use or manufacture of firearms, explosives, or fire-producing devices for the purpose of carrying out violent public demonstrations, with a fine of $5,000 and up to ten years in prison as the penalty. Another statute made it a crime, with a penalty of up to one year in jail, to place a burning cross on public property or the property of another without permission. In 1982, a law was passed increasing the penalties for civil rights violations when committed by a person or persons wearing a hood, mask, or other device, a crime made punishable with up to five years in prison and a $5,000 fine. (U.S. Civil Rights Commission, *Hate Groups and Acts of Bigotry: Connecticut's Response* (Washington, D.C.: U.S. Government Printing Office, October 1982), p. 33.

28. *New York Times,* February 3, 1984, p. 16.

29. *Miami Herald,* January 13, 1985, p. 6A.

30. *Klan Watch Law Report,* The Southern Poverty Law Center, September 1986, p. 1.

31. *Law Report,* Southern Poverty Law Center, Summer 1987, p. 1; also see Jesse Kornbluth, "The Woman Who Beat the Klan," *New York Times Magazine,* November 1, 1987, p. 26; and William E. Schmidt, "Black Takes Possession of Klan Headquarters," *New York Times,* May 20, 1987, p. A1. It was estimated that the UKA's membership had declined from about 30,000 in the 1960s to fewer

than 1,500 at the time of the jury award. The assessment of the fine against the Klan and the defendants, it was thought, probably dealt a death blow to the UKA. In 1989, Klansmen who had attacked black marchers in Decatur, Alabama, ten years earlier fended off a stiffer penalty by agreeing to take a course in race relations. The legal settlement was developed by the Southern Poverty Law Center, which represented the black plaintiffs. It also required the Klansmen to pay damages, perform community service, and refrain from harassing blacks or joining any white supremacist group for up to ten years. In a remarkable turn of history, one of those required to take the race relations course was Roger Handley, former Invisible Empire Grand Wizard. The course was to be taught by the Reverend Joseph Lowery, president of the Southern Christian Leadership Conference and the man who led the march in Decatur (*Law Report,* Southern Poverty Law Center, October 1989, pp. 1, 3). For a summary of major victories in the courts against the Klan from 1981 through 1988, see *Law Report,* Southern Poverty Law Center, July 1989, p. 5.

32. On the indictments, see *Klan Watch Intelligence Report,* Southern Poverty Law Center, May–June 1987, p. 1. On the order of Secretary of Defense Caspar Weinberger, see *Washington Report,* American Jewish Committee, 1, no. 4: 14.

33. Jack Craig, *Boston Globe,* May 9, 1987, p. 1.

34. Erin Maclellan, "Klan Marches Peacefully in Greensboro," *Boston Globe,* June 8, 1987, p. 3.

35. *Boston Globe,* July 13, 1986, p. 5.

36. *Boston Globe,* September 20, 1984, p. 41.

37. William K. Stevens, "White Philadelphian, 13, Is a Model to Those Combating Racist Incidents," *New York Times,* November 26, 1986, p. B14. In the first case, a thirteen-year-old white boy broke the code of silence and testified against the defendant.

38. U.S. Civil Rights Commission, *Hate Groups and Acts of Bigotry: Connecticut's Response,"* p. 54.

39. *Boston Sunday Globe,* February 8, 1987, p. 22. With passage in 1983 of the Massachusetts Racial and Religious Intimidation Act, imposing fines and jail terms for racially inspired acts of violence, the local police had a particularly effective statute for enforcement, one that undoubtedly served as a deterrent to racially motivated crime.

40. *Forum,* National Institute Against Prejudice and Violence, November 1986, p. 2, and February 1987, p. 2.

41. Fox Butterfield, "Boston Mayor Takes Action to Promote Racial Harmony," *New York Times,* March 15, 1984, p. 1. The previous police commissioner, Joseph M. Jordan, had been reluctant to discipline the officers involved (Gregory Witcher, *Boston Globe,* May 10, 1986, pp. 27, 31).

42. *New York Times,* December 22, 1986, p. A1.

43. Ibid., p. B4. The New York City police immediately put fifty investigators on the case, and twenty-four hours later arrested and charged four white teen-agers with assault. *New York Times,* December 23, 1986, p. A1.

44. National Conference of Christians and Jews, *Familiarity Breeds Respect* (National Conference of Christians and Jews, 1980).

45. The Anti-Defamation League was a model for many other organizations. Italians, Arabs, and others established antidefamation organizations of their own. The ADL's bulletin in the 1980s (published monthly except July and August) reported on new programs to deal with ethnic and religious bias. Many of those programs had nothing specific to do with Jews. See *A.D.L. Bulletin,* January 1989, for a

report on awards given by the ADL for human relations films and video productions to combat bigotry against blacks, the deaf, the retarded, etc.

46. Pat Jamison, "Teens Learn About Differences," *Chicago Tribune,* September 4, 1987, section 2, p. 5. The Center for Democratic Renewal, formed in Atlanta as a national organization to monitor the activities of the Ku Klux Klan, included more than sixty-five community, religious, and political organizations by the mid-1980s and concentrated on community organization and training to combat racist activities. The Southern Poverty Law Center, based in Montgomery, Alabama, published the *Klan Watch Law Report* to spotlight activities of the Klan and furnish legal assistance to those involved in litigation against the Klan and other hate groups.

The Baltimore-based National Institute Against Violence and Prejudice, the first center created to study and respond to racially motivated violence, went beyond the usual research, information, and assistance to those needing support to deal with racism and religious bigotry. It drafted and analyzed model legislation to combat crimes motivated by bigotry. Creating a new word, "ethno-violence," it began a national study of the effects of such violence on minority group victims. The Facing History and Ourselves Foundation in Brookline, Massachusetts, developed probably the most widely used and effective educational program to combat bigotry in the 1980s, presenting students with materials about the Holocaust and other examples of mass violence based on hate, such as the genocide of Armenians in the First World War period. On the ethno-violence project, see *The Ethno-Violence Project: Pilot Study,* Institute Report No. 1 (Baltimore: National Institute Against Prejudice and Violence, 1986). Many school systems, particularly the larger ones, developed courses on tolerance. New York City, which faced growing tensions in race relations after the Howard Beach and Bensonhurst murders and the rape of a young white woman by black and Hispanic youths in Central Park, implemented a $1 million multicultural curriculum in 1988 intended to develop interracial, ethnic, and religious understanding. The school chancellor, Bernard Mecklowitz, said that schools could not afford to let parents take the lead in teaching racial tolerance. The curriculum included four broad themes: equality; culture and diversity; migration and immigration; and contributions of ethnic groups. One of the handbooks used in several districts focused on twelve different groups (Felicia R. Lee, "Intolerance to Be Topic for Students," *New York Times,* September 18, 1989, p. B1).

47. A 1986 report of the U.S. Commission on Civil Rights focused on racially motivated violence, harassment, and intimidation directed against Asian and Pacific Island Americans. A hearing by the Criminal Justice Subcommittee of the House of Representatives Committee on the Judiciary in the same year heard testimony on "violence against Arab-Americans." *Forum,* National Institute Against Prejudice and Violence, November 1986, p. 2. It became commonplace for state human relations commissions to hold seminars for police officers and others to help them deal with ethnic conflict (Amy Linn, "A Lesson on Ethnic Conflicts," *Philadelphia Inquirer,* June 13, 1986, p. 6B).

48. John S. Workman, "Two Tales of a City," *Arkansas Gazette,* November 2, 1981, p. 10A. Groups like the one in Arkansas often were established immediately after a major incident of bigotry, as in 1980 when the Philadelphia Southwest Task Force was created to defuse tensions; working with the city's Commission on Human Relations, it remained in existence to help cope with subsequent episodes of violence (William K. Stevens, "Racial Tension Starts to Simmer Down," *New York Times,* December 1, 1985, p. 52). A few days after the Howard Beach tragedy, the Concerned Citizens of South Queens, an ecumenical, multiracial, and multi-

ethnic coalition, was formed to prevent further incidents of racial violence (George James, "After Howard Beach: Seeking Racial Peace," *New York Times,* March 10, 1987, pp. B1, B4).

49. Elizabeth Coonrod, "Change, Optimism Slowly Dispel Racial Tension in Woodburn," *The Oregonian,* August 11, 1985, p. 1.

50. *Welcome: Chao Mung,* an orientation booklet presented by the Greater New Orleans Section, National Council of Jewish Women and Associated Catholic Charities of New Orleans, 1979.

51. Eve Taylor Parks and Lois F. Parker, eds., *Memorable Quotations of Franklin D. Roosevelt* (New York: Thomas V. Crowell and Company, 1965), p. 64.

52. Dennis P. Ryan, *Beyond the Ballot Box: A Social History of the Boston Irish, 1848–1917* (Rutherford, N.J.: Fairleigh Dickinson University Press, 1983).

53. Lawrence H. Fuchs, *Hawaii Pono* (New York: Harcourt, Brace and World, 1961), p. 442.

54. *Boston Globe,* May 2, 1984, p. 15.

55. Martin Crutsinger, "Watt Offers Apology to Indian Leaders," *Boston Globe,* January 28, 1983, p. 3.

56. *New York Times,* September 23, 1983, p. B14.

57. Marianne Mele Hall was appointed as chairwoman of the three-member Copyright Tribunal, a department of the Library of Congress that had become increasingly important because it was responsible for setting the lucrative royalty rates cable television operators must pay. In the book she co-authored, American blacks were accused of avoiding personal responsibility and abhorring the work ethic (*Washington Post National Weekly Edition,* May 20, 1985, p. 27; *Boston Globe,* May 9, 1985, p. 3; *Boston Globe,* May 4, 1985, p. 36.)

58. *Senator Paul Tsongas Reports,* Autumn 1983, p. 2.

59. Lena Williams, "Senate Panel Hands Reagan First Defeat on Nominee for Judgeship," *New York Times,* June 6, 1986, p. 13.

60. "The Fascist Connection," editorial in the *Boston Globe,* September 14, 1988, p. 22. One essayist was surprised at the lack of public outrage over the revelation of anti-Semites in high places in the Bush campaign and over other recent incidents of anti-Semitism (Leonard Zakim, "Where is the Public Outrage?" *Boston Globe,* September 14, 1988, p. 23).

61. Andrew H. Malcolm, "Monitors Seeking to Calm Oratory," *New York Times,* February 8, 1987, p. 14.

62. *New York Times,* March 22, 1987, p. 45.

63. *New York Times,* May 13, 1983, p. A24.

64. Frances Frank Marcus, "Order on Halting Blacks is Rescinded in Louisiana," *New York Times,* December 4, 1986, p. A32.

65. Howard W. French, "Racial Slurs Barred Within Police Department," *New York Times,* October 7, 1987, p. B5.

66. *Boston Globe,* May 5, 1985, p. 22.

67. Wallace Turner, "Aide to Coast G.O.P. Candidate Resigns after Remarks on Racism," *New York Times,* October 14, 1982, p. 10.

68. *New York Times,* March 23, 1986, p. 2.

69. Fox Butterfield, "Trustee's Remark Renews Charges of Racial Insensitivity at Wellesley," *New York Times,* February 12, 1987, p. A20.

70. Jack Craig, *Boston Globe,* May 9, 1987, p. 1.

71. Jimmy the Greek, whose real name is Jimmy Snyder, was fired from CBS for his explanation of the presumed physical ability of blacks in football and basketball: "This goes all the way to the Civil War when during the slave trading . . . the owner, the slave owner, would breed his big black to his big woman so he could

have a big black kid, you see" (Richard Cohen, "The Greek's Offense," *Washington Post National Weekly Edition*, January 25–31, 1988, p. 28).

72. Esther Iverem, "Racist Remarks Force Recall of State Manual," *New York Times*, May 4, 1987, p. B3.

73. Robert D. McFadden, "Third Manual Says Whites are Racist," *New York Times*, May 16, 1987, p. 33.

74. *New York Times*, June 2, 1987, p. A18.

75. Mark A. Uhlig, "Affirmative Action Manual Defended," *New York Times*, May 7, 1987, p. B8.

76. James Barron, "Black Official Faults Tactics of Sharpton," *New York Times*, March 2, 1988, p. B1.

77. *Congressional Record*, 98th Cong., 2d sess., Vol. 130, No. 92, Washington, D.C., June 24, 1984, pp. S8671–8677.

78. Background on the Jackson-Farrakhan episode can be found in *Newsweek*, April 9, 1984, and April 23, 1984. Also see Timothy F. Hagan, "They Have Cause for Sadness," *Washington Post*, June 28, 1984, p. 16. As a delegate to the Democratic national convention, Hagan, a county commissioner from Cleveland, introduced a resolution condemning anti-Semitism and tried to persuade Jackson to support it.

79. One exception to the general absence of criticism of Farrakhan by black leaders was Bayard Rustin, the organizer of the 1965 March on Washington (Bayard Rustin, "Jackson, Repudiate Farrakhan," *New York Times*, June 17, 1984, p. E21). Sixty-nine percent of the black delegates to the Democratic convention who supported Jackson actually had a favorable view of Farrakhan, compared to only 19 percent with an unfavorable view. Of the total of 604 black delegates at the convention, 47 percent were favorable to Farrakhan, 38 percent unfavorable. (Nonblack delegates were strongly negative, with only 3 percent favorable.) See William Schneider, "How Farrakhan Issue Divides the Delegates," *National Journal Convention Special*, July 25, 1984, p. 1388.

That a double standard more forgiving to black politicians still obtained in 1988 was clear after an aide to the mayor of Chicago charged publicly that Jews were engaged in a conspiracy to control the world and that Jewish doctors had injected the AIDS virus into blacks. It took nearly a week for Chicago's black mayor, Eugene Sawyer, to dismiss the man, Steve Cokely. Cokely, long associated with Farrakhan, remained a hero among many blacks in the city, and was not denounced by Chicagoan Jesse Jackson for his remarks. The mayor of Atlanta, Andrew Young, denounced "the hatred and sickening garbage of anti-Semitism," but most other black political leaders were not heard from (Thomas C. Homburger and Michael C. Kotzin, "The Cokely Affair and Its Aftermath," *A.D.L. Bulletin*, Anti-Defamation League of B'nai B'rith (October 1988), pp. 3–5). A different approach was taken in 1988 by New York City's black mayoral candidate, David Dinkins, who promptly put pressure on a campaign aide to leave the campaign when the Anti-Defamation League revealed anti-Semitic remarks he had made in 1969, even though he claimed to have subsequently apologized to Jewish groups. See Celestine Bohlen, "Teacher Leaves Dinkins' Campaign: Critics Recall an Anti-Jewish Poem from the 60's," *New York Times*, October 12, 1989, p. B3.

80. So sensitive were political candidates to any possible accusation of condoning racism or anti-Semitism that a deputy chairman of the Republican National Committee and an adviser to Vice President George Bush was obliged to resign from his campaign position when it was discovered that he had done a check on the number of Jewish personnel in the Bureau of Labor Statistics at the behest of

President Richard Nixon. See Maureen Dowd, "Advisor to Bush quits G.O.P. Post Amid Anti-Semitism Allegations," *New York Times,* September 12, 1988, p. 1.

81. Anti-Defamation League in New England (Spring 1987), p. 2.

82. *San Francisco Chronicle,* September 25, 1986, p. 18. In 1988, Japan's prime minister, Noboru Takeshita, was obliged to apologize to the congressional Black Caucus for comments made by a senior Japanese politician suggesting that American blacks often go bankrupt to avoid paying debts. Takeshita, apparently adopting the etiquette of public discourse in the U.S., said, "There is no room or justification for racial discrimination." He did not respond to the Black Caucus's proposal that the Japanese government begin a public education program on racial incidents. When black organizations learned that Little Black Sambo figures were on sale in department stores in Japan, they threatened to boycott Japanese goods in the U.S., forcing a withdrawal of the items (David E. Sanger, "Japan Apologizes for a Racial Slur," *New York Times,* August 16, 1988, p. A11).

83. The failure to make up for the past was felt keenly by ethnic Hawaiians involved in the Hawaiian nationalist movement in the island state. Their kingdom had been destroyed with the complicity of the American government, their land occupied, and Hawaii was now a major military base for the U.S. and a playground for tourists from all over the world. Hawaiian nationalists, small in number but intense in feeling, claimed not only the right to survive as a culturally different group but also the right to a separate land base that they could control and that would be independent of the U.S. and recognized as a sovereign nation under international law. Although the congressionally appointed American Indian Policy Commission reasserted the principle of Indian self-determination and defined Indian tribes as "sovereign political bodies" in 1977, nothing comparable had ever been done for ethnic Hawaiians. Congress did create a Native Hawaiians Study Commission: a minority of its members called for restoration of the rights of Hawaiians to own common land and recognition of a relationship for ethnic Hawaiians to the American polity at least comparable to that of Native American Indian nations (Native Hawaiian Study Commission, *Report on the Culture, Needs and Concerns of Native Hawaiians,* submitted to the Committee on Energy and Natural Resources of the U.S. Senate, the Committee on Interior and Insular Affairs of the U.S. House of Representatives, vol. 2 (Honolulu: 1983).

84. John E. Rankin, a representative from Mississippi, argued that "the white man's civilization has come into conflict with Japanese barbarism" and that "Christianity has come into conflict with Shintoism, atheism, and infidelity," and concluded that "it is of vital importance that we get rid of every Japanese, whether in Hawaii or in the mainland" (Morton Grodzins, *Americans Betrayed: Politics and the Japanese Evacuation* [Chicago: University of Chicago Press, 1949], p. 86). The Supreme Court upheld the law imposing a curfew on Japanese-Americans, maintaining that the Court should not sit in review on the judgment of the military in time of war. The liberal Justice William O. Douglas wrote, "We must credit the military with as much good faith . . . as we would any other public official acting pursuant to his duties" (ibid., p. 353).

85. The Justice Department previously had petitioned a federal district court judge in San Francisco to set aside the conviction of one nisei who had been jailed and sentenced to five years' probation for failing to report to a center for evacuation to an internment camp, and the department acknowledged that his conviction was "part of an unfortunate episode in our nation's history." In another case, a district court judge overturned the conviction of a nisei because the government had suppressed evidence (*New York Times,* December 9, 1986, p. A23). Also see *New York Times,* June 21, 1985, p. A12.

86. See also *Summary of the Recommendations of the Commission on Wartime Relocation and Internment of Civilians,* Reprinted by the Library of Congress, Congressional Research Service, June 1983, pp. 7, 11.

87. Ibid., p. 12. The Japanese-American Evacuation Claims Act of 1984 gave persons of Japanese ancestry the right to claim from the government real and personal property losses that occurred as a consequence of the exclusion and evacuation, but the act provided nothing for lost income or any compensation for pain and suffering, and only about $37 million was paid in claims, an amount far below what would have been fair compensation for actual losses. Other federal and state legislation was passed to make amends, including a 1972 change in the Social Security Act providing that Japanese-Americans above the age of eighteen would be deemed to have earned and contributed to the Social Security system during their detention, and a 1977 amendment to the federal civil service retirement law to allow them civil service retirement credit for the time spent under detention orders. Each of these measures, and others taken by the state of California, acknowledged to some degree the wrongs inflicted during the war upon the Japanese. But the commission's recommendation that Congress and the president formally apologize and pay monetary compensation to those who had been wronged and still lived went far beyond the actions taken to that point.

    The commission's findings, and hearings in the House of Representatives on them, stirred additional activity in the states and localities. Washington state and the city of Seattle acted to reimburse public employees for lost wages. San Jose, California, created its own commission on the internment of local Japanese-Americans in order to document the experiences of Santa Clara Valley residents who had been interned, and its report was used to develop a curriculum for the city's high schools on the history of the internment. Katherine Bishop, "Settling a Debt from World War II," *New York Times,* February 16, 1986, Section 4, p. 4. Not all Japanese-Americans wanted their losses repaid through a congressional appropriation, but probably all of them sought a public apology from Congress and the president (Teresa Watanabe, "Redress Divides Japanese-Americans," *Los Angeles Times,* June 29, 1986, p. 12).

88. Robert Matsui is quoted in the *Boston Globe,* April 29, 1986, p. 8. The dilatory behavior of Congress in appropriating money to implement the payments caused Senator Daniel Inouye to speak to the Senate on September 28, 1989. Inouye also became tearful as he told his colleagues "what has been in my heart all these years" (Andrew Rosenthal, "Senate Would Speed Reparations to Survivors of Internment Camps," *New York Times,* September 30, 1989, p. 8). Representative Norman Y. Mineta, who, like Representative Matsui, had also been interned during the war, had pleaded earlier for Congress to keep faith with "those who had been wronged" (*New York Times,* July 18, 1989, p. A16).

89. David C. Ruffin, "The Reagan Court: Turning Back the Clock," *Focus,* July 1989, pp. 3, 4, for the view that 1989 decisions constituted a severe setback to civil rights. For the view that racial violence was increasing, see "Skinheads Lead Sharp Upswing in Racial Violence," *Law Report,* Southern Poverty Law Center, April 1989, p. 1. In fact, there were more cases of reported racial violence. In New York State, there was a growing backlog of discrimination complaints (Sam Howe Verhovek, "Case Backlog Is Swamping Rights Agency," *New York Times,* July 17, 1989, p. B7). It was unclear whether the increase in complaints was due to an actual increase in discrimination or to the willingness of more people to claim discrimination. It was also unclear whether the increase in reports of bigotry-motivated violence was due to better reporting systems and new laws or whether there actually was such an increase. In any case, public opinion polls

showed a marked decline in racist attitudes among whites even during the Reagan years. For example, the percentage of whites who said they believed blacks lacked the inborn ability to succeed intellectually and in other ways went down from 23 percent in 1981 to 14 percent in 1989. Whereas less than half of the whites surveyed thought it was wrong to refuse to sell their homes to blacks in 1981, three-quarters of the whites believed that it was wrong in 1989. A marked increase in cross-racial friendships was reported for the eight-year period (ABC's race relations survey, reported October 24, 1989).

90. James C. McKinley, Jr., "Minority Students Walk out over a Teacher's Remarks," *New York Times,* October 4, 1989, p. B3; Mireya Navarro, "Racial Tensions in New York Blamed for School Disruption," *New York Times,* October 5, 1989, p. B3. The white social studies teacher was reported as saying that American blacks were not sufficiently concerned about the subjugation of blacks in West African nations.

22. *"To Get Beyond Racism"*: *Integrating Education and Housing*

1. *Loving* v. *Virginia,* 338 U.S. 1010 (1967), p. 1017.
2. *Regents of the University of California* v. *Bakke,* 438 U.S. 265 (1978).
3. Ronald Takaki, "Reflections on Racial Patterns in America: An Historical Perspective," in Winston A. Van Horne, ed., *Ethnicity and Public Policy* (Milwaukee: University of Wisconsin System, American Ethnic Studies Coordinating Committee, 1982).
4. Terry Eastland and William J. Bennett, *Counting by Race: Equality from the Founding Fathers to Bakke and Weber* (New York: Basic Books, 1979); Nathan Glazer, *Affirmative Discrimination: Ethnic Inequality and Public Policy* (New York: Basic Books, 1975); and Nathan Glazer, *Ethnic Dilemmas* (Cambridge: Harvard University Press, 1983).
5. *Korematsu* v. *United States,* 323 U.S. 214 (1944), and *McLaughlin* v. *Florida,* 379 U.S. 184 (1964).
6. *Chronicle of Higher Education,* September 5, 1984, p. 1.
7. *The Robert Wood Johnson Minority Faculty Development Program,* pamphlet (Robert Wood Johnson Foundation, 1983).
8. Lori B. Miller, "Medical Schools Adding to Efforts on Minorities," *New York Times,* August 3, 1987, p. B3.
9. *Chronicle of Higher Education,* July 11, 1984, p. 2.
10. *Boston Globe,* August 5, 1984, pp. A103–104.
11. Edward B. Fiske, "Columbia to Pay Off Loans for Some Minority Students," *New York Times,* September 9, 1987, p. B1. The program was to be financed by income from a new endowment fund set up under a $25-million gift from John W. Kluge, chairman of Metromedia, Inc. The university also announced three other programs to be financed with income from the endowment. Academically able high school seniors from minority groups in fifteen cities were to be flown to New York to visit the Columbia campus along with their guidance counselors. Eight minority group undergraduates were to be designated as Kluge scholars, who would receive additional assistance in outright grants and some support in the form of jobs and loans. Funds were to be provided to minority group undergraduates for scholarly work in summer as an alternative to summer jobs.
12. *Editor and Publisher,* February 4, 1984, p. 23.
13. *Black Enterprise,* November 1983, p. 50.
14. *Black Enterprise,* December 1984, p. 24.

15. *Black Enterprise,* June 1985, pp. 222, 230.
16. *Black Enterprise,* December 1984, p. 24.
17. *Black Enterprise,* November 1983, p. 50.
18. Norman Hill and Leon Lynch, "Rustin Fought Quotas, Not Affirmative Action," *New York Times,* October 3, 1987, p. 26.
19. *Black Enterprise,* July 1985, pp. 36, 37.
20. *Black Enterprise,* November 1984, p. 32.
21. *Swann* v. *Charlotte Mecklenburg Board of Education,* 402 U.S. 1 (1971).
22. *Keyes* v. *School District No. 1, Denver,* 413 U.S. 189 (1973). In *Affirmative Discrimination,* Glazer was strongly critical of the blurring of the distinction between de jure and de facto school segregation, but the presumption that school segregation resulted in part from housing segregation that was caused in some measure by state action was not unreasonable. Glazer himself quotes former Attorney General Ramsey Clark as pointing out that the Federal Housing Authority required racially restricted covenants until 1948 (Glazer, *Affirmative Discrimination,* p. 93).
23. *Because It Is Right,* a report by the Governor's Commission on Racial Imbalance in the Public Schools of the Commonwealth of Massachusetts, 1964. The commission members, including the author, Richard Cardinal Cushing, and former Attorney General Edward McCormack, worked hard to produce an accurate and fair report. But none of us had children in the public schools of Boston.
24. *Milliken* v. *Bradley,* 418 U.S. 717 (1974). For a discussion of white flight, see "Educational Opportunity: Equal for Everyone?" *The American Experiment: E Pluribus Unum,* principal scholar Lawrence H. Fuchs (Newton, Mass.: Education Development Center, Inc., School and Society Programs, 1981), pp. 65–67.
25. Gary Orfield, "School Desegregation Needed Now: Support for Busing Grows but National Policy Has Been at a Stand-Still in the 1980s," *Focus,* the Joint Center for Political Studies, July 1987, p. 7. The most integrated were: Tampa–St. Petersburg, Florida; Wilmington, Delaware; Louisville, Kentucky; Greensboro, North Carolina; Indianapolis, Indiana; Columbus, Ohio; and Orlando, Florida.
26. Gary Orfield, *Public School Desegregation in the United States, 1968–1980* (Washington, D.C.: Joint Center for Political Studies, 1983), p. 40. The biggest reduction in segregation for Hispanics came in Austin, Texas, which implemented a major desegregation order, one of the few busing orders with the explicit goal of desegregating Hispanics (ibid., p. 5).
27. Lena Williams, "Desegregation Plans Said to Improve Race Balance in Schools," *New York Times,* May 20, 1987, p. A27. The Northeast, which was the most integrated in 1968, had become the most segregated by 1978. The results of desegregation in the South were extraordinary. In 1968, only 32 percent of southern blacks were in schools with whites. Ten years later, the percentage was 91 (Theodore M. Hesburgh, "The End of Apartheid in America," *George Washington Law Review* [January/March 1986], p. 250).
28. Orfield, "School Desegregation Needed Now," p. 6.
29. Christine H. Rossell and Willis D. Hawley, eds., *The Consequences of School Desegregation* (Philadelphia: Temple University Press, 1983), pp. 5–7. Integration worked best in large high schools with substantial minority populations, where students came from a variety of class and ethnic backgrounds. One such school was New Rochelle High School in New Rochelle, New York (1,850 students in 1987, 30 percent black and 5 percent Hispanic). Honors classes were overwhelmingly white, but black parents and students spoke glowingly of opportunities to participate in honors classes and to have access to good equipment and be taught by excellent teachers. Most of the students who were suspended were black (Sara

Riemer, "At 2 Schools, Stubborn Racial Divisions: In Suburbs, Mixed Results," *New York Times*, March 30, 1987, pp. A1–B4).

30. "Desegregated Schools Linked to College-Going by Blacks," *Chronicle of Higher Education*, October 30, 1985, p. 18. The study was made by the Rand Corporation and showed that 33 percent of the black male students who started attending desegregated schools in 1966 were enrolled full-time in college in 1982, while only 13 percent of their peers from segregated schools were in college. Also see Orfield, "School Desegregation Needed Now," pp. 6, 7.

31. Joe Mills, Henry Braddock II, Robert L. Crain, and James M. McPartland, "A Long-Term View of School Desegregation: Some Recent Studies of Graduates as Adults," *Phi Delta Kappan* (December 1984), pp. 260, 261. By 1978, most white adults expected that most children would, as a matter of course, be attending desegregated schools within five years (Jennifer L. Hochschild, *Thirty Years After Brown*, Joint Center for Political Studies, Washington, D.C., 1985, p. 14. Also see Hochschild on the benefits of successful desegregation, pp. 34, 35).

32. Neil R. Pierce and Jerry Hagstrom, *The Book of America: Inside Fifty States Today* (New York: W. W. Norton, 1983), pp. 464, 465. The percentage of blacks who wanted the federal government to ensure school desegregation actually decreased from 75 percent in 1964 to 60 percent in 1978, according to one survey, and a minority of black educators and journalists wrote critically about busing (Hochschild, *Thirty Years After Brown*, p. 11).

33. Orfield, "School Desegregation Needed Now," p. 6.

34. "Nashville: A Different Step for Desegregation," *Education U.S.A.*, June 2, 1980, reprinted in "Educational Opportunity: Equal for Everyone?" *The American Experiment: E Pluribus Unum*, p. 77.

35. David L. Kirp, *Just Schools: The Ideal of Racial Equality in American Education* (Berkeley: University of California Press, 1982), p. 7. Implementation of desegregation plans varied extensively because they resulted from different actions; many derived from court orders, others from federal, state, and local initiatives. Chicago, which could not do much integrating because of demographic limitations, negotiated an agreement that called for improvement in schools destined to stay black. Seattle adopted a modest busing plan and enlarged it on the initiative of the city itself. Cleveland was told by a federal district court that its plan to comply with desegregation was a failure, and the court took over the management of the system, just as a federal judge had done in Boston. Some desegregation plans were effectuated smoothly, as in Berkeley; others, as in Los Angeles, were badly managed and resulted in the departure of large numbers of white students from the public schools.

36. "Integration by Magnets," *Time*, June 15, 1975, reprinted in "Educational Opportunity: Equal for Everyone?" *The American Experiment: E Pluribus Unum*, p. 82; E. R. Shipp, "Cincinnati School Pact Embraced as a 'Model,'" *New York Times*, February 17, 1984, p. 4. To achieve integration, the state agreed to contribute $35 million in addition to regular budgetary allocations to the Cincinnati schools.

37. Ellen Coughlin, *Chronicle of Higher Education*, May 16, 1984, pp. 1, 14, 15. The best-known example of a voluntary metropolitan remedy was the "Wisconsin plan," which promoted interdistrict transfers by having the state pay for the transfer of students between schools and school districts to promote cultural and racial integration in education. All transfers were voluntary, however, and by 1980, when implementation of the plan was at its height, approximately one thousand children were exchanged between city and suburbs (U.S. Commission on Civil Rights, *School Desegregation in the St. Louis and Kansas City Areas:*

Metropolitan Interdistrict Options (Washington, D.C.: U.S. Government Printing Office, January 1981), p. 14. The report was prepared by the Missouri Advisory Committee to the U.S. Commission on Civil Rights.

38. "Suit on School Desegregation Against Milwaukee Has Begun," *New York Times,* May 21, 1987, p. A20. The headline is inaccurate, since Milwaukee initiated the suit against the suburbs.

39. Diego Ribadeneira, "Cambridge Desegregation Plan Praised," *Boston Sunday Globe,* April 5, 1987, p. 42. So successful was the plan that only five of the city's thirteen elementary schools had a minority enrollment of more than 50 percent. More than 90 percent of Cambridge students were placed in one of their top three choices and 70 percent in their first in 1987. Cambridge had achieved more voluntary desegregation than any school system in the state, with 62 percent of the students attending schools of choice outside their neighborhoods.

40. Edward B. Fiske, "School Integration Patterns Change," *New York Times,* June 23, 1988, p. A16. The information came from a study by Gary Orfield, *Racial Change and Desegregation in Large School Districts* (Washington, D.C.: The National School Boards Association, 1988). The typical Hispanic public school student attended a school that was 53 percent Hispanic, 30 percent black, 12 percent white, and 5 percent Asian. Asian students went to the most integrated schools; a typical Asian went to a school 30 percent white, 23 percent Asian, 28 percent Hispanic, and 19 percent black. The typical black student attended a school 60 percent black; Hispanics and Asians represented a significant part of the remaining 40 percent.

41. Alan R. Gold, "Boston Ready to Overhaul School Busing Policy," *New York Times,* December 28, 1988, p. B8.

42. Andrea Adelson, "Desegregation Law Suit Ending after Twenty-Five Years," *New York Times,* June 22, 1988.

43. Orfield, *Public School Desegregation in the U.S.,* pp. 12–20. The percentage of Hispanic students in predominantly minority schools rose from 55 to 68 percent between 1968 and 1980.

44. Ibid., p. 20.

45. Elizabeth Kolbert, "A New York Report Says Racism Creates Two School Systems," *New York Times,* October 22, 1988, pp. 1, 32. The primary recommendation of the task force was that the state education aid formula be revised to favor poorer school districts.

46. Lydia Chavez, "Two Bronx Schools: Study in Inequality," *New York Times,* July 2, 1987, pp. A1, B2. Poor schools throughout the Bronx had almost twice as many inexperienced teachers as the relatively well-to-do schools. The poorer schools were crowded. They operated at 140 percent of capacity, compared to 100 percent for the middle-class schools. The well-to-do schools received as much maintenance money as the poorer schools, which needed it much more. The most important attack on the system came in 1989, when the Texas Supreme Court ruled that the state system for financing public schools was unconstitutional because of the enormous gap in the quality of education between rich and poor schools. Nine other states also faced lawsuits or court orders concerning school financing: Alaska, Connecticut, Indiana, Minnesota, Montana, New Jersey, North Dakota, Oregon, and Tennessee. Since there was no federal constitutional right to establishing school districts that were financed equally, and since it was highly unlikely that legislatures would act on their own to equalize educational opportunities between rich and poor school districts, the only hope for significant change lay in the state courts. For a review of the challenges in nine states, see

Edward B. Fiske, "Historic Shift Seen in School Finance," *New York Times*, October 4, 1989, p. B9.

47. 42 U.S.C. No. 3601-19, 3631. The only exemptions to the Fair Housing Act were "single family homes sold or rented without the use of a broker and without discriminatory advertising; homes or units in dwellings containing living quarters for no more than four families provided that the owner lived in one of them and did not advertise or use a broker; and rooms in private clubs not open to the public." For a review of the implementation of the act in its first ten years, see U.S. Commission on Civil Rights, *The Federal Fair Housing Enforcement Effort* (Washington, D.C.: U.S. Government Printing Office, March 1979).

48. Harry M. Rosen and David H. Rosen, *But Not Next Door* (New York: Ivan Oblensky, Inc., 1962); Rose Helper, *Racial Policies and Practices of Real Estate Brokers* (Minneapolis: University of Minnesota Press, 1969); Arnold Hirsch, *Making the Second Ghetto* (Cambridge: Cambridge University Press, 1983); and Frank F. Lee, *Negro and White in a Connecticut Town* (New York: Bookman Associates, 1961).

49. John Lescott-Leszczynski, *The History of U.S. Ethnic Policy and Its Impact on European Ethnics* (Boulder, Colo.: Westview Press, 1984), p. 114.

50. *Devastation/Resurrection: The South Bronx* (New York: Bronx Museum of Arts, 1979), pp. 39–42.

51. Ibid., pp. 40–43.

52. Ibid., p. 54.

53. Mary T. Clark, *Discrimination Today: Guidelines for Civic Action* (New York: Hobbs, Dorman and Company, Inc., 1966), p. 127.

54. These practices are described in detail in Charles Bullock III and Charles M. Lamb, *Implementation of Civil Rights Policy* (Monterey, Calif.: Brookes/Cole Publishing Company, 1984).

55. Ibid., p. 38.

56. Roger Witherspoon with S. Lee Hilliard, "No Trespassing!" *Black Enterprise*, May 1985, p. 44. The realtors agreed to advertise the homes for sale in minority media and to send notice of all available housing to minority groups; to hire minority salesmen; and to state a realistic percentage of homes that they felt members of minority groups should be able to purchase.

57. Ibid.

58. Ibid., p. 42.

59. Karl Taeuber of the Center for Demography and Ecology at the University of Wisconsin measured the index of segregation on a continuum from blocks 100 percent black to those 0 percent black. The three cities with the most progress toward integrating neighborhoods were Jacksonville, Richmond, and Nashville (ibid., p. 40).

60. The Dallas stories are discussed in Annika Schildt, "Desegregating Public Housing: Deciphering Public Policy," senior honors thesis, Brandeis University, April 1986, p. 52.

61. "Housing Segregation: Newest Patterns Produce Old Results," *New York Times*, April 1, 1987, pp. B1, B4.

62. John Herbers, "Housing Barriers are Proving Hard to Pull Down," *New York Times*, December 1, 1985, p. E3.

63. Jerry Ackerman, "Easier Access: Officials Optimistic More Minorities are Finding Low-Income Housing in Suburbs," *Boston Globe*, January 27, 1988, p. 21. Under pressure of threats, agreements were sometimes negotiated by voluntary fair housing organizations, as in Quincy, Massachusetts, when litigation initiated by two black plaintiffs in 1982 resulted in a consent decree negotiated by the Greater

Boston Legal Services to place minorities in 25 percent of new public housing, with an independent monitor to oversee compliance. By 1988, the Quincy Housing Authority reported that 11 percent of the agency's 619 family units were occupied by minorities (mostly Asian), compared to 2.3 percent in 1982 (Jerry Taylor, "Quincy Agrees: Minorities to Get 25% of Rentals," *Boston Globe*, March 26, 1985, p. 1).

But a fair-housing test conducted in Framingham by the Massachusetts Commission Against Discrimination uncovered evidence of widespread discrimination against blacks, Hispanics, and poor women, who were steered away from rental properties or discouraged from applying for apartments (Diane E. Lewis, "Fair Housing Test Finds Bias," *Boston Globe*, November 17, 1988, p. 27). The pace of integration was slowed by the failure of communities to build low- and moderate-income housing. By 1988, only 28 of the state's 351 cities and towns met the targets set for them by law nearly twenty years after the legislation had been passed (Andrew J. Dabilis, "Many Communities Lag on Affordable Housing," *Boston Globe*, November 15, 1988, p. 1).

64. Michael T. Kaufman, "Forest Hills: From Rage to Tranquility," *New York Times*, September 15, 1988, pp. B1, B6.

65. Howard Kurtz, "Yonkers Housing Policy Cited in the School Bias Ruling," *Boston Globe*, November 21, 1985, p. 1. A plan that would have settled the case earlier had been approved by the board of education, but the Yonkers city council refused to finance the plan, which called for desegregation of the city's schools and creation of magnet schools.

66. James Feron, "High Court Rules and Yonkers Crisis Intensifies," *New York Times*, September 3, 1988, p. 26; James Feron, "Two Council Members in Yonkers Shift Stand on Housing," *New York Times*, September 10, 1988, pp. 1, 32. A federal appeals court set $1 million a day as the ceiling on the Yonkers fine. The U.S. Supreme Court suspended the penalties against the council members pending the submission of a request that the high court hear an argument on the constitutionality of the fines.

67. John Herbers, "Use of Private Suits in Housing Bias Cases in Federal Courts is Increasing," *New York Times*, February 16, 1986, p. 36.

68. *Fair Housing Newsletter*, Education/Instruction, Inc., Boston, Mass., July 1984, pp. 10, 11.

69. *New York Times*, November 11, 1984, p. 24. Under the Oak Park plan, the apartment was kept off the market if a tenant was not found immediately. For the first thirty days, the owner received no rent, but in the next ninety days he or she received 80 percent of the last rent received on the unit, and if the apartment had not been rented at the end of 120 days, the housing center and the landlord would have to agree on whether to continue the arrangement.

70. Schildt, "Desegregating Public Housing," pp. 65–72.

71. Ibid., p. 116.

72. Ibid., chapter 5.

73. The issue of affordable housing affected blacks and Puerto Ricans disproportionately because so many of them were poor and lived in cities. From 1937, when the first housing act was passed, until the Reagan years, the federal government had steadily increased its involvement in the development of affordable housing. Until the 1950s, all aid was in the form of public housing programs owned and operated by the government. The growth in publicly supported housing did not come until the 1970s, as HUD's housing-assistance budgets grew from $13 billion in 1975 to a peak of $32 billion in 1981, the last budget of President Jimmy Carter. Under Reagan, federal funds available for public housing fell sharply. Early programs provided for low-interest repayments for low-income families and for

interest payment supplements to developers and owners of housing built for low-income tenants. The major program, Section VIII under the Housing Act, provided for construction of new apartments as well as for rent supplements to families in existing housing. In the mid-1980s, Section VIII was seen by the Reagan administration as too expensive and was replaced by a system of vouchers given to the qualifying poor, which was supposed to cover the difference between the amount they paid for housing (up to 30 percent of their income) and the fair market rent established by HUD. Disagreements as to the best method of promoting affordable housing continued into the end of the decade, but there was no disagreement that the amount of such housing for the poor had shrunk substantially (Ann Mariano, "Does Reagan Want to Kill Housing Aid?" *Washington Post National Weekly Edition,* December 9, 1985, p. 6.

74. Leonard Buder, "Race Quotas Voided at Brooklyn Housing Complex," *New York Times,* May 6, 1987, pp. A1, B2; George James, "Starrett Residents Fault Decision Barring Quotas," *New York Times,* May 7, 1987, p. B3. The distribution of tenants in 1987 was 8.5 percent Hispanic, 5 percent Asian, 22 percent black, and the rest white. For an excellent discussion of the dilemma that Starrett City posed, see Jefferson Morley, "Double Reverse Discrimination," *New Republic,* July 29, 1985, pp. 14–18. Also see Linda Greenhouse, "High Court Voids Quotas on Races in Housing Units," *New York Times,* November 8, 1988, p. 1, and John Kifner, "Starrett City's Nightmare: End of Quotas," *New York Times,* November 14, 1988, p. B1.

75. William K. Stevens, "Scattered Low-Cost Housing Offers Renewed Hope to Poor and Minorities," *New York Times,* September 15, 1988, p. B6. The approach in Rockville called for purchase by a quasi-public body, the Housing Opportunities Commission, of 600 of more than 2,500 units built for low- and moderate-income families to provide low-interest financing.

23. *"To Get Beyond Racism": Political Access and Economic Opportunity*

1. Abigail M. Thernstrom, *Whose Votes Count? Affirmative Action and Minority Voting Rights,* a Twentieth Century Fund Study (Cambridge: Harvard University Press, 1987), p. 44.

2. Ibid., pp. 34–52. Thernstrom casts doubt on allegations of historic disenfranchisement of Mexican-Americans by whites, pointing out that Mexican-Americans usually held county offices, even in Texas, where there was a large Mexican-American voting-age population, a situation vastly different from that of blacks in the South (ibid., p. 56). Economic pressures, harassment, and intimidation against Mexican-Americans undoubtedly kept some from participating freely in politics.

3. Ibid., pp. 77, 80. The amendments passed by overwhelming margins of 389 to 24 in the House of Representatives and 86 to 8 in the Senate.

4. Peyton McCrairy, "Taking History to Court," *Focus,* The Joint Center for Political Studies, January 1988, pp. 4, 5, 8. After falling into disuse in the early 1980s, the intent standard was revived again toward the end of the decade as plaintiffs, with the help of historians, learned how to gather evidence of discriminatory intent.

5. Frank R. Parker, "The Voting Rights Act: Twenty Years Later," *Focus,* The Joint Center for Political Studies, August 1985, p. 5.

6. Lesley Oelsner, "U.S. High Court Backs Use of Racial Quotas for Voting Districts," *New York Times,* March 2, 1977, p. A1.

7. Thernstrom, *Whose Vote Counts?* pp. 158, 171. By June 1984, a total of 77,227 voting changes had been submitted to the attorney general.

8. Ibid., pp. 243, 244.

9. Robert Smith is quoted in *Focus*, May 1987, p. 4.
10. Thernstrom, *Whose Votes Count?* pp. 211–227. An outstanding example was the mayoral election in East Chicago, Indiana, in 1983, when the white incumbent took every Hispanic ward and a majority of the black vote even though a black lawyer was running, in a city 45 percent Hispanic and 30 percent black. At least a dozen examples of blacks being elected by white votes were cited.
11. "Voting Rights Cases: An Uphill Battle," MALDEF, January 1988, p. 2.
12. Ronald Smothers, "Suit Seeks to Alter Voting System in Birmingham," *New York Times*, November 10, 1987, p. A28.
13. *Boston Sunday Globe*, December 23, 1984, p. A21.
14. *Dupuy H. Anderson, et al., v. Wade O. Martin, Jr.* 375 U.S. 399 (1964), p. 433.
15. Thernstrom, *Whose Votes Count?* p. 122.
16. The conversations of freedmen with General Sherman and Secretary Stanton were reported in "The Freedmen in Georgia: Minutes of an Interview Between the Colored Ministers and Church Officers at Savannah with the Secretary of War and Major Gen. Sherman," *The National Freedman*, The New England Freedmen's Society, January 1865, p. 1.
17. For a full discussion of the evolution of the application of affirmative action, see Terry Eastland and William J. Bennett, *Counting by Race: Equality from the Founding Fathers to Bakke and Weber* (New York: Basic Books, 1979), pp. 131, 132ff. Also see Nathan Glazer, *Affirmative Discrimination: Ethnic Inequality and Public Policy* (New York: Basic Books, 1975), chapter 2.

   The designation of protected classes came mainly as a result of executive orders pursuant to civil rights legislation. The first and probably most important executive order was 11246 (Equal Employment Opportunity) in 1965. Then came 11478 (Equal Employment Opportunity in the Federal Government) in 1969; and 11764 (Nondiscrimination in Federally Assisted Programs) in 1974. Although the Civil Rights Act was enacted with blacks in mind, the Department of Labor and other agencies typically began to list Hispanics, Asians, Pacific Islanders, and American Indians or Alaskan natives as classes designated to receive the benefits of affirmative action in addition to blacks.
18. John Lescott-Leszczynski, *The History of U.S. Ethnic Policy and Its Impact on European Ethnics* (Boulder, Colo.: Westview Press, 1984), pp. 141, 145. The Office of Minority Business Enterprise was reorganized in 1979 into the Minority Business Development Agency.
19. Ibid., p. 146.
20. Dirk Johnson, "Women and Minorities Compete for Share of Highway Contracts," *New York Times*, March 5, 1988, p. 1. Congress also required the Defense Department to award 5 percent of its contracts to minority businesses and colleges (Edwin Dorn, "New Law Sets D.O.D. Contracting Goal," *Focus*, January 1987, pp. 5, 8). An escape hatch was provided for the Defense Department; it could avoid the requirement "for compelling national security" reasons.
21. Glazer, *Affirmative Discrimination*, chapter 2.
22. *Marco DeFunis et al. v. Charles Odegaard*, 416 U.S. 312 (1974), 40 L Ed 2d 164.
23. In a five-to-four decision, the case was declared moot because DeFunis attended law school after the Superior Court of King County, Washington, ordered him admitted. The only reason the case came before the U.S. Supreme Court was that the Supreme Court of Washington reversed the ruling. But by the time the U.S. Supreme Court was ready to rule, DeFunis was in his last quarter in law school. Four justices dissented, arguing that the case should not be considered moot, since any number of events might prevent the plaintiff's graduation at the end of the current school year, and he might once again be faced with the

law school's allegedly unlawful admissions policy. Only Justice Douglas expressed his views on the merits of the case, concluding that it should be remanded for a new trial to consider whether DeFunis had suffered invidious discrimination because of his race.

24. Ibid., pp. 183, 184.
25. Ibid., pp. 179, 183.
26. *United Steelworkers of America* v. *Weber*, 443 U.S. 193 (1979).
27. *Fullilove* v. *Klutznick*, 448 U.S. 448 (1981).
28. *Local 28, the Sheet Metal Workers* v. *Equal Employment Opportunity Commission*, 478 U.S. 421 (1986).
29. *Local 93 of the International Association of Firefighters* v. *City of Cleveland*, 478 U.S. 501 (1986).
30. Ibid.
31. *U.S.* v. *Paradise*, 48 U.S. 149 (1987).
32. *Johnson* v. *Transportation Agency, Santa Clara, California*, 480 U.S. 616 (1987).
33. *Regents of the University of California* v. *Bakke*, 438 U.S. 265 (1978).
34. *Firefighters Local Union No. 1784* v. *Stotts*, 464 U.S. 808 (1984).
35. *Wygant* v. *Jackson Board of Education*, 476 U.S. 267 (1986).
36. Excerpts of the opinions of the Supreme Court justices in *Croson* v. *Virginia* appeared in the *New York Times*, January 24, 1989, p. A16. For follow-up stories, see Martin Tolchin, "Officials in Cities and States Vow to Continue Minority Contractor Programs," *New York Times*, January 25, 1989, p. 18; Linda Greenhouse, "Signal on Job Rights: Court Doesn't Bar Affirmative Action, but Holds Plans to a Stringent Test," *New York Times*, January 25, 1989, pp. A1, A18; and B. Drummond Ayres, Jr., "Court Ruling Is a Bitter Irony for Richmond Blacks," *New York Times*, January 25, 1989, p. A18. The striking down of the Richmond set-aside program led other cities such as Atlanta to redraft their own program to meet the requirements set forth by the Supreme Court. Atlanta's program was struck down by the Georgia Supreme Court, but Atlanta felt it would have little trouble in drafting a program that demonstrated past discrimination ("Atlanta: Keeping Affirmative Action Alive," *Black Enterprise*, September 1989, p. 48).
37. In insisting on strict scrutiny of race-conscious programs, the Court showed that it was sensitive to the possibilities of the potential abuse of such programs and of reverse discrimination stemming from them. In 1989, it stretched the ability of white workers to obtain relief from such discrimination in a five-to-four ruling that court-approved counting-by-race settlements may be subject to legal complaint by white workers after the settlement had been put into effect. In this case, white firefighters in Birmingham, Alabama, were permitted to challenge a consent decree under which the fire department had settled a discrimination suit by agreeing to hire and promote more blacks (*Martin* v. *Wilks*, No. 87-1614 [1989]).
38. For a strong attack on counting by race, see Thomas W. Sowell, *Civil Rights: Rhetoric or Reality* (New York: Morrow, 1984). Also see Glazer, *Affirmative Discrimination*, and Robert M. O'Neil, *Discriminating Against Discrimination* (Bloomington: Indiana University Press, 1975). The philosophical case against goals and timetables may also be found in Eastland and Bennett, *Counting by Race*. A book-length attempt to develop a philosophical justification for counting by race through goals and timetables can be found in Robert K. Fullinwider, *The Reverse Discrimination Controversy: A Moral and Legal Analysis* (Totowa, N.J.: Rowman and Littlefield, 1980). See also Ronald Takaki, "Reflections on Racial Patterns in America: An Historical Perspective," in Winston A. Van Horne and Thomas V. Tonnesen, eds., *Ethnicity and Public Policy* (Madison: University of Wisconsin Press, 1982); and Marcy C. Segers, "Justifying Affirmative Action," in James C. Foster and Mary C. Segers, *Elusive Equality: Liberalism, Affirmative Action and*

Social Change in America (Port Washington, N.Y.: National University Publications, Association Faculty Press, 1983).

39. William Julius Wilson, *The Declining Significance of Race: Blacks and Changing American Institutions* (Chicago: University of Chicago Press, 1978), p. 103. Also see Finis Welch, "Affirmative Action and Discrimination," in Steven Shulman and William Darity, Jr., eds., *The Question of Discrimination* (Middletown, Conn., Wesleyan University Press, 1989).

40. William M. Taylor, "Affirmative Action in the United States," paper prepared for the International Conference on Affirmative Action, Bellagio, Italy, August 16–18, 1982, p. 32.

41. Wilson, *Declining Significance of Race*, p. 101.

42. Ibid., p. 103.

43. Potomac Institute, *A Decade of Opportunity: Affirmative Action in the 1970s* (Washington, D.C.: Potomac Institute, 1984), p. 39.

44. Ibid., pp. 43, 44.

45. "Progress Report on the Black Executive: the Top Spots Are Still Elusive," *Business Week,* February 24, 1984, p. 104.

46. *Washington Post,* April 11, 1982, p. A10.

47. Ibid.

48. *Indianapolis Star,* June 4, 1985.

49. *Black Americans in Defense of Our Nation,* Office of the Deputy Assistant Secretary of Defense for Equal Opportunity and Safety Policy, Department of Defense, 1982, pp. 46, 47.

50. Charles V. Willie, *Chronicle of Higher Education,* May 16, 1984, p. 12. See also U.S. Commission on Civil Rights, *Equal Opportunity: Affirmative Admissions Programs at Law and Medical Schools* (Washington, D.C.: U.S. Government Printing Office, 1978), pp. 74–75; *Journal of Medical Education* 51 (August 1976): 692; and *Journal of Medical Education* 55 (December 1980): 1042.

51. *A Study of Attitudes Toward Racial and Religious Minorities and Toward Women,* prepared for The National Conference of Christians and Jews, conducted by Louis Harris and Associates, Inc., 1978, pp. 15, 18.

52. Report of the National Advisory Commission on Civil Disorders, special introduction by Tom Wicker (New York: Bantam Books, 1968).

53. *New York Times,* July 10, 1984, p. A16.

54. *Washington Post National Weekly Edition,* October 7, 1985, p. 38. Surveys conducted by the Gallup organization show that between the 1960s and 1980s blacks became more satisfied with their lives. In 1963, 68 percent of whites and 38 percent of blacks said they were satisfied with their incomes, a gap of thirty points. By 1985, the spread was down to twenty points, with 65 percent of whites and 45 percent of blacks saying they were satisfied with their family incomes. In 1963, 76 percent of whites and only 43 percent of blacks—a gap of thirty-three points—said they were satisfied with their housing. By 1985, 83 percent of whites and 70 percent of blacks expressed satisfaction with their housing. Seventy-one percent of whites and 55 percent of blacks were satisfied with their jobs or the work they did in 1985, whereas twenty-two years earlier 90 percent of whites but only 54 percent of blacks were satisfied (*Washington Post National Weekly Edition,* March 4, 1985), p. 38). An earlier, 1978, finding from a *New York Times*/CBS poll showed that although 35 percent of blacks surveyed said they had grown up in lower-class homes, only 17 percent saw themselves as belonging to the lower class today, indicating some strong personal psychological mobility (*New York Times,* April 24, 1978, pp. 1, 3). A national survey in 1989 showed some slippage in the confidence of blacks that life for African-Americans was generally improving: 47

percent of blacks said the quality of life for black Americans had improved in the previous ten years; 60 percent had reported that in 1981. Whites in the survey tended to agree: 69 percent in 1989 said conditions had improved for blacks during the past decade, down from 77 percent in 1981. Clearly, the Reagan years were not viewed as a period of marked progress, compared to the previous decade. The questions cited above dealt with perceptions. The same survey and another national survey actually revealed a marked decline in racial prejudice and considerable progress in integration during the 1980s ("There's Still Room for Improvement in Racial Relations," *Washington Post National Weekly Edition,* October 30–November 5, 1989, p. 37).

55. Kenneth E. John, "Most People Don't Agree with the Justices on Affirmative Action," *Washington Post National Weekly Edition,* June 29, 1987, p. 37. The question asked was: "The U.S. Supreme Court recently ruled that employers may sometimes favor women and members of minorities over better qualified men and whites in hiring and promoting to achieve better balance in their work forces. Do you approve or disapprove of this decision?" Twenty-nine percent approved, 63 percent disapproved, and 8 percent expressed no opinion.

56. "Most in Poll Back Affirmative Action," *Boston Globe,* October 14, 1988, p. 7. This poll was conducted by the Louis Harris organization.

57. *Black Enterprise,* November 1983, p. 24. Several states adopted measures to guard against misrepresentation. Such laws made explicit the crime of hiring a black, a Hispanic, an Asian, or a woman to serve as a front for an enterprise actually controlled by others.

58. *Boston Globe,* February 28, 1985, p. 21.

59. Robert Pear, "U.S. Urged to End Aid to Businesses Run by Minorities," *New York Times,* April 8, 1988, pp. A1, A23.

60. "Setbacks for Minority Aid," *New York Times,* May 18, 1987, p. D2. Neither case dealt with the constitutionality of federal laws to establish set-asides in letting of contracts or subsidizing of business. Both decisions rested on the ground that local jurisdictions have no competence to address the subtle questions of inequity in society by such race-conscious remedies, amounting to quotas.

61. Peter S. Canellos, "Race Fraud Triggers Memories of Discord," *Boston Globe,* November 1, 1988, p. 15. In 1974, when a U.S. district court judge ruled that the standard fire-fighting exam discriminated against minorities, only 19 of more than 2,100 Boston fire fighters were black or Hispanic. By 1988, 21 percent were black or Hispanic, compared to 29 percent of Boston's population. In Los Angeles, where teachers were assigned to schools on the basis of their race and ethnicity, several started to claim new skin colors and ancestries to avoid reassignment. As a consequence, the Los Angeles board of education set up an ethnic review committee of five members, two of whom had to be from the race or ethnic background that the person requesting the change wished to change from and three from the race or ethnic background that he or she wished to change to (Eastland and Bennett, *Counting by Race,* pp. 168–169).

62. Howard W. French, "Wedtech's Challenge: Monsoon of Evidence," *New York Times,* July 24, 1988, p. 20.

63. Lena Williams, "Minority Contracts Program: Achievement Despite Scandal," *New York Times,* May 12, 1987, p. A20.

64. Douglass to Major Martin Delany, quoted in Philip S. Foner, ed., *The Life and Writings of Frederick Douglass* (New York: International Publishers, 1935), 4:280, 281.

65. Jonathan M. Chu, letter to the *Boston Globe,* January 15, 1985, p. 14.

66. For a full discussion of the Santa Clara case, see U.S. Commission on Civil

Rights, *Toward an Understanding of Johnson,* Clearing House Publication No. 94 (Washington, D.C., October 1987).

67. Glen C. Loury, "Goals or Quotas," *Washington Post National Weekly Edition,* March 26, 1986, p. 5.

68. Richard Rodriguez, *Hunger of Memory: The Education of Richard Rodriguez* (Boston: David R. Godine, 1982). pp. 151–153.

69. George Scher, "Justifying Reverse Discrimination," in Marshall Cohen and Thomas Scanlon, eds., *Equality and Preferential Treatment* (Princeton, N.J.: Princeton University Press, 1977), p. 163. For another vigorous defense of counting by race, see Herbert Hill, "Black Labor and Affirmative Action: An Historical Perspective," in Shulman and Darity, eds., *Question of Discrimination,* pp. 190–267.

70. The Santa Clara case gave a signal to companies that their written affirmative action plans, including hiring goals and timetables, were supported even by the Reagan Supreme Court. Such plans were extensively used by corporate America and private businesses. Nearly 70 percent of all manufacturing firms and over 60 percent of nonmanufacturing firms employed numerical goals and timetables. After the Richmond decision was handed down, the National Minority Supplier Development Council, Inc., said that although contractors would lose some public-sector contracts, minority suppliers would turn to private industry ("Affirmative Action," *Black Enterprise,* September 1989, p. 46).

71. Thomas Sowell, "The Civil Rights Industry's Misguided Ideas about Blacks," *Washington Post National Weekly Edition,* August 20, 1984, p. 23. One black mother in California was insulted and believed her son deprived of real opportunity when she was informed that he could not be given an intelligence test because the federal courts had ruled such tests racially and culturally biased. The absurdity of counting by race in this instance was made plain when educational officials encouraged her to bypass the test ban by declaring her son to be a Latino, since she was Hispanic, although he had identified himself as a black and his father was black. From her point of view, her son's right to compete had been denied (Jay Matthews, "A Mother Challenges California's Ban on IQ Tests for Blacks," *Washington Post National Weekly Edition,* July 20, 1987, p. 34).

72. Lescott-Leszczynski, *History of U.S. Ethnic Policy,* p. 141.

73. *Boston Globe,* October 8, 1985, p. 83.

74. This story was followed in the *New York Times,* August 31, 1984, pp. 1, B3, and November 18, 1985, p. A1.

75. Col. Wade S. Gatling, "Black Fliers," *Focus,* January 1985, pp. 1, 3–4A.

76. Beverly P. Cole, "Testing Blacks Out of Education and Employment," *Crisis,* November 1984, pp. 9, 10.

77. Failure generates the expectation of failure, continuing a vicious cycle that, according to a black sociologist and physician, can be broken only when blacks "overcome our fears, encourage competition, and support the kind of performance that will dispel the notion of black intellectual inferiority." This challenge sounds as if the authors were blaming the victims, but they acknowledged that many whites, including teachers and managers, perpetuated expectations of black inferiority. They did not discount the residual effects of discrimination or the subtle pressures of continuing racism. But they called upon blacks to learn to compete in tests and not to accept the status of victim. "Teachers, parents and other authority figures must encourage young blacks to attribute their intellectual success to ability (thereby boosting confidence) and their failure to lack of effort" (Jeff Howard and Ray Hammond, "Rumors of Inferiority: The Hidden Obstacles to Black Success," *New Republic,* September 9, 1985, p. 21).

78. *Indianapolis Star,* June 8, 1985, p. 1.
79. *Boston Globe,* February 27, 1985, p. 24.
80. *Chronicle of Higher Education,* February 28, 1985, p. 20.
81. Fox Butterfield, "Why Asians Are Going to the Head of the Class," *New York Times,* August 3, 1986, section 12, pp. 18–23. Asians, who were performing well in school, presented a problem because they invariably were included in the beneficiary classes and could be counted toward achieving numerical goals for all minorities, even though the average SAT scores for Asian-Americans in the 1980s was higher than for any other major population group.
82. William A. Clement, Jr., and A. Vernon Weave, Decision in the matter of: Application of Opportunity Development Association and Others for designation of Hasidic Jews as a socially and economically disadvantaged group pursuant to 13 C.F.R., Paragraph 124, 1-1(c) (3) (iii), Small Business Administration, April 9, 1980.
83. Arnold Shankman, *Ambivalent Friends: Afro-Americans View the Immigrants* (Westport, Conn.: Greenwood Press, 1982), pp. 76, 156.
84. *Morton* v. *Mancari,* 417 U.S. 538 (1974).
85. These data are from the work of economist Barry Chiswick, reported in *Working Women,* July 1986, p. 54. On disparities in wealth between white and black women, see the report of the U.S. Census Bureau study on wealth in the U.S., *New York Times,* July 19, 1986, p. 1.
86. Judy Goldsmith, "Testimony of the National Organization for Women" before the U.S. Commission on Civil Rights, March 6–7, 1985, in *Selected Affirmative Action Topics in Employment and Business Set-Asides* (Washington, D.C.: U.S. Government Printing Office, 1985), 1:228ff. As late as 1982, 46 percent of all employed women worked at only four occupations: clerks, hairdressers, saleswomen, and waitresses; by 1983, only 7 percent held managerial jobs.
87. Economist Victor Fuchs showed that trends in the feminization of poverty between 1959 and 1984 were much more severe for black women than for white women, but that in both cases "the feminization of poverty that did occur was *not* the result of worsening labor market conditions for women in comparison with men." Rather, the increase in the proportion of women in single-parent (overwhelmingly female) households was the principal source of the feminization of poverty and a major reason why the trend was more adverse for blacks than for whites (Victor R. Fuchs, *The Feminization of Poverty?,* Working Paper No. 1934, National Bureau of Economic Research, Inc., May 1986, pp. 10, 11, 19.
88. Robert B. Hill, "Comparative Socio-Economic Profiles of Caribbean and Non-Caribbean Blacks in the United States," paper presented at the International Conference on Immigration and the Changing Black Population in the United States, May 18–21, 1983, University of Michigan, Ann Arbor. Hill's results were based on a survey of 3,000 black households conducted by the National Urban League and its affiliates in the fall and winter of 1979. By the 1980s, almost one of every ten blacks in the U.S. were not descendants of American slaves but of Caribbean or West Indian extraction, and there was an increasing number of black immigrants. Also, the descendants of blacks who had been free before the Civil War inherited many generations of advantages over descendants of slaves. One study in Philadelphia showed that ex-slaves who had purchased their own freedom were more active in self-help societies, had fewer children, sent a considerably greater percentage of their children to school, and in many other ways behaved like immigrants, with a greater sense of control over their own lives (Theodore M. Hershberg, "Free Blacks in Ante-Bellum Philadelphia," in Allen F. Davis and Mark H. Haller, eds., *The Peoples of Philadelphia: A History of Ethnic*

Groups and Lower Class Life, 1790–1940 (Philadelphia: Temple University Press, 1973), pp. 120ff.).

89. William Julius Wilson, "Race, Class and Public Policy," *American Sociologist,* 16 (May 1981): 127.

90. Rodriguez, *Hunger of Memory,* p. 51.

91. Cyrena M. Pondrum, "The Carrot and the Stick: Twin Approaches to Achieving Minority Employment Equality," in *Ethnicity, Law and the Social Good,* ed. Winston A. Van Horne (Madison: University of Wisconsin System, 1983), p. 84. Sixty-eight percent of black families in 1947 were estimated to be living below the poverty level; by 1973 that percentage had dropped to 28. Most of the progress appears to have been made before counting-by-race remedies were commonplace. Some studies actually concluded that affirmative action had only a marginal impact on eliminating black-white wage differentials between 1940 and 1980. The most sophisticated of such studies concluded that "affirmative action apparently had no significant long-run effect, either positive or negative, on the male racial wage gap." Education and migration were deemed the primary causes of long-term economic improvement among blacks. See James P. Smith and Finis R. Welch, *Closing the Gap: Forty Years of Economic Progress for Blacks* (Santa Monica, Calif.: Rand, 1986), p. 99.

24. Respecting Diversity, Promoting Unity: The Language Issue

1. Noah Webster, *Dissertation on the English Language,* quoted in Susan Forbes and Peter Lemos, "History of American Language Policy and Immigration," *Papers on U.S. Immigration History,* in *Appendix A to the Final Report and Recommendations of the Select Commission on Immigration and Refugee Policy* (Washington, D.C.: U.S. Government Printing Office, April 30, 1981), p. 27.

2. Forbes and Lemos, "History of American Language Policy," p. 48.

3. Arnold H. Liebowitz, "The Official Character of Language in the United States: Literacy Requirements for Immigration, Citizenship and Entrance into American Life," *Papers on U.S. Immigration History,* p. 8.

4. Ibid., p. 9.

5. Ibid., p. 13.

6. Ibid., p. 15.

7. Forbes and Lemos, "History of American Language Policy," p. 92. The fight against the Chicago law by Germans, Poles, and Bohemians, most of whom were Catholics or Lutherans, constituted a classic case of ethnic-Americanization through participation in politics. The ethnic groups lobbied on the ground that the government had no business interfering with parochial schools as long as they met basic standards in teaching children fundamental skills. The immigrants, making the issue one of parental rights, won the political battle, and the law was repealed. As the scholar of the episode wrote, "in the battle to preserve their national identity, the immigrants were Americanized. Instead of passively submitting to the state, they resisted and learned the ways and means of participatory democracy" (Charles Shanabruch, "The Repeal of the Edwards Law: A Study of Religion and Ethnicity in Illinois Politics," *Ethnicity,* September 1980, p. 328).

8. Ibid., p. 38.

9. Ibid., p. 142.

10. Liebowitz, "Official Character of Language," p. 24.

11. *Meyer v. Nebraska,* 262 U.S. 320 (1923).

12. *Farrington v. Tokushige,* 273 U.S. 284 (1927).

13. Liebowitz, "Official Character of Language," p. 34.

14. 8 U.S.C. 1423 (1964). The requirement may have kept some persons desiring citizenship from applying, but probably it was more symbolic than an actual obstacle to citizenship, with a relatively small number of persons actually prevented from obtaining citizenship because they failed the test (Liebowitz, "Official Character of Language," p. 53).

15. *Lao v. Nichols,* 414 U.S. 563 (1974).

16. Liebowitz, "Official Character of Language," pp. 42, 45.

17. Ibid., p. 49.

18. Ibid., p. 46. Federal courts were divided as to whether Title VI of the Civil Rights Act required bilingual notices with respect to welfare and housing services, although they were not constitutional rights.

19. Theodore H. White, *America In Search of Itself: The Making of a President, 1956–1980* (New York: Harper and Row, 1982), p. 367.

20. John Lukacs, *Outgrowing Democracy: The History of the United States in the Twentieth Century* (Garden City, N.Y.: Doubleday, 1984), p. 56.

21. Barry Siegel, "Immigrants: Sizing Up the New Wave," *Los Angeles Times,* December 12, 1982, pp. 1, 23.

22. Kenji Hakuta, *Mirror of Language: The Debate on Bilingualism* (New York: Basic Books, 1986), p. 213.

23. Arlen J. Large, "Proliferation of Spanish in U.S. Inspires Action against Bilingualism," *The Wall Street Journal,* July 22, 1985, p. 1.

24. Elizabeth Llorente, "Official English: Law of the Land?" *Vista,* October 23, 1988, pp. 6–8.

25. On the Monterey story, see "A Melting Pot Heats Up," *Los Angeles Times,* July 18, 1986, p. 4. On the Korean street signs, see "Philadelphia Removes Korean Street Signs," *New York Times,* August 6, 1986, p. A12.

26. For results on the referenda, see the *New York Times,* November 10, 1988, pp. B10, B12. The Arizona proposition to require that the state government "act in English and no other language" won with only 51 percent of the votes. In Florida, 84 percent of the voters supported the declaration.

27. S. I. Hayakawa on the pro side and Paul Cejas and Rosa Castro Feinberg on the con side in "The English-Only Debate," *Vista,* February 8, 1987, pp. 11, 13, 14. Probably the most specific language explicating what was meant by English-only legislation came in 1980 in the ordinance passed in Dade County, which specified: "The expenditure of County funds for the purpose of utilizing any language other than English, or promoting any culture other than that of the United States is prohibited. All county government meetings, hearings, and publications shall be in English only." In approving the antibilingualism ordinance in a referendum, the voters overthrew a 1973 decision by the Metro Commission to make Dade County officially bilingual. For a fuller discussion, see Raymond A. Mohl, "The Politics of Ethnicity in Contemporary Miami," *Migration World,* 14, no. 3 (1986): 10, 11.

28. Joshua Fishman, *Language Loyalty in the United States: The Maintenance and Perpetuation of Non English Mother Tongues by American Ethnic and Religious Groups* (The Hague: Mouton, 1966). The quotation is in the epigraph. Fishman's book, written with three co-authors and six other scholars, is the most seminal and significant book on the history of efforts at language maintenance.

29. Geoffrey Nunberg, "An Official Language for California?" *New York Times,* October 2, 1986, p. A23.

30. American Slav Congress, *The Struggle for Peace and Democracy in U.S.A.: Tasks Before Slavic Americans* (1947).

31. The experience of Puerto Rican children can be found in Piri Thomas, "I Re-

member: Reminiscences of School Days in Spanish Harlem," *American Educator,* Spring 1978, p. 22. A poignant description of the alienation that can come from assaults on the language and culture of one's parents can be found in Morris U. Schappes, "Immigrant Education . . . Then and Now," *Genesis Two,* Winter 1987/88, pp. 24–28. Schappes describes how Yiddish had to be discredited for him to feel comfortable as a young American boy. His parents spoke little English and he was ashamed that his mother read a Yiddish newspaper in public. "I would sit as far away from her on the train as I possibly could. I didn't want to be sitting next to a woman who was reading a Yiddish newspaper" (ibid., p. 27). Schappes lived long enough to learn about the young college students who created a center for the revival of Yiddish in Amherst, Massachusetts, in the 1980s, and that several universities were teaching Yiddish.

32. Remarks by Miguel O. Martinez, *New York Times,* May 18, 1985, p. 27.

33. "Hispanic People Attack English-Language Bills," *New York Times,* August 2, 1987, p. 32. Coalitions that were formed to deflect the English-only movement emphasized the importance of learning English. In Florida, the organization was called "English Plus." In Arizona, it was called "Arizona English," which, like the group in Florida, focused not just on the importance of stopping a movement that could erode the rights of members of language minority groups but also on the need to promote proficiency in English. However, when Arizona English tried to obtain signatures to put on the referendum ballot a question that would establish the constitutional right to use languages in addition to English, it failed to get a sufficient number of signatures, and Arizona passed its English-only amendment in 1988 by a small margin (Llorente, "Official English: Law of the Land?" p. 6, and Cejas and Feinberg, "The English Only Debate," p. 13).

34. *U.S. News and World Report,* February 18, 1985, pp. 49–52.

35. Solomon Arbeiter, *Profiles: College-Bound Seniors, 1984* (New York: College Entrance Examination Board, 1984), p. 4.

36. Cordelia Ramires, "The Wage Structure of Hispanic Men: Implications for Policy," *Social Science Quarterly,* June 1984, p. 413.

37. Richard Rodriguez, *Hunger of Memory: The Education of Richard Rodriguez* (Boston: David R. Godine, 1982), pp. 19, 22.

38. Ibid., p. 79.

39. For a description of the language situation of the Amish, see John A. Hostetler, *Amish Society* (Baltimore: Johns Hopkins Press, 1963). Also see Donald A. Erickson, "Show-Down at an Amish School House," in Albert N. Keim, ed., *Compulsory Education and the Amish Right Not to Be Modern* (Boston: Beacon Press, 1975).

40. *Lau v. Nichols,* 414 U.S. 565 (1974), p. 788.

41. Quoted in Donald W. Larmouth, "Does Linguistic Heterogeneity Erode National Unity?" in *Ethnicity and Language,* Ethnicity and Public Policy Series, vol. 6 (Milwaukee: University of Wisconsin System Institute on Race and Ethnicity, 1987), p. 50.

42. *Forum,* National Clearinghouse for Bilingual Education, October/November 1984, p. 6, and December/January 1985, p. 2.

43. *Forum,* October/November 1984, p. 2.

44. See *U.S. v. State of Texas,* 506 F. Supp. 405 (e.d. Tex. 1981). U.S. Judge William Wayne Justice found that Texas was guilty of discrimination against the state's Hispanic children in violation of the Fourteenth Amendment and the Equal Educational Opportunities Act of 1974, and ordered a comprehensive, statewide bilingual education program. In *Castenada v. Pickard,* the Fifth Circuit Court of Appeals found that the Raymondville, Texas, independent school district's bilin-

gual education program was inadequate and therefore violated the EEO Act of 1974 (648 F. 2d 989 [5th Cir. 1981]). And a federal district court in Denver found that the rights of language minority students had been denied because School District No. 1 in Denver had failed to implement a transitional bilingual education program. As a result of the decision, the Denver public schools in 1984 entered into a consent decree to expand and improve its transitional bilingual program (*Keyes v. School District No. 1, Denver, Colorado,* 576 F. Supp. 1503 [D. Colo. 1983]).

45. Noel Epstein, "Language, Ethnicity and the Schools: Policy Alternatives for Bilingual-Bicultural Education" (Washington, D.C.: The George Washington University Institute for Educational Leadership, 1977), p. 70.

46. Tri Pham, quoted in "Vietnam's Children: Serious Achievers," *Washington Times,* April 24, 1984, p. 3B.

47. Malcolm N. Danoff, *Evaluation of the Impact of ESEA Title VII Spanish/English Bilingual Education Programs* (Palo Alto, Calif.: American Institute for Research, 1978).

48. Kenji Hakuta, "Mirror of Language: The Debate on Bilingualism," in *Ethnicity and Language,* p. 225. For a review of some of these studies, see Ricardo R. Fernández, "Legislation, Regulation, and Litigation: The Origins and Evolution of Public Policy on Bilingual Education in the United States," in *Ethnicity and Language,* pp. 110, 111. The 1980 study was conducted by Keith Baker and Adriana A. de Kanter, *Bilingual Education: A Reappraisal of Federal Policy* (Lexington, Mass.: D. C. Heath & Co., 1983). There were several rebuttals and criticisms of the book by Epstein, the AIR report, and the Baker–de Kanter survey and analysis (Fernández, "Legislation, Regulation, and Litigation," p. 110). Most of the experts in the General Accounting Office study disagreed with the department's interpretation that the evidence was too ambiguous to permit conclusions, and hence disagreed with the author's conclusion in the text. But there was sufficient disagreement even among the experts reporting for the GAO to cast doubt on the effectiveness of bilingual education (U.S. General Accounting Office, *Bilingual Education: A New Look at the Research Evidence* [Washington, D.C.: U.S. Government Printing Office, March 1987]).

49. Richard Ruiz, "Language, Ethnicity and Public Policy in the U.S.A." Working draft of a paper presented at the 10th Annual Colloquium on Ethnicity and Public Policy, Green Bay, Wisconsin, May 1989, p. 38.

50. Liza Jaipaul, "Success in Thirty-Two Languages," *Queens,* June 24, 1988, p. 1. Also see *Curriculum Materials Developed for Use at the International High School, La Guardia Community College: The International Approach, Learning English Through Content Area Study* (Long Island City, N.Y.: The International High School, 1988).

51. By 1986, seventeen states had legislation requiring special instruction for limited-English-proficient students, but not necessarily a bilingual educational program. Twenty-seven other states and territories had no legislation at all with respect to bilingual education, and only West Virginia still prohibited instruction in a language other than English (National Clearinghouse on Bilingual Education, *Statistical Files on S.E.A.s,* E.S.L. Information Packet [Rosslyn, Va.: National Clearinghouse on Bilingual Education, 1984]). *Forum,* the regular bimonthly of the National Clearinghouse for Bilingual Education, reported in the mid and late 1980s on a variety of demonstration projects using different approaches to bilingual education, teaching English as a second language, and to immersion; for example, see August/September 1985.

52. *Washington Post,* July 29, 1985, p. 9.

53. Mark Zambrano, "Language Teaching Format Borders on Controversial," *Chicago Tribune,* June 3, 1986, p. 1. The program, which took place in Bowie High School, was not nearly as threatening as it would have been if applied to elementary school students, since most high school students who knew and used Spanish were not likely to forget it.
54. Larry Rohter, "Two Systems of Bilingual Education, But Which Is Best?" *New York Times,* November 24, 1986, p. B1.
55. *New York Times,* August 21, 1988, pp. B1, B6.
56. Brad Pokorny, "Lowell Seeks Help in Educating Cambodian Immigrants," *Boston Globe,* June 6, 1985, p. 29.
57. "Saying No to Bilingual Education," *New York Times,* August 29, 1987, p. 26. California, Texas, and New York faced persistent shortages of bilingual teachers. In California the problem was particularly acute, since English-deficient students accounted for one of seven pupils in California's public schools by 1988, 75 percent of whom were Spanish-speaking, with the rest speaking fifty-nine languages. Sixty percent of California's teachers in bilingual instruction classes lacked formal bilingual teaching credentials (Louis Freedberg, "California Faces Teacher Shortage," *New York Times,* December 15, 1988, p. A33).
58. *U.S. News and World Report,* August 10, 1987, p. 48.
59. Llorente, "Official English: Law of the Land?" pp. 6–8.
60. MALDEF, January 1988, p. 4. Non-English-speaking immigrants and refugees needed language training, but there was nothing on the scale of the English programs in the earlier part of the century. The federal government provided small amounts of money for pilot projects, as when the New England Shrimp Company was given $24,000 for a six-month training program that provided classes three evenings a week for plant personnel, more than 85 percent of whom were Southeast Asian or Hispanic ("English Classes for New Workers," *Nuestro,* March 1987, p. 7). The federal government also provided assistance for refugees. But most efforts at English training were done by private agencies, sometimes with state and local assistance.
61. "Text of the 1984 Democratic Party platform," *Congressional Quarterly,* July 21, 1984, p. 1769.
62. Edith Abbott, *Immigration: Select Documents and Case Records* (Chicago: University of Chicago Press, 1924), pp. 522–523.
63. Ethan Bronner, "Justice Thwarted by Language Barrier," *Boston Globe,* June 29, 1986, p. A19.
64. Robert Reinhold, "Courts Seeking Translators for Alien Cases," *New York Times,* August 11, 1987, pp. 1, D22. The number of interpreters used in Manhattan County courts increased from 125 in 1975 to 400 in 1987. The number of sessions requiring interpreters by the federal courts in New York rose from 2,200 in 1982 to 4,087 in 1986.
65. Cora Bagley Marrett and Cheryl Leggon, *Research in Race and Ethnic Relations* (Greenwich, Conn.: Jai Press, Inc., 1982), 3:158–160.
66. Quoted in U.S. Select Commission on Immigration and Refugee Policy, *Immigration Policy and the National Interest. Staff Report, Supplement to the Final Report and Recommendations of the Select Commission on Immigration and Refugee Policy* (Washington, D.C.: U.S. Government Printing Office, April 30, 1981), p. 404.
67. Robert R. Brischetto and Rodolfo O. de la Garza, *The Mexican-American Electorate: Political Participation and Ideology,* Mexican-American Electorate Series, Occasional Paper No. 3, joint publication of the Southwest Voter Registration Education Project, San Antonio, and the Hispanic Studies Program of the Center

for Mexican-American Studies, University of Texas, Austin (Austin and San Antonio: 1983), p. 31. In a previous study, the authors found that 63 percent of the Spanish monolinguals in their sample read no newspaper at all, compared to less than 30 percent of the bilinguals. Four of five bilinguals watched the local evening news on English TV most of the time (Rodolfo O. de la Garza and Robert R. Brischetto, with the assistance of David Vaughn, *The Mexican-American Electorate: Information Sources and Policy Orientations,* Mexican-American Electorate Series, Occasional Paper No. 2, pp. 18–20. That one of ten monolingual citizens could not speak English also reflected the exemption given to older applicants from the English language requirement).

68. The naturalization English language examination often was applied in a lax way, as indicated by the fact that in the 1980s one in ten Mexican-American citizens spoke only Spanish (Liebowitz, "Official Character of Language," p. 53).

69. *Castro* v. *State of California,* 2 Cal. 3rd 223, 243 (1970).

70. Lori S. Orum, *The Education of Hispanics: Status and Implications* (Washington, D.C.: National Council of La Raza, 1986), p. 49.

71. Ibid., pp. 24–30. Dropout rates were highest for Mexican-Americans, Puerto Ricans, and non-English-speaking Hispanics generally. In 1985, 17.1 percent of Mexican-Americans twenty-five or older had completed less than five years of school, 12.8 percent of Puerto Ricans, 7.4 percent of Cubans (including the poorer and less educated Marielitos), and only 7.2 percent of Central and South Americans, compared to 6.1 percent of blacks and 2.2 percent of whites.

Older immigrant-ethnic groups had severe truancy and dropout rates at the turn of the century, but the failure to complete high school then was not nearly so punishing in an industrial economy as in an information-service economy. One estimate holds that as many as 10 percent of the Italian immigrant children in New York City at the turn of the century managed to avoid school altogether, and as late as 1930 only 11 percent of the Italian-Americans who entered high schools in New York City graduated, although over 40 percent of all the city's students did so. See Richard D. Alba, "The Twilight of Ethnicity among Americans of European Ancestry: The Case of Italians," *Ethnic and Racial Studies,* January 1985, p. 140.

72. Orum, *Education of Hispanics,* p. 35.

73. Ibid., p. 29.

74. Ibid., p. 43.

75. Ibid., p. 50.

76. "For Latinos, a Growing Divide," *U.S. News and World Report,* August 10, 1987, p. 47.

77. Arturo Vargas, "Illiteracy in the Hispanic Community" (Washington, D.C.: National Council of La Raza, 1986), pp. 19, 20. See also Lydia Chavez, "Encouraging Hispanic Students to Stay in School," *New York Times,* August 3, 1986, p. 28, and Cheryl M. Fields, "Colleges in California Seek New Ways to Expand Pool of Hispanic Students Prepared for Higher Education," *Chronicle of Higher Education,* September 30, 1987, p. A31.

25. Questions of Membership: Who Are the Outsiders?

1. In Brooklyn, the INS joined the Congress of Racial Equality and thousands of Caribbeans to celebrate "West Indian Day" to promote its legalization program (*Big Red News,* September 19, 1987, p. 1). In its western region, the INS sent seven red, white, and blue vans and a mobile home into remote areas to reach aliens

(Joe Gandelman, "I.N.S. Van Will Assist Migrants," *San Diego Union*, August 11, 1987, p. 12).

For a comparison with other countries' legalization programs, see Doris Meissner, Demetrios G. Papademetriou, and David North, *Legalization of Undocumented Aliens: Lessons from Other Countries*, report on a consultation on comparative legalization held at the Carnegie Endowment for International Peace (Washington, D.C.: Carnegie Endowment for International Peace, December 10, 1986). In every case, the number of illegal aliens who came forward for amnesty was smaller than expected. In Canada's 1973 program, of an estimated 200,000 to 300,000 illegal immigrants, 50,000 applied, even though the June 1973 law provided that all those who had been in Canada before November 1972 were allowed to become legalized. One requirement, that the illegal aliens show family ties in Canada, restricted the number eligible. Meissner, et al., *Legalization of Undocumented Aliens*, p. 13.

2. John F. Burns, "Canada Rejects Alien-Amnesty Plan," *New York Times*, December 31, 1988, p. 35.

3. Bruce Stannard, "Migration Wrangle Heats Up: Asian Inflow Revives Old Phobias," *The Bulletin*, November 24, 1987, pp. 72–76.

4. "The Struggle Against 'Economic Refugees' from Lebanon," *Refugees*, January 1985, p. 39; Erland Bergman, "A Swedish Dilemma—Ethnic Conflicts in Sweden," *Current Sweden*, The Swedish Institute, December 1982; and Johan Hirschfeldt, "An Ombudsman Against Ethnic Discrimination," *Current Sweden*, October 1986.

5. Henry Kamm, "Western Nations Raising Barriers to Refugees Trying to Flee Poverty," *New York Times*, March 27, 1989, p. A1.

6. For a fuller discussion of British citizenship laws, see R. Sondhi, "Immigration and Citizenship in Postwar Britain," in C. Fried, ed., *Minorities: Community and Identity* (New York: Springer Verlag, 1983), pp. 255–268. For consideration of the legal status of aliens and refugees in Germany, see R. Marx, "The Political, Social, and Legal Status of Aliens and Refugees in the Federal Republic of Germany," in Fried, *Minorities: Community and Identity*, pp. 269–281.

7. Even in the nineteenth century, the French imported outsiders to do menial jobs. In 1888, a French economist remarked, "The French are seldom willing to be simple laborers or street sweepers, to do certain of the exhausting or painful jobs in the textile mills of the north, in the refineries or oil processing plants of the south . . ." (Paul LeRoy-Beaulieu, quoted in Gary S. Cross, *Immigrant Workers in Industrial Plants: The Making of a New Laboring Class* [Philadelphia: Temple University Press, 1983], p. 8). Although the path to naturalization was much longer and more difficult than in the U.S., the children and grandchildren of pre-1930s southern European immigrants had generally acculturated to life in France by the 1980s, when the French faced the problem of digesting large numbers of newcomers from North Africa and the Middle East as well as southern Europe. A difference in the American approach toward immigrants in the early twentieth century can be seen by the fact that only 11 percent of the foreign population of France had been naturalized by 1930, compared to 55 percent in the U.S. (Cross, *Immigrant Workers in Industrial Plants*, p. 8). Also see S. Boulot and D. Fradet, "L'échec scolaire des enfants immigrés, un problème mal posé," *Les Temps Modernes*, March–April 1984, and H. Bastide, "Les enfants d'immigrés et l'ensignent du français," INED, Travaux et documents, No. 97, 1982. These French sources were brought to my attention by Gerard Noiriel in an unpublished paper, "Proposals for a Comparative Research Program in Immigration in France and the United States." Also see William Rogers Brubaker, ed., *Immigration and the Politics of Citizenship in Europe and North America* (Lanham:

University Press of America, 1989) and Tomas Hammer, ed., *European Immigration Policy: A Comparative Study* (Cambridge: Cambridge University Press, 1985).

8. *Afroyim* v. *Rusk*, 387 U.S. 253, p. 268. For consideration of the law on expatriation before 1967, see John P. Roche, "The Expatriation Cases: 'Breathes There a Man, with Soul so Dead . . . ?'" in Martin M. Shapiro, ed., *The Supreme Court and Constitutional Rights: Readings in Constitutional Law* (Atlanta: Scott Foresman and Company, 1967). As discussed in chapter 20, Nazis or other persons who defrauded the government in order to obtain immigrant status and who were subsequently naturalized were subject to denaturalization and deportation (Richard D. Steel, "Denaturalization: Material Fact and Willful Misrepresentation," *Immigration Journal*, January–March 1987, p. 1).

9. Richard Halloran, "Judge Gives Naturalized Citizens Right to U.S. Security Clearances," *New York Times*, February 15, 1988, p. A10.

10. Reed Ueda, "New Citizens and the American Civic Tradition: Naturalization, Americanization, and Americanism in the European and Asian Immigration, 1870–1950," unpublished essay, p. 9, cited with the permission of the author. Many states prohibited aliens from employment in civic service and on public works in the 1920s and 1930s and sharply restricted aliens from obtaining fishing and gaming licenses. Also see Elizabeth Hull, *Without Justice for All: The Constitutional Rights of Aliens* (Westport, Conn.: Greenwood Press, 1985), chapter 2, "Resident Aliens."

11. Hull, *Without Justice for All*, p. 40.

12. *Graham* v. *Richardson*, 403 U.S. 365 (1971).

13. Hull, *Without Justice for All*, p. 42.

14. Ibid., p. 49. Elizabeth Hull is one of those scholars who deplored the continuation of most distinctions in law between resident aliens and citizens. So did T. Alexander Aleinikoff, who argued that many distinctions were arbitrary and not valid because they were based on the assumption that membership in the national community was equivalent to citizenship ("Aliens, Citizens and Constitutional Membership," unpublished essay, November 1987).

15. Robert Reinhold, "Judge Voids Sections of 1952 Alien Law in Deportation Case," *New York Times*, December 23, 1988, p. 1.

16. *Plyler* v. *Doe*, 457 U.S. 202 (1982).

17. Ibid., p. 215.

18. Stuart Taylor, Jr., "Court Backs Illegal Aliens in a Deportation Case," *New York Times*, May 27, 1987, p. A21.

19. *New York Times*, June 26, 1984, p. 85.

20. *Annual Report of the Mexican-American Legal Defense and Education Fund*, May 1987–April 1988, p. 10.

21. "Illegal Aliens Are Eligible for Medicaid," *New York Times*, July 20, 1986, p. 6.

22. Marvin E. Howe, "I.N.S. Ruling Benefits Illegal Immigrant Children," *New York Times*, March 26, 1988, p. 35.

23. For a strong criticism of the tendency to extend rights to the children of illegal aliens and to break down distinctions in membership rights between illegal aliens and citizens and resident aliens, see Peter H. Schuck and Roger M. Smith, *Citizenship without Consent: Illegal Aliens in the American Polity* (New Haven: Yale University Press, 1985).

24. One constriction of the rights of aliens out of status was a ruling that allowed the U.S. attorney general to apply a strict interpretation of that portion of the law that enable him or her to deport aliens who have been in the U.S. continuously for seven years. The law provides that illegal aliens who have been in the country continuously for seven years are eligible for a stay of deportation if they

can demonstrate that their deportation would lead to "extreme hardship" (often meaning separation from an American-born child). It was ruled that any brief absence from the U.S., however innocent, would interrupt the seven years "continuous physical presence" requirement (Francesco Isgro, "Review of Significant Cases Decided by the Federal Courts in 1984," *Migration Today*, 12, no. 4/5 (1984): 35.

25. Alfonso A. Narvaez, "Illegal Aliens Find Freedom at Immigration Center," *New York Times*, August 9, 1987, p. 44.
26. L. A. Jolidom, "Amnesty Day: 'This Is Our Country Now,'" *U.S.A. Today*, May 5, 1987, p. 1.
27. Doris Sue Wong, "Immigrants Feeling Good about Amnesty," *Boston Globe*, August 27, 1987, p. 46.
28. William Julius Wilson, *The Declining Significance of Race: Blacks and Changing American Institutions* (Chicago: University of Chicago Press, 1978), p. 128.
29. U.S. Bureau of the Census, *Statistical Abstract of the United States, 1985*, 105th edition (Washington, D.C.: U.S. Government Printing Office), p. 402. Blacks comprised 12.7 percent of health technologists and technicians, 17.7 percent of licensed practical nurses, 7.7 percent of physicians' assistants, 11.1 percent of elementary school teachers, 7.9 percent of librarians, and 26.2 percent of all postal clerks (not counting mail carriers). The percentage of physicians had risen to 3.2, of dentists to 2.4, and of college and university teachers to 4.4 percent. The whole point of caste had been destroyed. It was not uncommon by 1990 to see whites serving blacks in restaurants or carrying bags for them in hotels, even in such cities as Atlanta, the heart of the old Confederacy.

The biggest expansion of the black middle class actually came in the 1960s and 1970s. It was between 1961 and 1982 that the proportion of blacks in professional jobs increased from 4.6 percent to 13.0 percent and in managerial jobs from 2.5 to 5.5 percent (*Current Population Reports*, Bureau of the Census, May 1982). Gains were made by blacks at the executive level of the federal government. Blacks and other minorities in such positions increased from 2.3 percent to 7.0 percent, and in the general schedule rank of GS-15 jobs from 3.3 percent to 8.0 percent (Spencer Rich, "Minorities, Women Gain in Top Jobs: Affirmative Action Cited as Major Factor," *Washington Post National Weekly Edition*, November 15, 1985, p. 34).
30. James Smith and Finis Welch, "Black-White Male Wage Ratios: 1960–1970," *American Economic Review*, June 1977.
31. Reynolds Farley and Walter Allen, *Color Line and the Quality of Life in America* (New York: Russell Sage Foundation, 1987), p. 275. Farley and Allen present a comprehensive, detailed analysis of the statistics of the 1980 census along the color line and a survey of the literature analyzing characteristics of the black underclass.
32. Richard Bernstein, "Twenty Years after the Kerner Report: Three Societies, All Separate," *New York Times*, February 29, 1988, p. B8.
33. Robert McNatt, "Are You a BUPPY? No? Want to Bet?" *Black Enterprise*, August 1984, p. 76. For a book-length analysis, see Bart Landry, *The New Black Middle Class* (Berkeley: University of California Press, 1987). Buppies tended to move out of the cities. According to one study, over 65 percent of blacks with four or more years of college who moved in the 1970s went to suburban census tracts that were less than 10 percent black ("Blacks on the Move: A Decade of Demographic Change," from a report by William P. O'Hare et al., abridged by Phillip Sawicki (Washington, D.C.: Joint Center for Political Studies, 1982, p. 64). In the Washington metropolitan area, a majority of the 650,000 blacks

lived in the suburbs in 1988, not the District of Columbia. Of the area's 300,000 prosperous blacks, almost twice as many lived in white neighborhoods as in mostly black ones (Joel Garreau, "The Integration of the American Dream," *Washington Post National Weekly Edition,* February 8–14, 1988, p. 6).

34. Margaret C. Simms, "Incomes for Black Families Continue to Rise," *Focus,* The Joint Center for Political Studies, October 1987, pp. 4, 8. Blacks represented 28 percent of all Americans in poverty.

35. Farley and Allen, *Color Line,* pp. 412, 418.

36. Kenneth B. Clark, *Dark Ghetto* (New York: Harper and Row, 1965). For a reprint of the Moynihan Report and discussion of the attacks on it, see Lee Rainwater and William C. Yancey, eds., *The Moynihan Report and the Politics of Controversy* (Cambridge: MIT Press, 1967). Rainwater also wrote on how family stress leading to family disorganization was a source of weakened identity and self-esteem for poor ghetto blacks ("Crucible of Identity: The Negro Lower Class Family," *Daedalus* 95 [Winter 1966]: 172–216). Two historians wrote about the strengths of black families prior to the major migrations from the South to the North (Herbert Gutman, *The Black Family in Slavery and Freedom, 1750–1925* [New York: Pantheon Books, 1976], and Leon F. Litwak, *Been in the Storm So Long: The Aftermath of Slavery* [New York: Knopf, 1979]).

The attacks on Moynihan's thesis—that serious behavioral problems in the ghetto were linked to stressed black families—were born in part out of deep resentment that a white Irish-American seemed to be blaming the victim by characterizing black families as subject to a "tangle of pathology." The black sociologist Andrew Billingsley argued that Moynihan and others who shared his views were wrong to think there was a single standard of healthy family life based on white European cultural norms (Andrew Billingsley, *Black Families in White America* [Englewood Cliffs, N.J.: Prentice-Hall, 1968], pp. 198–201). A white sociologist, Carol Stack, showed how blacks created extended family networks to give support to mothers as care-givers for small children (*All Our Kin* [New York: Harper and Row, 1975]). By the late 1980s, the major points made by Moynihan and Clark were generally acknowledged as valid.

37. Wilson, *Declining Significance of Race,* p. 134.

38. Victor Fuchs, *How We Live* (Cambridge: Harvard University Press, 1983). Whites showed increases in the percentages of babies born to unwed mothers and of female-headed households, but these developments were much more characteristic of blacks, and by 1980 four times the proportion of black families were headed by women as white families and five time the proportion of black babies were born to unmarried mothers, compared to white babies.

39. Eddie M. Williams, "Perspective," *Focus,* The Joint Center for Political Studies, September 1985, p. 2.

40. Wilson, *Declining Significance of Race,* p. 108.

41. Elliot Liebow, *Talley's Corner* (Boston: Little, Brown & Company, 1967).

42. William Julius Wilson, "Race, Class and Public Policy," *The American Sociologist,* 16 (May 1981): 125, 126.

43. Ibid., p. 127.

44. Joint Center for Political Studies, *A Policy Framework for Racial Justice,* with a foreword by John Hope Franklin and Kenneth B. Clark (Washington, D.C.: Joint Center for Political Studies, 1983), p. 10. The participants in the three conferences read like a Who's Who in black America, including top scholars, lawyers, and leaders of major black organizations. William J. Wilson attended all three, along with Bernard Anderson, then director of the Division of Social Sciences at the Rockefeller Foundation.

45. Ibid., p. 12. As the conferees met in 1982, data appeared that showed that one of every five nonwhite babies born in 1982 had a teen-age mother. Where data existed for blacks only (California, Georgia, Indiana, Michigan, New Jersey, Nevada, and Oklahoma), the percentage was closer to one of every four, or slightly more (Marian Wright Edelman, "Caring for Young Mothers," *Focus,* April 1985, p. 5).

46. Glenn C. Loury, *Imprints,* 2, no. 2 (February 1983): 4.

47. *Focus,* March 1984, pp. 5, 6.

48. *Black Enterprise,* January 1985, p. 50; *New York Times,* May 17, 1985, p. 26.

49. Robert L. Woodson, *Washington Post National Weekly Edition,* May 27, 1985, p. 25.

50. Andrew F. Brimmer, *Trends, Prospects and Strategies for Black Economic Progress* (Washington, D.C.: The Joint Center for Political Studies, 1985), p. 19.

51. Dorothy I. Height, "What Must Be Done About Children Having Children," *Ebony,* March 1985, p. 76.

52. Committee on Policy for Racial Justice, *Black Initiative and Governmental Responsibility,* with an introduction by John Hope Franklin and Eleanor Holmes Norton (Washington, D.C.: Joint Center for Political Studies, Inc., 1987).

53. Ibid., pp. 12, 13.

54. Ibid., pp. vi, vii.

55. Ibid., p. 7.

56. W. E. B. Du Bois, *The Philadelphia Negro: A Social Study* (New York: Schocken Books, 1967), p. 390.

57. Katherine McFate, "Defining the Underclass," *Focus,* June 1987, pp. 8, 9. In March 1987, the Joint Center for Political Studies sponsored a conference that began with a presentation by William J. Wilson that the poverty population of the nation's five largest cities (New York, Chicago, Los Angeles, Philadelphia, and Detroit) had increased by 22 percent between 1970 and 1980, even though their total population had decreased by 9 percent. By 1984, 46.2 percent of all black children were living below the poverty line, compared to 16.1 percent of all white children. In female-headed households, 66.2 percent of black children were below the poverty line, compared to 45.9 percent of white children in female-headed households (U.S. Bureau of the Census, *Current Population Reports,* Series P-60, No. 152).

58. Nicholas Lemann, "The Origins of the Underclass," *The Atlantic,* July 1986. The Kerner Report (1968), looking beyond the riots just past, warned that the nation was moving toward two societies, "one black, one white—separate and unequal." Twenty years later, it was clear that race and ethnicity in American society were much more complicated than that. Racial and ethnic boundaries in the American kaleidoscope were more fluid than they had ever been (see chapters 16 and 17). African-American professionals often had more in common with white, Hispanic, and Asian-American professionals than with the black of the underclass, whose situation was actually worse in 1988 than twenty years earlier.

 Another discussion of the black underclass appeared in Fred R. Harris and Roger W. Wilkins, *Quiet Riots: Race and Poverty in the United States* (New York: Pantheon, 1988). The authors ignored the complexities of ethnicity and race in the American kaleidoscope, but underscored the isolation of a large and growing ghetto underclass in the nation's largest cities. The best discussion of the underclass appears in William J. Wilson, *The Truly Disadvantaged: The Inner City, the Underclass and Public Policy* (Chicago: University of Chicago Press, 1987).

59. Oscar Lewis, *La Vida* (London: Secker and Warburg, 1967).

60. Nathan Glazer and Daniel P. Moynihan, *Beyond the Melting Pot,* 2d ed. (Cambridge: MIT Press, 1970), pp. 116–129. A random sample of New York City

households in 1952 showed 13 percent of Puerto Ricans unemployed and 6 percent of nonwhites. In the 1950 census, 17 percent of Puerto Ricans were unemployed, compared to 12 percent of blacks. By 1970, half of all the families of the city receiving supplemental assistance from the Department of Welfare were Puerto Rican, and one-quarter of all Puerto Rican children in the city were on some form of assistance.

61. Board of Education of the City of New York, *Toward Greater Opportunity* (New York: 1960), p. 16.
62. Commonwealth of Puerto Rico, *Puerto Ricans and Other Hispanics in New York City's Public Schools and Universities* (New York: 1975), p. 157.62.
63. Alejandro Portes and Cynthia Truelove, "Making Sense of Diversity: Research on Hispanic Minorities in the United States," *The Annual Review of Sociology,* 1987, p. 365.
64. Frank Bonilla, "Ethnic Orbits: The Circulation of Capital and People," paper, April 1984; see Tables I and II. Only in California did the proportion of Puerto Ricans with four years of high school exceed 25 percent. In California, 16.5 percent of Puerto Ricans were living in poverty, compared to 39.0 percent in New York, 36.5 percent in New Jersey, and 25.7 percent in Illinois. Although the Puerto Rican population of California grew considerably in the 1970s, and even more rapidly in Texas, Massachusetts, Florida, Virginia, and Connecticut, almost half of all Puerto Ricans still lived in New York State (mostly New York City) and more in New Jersey and Illinois than in the next four states combined.
65. Sandra H. Berry, *Los Angeles Today and Tomorrow: Results of the Los Angeles 2000 Community Survey* (Santa Monica: Rand Corporation, 1988), pp. 7, 29. A higher percentage of Hispanics in Los Angeles (21 percent) than whites (15 percent) actually listed employment opportunities as what they liked best about the city.
66. Portes and Truelove, "Making Sense of Diversity," pp. 365, 370.
67. Juan Gonzalez, "Puerto Ricans in the U.S.: A Community Battling a Negative Image with the Force of Positive Action," *Vista,* May 2, 1987, p. 11. One factor accounting for the lower income of Puerto Ricans was that Mexicans engaged in entrepreneurial activities. The proportions of Mexicans owning businesses was twice as high as for Puerto Ricans (1,468 versus 740 per 100,000 of each group) (Portes and Truelove, "Making Sense of Diversity," p. 369). For excellent brief discussions of the special problems of Puerto Ricans, see Marta Tienda and William A. Diaz, "Puerto Ricans' Special Problems," *New York Times,* August 28, 1987, p. A31, and Marta Tienda and William A. Diaz, "What's Behind Growing Puerto Rican Poverty?" *New York Times,* October 10, 1987, p. 30. Tienda and Diaz emphasize the disproportionate drop in participation in the labor force by Puerto Rican men, even compared to blacks and Mexicans, which they explain by the circular migration between Puerto Rico and the mainland, resulting in a loss of income, high dropout rates, and other problems. One result is a heavy dependence on welfare. Between 1969 and 1984, the use of public assistance by Puerto Rican families headed by couples increased 115 percent, but it increased 291 percent among those headed by single women. By contrast, husband-and-wife-headed Mexican families on welfare actually declined 12 percent, while those headed by single women rose only 23 percent.
68. It was impossible to determine how many illegal aliens had settled in the U.S. who were not covered by the legalization programs of the 1986 law, but it was a substantial number, and illegal aliens continued to come to the U.S. to work despite that law. There were some estimates (more like guesstimates) that a majority of 400,000 Dominicans in New York City were out of status in 1986, and perhaps more than half of the 500,000 Salvadoreans in the U.S. also were

illegal aliens (Jean Molesky, "The Exiled: Pathology of Central American Refugees," *Migration World*, 15, no. 4 [1986]: 19).

69. Ellen K. Coughlin, "Worsening Plight of the 'Underclass' Catches Attention of Researchers," *Chronicle of Higher Education*, March 30, 1988, p. 7. Coughlin reported on data from Robert D. Reischauer, a senior fellow in economics at the Brookings Institution.

70. Michael A. Lawrence, "Wealth: Getting It and Keeping It," *The Crisis*, March 1985, p. 22. The author urged blacks to invest in savings accounts and certificates of deposit, and to look at houses and other properties as investments. In the same issue, Bayard Rustin, the great civil rights strategist, pointed to the entrepreneurship of Koreans and other immigrants in a special interview. Rustin, who had always maintained that the key to power was economic mobility, decried the emphasis in the black movement in the 1970s on black studies and black dormitories. Rustin had been called an Uncle Tom when he spoke out in that way in the 1970s, but by the middle of the 1980s he was considered a prophet by many and given the pages of *The Crisis* to preach his message of strong family solidarity and entrepreneurship (pp. 28, 29).

71. Gerald David Jaynes and Robin Williams, eds., *A Common Destiny: Blacks and American Society* (Washington, D.C.: The National Academy Press, 1989). The 600-page report, based on six years of study, was built on the work of nearly one hundred scholars. The report acknowledges the substantial economic progress of blacks between 1940 and 1973 as a result of the migration of southern blacks to centers of industrial activity at a time of sustained economic growth. But it emphasizes the relative lack of progress since that time and predicts that in the near future roughly one-third of the black population will continue to be poor, and that the relative employment and earnings of black men is likely to deteriorate further.

72. Scholars argued intensely over the basic causes of chronic intergenerational poverty and the attendant problems of crime, female-headed families, etc. Charles Murray, in a provocative book, *Losing Ground*, put the blame on the welfare system (Charles Murray, *Losing Ground: American Social Policy, 1950–1980* [New York: Basic Books, 1984]), even though, as Lisbeth B. Schorr pointed out, other countries with larger social welfare programs had much lower rates of teen-age births and teen-age crime (Lisbeth B. Schorr with Daniel Schorr, *Within Our Reach: Breaking the Cycle of Disadvantage* [New York: Doubleday, 1988], p. xxv). Others argued that the extremely poor would be worse off were it not for welfare programs (Peter B. Edelman, "The Next Century of Our Constitution: Rethinking Our Duty to the Poor," *Hastings Law Journal* [November 1987]). Lisbeth Schorr's contribution was to identify a variety of programs that worked to break the cycle of disadvantage by preventing severe damage to children and adolescents.

Index

ABOUT THE AUTHOR

Lawrence H. Fuchs, Meyer and Walter Jaffee Professor of American Civilization & Politics at Brandeis University, was appointed by President Carter and the Congress as executive director of the Select Commission on Immigration and Refugee Policy. The Commission's 1981 report became the basis for the Immigration Reform and Control Act of 1986, the first major reform of U.S. immigration policy since 1965. Fuchs frequently has testified before the House and Senate on immigration and refugee policy.

He is the author of *Family Matters, American Ethnic Politics, Those Peculiar Americans: The Peace Corps and American National Character, John F. Kennedy and American Catholicism, Hawaii Pono: A Social History,* and *The Political Behavior of American Jews.* He is also the originator of a four-volume high school text, *Black in White America: The Struggle for Identity and Power.*

A graduate of New York University (B.A. 1950) and Harvard University (Ph.D. 1955), Fuchs has taught at Brandeis since 1952. He was director of the Peace Corps in the Philippines from 1961 to 1963. His home is in Weston, Massachusetts.

ABOUT THE BOOK

The American Kaleidoscope was composed on the Mergenthaler 202 in Galliard, a contemporary rendering of a classic typeface prepared for Mergenthaler in 1978 by the British type designer Matthew Carter. The book was composed by Brevis Press of Bethany, Connecticut, and designed and produced by Kachergis Book Design of Pittsboro, North Carolina.

Wesleyan University Press, 1990.